GIVE ME LIBERTY!

An American History

Second Edition

VOLUME 1: TO 1877

W · W · NORTON & COMPANY · NEW YORK · LONDON

GIVE ME LIBERTY!

AN AMERICAN HISTORY

Second Edition

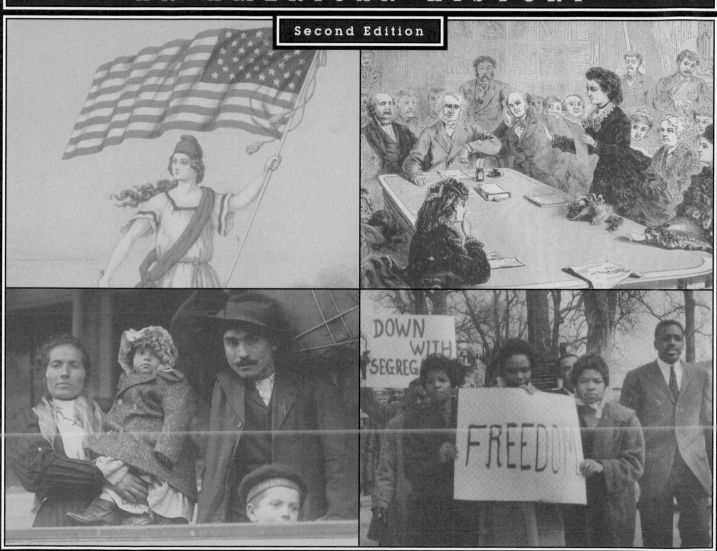

by ERIC FONER

For my mother, Liza Foner (1909–2005), an accom-
plished artist who lived through most of the twentieth
century and into the twenty-first

W. W. Norton & Company has been independent since its founding in 1923, when William Warder Norton and Mary D. Herter Norton first published lectures delivered at the People's Institute, the adult education division of New York City's Cooper Union. The Nortons soon expanded their program beyond the Institute, publishing books by celebrated academics from America and abroad. By mid-century, the two major pillars of Norton's publishing program—trade books and college texts—were firmly established. In the 1950s, the Norton family transferred control of the company to its employees, and today—with a staff of four hundred and a comparable number of trade, college, and professional titles published each year—W. W. Norton & Company stands as the largest and oldest publishing house owned wholly by its employees.

Editor: Steve Forman
Associate Managing Editor, College: Kim Yi
Editorial Assistant: Rebecca Arata
Copy Editor: Alice Vigliani
Managing Editor, College: Marian Johnson
Manufacturing by RR Donnelley, Willard
Composition by Matrix Publishing Services
Book design by Antonina Krass
Production Manager: Chris Granville
Photo Researchers: Rebecca Arata, Stephanie Romeo
Associate Director, Electronic Media: Steven S. Hoge
Cartographer: Martha Bostwick, Maps.com

Acknowledgments and copyrights continue on the Credits pages, which serve as a continuation of the copyright page.

Library of Congress Cataloging-in-Publication Data
Foner, Eric.
    Give me liberty! : an American history / by Eric Foner. — 2nd ed.
        p. cm.
    Includes bibliographical references and index.
    ISBN 978-0-393-93027-6 (pbk.)
    1. United States—History. 2. United States—Politics and government. 3. Democracy—United States—History. 4. Liberty—History. I. Title.

E178.F66 2007
973—dc22

                                                                2007001292

W. W. Norton & Company, Inc., 500 Fifth Avenue, New York, N. Y. 10110
www.wwnorton.com
W. W. Norton & Company Ltd., Castle House, 75/76 Wells Street, London W1T 3QT
1 2 3 4 5 6 7 8 9 0

Contents

Part 1 American Colonies to 1763

vi   Contents

Part 2 A New Nation, 1763–1840

Contents

Part 3 Slavery, Freedom, and the Crisis of the Union, 1840–1877

APPENDIX

DOCUMENTS

TABLES AND FIGURES

LIST OF MAPS, TABLES, AND FIGURES

TABLES AND FIGURES

ABOUT THE AUTHOR

ERIC FONER is DeWitt Clinton Professor of History at Columbia University, where he earned his B.A. and Ph.D. In his teaching and scholarship, he focuses on the Civil War and Reconstruction, slavery, and nineteenth-century America. Professor Foner's publications include *Free Soil, Free Labor, Free Men: The Ideology of the Republican Party Before the Civil War; Tom Paine and Revolutionary America; Politics and Ideology in the Age of the Civil War; Nothing But Freedom: Emancipation and Its Legacy; Reconstruction: America's Unfinished Revolution, 1863–1877; Freedom's Lawmakers: A Directory of Black Officeholders During Reconstruction; The Story of American Freedom; Who Owns History? Rethinking the Past in a Changing World;* and *Forever Free: The Story of Emancipation and Reconstruction.* His history of Reconstruction won the *Los Angeles Times* Book Award for History, the Bancroft Prize, and the Parkman Prize. He has been co-curator for two historical exhibits, "A House Divided" at the Chicago Historical Society, and "America's Reconstruction" at the Virginia Historical Society. He has served as president of the Organization of American Historians (1993–1994) and the American Historical Association (2000). In 2006 he received the Presidential Award for Outstanding Teaching from Columbia University.

Preface

Give Me Liberty! An American History is a survey of American history from the earliest days of European exploration and conquest of the New World to the first years of the twenty-first century. It offers students a clear, concise narrative whose central theme is the changing contours of American freedom.

I am extremely gratified by the response to the First Edition of *Give Me Liberty!*, which has been used in survey courses at many hundreds of two- and four-year colleges and universities throughout the country. The comments I have received from instructors and students encourage me to think that *Give Me Liberty!* has worked well in their classrooms. Their comments have also included many valuable suggestions for revisions, which I greatly appreciate. These have ranged from corrections of typographical and factual errors that crept into the First Edition (perhaps most embarrassingly, I misstated the year of the sinking of the *Titanic*), to thoughts about subjects that needed more extensive treatment. In making revisions for this Second Edition, I have tried to take these suggestions into account. I have also incorporated the findings and insights of new scholarship that has appeared since the original edition was written.

The most significant changes in the Second Edition are as follows:

Throughout the book, I have revised and added material about the history of Native Americans, an area of American history that has received significant new attention in the past few years. For example, Chapter 1 opens with an expanded treatment of Native American life before European contact; Chapter 4 contains new material on Indian slavery in the colonial era; Chapter 10 devotes increased attention to Supreme Court decisions of the Jacksonian era related to the status of Indians; Chapter 16 includes a new discussion of issues surrounding Indian citizenship in the late nineteenth century, Chapter 18 includes a new examination of Native American Progressivism; and Chapter 25 provides further coverage of the movement for greater rights for American Indians that emerged during the turbulent 1960s.

The history of immigration and the controversies surrounding it receive greater attention throughout this edition. Chapter 9 now includes an expanded section on immigration and nativism in the era before the Civil War; Chapter 18 devotes increased attention to Asian immigration in the early twentieth century; and the final two chapters discuss at length recent shifts in immigration patterns and the way immigration, especially from Latin America, has again become a controversial political issue. The discussion of the evolution of citizenship rights for immigrant groups and racial minorities more broadly has also been expanded, as in discussions of efforts to "colonize" African-Americans outside the United States, in Chapter 12; movements among Chinese and Mexican immigrants for equal rights, in Chapters 17 and 22; and an expanded treatment of the implications of changes in immigration policies in the 1920s, in Chapter 20.

I have strengthened at many points the discussion of the history of the American West, including additional coverage in Chapter 16 of western farming and the role of women in the trans-Mississippi West, a new discussion in Chapter 21 of New Deal agricultural and resource management policies, and a new treatment of the Sagebrush Rebellion as part of the growth of conservatism in the 1970s, in Chapter 26.

Throughout the book, I have strengthened the presentation of American history in a global context. Thus, Chapter 2 examines the impact of the English Civil War of the 1640s on the American colonies, with special attention to how new ideas about English liberty circulated in the New World; Chapter 3 discusses how the colonies participated in an Atlantic world of commerce and ideas; Chapter 6 contains a new section on the fate of the thousands of slaves who left with the British after the War of Independence for new lives in Canada, Britain, and West Africa; Chapter 14 points to changes in world production of cotton stimulated by the cotton embargo during the American Civil War; Chapter 18 places American immigration in the context of worldwide population flows; and Chapter 28 examines the country's relationship with the rest of the world in the aftermath of the terrorist attacks of September 11, 2001 and the war in Iraq.

A number of chapters have been reorganized to achieve greater focus and clarity. Most notably, I have completely restructured Chapters 1–4 covering the colonial period. The first now concentrates on Native American life before European contact and the establishment of the Spanish, French, and Dutch American empires in the New World. Chapter 2 now deals entirely with English America. Chapter 3 explores the making of a distinctive Anglo-American society, culture, and politics, and the diverse ethnic and religious groups that populated the colonies in the eighteenth century. Chapter 4 now includes a more developed treatment of the early history of American slavery, bringing together material previously scattered in the early chapters. In another reorganization, sections on conservative thought and politics in the 1950s and 1960s have been moved from Chapter 26 to their appropriate chronological placement.

The Voices of Freedom sections in each chapter now include two document excerpts instead of one. The excerpts are juxtaposed to suggest differing ideas about American freedom at each historical moment. This pairing allows for the inclusion of a more diverse group of authors, especially a larger number of women than in the first edition. I have also added a series of questions at the end of the sections to further discussion.

This Second Edition also includes a number of new images in each chapter. I have added new photos and figures in order to expand the visual representation of key ideas and personalities in the text.

I have greatly expanded the final chapter, which deals with the momentous events of the early twenty-first century, and especially how ideas and practices concerning freedom have come under strain since the terrorist attacks of September 11, 2001. In addition to adding material on historical developments since the publication of the first edition—the war in Iraq, the reelection of President Bush, the devastation caused by Hurricane Katrina, and the emergence of immigration as a major political issue, for example—I examine current debates over the balance between liberty and security in wartime, whether the United States should be bound by international standards concerning the treatment of prisoners of war, and whether the president, Congress, or the courts has the right to determine the rights of those accused of crimes related to terrorism.

Other improvements in the text intended to make it more accessible to students include an increase in each chapter in the number of subheadings, expanded timelines at the opening of chapters, and a list of key terms in the chapter review pages, with definitions available to students on the companion website and in the Study Guide.

These changes, I believe, enhance the purpose of *Give Me Liberty!*: to offer students a clear, concise, and thematically enriched introduction to American history.

Americans have always had a divided attitude toward history. On the one hand, they tend to be remarkably future-oriented, dismissing events of even the recent past as "ancient history" and sometimes seeing history as a burden to be overcome, a prison from which to escape. On the other hand, like many other peoples, Americans have always looked to history for a sense of personal or group identity and of national cohesiveness. This is why so many Americans devote time and energy to tracing their family trees and why they visit historical museums and National Park Service historical sites in ever-increasing numbers. My hope is that this book will help to convince readers with all degrees of interest that history does matter to them.

The novelist and essayist James Baldwin once observed that history "does not refer merely, or even principally, to the past. On the contrary, the great force of history comes from the fact that we carry it within us, . . . [that] history is literally present in all that we do." As Baldwin recognized, the force of history is evident in our own world. Especially in a political democracy like the United States, whose government is designed to rest on the consent of informed citizens, knowledge of the past is essential—not only for those of us whose profession is the teaching and writing of history, but for everyone. History, to be sure, does not offer simple lessons or immediate answers to current questions. Knowing the history of immigration to the United States, and all of the tensions, turmoil, and aspirations associated with it, for example, does not tell us what current immigration policy ought to be. But without that knowledge, we have no way of understanding which approaches have worked and which have not—essential information for the formulation of future public policy.

History, it has been said, is what the present chooses to remember about the past. Rather than a fixed collection of facts, or a group of interpretations that cannot be challenged, our understanding of history is constantly changing. There is nothing unusual in the fact that each generation rewrites history to meet its own needs, or that scholars disagree among themselves on basic questions like the causes of the Civil War or the reasons for the Great Depression. Precisely because each generation asks different questions of the past, each generation formulates different answers. The past thirty years have witnessed a remarkable expansion of the scope of historical study. The experiences of groups neglected by earlier scholars, including women, African-Americans, working people, and others, have received unprecedented attention from historians. New subfields—social history, cultural history, and family history among them—have taken their place alongside traditional political and diplomatic history.

Give Me Liberty! draws on this voluminous historical literature to present an up-to-date and inclusive account of the American past, paying due attention to the experience of diverse groups of Americans while in no way neglecting the events and processes Americans have experienced in common. It devotes serious attention to political, social, cultural, and economic history, and to their interconnections. The narrative brings together major events and prominent leaders with the many groups of ordinary people who make up American society. *Give Me Liberty!* has a rich cast of characters, from Thomas Jefferson to campaigners for woman suffrage, from Franklin D. Roosevelt to former slaves seeking to breathe meaning into emancipation during and after the Civil War.

Aimed at an audience of undergraduate students with little or no detailed knowledge of American history, *Give Me Liberty!* guides readers through the complexities of the subject without overwhelming them with excessive detail. The unifying theme of freedom that runs through the text gives shape to the narrative and integrates the numerous strands that make up the American experience. This approach builds on that of my earlier book, *The Story of American Freedom* (1998), although *Give Me Liberty!* places events and personalities in the foreground and is more geared to the structure of the introductory survey course.

Freedom, and battles to define its meaning, has long been central to my own scholarship and undergraduate teaching, which focuses on the nineteenth century and especially the era of Civil War and Reconstruction (1850–1877). This was a time when the future of slavery tore the nation apart and emancipation produced a national debate over what rights the former slaves, and all Americans, should enjoy as free citizens. I have found that attention to clashing definitions of freedom and the struggles of different groups to achieve freedom as they understood it offers a way of making sense of the bitter battles and vast transformations of that pivotal era. I believe that the same is true for American history as a whole.

No idea is more fundamental to Americans' sense of themselves as individuals and as a nation than freedom. The central term in our political language, freedom—or liberty, with which it is almost always used interchangeably—is deeply embedded in the record of our history and the language of everyday life. The Declaration of Independence lists liberty among mankind's inalienable rights; the Constitution announces its purpose as securing liberty's blessings. The United States fought the Civil War to bring about a new birth of freedom, World War II for the Four Freedoms, and the Cold War to defend the Free World. Americans' love of liberty has been represented by liberty poles, liberty caps, and statues of liberty, and acted out by burning stamps and burning draft cards, by running away from slavery, and by demonstrating for the right to vote. "Every man in the street, white, black, red, or yellow," wrote the educator and statesman Ralph Bunche in 1940, "knows that this is 'the land of the free' . . . 'the cradle of liberty.'"

The very universality of the idea of freedom, however, can be misleading. Freedom is not a fixed, timeless category with a single unchanging definition. Indeed, the history of the United States is, in part, a story of debates, disagreements, and struggles over freedom. Crises like the American Revolution, the Civil War, and the Cold War have permanently transformed the idea of freedom. So too have demands by various groups of Americans to enjoy greater freedom. The meaning of freedom has been constructed not only in congressional debates and political treatises, but on plantations and picket lines, in parlors and even bedrooms.

Over the course of our history, American freedom has been both a reality and a mythic ideal—a living truth for millions of Americans, a cruel mockery for others. For some, freedom has been what some scholars call a "habit of the heart," an ideal so taken for granted that it is lived out but rarely analyzed. For others, freedom is not a birthright but a distant goal that has inspired great sacrifice.

Give Me Liberty! draws attention to three dimensions of freedom that have been critical in American history: (1) the *meanings* of freedom; (2) the *social conditions* that make freedom possible; and (3) the *boundaries* of freedom that determine who is entitled to enjoy freedom and who is not. All have changed over time.

In the era of the American Revolution, for example, freedom was primarily a set of rights enjoyed in public activity—the right of a community to be governed by laws to which its representatives had consented and of individuals to engage in religious worship without governmental interference. In the nineteenth century, freedom came to be closely identified with each person's opportunity to develop to the fullest his or her innate talents. In the twentieth, the "ability to choose," in both public and private life, became perhaps the dominant understanding of freedom. This development was encouraged by the explosive growth of the consumer marketplace (a development that receives considerable attention in *Give Me Liberty!*), which offered Americans an unprecedented array of goods with which to satisfy their needs and desires. During the 1960s, a crucial chapter in the history of American freedom, the idea of personal freedom was extended into virtually every realm, from attire and "lifestyle" to relations between the sexes. Thus, over time, more and more areas of life have been drawn into Americans' debates about the meaning of freedom.

A second important dimension of freedom focuses on the social conditions necessary to allow freedom to flourish. What kinds of economic institutions and relationships best encourage individual freedom? In the colonial era and for more than a century after independence, the answer centered on economic autonomy, enshrined in the glorification of the independent small producer—the farmer, skilled craftsman, or shopkeeper—who did not have to depend on another person for his livelihood. As the industrial economy matured, new conceptions of economic freedom came to the fore: "liberty of contract" in the Gilded Age, "industrial freedom" (a say in corporate decision-making) in the Progressive era, economic security during the New Deal, and, more recently, the ability to enjoy mass consumption within a market economy.

The boundaries of freedom, the third dimension of this theme, have inspired some of the most intense struggles in American history. Although founded on the premise that liberty is an entitlement of all humanity, the United States for much of its history deprived many of its own people of freedom. Non-whites have rarely enjoyed the same access to freedom as white Americans. The belief in equal opportunity as the birthright of all Americans has coexisted with persistent efforts to limit freedom by race, gender, class, and in other ways.

Less obvious, perhaps, is the fact that one person's freedom has frequently been linked to another's servitude. In the colonial era and nineteenth century, expanding freedom for many Americans rested on the lack of freedom—slavery, indentured servitude, the subordinate position of women—for others. By the same token, it has been through battles at the boundaries—the efforts of racial minorities, women, and others to secure greater freedom—that the meaning and experience of freedom have been deepened and the concept extended into new realms.

Time and again in American history, freedom has been transformed by the demands of excluded groups for inclusion. The idea of freedom as a universal birthright owes much both to abolitionists who sought to extend the blessings of liberty to blacks and to immigrant groups who insisted on full recognition as American citizens. The principle of equal protection of the law without regard to race, which became a central element of American freedom, arose from the antislavery struggle and Civil War and was reinvigorated by the civil rights revolution of the 1960s, which called itself the "freedom movement." The battle for the right of free speech by labor radicals and birth control advocates in the first part of the twentieth century helped to make civil liberties an essential element of freedom for all Americans.

While concentrating on events within the United States, *Give Me Liberty!* also, as indicated above, situates American history in the context of developments in other parts of the world. Many of the forces that shaped American history, including the international migration of peoples, the development of slavery, the spread of democracy, and the expansion of capitalism, were worldwide processes, not confined to the United States. Today, American ideas, culture, and economic and military power exert unprecedented influence throughout the world. But beginning with the earliest days of settlement, when European empires competed to colonize North America and enrich themselves from its trade, American history cannot be understood in isolation from its global setting.

Readers will find a number of recurring elements in *Give Me Liberty!*, intended to make the book accessible and to highlight the theme of freedom. The book is divided into six parts, each of which opens with a brief introduction and a portfolio of visual images of freedom taken from the chapters of that part. Each chapter begins with a specific historical moment or incident that illuminates some of the major themes that follow. Each contains two brief documentary excerpts called "Voices of Freedom" that illustrate how Americans at various times have understood the idea of freedom. Many of these excerpts are taken from the companion reader to *Give Me Liberty!*, also called *Voices of Freedom*, a documentary history of American freedom. (A Second Edition of that collection has also been prepared, which considerably increases the number and range of documents included.) All these documents, as well as a selection of documents included in the Appendix to the textbook, are what historians call "primary sources"—that is, they were written or spoken by men and women enmeshed in the events of the past, rather than by later historians. They therefore offer students the opportunity to encounter ideas about freedom in the actual words of participants in the drama of American history. Also included with every chapter is a brief, annotated Suggested Reading list. These lists are meant to direct students to the most important works of historical scholarship on that period.

Freedom is the oldest of clichés and the most modern of aspirations. At various times in our history, it has served as the rallying cry of the powerless and as a justification of the status quo. Freedom helps to bind our culture together and exposes the contradictions between what America claims to be and what it sometimes has been. American history is not a narrative of continual progress toward greater and greater freedom. As the abolitionist Thomas Wentworth Higginson noted after the Civil War, "revolutions may go backward." While freedom can be achieved, it may also be taken away. This happened, for example, when the equal rights granted to former slaves immediately after the Civil War were essentially nullified during the era of segregation. As was said in the eighteenth century, the price of freedom is eternal vigilance.

In the early twenty-first century, freedom continues to play a central role in our political and social life and thought. It is invoked by individuals and groups of all kinds, from critics of economic globalization to those who seek to secure American freedom at home and export it abroad. I hope that *Give Me Liberty!* will offer beginning students a clear account of the course of American history, and of its central theme, freedom, which today remains as varied, contentious, and ever-changing as America itself.

ACKNOWLEDGMENTS

All works of history are, to a considerable extent, collaborative books, in that every writer builds on the research and writing of previous scholars. This is especially true of a textbook that covers the entire American experience over more than five centuries. My greatest debt is to the innumerable historians on whose work I have drawn in preparing this volume. The Suggested Reading list at the end of each chapter offers only a brief introduction to the vast body of historical scholarship that has influenced and informed this book.

More specifically, however, I wish to thank the following scholars, who generously read portions of this work and offered valuable comments, criticisms, and suggestions:

For the First Edition:
   Valerie Adams, Embry-Riddle Aeronautical University
   Terry Alford, Northern Virginia Community College
   Tyler Anbinder, George Washington University
   Eric Arnesen, University of Illinois, Chicago
   Ira Berlin, University of Maryland
   Nikki Brown, Kent State University
   Jon Butler, Yale University
   Diane S. Clemens, University of California, Berkeley
   Paul G. E. Clemens, Rutgers University
   Jane Dailey, Johns Hopkins University
   Douglas Deal, State University of New York, Oswego
   Ricky Dobbs, Texas A&M University, Commerce
   Thomas Dublin, State University of New York, Binghamton
   Joel Franks, San Jose State University
   Kirsten Gardner, University of Texas at San Antonio
   Lawrence B. Glickman, University of South Carolina
   Colin Gordon, University of Iowa
   Sam Haynes, University of Texas at Arlington
   Rebecca Hill, Borough of Manhattan Community College
   Jesse Hingson, Manatee Community College
   Wallace Hutcheon, Northern Virginia Community College
   Kevin Kenny, Boston College
   Peter Kolchin, University of Delaware
   Bruce Laurie, University of Massachusetts, Amherst
   Daniel Letwin, Pennsylvania State University
   Peter Mancall, University of Southern California
   Louis Masur, City College, City University of New York
   Alan McPherson, Howard University
   Don Palm, Sacramento City College
   Larry Peterson, North Dakota State University
   John Recchiuti, Mount Union College
   Scott Sandage, Carnegie-Mellon University
   Bryant Simon, University of Georgia
   Brooks Simpson, Arizona State University
   Judith Stein, City College, City University of New York
   George Stevens, Dutchess Community College
   Thomas Sugrue, University of Pennsylvania
   Alan Taylor, University of California, Davis
   Daniel B. Thorp, Virginia Polytechnic Institute
   Helena Wall, Pomona College
   Jon Wiener, University of California, Irvine.

For the Second Edition:
   Marsha Ackermann, Eastern Michigan University
   Valerie Adams, Embry-Riddle Aeronautical University

Omar Ali, Towson University
Ellen Baker, Columbia University
Ruth Bloch, University of California, Los Angeles
Roger Bromert, Southern Oklahoma State University
Charlotte Brooks, University at Albany, State University of New York
Barbara Calluori, Montclair State University
Robert Cassanello, University of Central Florida
Thomas Clarkin, San Antonio College
Gerard Clock, Pace University
Ronald Dufour, Rhode Island College
Mike Green, Community College of Southern Nevada
Maurine Greenwald, University of Pittsburgh
Evan Haefeli, Columbia University
Sharon A. Roger Hepburn, Radford College
Tam Hoskisson, Northern Arizona University
David Hsiung, Juniata College
Jeanette Keith, Bloomsburg University of Pennsylvania
Daniel Kotzin, Kutztown University
Robert M. S. McDonald, U.S. Military Academy
Stephen L. McIntyre, Missouri State University
Cynthia Northrup, University of Texas at Arlington
Kathleen Banks Nutter, Stony Brook University, State University of
    New York
John Paden, Rappahannock Community College
Sarah Phillips, Columbia University
Charles K. Piehl, Minnesota State University, Mankato
Ann Planc, University of California, Santa Barbara
Charles Postel, California State University, Sacramento
John Recchiuti, Mount Union College
Rob Risko, Trinity Valley Community College, Athens
Wade Shaffer, West Texas A&M University
Silvana R. Siddali, Saint Louis University
Judith Stein, The City College of the City University of New York
George Stevens, Dutchess Community College
Matthew A. Sutton, Oakland University
Timothy Thurber, Virginia Commonwealth University
David Voelker, University of Wisconson—Green Bay
Peter Way, Bowling Green State University
Richard Weiner, Indiana University—Purdue University Fort Wayne
Barbara Welke, University of Minnesota

I am particularly grateful to my colleagues in the Columbia University
Department of History: Even Haefeli and Ellen Baker, who read and made
many suggestions for improvements in their respective areas of expertise
(colonial America, and the history of the West), and Sarah Phillips, who
offered advice on treating the history of the environment.

I am also deeply indebted to graduate students at Columbia University's
Department of History who helped with this project. James Delbourgo conducted research for the chapters on the colonial era. Beverly Gage did the
same for the twentieth century. Daniel Freund provided all-round research

assistance. Victoria Cain did a superb job of locating visual images. And many thanks to Valerie Adams and Thomas Clarkin for their good and untiring work on the end-of-chapter materials. I also want to thank my colleagues Elizabeth Blackmar and Alan Brinkley for offering advice and encouragement throughout the writing of this book.

At W. W. Norton & Company, Steve Forman was an ideal editor—patient, encouraging, always ready to offer sage advice, and quick to point out lapses in grammar and logic. His assistant, Rebecca Arata, also did extraordinarily valuable work on this project. Antonina Krass created a beautiful and unobtrusive book design. Debra Morton Hoyt is responsible for the splendid covers. Kim Yi was the center of gravity for the many pieces of this project. She, Chris Granville, and Marian Johnson skillfully guided the project as it moved from final manuscript to bound book. Steve Hoge did the same as *Give Me Liberty!* entered cyberspace.

Many students may have heard stories of how publishing companies alter the language and content of textbooks in an attempt to maximize sales and avoid alienating any potential reader. In this case, I can honestly say that W. W. Norton allowed me a free hand in writing the book and, apart from the usual editorial corrections, did not try to influence its content at all. For this I thank them, while I accept full responsibility for the interpretations presented and for any errors the book may contain. Since no book of this length can be entirely free of mistakes, I welcome readers to send me corrections at ef17@columbia.edu.

My greatest debt, as always, is to my family—my wife, Lynn Garafola, for her good-natured support while I was preoccupied by a project that consumed more than its fair share of my time and energy, and my daughter, Daria, who while a ninth and tenth grader read every chapter as it was written and offered invaluable suggestions about improving the book's clarity, logic, and grammar.

Eric Foner
New York City
July 2007

TO THE STUDENT, FROM THE PUBLISHER

Eric Foner's *Give Me Liberty! An American History*, Second Edition, provides you with all of the tools you need to succeed in your American history course.

A CONCISE, COHESIVE NARRATIVE

The book itself covers the key events in American history in a concise, clear narrative that is not clogged with dense detail. The narrative is cohesive throughout because it was written entirely by a single author and is driven by a strong theme. That theme—freedom and the continuing efforts of Americans to define it and achieve it—goes to the core of American history. As important today as it has been throughout our history, the theme of American freedom gives you an immediate point of contact with the history you will read in this text. The author, Eric Foner, has earned widespread acclaim for his books on the Civil War and Reconstruction periods and beyond. He has written an authoritative narrative that you can rely on. His narrative also provides you with a fine introduction to the field of history as it is broadly written and taught today. Whether you are a prospective history major or are taking the survey as your only history course, Foner's *Give Me Liberty!* suits your needs.

HELPFUL FEATURES

Give Me Liberty! includes the following features aimed at helping you master the material it presents:

Chapter outlines and chapter chronologies appear in each chapter-opening sequence.

Focus Questions are listed in the chapter openings and then repeated individually above the relevant text in the running heads of right-hand pages. These questions are meant to remind you, at a glance, of the larger issues at stake in the discussion on the page.

Chapter Review page: Each chapter ends with a review page that includes a list of key terms with page references, a series of review questions, and a review table of major events or developments discussed in the chapter.

Voices of Freedom Boxes: Each chapter of the text includes excerpts from two paired primary sources that address the theme of American freedom. (See the Contents for a list of these Voices of Freedom boxes.) Eric Foner chose these excerpts to illustrate key ideas and arguments about American freedom. He has written headnotes and questions for each Voices of Freedom feature.

Part Openers: The book is divided into six chronological Parts, and each one opens with a brief but substantive overview of the major events and developments covered in the section. Don't skip these— they are worth reading!

Suggested Readings: These annotated end-of-chapter lists include sources for the chapter discussions and readings to get you started on projects and research papers.

Appendix with Documents and Tables: The Appendix to *Give Me Liberty* includes a small collection of primary documents ranging from the Declaration of Independence and the Constitution to Frederick Douglass's speech, "What, to the slave, Is the Fourth of July?," the Seneca Falls Declaration and Resolutions, the Omaha Platform of the Populist Party, Martin Luther King Jr.'s "I Have A Dream" speech, and Ronald Reagan's first inaugural address. The tables give you accurate data on broad social and political developments in American history. For a full listing of these documents and the Appendix Tables, see the Contents.

THE WEBSITE

ORGANIZE, LEARN, AND CONNECT WITH STUDYSPACE

wwnorton.com/studyspace
Free and open, the StudySpace website helps you organize, learn, and connect review materials, textbook coverage, and online research. Whether accessing freedom-oriented primary-source documents, reviewing their reading, or interactively testing your grasp of history and geography, you can access a full range of multi-media resources organized within a coherent, assignment-driven study plan.

ORGANIZE

Chapter outlines help you navigate the text as you read.

Eric Foner's brief *Questioning Freedom* podcasts provide a thematic context for every chapter. These interview segments are available in both audio and video streaming formats and each question and answer is transcribed and printer-friendly.

LEARN

Interactive maps allow you to explore the geography, historical context, and demographics of specific regions. These iMaps can also be printed without labels for offline re-labeling exercises.

Interactive Chrono-Sequencers challenge students' understanding of the flow of history. These interactive chapter chronologies allow you to reassemble sequences of events and help reinforce your understanding.

Flashcards help you recall and master important events and terms.

CONNECT

Sources of Freedom primary source documents amplify chapter themes. Ideal for brief research projects, the sources are organized by topic, complete with introductions, head notes, and media analysis worksheets, which can be submitted to the instructor via email.

***Give Me Liberty!* Soundtrack includes many lasting and controversial freedom songs.** This unique collection of folk and popular songs is sure to spark discussion and provide provocative classroom examples.

PRINT SUPPLEMENTS

Voices of Freedom: A Documentary History
Edited by Eric Foner, this companion reader to *Give Me Liberty!* includes hundreds of primary-source documents touching upon the theme of American freedom. In chapters corresponding to the text chapters, the freedom theme is fleshed out in the words of well-known historical figures and ordinary Americans. Each document is accompanied by an introductory headnote and study questions.

Study Guide in two volumes
Prepared by Daniel Letwin (Pennsylvania State University), John Recchiuti (Mount Union College) and Thomas Clarkin (San Antonio College), the *Study Guide* accompanying *Give Me Liberty!* includes chapter objectives, detailed chapter outlines, chronologies, many study questions in multiple-choice, true/false, and essay form, definitions of the Key Terms in the end-of-chapter review page lists, and suggested readings, film, video, and Web resources.

For more information on Eric Foner's *Give Me Liberty! An American History*, please visit us at www.wwnorton.com/foner.

Part 1

AMERICAN COLONIES TO 1763

he colonial period of American history was a time of enormous change, as the people of four continents—North America, South America, Europe, and Africa—were suddenly and unexpectedly thrown into contact with one another. The period also initiated a new era in the history of freedom. It was not, however, a desire for freedom that drove early European explorations of North and South America. Contact between Europe and the Americas began as a byproduct of the quest for a sea route for trade with Asia. But it quickly became a contest for power between rival empires, who moved to conquer, colonize, and exploit the resources of the New World.

At the time of European contact, the Western Hemisphere was home to tens of millions of people. Within the present border of the United States there existed Indian societies based on agriculture, hunting, or fishing, with their own languages, religious practices, and forms of government. All experienced wrenching changes after Europeans arrived, including incorporation into the world market and epidemics of disease that devastated many native groups.

The colonies that eventually came to form the United States originated in very different ways. Virginia, the first permanent colony to be established, was created by a private company that sought to earn profits through exploration for gold and the development of transatlantic trade. Individual proprietors—well-connected Englishmen given large grants of land by the king—established Maryland and Pennsylvania. New York, which had been founded by the Dutch, came into British hands as the result of a war. Religious groups seeking escape from persecution in England and hoping to establish communities rooted in their understanding of the principles of the Bible founded colonies in New England.

In the seventeenth century, all the British colonies experienced wrenching social conflicts as groups within them battled for control. Relations with Indians remained tense and sometimes violent. Religious and political divisions in England, which experienced a civil war in the 1640s and the ouster of the king in 1688, reverberated in the colonies. So did wars between European powers, which spilled over into North America. Nonetheless, after difficult beginnings, Britain's mainland colonies experienced years of remarkable growth in population and economic activity. By the eighteenth century, the non-Indian population of Britain's North American colonies had far outstripped that of the colonies of France and Spain.

In every colony in British America, well-to-do landowners and merchants dominated economic and political life. Nonetheless, emigration to the colonies offered numerous settlers opportunities they had not enjoyed at home, including access to land, the freedom to worship as they pleased, and the right to vote. Every British colony had an elected assembly that shared power with a governor, who was usually appointed from London. Even this limited degree of self-government contrasted sharply with the lack of representative institutions in the Spanish and French empires. All these circumstances drew thousands of English emigrants to North America in the seventeenth century, and thousands more from Ireland, Scotland, and the European continent in the eighteenth century.

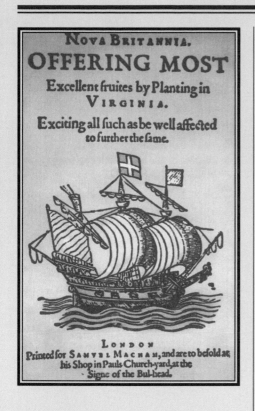

Nova Britannia,
OFFERING MOST
Excellent fruites by Planting in
VIRGINIA.

Exciting all such as be well affected
to further the same.

LONDON
Printed for SAMVEL MACHAM, and are to be sold at
his Shop in Pauls Church-yard, at the
Signe of the Bul-head.

Yet the conditions that allowed colonists to enjoy such freedoms were made possible by lack of freedom for millions of others. For the native inhabitants of the Western Hemisphere, European colonization brought the spread of devastating epidemics and either dispossession from the land or forced labor for the colonizers. Millions of Africans were uprooted from their homes and transported to the New World to labor on the plantations of Brazil, the Caribbean, and England's North American colonies. Even among European immigrants, the majority arrived not as completely free individuals but as indentured servants, who owed a prearranged number of years of labor to those who paid their passage.

In colonial America, many modern ideas of freedom did not exist, or existed in very different forms than today. Equality before the law was unknown—women, non-whites, and propertyless men enjoyed far fewer rights than landowning white male citizens. Economic freedom, today widely identified with participation in an unregulated market, meant independence—owning land or a shop and not relying on another person for a livelihood. Most colonies had official churches, and even many colonists who sought religious liberty for themselves refused to extend it to others. Speaking or writing critically of public authorities could land a person in jail.

Nonetheless, ideas about freedom played a major role in justifying European colonization. The Spanish and French claimed to be liberating Native Americans by bringing them advanced civilization and Roman Catholicism. England insisted that true freedom for Indians meant adopting English ways, including Protestantism. Moreover, the expansion of England's empire occurred at a time when freedom came to be seen as the defining characteristic of the English nation. Slavery existed in every New World colony. In many, it became the basis of economic life. Yet most Britons, including colonists, prided themselves on enjoying "British liberty," a common set of rights including protection from the arbitrary exercise of governmental power.

Thus, freedom and lack of freedom expanded together in the colonies of British North America that would eventually form the United States.

CHAPTER 1

Their greene corne.

Corne newly sprong.

A New World

The Village of Secoton, by John White, an English artist who spent a year on the Outer Banks of North Carolina in 1585–1586 as part of an expedition sponsored by Sir Walter Raleigh. A central street links houses surrounded by fields of corn. In the lower part, dancing Indians take part in a religious ceremony.

FOCUS QUESTIONS

- What were the major patterns of Native American life in North America before Europeans arrived?

- How did Indian and European ideas of freedom differ on the eve of contact?

- What impelled European explorers to look west across the Atlantic?

- What happened when the peoples of the Americas came in contact with Europeans?

- What were the chief features of the Spanish empire in America?

- What were the chief features of the French and Dutch empires in North America?

"The discovery of America," the British writer Adam Smith announced in his celebrated work *The Wealth of Nations* (1776), was one of "the two greatest and most important events recorded in the history of mankind." Historians no longer use the word "discovery" to describe the European exploration, conquest, and colonization of a hemisphere already home to millions of people. But there can be no doubt that when Christopher Columbus made landfall in the West Indian islands in 1492, he set in motion some of the most pivotal developments in human history. Immense changes soon followed in both the Old and New Worlds; the consequences of these changes are still with us today.

The peoples of the American continents and Europe, previously unaware of each other's existence, were thrown into continuous interaction. Crops new to each hemisphere crossed the Atlantic, reshaping diets and transforming the natural environment. Because of their long isolation, the inhabitants of North and South America had developed no immunity to the germs that also accompanied the colonizers. As a result, they suffered a series of devastating epidemics, the greatest population catastrophe in human history. Within a decade of Columbus's voyage, a fourth continent—Africa—found itself drawn into the new Atlantic system of trade and population movement. In Africa, Europeans found a supply of unfree labor that enabled them to exploit the fertile lands of the Western Hemisphere. Indeed, of approximately 10 million men, women, and children who crossed from the Old World to the New between 1492 and 1820, the vast majority, about 7.7 million, were African slaves.

From the vantage point of 1776, the year the United States declared itself an independent nation, it seemed to Adam Smith that the "discovery" of America had produced both great "benefits" and great "misfortunes." To the nations of western Europe, the development of American colonies brought an era of "splendor and glory." The emergence of the Atlantic as the world's major avenue for trade and population movement, Smith noted, enabled millions of Europeans to increase the "enjoyments" of life. To the "natives" of the Americas, however, Smith went on, the years since 1492 had been ones of "dreadful misfortunes" and "every sort of injustice." And for millions of Africans, the settlement of America meant a descent into the abyss of slavery.

Long before Columbus sailed, Europeans had dreamed of a land of abundance, riches, and ease beyond the western horizon. Once the "discovery" of this New World had taken place, they invented an America of the imagination, projecting onto it their hopes for a better life. Here, many believed, would arise unparalleled opportunities for riches, or at least liberation from poverty. Europeans envisioned America as a religious refuge, a society of equals, a source of power and glory. They searched the New World for golden cities and fountains of eternal youth.

Some sought to establish ideal communities based on the lives of the early Christian saints or other blueprints for social justice.

Some of these dreams of riches and opportunity would indeed be fulfilled. To many European settlers, America offered a far greater chance to own land and worship as they pleased than existed in Europe, with its rigid, unequal social order and official churches. Yet the conditions that enabled millions of settlers to take control of their own destinies were made possible by the debasement of millions of others. The New World became the site of many forms of unfree labor, including indentured

A 1544 engraving of the Western Hemisphere by Sebastian Cabot, the son of the Italian-born explorer John Cabot and, like his father, an accomplished mariner. In the early sixteenth century, sailing for England and then Spain, Sebastian Cabot led several expeditions to the New World. The ships depicted are caravels, the first European vessels capable of long-distance travel, and the map also shows stylized scenes of Native Americans, including a battle with Spanish conquistadores.

servitude, forced labor by Indians, and one of the most brutal and unjust systems ever devised by man, plantation slavery. The conquest and settlement of the Western Hemisphere opened new chapters in the long histories of both freedom and slavery.

There was a vast human diversity among the peoples thrown into contact with one another in the New World. Exploration and settlement took place in an era of almost constant warfare among European nations, each racked by internal religious, political, and regional conflicts. Native Americans and Africans consisted of numerous groups with their own languages and cultures. They were as likely to fight one another as to unite against the European newcomers. All these peoples were changed by their integration into the new Atlantic economy. The complex interactions of Europeans, American Indians, and Africans would shape American history during the colonial era.

THE FIRST AMERICANS

THE SETTLING OF AMERICA

The residents of the Americas were no more a single group than Europeans or Africans. They spoke hundreds of different languages and lived in numerous kinds of societies. Most, however, were descended from bands of hunters and fishers who had crossed the Bering Strait via a land bridge at various times between 15,000 and 60,000 years ago—the exact dates are hotly debated by archaeologists. Others may have arrived by sea from Asia or Pacific islands. Around 14,000 years ago, when glaciers melted at the end of the Ice Age, the land link became submerged under water, permanently separating the Western Hemisphere from Asia.

History in North and South America did not begin with the coming of Europeans. The New World was new to Europeans but an ancient homeland to those who already lived there. The hemisphere had witnessed many changes during its human history. First, the early inhabitants and their descendants spread across the two continents, reaching the tip of South America perhaps 11,000 years ago. As the climate warmed, they faced a food crisis as the immense animals they had hunted, including wooly mammoths and giant bison, became extinct. Around 9,000 years ago, at the same time that agriculture was being invented in the Near East, it also emerged in modern-day Mexico and the Andes, and then spread to other parts of the Americas, making settled civilizations possible. Throughout the hemisphere, maize (corn), squash, and beans formed the basis of agriculture. The absence of livestock in the Western Hemisphere, however, limited farming by preventing the plowing of fields and the application of natural fertilizer.

THE FIRST AMERICANS

A map illustrating the probable routes by which the first Americans settled the Western Hemisphere at various times between 15,000 and 60,000 years ago.

INDIAN SOCIETIES OF THE AMERICAS

North and South America were hardly an empty wilderness when Europeans arrived. The hemisphere contained cities, roads, irrigation systems, extensive trade networks, and large structures such as the pyramid-temples whose beauty still inspires wonder. With a population close to 250,000,

Map of the Aztec capital Tenochtitlán and the Gulf of Mexico, probably produced by a Spanish conquistador and published in 1524 in an edition of the letters of Hernán Cortés. The map shows the city's complex system of canals, bridges, and dams, with the Great Temple at the center. Gardens and a zoo are also visible.

Tenochtitlán, the capital of the Aztec empire in what is now Mexico, was one of the world's largest cities. Its great temple, splendid royal palace, and central market comparable to that of European capitals made the city seem "like an enchanted vision," according to one of the first Europeans to encounter it. Further south lay the Inca kingdom, centered in modern-day Peru. Its population of perhaps 12 million was linked by a complex system of roads and bridges that extended 2,000 miles along the Andes mountain chain.

When Europeans arrived, a wide variety of native peoples lived within the present borders of the United States. Indian civilizations in North America had not developed the scale, grandeur, or centralized organization of the Aztec and Inca to their south. North American Indians lacked the technologies Europeans had mastered, such as metal tools and machines, gunpowder, and the scientific knowledge necessary for long-distance navigation. No society north of Mexico had achieved literacy (although some made maps on bark and animal hides). They also lacked wheeled vehicles, since they had no domestic animals like horses or oxen to pull them. Their "backwardness" became a central justification for European conquest. But, over time, Indian societies had perfected techniques of farming, hunting, and fishing, developed structures of political power and religious belief, and engaged in far-reaching networks of trade and communication.

MOUND BUILDERS OF THE MISSISSIPPI VALLEY

Remarkable physical remains still exist from some of the early civilizations in North America. Around 3,500 years ago, before Egyptians built the pyramids, Native Americans constructed a large community centered on a series of giant semicircular mounds on a bluff overlooking the Mississippi River in present-day Louisiana. Known today as Poverty Point, it was a commercial and governmental center whose residents established trade routes throughout the Mississippi and Ohio River valleys. Archaeologists have found there copper from present-day Minnesota and Canada, and flint mined in Indiana.

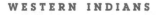

A modern aerial view of Poverty Point, where thousands of years ago early Americans built a large community centered on giant semicircular mounds.

Over a thousand years before Columbus sailed, Indians of the Ohio River valley, called "mound builders" by eighteenth-century settlers who encountered the large earthen burial mounds they created, had traded across half the continent. After their decline another culture flourished in the Mississippi River valley, centered on the city of Cahokia near present-day St. Louis, a fortified community with between 10,000 and 30,000 inhabitants in the year 1200. Its residents, too, built giant mounds, the largest of which stood 100 feet high, topped by a temple. Little is known of Cahokia's political and economic structure. But it stood as the largest settled community in what is now the United States until surpassed in population by New York and Philadelphia around 1800.

WESTERN INDIANS

In the arid northeastern area of present-day Arizona, the Hopi and Zuni and their ancestors engaged in settled village life for over 3,000 years. During the peak of the region's culture, between the years 900 and 1200, these peoples built great planned towns with large multiple-family dwellings in local canyons, constructed dams and canals to gather and distribute water, and conducted trade with groups as far away as central Mexico and the Mississippi valley. The largest of their structures, Pueblo Bonita, in Chaco Canyon, New Mexico, stood five stories high and had over 600 rooms. Not until the 1880s was a dwelling of comparable size constructed in the United States.

After the decline of these communities, probably because of drought, survivors moved to the south and east, where they established villages and perfected the techniques of desert farming, complete with irrigation systems to provide water for crops of corn, beans, and cotton. These were the people Spanish explorers called the Pueblo Indians (because they lived in small villages, or *pueblos*) when the Spanish first encountered them in the sixteenth century.

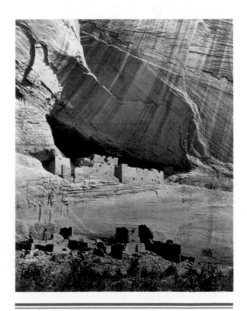

Cliff dwellings in Cañon de Chelly, in the area of modern-day Arizona, built sometime between 300 and 1300 and photographed in 1873.

Indian Conjuror, *another drawing by the artist John White, shows a religious figure in a dancing posture.*

On the Pacific coast, another densely populated region, hundreds of distinct groups resided in independent villages and lived primarily by fishing, hunting sea mammals, and gathering wild plants and nuts. As many as 25 million salmon swam up the Columbia River each year, providing Indians with abundant food. On the Great Plains, with its herds of buffalo—descendants of the prehistoric giant bison—many Indians were hunters (who tracked animals on foot before the arrival of horses with the Spanish), but others lived in agricultural communities.

INDIANS OF EASTERN NORTH AMERICA

In eastern North America, hundreds of tribes inhabited towns and villages scattered from the Gulf of Mexico to present-day Canada. They lived on corn, squash, and beans, supplemented by fishing and hunting deer, turkeys, and other animals. Indian trade routes crisscrossed the eastern part of the continent. Tribes frequently warred with one another to obtain goods, seize captives, or take revenge for the killing of relatives. They conducted diplomacy and made peace. Little in the way of centralized authority existed until, in the fifteenth century, various leagues or confederations emerged in an effort to bring order to local regions. In the Southeast, the Choctaw, Cherokee, and Chickasaw each united dozens of towns in loose alliances. In present-day New York and Pennsylvania, five Iroquois peoples—the Mohawk, Oneida, Cayuga, Seneca, and Onondaga—formed a Great League of Peace, bringing a period of stability to the area. Each year a Great Council, with representatives from the five groupings, met to coordinate behavior toward outsiders.

The most striking feature of Native American society at the time Europeans arrived was its sheer diversity. Each group had its own political system and set of religious beliefs, and North America was home to literally hundreds of mutually unintelligible languages. Indians had no sense of "America" as a continent or hemisphere. They did not think of themselves as a single unified people, an idea invented by Europeans and only many years later adopted by Indians themselves. Indian identity centered on the immediate social group—a tribe, village, chiefdom, or confederacy. When Europeans first arrived, many Indians saw them as simply one group among many. Their first thought was how to use the newcomers to enhance their standing in relation to other native peoples, rather than to unite against them. The sharp dichotomy between Indians and "white" persons did not emerge until later in the colonial era.

NATIVE AMERICAN RELIGION

Nonetheless, the diverse Indian societies of North America did share certain common characteristics. Their lives were steeped in religious ceremonies often directly related to farming and hunting. Spiritual power, they believed, suffused the world, and sacred spirits could be found in all kinds of living and inanimate things—animals, plants, trees, water, and wind. Through religious ceremonies, they aimed to harness the aid of powerful supernatural forces to serve the interests of man. In some tribes, hunters performed rituals to placate the spirits of animals they had killed. Other religious ceremonies sought to engage the spiritual power of nature to

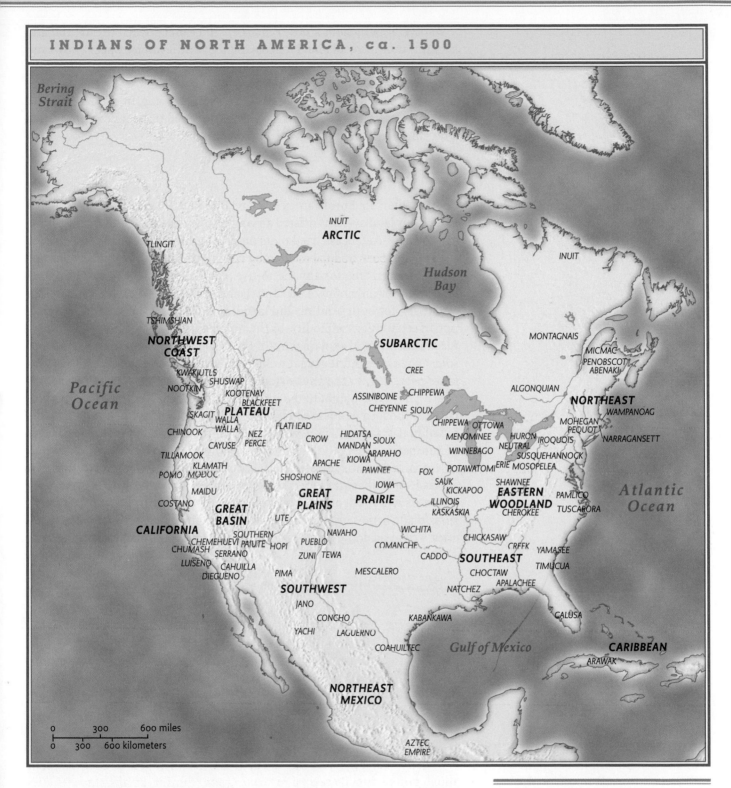

INDIANS OF NORTH AMERICA, ca. 1500

secure abundant crops or fend off evil spirits. Indian villages also held elaborate religious rites, participation in which helped to define the boundaries of community membership. In all Indian societies, those who seemed to possess special abilities to invoke supernatural powers—shamans, medicine men, and other religious leaders—held positions of respect and authority.

The native population of North America at the time of first contact with Europeans consisted of numerous tribes with their own languages, religious beliefs, and economic and social structures.

Indian religion did not pose a sharp distinction between the natural and supernatural, or secular and religious activities. In some respects, however, Indian religion was not that different from popular spiritual beliefs in Europe. Most Indians held that a single Creator stood atop the spiritual hierarchy. Nonetheless, nearly all Europeans arriving in the New World quickly concluded that Indians were in dire need of being converted to a true, Christian faith.

LAND AND PROPERTY

Equally alien in European eyes were Indian attitudes toward property. Numerous land systems existed among Native Americans. Generally, however, village leaders assigned plots of land to individual families to use for a season or more, and tribes claimed specific areas for hunting. Unclaimed land remained free for anyone to use. Families "owned" the right to use land, but they did not own the land itself. Indians saw land, the basis of economic life for both hunting and farming societies, as a common resource, not an economic commodity. In the nineteenth century, the Indian leader Black Hawk would explain why, in his view, land could not be bought and sold: "The Great Spirit gave it to his children to live upon, and cultivate as far as necessary for their subsistence; and so long as they occupy and cultivate it, they have a right to the soil." Few if any Indian societies were familiar with the idea of a fenced-off piece of land belonging forever to a single individual or family. There was no market in real estate before the coming of Europeans.

Nor were Indians devoted to the accumulation of wealth and material goods. Especially east of the Mississippi River, where villages moved every few years when soil or game became depleted, acquiring numerous possessions made little sense. However, status certainly mattered in Indian societies. Tribal leaders tended to come from a small number of families, and

A Catawba map illustrates the differences between Indian and European conceptions of landed property. The map depicts not possession of a specific territory, but trade and diplomatic connections between various native groups and with the colony of Virginia, represented by the rectangle on the lower right.

chiefs lived more splendidly than average members of society. But their reputation often rested on their willingness to share goods with others rather than hoarding them for themselves.

A few Indian societies had rigid social distinctions. Among the Natchez, descendants of the mound-building Mississippian culture, a chief, or "Great Sun," occupied the top of the social order, with nobles, or "lesser suns," below him, and below them, the common people. In general, however, wealth mattered far less in Indian society than in European society at the time. Generosity was among the most valued social qualities, and gift giving was essential to Indian society. Trade, for example, meant more than a commercial transaction—it was accompanied by elaborate ceremonies of gift exchange. A central part of Indian economies, gift giving bound different groups in webs of mutual obligation. Although Indians had no experience of the wealth enjoyed at the top of European society, under normal circumstances no one in Indian societies went hungry or experienced the extreme inequalities of Europe. "There are no beggars among them," reported the English colonial leader Roger Williams of New England's Indians.

GENDER RELATIONS

The system of gender relations in most Indian societies also differed markedly from that of Europe. Membership in a family defined women's lives, but they openly engaged in premarital sexual relations and could even choose to divorce their husbands. Most, although not all, Indian societies were matrilineal—that is, centered on clans or kinship groups in which children became members of the mother's family, not the father's. Tribal leaders were almost always men, but women played an important part in certain religious ceremonies, and female elders often helped to

Indians fishing, in a 1585 drawing by John White. The canoe is filled with fish, while two men harpoon others in the background. Among the wildlife illustrated are hammerhead sharks and catfish.

select male village leaders and took part in tribal meetings. Under English law, a married man controlled the family's property and a wife had no independent legal identity. In contrast, Indian women owned dwellings and tools, and a husband generally moved to live with the family of his wife. In Indian societies, men contributed to the community's well-being and demonstrated their masculinity by success in hunting or, in the Pacific Northwest, by catching fish with nets and harpoons. Because men were frequently away on the hunt, women took responsibility not only for household duties but for most agricultural work as well. Among the Pueblo of the Southwest, however, where there was less hunting than in the East, men were the primary cultivators.

EUROPEAN VIEWS OF THE INDIANS

Europeans tended to view Indians in extreme terms. They were regarded either as "noble savages," gentle, friendly, and superior in some ways to Europeans, or as uncivilized and brutal savages. Giovanni da Verrazano, a Florentine navigator who sailed up and down the east coast of North America in 1524, described Indians he encountered as "beautiful of stature and build." (For their part, many Indians, whose diet was probably more nutritious than that of most Europeans, initially found the newcomers weak and ugly.)

Over time, however, negative images of Indians came to overshadow positive ones. Early European descriptions of North American Indians as barbaric centered on three areas—religion, land use, and gender relations. Whatever their country of origin, European newcomers concluded that Indians lacked genuine religion, or in fact worshiped the devil. Their shamans and herb healers were called "witch doctors," their numerous ceremonies and rituals at best a form of superstition, their belief in a world alive with spiritual power a worship of "false gods." Christianity presented no obstacle to the commercial use of the land, and indeed in some ways encouraged it, since true religion was thought to promote the progress of civilization. Whereas the Indians saw nature as a world of spirits and souls, the Europeans viewed it as a collection of potential commodities, a source of economic opportunity.

Europeans invoked the Indians' distinctive pattern of land use and ideas about property to answer the awkward question raised by a British minister at an early stage of England's colonization: "By what right or warrant can we enter into the land of these Savages, take away their rightful inheritance from them, and plant ourselves in their places?" While the Spanish claimed title to land in America by right of conquest and papal authority, the English, French, and Dutch came to rely on the idea that Indians had not actually "used" the land and thus had no claim to it. Despite the Indians' highly developed agriculture and well-established towns, Europeans frequently described them as nomads without settled communities. The land was thus deemed to be a vacant wilderness ready to be claimed by newcomers who would cultivate and improve it. European settlers believed that mixing one's labor with the earth, which Indians supposedly had failed to do, gave one title to the soil.

In the Indians' sexual division of labor and matrilineal family structures, Europeans saw weak men and mistreated women. Hunting and fishing, the

A seventeenth century engraving by a French Jesuit priest illustrates many Europeans' view of Indian religion. A demon hovers over an Iroquois longhouse, suggesting that Indians worship the devil.

primary occupations of Indian men, were considered leisure activities in much of Europe, not "real" work. Because Indian women worked in the fields, Europeans often described them as lacking freedom. They were "not much better than slaves," in the words of one English commentator. Europeans considered Indian men "unmanly"—too weak to exercise authority within their families and restrain their wives' open sexuality, and so lazy that they forced their wives to do most of the productive labor. Throughout North America, Europeans promoted the ideas that women should confine themselves to household work and that men ought to exercise greater authority within their families. Europeans insisted that by subduing the Indians, they were actually bringing them freedom—the freedom of true religion, private property, and the liberation of both men and women from uncivilized and unchristian gender roles.

Indian women planting crops while men break the sod. An engraving by Theodor de Bry, based on a painting by Jacques Le Moyne de Morgues. Morgues was part of an expedition of French Huguenots to Florida in 1564; he escaped when the Spanish destroyed the outpost in the following year.

INDIAN FREEDOM, EUROPEAN FREEDOM

INDIAN FREEDOM

And what of liberty as the native inhabitants of the New World understood it? Many Europeans saw Indians as embodying freedom. The Iroquois, wrote one colonial official, held "such absolute notions of liberty that they allow of no kind of superiority of one over another, and banish all servitude from their territories." But most colonizers quickly concluded that the notion of "freedom" was alien to Indian societies. Early English and French dictionaries of Indian languages contained no entry for "freedom" or *liberté*. Nor, wrote one early trader, did Indians have "words to express despotic power, arbitrary kings, oppressed or obedient subjects."

Indeed, Europeans considered Indians barbaric in part because they did not appear to live under established governments or fixed laws, and had no respect for authority. "They are born, live, and die in a liberty without restraint," wrote one religious missionary. In a sense, they were *too* free, lacking the order and discipline that Europeans considered the hallmarks of civilization. Even slavery, wrote Richard Eden, an English writer of the mid-sixteenth century, was preferable to the Indians' condition before European contact, which he described as "rather a horrible licentiousness than a liberty." When Giovanni da Verrazano described the Indians as living in "absolute freedom," he did not intend this as a compliment.

The familiar modern understanding of freedom as personal independence, often based on ownership of private property, had little meaning in most Indian societies. But Indians certainly had their own ideas of freedom. While the buying and selling of slaves was unknown, small-scale slavery existed in some Indian societies. So too did the idea of personal liberty as the opposite of being held as a slave. Indians would bitterly resent the efforts of some Europeans to reduce them to slavery.

Although individuals were expected to think for themselves and did not always have to go along with collective decision making, Indian men and women judged one another according to their ability to live up to widely understood ideas of appropriate behavior. Far more important than individual autonomy were kinship ties, the ability to follow one's spiritual values, and the well-being and security of one's community. In Indian culture, group autonomy and self-determination, and the mutual obligations that came with a sense of belonging and connectedness, took precedence over individual freedom. Ironically, the coming of Europeans, armed with their own language of liberty, would make freedom a preoccupation of American Indians, as part and parcel of the very process by which they were reduced to dependence on the colonizers.

CHRISTIAN LIBERTY

On the eve of colonization, Europeans held numerous ideas of freedom. Some were as old as the city-states of ancient Greece, others arose during the political struggles of the early modern era. Some laid the foundations for modern conceptions of freedom, others are quite unfamiliar today. Freedom was not a single idea but a collection of distinct rights and privileges, many enjoyed only by a small portion of the population.

One conception common throughout Europe understood freedom less as a political or social status than as a moral or spiritual condition. Freedom meant abandoning the life of sin to embrace the teachings of Christ. "Where the Spirit of the Lord is," declares the New Testament, "there is liberty." In this definition, servitude and freedom were mutually reinforcing, not contradictory states, since those who accepted the teachings of Christ simultaneously became "free from sin" and "servants to God."

"Christian liberty" had no connection to later ideas of religious toleration, a notion that scarcely existed anywhere on the eve of colonization. Every nation in Europe had an established church that decreed what forms of religious worship and belief were acceptable. Dissenters faced persecution by the state as well as condemnation by church authorities. Religious uniformity was thought to be essential to public order; the modern idea that a person's religious beliefs and practices are a matter of private choice, not legal obligation, was almost unknown. The religious wars that racked Europe in the sixteenth and seventeenth centuries centered on which religion would predominate in a kingdom or region, not the right of individuals to choose which church in which to worship.

FREEDOM AND AUTHORITY

In its secular form, the equation of liberty with obedience to a higher authority suggested that freedom meant not anarchy but obedience to law. Aristotle had described the law as liberty's "salvation," not its enemy. The identification of freedom with the rule of law did not, however, mean that all subjects of the crown enjoyed the same degree of freedom. Early modern European societies were extremely hierarchical, with marked gradations of social status ranging from the king and hereditary aristocracy down to the urban and rural poor. Inequality was built into virtually every social relationship. The king claimed to rule by the authority of God. Persons of high rank demanded deference from those below them. Less than 5 percent of the population monopolized English economic wealth and political power.

Within families, men exercised authority over their wives and children. According to the widespread legal doctrine known as "coverture," when a woman married she surrendered her legal identity, which became "covered" by that of her husband. She could not own property or sign contracts in her own name, control her wages if she worked, write a separate will, or, except in the rarest of circumstances, go to court seeking a divorce. The husband conducted business and testified in court for the entire family. He had the exclusive right to his wife's "company," including domestic labor and sexual relations.

Everywhere in Europe, family life depended on man's dominance and woman's submission. Indeed, political writers of the sixteenth century explicitly compared the king's authority over his subjects with the husband's over his family. Both were ordained by God. To justify this argument, they referred to a passage in the New Testament: "As the man is the head of the woman, so is Christ the head of the Church." Neither kind of authority could be challenged without threatening the fabric of social order.

LIBERTY AND LIBERTIES

In this hierarchical society, liberty came from knowing one's social place and fulfilling the duties appropriate to one's rank. Most men lacked the freedom that came with economic independence. Property qualifications and other restrictions limited the electorate to a minuscule part of the adult male population. The law required strict obedience of employees, and breaches of labor contracts carried criminal penalties.

European ideas of freedom still bore the imprint of the Middle Ages, when "liberties" meant formal, specific privileges such as self-government, exemption from taxation, or the right to practice a particular trade, granted to individuals or groups by contract, royal decree, or purchase. One legal dictionary defined a liberty as "a privilege . . . by which men may enjoy some benefit beyond the ordinary subject." Only those who enjoyed the "freedom of the city," for example, could engage in certain economic activities. Numerous modern civil liberties did not exist. The law decreed acceptable forms of religious worship. The government regularly suppressed publications it did not like, and criticism of authority could lead to imprisonment. In England, members of the House of Commons enjoyed freedom of speech during parliamentary sessions, but the right did not extend to ordinary citizens. Personal independence was reserved for a small part of the population, and this was one reason why authorities found "masterless men"—those without regular jobs or otherwise outside the control of their social superiors—so threatening. Nonetheless, every European country that colonized the New World claimed to be spreading freedom—for its own population and for Native Americans.

THE EXPANSION OF EUROPE

It is fitting that the second epochal event that Adam Smith linked to Columbus's voyage of 1492 was the discovery by Portuguese navigators of a sea route from Europe to Asia around the southern tip of Africa. The European conquest of America began as an offshoot of the quest for a sea route

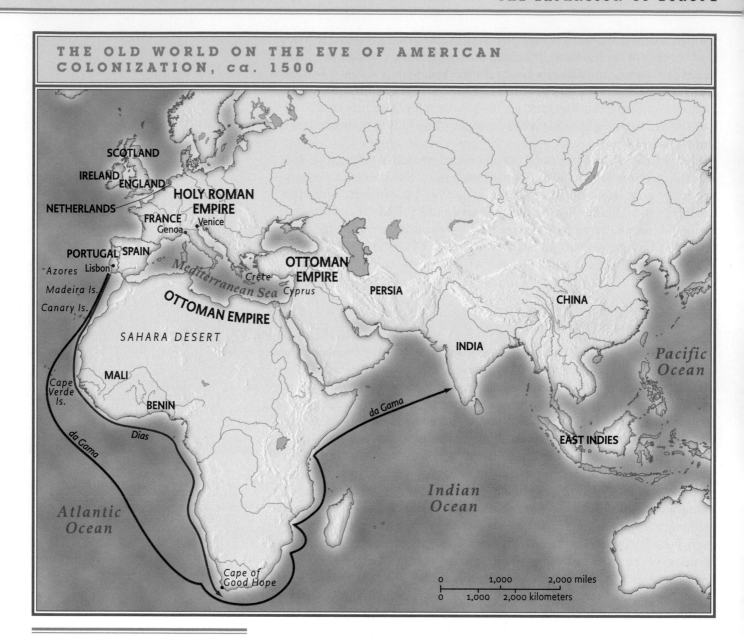

THE OLD WORLD ON THE EVE OF AMERICAN COLONIZATION, ca. 1500

In the fifteenth century, the world known to Europeans was limited to Europe, parts of Africa, and Asia. Explorers from Portugal sought to find a sea route to the East in order to circumvent the Italian city-states and Middle Eastern rulers who controlled the overland trade.

to India, China, and the islands of the East Indies, the source of the silk, tea, spices, porcelain, and other luxury goods on which international trade in the early modern era centered. For centuries, this commerce had been conducted across land, from China and South Asia to the Middle East and the Mediterranean region. Profit and piety—the desire to eliminate Islamic middlemen and win control of the lucrative trade for Christian western Europe—combined to inspire the quest for a direct route to Asia.

PORTUGUESE NAVIGATION

At the beginning of the fifteenth century, one might have predicted that China would establish the world's first global empire. Chinese ships, far larger than those of any European nation, explored the Indian Ocean and East African coast. Had they continued westward they might have reached North America. But as a wealthy, land-based empire, China did not feel the need for overseas expansion, and after 1433 the government ended support for long-distance maritime expeditions. It fell to Portugal, situated on the western corner of the Iberian Peninsula, far removed from the overland route to Asia, to take advantage of new techniques of sailing and navigation to begin exploring the Atlantic.

The development of the caravel, a ship capable of long-distance travel, and the compass and quadrant, devices that enabled sailors to determine their location and direction with greater accuracy than in the past, made it possible to sail down the coast of Africa and return to Portugal. Portuguese seafarers initially hoped to locate the source of gold that for centuries had been transported in caravans across the Sahara Desert to North Africa and Europe. This commerce, which passed through the African kingdom of Mali on the southern edge of the Sahara, provided Europe with most of its gold. Around 1400, it rivaled trade with the East in economic importance. And like trade with Asia, it was controlled by Muslim merchants.

PORTUGAL AND WEST AFRICA

Today, Africa is the world's poorest continent. In the fifteenth century, it was known for its wealth. Mansa Mūsā, the ruler of Mali, had literally put his realm on the map in 1324 when he led a great pilgrimage to Mecca, distributing so much gold along the way that its price was depressed for a decade. Until 1434, however, no European sailor had seen the coast of Africa below the Sahara, or the forest kingdoms south of Mali that contained the actual gold fields. But in that year, a Portuguese ship brought a sprig of rosemary from West Africa, proof that one could sail beyond the desert and return. Little by little, Portuguese ships moved farther down the coast. In 1485, they reached Benin, an imposing city whose craftsmen produced bronze sculptures that still inspire

An engraving, published in 1668, of a procession of the oba (king) outside Benin on the western coast of Africa. The image suggests the extent of the city, a center of government, trade, and the arts.

admiration for their artistic beauty and superb casting techniques. The Portuguese established fortified trading posts on the western coast of Africa. The profits reaped by these Portuguese "factories"—so named because merchants were known as "factors"—inspired other European powers to follow in their footsteps.

Portugal also began to colonize Madeira, the Azores, and the Canary and Cape Verde Islands, which lie in the Atlantic off the African coast. Sugar plantations worked by Muslim captives and slaves from Slavic areas of eastern Europe had flourished in the Middle Ages on Mediterranean islands like Cyprus, Malta, and Crete. Now, the Portuguese established plantations on the Atlantic islands, eventually replacing the native population with thousands of slaves shipped from Africa—an ominous precedent for the New World. Soon, the center of sugar production would shift again, to the Western Hemisphere.

FREEDOM AND SLAVERY IN AFRICA

Slavery in Africa long predated the coming of Europeans. Traditionally, African slaves tended to be criminals, debtors, and captives in war. They worked within the households of their owners and had well-defined rights, such as possessing property and marrying free persons. It was not uncommon for African slaves to acquire their freedom. Slavery was one of several forms of labor, not the basis of the economy as it would become in large parts of the New World. The coming of the Portuguese, soon followed by traders from other European nations, accelerated the buying and selling of slaves within Africa. At least 100,000 African slaves were transported to Spain and Portugal between 1450 and 1500. In 1502, the first African slaves were transported to islands in the Caribbean. The transatlantic slave trade, and its impact on Africa, will be discussed in Chapter 4.

Having reached West Africa, Portuguese mariners pushed their explorations ever southward along the coast. Bartholomeu Dias reached the Cape of Good Hope at the continent's southern tip in 1487. In 1498, Vasco da Gama sailed around it to India, demonstrating the feasibility of a sea route to the East. With a population of under 1 million, Portugal established a vast trading empire, with bases in India, southern China, and Indonesia. It replaced the Italian city-states as the major European commercial partner of the East. But six years before da Gama's voyage, Christopher Columbus had, he believed, discovered a new route to China and India by sailing west.

THE VOYAGES OF COLUMBUS

A seasoned mariner and fearless explorer from Genoa, a major port in northern Italy, Columbus had for years sailed the Mediterranean and North Atlantic, studying ocean currents and

A detail from the Cantino World Map *depicting the western coast of Africa at the beginning of the Atlantic slave trade. Created by an anonymous Portuguese mapmaker in 1502, the map included Europe, Africa, and a small part of the Western Hemisphere, described as "the islands lately discovered in the parts of India." It was smuggled out of Portugal by Alberto Cantino, a diplomat representing an Italian city-state.*

wind patterns. Like nearly all navigators of the time, Columbus knew the earth was round. But he drastically underestimated its size. He believed that by sailing westward he could relatively quickly cross the Atlantic and reach Asia. No one in Europe knew that there were two giant continents 3,000 miles to the west. The Vikings, to be sure, had sailed from Greenland to Newfoundland around the year 1000 and established a settlement, Vinland, at a site now known as L'Anse aux Meadows. But this was abandoned after a few years and had been forgotten, except in Norse legends.

A fifteenth-century engraving depicts a slave at work in a Portuguese home. Even before Columbus's voyages to the Western Hemisphere, tens of thousands of slaves were brought from Africa to Spain and Portugal.

Columbus sought financial support throughout Europe for the planned voyage. His brother Bartholomew even visited Henry VII of England to ask for assistance. Most of Columbus's contemporaries, however, knew that he considerably underestimated the earth's size, which helps explain why he had trouble gaining backers for his expedition. Eventually, King Ferdinand and Queen Isabella of Spain agreed to become sponsors. Their marriage in 1469 had united the warring kingdoms of Aragon and Castile. In 1492, they completed the *reconquista*—the "reconquest" of Spain from the Moors, African Muslims who had occupied part of the Iberian Peninsula for centuries. The capture of Grenada, the Moors' last stronghold, accomplished Spain's territorial unification. To ensure its religious unification, Ferdinand and Isabella ordered all Muslims and Jews to convert to Catholicism or leave the country. Along with the crown, much of Columbus's financing came from bankers and merchants of Spain and the Italian city-states, who desperately desired to circumvent the Muslim stranglehold on the eastern trade. Columbus set sail with royal letters of introduction to Asian rulers, authorizing him to negotiate trade agreements.

CONTACT

COLUMBUS IN THE NEW WORLD

On October 12, 1492, after only thirty-three days of sailing from the Canary Islands, where he had stopped to resupply his three ships, Columbus and his expedition arrived at the Bahamas. His exact landing site remains in dispute, but it was probably San Salvador, a tiny spot of land known today as Watling Island. Soon afterwards, he encountered the far larger islands of Hispaniola (today the site of Haiti and the Dominican Republic) and Cuba. When one of his ships ran aground, he abandoned it and left thirty-eight men behind on Hispaniola. But he found room to bring ten inhabitants of the island back to Spain for conversion to Christianity.

In the following year, 1493, European colonization of the New World began. Columbus returned with seventeen ships and over 1,000 men to

Columbus's Landfall, *an engraving from* La lettera dell'isole *(Letter from the Islands). This 1493 pamphlet reproduced, in the form of a poem, Columbus's first letter describing his voyage of the previous year. Under the watchful eye of King Ferdinand of Spain, Columbus and his men land on a Caribbean island, while local Indians flee.*

explore the area and establish a Spanish outpost. Columbus's settlement on the island of Hispaniola, which he named La Isabella, failed, but in 1502 another Spanish explorer, Nicolás de Ovando, arrived with 2,500 men and established a permanent base, the first center of the Spanish empire in America. Before he died in 1506, Columbus made two more voyages to the New World, in 1498 and 1502. He went to his grave believing that he had discovered a westward route to Asia. The explorations of another Italian, Amerigo Vespucci, along the coast of South America between 1499 and 1502 made plain that a continent entirely unknown to Europeans had been encountered. The New World would come to bear not Columbus's name but one based on Vespucci's—America. Vespucci also realized that the native inhabitants were distinct peoples, not residents of the East Indies as Columbus had believed, although the name "Indians," applied to them by Columbus, has endured to this day.

EXPLORATION AND CONQUEST

The speed with which European exploration proceeded in the aftermath of Columbus's first voyage is remarkable. The technique of printing with movable type, invented in the 1430s by the German craftsman Johannes Gutenberg, had made possible the rapid spread of information in Europe, at least among the educated minority. News of Columbus's achievement traveled quickly. One writer hailed him as "a hero such as the ancients made gods of." Others were inspired to follow in his wake. John Cabot, a Genoese merchant who had settled in England, reached Newfoundland in 1497. Soon, scores of fishing boats from France, Spain, and England were active in the region. Pedro Cabral claimed Brazil for Portugal in 1500.

But the Spanish took the lead in exploration and conquest. Inspired by a search for wealth, national glory, and the desire to spread Catholicism, Spanish conquistadores, often accompanied by religious missionaries and carrying flags emblazoned with the sign of the cross, radiated outward from Hispaniola. In 1513, Vasco Núñez de Balboa trekked across the isthmus of Panama and became the first European to gaze upon the Pacific Ocean. Between 1519 and 1522, Ferdinand Magellan led the first expedition to sail around the world, encountering Pacific islands and peoples previously unknown to Europe. Magellan was killed in the Philippines, but his fleet completed the journey, correcting once and for all Columbus's erroneous assessment of the earth's size.

The first explorer to encounter a major American civilization was Hernán Cortés, who in 1519 arrived at Tenochtitlán, the nerve center of the Aztec empire, whose wealth and power rested on domination of numerous subordinate peoples nearby. The Aztecs were violent warriors who engaged in the ritual sacrifice of captives and others, sometimes thousands at a time. This practice thoroughly alienated their neighbors and reinforced the Spanish view of America's native inhabitants as barbarians, even though in Europe at this time thousands of men and women were burned at the stake as witches or religious heretics, and criminals were executed in public spectacles that attracted throngs of onlookers.

VOYAGES OF DISCOVERY

With only a few hundred European men, the daring Cortés conquered the Aztec city, relying on superior military technology including iron weapons and gunpowder, as well as shrewdness in enlisting the aid of some of the Aztecs' subject peoples, who supplied him with thousands of warriors. His most powerful ally, however, was disease—a smallpox epidemic that devastated Aztec society. A few years later, Francisco Pizarro

Christopher Columbus's first Atlantic crossing, in 1492, was soon followed by voyages of discovery by English, Portuguese, Spanish, and Italian explorers.

Engravings, from the Florentine Codex, *of the forces of Cortés marching on Tenochtitlán and assaulting the city with cannon fire. The difference in military technology between the Spanish and Aztecs is evident. Indians who allied with Cortés had helped him build vessels and carry them in pieces over mountains to the city. The codex (a volume formed by stitching together manuscript pages) was prepared under the supervision of a Spanish missionary in sixteenth-century Mexico.*

conquered the great Inca kingdom centered in modern-day Peru. Pizarro's tactics were typical of the conquistadores. He captured the Incan king, demanded and received a ransom, and then proceeded to kill the king anyway. Soon, treasure fleets carrying cargoes of gold and silver from the mines of Mexico and Peru traversed the Atlantic to enrich the Spanish crown.

THE DEMOGRAPHIC DISASTER

The transatlantic flow of goods and people, sometimes called the Columbian Exchange, reversed millions of years of evolution. Plants, animals, and cultures that had evolved independently on separate continents were now thrown together. Products introduced to Europe from America included corn, tomatoes, potatoes, peanuts, tobacco, and cotton, while to the New World from the Old came wheat, rice, sugar cane, horses, cattle, pigs, and sheep. But Europeans also brought with them germs previously unknown in the Americas.

No one knows exactly how many people lived in North and South America at the time of Columbus's voyages—the most current estimates range between 90 million and 110 million. The European population in 1492 was about 70 million, the African population around 50 million, and about 170 million lived in China and modern-day India. Most natives of the New World lived in Central and South America. In 1492, the Indian population within what are now the borders of the United States was between 2 million and 10 million.

Whatever their numbers, the Indian population suffered a catastrophic decline because of contact with Europeans and their wars, enslavement, and especially diseases like smallpox, influenza, and measles. Never having encountered these diseases, Indians had not developed antibodies to fight

Another scene from the Florentine Codex *depicts the smallpox epidemic that ravaged the Aztec capital after the arrival of Cortés.*

them. The result was devastating. Many West Indian islands were all but depopulated. On Hispaniola, the native population, estimated at between 300,000 and 1 million in 1492, had nearly disappeared fifty years later. The population of Mexico would fall by more than 90 percent in the sixteenth century, from perhaps 20 million to under 2 million. As for the area that now forms the United States, its Native American population fell continuously. It reached its lowest point around 1900, at only 250,000.

Overall, the death of perhaps 80 million people—close to one-fifth of mankind—in the first century and a half of contact with Europeans represents the greatest loss of life in human history. It was disease as much as military prowess and more advanced technology that enabled Europeans to conquer the Americas.

THE SPANISH EMPIRE *reread*

By the middle of the sixteenth century, Spain had established an immense empire that reached from Europe to the Americas and Asia. The Atlantic and Pacific oceans, once barriers separating different parts of the world, now became highways for the exchange of goods and the movement of people. Spanish galleons carried gold and silver from Mexico and Peru eastward to Spain and westward to Manila in the Philippines and on to China.

The Spanish empire included the most populous parts of the New World and the regions richest in natural resources. Stretching from the Andes Mountains of South America through present-day Mexico and the Caribbean and eventually into Florida and the southwestern United States, Spain's empire exceeded in size the Roman empire of the ancient world. Its center in North America was Mexico City, a magnificent capital built on the ruins of the Aztec city of Tenochtitlán and boasting churches, hospitals, monasteries, government buildings, and the New World's first university. Unlike the English and French New World empires, Spanish America was essentially an urban civilization, an "empire of towns." For centuries, its great cities, notably Mexico City, Quito, and Lima, far outshone any urban centers in North America and most of those in Europe.

GOVERNING SPANISH AMERICA

Spain's system of colonial government rivaled that of ancient Rome. Alarmed by the destructiveness of the conquistadores, the Spanish crown replaced them with a more stable system of government headed by lawyers and bureaucrats. At least in theory, the government of Spanish America reflected the absolutism of the newly unified nation at home. Authority originated with the king and flowed downward through the Council of the Indies—the main body in Spain for colonial administration—and then to viceroys in Mexico and Peru and other local officials in America. The Catholic Church also played a significant role in the administration of Spanish colonies, frequently exerting its authority on matters of faith, morals, and treatment of the Indians.

An illustration from the Huexotzinco Codex *(1531) depicts Mexicans providing products and services as taxes to the Spanish conquerors. The banner of the Virgin Mary and baby Jesus reflects the early spread of Christianity. The people of Huexotzinco, a town near Mexico City, had aided Hernán Cortés in his conquest of the Aztec empire. The codex was part of a successful lawsuit, endorsed by Cortés, in which the Indians challenged excessive taxation by colonial officials.*

Successive kings kept elected assemblies out of Spain's New World empire. Royal officials were generally appointees from Spain, rather than *criollos*, as persons born in the colonies of European ancestry were called. The imperial state was a real and continuous presence in Spanish America. But as its power declined in Europe beginning in the seventeenth century, the local elite came to enjoy more and more effective authority over colonial affairs. Given the vastness of the empire, local municipal councils, universities, merchant organizations, and craft guilds enjoyed considerable independence.

COLONISTS IN SPANISH AMERICA

Despite the decline in the native population, Spanish America remained populous enough that, with the exception of the West Indies and a few cities, large-scale importations of African slaves were unnecessary. Instead, the Spanish forced tens of thousands of Indians to work in gold and silver mines, which supplied the empire's wealth, and on large-scale farms, or *haciendas*, controlled by Spanish landlords. In Spanish America, unlike other New World empires, Indians performed most of the labor, and although the Spanish introduced livestock, wheat, and sugar, the main agricultural crops were the same ones grown before colonization—corn, beans, and squash.

"The maxim of the conqueror must be to settle," said one Spanish official. The government barred non-Spaniards from emigrating to its American domains, as well as non-Christian Spaniards, including Jews and Moors. But the opportunity for social advancement drew numerous colonists from Spain—225,000 in the sixteenth century and a total of 750,000 in the three centuries of Spain's colonial rule. Eventually, a significant number came in families, but at first the large majority were young, single men, many of them laborers, craftsmen, and soldiers. Many also came as government officials, priests, professionals, and minor aristocrats, all ready to direct the manual work of Indians, since living without having to labor was a sign of noble status. The most successful of these colonists enjoyed lives of luxury similar to those of the upper classes at home.

COLONISTS AND INDIANS

Although persons of European birth, called *peninsulares*, stood atop the social hierarchy, they never constituted more than a tiny proportion of the population of Spanish America. Unlike in the later British empire, Indian inhabitants always outnumbered European colonists and their descendants in Spanish America, and large areas remained effectively under Indian control for many years. Like the later French empire and unlike the

Four Racial Groups, *taken from a series of paintings by the eighteenth-century Mexican artist Andrés de Islas, illustrates the racial mixing that took place in the Spanish empire and the new vocabulary invented to describe it. Top left: The offspring of a Spaniard and Indian is a* mestizo. *Right: A Spaniard and a* mestiza *produce a* castizo. *Bottom left: The child of an Indian and a* mestiza *is a* coyote. *Right: And the child of an Indian man and African woman is a* chino.

English, Spanish authorities granted Indians certain rights within colonial society and looked forward to their eventual assimilation. Indeed, the success of the Spanish empire depended on the nature of the native societies on which it could build. In Florida, the Amazon, and Caribbean islands like Jamaica, which lacked major Indian cities and large native populations, Spanish rule remained tenuous.

The Spanish crown ordered wives of colonists to join them in America and demanded that single men marry. But with the population of Spanish women remaining low, the intermixing of the colonial and Indian peoples soon began. As early as 1514, the Spanish government formally approved of such marriages, partly as a way of bringing Christianity to the native population. By 1600, *mestizos* (persons of mixed origin) made up a large part of the urban population of Spanish America. In the century that followed, *mestizos* repopulated the Valley of Mexico, where disease had decimated the original inhabitants. Over time, Spanish America evolved into a hybrid culture, part Spanish, part Indian, and in some areas part African, but with a single official faith, language, and governmental system. In 1531, a poor Indian, Juan Diego, reported seeing a vision of the Virgin Mary, looking very much like a dark-skinned Indian, near a Mexican village. Miracles began to be reported, and a shrine was built in her honor. The Virgin of Guadalupe would come to be revered by millions as a symbol of the mixing of Indian and Spanish cultures, and later of the modern nation of Mexico.

JUSTIFICATIONS FOR CONQUEST

What allowed one nation, the seventeenth-century Dutch legal thinker Hugo Grotius wondered, to claim possession of lands that "belonged to someone else"? This question rarely occurred to most of the Europeans who crossed the Atlantic in the wake of Columbus's voyage, or to rulers in the Old World. They had immense confidence in the superiority of their own cultures to those they encountered in America. They expected these societies to abandon their own beliefs and traditions and embrace those of the newcomers. Failure to do so reinforced the conviction that these people were uncivilized "heathens" (non-Christians).

Europeans brought with them not only a long history of using violence to subdue their internal and external foes but also missionary zeal to spread the benefits of their own civilization to others, while reaping the rewards of empire. Spain was no exception. The establishment of its empire in America took place in the wake of Spain's own territorial unification, the rise of a powerful royal government, and the enforcement of religious orthodoxy by the expulsion of Muslims and Jews in 1492. To further legitimize Spain's claim to rule the New World, a year after Columbus's first voyage Pope Alexander VI divided the non-Christian world between Spain and Portugal. The line was subsequently adjusted to give Portugal control of Brazil, with the remainder of the Western Hemisphere falling under Spanish authority.

SPREADING THE FAITH

Not surprisingly, the pope justified this pronouncement by requiring Spain and Portugal to spread Catholicism among the native inhabitants of the

A banner carried by the forces of Cortés, conqueror of the Aztec kingdom, features an image of the Virgin Mary, illustrating how the desire to spread the Roman Catholic faith provided a justification for conquest.

A benign view of Spanish colonization. This engraving from a 1621 book depicts Spanish missionaries bringing Christianity to New World natives while priests do construction work. A fortified colonial town is visible in the background.

Americas. The missionary element of colonization, already familiar because of the long holy war against Islam within Spain itself, was powerfully reinforced in the sixteenth century, when the Protestant Reformation divided the Catholic Church. In 1517, Martin Luther, a German priest, posted his Ninety-Five Theses, which accused the Church of worldliness and corruption. Luther wanted to cleanse the Church of abuses such as the sale of indulgences (official dispensations forgiving sins). He insisted that all believers should read the Bible for themselves, rather than relying on priests to interpret it for them. His call for reform led to the rise of new Protestant churches independent of Rome and plunged Europe into more than a century of religious and political strife.

Spain, the most powerful bastion of orthodox Catholicism, redoubled its efforts to convert the Indians to the "true faith." National glory and religious mission went hand in hand. Convinced of the superiority of Catholicism to all other religions, Spain insisted that the primary goal of colonization was to save the Indians from heathenism and prevent them from falling under the sway of Protestantism. The aim was neither to exterminate nor to remove the Indians, but to transform them into obedient, Christian subjects of the crown. Indeed, lacking the later concept of "race" as an unchanging, inborn set of qualities and abilities, many Spanish writers insisted that Indians could in time be "brought up" to the level of European civilization. Of course, this meant not only the destruction of existing Indian political structures but also a transformation of their economic and spiritual lives.

PIETY AND PROFIT

To the Spanish colonizers, the large native populations of the Americas were not only souls to be saved but also a labor force to be organized to extract gold and silver that would enrich the mother country. The tension between these two outlooks would mark Spanish rule in America for three centuries. On the one hand, Spanish rulers proclaimed the goal of bringing true "freedom" to the Indians by instructing them in Christianity. Even enslaving the natives was justified as a means of liberating them from their own backwardness and savagery and enabling them to become part of Christian civilization. Religious orders established missions throughout the empire, and over time millions of Indians were converted to Catholicism.

On the other hand, Spanish rule, especially in its initial period, witnessed a disastrous fall in Indian population, not only because of epidemics but also because of the brutal conditions of labor to which Indians were subjected. The conquistadores and subsequent governors, who required conquered peoples to acknowledge the Catholic Church and provide gold and silver, saw no contradiction between serving God and enriching themselves. Others, however, did.

LAS CASAS'S COMPLAINT

As early as 1537, Pope Paul III, who hoped to see Indians become devout subjects of Catholic monarchs, outlawed their enslavement (an edict never extended to apply to Africans). His decree declared Indians to be "truly men," who must not be "treated as dumb beasts." Fifteen years later, the Dominican priest Bartolomé de Las Casas published an account of the decimation of the Indian population with the compelling title *A Very Brief Account of the Destruction of the Indies*. Las Casas's father had sailed on Columbus's second voyage, and he himself had participated in the plunder of Peru and the exploitation of Indian labor on Hispaniola and Cuba. But in 1514 Las Casas freed his own Indian slaves and began to preach against the injustices of Spanish rule.

Las Casas's writings denounced Spain for causing the death of millions of innocent people. "It has been Spain's practice," he reported, "in every land they have discovered to stage a massacre" in order to make the inhabitants "tremble with fear." He narrated in shocking detail the "strange cruelties" carried out by "the Christians," including the burning alive of men, women, and children and the imposition of forced labor. The Indians, he wrote, had been "totally deprived of their freedom and were put in the harshest, fiercest, most terrible servitude and captivity." Long before the idea was common, Las Casas insisted that Indians were rational beings, not barbarians, and that Spain had no grounds on which to deprive them of their lands and liberty. "The entire human race is one," he proclaimed, and while he continued to believe that Spain had a right to rule in America, largely on religious grounds, he called for Indians to enjoy "all guarantees of liberty and justice" from the moment they became subjects of Spain. "Nothing is certainly more precious in human affairs, nothing more esteemed," he wrote, "than freedom." Yet Las Casas also suggested that importing slaves from Africa would help to protect the Indians from exploitation.

Spanish conquistadores murdering Indians at Cuzco, in modern-day Peru. The Dutch-born engraver Theodor de Bry and his sons illustrated ten volumes about New World exploration published between 1590 and 1618. A Protestant, de Bry created vivid images that helped to spread the Black Legend of Spain as a uniquely cruel colonizer.

REFORMING THE EMPIRE

Like other Spaniards, Las Casas believed that the main justification for empire was converting the Indians to Christianity. Spanish cruelty, he feared, undermined this effort. Largely because of Las Casas's efforts, Spain in 1542 promulgated the New Laws, commanding that Indians no longer be enslaved. Not everyone welcomed the change. Gonzalo Pizarro, brother of the conqueror of Peru, organized an unsuccessful rebellion in protest. In 1550, Spain abolished the *encomienda* system, under which the first settlers had been granted authority over conquered Indian lands with the right to extract forced labor from the native inhabitants. In its place, the government established the *repartimiento* system, whereby residents of Indian villages remained legally free and entitled to wages, but were still required to perform a fixed amount of labor each year. The Indians were not slaves—they had access to land, were paid wages, and could not be bought and sold. But since the requirement that they work for the Spanish remained the essence of the system, it still allowed for many abuses by Spanish landlords and by priests who required Indians to toil on mission lands as part of the conversion process. Indeed, a long struggle ensued among settlers, missionaries, and colonial authorities for control of Indian labor. Each party proclaimed itself a humane overlord and denounced the others for exploiting the native population.

By the end of the sixteenth century, work in the Spanish empire consisted largely of forced wage labor by native inhabitants and slave labor by Africans on the West Indian islands and a few parts of the mainland. Like all empires, Spain's always remained highly exploitative. Over time, the initial brutal treatment of Indians improved somewhat. But Las Casas's writings, translated almost immediately into several European languages, contributed to the spread of the Black Legend—the image of Spain as a uniquely brutal and exploitative colonizer. This would provide a potent justification for other European powers to challenge Spain's predominance in the New World.

A 1791 view of Mission San Carlos in what is now California depicts the Indian community and a corral in the background, while missionaries and Spanish explorers greet each other in the foreground.

EXPLORING NORTH AMERICA

While the Spanish empire centered on Mexico, Peru, and the West Indies, the hope of finding a new kingdom of gold soon led Spanish explorers into territory that now forms part of the United States. Juan Ponce de León, who had conquered Puerto Rico, entered Florida in 1513 in search of slaves, wealth, and a fabled fountain of youth, only to be repelled by local Indians. In 1528, another expedition seeking plunder in Florida embarked from Spain, but after a series of storms only a handful of men reached the Gulf coast. For seven years they traversed the Southwest until a few survivors arrived in Mexico in 1536. One, Álvar Núñez Cabeza de Vaca, wrote an

By around 1600, New Spain had become a vast empire stretching from the modern-day American Southwest through Mexico, Central America, and into the former Inca kingdom in South America. This map shows early Spanish exploration in the present-day United States.

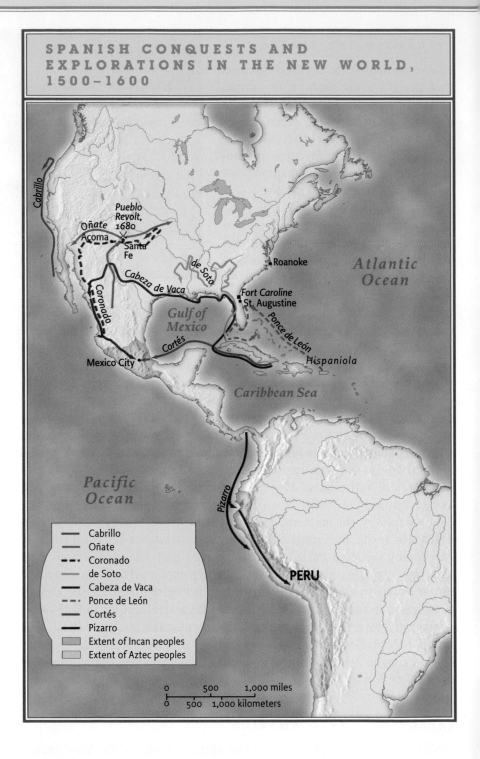

SPANISH CONQUESTS AND EXPLORATIONS IN THE NEW WORLD, 1500–1600

account of his adventures, including tales told by native inhabitants (possibly to persuade the newcomers to move on) of the seven golden cities of Cibola, somewhere over the horizon.

In the late 1530s and 1540s, Juan Rodriguez Cabrillo explored the Pacific coast as far north as Oregon, and expeditions led by Hernando deSoto, Cabeza de Vaca, Francisco Vásquez de Coronado, and others marched through the Gulf region and the Southwest, fruitlessly searching for another Mexico or Peru. Coronado explored much of the interior of the continent, reaching as far north as the Great Plains, and became the first European to encounter the immense herds of buffalo that roamed the West. These expeditions, really mobile communities with hundreds of adventurers, priests, potential settlers, slaves, and livestock, spread disease and devastation among Indian communities. DeSoto's was particularly brutal. His men tortured, raped, and enslaved countless Indians and transmitted deadly diseases. When Europeans in the seventeenth century returned to colonize the area traversed by deSoto's party, little remained of the societies he had encountered. Where large towns had existed, explorers found only herds of grazing bison.

SPANISH FLORIDA

Nonetheless, these explorations established Spain's claim to a large part of what is now the American South and Southwest. The first region to be colonized within the present-day United States was Florida. Spain hoped to establish a military base there to combat pirates who threatened the treasure fleet that each year sailed from Havana for Europe loaded with gold and silver from Mexico and Peru. Spain also wanted to forestall French incursions in the area. In 1565, Philip II of Spain authorized the nobleman Pedro Menéndez de Avilés to lead a colonizing expedition to Florida. Menéndez destroyed a small outpost at Fort Caroline, which a group of Huguenots (French Protestants) had established in 1562 near present-day Jacksonville. Menéndez and his men massacred the 500 colonists and went on to establish Spanish forts on St. Simons Island, Georgia, and at St. Augustine, Florida. The latter remains the oldest site in the United States continuously inhabited by European settlers and their descendants.

Spanish expeditions soon established forts from present-day Miami into South Carolina, and Spanish religious missionaries set up outposts in Florida and on the Sea Islands, hoping to convert the local Indians to Christianity. Most of the forts fell into disuse, and many of the missions were destroyed by local Guale Indians in an uprising that began in 1597. The Indians explained their revolt by noting that the missionaries had sought to eliminate "our dances, banquets, feasts, celebrations, and wars. . . . They persecute our old people by calling them witches." The missions were soon rebuilt, only to be devastated again a century later, this time by English and Indian forces from South Carolina. In general, Florida failed to attract settlers, remaining an isolated military settlement, in effect a fortified outpost of Cuba. As late as 1763, Spanish Florida had only 4,000 inhabitants of European descent.

SPAIN IN THE SOUTHWEST

Spain took even longer to begin the colonization of the American Southwest. Although Spanish adventurers and exploring parties made incursions into the area in the sixteenth century, it was not until 1598 that Juan de Oñate led a group of 400 soldiers, colonists, and missionaries north from Mexico to establish a permanent settlement. While searching for fabled deposits of precious metals, Oñate's nephew and fourteen soldiers were

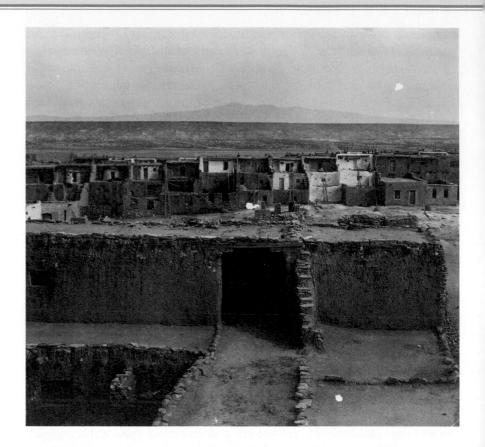

Acoma, the "sky city," as it appeared in 1904.

killed by inhabitants of Acoma, the "sky city" located on a high bluff in present-day New Mexico.

Oñate decided to teach the local Indians a lesson. After a two-day siege, his forces scaled the seemingly impregnable heights and destroyed Acoma, killing over 800 of its 1,500 or so inhabitants, including 300 women. Of the 600 Indians captured, the women and children were consigned to servitude in Spanish families, while adult men were punished by the cutting off of one foot. Not until the 1640s was Acoma, which had been inhabited since the thirteenth century, rebuilt. Oñate's message was plain—any Indians who resisted Spanish authority would be crushed. But his method of rule, coupled with his failure to locate gold, alarmed authorities in Mexico City. In 1606, Oñate was ordered home and punished for his treatment of New Mexico's Indians. In 1610, Spain established the capital of New Mexico at Santa Fe, the first permanent European settlement in the Southwest.

THE PUEBLO REVOLT

In 1680, New Mexico's small and vulnerable colonist population numbered less than 3,000. Most were *mestizos* (persons of mixed Spanish and Indian origin), since few European settlers came to the region. Relations between the Pueblo Indians and colonial authorities had deteriorated throughout the seventeenth century, as governors, settlers, and missionaries sought to exploit the labor of an Indian population that declined from about 60,000 in 1600 to some 17,000 eighty years later. Franciscan friars worked relentlessly to convert Indians to Catholicism, often using intimidation and violence. Their spiritual dedication and personal courage impressed many Indians, however, as did the European goods and technologies they introduced. Some natives welcomed them as a counterbalance to the depredations of soldiers and settlers and accepted baptism, even as they continued to practice their old religion, adding Jesus, Mary, and the Catholic saints to their already rich spiritual pantheon. But as the Inquisition—the persecution of non-Catholics—became more and more intense in Spain, so did the friars' efforts to stamp out traditional religious ceremonies in New Mexico. By burning Indian idols, masks, and other sacred objects, the missionaries alienated far more Indians than they converted. A prolonged drought that began around 1660 and the authorities' inability to protect the villages and missions from attacks by marauding Navajo and Apache Indians added to local discontent.

The Pueblo peoples had long been divided among themselves. The Spanish assumed that the Indians could never unite against the colonizers. In August 1680, they were proven wrong.

Little is known about the life of Popé, who became the main organizer of an uprising that aimed to drive the Spanish from the colony and restore the Indians' traditional autonomy. A religious leader born around 1630 in San Juan Pueblo in present-day New Mexico, Popé first appears in the historical record in 1675, when he was one of forty-seven Pueblo Indians arrested for "sorcery"—that is, practicing their traditional religion. Four of the prisoners were hanged, and the rest, including Popé, were brought to Santa Fe to be publicly whipped. After this humiliation, Popé returned home and began holding secret meetings in Pueblo communities.

Under Popé's leadership, New Mexico's Indians joined in a coordinated uprising. Ironically, because the Pueblos spoke six different languages, Spanish became the revolt's "lingua franca" (a common means of communication among persons of different linguistic backgrounds). Some 2,000 warriors destroyed isolated farms and missions, killing 400 colonists, including 21 Franciscan missionaries. They then surrounded Santa Fe. The Spanish resisted fiercely but eventually had no choice but to abandon the town. Most of the Spanish survivors, accompanied by several hundred Christian Indians, made their way south out of New Mexico. Within a few weeks, a century of colonization in the area had been destroyed. From their own point of view, the Pueblo Indians had triumphantly reestablished the freedom lost through Spanish conquest.

The Pueblo Revolt was the most complete victory for Native Americans over Europeans and the only wholesale expulsion of settlers in the history of North America. According to a royal attorney who interviewed the Spanish survivors in Mexico City, the revolt arose from the "many oppressions" the Indians had suffered. The victorious Pueblos turned with a vengeance on all symbols of European culture, uprooting fruit trees, destroying cattle, burning churches and images of Christ and the Virgin Mary, and wading into rivers to wash away their Catholic baptisms. They rebuilt their places

St. Anthony and the Infant Jesus, painted on a tanned buffalo hide by a Franciscan priest in New Mexico in the early eighteenth century. This was not long after the Spanish reconquered the area, from which they had been driven by the Pueblo Revolt.

VOICES OF FREEDOM

FROM BARTOLOMÉ DE LAS CASAS, *History of the Indies* (1528)

Las Casas was the Dominican priest who condemned the treatment of Indians in the Spanish empire. His widely disseminated *History of the Indies* helped to establish the Black Legend of Spanish cruelty.

The Indians [of Hispaniola] were totally deprived of their freedom and were put in the harshest, fiercest, most horrible servitude and captivity which no one who has not seen it can understand. Even beasts enjoy more freedom when they are allowed to graze in the fields. But our Spaniards gave no such opportunity to Indians and truly considered them perpetual slaves, since the Indians had not the free will to dispose of their persons but instead were disposed of according to Spanish greed and cruelty, not as men in captivity but as beasts tied to a rope to prevent free movement. When they were allowed to go home, they often found it deserted and had no other recourse than to go out into the woods to find food

and to die. When they fell ill, which was very frequently because they are a delicate people unaccustomed to such work, the Spaniards did not believe them and pitilessly called them lazy dogs and kicked and beat them; and when illness was apparent they sent them home as useless. . . . They would go then, falling into the first stream and dying there in desperation; others would hold on longer but very few ever made it home. I sometimes came upon dead bodies on my way, and upon others who were gasping and moaning in their death agony, repeating "Hungry, hungry." And this was the freedom, the good treatment and the Christianity the Indians received.

About eight years passed under [Spanish rule] and this disorder had time to grow; no one gave it a thought and the multitude of people who originally lived on the island . . . was consumed at such a rate that in these eight years 90 per cent had perished. From here this sweeping plague went to San Juan, Jamaica, Cuba and the continent, spreading destruction over the whole hemisphere.

FROM "DECLARATION OF JOSEPHE,"
DECEMBER 19, 1681

Josephe was a Spanish-speaking Indian questioned by a royal attorney in Mexico City investigating the Pueblo Revolt. The revolt of the Indian population, in 1680, temporarily drove Spanish settlers from modern-day New Mexico.

Asked what causes or motives the said Indian rebels had for renouncing the law of God and obedience to his Majesty, and for committing so many of crimes, [he answered] the causes they have were alleged ill treatment and injuries received from [Spanish authorities], because they beat them, took away what they had, and made them work without pay. Thus he replies.

Asked if he has learned if it has come to his notice during the time that he has been here the reason why the apostates burned the images, churches, and things pertaining to divine worship, making a mockery and a trophy of them, killing the priests and doing the other things they did, he said that he knows and had heard it generally stated that while they were besieging the villa the rebellious traitors burned the church and shouted in loud voices, "Now the God of the Spaniards, who was their father, is dead, and Santa Maria, who was their mother, and the saints, who were pieces of rotten wood," saying that only their own god lived. Thus they ordered all the temples and images, crosses and rosaries burned, and their function being over, they all went to bathe in the rivers, saying that they thereby washed away the water of baptism. For their churches, they placed on the four sides and in the center of the plaza some small circular enclosures of stone where they went to offer flour, feathers, and the seed of maguey [a local plant], maize, and tobacco, and performed other superstitious rites, giving the children to understand that they must all do this in the future. The captains and the chiefs ordered that the names of Jesus and Mary should nowhere be uttered. . . . He has seen many houses of idolatry which they have built, dancing the dance of the cachina [part of a traditional Indian religious ceremony], which this declarant has also danced. Thus he replies to the question.

QUESTIONS

1. Why does Las Casas, after describing the ill treatment of Indians, write, "And this was the freedom, the good treatment and the Christianity the Indians received"?

2. What role did religion play in the Pueblo Revolt?

3. What ideas of freedom are apparent in the two documents?

of worship, called "kivas," and resumed sacred dances the friars had banned. "The God of the Spaniards," they shouted, "is dead."

Cooperation among the Pueblo peoples, however, soon evaporated. By the end of the 1680s, warfare had broken out among several villages, even as Apache and Navajo raids continued. Popé died around 1690. In 1692, the Spanish launched an invasion that reconquered New Mexico. Some communities welcomed them back as a source of military protection. But Spain had learned a lesson. In the eighteenth century, colonial authorities adopted a more tolerant attitude toward traditional religious practices and made fewer demands on Indian labor.

THE FRENCH AND DUTCH EMPIRES

If the Black Legend inspired a sense of superiority among Spain's European rivals, the precious metals that poured from the New World into the Spanish treasury aroused the desire to try to match Spain's success. The establishment of Spain's American empire transformed the balance of power in the world economy. The Atlantic replaced the overland route to Asia as the major axis of global trade. During the seventeenth century, the French, Dutch, and English established colonies in North America. England's mainland colonies, to be discussed in the next chapter, consisted of agricultural settlements with growing populations whose hunger for land produced incessant conflict with native peoples. New France and New Netherland were primarily commercial ventures that never attracted large numbers of colonists. More dependent on Indians as trading partners and military allies, these settlements allowed them greater freedom than the English.

FRENCH COLONIZATION

The first of Spain's major European rivals to embark on New World explorations was France. The French initially aimed to find gold and to locate a Northwest Passage—a sea route directly to the Pacific Ocean. But the hopes of the early French explorers were soon disappointed, and North America came to seem little more than a barrier to be crossed, not a promising site for settlement or exploitation. For most of the sixteenth century, only explorers, fishermen, pirates preying on Spanish shipping farther south, and, as time went on, fur traders visited the East Coast. French efforts to establish settlements in Newfoundland and Nova Scotia failed, beset by native resistance and inadequate planning and financing. Not until the seventeenth century would France, as well as England and the Netherlands, establish permanent settlements in North America.

The explorer Samuel de Champlain, sponsored by a French fur-trading company, founded Quebec in 1608. In 1643, the Jesuit priest Jacques Marquette and the fur trader Louis Joliet located the Mississippi River, and by 1681 René-Robert Cavelier, Sieur de La Salle, had descended to the Gulf of Mexico, claiming the entire Mississippi River valley for France. New France

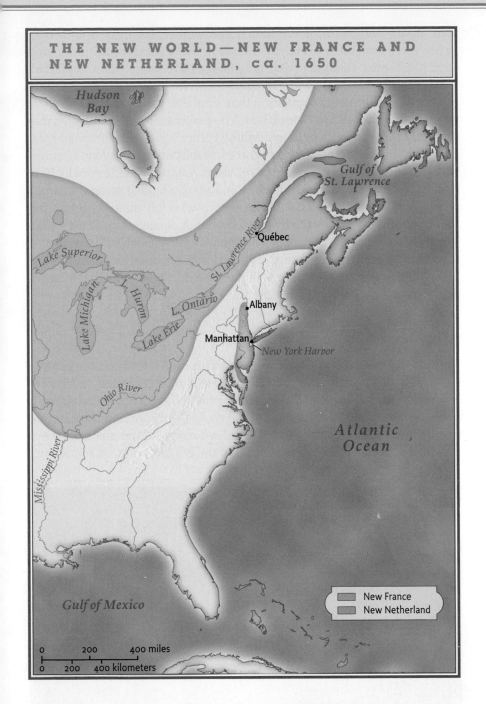

New France and New Netherland.

eventually formed a giant arc along the St. Lawrence, Mississippi, and Ohio rivers.

Until 1663, when the population of European origin was fewer than 3,000, French Canada was ruled by the Company of New France through a governor-general appointed in Paris. There was no representative assembly. In that year, the French government established a new company. It granted land along the St. Lawrence River in *seigneuries* to well-connected nobles and army officers who would transport colonists to take their place in a feudal society. But most of the *engagés*, or indentured servants, returned home after their contracts expired. Over 80 percent of the migrants were men. Apart from nuns, fewer than 1,800 women (compared with over 12,000 men) emigrated to French Canada in the seventeenth century. And during the entire colonial period, only about 250 complete families did so.

By 1700, the number of white inhabitants of New France had risen to only 19,000. With a far larger population than England, France sent many fewer emigrants to the Western Hemisphere. The government at home feared that significant emigration would undermine France's role as a European great power and might compromise its effort to establish trade and good relations with the Indians. Unfavorable reports about America circulated widely in France. Canada was widely depicted as an icebox, a land of savage Indians, a dumping ground for criminals. Most French who left their homes during these years preferred to settle in the Netherlands, Spain, or the West Indies. The revocation in 1685 of the Edict of Nantes, which had extended religious toleration to French Protestants, led well over 100,000 Huguenots to flee their country. But they were not welcome in New France, which the crown desired to remain an outpost of Catholicism.

NEW FRANCE AND THE INDIANS

With its small white population and emphasis on the fur trade rather than agricultural settlement, the viability of New France depended on friendly relations with local Indians. The French prided themselves on adopting a more humane policy than their imperial rivals. "Only our nation," declared one French writer, "knows the secret of winning the Indians' affection." Lacking the voracious appetite for land of the English colonies and relying

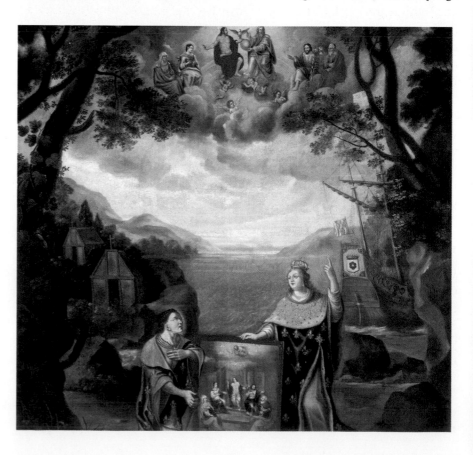

France Bringing the Faith to the Indians of New France. *This painting from the 1670s, attributed to a Franciscan missionary, offers a religious justification for colonization. A Native American in a French robe kneels before a female representation of France. Both hold a painting of the Trinity, suggesting Indians' eager acceptance of Catholicism, while France points skyward, to where God hands the earth to Christ.*

on Indians to supply furs to trading posts, the French worked out a complex series of military, commercial, and diplomatic connections, the most enduring alliances between Indians and settlers in colonial North America. They neither appropriated substantial amounts of Indian land, like the English, nor conquered native inhabitants militarily and set them to forced labor, as in Spanish America. The Jesuits, a missionary religious order, did seek, with some success, to convert Indians to Catholicism. But unlike Spanish missionaries in early New Mexico, they allowed Christian Indians to retain a high degree of independence and much of their traditional social structure, and they did not seek to suppress all traditional religious practices.

Like other colonists throughout North America, however, the French brought striking changes in Indian life. Contact with Europeans was inevitably followed by the spread of disease. Participation in the fur trade drew natives into the burgeoning Atlantic economy, introducing new goods and transforming hunting from a search for food into a quest for marketable commodities. Indians were soon swept into the rivalries among European empires, and Europeans into conflicts among Indians. As early as 1615, the Huron of present-day southern Ontario and upper New York State forged a trading alliance with the French and many converted to Catholicism. In the 1640s, however, after being severely weakened by a smallpox epidemic, the tribe was virtually destroyed in a series of attacks by Iroquois armed by the Dutch.

As in the Spanish empire, New France witnessed considerable cultural exchange and intermixing between colonial and native populations. On the "middle ground" of the upper Great Lakes region in French America, Indians and whites encountered each other for many years on a basis of relative equality. And *métis*, or children of marriages between Indian women and French traders and officials, became guides, traders, and interpreters. Like the Spanish, the French seemed willing to accept Indians as part of colonial society. They encouraged Indians to adopt the European division of labor between men and women, and to speak French. Indians who converted to Catholicism were promised full citizenship. In fact, however, it was far rarer for natives to adopt French ways than for French settlers to become attracted to the "free" life of the Indians. "It happens more commonly," one official complained, "that a Frenchman becomes savage than a savage becomes a Frenchman."

THE DUTCH EMPIRE

In 1609, Henry Hudson, an Englishman employed by the Dutch East India Company, sailed into New York Harbor searching for a Northwest Passage to Asia. He claimed the area for the Netherlands. By 1614, Dutch traders had established an outpost at Fort Orange, near present-day Albany. Twelve years later, the Dutch West India Company, which had been awarded a monopoly of Dutch trade with America, settled colonists on Manhattan Island.

These ventures formed one small part in the rise of the Dutch overseas empire. In the early seventeenth century, the Netherlands dominated international commerce and Amsterdam was Europe's foremost shipping and

A silver medal awarded to Canadian Indian chiefs by Louis XV of France, symbolizing the French-Algonquian alliance on the "middle ground" of the Great Lakes region.

banking center. The small nation had entered a golden age of rapidly accumulating wealth and stunning achievements in painting, philosophy, and the sciences. The Dutch invented the joint stock company, a way of pooling financial resources and sharing the risk of maritime voyages, which proved central to the development of modern capitalism. With a population of only 2 million, the Netherlands established a far-flung empire that reached from Indonesia to South Africa and the Caribbean and temporarily wrested control of Brazil from Portugal.

DUTCH FREEDOM

The Dutch prided themselves on their devotion to liberty. Indeed, in the early seventeenth century they enjoyed two freedoms not recognized elsewhere in Europe—freedom of the press and broad religious toleration. Even though there was an established church, the Dutch Reformed, individuals could hold whatever religious beliefs they wished. Amsterdam had become a haven for persecuted Protestants from all over Europe, including French Huguenots, German Calvinists, and those, like the Pilgrims, who desired to separate from the Church of England. Jews, especially those fleeing from Spain, also found refuge there. Other emigrants came to the Netherlands in the hope of sharing in the country's prosperity. During the seventeenth century, the nation attracted about half a million migrants from elsewhere in Europe. Many of these newcomers helped to populate the Dutch overseas empire.

FREEDOM IN NEW NETHERLAND

Despite the Dutch reputation for cherishing freedom, New Netherland was hardly governed democratically. New Amsterdam, the main population center, was essentially a fortified military outpost controlled by appointees of the West India Company. Although the governor called on prominent citizens for advice from time to time, neither an elected assembly nor a town council, the basic unit of government at home, was established.

In other ways, however, the colonists enjoyed more liberty, especially in religious matters, than their counterparts elsewhere in North America. Even their slaves possessed rights. The Dutch dominated the Atlantic slave trade in the early seventeenth century, and they introduced slaves into New Netherland as a matter of course. By 1650, the colony's 500 slaves outnumbered those in the Chesapeake. Some enjoyed "half-freedom"—they were required to pay an annual fee to the company and work for it when called upon, but they were given land to support their families. Settlers employed slaves on family farms or for household or craft labor, not on large plantations as in the West Indies.

An engraving of New Amsterdam made around 1650 depicts ships involved in transatlantic trade and slaves at work.

Women in the Dutch settlement enjoyed far more independence than in other colonies. According to Dutch law, married women retained their separate legal identity. They could go to court, borrow money, and own property. Men were used to sharing property with their wives. Their wills generally left their possessions to their widows and daughters as well as sons. Margaret Hardenbroeck, the widow of a New Amsterdam merchant, expanded her husband's business and became one of the town's richest residents after his death in 1661.

Most striking was the religious toleration that attracted to New Netherland a remarkably diverse population. As early as the 1630s, at least eighteen languages were said to be spoken in New Amsterdam, whose residents included not only Dutch settlers but also Africans, Belgians, English, French, Germans, Irish, and Scandinavians. Meanwhile, Puritan emigrants from New England established towns on Long Island. Religious toleration extended not only to Protestants but also to Catholics and, grudgingly, to Jews. Twenty-three Jews arrived in New Amsterdam in 1654 from Brazil and the Caribbean. Referring to them as "members of a deceitful race," Governor Peter Stuyvesant ordered the newcomers to leave. But the company overruled him, noting that Jews at home had invested "a large amount of capital" in its shares.

A painting of New Amsterdam in 1650 illustrates the tiny size of the outpost. A gallows stands prominently by the waterfront. Immediately to its right is a tall mechanism for loading and unloading ships.

SETTLING NEW NETHERLAND

In an attempt to attract settlers to North America, the Dutch West India Company promised colonists not only religious toleration but also cheap livestock and free land after six years of labor. Eventually, it even surrendered its monopoly of the fur trade, opening this profitable commerce to all comers. Many settlers, Stuyvesant complained, had been lured by "an imaginary liberty" and did not display much respect for the company's authority.

In 1629, the company adopted a plan of "Freedoms and Exemptions," offering large estates to *patroons*—shareholders who agreed to transport tenants for agricultural labor. The patroon was required to purchase title to the land from Indians, but otherwise his "freedoms" were like those of a medieval lord, including the right to 10 percent of his tenants' annual income and complete authority over law enforcement within his domain. Only one patroonship became a going concern, that of Kiliaen van Rensselaer, who acquired some 700,000 acres in the Hudson Valley. His family's autocratic rule over the tenants, as well as its efforts to extend its domain to include lands settled by New Englanders who claimed that they owned their farms, would inspire sporadic uprisings into the mid-nineteenth century.

During the seventeenth century, the Netherlands sent 1 million people overseas (many of them recent immigrants who were not in fact Dutch) to populate and govern their far-flung colonies. Very few, however, made North America their destination. By the mid-1660s, the European population of New Netherland numbered only 9,000. New Netherland remained a tiny backwater in the Dutch empire. So did an even smaller outpost near present-day Wilmington, Delaware, established in 1638 by a group of Dutch merchants. To circumvent the West India Company's trade monopoly, they claimed to be operating under the Swedish flag and called their settlement New Sweden. There were only 300 settlers when New Netherland seized the colony in 1655.

NEW NETHERLAND AND THE INDIANS

The Dutch came to North America to trade, not to conquer. They were less interested in settling the land than in exacting profits from it. Mindful of the Black Legend of Spanish cruelty, the Dutch determined to treat the native inhabitants more humanely than the Spanish. Having won their own independence from Spain after the longest and bloodiest war of sixteenth-century Europe, many Dutch identified with American Indians as fellow victims of Spanish oppression. They justified their imperial ambitions, in part, as an effort to liberate the New World from the tyranny of Spain and the Catholic Church. Initially, however, they aimed less to convert the Indian population than to employ it in the profitable fur trade.

From the beginning, Dutch authorities recognized Indian sovereignty over the land and forbade settlement in any area until it had been purchased. But they also required tribes to make payments to colonial authorities. Near the coast, where most newcomers settled, New Netherland was hardly free of conflict with the Indians. The expansionist ambitions of Governor William Kieft, who in the 1640s began seizing fertile farmland from the nearby Algonquian Indians, sparked a three-year war that resulted in the death of 1,000 Indians and over 200 colonists. With the powerful Iroquois Confederacy of the upper Hudson Valley, however, the Dutch established friendly commercial and diplomatic relations.

Thus, before the planting of English colonies in North America, other European nations had established various kinds of settlements in the New World. Despite their differences, the Spanish, French, and Dutch empires shared certain features. All brought Christianity, new forms of technology and learning, new legal systems and family relations, new forms of economic enterprise and wealth creation. They also brought savage warfare and widespread disease. These empires were aware of one another's existence. They studied and borrowed from one another, each lauding itself as superior to the others.

From the outset, dreams of freedom—for Indians, for settlers, for the entire world through the spread of Christianity—inspired and justified colonization. It would be no different when, at the beginning of the seventeenth century, England entered the struggle for empire in North America.

The seal of New Netherland, adopted by the Dutch West India Company in 1630, suggests the centrality of the fur trade to the colony's prospects. Surrounding the beaver is wampum, a string of beads used by Indians in religious rituals and as currency.

AMERICAE SIVE NOVI ORBIS, NOVA DESCRIPTIO.

A map of the Western Hemisphere, published in 1592 in Antwerp, then ruled by Spain and now part of Belgium. It shows North America divided between New France and New Spain before the coming of the English.

SUGGESTED READING

Bailyn, Bernard. *Atlantic History: Concept and Contours* (2005). Argues for writing the history of the entire Atlantic region, rather than any particular nation or empire.

Bender, Thomas. *A Nation among Nations: America's Place in World History* (2006). Attempts to place American history in an international global context; the opening chapters offer a global portrait of the age of exploration and conquest.

Calloway, Colin G. *One Vast Winter County: The American West before Lewis and Clark* (2003). A comprehensive portrait of Indian life in one key region of North America.

Crosby, Alfred J. *The Columbian Exchange: Biological and Cultural Consequences of 1492* (1972). Examines the flow of goods and diseases across the Atlantic and their consequences.

Eccles, W. J. *France in America* (1990). Presents the history of French colonization in North America.

Elliott, J. H. *Empires of the Atlantic World: Britain and Spain in America 1492–1830* (2006). A fascinating comparison of the development of two New World empires.

Fernández-Armesto, Felipe. *The Americas: A Hemispheric History* (2003). A brief history that identifies common patterns in the development of North and South America.

Gibson, Charles. *Spain in America* (1966). Surveys the history of Spain's American empire.

Gutiérrez, Ramón A. *When Jesus Came, the Corn Mothers Went Away: Marriage, Sexuality, and Power in New Mexico, 1500–1846* (1991). Discusses the changes in Indian life in New Mexico as a result of Spanish colonization.

Knaut, Andrew L. *The Pueblo Revolt of 1680: Conquest and Resistance in Seventeenth-Century New Mexico* (1997). A recent account of the largest revolt of native peoples.

Mann, Charles C. *1491: New Revelations of the Americas before Columbus* (2005). A comprehensive account of life in the Western Hemisphere before the arrival of Europeans.

Parry, J. H. *The Age of Reconnaissance* (1981). A global history of the era of European exploration and colonization.

Richter, Daniel K. *Facing East from Indian Country* (2001). Examines the era of exploration and settlement as viewed through the experience of Native Americans.

———. *The Ordeal of the Longhouse: The Peoples of the Iroquois League in the Era of European Colonization* (1992). Describes life among one of the most important Indian groups before and after the arrival of Europeans.

Schama, Simon. *Embarrassment of Riches: An Interpretation of Dutch Culture in the Golden Age* (1987). A portrait of Dutch society in the age of empire.

CHAPTER REVIEW **Study and Review at wwnorton.com/studyspace**

REVIEW QUESTIONS

1. Describe why the "discovery" of America was one of the "most important events recorded in the history of mankind," according to Adam Smith.

2. One of the most striking features of the Native American society at the time of European discovery was its sheer diversity. Support this statement.

3. Compare and contrast European values and ways of life to that of the Indians. Be sure to look at religion, views on property ownership, gender relations, and views of freedom.

4. What were the main factors fueling the European age of expansion?

5. Describe the political, religious, and economic motivations for Spanish conquest.

KEY TERMS

Cahokia (p. 11)

caravel (p. 21)

Vinland (p. 23)

reconquista (p. 23)

Columbian Exchange (p. 26)

mestizos (p. 30)

encomienda system (p. 33)

Pueblo Revolt (p. 36)

REVIEW TABLE

Early Explorers of the New World

Explorer	Dates	Area Explored
Christopher Columbus	1492	Caribbean and Central America
John Cabot	1497	Newfoundland
Amerigo Vespucci	1499–1502	Coast of Brazil, Gulf of Mexico
Pedro Cabral	1500	South America (Brazil)
Juan Ponce de León	1513	Florida
Ferdinand Magellan	1519–1522	Sailed around the world
Juan Oñate	1598	American Southwest
Nicolás de Ovando	1502	Hispaniola
Vasco Núñez de Balboa	1513	Panama Isthmus
Francisco Pizarro	1530s	Peru

CHAPTER 2

Beginnings of English America, 1607–1660

A self-portrait from around 1680, painted by Thomas Smith. A sailor who came to New England from Bermuda around 1650, Smith acquired considerable wealth, as evidenced by his fashionable clothing. The background depicts a naval battle involving Dutch and English ships (possibly a reference to their joint attack on a North African port in 1670). In the foreground is a poem with Smith's initials. This is the earliest-known American self-portrait.

FOCUS QUESTIONS

- What were the main contours of English colonization in the seventeenth century?

- How did English settlers gain a foothold in the early Chesapeake colonies?

- How did Virginia and Maryland develop in their early years?

- What made the English settlement of New England distinctive?

- What were the main sources of discord in early New England?

- How did the English Civil War affect the colonies in America?

On April 26, 1607, three small ships carrying colonists from England sailed out of the morning mist at what is now called Cape Henry into the mouth of Chesapeake Bay. After exploring the area for a little over two weeks, they chose a site sixty miles inland on the James River for their settlement, hoping to protect themselves from marauding Spanish warships. Here they established Jamestown (named for the king of England) as the capital of the colony of Virginia (named for his predecessor, Elizabeth I, the "virgin queen"). But despite these bows to royal authority, the voyage was sponsored not by the English government, in 1607 hard-pressed for funds, but by the Virginia Company, a private business organization whose shareholders included merchants, aristocrats, and members of Parliament, and to which the queen gave her blessing.

When the three ships returned home, 104 settlers remained in Virginia. All were men, for the Virginia Company had more interest in searching for gold and in other ways exploiting the area's natural resources than in establishing a functioning society. Nevertheless, Jamestown became the first permanent English settlement in the area that is now the United States. The settlers were the first of tens of thousands of Europeans who crossed the Atlantic during the seventeenth century to live and work in North America. They led the way for new empires that mobilized labor and economic resources, reshaped societies throughout the Atlantic world, and shifted the balance of power at home from Spain and Portugal to the nations of northwestern Europe.

The founding of Jamestown took place at a time of heightened European involvement in North America. Interest in colonization was spurred by national and religious rivalries and the growth of a merchant class eager to invest in overseas expansion and to seize for itself a greater share of world trade. As noted in Chapter 1, it was quickly followed by the founding of Quebec by France in 1608, and Henry Hudson's exploration in 1609 of the river that today bears his name, leading to the founding of the Dutch colony of New Netherland. In 1610, the Spanish established Santa Fe as the capital of New Mexico. Over a century after the voyages of Columbus, the European penetration of North America had finally begun in earnest. It occurred from many directions at once—from east to west at the Atlantic coast, north to south along the St. Lawrence and Mississippi rivers, and south to north in what is now the American Southwest.

English North America in the seventeenth century was a place where entrepreneurs sought to make fortunes, religious minorities hoped to worship without governmental interference and to create societies based on biblical teachings, and aristocrats dreamed of re-creating a vanished world of feudalism. Those who drew up blueprints for settlement expected to reproduce the social structure with which they were familiar, with all its hierarchy and inequality. The lower orders would occupy the same less-than-fully-free status as in England, subject to laws regulating their labor and depriving them of a role in politics. But for ordinary men and women, emigration offered an escape from lives of deprivation and inequality. "No man," wrote John Smith, an early leader of Jamestown, "will go from [England] to have less freedom" in America. The charter of the Virginia Company, granted by James I in 1606, promised that colonists would enjoy "all liberties" of those residing in "our realm of England." The settlers of English America came to enjoy greater rights than colonists of other empires, including the power to choose members of elected assemblies, protections of the common law such as the right to trial by jury, and access to land, the key to economic independence.

Many degrees of freedom coexisted in seventeenth-century North America, from the slave, stripped completely of liberty, to the independent landowner, who enjoyed a full range of rights. During a lifetime, a person might well occupy more than one place on this spectrum. The settlers' success, however, rested on depriving Native Americans of their land and, in some colonies, on importing large numbers of African slaves as laborers. Freedom and lack of freedom expanded together in seventeenth-century America.

ENGLAND AND THE NEW WORLD

UNIFYING THE ENGLISH NATION

Although John Cabot, sailing from England in 1497, had been the first European since the Vikings to encounter the North American continent, English exploration and colonization would wait for many years. As the case of Spain suggests, early empire building was, in large part, an extension of the consolidation of national power in Europe. But during the sixteenth century, England was a second-rate power racked by internal disunity. Henry VII, who assumed the throne in 1485, had to unify the kingdom after a long period of civil war. His son and successor, Henry VIII, launched the Reformation in England. When the Pope refused to annul his marriage to Catherine of Aragon, Henry severed the nation from the Catholic Church. In its place he established the Church of England, or Anglican Church, with himself at the head. Decades of religious strife followed. Under Henry's son Edward VI, who became king at the age of ten in 1547, the regents who governed the country persecuted Catholics. When Edward died in 1553, his stepsister Mary became queen. Mary temporarily restored Catholicism as the state religion and executed a number of Protestants. Her rule was so unpopular that reconciliation with Rome became impossible. Mary's successor, Elizabeth I (reigned

Mary, the queen who attempted to restore Catholicism in England, as painted by an unknown artist.

1558–1603), restored the Anglican ascendancy and executed over 100 Catholic priests.

ENGLAND AND IRELAND

England's long struggle to conquer and pacify Ireland, which lasted well into the seventeenth century, absorbed money and energy that might have been directed toward the New World. In subduing Ireland, whose Catholic population was deemed a threat to the stability of Protestant rule in England, the government employed a variety of approaches, including military conquest, the slaughter of civilians, the seizure of land and introduction of English economic practices, and the dispatch of large numbers of settlers. Rather than seeking to absorb the Irish into English society, the English excluded the native population from a territory of settlement known as the Pale, where the colonists created their own social order.

Just as the "reconquest" of Spain from the Moors established patterns that would be repeated in Spanish New World colonization, the methods used in Ireland anticipated policies England would undertake in America. Some sixteenth-century English writers directly compared the allegedly barbaric "wild Irish" with American Indians. Like the Indians, the Irish supposedly confused liberty and license. They refused to respect English authority and resisted conversion to English Protestantism. The early English colonies in North America and the West Indies were known as "plantations" (that is, communities "planted" from abroad among an alien population); the same term was originally used to describe Protestant settlements in Ireland.

ENGLAND AND NORTH AMERICA

Not until the reign of Elizabeth I did the English turn their attention to North America, although sailors and adventurers still showed more interest in raiding Spanish cities and treasure fleets in the Caribbean than establishing settlements. The government granted charters (grants of exclusive rights and privileges) to Sir Humphrey Gilbert and Sir Walter Raleigh, authorizing them to establish colonies in North America at their own expense.

With little or no support from the crown, both ventures failed. Gilbert, who had earned a reputation for brutality in the Irish wars by murdering civilians and burning their crops, established a short-lived settlement on Newfoundland in 1582. Three years later, Raleigh dispatched a fleet of five ships with some 100 colonists (many of them his personal servants) to set up a base on Roanoke Island, off the North Carolina coast, partly to facilitate continuing raids on Spanish shipping. But the colonists, mostly young men under military leadership, abandoned the venture in 1586 and returned to England. A second group of 100 settlers, composed of families who hoped to establish a permanent colony, was dispatched that year. Their fate remains a mystery. When a ship bearing supplies arrived in 1590, the sailors found the colony abandoned, with the inhabitants evidently having moved to live among the Indians. The word "Croaton," the Indian

The Armada Portrait *of Queen Elizabeth I, by the artist George Gower, commemorates the defeat of the Spanish Armada in 1588 and appears to link it with English colonization of the New World. England's victorious navy is visible through the window, while the queen's hand rests on a globe, with her fingers pointing to the coast of North America.*

name for a nearby island or tribe, had been carved on a tree. Raleigh, by now nearly bankrupt, lost his enthusiasm for colonization. To establish a successful colony, it seemed clear, would require more planning and economic resources than any individual could provide.

SPREADING PROTESTANTISM

As in the case of Spain, national glory, profit, and religious mission merged in early English thinking about the New World. The Reformation heightened the English government's sense of Catholic Spain as its mortal enemy (a belief reinforced in 1588 when a Spanish naval armada unsuccessfully attempted to invade the British Isles). Just as Spain justified its empire in part by claiming to convert Indians to Catholicism, England expressed its imperial ambitions in terms of an obligation to liberate the New World from the tyranny of the Pope. By the late sixteenth century, anti-Catholicism had become deeply ingrained in English popular culture. Reports of the atrocities of Spanish rule were widely circulated. English translations of Bartolomé de Las Casas's writings appeared during Elizabeth's reign. One, using a common Protestant term for the Catholic Church, bore the title, "Popery Truly Displayed."

Although atrocities were hardly confined to any one nation—as England's own conduct in Ireland demonstrated—the idea that the empire of Catholic Spain was uniquely murderous and tyrannical enabled the English to describe their own imperial ambitions in the language of freedom. In *A Discourse Concerning Western Planting*, written in 1584 at the request of Sir Walter Raleigh, the Protestant minister and scholar Richard Hakluyt

know him

listed twenty-three reasons why Queen Elizabeth I should support the establishment of colonies. Among them was the idea that English settlements would strike a blow against Spain's empire and therefore form part of a divine mission to rescue the New World and its inhabitants from the influence of Catholicism and tyranny. "Tied as slaves" under Spanish rule, he wrote, the Indians of the New World were "crying out to us . . . to come and help." They would welcome English settlers and "revolt clean from the Spaniard," crying "with one voice, Liberia, Liberia, as desirous of liberty and freedom." England would repeat much of Spain's behavior in the New World. But the English always believed that they were unique. In their case, empire and freedom would go hand in hand.

MOTIVES FOR COLONIZATION

But bringing freedom to Indians was hardly the only argument Hakluyt marshaled as England prepared to step onto the world stage. National power and glory were never far from the minds of the era's propagandists of empire. Through colonization, Hakluyt and other writers argued, England, a relatively minor power in Europe at the end of the sixteenth century, could come to rival the wealth and standing of great nations like Spain and France.

Other considerations also weighed heavily in their arguments. Spanish claims to the south and French explorations in the area of present-day Canada left to England the middle part of North America, a region deemed worthless by other powers because it lacked precious metals and was unsuitable for sugar cultivation, the two paths to riches in early American empires. This did not, however, prevent promoters of colonization from painting a portrait of a fertile land of "great plenty." Its animals were supposedly so abundant and its climate and soil so favorable that colonists could enrich the mother country and themselves by providing English consumers with goods now supplied by foreigners and opening a new market for English products. Unlike early adventurers such as Raleigh, who thought of wealth in terms of deposits of gold, Hakluyt insisted that trade would be the basis of England's empire.

THE SOCIAL CRISIS

Equally important, America could be a refuge for England's "surplus" population, benefiting mother country and emigrants alike. The late sixteenth century was a time of social crisis in England, with economic growth unable to keep pace with the needs of a population that grew from 3 million in 1550 to about 4 million in 1600. For many years, English peasants had enjoyed a secure hold on their plots of land. But in the sixteenth and seventeenth centuries, landlords sought profits by raising sheep for the expanding trade in wool and introducing more modern farming practices such as crop rotation. They evicted small farmers and fenced in "commons" previously open to all.

While many landlords, farmers, and town merchants benefited from the "enclosure" movement, as this process was called, thousands of persons were uprooted from the land. Many flooded into England's cities, where

An engraving by Theodor de Bry depicts colonists hunting and fishing in Virginia. Promotional images such as this emphasized the abundance of the New World and suggested that colonists could live familiar lives there.

wages fell dramatically. Others, denounced by authorities as rogues, vagabonds, and vagrants, wandered the roads in search of work. Their situation grew worse as prices throughout Europe rose, buoyed by the influx of gold and silver from the mines of Latin America into Spain. A pioneering study of English society conducted at the end of the seventeenth century estimated that half the population lived at or below the poverty line. The cost of poor relief fell mainly on local communities. "All our towns," wrote the Puritan leader John Winthrop in 1629, shortly before leaving England for Massachusetts, "complain of the burden of poor people and strive by all means to rid any such as they have." England, he added somberly, "grows weary of her inhabitants."

The government struggled to deal with this social crisis. Under Henry VIII, those without jobs could be whipped, branded, forced into the army, or hanged. During Elizabeth's reign, a law authorized justices of the peace to regulate hours and wages and put the unemployed to work. "Vagrants" were required to accept any job offered to them and could be punished if they sought to change employment. Another solution was to encourage the unruly poor to leave for the New World. Richard Hakluyt wrote of the advantages of settling in America "such needy people of our country who now trouble the commonwealth and . . . commit outrageous offenses." As colonists, they could become productive citizens, contributing to the nation's wealth.

MASTERLESS MEN

As early as 1516, when Thomas More published *Utopia*, a novel set on an imaginary island in the Western Hemisphere, the image of America as a place where settlers could escape from the economic inequalities of Europe had been circulating in England. This ideal coincided with the goals of ordinary Englishmen. Although authorities saw wandering or unemployed "masterless men" as a danger to society and tried to force them to accept jobs, popular attitudes viewed economic dependence as itself a form of servitude. Working for wages was widely associated with servility and loss of liberty. Only those who controlled their own labor could be regarded as truly free. Indeed, popular tales and ballads romanticized the very vagabonds, highwaymen, and even beggars denounced by the propertied and powerful, since despite their poverty they at least enjoyed freedom from wage work.

The image of the New World as a unique place of opportunity, where the English laboring classes could regain economic independence by acquiring land and where even criminals would enjoy a second chance, was deeply rooted from the earliest days of settlement. John Smith had scarcely landed in Virginia in 1607 when he wrote that in America "every man may be the master and owner of his own labor and land." In 1623, the royal letter approving the recruitment of emigrants to New England promised that any

GIN LANE.

William Hogarth's well-known engraving Gin Lane (1751) offers a satiric glimpse of lower-class life in London. Hogarth was particularly concerned about the abuse of alcohol. A drunken woman allows her baby to fall from her arms while, on the left, a man and his wife pawn their coats, tools, and cooking utensils for money for liquor.

Know:
John Winthrop

settler could easily become "lord of 200 acres of land"—an amount far beyond the reach of most Englishmen. The main lure for emigrants from England to the New World was not so much riches in gold and silver as the promise of independence that followed from owning land. Economic freedom and the possibility of passing it on to one's children attracted the largest number of English colonists.

THE COMING OF THE ENGLISH

ENGLISH EMIGRANTS

Seventeenth-century North America was an unstable and dangerous environment. Diseases decimated Indian and settler populations alike. Colonies were racked by religious, political, and economic tensions and drawn into imperial wars and conflict with Indians. They remained dependent on the mother country for protection and economic assistance. Without sustained immigration, most settlements would have collapsed. With a population of between 4 million and 5 million, about half of Spain and a quarter of that of France, England produced a far larger number of men, women, and children willing to brave the dangers of emigration to the New World. In large part, this was because economic conditions in England were so bad.

Between 1607 and 1700, over half a million people left England. North America was not the destination of the majority of these emigrants. Approximately 180,000 settled in Ireland, and about the same number migrated to the West Indies, where the introduction of sugar cultivation promised riches for those who could obtain land. Nonetheless, the population of England's mainland colonies quickly outstripped that of their rivals. The Chesapeake area, where the tobacco-producing colonies Virginia and Maryland developed a constant demand for cheap labor, received about 120,000 settlers, most of whom landed before 1660. New England attracted 21,000 emigrants, nearly all of them arriving before 1640. In the second part of the seventeenth century, the Middle Colonies (New York, New Jersey, and Pennsylvania) attracted about 23,000 settlers. Although the arrivals to New England and the Middle Colonies included many families, the majority of newcomers were young, single men from the bottom rungs of English society, who had little to lose by emigrating. Many had already moved from place to place in England. Colonial settlement was in many ways an extension of the migration at home of an increasingly mobile English population.

INDENTURED SERVANTS

Settlers who could pay for their own passage—government officials, clergymen, merchants, artisans, landowning farmers, and members of the lesser nobility—arrived in America as free persons. Most quickly acquired land. In the seventeenth century, however, nearly two-thirds of English settlers came as indentured servants, who voluntarily surrendered their

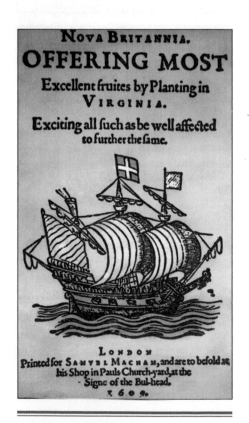

A pamphlet published in 1609 promoting emigration to Virginia.

freedom for a specified time (usually five to seven years) in exchange for passage to America.

Like slaves, servants could be bought and sold, could not marry without the permission of their owner, were subject to physical punishment, and saw their obligation to labor enforced by the courts. To ensure uninterrupted work by female servants, the law lengthened the term of their indenture if they became pregnant. "Many Negroes are better used," complained Elizabeth Sprigs, an indentured servant in Maryland who described being forced to work "day and night . . . then tied up and whipped." But, unlike slaves, servants could look forward to a release from bondage. Assuming they survived their period of labor, servants would receive a payment known as "freedom dues" and become free members of society.

For most of the seventeenth century, however, indentured servitude was not a guaranteed route to economic autonomy. Given the high death rate, many servants did not live to the end of their terms. Freedom dues were sometimes so meager that they did not enable recipients to acquire land. Many servants found the reality of life in the New World less appealing than they had anticipated. Employers constantly complained of servants running away, not working diligently, or being unruly, all manifestations of what one commentator called their "fondness for freedom."

LAND AND LIBERTY

Access to land played many roles in seventeenth-century America. Land, English settlers believed, was the basis of liberty. Owning land gave men control over their own labor and, in most colonies, the right to vote. The promise of immediate access to land lured free settlers, and freedom dues that included land persuaded potential immigrants to sign contracts as indentured servants. Land in America also became a way for the king to reward relatives and allies. Each colony was launched with a huge grant of land from the crown, either to a company or to a private individual known as a proprietor. Some grants, if taken literally, stretched from the Atlantic Ocean to the Pacific.

Land was a source of wealth and power for colonial officials and their favorites, who acquired enormous estates. Without labor, however, land would have little value. Since emigrants did not come to America intending to work the land of others (except temporarily in the case of indentured servants), the very abundance of "free" land eventually led many property owners to turn to slaves as a workforce.

ENGLISHMEN AND INDIANS

Land in North America, of course, was already occupied. And the arrival of English settlers presented the native inhabitants of eastern North America with the greatest crisis in their history. Unlike the Spanish, English colonists did not call themselves "conquerors." They wanted land, not dominion over the existing population. They were chiefly interested in displacing the Indians and settling on their land, not intermarrying with

An indenture (a contract for labor for a period of years) signed by James Mahoney, who emigrated from Ireland to North America in 1723.

them, organizing their labor, or making them subjects of the crown. The marriage between John Rolfe and Pocahontas, the daughter of Virginia's leading chief, discussed below, is well known but almost unique. No such mixed marriage took place in seventeenth-century Massachusetts and only two more in Virginia before the legislature outlawed the practice in 1691. The English exchanged goods with the native population, and Indians often traveled through colonial settlements. Fur traders on the frontiers of settlement sometimes married Indian women, partly as a way of gaining access to native societies and the kin networks essential to economic relationships. Most English settlers, however, remained obstinately separate from their Indian neighbors.

Despite their insistence that Indians had no real claim to land since they did not cultivate or improve it, most colonial authorities in practice recognized Indians' title based on occupancy. They acquired land by purchase, often in treaties forced upon Indians after they had suffered military defeat. Colonial courts recorded numerous sales of Indian land to governments or individual settlers. To keep the peace, some colonial governments tried to prevent the private seizure or purchase of Indian lands, or they declared certain areas off-limits to settlers. But these measures were rarely enforced and ultimately proved ineffective. New settlers and freed servants sought land for themselves, and those who established families in America needed land for their children.

The seventeenth century was marked by recurrent warfare between colonists and Indians. These conflicts generated a strong feeling of superiority among the colonists and left them intent on maintaining the real and imagined boundaries separating the two peoples. In the initial stages of settlement, English colonists often established towns on sites Indians had cleared, planted Indian crops, and adopted Indian technology such as snowshoes and canoes, which were valuable for travel in the American

An engraving by John White of an Indian village surrounded by a stockade.

wilderness. But over time the English displaced the original inhabitants more thoroughly than any other European empire.

THE TRANSFORMATION OF INDIAN LIFE

Many eastern Indians initially welcomed the newcomers, or at least their goods, which they appreciated for their practical advantages. Items like woven cloth, metal kettles, iron axes, fishhooks, hoes, and guns were quickly integrated into Indian life. Indians also displayed a great desire for goods like colorful glass beads and copper ornaments that could be incorporated into their religious ceremonies.

As Indians became integrated into the Atlantic economy, subtle changes took place in Indian life. European metal goods changed their farming, hunting, and cooking practices. Men devoted more time to hunting beaver for fur trading. Older skills deteriorated as the use of European products expanded, and alcohol became increasingly common and disruptive. Indians learned to bargain effectively and to supply items that Europeans desired. Later observers would describe this trade as one in which Indians exchanged valuable commodities like furs and animal skins for worthless European trinkets. In fact, both Europeans and Indians gave up goods they had in abundance in exchange for items in short supply in their own society. But as the colonists achieved military superiority over the Indians, the profits of trade mostly flowed to colonial and European merchants. Growing connections with Europeans stimulated warfare among Indian tribes, and the overhunting of beaver and deer forced some groups to encroach on territory claimed by others. And newcomers from Europe brought epidemics that decimated Indian populations.

CHANGES IN THE LAND

Traders, religious missionaries, and colonial authorities all sought to reshape Indian society and culture. But as settlers spread over the land, they threatened Indians' ways of life more completely than any company of soldiers or group of bureaucrats. As settlers fenced in more and more land and introduced new crops and livestock, the natural environment changed in ways that undermined traditional Indian agriculture and hunting. Pigs and cattle roamed freely, trampling Indian cornfields and gardens. The need for wood to build and heat homes and export to England depleted forests on which Indians relied for hunting. The rapid expansion of the fur trade diminished the population of beaver and other animals. "Since you are here strangers, and come into our country," one group of Indians told early settlers in the Chesapeake, "you should rather conform yourselves to the customs of our country, than impose yours on us." But it was the Indians whose lives were most powerfully altered by the changes set in motion in 1607 when English colonists landed at Jamestown.

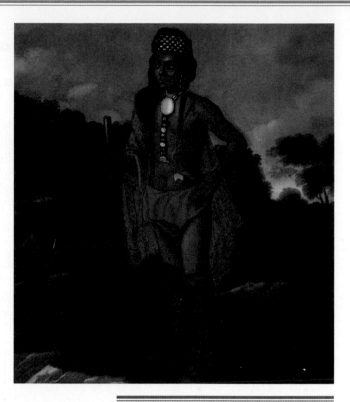

The only known contemporary portrait of a New England Indian, this 1681 painting by an unnamed artist was long thought to represent Ninigret II, a leader of the Narragansetts of Rhode Island. It has been more recently identified as David, an Indian who saved the life of John Winthrop II, a governor of colonial Connecticut. Apart from the wampum beads around his neck, everything the Indian wears is of English manufacture.

SETTLING THE CHESAPEAKE

THE JAMESTOWN COLONY

The early history of Jamestown was, to say the least, not promising. The colony's leadership changed repeatedly, its inhabitants suffered an extraordinarily high death rate, and, with the company seeking a quick profit, supplies from England proved inadequate. The hopes of locating riches such as the Spanish had found in Mexico were quickly dashed. "Silver and gold they have none," one Spanish observer commented, their local resources were "not much to be regarded," and they had "no commerce with any nation." The first settlers were "a quarrelsome band of gentlemen and servants." They included few farmers and laborers and numerous sons of English gentry and high-status craftsmen (jewelers, stonecutters, and the like), who preferred to prospect for gold rather than farm. They "would rather starve than work," declared John Smith, one of the colony's first leaders.

Jamestown lay beside a swamp containing malaria-carrying mosquitoes, and the garbage settlers dumped into the local river bred germs that caused dysentery and typhoid fever. Disease and lack of food took a heavy toll. By the end of the first year, the original population of 104 had fallen by half. New arrivals (including the first two women, who landed in 1608) brought the numbers up to 400 in 1609, but by 1610, after a winter long remembered as the "starving time," only 65 settlers remained alive. At one point, the survivors abandoned Jamestown and sailed for England, only to be intercepted and persuaded to return to Virginia by ships carrying a new governor, 250 colonists, and supplies. By 1616, about 80 percent of the immigrants who had arrived in the first decade were dead.

Only rigorous military discipline held the colony together. John Smith was a forceful man whose career before coming to America included a period fighting the Turks in Hungary, where he was captured and for a time enslaved. He imposed a regime of forced labor on company lands. "He that will not work, shall not eat," Smith declared. Smith's autocratic mode of governing alienated many of the colonists. After being injured in an accidental gunpowder explosion in 1609, he was forced to return to England. But his immediate successors continued his iron rule.

FROM COMPANY TO SOCIETY

The Virginia Company slowly realized that for the colony to survive it would have to abandon the search for gold, grow its own food, and find a marketable commodity. It would also have to attract more settlers. With this end in view, it announced new policies in 1618 that powerfully

By 1650, English settlement in the Chesapeake had spread well beyond the initial colony at Jamestown, as tobacco planters sought fertile land near navigable waterways.

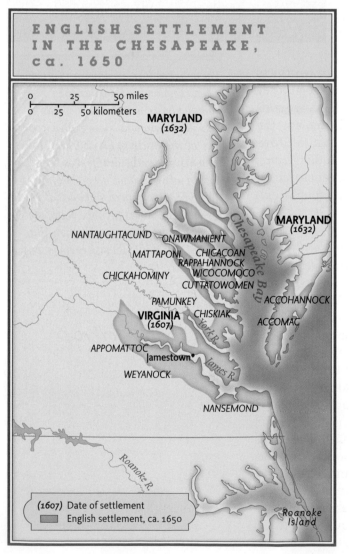

ENGLISH SETTLEMENT IN THE CHESAPEAKE, ca. 1650

MARYLAND (1632)

MARYLAND (1632)

NANTAUGHTACUND
ONAWMANIENT
MATTAPONI
CHICACOAN
RAPPAHANNOCK
CHICKAHOMINY
WICOCOMOCO
CUTTATOWOMEN
PAMUNKEY
ACCOHANNOCK
VIRGINIA (1607)
CHISKIAK
ACCOMAC
York R.
APPOMATTOC
Jamestown
James R.
WEYANOCK
NANSEMOND
Chesapeake Bay

Roanoke R.

(1607) Date of settlement
English settlement, ca. 1650

Roanoke Island

shaped Virginia's development as a functioning society rather than the outpost of London-based investors. Instead of retaining all the land for itself, the company introduced the headright system, awarding fifty acres of land to any colonist who paid for his own or another's passage. Thus, anyone who brought in a sizable number of servants would immediately acquire a large estate. In place of the governor's militaristic regime, a "charter of grants and liberties" was issued, including the establishment of a House of Burgesses. When it convened in 1619, this became the first elected assembly in colonial America.

The House of Burgesses was hardly a model of democracy—only landowners could vote, and the company and its appointed governor retained the right to nullify any measure the body adopted. But its creation established a political precedent that all English colonies would eventually follow. Also in 1619, the first twenty blacks arrived in Virginia on a Dutch vessel. The full significance of these two events would not be apparent until years later. But they laid the foundation for a society that would one day be dominated economically and politically by slaveowning planters.

POWHATAN AND POCAHONTAS

When the English arrived at Jamestown, they landed in an area inhabited by some 15,000 to 25,000 Indians living in numerous small agricultural villages. Most acknowledged the rule of Wahunsonacock, a shrewd and forceful leader who had recently consolidated his authority over the region and collected tribute from some thirty subordinate tribes. Called Powhatan by the settlers after the Indian word for both his tribe and his title of paramount chief, he quickly realized the advantages of trade with the newcomers. For its part, mindful of Las Casas's condemnation of Spanish behavior, the Virginia Company instructed its colonists to treat local Indians kindly and to try to convert them to Christianity. Realizing that the colonists depended on the Indians for food, John Smith tried to stop settlers from seizing produce from nearby villages, lest the Indians cut off all trade.

In the first two years of Jamestown's existence, relations with Indians were mostly peaceful and based on a fairly equal give-and-take. At one point, Smith was captured by the Indians and threatened with execution by Powhatan, only to be rescued by Pocahontas, reputedly the favorite among his many children by dozens of wives. The incident has come down in legend (most recently a popular animated film) as an example of a rebellious, love-struck teenager defying her father. In fact, it was probably part of an elaborate ceremony designed by Powhatan to demonstrate his power over the colonists and incorporate them into his realm. Pocahontas subsequently became an intermediary between the two peoples, bringing food and messages to Jamestown.

John Smith's return to England raised tensions between the two groups and a period of sporadic conflict began in 1610, with the English massacring villagers indiscriminately and destroying Indian crops. Pocahontas herself was captured and held as a hostage by the settlers in 1613. While confined to Jamestown, she converted to Christianity. As part of the restoration of peace in 1614, she married the English colonist John Rolfe. Two years later, she accompanied her husband to England, where she

A portrait of John Smith, the leader of the early Virginia colony, engraved on a 1624 map of New England.

The only portrait of Pocahontas during her lifetime was engraved by Simon van de Passe in England in 1616. After converting to Christianity, Pocahontas took the name Rebecca.

POWHATAN

Appamatuck

In folcher Maieſtät hat ſich der
Konig für dem gefangenen Capitain
Schmidt erzeigt und ſehen laſſen.

Powhatan, the most prominent Indian leader in the original area of English settlement in Virginia. This image, showing Powhatan and his court, was engraved on John Smith's map of Virginia and included in Smith's General History of Virginia, *published in 1624.*

caused a sensation in the court of James I as a symbol of Anglo-Indian harmony and missionary success. But she succumbed to disease in 1617. Her father died the following year.

THE UPRISING OF 1622

Once it became clear that the English were interested in establishing a permanent and constantly expanding colony, not a trading post, conflict with local Indians was inevitable. The peace that began in 1614 ended abruptly in 1622 when Powhatan's brother and successor, Opechancanough, led a brilliantly planned surprise attack that in a single day wiped out one-quarter of Virginia's settler population of 1,200. The surviving 900 colonists organized themselves into military bands, which then massacred scores of Indians and devastated their villages. A spokesman for the Virginia Company explained the reason behind the Indian assault: "The daily fear that . . . in time we by our growing continually upon them would dispossess them of this country." But by going to war, declared Governor Francis Wyatt, the Indians had forfeited any claim to the land. Virginia's policy, he continued, must now be nothing less than the "expulsion of the savages to gain the free range of the country."

Indians remained a significant presence in Virginia, and trade continued throughout the century. But the unsuccessful uprising of 1622 fundamentally shifted the balance of power in the colony. The settlers' supremacy was reinforced in 1644 when a last desperate rebellion led by Opechancanough, now said to be 100 years old, was crushed after causing the deaths of some 500 colonists. Virginia forced a treaty on the surviving coastal Indians, who now numbered less than 2,000, that acknowledged their subordination to the government at Jamestown and required them to move to tribal reservations to the west and not enter areas of European settlement without permission. This policy of separation followed the precedent already established in Ireland. Settlers spreading inland into the Virginia countryside continued to seize Indian lands.

The destruction caused by the uprising of 1622 was the last in a series of blows suffered by the Virginia Company. Two years later, it surrendered its charter and Virginia became the first royal colony, its governor now appointed by the crown. Virginia had failed to accomplish any of its goals for either the company or the settlers. Investors had not turned a profit, and although the company had sent 6,000 settlers to Virginia, its white population numbered only 1,200 when the king assumed control. Preoccupied with affairs at home, the government in London for years paid little attention to Virginia. Henceforth, the local elite, not a faraway company, controlled the colony's development. And that elite was growing rapidly in wealth and power thanks to the cultivation of a crop introduced from the West Indies by John Rolfe—tobacco.

A TOBACCO COLONY

King James I considered tobacco "harmful to the brain and dangerous to the lungs" and issued a spirited warning against its use. But increasing numbers of Europeans enjoyed smoking and believed the tobacco plant had medicinal

Theodor de Bry's engraving of the 1622 Indian uprising in Virginia depicts the Indians massacring defenseless colonists (who are shown unarmed although many in fact owned guns).

benefits. As a commodity with an ever-expanding mass market in Europe, tobacco became Virginia's substitute for gold. It enriched an emerging class of tobacco planters, as well as members of the colonial government who assigned good land to themselves. The crown profited from customs duties (taxes on tobacco that entered or left the kingdom). By 1624, over 200,000 pounds were being grown, producing startling profits for landowners. Forty years later, the crop totaled 15 million pounds, and it doubled again by the 1680s. The spread of tobacco farming produced a dispersed society with few towns and little social unity. It inspired a get-rich-quick attitude and a frenzied scramble for land and labor. By the middle of the seventeenth century, a new influx of immigrants with ample financial resources—sons of merchants and English gentlemen—had taken advantage of the headright system and governmental connections to acquire large estates along navigable rivers. They established themselves as the colony's social and political elite.

The expansion of tobacco cultivation also led to an increased demand for field labor, met for most of the seventeenth century by young, male indentured servants. Despite harsh conditions of work in the tobacco fields, a persistently high death rate, and laws mandating punishments from whipping to an extension of service for those who ran away or were unruly, the abundance of land continued to attract migrants. Of the 120,000 English immigrants who entered the Chesapeake region during the seventeenth century, three-quarters came as servants. Virginia's white society increasingly came to resemble that of England, with a wealthy landed gentry at

An advertisement for tobacco, including the image of Sir Walter Raleigh. At the bottom, slaves handle barrels and a tobacco plant.

the top; a group of small farmers, mostly former indentured servants who had managed to acquire land, in the middle; and an army of poor laborers—servants and landless former indentured servants—at the bottom. By 1700, the region's white population had grown to nearly 90,000.

WOMEN AND THE FAMILY

Virginia, however, lacked one essential element of English society—stable family life. The colony avidly promoted the immigration of women, including several dozen "tobacco brides" who arrived in 1620 and 1621 for arranged marriages. But given the demand for male servants to work in the tobacco fields, men in the Chesapeake outnumbered women for most of the seventeenth century by four or five to one. The vast majority of women who emigrated to the region came as indentured servants. Since they usually had to complete their terms of service before marrying, they did not begin to form families until their mid-twenties. The high death rate, unequal ratio between the sexes, and late age of marriage for those who found partners retarded population growth and produced a society with large numbers of single men, widows, and orphans. Although patriarchal ideals remained intact in Virginia, in practice the traditional authority of husbands and fathers was weakened. Because of their own low life expectancy, fathers found it difficult to supervise the careers and marriages of their children.

In the colonies as in England, a married woman possessed certain rights before the law, including a claim to "dower rights" of one-third of her husband's property in the event that he died before she did. When the widow died, however, the property passed to the husband's male heirs. (English law was far less generous than in Spain, where a woman could hold inde-

Processing tobacco was as labor-intensive as caring for the plant in the fields. Here scantily clad slaves and female indentured servants work with the crop after it has been harvested.

pendently any property inherited from her parents, and a man and wife owned jointly all the wealth accumulated during a marriage.)

Social conditions in the colonies, however, opened the door to roles women rarely assumed in England. Widows and the few women who never married took advantage of their legal status as femme sole (a woman alone, who enjoyed an independent legal identity denied to married women) to make contracts and conduct business. Margaret Brent, who emigrated to the Chesapeake in 1638, acquired land, managed her own plantation, and acted as a lawyer in court. Some widows were chosen to administer their husbands' estates or were willed their husbands' property outright, rather than receiving only the one-third "dower rights." But because most women came to Virginia as indentured servants, they could look forward only to a life of hard labor in the tobacco fields and early death. Servants were frequently subjected to sexual abuse by their masters. Those who married often found themselves in poverty when their husbands died.

THE MARYLAND EXPERIMENT

Although it began under very different sponsorship and remained much smaller than Virginia during the seventeenth century, the second Chesapeake colony, Maryland, followed a similar course of development. As in Virginia, tobacco came to dominate the economy and tobacco planters the society. But in other ways, Maryland's history was strikingly different.

Maryland was established in 1632 as a proprietary colony, that is, a grant of land and governmental authority to a single individual. This was Cecilius Calvert, the son of a recently deceased favorite of King Charles I. The charter made Calvert proprietor of the colony and granted him "full, free, and absolute power," including control of trade and the right to initiate all legislation, with an elected assembly confined to approving or disapproving his proposals. Calvert imagined Maryland as a feudal domain. Land would be laid out in manors with the owners paying "quitrents" to the proprietor. Calvert disliked representative institutions and believed ordinary people should not meddle in governmental affairs. On the other hand, the charter also guaranteed to colonists "all privileges, franchises, and liberties" of Englishmen. While these were not spelled out, they undoubtedly included the idea of a government limited by the law. Here was a recipe for conflict, and Maryland had more than its share during the seventeenth century.

RELIGION IN MARYLAND

Further aggravating instability in the colony was the fact that Calvert, a Catholic, envisioned Maryland as a refuge for his persecuted coreligionists in England, especially the younger sons of Catholic gentry who had few economic or political prospects in England. In Maryland, he hoped, Protestants and Catholics could live in a harmony unknown in Europe. The first group of 130 colonists included a number of Catholic gentlemen and two priests. Most appointed officials were also Catholic, including relatives of the proprietor, as were those to whom he awarded the choicest land grants.

But Protestants always formed a majority of the settlers. Most, as in Virginia, came as indentured servants, but others took advantage of Maryland's generous headright system to acquire land by transporting workers to the colony.

As in Virginia, the death rate remained very high. In one county, half the marriages during the seventeenth century lasted fewer than eight years before one partner died. Almost 70 percent of male settlers in Maryland died before reaching the age of fifty, and half the children born in the colony did not live to adulthood. But at least initially, Maryland seems to have offered servants greater opportunity for landownership than Virginia. Unlike in the older colony, freedom dues in Maryland included fifty acres of land. As tobacco planters engrossed the best land later in the century, however, the prospects for landless men diminished.

THE NEW ENGLAND WAY

THE RISE OF PURITANISM

As Virginia and Maryland evolved toward societies dominated by a small aristocracy ruling over numerous bound laborers, a very different social order emerged in seventeenth-century New England. The early history of that region is intimately connected to the religious movement known as "Puritanism," which arose in England late in the sixteenth century. The term was initially coined by opponents to ridicule those not satisfied with the progress of the Protestant Reformation in England, who called themselves not Puritans but "godly" or "true Protestants." Puritanism came to define a set of religious principles and a view of how society should be organized. Puritans differed among themselves on many issues. But all shared the conviction that the Church of England retained too many elements of Catholicism in its religious rituals and doctrines. Puritans saw elaborate church ceremonies, the rule that priests could not marry, and ornate church decorations as vestiges of "popery." Many rejected the Catholic structure of religious authority descending from a pope or king to archbishops, bishops, and priests. Only independent local congregations, they believed, should choose clergymen and determine modes of worship. These Puritans were called "Congregationalists." All Puritans shared many of the beliefs of the Church of England and the society as a whole, including a hatred of Catholicism and a pride in England's greatness as a champion of liberty. But they believed that neither the Church nor the nation was living up to its ideals.

Puritans considered religious belief a complex and demanding matter and urged believers to seek the truth by reading the Bible and listening to sermons by educated ministers, rather than devoting themselves to sacraments administered by priests and to what Puritans considered formulaic prayers. The sermon was the central rite of Puritan practice. In the course of a lifetime, according to one estimate, the average Puritan listened to some 7,000 sermons. In their religious beliefs, Puritans followed the ideas of the French-born Swiss theologian John Calvin. The world, Calvin taught,

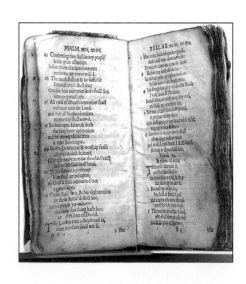

was divided between the elect and the damned. All persons sought salvation, but whether one was among the elect destined to be saved had already been determined by God. His will, ultimately, was unknowable, and nothing one did on earth including prayers, good works, and offerings would make any difference. But while there were no guarantees of salvation, worldly success—leading a good life, prospering economically—might well be indications of God's grace. Idleness and immoral behavior were sure signs of damnation.

MORAL LIBERTY

Puritanism, however, was not simply a set of ideas but a state of mind, a zealousness in pursuing the true faith that alienated many who held differing religious views. A minority of Puritans (such as those who settled in Plymouth Colony) became separatists, abandoning the Church of England entirely to form their own independent churches. Most, however, hoped to purify the Church from within. But in the 1620s and 1630s, as Charles I seemed to be moving toward a restoration of Catholic ceremonies and the Church of England dismissed Puritan ministers and censored their writings, many Puritans decided to emigrate. "Popish" practices, one minister complained, had grown to such "an intolerable height" in England that "the consciences of God's saints . . . could no longer bear them." By the same token, Puritans blamed many of England's social problems on the wandering poor, whom they considered indolent and ungodly. When Puritans emigrated to New England, they hoped to escape what they believed to be the religious and worldly corruptions of English society. They would establish a "city set upon a hill," a Bible Commonwealth whose influence would flow back across the Atlantic and rescue England from godlessness and social decay.

Like so many other emigrants to America, Puritans came in search of liberty, especially the right to worship and govern themselves in what they deemed a truly Christian manner. Freedom for Puritans was primarily a spiritual affair. It implied the opportunity and the responsibility to obey God's will through self-government and self-denial. It certainly did not mean unrestrained action, improper religious practices, or sinful behavior, of which, Puritans thought, there were far too many examples in England. In a 1645 speech to the Massachusetts legislature explaining the Puritan conception of freedom, John Winthrop, the colony's governor, distinguished sharply between two kinds of liberty. "Natural" liberty, or acting without restraint, suggested "a liberty to do evil." This was the false idea of freedom supposedly adopted by the Irish, Indians, and bad Christians generally. Genuine "moral" liberty—the Christian liberty described in Chapter 1—meant "a liberty to that only which is good." It was quite compatible with severe restraints on speech, religion, and personal behavior. True freedom, Winthrop insisted, depended on "subjection to authority," both religious and secular; otherwise, anarchy was sure to follow. To Puritans, liberty meant that the elect had a right to establish churches and govern society, not that others could challenge their beliefs or authority.

A portrait of John Winthrop, first governor of the Massachusetts Bay Colony, painted in the 1640s.

THE PILGRIMS AT PLYMOUTH

The first Puritans to emigrate to America were a group of separatists known as the Pilgrims. They had already fled to the Netherlands in 1608, believing that Satan had begun "to sow errors, heresies and discords" in England. A decade later, fearing that their children were being corrupted by being drawn into the surrounding culture, they decided to emigrate to Virginia. The expedition was financed by a group of English investors who hoped to establish a base for profitable trade. In September 1620, the *Mayflower*, carrying 150 settlers and crew (among them many non-Puritans), embarked from England. Blown off course, they landed not in Virginia but hundreds of miles to the north, on Cape Cod. Here the 102 who survived the journey established the colony of Plymouth. Before landing, the Pilgrim leaders drew up the Mayflower Compact, in which the adult men going ashore agreed to obey "just and equal laws" enacted by representatives of their own choosing. This was the first written frame of government in what is now the United States.

A century earlier, when Giovanni da Verrazano explored the Atlantic coast of North America, he encountered thickly settled villages and saw the smoke of innumerable Indian bonfires. By the time the Pilgrims landed, hundreds of European fishing vessels had operated off New England, landing to trade with Indians and bringing, as elsewhere, epidemics. The Pilgrims arrived in an area whose native population had recently been decimated by smallpox. They established Plymouth on the site of an abandoned Indian village whose fields had been cleared before the epidemic and were ready for cultivation. Nonetheless, the settlers arrived six weeks before winter without food or farm animals. Half died during the first winter. The colonists only survived through the help of local Indians, notably Squanto, who with twenty other Indians had been kidnapped and brought to Spain in 1614 by the English explorer Thomas Hunt, who planned to sell them as slaves. Rescued by a local priest, Squanto somehow made his way to London, where he learned English. He returned to Massachusetts in 1619 only to find that his people, the Patuxet, had succumbed to disease. He served as interpreter for the Pilgrims, taught them where to fish and how to plant corn, and helped in the forging of an alliance with Massasoit, a local chief. In the autumn of 1621, the Pilgrims invited their Indian allies to a harvest feast celebrating their survival, the first Thanksgiving.

The Pilgrims hoped to establish a society based on the lives of the early Christian saints. Their government rested on the principle of consent, and voting was not restricted to church members. All

An engraving by Theodore de Bry depicts an encounter between an English explorer and the Wampanoag Indians on Cape Cod or Martha's Vineyard in 1602. The region's Indians had much experience with Europeans before Pilgrims settled there.

land was held in common until 1627, when it was divided among the settlers. Plymouth survived as an independent colony until 1691, but it was soon overshadowed by Massachusetts Bay to its north.

THE GREAT MIGRATION

Chartered in 1629, the Massachusetts Bay Company was founded by a group of London merchants who hoped to further the Puritan cause and turn a profit through trade with the Indians. The first five ships sailed from England in 1629, and by 1642 some 21,000 Puritans had emigrated to Massachusetts. Long remembered as the Great Migration, this flow of population represented less than one-third of English emigration in the 1630s. Far more English settlers arrived in Ireland, the Chesapeake, and the Caribbean. After 1640, migration to New England virtually ceased, and in some years more colonists left the region than arrived. Nonetheless, the Great Migration established the basis for a stable and thriving society.

In many ways, the settling of New England was unique. Although servants represented about one-quarter of the Great Migration, most settlers arrived in Massachusetts in families. They came for many reasons, including the desire to escape religious persecution, anxiety about the future of England, and the prospect of economic betterment. Compared with colonists in Virginia and Maryland, they were older and more prosperous, and the number of men and women more equally balanced. Because of the even sex ratio and New England's healthier climate, the population grew rapidly, doubling every twenty-seven years. Although the region received only a small fraction of the century's migration, by 1700 New England's white population of 91,000 outnumbered that of both the Chesapeake and the West Indies. Nearly all were descendants of those who crossed the Atlantic during the Great Migration.

Seal of the Massachusetts Bay Colony. The Indian's scanty attire suggests a lack of civilization. His statement "Come Over and Help Us," based on an incident in the Bible, illustrates the English conviction that they were liberating the native population, rather than exploiting them as other empires had.

THE PURITAN FAMILY

While the imbalance between male and female migrants made it difficult for patriarchal family patterns fully to take root in the Chesapeake until the end of the seventeenth century, they emerged very quickly in New England. Whatever their differences with other Englishmen on religious matters, Puritans shared with the larger society a belief in male authority within the household as well as an adherence to the common-law tradition that severely limited married women's legal and economic rights. Puritans in America carefully emulated the family structure of England, insisting that the obedience of women, children, and servants to men's will was the foundation of social stability. The father's authority was all the more vital because in a farming society without large numbers of slaves or servants, control over the labor of one's family was essential to a man's economic success.

To be sure, Puritans deemed women to be the spiritual equals of men, and women were allowed to become full church members. Although all ministers were men, the Puritan belief in the ability of believers to interpret the Bible opened the door for some women to claim positions of religious leadership. The ideal Puritan marriage was based on reciprocal affection and companionship, and divorce was legal. Yet within the

The Savage Family, *a 1779 painting by the New England painter Edward Savage, depicts several generations of a typically numerous Puritan family.*

household, the husband's authority was virtually absolute. Indeed, a man's position as head of his family was thought to replicate God's authority in spiritual matters and the authority of the government in the secular realm. Magistrates sometimes intervened to protect wives from physical abuse, but they also enforced the power of fathers over their children and husbands over their wives. Moderate "correction" was considered appropriate for women who violated their husbands' sense of proper behavior.

Their responsibilities as wives and mothers defined women's lives. In his 1645 speech on liberty quoted above, John Winthrop noted that woman achieved genuine freedom by fulfilling her prescribed social role and embracing "subjection to her husband's authority." The family was the foundation of strong communities, and unmarried adults seemed a danger to the social fabric. An early law of Plymouth declared that "no single person be suffered to live of himself." The typical New England woman married at twenty-two, a younger age than her English counterpart, and gave birth seven times. Because New England was a far healthier environment than the Chesapeake, more children survived infancy. Thus, much of a woman's adult life was devoted to bearing and rearing children.

GOVERNMENT AND SOCIETY IN MASSACHUSETTS

In a sermon aboard the *Arabella*, on which he sailed for Massachusetts in 1630, John Winthrop spoke of the settlers binding themselves together "in the bond of brotherly affection" in order to promote the glory of God and their own "common good." Puritans feared excessive individualism and lack of social unity. Unlike the dispersed plantation-centered society of the Chesapeake, the leaders of Massachusetts organized the colony in self-governing towns. Groups of settlers received a land grant from the colony's government and then subdivided it, with residents awarded house lots in a central area and land on the outskirts for farming. Much land remained in commons, either for collective use or to be divided among later settlers or the sons of the town's founders. Each town had its own Congregational church. Each, according to a law of 1647, was required to establish a school, since the ability to read the Bible was central to Puritan belief. To train an educated ministry, Harvard College was established in 1636 (nearly a century after the Royal University of Mexico, founded in 1551), and two years later the first printing press in English America was established in Cambridge.

The government of Massachusetts reflected the Puritans' religious and social vision. Wishing to rule the colony without outside interference and to prevent non-Puritans from influencing decision making, the shareholders of the Massachusetts Bay Company emigrated to America, taking the charter with them and transforming a commercial document into a form of government. At first, the eight shareholders chose the men who ruled the colony. In 1634, a group of deputies elected by freemen (landowning church members) was added to form a single ruling body, the General Court. Ten years later, company officers and elected deputies were divided into two legislative houses. Unlike Virginia, whose governors were appointed first by a faraway company and, after 1624, by the crown, or Maryland, where authority rested with a single proprietor, the freemen of Massachusetts elected their governor.

The principle of consent was central to Puritanism. Church government was decentralized—each congregation, as one minister put it, had "complete liberty to stand alone." Churches were formed by voluntary agreement among members, who elected the minister. No important church decision was made without the agreement of the male members. Towns governed themselves, and local officials, delegates to the General Court, and the colonial governor were all elected. Puritans, however, were hardly believers in equality. Church membership, a status that carried great prestige and power, was a restrictive category. Anyone could worship at a church, or, as the Puritans preferred to call it, meeting house, but to be a full member required demonstrating that one had experienced divine grace and could be considered a "visible saint," usually by testifying about a conversion experience. Although male property holders generally chose local officials, voting in colony-wide elections was limited to men who had been accepted as full church members. This requirement at first made for a broad electorate, especially compared with England. But as time went on, it meant that a smaller and smaller percentage of the population controlled the government. Puritan democracy was for those within the circle of church membership; those outside the boundary occupied a secondary place in the Bible Commonwealth.

An embroidery banner depicting the main building at Harvard, the first college established in the English colonies. It was probably made by a Massachusetts woman for a husband or son who attended Harvard.

PURITAN LIBERTIES

Seventeenth-century New England was a hierarchical society in which socially prominent families were assigned the best lands and the most desirable seats in church. "Some must be rich and some poor, some high and eminent in power and dignity; others mean and in subjection" declared John Winthrop. This was part of God's plan, reinforced by man-made law and custom. The General Court forbade ordinary men and women from wearing "the garb of gentlemen." Ordinary settlers were addressed as "goodman" and "goodwife," while the better sort were called "gentleman" and "lady" or "master" and "mistress." When the General Court in 1641 issued a Body of Liberties outlining the rights and responsibilities of Massachusetts colonists, it adopted the traditional understanding of liberties as privileges that derived from one's place in the social order. Inequality was considered an expression of God's will, and while some liberties applied to all inhabitants, there were separate lists of rights for freemen, women, children, and servants. The Body of Liberties also allowed for slavery. The first African slave appears in the records of Massachusetts Bay in 1640.

Massachusetts forbade ministers from holding office so as not to interfere with their spiritual responsibilities. But church and state were closely interconnected. The law required each town to establish a church and to levy a tax to support the minister. There were no separate church courts, but the state enforced religious devotion. The Body of Liberties affirmed the rights of free speech and assembly and equal protection of the law for all within the colony, but the laws of Massachusetts prescribed the death penalty for, among other things, worshiping "any god, but the lord god," practicing witchcraft, or committing blasphemy.

NEW ENGLANDERS DIVIDED

The Puritans exalted individual judgment—hence their insistence on reading the Bible. The very first item printed in English America was a broadside, *The Oath of a Freeman* (1638), explaining the rights and duties of citizens of Massachusetts and emphasizing that men should vote according to their "own conscience . . . without respect of persons, or favor of any men." Yet modern ideas of individualism, privacy, and personal freedom would have struck Puritans as quite strange. They considered too much emphasis on the "self" dangerous to social harmony and community stability. In the closely knit towns of New England, residents carefully monitored one another's behavior and chastised or expelled those who violated communal norms. In the Puritan view, as one colonist put it, the main freedom possessed by dissenters was the "liberty to keep away from us." Towns banished individuals for such offenses as criticizing the church or government, complaining about the colony in letters home to England, or, in the case of one individual, Abigail Gifford, for being "a very burdensome woman." Tolerance of difference was not high on the list of Puritan values.

ROGER WILLIAMS

Differences of opinion about how to organize a Bible Commonwealth, however, emerged almost from the founding of Massachusetts. With its emphasis on individual interpretation of the Bible, Puritanism contained the seeds of its own fragmentation. The first sustained criticism of the existing order came from the young minister Roger Williams, who arrived in Massachusetts in 1631 and soon began to insist that its congregations withdraw from the Church of England and that church and state be separated. "Soul liberty," Williams believed, required that individuals be allowed to follow their consciences wherever they led. To most Puritans, the social fabric was held together by certain religious truths, which could not be questioned. To Williams, any law-abiding citizen should be allowed to practice whatever form of religion he chose. For the government to "molest any person, Jew or Gentile, for either professing doctrine or practicing worship" violated the principle that genuine religious faith is voluntary.

Williams aimed to strengthen religion, not weaken it. The embrace of government, he insisted, corrupted the purity of Christian faith and drew believers into endless religious wars like those that racked Europe. To leaders like John Winthrop, the outspoken minister's attack on the religious-political establishment of Massachusetts was bad enough, but Williams compounded the offense by rejecting the conviction that Puritans were an elect people on a divine mission to spread the true faith. Williams denied that God had singled out any group as special favorites.

RHODE ISLAND AND CONNECTICUT

Banished from Massachusetts in 1636, Williams and his followers moved south, where they established the colony of Rhode Island, which eventu-

By the mid-seventeenth century, English settlement in New England had spread well inland and up and down the Atlantic coast.

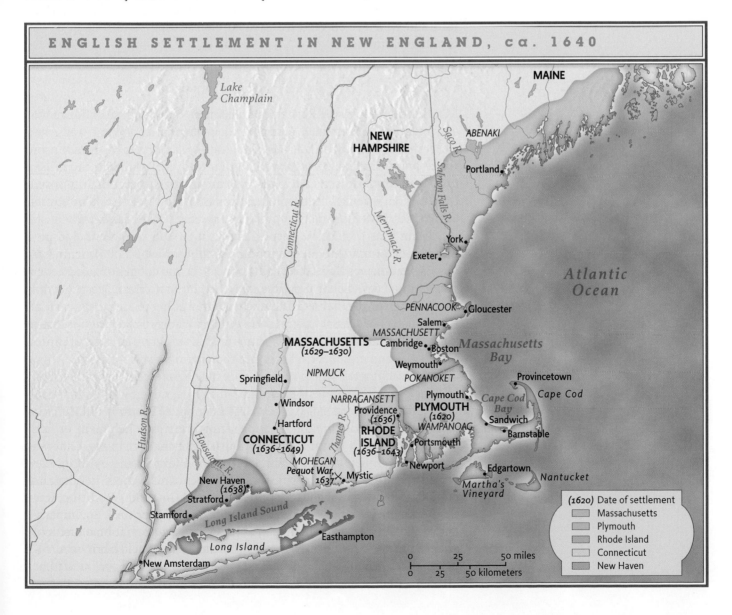

ENGLISH SETTLEMENT IN NEW ENGLAND, ca. 1640

(1620) Date of settlement
Massachusetts
Plymouth
Rhode Island
Connecticut
New Haven

ally received a charter from London. In a world in which the right of individuals to participate in religious activities without governmental interference barely existed, Rhode Island became a beacon of religious freedom. It had no established church, no religious qualifications for voting until the eighteenth century, and no requirement that citizens attend church. It became a haven for Dissenters (Protestants who belonged to denominations other than the established church) and Jews persecuted in other colonies. Rhode Island's frame of government was also more democratic. The assembly was elected twice a year, the governor annually, and town meetings were held more frequently than elsewhere in New England.

Religious disagreements in Massachusetts generated other colonies as well. In 1636, the minister Thomas Hooker established a settlement at Hartford. Its system of government, embodied in the Fundamental Orders of 1639, was modeled on that of Massachusetts—with the significant exception that men did not have to be church members to vote. Quite different was the colony of New Haven, founded in 1638 by emigrants who wanted an even closer connection between church and state. In 1662, Hartford and New Haven received a royal charter that united them as the colony of Connecticut.

THE TRIALS OF ANNE HUTCHINSON

More threatening to the Puritan establishment both because of her gender and because she attracted a large and influential following was Anne Hutchinson. A midwife and the daughter of a clergyman, Hutchinson, wrote John Winthrop, was "a woman of a ready wit and bold spirit." She arrived in Massachusetts with her husband in 1634 to join their minister, John Cotton, who had been expelled from his pulpit in England by church authorities. Hutchinson began holding meetings in her home, where she led discussions of religious issues among men and women, including a number of prominent merchants and public officials. In Hutchinson's view, salvation was God's direct gift to the elect and could not be earned by good works, devotional practices, or other human effort. Most Puritans shared this belief. What set Hutchinson apart was her charge that nearly all the ministers in Massachusetts were guilty of faulty preaching for distinguishing "saints" from the damned on the basis of activities such as church attendance and moral behavior rather than an inner state of grace.

In Massachusetts, where church and state reinforced each other, both ministers and magistrates were intent on suppressing any views that challenged their own leadership. Their critics denounced Cotton and Hutchinson for Antinomianism (a term for putting one's own judgment or faith above both human law and the teachings of the church). In 1637, she was placed on trial before a civil court for sedition (expressing opinions dangerous to authority). Her position as a "public woman" made her defiance seem even more outrageous. Her meetings, said Governor Winthrop, were neither "comely in the sight of God nor fitting to your sex." A combative and articulate woman, Hutchinson ably debated interpretation of the Bible with her university-educated accusers. She more than held her own during her trial. But when she spoke of divine revelations, of God speaking to her directly rather than through ministers or the Bible, she violated Puritan doctrine and sealed her own fate. Such a claim, the colony's leaders felt, posed a threat to the very existence of organized churches—and, indeed, to all authority. Hutchinson and a number of her followers were banished. Her family made its way to Rhode Island and then to Westchester, north of what is now New York City, where Hutchinson and most of her relatives perished during an Indian war.

Anne Hutchinson lived in New England for only eight years, but she left her mark on the region's religious culture. As in the case of Roger Williams, her career showed how the Puritan belief in each individual's ability to interpret the Bible could easily lead to criticism of the religious and political establishment. It would take many years before religious toleration—which violated the Puritans' understanding of "moral liberty" and social harmony—came to Massachusetts.

PURITANS AND INDIANS

Along with disruptive religious controversies, New England, like other colonies, had to deal with the difficult problem of relations with Indians. The native population of New England numbered perhaps 100,000 when the Puritans arrived. But because of recent epidemics, the migrants encountered fewer Indians near the coast than in other parts of eastern North America. In areas of European settlement, colonists quickly outnumbered the native population. Some settlers, notably Roger Williams, sought to treat the Indians with justice. Williams learned complex Indian languages, and he insisted that the king had no right to grant land already belonging to someone else. No town, said Williams, should be established before its site had been purchased. While John Winthrop believed uncultivated land could legitimately be taken by the colonists, he recognized the benefits of buying land rather than simply seizing it. But he insisted that such purchases (usually completed after towns had already been settled) must carry with them Indian agreement to submit to English authority and pay tribute to the colonists.

To New England's leaders, the Indians represented both savagery and temptation. In Puritan eyes, they resembled Catholics, with their false gods and deceptive rituals. They enjoyed freedom, but of the wrong kind—what Winthrop condemned as undisciplined "natural liberty" rather than the "moral liberty" of the civilized Christian. Always concerned that sinful persons might prefer a life of ease to hard work, Puritans feared that Indian society might prove attractive to colonists who lacked the proper moral fiber. In 1642, the Connecticut General Court set a penalty of three years at hard labor for any colonist who abandoned "godly society" to live with the Indians. To counteract the attraction of Indian life, the leaders of New England also encouraged the publication of "captivity" narratives by those captured by Indians. The most popular was *The Sovereignty and Goodness of God* by Mary Rowlandson, who had emigrated with her parents as a child in 1639 and was seized along with a group of other settlers and held for three months until ransomed during an Indian war in the 1670s. Rowlandson acknowledged that she had been well treated and suffered "not the least abuse or unchastity," but her book's overriding theme was her determination to return to Christian society.

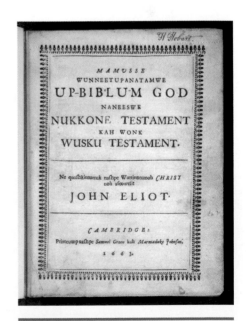

The title page of a translation of the Bible into the Massachusett language, published by John Eliot in 1663.

An engraving from John Underhill's News from America, *published in London in 1638, shows the destruction of the Pequot village on the Mystic River in 1637. The colonial forces, firing guns, are aided by Indian allies with bows and arrows.*

Puritans announced that they intended to bring Christian faith to the Indians, but they did nothing in the first two decades of settlement to accomplish this. They generally saw Indians as an obstacle to be pushed aside, rather than as potential converts.

THE PEQUOT WAR

Indians in New England lacked a paramount chief like Powhatan in Virginia. Coastal Indian tribes, their numbers severely reduced by disease, initially sought to forge alliances with the newcomers to enhance their own position against inland rivals. But as the white population expanded and new towns proliferated, conflict with the region's Indians became unavoidable. The turning point came in 1637 when a fur trader was killed by Pequots—a powerful tribe who controlled southern New England's fur trade and exacted tribute from other Indians. A force of Connecticut and Massachusetts soldiers, augmented by Narragansett allies, surrounded the main Pequot fortified village at Mystic and set it ablaze, killing those who tried to escape. Over 500 men, women, and children lost their lives in the massacre. By the end of the war a few months later, most of the Pequot had been exterminated or sold into Caribbean slavery. The treaty that restored peace decreed that their name be wiped from the historical record.

The destruction of one of the region's most powerful Indian groups not only opened the Connecticut River valley to rapid white settlement but also persuaded other Indians that the newcomers possessed a power that could not be resisted. The colonists' ferocity shocked their Indian allies, who considered European military practices barbaric. A few Puritans agreed. "It was a fearful sight to see them frying in the fire," the Pilgrim leader William Bradford wrote of the raid on Mystic. But to most Puritans, including Bradford, the defeat of a "barbarous nation" by "the sword of the Lord" offered further proof that they were on a sacred mission and that Indians were unworthy of sharing New England with the visible saints of the church.

THE NEW ENGLAND ECONOMY

The leaders of the New England colonies prided themselves on the idea that religion was the primary motivation for emigration. "We all came into these parts of America," proclaimed an official document of the 1640s, "with one and the same end and aim, namely, to advance the kingdom of our Lord Jesus Christ and to enjoy the liberties of the Gospel in purity with peace." But economic motives were hardly unimportant. One promotional pamphlet of the 1620s spoke of New England as a place "where religion and profit jump together."

Most Puritans came to America from East Anglia, an internationally renowned cloth-producing region. One of the most economically advanced areas of England, East Anglia in the 1620s and 1630s was suffering from a series of poor harvests and the dislocations caused by a decline in the cloth trade. A majority of the emigrants from this area were weavers, tailors, or farmers. But while they were leaving a depressed region, they were relatively well-off. Most came from the middle ranks of society and paid for their family's passage rather than indenturing themselves to labor. They sought in New England not only religious liberty but also economic advancement—if not riches, then at least a "competency," the economic independence that came with secure landownership or craft status. When one preacher proclaimed that the "main end" of settlement was to honor God, a man in the congregation cried out, "Sir, you are mistaken . . . our main end was to catch fish." But to Puritans no contradiction existed between piety and profit so long as one did not forget the needs of the larger community. Success in one's calling might be taken as a sign of divine grace.

Lacking a marketable staple like sugar or tobacco, New Englanders turned to fishing and timber for exports. But the economy centered on family farms producing food for their own use and a small marketable surplus. Although the Body of Liberties of 1641, as noted above, made provision for slavery in the Bible Commonwealth, there were very few slaves in seventeenth-century New England. Nor were indentured servants as central to the economy as in the Chesapeake. Most households relied on the labor of their own members, including women in the home and children in the fields. Sons remained unmarried into their mid-twenties, when they could expect to receive land from their fathers, from local authorities, or by moving to a new town. Indeed, while religious divisions spawned new settlements, the desire for land among younger families and newcomers was the major motive for New England's expansion. In Sudbury, Massachusetts, for example, one resident proposed in 1651 that every adult man be awarded an equal parcel of land. When a town meeting rejected the idea, a group of young men received a grant from the General Court to establish their own town farther west.

THE MERCHANT ELITE

Per capita wealth in New England lagged far behind that of the Chesapeake, but it was much more equally distributed. A majority of New England families achieved the goal of owning their own land, the foundation for a comfortable independence. Nonetheless, as in the Chesapeake, economic development produced a measure of social inequality. On completing their terms, indentured servants rarely achieved full church membership or received grants of land. Most became disenfranchised wage earners.

New England gradually assumed a growing role within the British empire based on trade. As early as the 1640s, New England merchants shipped and marketed the staples of other colonies to markets in Europe and Africa. They engaged in a particularly profitable trade with the West

Mrs. Elizabeth Freake and Baby Mary.
Painted by an anonymous artist in the
1670s, this portrait depicts the wife and
daughter of John Freake, a prominent
Boston merchant and lawyer. To illustrate
the family's wealth, Mrs. Freake wears a
triple strand of pearls, a garnet bracelet,
and a gold ring, and her child wears a
yellow silk dress.

Indies, whose growing slave plantations they supplied with fish, timber, and agricultural produce gathered at home. Especially in Boston, a powerful class of merchants arose who challenged some key Puritan policies, including the subordination of economic activity to the common good. As early as the 1630s, when the General Court established limits on prices and wages—measures common in England—and gave a small group of merchants a monopoly on imports from Europe, others protested. Indeed, merchants were among the most prominent backers of Anne Hutchinson's challenge to colonial authority. Some left Boston to establish a new town at Portsmouth, in the region eventually chartered as the royal colony of New Hampshire. Others remained to fight, with increasing success, for the right to conduct business as they pleased. By the 1640s, Massachusetts had repealed many of its early economic regulations.

While Puritans never abandoned the idea that economic activity should serve the general welfare, Boston merchants soon came to exercise a decisive influence in public affairs. The government of Massachusetts Bay Colony actively promoted economic development, building roads and bridges, offering bounties to economic enterprises, and abandoning laws limiting prices. Eventually, the Puritan experiment would evolve into a merchant-dominated colonial government.

THE HALF-WAY COVENANT

In the mid-seventeenth century, some Puritan leaders began to worry about their society's growing commercialization and declining piety, or "declension." By 1650, less than half the population of Boston had been admitted to full church membership. Massachusetts churches were forced to deal with a growing problem—the religious status of the third generation. Children of the elect could be baptized, but many never became full church members since they were unable to demonstrate the necessary religious commitment or testify to a conversion experience. What was the status of their children? New Englanders faced a difficult choice. They could uphold rigorous standards of church admission, which would limit the size and social influence of the Congregational Church. Or they could make admission easier, which would keep the church connected with a larger part of the population but would raise fears about a loss of religious purity.

The Half-Way Covenant of 1662 tried to address this problem by allowing for the baptism and a kind of subordinate, or "half-way," membership for grandchildren of those who emigrated during the Great Migration. In a significant compromise of early Puritan beliefs, ancestry, not religious conversion, became the pathway to inclusion among the elect. But church membership continued to stagnate.

By the 1660s and 1670s, ministers were regularly castigating the people for selfishness, manifestations of pride, violations of the Sabbath, and a "great backsliding" from the colony's original purposes. These warnings, called "jeremiads" after the ancient Hebrew prophet Jeremiah, interpreted crop failures and disease as signs of divine disapproval and warned of further punishment to come if New Englanders did not mend their ways. Yet hard work and commercial success in one's chosen calling had always been central Puritan values. In this sense, the commercialization of New

England was as much a fulfillment of the Puritan mission in America as a betrayal.

RELIGION, POLITICS, AND FREEDOM

THE RIGHTS OF ENGLISHMEN

Even as English emigrants began the settlement of colonies in North America, England itself became enmeshed in political and religious conflict, in which ideas of liberty played a central role. The struggle over English liberty in the first half of the seventeenth century expanded the definition of freedom at home and spilled over into early English North America.

By 1600, the traditional definition of "liberties" as a set of privileges confined to one or another social group still persisted, but alongside it had arisen the idea that certain "rights of Englishmen" applied to all within the kingdom. This tradition rested on the Magna Carta (or Great Charter) of 1215. An agreement between King John and a group of barons—local lords whose private armies frequently fought against each other and the crown—the Magna Carta attempted to put an end to a chronic state of civil unrest. It listed a series of "liberties" granted by the king to "all the free men of our realm." This was a restricted group at the time, since a large part of the English population still lived as serfs—peasants working land owned by feudal lords and legally bound to provide labor and other services. The liberties mentioned in the Magna Carta included protection against arbitrary imprisonment and the seizure of one's property without due process of law.

The principal beneficiaries of the Magna Carta were the barons, who obtained the right to oversee the king's conduct and even revolt if he violated their privileges. But over time, the document came to be seen as embodying the idea of "English freedom"—that the king was subject to the rule of law, and that all persons should enjoy security of person and property. These rights were embodied in the common law, whose provisions, such as habeas corpus (a protection against being imprisoned without a legal charge), the right to face one's accuser, and trial by jury came to apply to all free subjects of the English crown. And as serfdom slowly disappeared, the number of Englishmen considered "freeborn," and therefore entitled to these rights, expanded enormously.

The Court of Common Pleas. *Trial by jury was a central element in the definition of "English liberty." This watercolor appeared in a three-volume series,* The Microcosm of London *(1808–1810).*

THE ENGLISH CIVIL WAR

At the beginning of the seventeenth century, when English emigrants began

The execution of Charles I in 1649, a central event of the English Civil War.

arriving in the New World, "freedom" still played only a minor role in England's political debates. But the political upheavals of that century elevated the notion of "English freedom" to a central place. The struggle for political supremacy between Parliament and the Stuart monarchs James I and Charles I culminated in the English Civil War of the 1640s. This long-running battle arose from religious disputes about how fully the Church of England should distance its doctrines and forms of worship from Catholicism. Conflict also developed over the respective powers of the king and Parliament, a debate that produced numerous invocations of the idea of the "freeborn Englishman" and led to a great expansion of the concept of English freedom.

The leaders of the House of Commons (the elective body that, along with the hereditary aristocrats of the House of Lords, makes up the English Parliament) accused the Stuart kings of endangering liberty by imposing taxes without parliamentary consent, imprisoning political foes, and leading the nation back toward Catholicism. Civil war broke out in 1642, resulting in a victory for the forces of Parliament. In 1649, Charles I was beheaded, the monarchy abolished, and England declared "a Commonwealth and Free State"—a nation governed by the will of the people. Oliver Cromwell, the head of the victorious Parliamentary army, ruled for almost a decade after the execution of the king. In 1660, the monarchy was restored and Charles II assumed the throne. But by then, the breakdown of authority had stimulated intense discussions of liberty, authority, and what it meant to be a "freeborn Englishman."

ENGLAND'S DEBATE OVER FREEDOM

The idea of freedom suddenly took on new and expanded meanings between 1640 and 1660. The writer John Milton, who in 1649 called London "the mansion-house of liberty," called for freedom of speech and of the press. New religious sects sprang up, demanding the end of public financing and special privileges for the Anglican Church and religious toleration for all Protestants. The Levellers, history's first democratic political movement, proposed a written constitution, the Agreement of the People, which began by proclaiming "at how high a rate we value our just freedom." At a time when "democracy" was still widely seen as the equivalent of anarchy and disorder, the document proposed to abolish the monarchy and House of Lords and to greatly expand the right to vote. "The poorest he that lives in England hath a life to live as the greatest he," declared the Leveller Thomas Rainsborough, and therefore "any man that is born in England . . . ought to have his voice in election." Rainsborough even condemned African slavery.

The Levellers offered a glimpse of the modern definition of freedom as a universal entitlement in a society based on equal rights, not a function of social class. Another new group, the Diggers, went even further, hoping to give freedom an economic underpinning through the common ownership of land. Previous discussion of freedom, declared Gerard Winstanley, the Diggers' leader, had been misguided: "You are like men in a mist, seeking for freedom and know not what it is." True freedom applied equally "to the poor as well as the rich"; all were entitled to "a comfortable livelihood in this their own land." Even before the restoration of the monarchy, the Levellers, Diggers, and other radical movements spawned by the English Civil War had been crushed or driven underground. But some of the ideas of liberty that flourished during the 1640s and 1650s would be carried to America by English emigrants.

ENGLISH LIBERTY

These struggles elevated the notion of "English liberty" to a central place in Anglo-American political culture. It became a major building block in the assertive sense of nationhood then being consolidated in England. The medieval idea of liberties as a collection of limited entitlements enjoyed by specific groups did not suddenly disappear. But it was increasingly overshadowed by a more general definition of freedom grounded in the common rights of all individuals within the English realm. By self-definition, England was a community of free individuals and its past a "history of liberty." All Englishmen were governed by a king, but "he rules over free men," according to the law, unlike the autocratic monarchs of France, Spain, Russia, and other countries.

By 1680, in his book *English Liberties, or, The Free-Born Subject's Inheritance,* the writer Henry Care described the English system of government as a "qualified Monarchy," the best political structure in the world because even though the "nobility" enjoyed privileges not available to others, all citizens were "guarded in their persons and properties by the fence of law, [which] renders them Freemen, not Slaves." The belief in freedom as the common heritage of all Englishmen and the conception of the British empire as the world's guardian of liberty helped to legitimize English colonization in the Western Hemisphere and to cast its imperial wars against Catholic France and Spain as struggles between freedom and tyranny.

Meeting of the General Council of the Army at Putney, *scene of the debate in 1647 over liberty and democracy between Levellers and more conservative army officers.*

VOICES OF FREEDOM

FROM JOHN WINTHROP,
Speech to the Massachusetts General Court
(July 3, 1645)

Winthrop, governor of the Massachusetts Bay Colony, describes two very different definitions of liberty in this speech.

The great questions that have troubled the country, are about the authority of the magistrates and the liberty of the people. . . . Concerning liberty, I observe a great mistake in the country about that. There is a twofold liberty, natural (I mean as our nature is now corrupt) and civil or federal. The first is common to man with beasts and other creatures. By this, man, as he stands in relation to man simply, hath liberty to do what he lists; it is a liberty to do evil as well as to [do] good. This liberty is incompatible and inconsistent with authority, and cannot endure the least restraint of the most just authority. The exercise and maintaining of this liberty makes men grow more

evil, and in time to be worse than brute beasts. . . . This is that great enemy of truth and peace, that wild beast, which all the ordinances of God are bent against, to restrain and subdue it.

The other kind of liberty I call civil or federal, it may also be termed moral. . . . This liberty is the proper end and object of authority, and cannot subsist without it; and it is a liberty to that only which is good, just, and honest. . . . This liberty is maintained and exercised in a way of subjection to authority; it is of the same kind of liberty wherewith Christ hath made us free. The woman's own choice makes . . . a man her husband; yet being so chosen, he is her lord, and she is to be subject to him, yet in a way of liberty, not of bondage; and a true wife accounts her subjection her honor and freedom, and would not think her condition safe and free, but in her subjection to her husband's authority. Such is the liberty of the church under the authority of Christ.

From Henry Care,
English Liberties, or,
The Free-Born Subject's Inheritance (1680)

Care's book was an influential example of seventeenth-century English ideas of liberty, especially of how a "balanced" constitution was essential to preserving individual rights.

The Constitution of our English government (the best in the world) is no arbitrary tyranny like the Turkish Grand Seignior's, or the French King's, whose wills (or rather lusts) dispose of the lives and fortunes of their unhappy subjects; nor an Oligarchy where the great men (like fish in the ocean) prey upon, and live by devouring the lesser at their pleasure. Nor yet a Democracy or popular State, much less an Anarchy, where all confusedly are hail fellows well met, but a most excellently mixt or qualified Monarchy, where the King is vested with large prerogatives sufficient to support majesty; and restrained only from power of doing himself and his people harm, which would be contrary to the end of all government . . . the nobility adorned with privileges to be a screen to majesty, and a refreshing shade to their inferiors, and the commonality, too, so guarded in their persons and properties by the fence of law, [which] renders them Freemen, not Slaves.

In France and other nations the mere will of the prince is law, his word takes off any . . . head, imposes taxes, or seizes any man's estate, when, how, and as often as he wishes. . . . But in England, the law is both the measure and the bond of every subject's duty and allegiance, each man having a fixed fundamental right born with him as to the freedom of his person and property in his estate, which he cannot be deprived of, but either by his consent, or some crime for which the law has imposed . . . a penalty. . . .

This original happy frame of government is truly and properly called an Englishman's liberty, a privilege not to [be] exempt from the law, but to be freed in person and estate, from arbitrary violence and oppression.

QUESTIONS

1. Why does Winthrop consider "natural" liberty dangerous?

2. Why does Care consider the English system of government the best in the world?

3. How do the two authors view the relationship between liberty and political authority?

THE CIVIL WAR AND ENGLISH AMERICA

These struggles, with their vigorous discussion of the rights of freeborn Englishmen, inevitably reverberated in England's colonies, dividing them from one another and internally. Most New Englanders sided with Parliament in the Civil War of the 1640s. Some returned to England to join the Parliamentary army or take up pulpits to help create a godly commonwealth at home. But Puritan leaders were increasingly uncomfortable as the idea of religious toleration for Protestants gained favor in England. It was the revolutionary Parliament that in 1644 granted Roger Williams his charter for the Rhode Island colony he had founded after being banished from Massachusetts.

Meanwhile, a number of followers of Anne Hutchinson became Quakers, one of the sects that sprang up in England during the Civil War. Quakers held that the spirit of God dwelled within every individual, not just the elect, and that this "inner light," rather than the Bible or teachings of the clergy, offered the surest guidance in spiritual matters. When Quakers appeared in Massachusetts, colonial officials had them whipped, fined, and banished. In 1659 and 1660, four Quakers who returned from exile were hanged, including Mary Dyer, a former disciple of Hutchinson. The treatment of Quakers gave Massachusetts a reputation in England as a hotbed of religious persecution. When Charles II, after the restoration of the monarchy in 1660, reaffirmed the Massachusetts charter, he ordered the colony to recognize the "liberty of conscience" of all Protestants. But while hangings ceased, efforts to suppress the Quakers continued, as did attacks on Baptists, whose disdain for a learned ministry also seemed to threaten Puritan beliefs.

THE CRISIS IN MARYLAND

Unlike the New England colonies, Virginia sided with Charles I. Its leaders even proclaimed Charles II king after his father's execution in 1649, although Oliver Cromwell's government in London soon brought the rebellious colony under control. In Maryland, the combination of the religious and political battles of the Civil War, homegrown conflict between Catholic and Protestant settlers, and anti-proprietary feeling produced a violent civil war within the colony, later recalled as the "plundering time." Indeed, Maryland in the 1640s verged on total anarchy, with a pro-Parliament force assaulting those loyal to Charles I. The emerging Protestant planter class longed to seize power from the Catholic elite created by Cecelius Calvert. The assembly's Protestant majority rejected laws proposed by the proprietor and claimed the same power to legislate and levy taxes enjoyed by the House of Commons in England.

To stabilize the colony and attract more settlers, Calvert appointed a Protestant governor and offered refuge to Protestant Dissenters being persecuted in Virginia, where Anglicanism was the established religion and laws restricted the religious and political rights of others. In 1649, Maryland adopted an Act Concerning Religion, which institutionalized the principle of toleration that had prevailed from the colony's beginning. All Christians were guaranteed the "free exercise" of religion. The Act did not establish religious liberty in a modern sense, since it punished those who denied the divinity of Jesus Christ or the doctrine of the Holy Trinity. Indeed, a Jewish physician was soon arrested under its provisions. Nonetheless, the law was a milestone in the history of religious freedom in colonial America.

Turmoil, however, continued. During the 1650s, the Commonwealth government in London placed Maryland under the control of a Protestant council, which repealed the Toleration Act and forbade Catholics from openly practicing their religion. In 1657, however, Calvert's authority was restored and with it Maryland's experiment in religious freedom.

CROMWELL AND THE EMPIRE

Oliver Cromwell, who ruled England from 1649 until his death in 1658, undertook an aggressive policy of colonial expansion, the promotion of Protestantism, and commercial empowerment in the British Isles and the Western Hemisphere. His army forcibly extended English control over Ireland, massacring civilians, banning the public practice of Catholicism, and seizing land owned by Catholics. In the Caribbean, England seized Jamaica, a valuable sugar island, from Spain. In 1651, as will be related in Chapter 3, Parliament passed the first Navigation Act, which sought to challenge the Dutch hold on international commerce by confining colonial trade to English ships and ports.

Thus, by the middle of the seventeenth century, several English colonies existed along the Atlantic coast of North America. Established as part of an ad hoc process rather than arising under any coherent national plan, they differed enormously in economic, political, and social structure. The seeds had been planted, in the Chesapeake, for the development of plantation societies based on unfree labor, and in New England, for settlements centered on small towns and family farms. Throughout the colonies, many residents enjoyed freedoms they had not possessed at home, especially access to land and the right to worship as they desired. Others found themselves confined to unfree labor for many years or an entire lifetime.

The next century would be a time of crisis and consolidation as the population expanded, social conflicts intensified, and Britain moved to exert greater control over its flourishing North American colonies.

A portrait of Oliver Cromwell, who ruled England after the execution of Charles I, by the artist Sir Peter Lely.

SUGGESTED READING

Anderson, Victoria D. *New England's Generation: The Great Migration and the Formation of Society and Culture in the Seventeenth Century* (1991). A careful study of emigration from England to New England.

Banner, Stuart. *How the Indians Lost Their Land: Law and Power on the Frontier* (2005). Argues that most Indian land came into settlers' hands by legal processes rather than conquest.

Bonomi, Patricia. *Under the Cope of Heaven: Religion, Society, and Politics in Colonial America* (1986). Traces the interrelationship of religion and politics and the rise of religious diversity in the colonies.

Brown, Kathleen. *Good Wives, Nasty Wenches, and Anxious Patriarchs: Gender, Race, and Power in Colonial Virginia* (1996). A pioneering study of gender relations and their impact on Virginia society.

Cronon, William. *Changes in the Land: Colonists and the Ecology of New England* (1983). A path-breaking examination of how English colonization affected the natural environment in New England.

Gleach, Frederic W. *Powhatan's World and Colonial Virginia: A Conflict of Cultures* (1997). A study of Indian culture and the impact of European colonization upon it.

Hill, Christopher. *The Century of Revolution* (1961). A survey stressing the causes and consequences of the English Civil War.

Horn, James. *Adapting to a New World: English Society in the Seventeenth-Century Chesapeake* (1994). A detailed examination of the lives of early settlers in England and later in Virginia.

Innes, Stephen. *Creating the Commonwealth: The Economic Culture of Puritan New England* (1995). Explores economic life and its impact on the development of New England society.

Morgan, Edmund S. *The Puritan Family* (1944). An early examination of family life and gender relations in colonial America.

Pestana, Carla G. *The English Atlantic in an Age of Revolution, 1640–1661* (2001). Analyzes how the English Civil War reverberated in the American colonies.

Price, David A. *Love and Hate in Jamestown: John Smith, Pocahontas, and the Start of a New Nation* (2003). Presents the legend and reality of John Smith, Pocahontas, and early Virginia.

Richter, Daniel K. *Facing East from Indian Country: A Native History of Early America* (2001). Recounts colonization as experienced and viewed by Native Americans.

Taylor, Alan. *American Colonies* (2001). A comprehensive survey of the history of North American colonies from their beginnings to 1763.

Winship, Michael. *Making Heretics: Militant Protestantism and Free Grace in Massachusetts, 1636–1641* (2002). The most recent account of Anne Hutchinson and the Antinomian controversy.

REVIEW QUESTIONS

1. Compare and contrast England's settlement history in the Americas to Spain's. Consider the treatment of Indians, the role of the Church, the significance of women, and economic development.

2. For the English, land was the basis of liberty. Explain the reasoning behind that concept and how it was markedly different from the Indians' conception of land.

3. The Puritans came to America seeking religious freedom, but they were extremely intolerant of other beliefs. How do you explain this?

4. Describe who was choosing to immigrate to America in the seventeenth century and explain their reasons.

5. In what ways did the New England economy differ from the Chesapeake economy?

KEY TERMS

Virginia Company (p. 52)

Roanoke Colony (p. 54)

uprising of 1622 (p. 64)

Puritans (p. 68)

Pilgrims (p. 70)

Mayflower Compact (p. 70)

captivity narratives (p. 77)

Pequot War (p. 78)

REVIEW TABLE

Early Colonial British Settlements

Colony	Date Established	Sponsor	Founder/ Governor	Major Religion
Virginia	1607	Virginia Company	John Smith	Anglican
Plymouth	1620	English investors	William Bradford	Pilgrims (Puritan Separatists)
Massachusetts	1630	Massachusetts Bay Company	John Winthrop	Puritan/ Congregationalists
Maryland	1632	Proprietary colony	Cecilius Calvert	Protestant and Catholic
Rhode Island	1636	Royal charter	Roger Williams	Haven for all religions

CHAPTER 3

Creating Anglo-America, 1660–1750

Charles Town Harbor, *a watercolor painted around 1740 by the artist Bishop Roberts, depicts the flourishing major port city of South Carolina. The ships all fly British flags, since the Navigation Acts prevented foreign vessels from carrying the colony's main export, rice. South Carolina was home to the wealthiest elite in Britain's mainland colonies, and ships carried imported luxury goods for them from Great Britain.*

FOCUS QUESTIONS

- How did the English empire in America expand in the mid-seventeenth century?

- How did slavery take root in the Atlantic World?

- What major social and political crises rocked the colonies in the late seventeenth century?

- What were the directions of social and economic change in the eighteenth-century colonies?

- How did patterns of class and gender roles change in eighteenth-century America?

In the last quarter of the seventeenth century, a series of crises rocked the European colonies of North America. Social and political tensions boiled over in sometimes ruthless conflicts between rich and poor, free and slave, settler and Indian, and members of different religious groups. At the same time, struggles within and between European empires echoed in the colonies. Aggrieved groups seized upon the language of freedom to advance their goals. Although each conflict had its own local causes, taken together they added up to a general crisis of colonial society in the area that would become the United States.

The bloodiest and most bitter conflict occurred in southern New England, where in 1675 an Indian alliance launched attacks on farms and settlements that were encroaching on Indian lands. It was the most dramatic and violent warfare in the region in the entire seventeenth century.

New Englanders described the Wampanoag leader Metacom (known to the colonists as King Philip) as the uprising's mastermind, although in fact most tribes fought under their own leaders. By this time, the white population considerably outnumbered the Indians. But the fate of the New England colonies for several months hung in the balance. By 1676, Indian forces had attacked nearly half of New England's ninety towns. Twelve in Massachusetts were destroyed. As refugees fled eastward, the line of settlement was pushed back almost to the Atlantic coast. Some

A scene from King Philip's War, included on a 1675 map of New England.

1,000 settlers, of a population of 52,000, and 3,000 of New England's 20,000 Indians, perished in the fighting.

In mid-1676, the tide of battle turned and a ferocious counterattack broke the Indians' power once and for all. Although the uprising united numerous tribes, others remained loyal to the colonists. The role of the Iroquois in providing essential military aid to the colonists helped to solidify their developing alliance with the government of New York. Together, colonial and Indian forces inflicted devastating punishment on the rebels. Metacom was captured and executed, Indian villages destroyed, and captives, including men, women, and children, killed or sold into slavery in the West Indies. Most of the survivors fled to Canada or New York. Even the "praying Indians"—about 2,000 Indians who had converted to Christianity and lived in autonomous communities under Puritan supervision—suffered. Removed from their towns to Deer Island in Boston Harbor, supposedly for their own protection, many perished from disease and lack of food. Both sides committed atrocities in this merciless conflict, but in its aftermath the image of Indians as bloodthirsty savages became firmly entrenched in the New England mind.

In the long run, King Philip's war produced a broadening of freedom for white New Englanders by expanding their access to land. But this freedom rested on the final dispossession of the region's Indians.

THE EXPANSION OF ENGLAND'S EMPIRE

THE MERCANTILIST SYSTEM

As the New World became a battleground in European nations' endless contests for wealth and power, England moved to seize control of Atlantic trade, solidify its hold on North America's eastern coast, and exert greater control over its empire. By the middle of the seventeenth century, it was apparent that the colonies could be an important source of wealth for the mother country. According to the prevailing theory known as "mercantilism," the government should regulate economic activity so as to promote national power. It should encourage manufacturing and commerce by special bounties, monopolies, and other measures. Above all, trade should be controlled so that more gold and silver flowed into the country than left it. That is, exports of goods, which generated revenue from abroad, should exceed imports, which required paying foreigners for their products. In the mercantilist outlook, the role of colonies was to serve the interests of the mother country by producing marketable raw materials and importing manufactured goods from home. "Foreign trade," declared an influential work written in 1664 by a London merchant, formed the basis of "England's treasure." Commerce, not territorial plunder, was the foundation of empire.

EASTERN NORTH AMERICA IN THE SEVENTEENTH AND EARLY EIGHTEENTH CENTURIES

Lake Superior

Gulf of St. Lawrence

Lake Michigan

Lake Huron

Quebec (1608)

PENOBSCOT

NEW FRANCE

Montreal

ABENAKI

Port Royal (1606)

Bay of Fundy

HURON

OTTAWA

St. Lawrence R.

Lake Champlain

KENNEBEC

OTTAWA

MOHAWK

NEW HAMPSHIRE

Lake Ontario

ONEIDA

ONONDAGA

Fort Orange

NARRAGANSETT

MASSACHUSETTS BAY (1629–1630)

CAYUGA

Van Rensellaer Estate ★

Boston

SENECA

Lake Erie

NEW NETHERLAND (1624)

PEQUOT

PLYMOUTH (1620)

TUSCARORA IROQUOIS

Hartford

Providence (1636)

DELAWARE

New Haven (1638)

Narragansett Bay

RHODE ISLAND (1636–1643)

WESTERN DELAWARE

New Amsterdam

West Mystic (May 26, 1637)

PENNSYLVANIA (1681)

NEW YORK (1664)

CONNECTICUT (1636–1639)

Wilmington (Fort Christina)

Philadelphia

SHAWNEE

Baltimore

MARYLAND (1632)

THE CHESAPEAKE

Henrico

James R.

Williamsburg

Jamestown

UPPER CHEROKEE

VIRGINIA (1607)

CATAWBA

Raleigh expedition to Roanoke Island (1585)

MIDDLE CHEROKEE

YAMASEE

Atlantic Ocean

LOWER CHEROKEE

CAROLINA (1663)

UPPER NATCHEZ

LOWER NATCHEZ

Charles Town (Charleston)

GEORGIA (1732) Savannah

CREEK

(1585) Date of settlement
Dutch settlement *English from 1664
English settlement
French settlement
Spanish settlement

0   100   200 miles
0   100   200 kilometers

By the early eighteenth century, numerous English colonies populated eastern North America, while the French had established their own presence to the north and west.

Under Oliver Cromwell, as noted in Chapter 2, Parliament passed the first Navigation Act, which aimed to wrest control of world trade from the Dutch, whose merchants profited from free trade with all parts of the world and all existing empires. Additional measures followed in 1660 and 1663. England's new economic policy, mercantilism, rested on the idea that England should enjoy the profits arising from the English empire.

According to the Navigation laws, certain "enumerated" goods—essentially the most valuable colonial products, such as tobacco and sugar—had to be transported in English ships and sold initially in English ports, although they could then be re-exported to foreign markets. Similarly, most European goods imported into the colonies had to be shipped through England, where customs duties were paid. This enabled English merchants, manufacturers, shipbuilders, and sailors to reap the benefits of colonial trade, and the government to enjoy added income from taxes. As members of the empire, American colonies would profit as well, since their ships were considered English. Indeed, the Navigation Acts stimulated the rise of New England's shipbuilding industry.

THE CONQUEST OF NEW NETHERLAND

The restoration of the English monarchy when Charles II assumed the throne in 1660 sparked a new period of colonial expansion. The government chartered new trading ventures, notably the Royal African Company, with a monopoly of the slave trade. Within a generation, the number of English colonies in North America doubled. First to come under English control was New Netherland, seized in 1664 during an Anglo-Dutch war that also saw England gain control of Dutch trading posts in Africa. King Charles II awarded the colony to his younger brother James, the duke of York, with "full and absolute power" to govern as he pleased. (Hence the colony's name became New York.)

New Netherland always remained peripheral to the far-flung Dutch empire. The Dutch fought to retain their holdings in Africa, Asia, and South America, but they surrendered New Netherland in 1664 without a fight. English rule transformed a minor military base into an important imperial outpost, a seaport trading with the Caribbean and Europe, and a launching pad for military operations against the French. New York's European population, around 9,000 when the English assumed control, rose to 20,000 by 1685.

NEW YORK AND THE RIGHTS OF ENGLISHMEN AND ENGLISHWOMEN

English rule expanded the freedom of some New Yorkers, while reducing that of others. The terms of surrender guaranteed that the English would respect the religious toleration and property holdings of the colony's many ethnic communities. But English law ended the Dutch tradition by which married women conducted business in their own name and inherited some of the property acquired during a marriage. As colonists of Dutch origin adapted to English rule, their wills directed more attention to advancing the fortunes of their sons than providing for their wives and daughters. There had been many female traders in New Amsterdam (often widows who had inherited a deceased husband's property), but few remained by the end of the seventeenth century.

The English also introduced more restrictive attitudes toward blacks. In colonial New York City, as in New Amsterdam, those residents who

An engraving representing the Grand Council of the Five Iroquois Nations of the area of present-day upstate New York. From a book about American Indians published in Paris by a Jesuit missionary, who depicts the Indians in the attire of ancient Romans. Note the prevalence of wampum belts in the image, in the foreground and in the hand and at the feet of the central figure. Wampum was used to certify treaties and other transactions.

enjoyed the status of "freeman," obtained by birth in the city or by an act of local authorities, enjoyed special privileges compared to others, including the right to work in various trades. But the English, in a reversal of Dutch practice, expelled free blacks from many skilled jobs.

Others benefited enormously from English rule. The duke of York and his appointed governors continued the Dutch practice of awarding immense land grants to favorites, including 160,000 acres to Robert Livingston and 90,000 to Frederick Philipse. By 1700, nearly 2 million acres of land were owned by only five New York families who intermarried regularly, exerted considerable political influence, and formed one of colonial America's most tightly knit landed elites.

NEW YORK AND THE INDIANS

Initially, English rule also strengthened the position of the Iroquois Confederacy of upstate New York. After a complex series of negotiations in the mid-1670s, Sir Edmund Andros, who had been appointed governor of New York after fighting the French in the Caribbean, formed an alliance known as the Covenant Chain, in which the imperial ambitions of the English and Indians reinforced one another. The Five Iroquois Nations assisted Andros in clearing parts of New York of rival tribes and helped the British in attacks on the French and their Indian allies. Andros, for his part, recognized the Iroquois claim to authority over Indian communities in the vast area stretching to the Ohio River valley. But beginning in the 1680s, Indians around the Great Lakes and Ohio valley regrouped and with French aid attacked the Iroquois, pushing them to the east. By the end of the century, the Five Nations adopted a policy of careful neutrality, seeking to play the European empires off against one another while continuing to profit from the fur trade.

THE CHARTER OF LIBERTIES

Many colonists, meanwhile, began to complain that they were being denied the "liberties of Englishmen," especially the right to consent to taxation. There had been no representative assembly under the Dutch, and governors appointed by the duke of York at first ruled without one. Discontent was especially strong on Long Island, which had been largely settled by New Englanders used to self-government.

In 1683, the duke agreed to call an elected assembly, whose first act was to draft a Charter of Liberties and Privileges. The Charter required that elections be held every three years among male property owners and the freemen of New York City; it also reaffirmed traditional English rights such as trial by jury and security of property, as well as religious toleration for all Protestants. In part, the Charter reflected an effort by newer English colonists to assert dominance over older Dutch settlers by establishing the principle that the "liberties" to which New Yorkers were entitled were those enjoyed by Englishmen at home.

THE FOUNDING OF CAROLINA

For more than three decades after the establishment of Maryland in 1634, no new English settlement was planted in North America. Then, in 1663, Charles II awarded to eight proprietors the right to establish a colony to the north of Florida, as a barrier to Spanish expansion. Not until 1670 did the first settlers arrive to found Carolina. In its early years, Carolina was the "colony of a colony." It began as an offshoot of the tiny island of Barbados. In the mid-seventeenth century, Barbados was the Caribbean's richest plantation economy, but a shortage of available land led wealthy planters to seek opportunities in Carolina for their sons. At first, Carolinians armed friendly Indians, employing them on raids into Spanish Florida, and enslaved others, shipping them to other mainland colonies and the West Indies. Indeed, between 1670 and 1720, the number of Indian slaves exported from Charleston was larger than the number of African slaves imported. In 1715, the Yamasee and Creek, alarmed by the enormous debts they had incurred in trade with the settlers and by slave traders' raids into their territory, rebelled. The uprising was crushed, and most of the remaining Indians were enslaved or driven out of the colony into Spanish Florida, from where they occasionally launched raids against English settlements.

The Fundamental Constitutions of Carolina, issued by the proprietors in 1669, proposed to establish a feudal society with a hereditary nobility (with strange titles like landgraves and caciques), serfs, and slaves. Needing to attract settlers quickly, however, the proprietors also provided for an elected assembly and religious toleration—by now recognized as essential to enticing migrants to North America. They also instituted a generous headright system, offering 150 acres for each member of an arriving family (in the case of indentured servants, of course, the land went to the employer) and 100 acres to male servants who completed their terms.

None of the baronies envisioned in the Fundamental Constitutions was actually established. Slavery, not feudalism, made Carolina an extremely hierarchical society. The proprietors instituted a rigorous legal code that

William Penn, member of a leading English Quaker family and the founder of Pennsylvania.

promised slaveowners "absolute power and authority" over their human property and included imported slaves in the headright system. This allowed any persons who settled in Carolina and brought with them slaves, including planters from Barbados who resettled in the colony, instantly to acquire large new landholdings. In its early days, however, the economy centered on cattle raising and trade with local Indians, not agriculture. Carolina grew slowly until planters discovered the staple—rice—that would make them the wealthiest elite in English North America and their colony an epicenter of mainland slavery.

THE HOLY EXPERIMENT

The last English colony to be established in the seventeenth century was Pennsylvania. The proprietor, William Penn, envisioned it as a place where those facing religious persecution in Europe could enjoy spiritual freedom, and colonists and Indians would coexist in harmony. Penn's late father had been a supporter and creditor of Charles II. To cancel his debt to the Penn family and bolster the English presence in North America, the king in 1681 granted Penn a vast tract of land south and west of New York, as well as the old Swedish-Dutch colony that became Delaware.

A devout member of the Society of Friends, or Quakers, Penn was particularly concerned to establish a refuge for his coreligionists, who faced increasing persecution in England. He had already assisted a group of English Quakers in purchasing half of what became the colony of New Jersey from Lord John Berkeley, who had received a land grant from the duke of York. Penn was largely responsible for the frame of government announced in 1677, the West Jersey Concessions, one of the most liberal of the era. Based on Quaker ideals, it created an elected assembly with a broad suffrage, established religious liberty, and divided the proprietors' investment into 100 shares in the hope of promoting the development of a society of small farmers.

QUAKER LIBERTY

Like the Puritans, Penn considered his colony a "holy experiment," but of a different kind—"a free colony for all mankind that should go hither." He hoped that Pennsylvania could be governed according to Quaker principles, among them the equality of all persons (including women, blacks, and Indians) before God and the primacy of the individual conscience. To Quakers, liberty was a universal entitlement, not the possession of any single people—a position that would eventually make them the first group of whites to repudiate slavery. Penn also treated Indians with a consideration almost unique in the colonial experience, arranging to purchase land before reselling it to colonists and offering refuge to tribes driven out of other colonies by warfare. Sometimes, he even purchased the same land twice, when more than one Indian tribe claimed it. Since Quakers were pacifists who came to America unarmed and did not even organize a militia until the 1740s, peace with the native population was essential. Penn's Chain of Friendship appealed to the local Indians, promising protection from rival tribes who claimed domination over them.

Religious freedom was Penn's most fundamental principle. He condemned attempts to enforce "religious Uniformity" for depriving thousands of "free inhabitants" of England of the right to worship as they desired. His Charter of Liberty, approved by the assembly in 1682, offered "Christian liberty" to all who affirmed a belief in God and did not use their freedom to promote "licentiousness." There was no established church in Pennsylvania, and attendance at religious services was entirely voluntary, although Jews were barred from office by a required oath affirming belief in the divinity of Jesus Christ. At the same time, the Quakers upheld a strict code of personal morality. Penn's Frame of Government prohibited swearing, drunkenness, and adultery, as well as popular entertainments of the era such as "revels, bull-baiting, and cock-fighting." Private religious belief may not have been enforced by the government, but moral public behavior certainly was. Not religious uniformity but a virtuous citizenry would be the foundation of Penn's social order.

A Quaker Meeting, *a painting by an unidentified British artist, dating from the late eighteenth or early nineteenth century. It illustrates the prominent place of women in Quaker gatherings.*

LAND IN PENNSYLVANIA

Given the power to determine the colony's form of government, Penn established an appointed council to originate legislation and an assembly elected by male taxpayers and "freemen" (owners of 100 acres of land for free immigrants and 50 acres for former indentured servants). These rules made a majority of the male population eligible to vote. Penn owned all the colony's land and sold it to settlers at low prices rather than granting it outright. Like other proprietors, he expected to turn a profit, and like most of them, he never really did. But if Penn did not prosper, Pennsylvania did. A majority of the early settlers were Quakers from the British Isles. But Pennsylvania's religious toleration, healthy climate, and inexpensive land, along with Penn's aggressive efforts to publicize the colony's advantages, soon attracted immigrants from all over western Europe.

Ironically, the freedoms Pennsylvania offered to European immigrants contributed to the deterioration of freedom for others. The colony's successful efforts to attract settlers would eventually come into conflict with Penn's benevolent Indian policy. And the opening of Pennsylvania led to an immediate decline in the number of indentured servants choosing to sail for Virginia and Maryland, a development that did much to shift those colonies toward reliance on slave labor.

ORIGINS OF AMERICAN SLAVERY

No European nation, including England, embarked on the colonization of the New World with the intention of relying on African slaves for the bulk of its labor force. But the incessant demand for workers spurred by the spread of tobacco cultivation eventually led Chesapeake planters to turn to the transatlantic trade in slaves. Compared with indentured servants, slaves offered planters many advantages. As Africans, they could not claim the protections of English common law. Slaves' terms of service never expired, and they therefore did not become a population of unruly landless men. Their children were slaves, and their skin color made it more difficult for them to escape into the surrounding society. African men, moreover, unlike their Native American counterparts, were accustomed to intensive agricultural labor, and they had encountered many diseases known in Europe and developed resistance to them, so were less likely to succumb to epidemics.

ENGLISHMEN AND AFRICANS

The English had long viewed alien peoples with disdain, including the Irish, Native Americans, and Africans. They described these strangers in remarkably similar language as savage, pagan, and uncivilized, often comparing them to animals. "Race"—the idea that humanity is divided into well-defined groups associated with skin color—is a modern concept that had not fully developed in the seventeenth century. Nor had "racism"—an ideology based on the belief that some races are inherently superior to others and entitled to rule over them. The main lines of division within humanity were thought to be civilization versus barbarism or Christianity versus heathenism, not color or race.

Nonetheless, anti-black stereotypes flourished in seventeenth-century England. Africans were seen as so alien—in color, religion, and social practices—that they were "enslavable" in a way that poor Englishmen were not. Most English also deemed Indians to be uncivilized. But the Indian population declined so rapidly, and it was so easy for Indians, familiar with the countryside, to run away, that Indian slavery never became viable. Some Indians were sold into slavery in the Caribbean. But it is difficult to enslave a people on their native soil. Slaves are almost always outsiders, transported from elsewhere to their place of labor.

SLAVERY IN HISTORY

Slavery has existed for nearly the entire span of human history. It was central to the societies of ancient Greece and Rome. Slavery survived for centuries in northern Europe after the collapse of the Roman Empire. Germans, Vikings, and Anglo-Saxons all held slaves. Slavery persisted even longer in the Mediterranean world, where a slave trade in Slavic peoples survived into the fifteenth century. (The English word "slavery" derives from "Slav.") Pirates from the Barbary Coast of North Africa regularly seized Christians from ships and enslaved them. In West Africa, as noted in Chapter 1, slavery and a slave trade predated the coming of Europeans, and small-scale slavery existed among Native Americans. But slavery in nearly all these instances differed greatly from the institution that developed in the New World.

In the Americas, slavery was based on the plantation, an agricultural enterprise that brought together large numbers of workers under the control of a single owner. This imbalance magnified the possibility of slave resistance and made it necessary to police the system rigidly. It encouraged the creation of a sharp boundary between slavery and freedom. Labor on slave plantations was far more demanding than in the household slavery common in Africa, and the death rate among slaves much higher. In the New World, slavery would come to be associated with race, a concept that drew a permanent line between whites and blacks. Unlike in Africa, slaves who became free always carried with them in their skin color the mark of bondage—a visible sign of being considered unworthy of incorporation as equals into free society.

SLAVERY IN THE WEST INDIES

A sense of Africans as alien and inferior made their enslavement by the English possible. But prejudice by itself did not create North American slavery. For that institution to take root, planters and government authorities had to be convinced that importing African slaves was the best way to solve their persistent shortage of labor. During the seventeenth century, the shipping of slaves from Africa to the New World became a major international business. But only a relative handful were brought to England's mainland colonies. By the time plantation slavery became a major feature of life in English North America, it was already well entrenched elsewhere in the Western Hemisphere. By 1600, huge sugar plantations worked by slaves from Africa had made their appearance in Brazil, a colony of Portugal. In the seventeenth century, England, Holland, Denmark, and France joined Spain as owners of West Indian islands. English emigrants to the West Indies outnumbered those to North America in the first part of the seventeenth century. In 1650, the English population of the West Indies exceeded that in all of North America. Generally, the first settlers

Cutting Sugar Cane *an engraving from* Ten Views in Antigua, *published in 1823. Male and female slaves harvest and load the sugar crop while an overseer on horseback addresses a slave. During the eighteenth century, sugar was the chief crop produced by Western Hemisphere slaves.*

An engraving from Charles de Rochefort's Histoire Naturelle et Morale des Îles Antilles de l'Amerique *(1665), depicts a sugar mill powered by cattle, with slaves feeding the cane into rollers, which grind it to crush out the juice. The text describes how the various parts of the machinery work.*

established mixed economies with small farms worked by white indentured servants. But as sugar planters engrossed the best land, they forced white farmers off island after island. White indentured servants proved as discontented as elsewhere. In 1629, when a Spanish expedition attacked the British island of Nevis, servants in the local militia jointed them shouting, "Liberty, joyful liberty!"

With the Indian population having been wiped out by disease and white indentured servants unwilling to do the back-breaking, monotonous work of sugar cultivation, the massive importation of slaves from Africa began. In 1645, for example, Barbados, a tiny island owned by England, was home to around 11,000 white farmers and indentured servants and 5,000 slaves. As sugar cultivation intensified, planters turned increasingly to slave labor. By 1660, the island's population had grown to 40,000, half European and half African. Ten years later, the slave population had risen to 82,000, concentrated on some 750 sugar plantations. Meanwhile, the white population stagnated. By the end of the seventeenth century, huge sugar plantations manned by hundreds of slaves dominated the West Indian economy, and on most of the islands the African population far outnumbered that of European origin.

Sugar was the first crop to be mass-marketed to consumers in Europe. Before its emergence, international trade consisted largely of precious metals like gold and silver, and luxury goods aimed at an elite market, like the spices and silks imported from Asia. Sugar was by far the most important product of the British, French, and Portugese empires, and New World sugar plantations pro-

In this scene depicted on an English handkerchief, male and female slaves work in the tobacco fields alongside a white indentured servant (right).

duced immense profits for planters, merchants, and imperial governments. Saint Domingue, today's Haiti, was the jewel of the French empire. In 1660, Barbados generated more trade than all the other English colonies combined.

Compared to its rapid introduction in Brazil and the West Indies, slavery developed slowly in North America. Slaves cost more than indentured servants, and the high death rate among tobacco workers made it economically unappealing to pay for a lifetime of labor. For decades, servants from England formed the backbone of the Chesapeake labor force, and the number of Africans remained small. As late as 1680, there were only 4,500 blacks in the Chesapeake, a little over 5 percent of the region's population. The most important social distinction in the seventeenth-century Chesapeake was not between black and white but between the white plantation owners who dominated politics and society and everybody else—small farmers, indentured servants, and slaves.

SLAVERY AND THE LAW

Centuries before the voyages of Columbus, Spain had enacted *Las Siete Partidas*, a series of laws granting slaves certain rights relating to marriage, the holding of property, and access to freedom. These laws were transferred to Spain's American empire. They were often violated, but nonetheless gave slaves opportunities to claim rights under the law. Moreover, the Catholic Church often encouraged masters to free individual slaves. The law of slavery in English North America would become far more repressive than in the Spanish empire, especially on the all-important question of whether avenues existed by which slaves could obtain freedom.

For much of the seventeenth century, however, the legal status of Chesapeake blacks remained ambiguous and the line between slavery and freedom more permeable than it would later become. The first Africans, twenty in all, arrived in Virginia in 1619. British pirates sailing under the Dutch flag had seized them from a Portuguese ship carrying slaves from Angola, on the southwestern coast of Africa, to modern-day Mexico. Small numbers followed in subsequent years. Although the first black arrivals were almost certainly treated as slaves, it appears that at least some managed to become free after serving a term of years. To be sure, racial distinctions were enacted into law from the outset. As early as the 1620s, the law barred blacks from serving in the Virginia militia. The government punished sexual relations outside of marriage between Africans and Europeans more severely than the same acts involving two white persons. In 1643, a poll tax (a tax levied on individuals) was imposed on African but not white women. In both Virginia and Maryland, however, free blacks could sue and testify in court, and some even managed to acquire land and purchase white servants or African slaves. It is not known exactly how Anthony Johnson, who apparently arrived in Virginia as a slave during the 1620s, obtained his freedom. But by the 1640s, he was the owner of slaves and of several hundred acres of land on Virginia's eastern shore. Blacks and whites labored side by side in the tobacco fields, sometimes ran away together, and established intimate relationships.

THE RISE OF CHESAPEAKE SLAVERY

Evidence of blacks being held as slaves for life appears in the historical record of the 1640s. In registers of property, for example, white servants are listed by the number of years of labor, while blacks, with higher valuations, have no terms of service associated with their names. Not until the 1660s, however, did the laws of Virginia and Maryland refer explicitly to slavery. As tobacco planting spread and the demand for labor increased, the condition of black and white servants diverged sharply. Authorities sought to improve the status of white servants, hoping to counteract the widespread impression in England that Virginia was a death trap. At the same time, access to freedom for blacks receded.

A Virginia law of 1662 provided that in the case of a child one of whose parents was free and one slave, the status of the offspring followed that of the mother. (This provision not only reversed the European practice of defining a child's status through the father but also made the sexual abuse of slave women profitable for slaveholders, since any children that resulted remained the owner's property.) In 1667, the Virginia House of Burgesses decreed that religious conversion did not release a slave from bondage. Thus, Christians could own other Christians as slaves. Moreover, authorities sought to prevent the growth of the free black population by defining all offspring of interracial relationships as illegitimate, severely punishing white women who begat children with black men, and prohibiting the freeing of any slave unless he or she were transported out of the colony. By 1680, even though the black population was still small, notions of racial difference were well entrenched in the law. In England's American empire, wrote one contemporary, "these two words, Negro and Slave [have] by custom grown homogenous and convertible." In British North America, unlike the Spanish empire, no distinctive mulatto, or mixed-race, class existed; the law treated everyone with African ancestry as black.

BACON'S REBELLION:
LAND AND LABOR IN VIRGINIA

Virginia's shift from white indentured servants to African slaves as the main plantation labor force was accelerated by one of the most dramatic confrontations of this era, Bacon's Rebellion of 1676. Governor William Berkeley had for thirty years run a corrupt regime in alliance with an inner circle of the colony's wealthiest tobacco planters. He rewarded his followers with land grants and lucrative offices. At first, Virginia's tobacco boom had benefited not only planters but also smaller farmers, some of them former servants who managed to acquire farms. But as tobacco farming spread inland, planters connected with the governor engrossed the best lands, leaving freed servants (a growing population, since Virginia's death rate was finally falling) with no options but to work as tenants or to move to the frontier. At the same time, heavy taxes on tobacco and falling prices because of overproduction reduced the prospects of small farmers. By the 1670s, poverty among whites had reached levels reminiscent of England. In addition, the right to vote, previously enjoyed by all adult men, was confined to landowners in 1670. Governor Berkeley maintained peaceful relations with Virginia's remaining native population. His refusal to allow white settlement in areas reserved for Indians angered many land-hungry colonists.

As early as 1661, a Virginia indentured servant was accused of planning an uprising among those "who would be for liberty and free from bondage." Fifteen years later, long-simmering social tensions coupled with widespread resentment against the injustices of the Berkeley regime erupted in Bacon's Rebellion. The spark was a minor confrontation between Indians and colonists on Virginia's western frontier. Settlers now demanded that the governor authorize the extermination or removal of the colony's Indians, to open more land for whites. Fearing all-out warfare and continuing to profit from the trade with Indians in deerskins, Berkeley refused. An uprising followed that soon careened out of control. Beginning with a series of Indian massacres, it quickly grew into a full-fledged rebellion against Berkeley and his system of rule.

To some extent, Bacon's Rebellion was a conflict within the Virginia elite. The leader, Nathaniel Bacon, a wealthy and ambitious planter who had arrived in Virginia in 1673, disdained Berkeley's coterie as men of "mean education and employments." His backers included men of wealth outside the governor's circle of cronies. But Bacon's call for the removal of all Indians from the colony, a reduction of taxes at a time of economic recession, and an end to rule by "grandees" rapidly gained support from small farmers, landless men, indentured servants, and even some Africans. The bulk of his army consisted of discontented men who had recently been servants.

Sir William Berkeley, governor of colonial Virginia, 1641–1652 and 1660–1677, in a portrait by Sir Peter Lely. Berkeley's authoritarian rule helped to spark Bacon's Rebellion.

THE END OF THE REBELLION, AND ITS CONSEQUENCES

Bacon promised freedom (including access to Indian lands) to all who joined his ranks. His supporters invoked the tradition of "English liberties" and spoke of the poor being "robbed" and "cheated" by their social superiors. In 1676, Bacon gathered an armed force for an unauthorized and indiscriminate campaign against those he called the governor's "protected and darling Indians." He refused Berkeley's order to disband and marched on Jamestown, burning it to the ground. The governor fled, and Bacon became the ruler of Virginia. His forces plundered the estates of Berkeley's supporters. Only the arrival of a squadron of warships from England restored order. Bacon's Rebellion was over. Twenty-three of his supporters were hanged (Bacon himself had taken ill and died shortly after Berkeley's departure).

The specter of a civil war among whites greatly frightened Virginia's ruling elite, who took dramatic steps to consolidate their power and improve their image. They restored property qualifications for voting, which Bacon had rescinded. At the same time, planters developed a new political style in which they cultivated the support of poorer neighbors. Meanwhile, the authorities reduced taxes and adopted a more aggressive Indian policy, opening western areas to small farmers, many of whom prospered from a rise in tobacco prices after 1680. To avert the further rise of a rebellious population of landless former indentured servants, Virginia's authorities accelerated the shift to slaves (who would never become free) on the tobacco plantations. As Virginia reduced the number of indentured servants, it redefined their freedom dues to include fifty acres of land.

A SLAVE SOCIETY

Between 1680 and 1700, slave labor began to supplant indentured servitude on Chesapeake plantations. Bacon's Rebellion was only one among several factors that contributed to this development. As the death rate finally began to fall, it became more economical to purchase a laborer for life. Improving conditions in England reduced the number of transatlantic migrants, and the opening of Pennsylvania, where land was readily available, attracted those who still chose to leave for America. Finally, the ending of a monopoly on the English slave trade previously enjoyed by the Royal Africa Company opened the door to other traders and reduced the price of imported African slaves.

By 1700, blacks constituted over 10 percent of Virginia's population. Fifty years later, they made up nearly half. Recognizing the growing importance of slavery, the House of Burgesses in 1705 enacted a new slave code, bringing together the scattered legislation of the previous century and adding new provisions that embedded the principle of white supremacy in the law. Slaves were property, completely subject to the will of their masters and, more generally, of the white community. They could be bought and sold, leased, fought over in court, and passed on to one's descendants. Henceforth, blacks and whites were tried in separate courts. No black, free or slave, could own arms, strike a white man, or employ a white servant. Any white person could apprehend any black to demand a certificate of freedom or a pass from the owner giving permission to be off the plantation. Virginia had changed from a "society with slaves," in which slavery was one system of labor among others, to a "slave society," where slavery stood at the center of the economic process.

NOTIONS OF FREEDOM

One sentiment shared by Europeans, Native Americans, and Africans was fear of enslavement. Throughout history, slaves have run away and in other ways resisted bondage. They did the same in the colonial Chesapeake. Colonial newspapers were filled with advertisements for runaway slaves. These notices described the appearance and skills of the fugitive and included such comments as "ran away without any cause" or "he has great notions of freedom." Some of the blacks brought to the region during the seventeenth century were the offspring of encounters between European traders and Africans on the western coast of Africa or the Caribbean. Familiar with European culture and fluent in English, they turned to the colonial legal system in their quest for freedom. Throughout the seventeenth century, blacks appeared in court claiming their liberty, at first on the basis of conversion to Christianity or having a white father. This was one reason Virginia in the 1660s closed these pathways to freedom. But although legal avenues to liberty receded, the desire for freedom did not. After the suppression of a slave conspiracy in 1709, Alexander Spotswood, the governor of Virginia, warned planters to be vigilant. The desire for freedom, he reminded them, can "call together all those who long to shake off the fetters of slavery."

COLONIES IN CRISIS

King Philip's War of 1675 and Bacon's Rebellion the following year coincided with disturbances in other colonies. In Maryland, where the proprietor, Lord Baltimore, in 1670 had suddenly restricted the right to vote to owners of fifty acres of land or a certain amount of personal property, a Protestant uprising unsuccessfully sought to oust his government and restore the suffrage for all freemen. In several colonies, increasing settlement on the frontier led to resistance by alarmed Indians. A rebellion by Westo Indians was suppressed in Carolina in 1680. The Pueblo Revolt of the same year (discussed in Chapter 1) indicated that the crisis of colonial authority was not confined to the British empire.

THE GLORIOUS REVOLUTION

Turmoil in England also reverberated in the colonies. In 1688, the long struggle for domination of English government between Parliament and the crown reached its culmination in the Glorious Revolution, which established parliamentary supremacy once and for all and secured the Protestant succession to the throne. Under Charles II, Parliament had asserted its authority in the formation of national policy. It expanded its control of finance, influenced foreign affairs, and excluded from political and religious power Catholics and Dissenters (Protestants who belonged to a denomination other than the official Anglican Church).

When Charles died in 1685, he was succeeded by his brother James II (formerly the duke of York), a practicing Catholic and a believer that kings ruled by divine right. In 1687, James decreed religious toleration for both Protestant Dissenters and Catholics. The following year, the birth of James's son raised the prospect of a Catholic succession, alarming those who equated "popery" with tyranny. A group of English aristocrats invited the Dutch nobleman William of Orange, the husband of James's Protestant daughter Mary, to assume the throne in the name of English liberties. William arrived in England with a small army in November 1688. As the landed elite and leaders of the Anglican Church rallied to William's cause, James II fled and the revolution was complete.

Unlike the broad social upheaval that marked the English Civil War of the 1640s, the Glorious Revolution was in effect a coup engineered by small group of aristocrats in alliance with an ambitious Dutch prince. They had no intention of challenging the institution of the monarchy. But the overthrow of James II entrenched more firmly than ever the notion that liberty was the birthright of all Englishmen and that the king was subject to the rule of law. To justify the ouster of James II, Parliament in 1689 enacted a Bill of Rights, which listed parliamentary powers such as control over taxation as well as rights of individuals including trial by jury. These were the "ancient" and "undoubted . . . rights and liberties" of all Englishmen. In the following year, the Toleration Act allowed Protestant Dissenters (but not

King William III, a portrait by an unknown artist, painted around 1697. William, who came to power in England as a result of the Glorious Revolution, wears an ermine cape.

Catholics) to worship freely, although only Anglicans could hold public office. In fact, despite the new regime's language of liberty, religious freedom was far more advanced in some American colonies, such as Rhode Island, Pennsylvania, and Carolina, than in England. Nonetheless, throughout English America the Glorious Revolution powerfully reinforced among the colonists the sense of sharing a proud legacy of freedom and Protestantism with the metropolis.

THE GLORIOUS REVOLUTION IN AMERICA

The Glorious Revolution exposed fault lines in colonial society and offered local elites an opportunity to regain authority that had recently been challenged. Until the mid-1670s, the North American colonies had essentially governed themselves, with little interference from England. Governor Berkeley ran Virginia as he saw fit; proprietors in New York, Maryland, and Carolina governed in any fashion they could persuade colonists to accept; and New England colonies elected their own officials and openly flouted trade regulations. In 1675, England established the Lords of Trade to oversee colonial affairs. Three years later, the Lords questioned the Massachusetts government about its compliance with the Navigation Acts. They received the surprising reply that since the colony had no representatives in Parliament, the Acts did not apply to it unless the Massachusetts General Court approved.

In the 1680s, England moved to reduce colonial autonomy. Shortly before his death, Charles II revoked the Massachusetts charter, citing wholesale violations of the Navigation Acts. Hoping to raise more money from America in order to reduce his dependence on Parliament, James II between 1686 and 1688 combined Connecticut, Plymouth, Massachusetts, New Hampshire, Rhode Island, New York, and East and West Jersey into a single super-colony, the Dominion of New England. It was ruled by the former New York governor Sir Edmund Andros, who did not have to answer to an elected assembly. These events reinforced the impression that James II was an enemy of freedom. In New England, Andros's actions alienated nearly everyone not dependent on his administration for favors. He appointed local officials in place of elected ones, imposed taxes without the approval of elected representatives, declared earlier land grants void unless approved by him, and enforced religious toleration for all Protestants. His rule threatened both English liberties and the church-state relationship at the heart of the Puritan order.

THE MARYLAND UPRISING

In 1689, news of the overthrow of James II triggered rebellions in several American colonies. In April, the Boston militia seized and jailed Edmund Andros and other officials, whereupon the New England colonies reestablished the governments abolished when the Dominion of New England was created. In May, a rebel militia headed by Captain Jacob Leisler established a Committee of Safety and took control of New York. Two months later, Maryland's Protestant Association overthrew the government of the colony's Catholic proprietor, Lord Baltimore.

All of these new regimes claimed to have acted in the name of English liberties and looked to London for approval. But the degrees of success of these coups varied markedly. Most triumphant were the Maryland rebels. Concluding that Lord Baltimore had mismanaged the colony, William revoked his charter (although the proprietor retained his land and rents) and established a new, Protestant-dominated government. Catholics retained the right to practice their religion but were barred from voting and holding office. In 1715, after the Baltimore family had converted to Anglicanism, proprietary power was restored. But the events of 1689 transformed the ruling group in Maryland and put an end to the colony's unique history of religious toleration.

LEISLER'S REBELLION

The outcome in New York was far different. The German-born Leisler, one of the wealthiest merchants in the city, was a fervent Calvinist who feared that James II intended to reduce England and its empire to "popery and slavery." Although it was not his intention, Leisler's regime divided the colony along ethnic and economic lines. Members of the Dutch majority seized the opportunity to reclaim local power after more than two decades of English rule, while bands of rebels ransacked the homes of wealthy New Yorkers. Prominent English colonists, joined by some wealthy Dutch merchants and fur traders, protested to London that Leisler was a tyrant. William refused to recognize Leisler's authority and dispatched a new governor, backed by troops. Many of Leisler's followers were imprisoned, and he himself was condemned to be executed. The grisly manner of his death—Leisler was hanged and then had his head cut off and body cut into four parts—reflected the depths of hatred the rebellion had inspired. For generations, the rivalry between Leisler and anti-Leisler parties polarized New York politics.

CHANGES IN NEW ENGLAND

After deposing Edmund Andros, the New England colonies lobbied hard in London for the restoration of their original charters. Most were successful, but Massachusetts was not. In 1691, the crown issued a new charter that absorbed Plymouth into Massachusetts and transformed the political structure of the Bible Commonwealth. Town government remained intact, but henceforth property ownership, not church membership, would be the requirement to vote in elections for the General Court. The governor was now appointed in London rather than elected. Thus, Massachusetts became a royal colony, the majority of whose voters were no longer Puritan "saints." Moreover, it was required to abide by the English Toleration Act of 1690—that is, to allow all Protestants to worship freely. The demise of the "New England way" greatly benefited non-Puritan merchants and large landowners, who came to dominate the new government.

These events produced an atmosphere of considerable tension in Massachusetts, exacerbated by raids by French troops and their Indian allies on the northern New England frontier. The advent of religious toleration heightened anxieties among the Puritan clergy, who considered other Protestant denominations a form of heresy. "I would not have a hand in setting up their

Devil worship," one minister declared of the Quakers. Indeed, not a few Puritans thought they saw the hand of Satan in the events of 1690 and 1691.

THE PROSECUTION OF WITCHES

Belief in magic, astrology, and witchcraft was widespread in seventeenth-century Europe and America, existing alongside the religion of the clergy and churches. Many Puritans believed in supernatural interventions in the affairs of the world. They interpreted as expressions of God's will such events as lightning that struck one house but spared another, and epidemics that reduced the population of their Indian enemies. Evil forces could also affect daily life. Witches were individuals, usually women, who were accused of having entered into a pact with the devil to obtain supernatural powers, which they used to harm others or to interfere with natural processes. When a child was stillborn or crops failed, many believed that witchcraft was at work.

In Europe and the colonies, witchcraft was punishable by execution. It is estimated that between the years 1400 and 1800, over 50,000 people were executed in Europe after being convicted of witchcraft. Witches were, from time to time, hanged in seventeenth-century New England. Most were women beyond childbearing age who were outspoken, economically independent, or estranged from their husbands, or who in other ways violated traditional gender norms. The witch's alleged power challenged both God's will and the standing of men as heads of family and rulers of society.

Women hanged as witches in seventeenth-century England. The letters identify local officials: A is the hangman, B the town crier, C the sheriff, and D a magistrate. An engraving from Ralph Gardiner's England's Grievance Discovered, *published in 1655.*

THE SALEM WITCH TRIALS

Until 1692, the prosecution of witches had been local and sporadic. But in the heightened anxiety of that year, a series of trials and executions took place in the town of Salem that made its name to this day a byword for fanaticism and persecution. The crisis began late in 1691 when several young girls began to suffer fits and nightmares, attributed by their elders to witchcraft. Soon, three witches had been named, including Tituba, an Indian from the Caribbean, a slave in the home of one of the girls. Since the only way to avoid prosecution was to confess and name others, accusations of witchcraft began to snowball. By the middle of 1692, hundreds of residents of Salem had come forward to accuse their neighbors. Some, it appears, used the occasion to settle old scores within the Salem community. Local authorities took legal action against nearly 150 persons, the large majority of them women. Many confessed to save their lives, but fourteen women and five men were hanged, protesting their innocence to the end. One man was pressed to death (crushed under a weight of stones) for refusing to enter a plea.

In Salem, accusations of witchcraft spread far beyond the usual profile of middle-aged women to include persons of all ages (one was a child of four) and those with no previous history of assertiveness or marital discord. As accusations and executions multiplied, it became clear that something was seriously wrong with the colony's system of justice. Toward the end of 1692, the governor of Massachusetts dissolved the Salem court and ordered the remaining prisoners released. At the same time, the prominent clergyman Increase Mather published an influential treatise, *Cases of Conscience Concerning Evil Spirits*, warning that juries should not take seriously either the testimony of those who claimed to be possessed or the confessions and accusations of persons facing execution. The events in Salem discredited the tradition of prosecuting witches and accelerated a commitment among prominent colonists to finding scientific explanations for natural events like comets and illnesses, rather than attributing them to magic. In future years, only two accused witches would be brought to trial in Massachusetts, and both were found not guilty.

THE GROWTH OF COLONIAL AMERICA

The Salem witch trials took place precisely two centuries after Columbus's initial voyage. The Western Hemisphere was dramatically different from the world he had encountered. Powerful states had been destroyed and the native population decimated by disease and in some areas deprived of its land. In North America, three new and very different empires had arisen, competing for wealth and power. The urban-based Spanish empire, with a small settler elite and growing mestizo population directing the labor of a large Indian population, still relied for wealth primarily on the gold and silver mines of Mexico and South America. The French empire centered on Saint Domingue, Martinique, and Guadeloupe, plantation islands of the West Indies. On the mainland, it consisted of a thinly settled string of farms and trading posts in the St. Lawrence Valley. In North America north of the Rio Grande, the English colonies had far outstripped their rivals in population and trade.

As stability returned after the crises of the late seventeenth century, English North America experienced an era of remarkable growth. Between 1700 and 1770, crude backwoods settlements became bustling provincial capitals. Even as epidemics continued in Indian country, the hazards of disease among colonists diminished, agricultural settlement pressed westward, and hundreds of thousands of newcomers arrived from the Old World. Thanks to a high birthrate and continuing immigration, the population of England's mainland colonies, 265,000 in 1700, grew nearly tenfold, to over 2.3 million seventy years later. (It is worth noting, however, that because of the decline suffered by the Indians, the North American population was considerably lower in 1770 than it had been in 1492.)

A DIVERSE POPULATION

Probably the most striking characteristic of colonial American society in the eighteenth century was its sheer diversity. In 1700, the colonies were essentially English outposts. Relatively few Africans had yet been brought

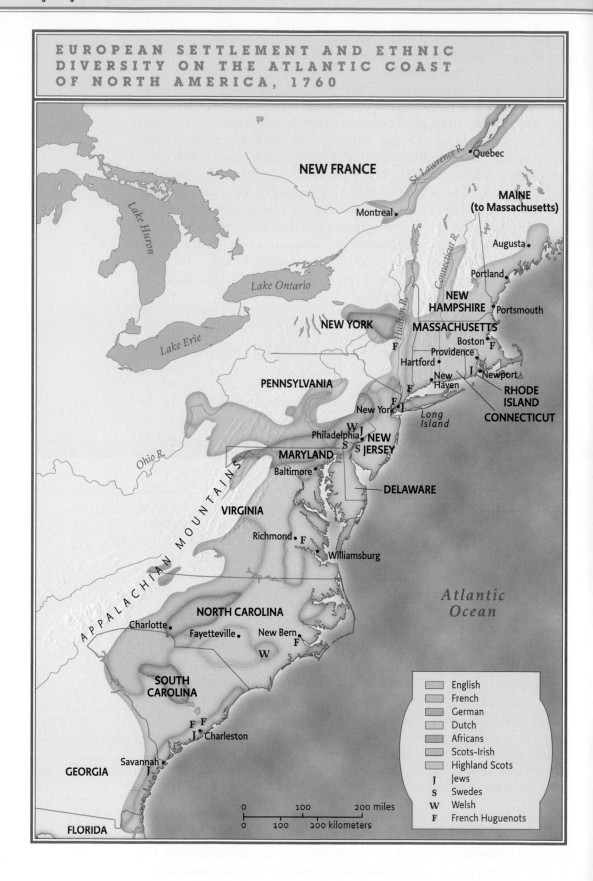

EUROPEAN SETTLEMENT AND ETHNIC DIVERSITY ON THE ATLANTIC COAST OF NORTH AMERICA, 1760

Table 3.1 ORIGINS AND STATUS OF MIGRANTS TO BRITISH NORTH AMERICAN COLONIES, 1700–1775

	Total	*Slaves*	*Indentured Servants*	*Convicts*	*Free*
Africa	278,400	278,400	—	—	—
Ireland	108,600	—	39,000	17,500	52,100
Germany	84,500	—	30,000	—	54,500
England/Wales	73,100	—	27,200	32,500	13,400
Scotland	35,300	—	7,400	2,200	25,700
Other	5,900	—	—	—	5,900
Total	585,800	278,400	103,600	52,200	151,600

to the mainland, and the overwhelming majority of the white population—close to 90 percent—was of English origin. In the eighteenth century, African and non-English European arrivals skyrocketed, while the number emigrating from England declined (see Table 3.1).

As economic conditions in England improved, the government began to rethink the policy of encouraging emigration. No longer concerned with an excess population of vagabonds and "masterless men," authorities began to worry that large-scale emigration was draining labor from the mother country. About 40 percent of European immigrants to the colonies during the eighteenth century continued to arrive as bound laborers who had temporarily sacrificed their freedom to make the voyage to the New World. But as the colonial economy prospered, poor indentured migrants were increasingly joined by professionals and skilled craftsmen—teachers, ministers, weavers, carpenters—whom England could ill afford to lose. This brought to an end official efforts to promote English emigration.

ATTRACTING SETTLERS

Yet while worrying about losing desirable members of its population, the government in London remained convinced that colonial development enhanced the nation's power and wealth. To bolster the Chesapeake labor force, nearly 50,000 convicts (a group not desired in Britain) were sent to work in the tobacco fields. Officials also actively encouraged Protestant immigration from the non-English (and less prosperous) parts of the British Isles and from the European continent, promising newcomers easy

Among the most striking features of eighteenth-century colonial society was the racial and ethnic diversity of the population. This resulted from increased immigration from the non-English parts of the British Isles and from mainland Europe, as well as the rapid expansion of the slave trade from Africa.

A German-language illustrated family record from late seventeenth-century Pennsylvania. Numerous Germans settled in the colony, attracted by William Penn's generous policies about acquiring land and his promise of religious freedom.

access to land and the right to worship freely. A law of 1740 even offered European immigrants British citizenship after seven years of residence, something that in the mother country could only be obtained by a special act of Parliament. The widely publicized image of America as an asylum for those "whom bigots chase from foreign lands," in the words of a 1735 poem, was in many ways a byproduct of Britain's efforts to attract settlers from non-English areas to its colonies.

Among eighteenth-century migrants from the British Isles, the 80,000 English newcomers (a majority of them convicted criminals) were considerably outnumbered by 145,000 from Scotland and Ulster, the northern part of Ireland, where many Scots had settled as part of England's effort to subdue the island. Scottish and Scotch-Irish immigrants had a profound impact on colonial society. Mostly Presbyterians, they added significantly to religious diversity in North America. Their numbers included not only poor farmers seeking land but also numerous merchants, teachers, and professionals (indeed, a large majority of the physicians in eighteenth-century America were of Scottish origin).

THE GERMAN MIGRATION

Germans, 110,000 in all, formed the largest group of newcomers from the European continent. Most came from the valley of the Rhine River, which stretches through present-day Germany into Switzerland. In the eighteenth century, Germany was divided into numerous small states, each with a ruling prince who determined the official religion. Those who found themselves worshiping the "wrong" religion—Lutherans in Catholic areas, Catholics in Lutheran areas, and everywhere, followers of small Protestant sects such as Mennonites, Moravians, and Dunkers—faced persecution. Many decided to emigrate. Other migrants were motivated by persistent agricultural crises and the difficulty of acquiring land. Indeed, the emigration to America represented only a small part of a massive reshuffling of the German population within Europe. Millions of Germans left their homes during the eighteenth century, most of them migrating eastward to Austria-Hungary and the Russian empire, which made land available to newcomers.

Wherever they moved, Germans tended to travel in entire families. English and Dutch merchants created a well-organized system whereby "redemptioners" (as indentured families were called) received passage in exchange for a promise to work off their debt in America. Most settled in frontier areas—rural New York, western Pennsylvania, and the southern backcountry—where they formed tightly knit farming communities in which German for many years remained the dominant language. Their arrival greatly enhanced the ethnic and religious diversity of Britain's colonies.

RELIGIOUS DIVERSITY

Eighteenth-century British America was not a "melting pot" of cultures. Ethnic groups tended to live and worship in relatively homogeneous communities. But outside of New England, which received few immigrants and retained its overwhelmingly English ethnic character, American society had a far more diverse population than Britain. Nowhere was this more evident than in the practice of religion. In 1700, nearly all the churches in the colonies were either Congregational (in New England) or Anglican. In the eighteenth century, the Anglican presence expanded considerably. New churches were built and new ministers arrived from England. But the number of Dissenting congregations also multiplied.

Apart from New Jersey (formed from East and West Jersey in 1702), Rhode Island, and Pennsylvania, the colonies did not adhere to a modern separation of church and state. Nearly every colony levied taxes to pay the salaries of ministers of an established church, and most barred Catholics and Jews from voting and holding public office. But increasingly, de facto toleration among Protestant denominations flourished, fueled by the establishment of new churches by immigrants, as well as new Baptist, Methodist, and other congregations created as a result of the Great Awakening, a religious revival that will be discussed in Chapter 4. By the mid-eighteenth century, dissenting Protestants in most colonies had gained the right to worship as they pleased and own their churches, although many places still barred them from holding public office and taxed them to support the official church. A visitor to Pennsylvania in 1750 described the colony's religious diversity: "We find there Lutherans, Reformed, Catholics, Quakers, Menonists or Anabaptists, Herrnhuters or Moravian Brethren, Pietists, Seventh Day Baptists, Dunkers, Presbyterians, . . . Jews, Mohammedans, Pagans."

Baptists were among the numerous religious denominations in the eigthteenth-century colonies. In this engraving, from a history of American Baptists published in 1770, a minister baptizes a new member in the Schuylkill River in Pennsylvania, while members of the congregation look on.

VOICES OF FREEDOM

From Letter by a Female Indentured Servant
(September 22, 1756)

Only a minority of emigrants from Europe to British North America were fully free. Indentured servants were men and women who surrendered their freedom for a specified period of time in exchange for passage to America. The letter by Elizabeth Springs from Maryland to her father in England expresses complaints voiced by many indentured servants.

Honored Father,

My being forever banished from your sight, will I hope pardon the boldness I now take of troubling you with these. My long silence has been purely owing to my undutifulness to you, and well knowing I had offended in the highest degree, put a tie on my tongue and pen, for fear I should be extinct from your good graces and add a further trouble to you. . . .

O Dear Father, believe what I am going to relate the words of truth and sincerity and balance my former bad conduct [to] my sufferings here, and then I am sure you'll pity your distressed daughter. What we unfortunate English people suffer here is beyond the probability of you in England to conceive. Let it suffice that I am one of the unhappy number, am toiling almost day and night, and very often in the horse's drudgery, with only this comfort that you bitch you do not do half enough, and then tied up and whipped to that degree that you now serve an animal. Scarce any thing but Indian corn and salt to eat and that even begrudged nay many Negroes are better used, almost naked no shoes nor stockings to wear, and the comfort after slaving during master's pleasure, what rest we can get is to wrap ourselves up in a blanket and lie upon the ground. This is the deplorable condition your poor Betty endures, and now I beg if you have any bowels of compassion left show it by sending me some relief. Clothing is the principal thing wanting, which if you should condescend to, may easily send them to me by any of the ships bound to Baltimore town, Patapsco River, Maryland. And give me leave to conclude in duty to you and uncles and aunts, and respect to all friends. . . .

Elizabeth Sprigs

FROM Letter by a Swiss-German Immigrant to Pennsylvania (August 23, 1769)

Germans were among the most numerous immigrants to the eighteenth-century colonies. Many wrote letters to family members at home, relating their experiences and impressions.

Dearest Father, Brother, and Sister and Brother-in-law,

I have told you quite fully about the trip, and I will tell you what will not surprise you—that we have a free country. Of the sundry craftsmen, one may do whatever one wants. Nor does the land require payment of tithes [taxes to support a local landlord, typical in Europe]. . . . The land is very big from Canada to the east of us to Carolina in the south and to the Spanish border in the west. . . . One can settle wherever one wants without asking anyone when he buys or leases something. . . .

I have always enough to do and we have no shortage of food. Bread is plentiful. If I work for two days I earn more bread than in eight days [at home]. . . . Also I can buy many things so reasonably [for example] a pair of shoes for [roughly] seven Pennsylvania shillings. . . . I think that with God's help I will obtain land. I am not pushing for it until I am in a better position.

I would like for my brother to come . . . and it will then be even nicer in the country. . . . I assume that the land has been described to you sufficiently by various people and it is not surprising that the immigrant agents [demand payment]. For the journey is long and it costs much to stay away for one year. . . .

Johannes Hänner

QUESTIONS

1. Why does Elizabeth Sprigs compare her condition unfavorably to that of blacks?

2. What does Johannes Hänner have in mind when he calls America a "free country"?

3. What factors might explain the different experiences of these two emigrants to British North America?

"Liberty of conscience," wrote a German newcomer in 1739, was the "chief virtue" of British North America, "and on this score I do not repent my immigration." Equally important to eighteenth-century immigrants, however, were other elements of freedom, especially the availability of land, the lack of a military draft, and the absence of restraints on economic opportunity common in Europe. Skilled workers were in great demand. "They earn what they want," one emigrant wrote to his brother in Switzerland in 1733. Letters home by immigrants spoke of low taxes, the right to enter trades and professions without paying exorbitant fees, and freedom of movement. "In this country," one wrote, "there are abundant liberties in just about all matters."

INDIAN LIFE IN TRANSITION

The tide of newcomers, who equated liberty with secure possession of land, threatened to engulf the surviving Indian populations. By the eighteenth century, Indian communities were well integrated into the British imperial system. Indian warriors did much of the fighting in the century's imperial wars. Their cultures were now quite different from what they had been at the time of first contact. Indian societies that had existed for centuries had disappeared, the victims of disease and warfare. New tribes, like the Catawba of South Carolina and the Creek Confederacy, which united dozens of Indian towns in South Carolina and Georgia, had been created from their remnants. Few Indians chose to live among whites rather than in their own communities. But they had become well accustomed to using European products like knives, hatchets, needles, kettles, and firearms. Alcohol introduced by traders created social chaos in many Indian communities. One Cherokee told the governor of South Carolina in 1753, "The clothes we wear, we cannot make ourselves, they are made to us. We use their ammunition with which we kill deer. . . . Every necessary thing we must have from the white people."

While traders saw in Indian villages potential profits and British officials saw allies against France and Spain, farmers and planters viewed Indians as little more than an obstruction to their desire for land. They expected Indians to give way to white settlers. The native population of the Virginia and South Carolina frontier had already been displaced when large numbers of settlers arrived. In Pennsylvania, however, the flood of German and Scotch-Irish settlers into the backcountry upset the relatively peaceful Indian-white relations constructed by William Penn. At a 1721 conference, a group of colonial and Indian leaders reaffirmed Penn's Chain of Friendship. But conflicts over land soon multiplied. The infamous Walking Purchase of 1737 brought the fraudulent dealing so common in other colonies to Pennsylvania. The Lenni Lanape Indians agreed to an arrangement to cede a tract of land bounded by the distance a man could walk in thirty-six hours. To their amazement, Governor James Logan hired a team of swift runners, who marked out an area far in excess of what the Indians had anticipated.

By 1760, when Pennsylvania's population, a mere 20,000 in 1700, had grown to 220,000, Indian-colonist relations, initially the most harmonious in British North America, had become poisoned by suspicion and hostility. One group of Susquehanna Indians declared "that the white people had abused them and taken their lands from them, and therefore they had no reason to think that they were now concerned for their happiness." They longed for the days when "old William Penn" treated them with fairness and respect.

REGIONAL DIVERSITY

By the mid-eighteenth century, the different regions of the British colonies had developed distinct economic and social orders. Small farms tilled by family labor and geared primarily to production for local consumption predominated in New England and the new settlements of the backcountry (the area stretching from central Pennsylvania southward through the Shenandoah Valley of Virginia and into upland North and South Carolina). The backcountry was the most rapidly growing region in North America. In 1730, the only white residents in what was then called "Indian country" were the occasional hunter and trader. By the eve of the American Revolution, the region contained one-quarter of Virginia's population and half of South Carolina's. Most were farm families raising grain and livestock, but slaveowning planters, seeking fertile soil for tobacco farming, also entered the area.

In the older portions of the Middle Colonies of New York, New Jersey, and Pennsylvania, farmers were more oriented to commerce than on the frontier, growing grain both for their own use and for sale abroad and supplementing the work of family members by employing wage laborers, tenants, and in some instances slaves. Because large landlords had engrossed so much desirable land, New York's growth lagged behind that of neighboring colonies. "What man will be such a fool as to become a base tenant," wondered Richard Coote, New York's governor at the beginning of the eighteenth century, "when by crossing the Hudson river that man can for a song purchase a good freehold?" With its fertile soil, favorable climate, initially

William Penn's Treaty with the Indians. *Penn's grandson, Thomas, the proprietor of Pennsylvania, commissioned this romanticized painting from the artist Benjamin West in 1771, by which time harmony between Indians and colonists had long since turned to hostility. In the nineteenth century, many reproductions of this image circulated, reminding Americans that Indians had once been central figures in their history.*

This 1772 broadside offers a rare view of the interior of a Philadelphia shop and lists some of the many European and West Indian goods on sale, including rum, tea, spices, and gun powder—a sign of the ongoing consumer revolution linked to international trade.

peaceful Indian relations, generous governmental land distribution policy, and rivers that facilitated long-distance trading, Pennsylvania came to be known as "the best poor man's country." Ordinary colonists there enjoyed a standard of living unimaginable in Europe.

THE CONSUMER REVOLUTION

During the eighteenth century, Great Britain eclipsed the Dutch as the leading producer and trader of inexpensive consumer goods, including colonial products like coffee and tea, and such manufactured goods as linen, metalware, pins, ribbons, glassware, ceramics, and clothing. Trade integrated the British empire. As the American colonies were drawn more and more fully into the system of Atlantic commerce, they shared in the era's consumer revolution. In port cities and small inland towns, shops proliferated and American newspapers were filled with advertisements for British goods. British merchants supplied American traders with loans to enable them to import these products, and traveling peddlers carried them into remote frontier areas.

Consumerism in a modern sense—the mass production, advertising, and sale of consumer goods—did not exist in colonial America. Nonetheless, eighteenth-century estate inventories—records of people's possessions at the time of death—revealed the wide dispersal in American homes of English and even Asian products. In the seventeenth century, most colonists had lived in a pioneer world of homespun clothing and homemade goods. Now, even modest farmers and artisans owned books, ceramic plates, metal cutlery, and items made of imported silk and cotton. Tea, once a luxury enjoyed only by the wealthy, became virtually a necessity of life. "People that are least able to go to the expense," one New Yorker noted, "must have their tea though their families want bread."

COLONIAL CITIES

Britain's mainland colonies were overwhelmingly agricultural. Nine-tenths of the population resided in rural areas and made their livelihood from farming. Colonial cities like Boston, New York, Philadelphia, and Charleston were quite small by the standards of Europe or Spanish America. In 1700, when the population of Mexico City stood at 100,000, Boston had 6,000 residents and New York 4,500. As late as 1750, eight cities in Spanish America exceeded in size any in English North America.

English American cities served mainly as gathering places for agricultural goods and for imported items to be distributed to the countryside. Nonetheless, the expansion of trade encouraged the rise of port cities, home to a growing population of colonial merchants and artisans (skilled craftsmen) as well as an increasing number of poor. In 1770, with some 30,000 inhabitants, Philadelphia was "the capital of the New World," at least its British component, and, after London and Liverpool, the empire's third busiest port. The financial, commercial, and cultural center of British America, its growth rested on economic integration with the rich agricultural region nearby. Philadelphia merchants organized the collection of farm goods, supplied rural storekeepers, and extended credit to consumers. They exported flour, bread, and meat to the West Indies and Europe.

COLONIAL ARTISANS

The city was also home to a large population of furniture makers, jewelers, and silversmiths serving wealthier citizens, and hundreds of lesser artisans like weavers, blacksmiths, coopers, and construction workers. The typical artisan owned his own tools and labored in a small workshop, often his home, assisted by family members and young journeymen and apprentices learning the trade. The artisan's skill, which set him apart from the common laborers below him in the social scale, was the key to his existence, and it gave him a far greater degree of economic freedom than those dependent on others for a livelihood. "He that hath a trade, hath an estate," wrote Benjamin Franklin, who had worked as a printer before achieving renown as a scientist and statesman.

Despite the influx of British goods, American craftsmen benefited from the expanding consumer market. Most journeymen enjoyed a reasonable chance of rising to the status of master and establishing a workshop of their own. Some achieved remarkable success. Born in New York City in 1723, Myer Myers, a Jewish silversmith of Dutch ancestry, became one of the city's most prominent artisans. Myers produced jewelry, candlesticks, coffeepots, tableware, and other gold and silver objects for the colony's elite, as well as religious ornaments for both synagogues and Protestant churches in New York and nearby colonies. He used some of his profits to acquire land in New Hampshire and Connecticut. Myers's career reflected the opportunities colonial cities offered to skilled men of diverse ethnic and religious backgrounds.

AN ATLANTIC WORLD

People, ideas, and goods flowed back and forth across the Atlantic, knitting together the empire and its diverse populations—British merchants and consumers, American colonists, African slaves, and surviving Indians—and created webs of interdependence among the European empires. Sugar, tobacco, and other products of the Western Hemisphere were marketed as far away as eastern Europe. London bankers financed the slave trade between Africa and Portugese Brazil. Spain spent its gold and silver importing goods from other countries. As trade expanded, the North American and West Indian colonies became the major overseas market for British manufactured goods. Although most colonial output was consumed at home, North Americans shipped farm products to Britain, the West Indies, and with the exception of goods like tobacco "enumerated" under the Navigation Acts, outside the empire. Virtually the entire Chesapeake tobacco crop was marketed in Britain, with most of it then re-exported to Europe by British merchants. Most of the bread and flour exported from the colonies was destined for the West Indies. African slaves there grew sugar that could be distilled into rum, a product increasingly popular among both North American colonists and Indians, who obtained it by trading furs and deerskins that were then shipped to Europe. The mainland colonies carried on a flourishing trade in fish and grains with southern Europe. Ships built in New England made up one-third of the British empire's trading fleet.

Membership in the empire had many advantages for the colonists. Most Americans did not complain about British regulation of their trade because

As Atlantic trade expanded, shipbuilding became a major enterprise in the colonies. This painting from around 1750 by an unknown artist depicts vessels under construction at the Grey's Inn Creek Shipyard in Maryland.

commerce enriched the colonies as well as the mother country and lax enforcement of the Navigation Acts allowed smuggling to flourish. In a dangerous world, moreover, the Royal Navy protected American shipping. And despite the many differences between life in England and its colonies, eighteenth-century English America drew closer and closer to, and in some ways became more and more similar to, the mother country across the Atlantic.

SOCIAL CLASSES IN THE COLONIES

THE COLONIAL ELITE

Most free Americans benefited from economic growth, but as colonial society matured an elite emerged that, while neither as powerful or wealthy as the aristocracy of England, increasingly dominated politics and society. Indeed, the gap between rich and poor probably grew more rapidly in the eighteenth century than in any other period of American history. In New England and the Middle Colonies, expanding trade made possible the emergence of a powerful upper class of merchants, often linked by family or commercial ties to great trading firms in London. There were no banks in colonial America. Credit and money were in short supply, and mercantile success depended on personal connections as much as business talent. By 1750, the colonies of the Chesapeake and Lower South were dominated by slave plantations producing staple crops, especially tobacco and rice, for the world market. Here great planters accumulated enormous wealth. The colonial elite also included the rulers of proprietary colonies like Pennsylvania and Maryland.

America had no titled aristocracy as in Britain. It had no system of legally established social ranks or family pedigrees stretching back to medieval times. Apart from the De Lanceys, Livingstons, and Van Rensselaers of New York, the Penn family in Pennsylvania, and a few southern planters, it had no one whose landholdings, in monetary value, rivaled those of the British aristocracy. But throughout British America, men of prominence controlled colonial government. In Virginia, the upper class was so tight-knit and intermarried so often that the colony was said to be governed by a "cousinocracy." Members of the gentry controlled the vestries, or local governing bodies, of the established Anglican Church, dominated the county courts (political as well as judicial institutions that levied taxes and enacted local ordinances), and were prominent in Virginia's legislature. In the 1750s, seven members of the same generation of the Lee family sat in the House of Burgesses.

Eighteenth-century Virginia was a far healthier environment than in the early days of settlement. Planters could expect to pass their wealth down to the next generation, providing estates for their sons and establishing family dynasties. Nearly every Virginian of note achieved prominence through family connections. The days when self-made men could rise into the Virginia gentry were long gone; by 1770, nearly all upper-class Virginians had inherited their wealth. Thomas Jefferson's grandfather was a justice of the peace (an important local official), militia captain, and sheriff, and his father was a member of the House of Burgesses. George Washington's father, grandfather, and great-grandfather had been justices of the peace. The Virginia gentry used its control of provincial government to gain possession of large tracts of land as western areas opened for settlement. Grants of 20,000 to 40,000 acres were not uncommon. Robert "King" Carter, a speaker of the House of Burgesses, acquired 300,000 acres of land and 1,000 slaves by the time of his death in 1732.

A 1753 portrait of Robert Carter, a member of one of Virginia's most prominent families, in the attire of a gentleman.

ANGLICIZATION

For much of the eighteenth century, the American colonies had more regular trade and communications with Britain than among themselves. Elites in different regions slowly developed a common lifestyle and sense of common interests. But rather than thinking of themselves as distinctively American, they became more and more English—a process historians call "Anglicization."

Wealthy Americans tried to model their lives on British etiquette and behavior. Somewhat resentful at living in provincial isolation—"at the end of the world," as one Virginia aristocrat put it—they sought to demonstrate their status and legitimacy by importing the latest London fashions and literature, sending their sons to Britain for education, and building homes equipped with fashionable furnishings modeled on the country estates and town houses of the English gentry. Their residences included large rooms for entertainment, display cases for imported luxury goods, and elaborate formal gardens. Some members of the colonial elite, like George Washington, even had coats of arms designed for their families, in imitation of English upper-class practice.

Desperate to follow an aristocratic lifestyle, many planters fell into debt. William Byrd III lived so extravagantly that by 1770 he had accumulated a debt of £100,000, an amount almost unheard of in England or America. But so long as the world market for tobacco thrived, so did Virginia's gentry.

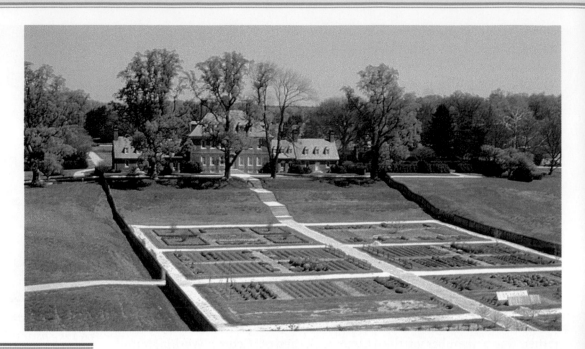

Built in the 1750s by Carter Burwell, grandson of the original Robert "King" Carter, Carter's Grove, near Williamsburg, Virginia, was a grand plantation mansion with large formal gardens, in imitation of English landscape design.

THE SOUTH CAROLINA ARISTOCRACY

The richest group of mainland colonists were South Carolina planters (although planters in Jamaica far outstripped them in wealth). Elite South Carolinians often traveled north to enjoy summer vacations in the cooler climate of Newport, Rhode Island, and they spent much of the remainder of their time in Charleston, the only real urban center south of Philadelphia and the richest city in British North America. Here aristocratic social life flourished, centered on theaters, literary societies, and social events. Like their Virginia counterparts, South Carolina grandees lived a lavish lifestyle amid imported furniture, fine wines, silk clothing, and other items from England. They surrounded themselves with house slaves dressed in specially designed uniforms. In 1774, the per capita wealth in the Charleston District was £2,300, more than four times that of tobacco areas in Virginia and eight times the figure for Philadelphia or Boston. But wealth in South Carolina was highly concentrated. The richest 10 percent of the colony owned half the wealth in 1770, the poorest quarter less than 2 percent.

Throughout the colonies, elites emulated what they saw as England's balanced, stable social order. Liberty, in their eyes, meant, in part, the power to rule—the right of those blessed with wealth and prominence to dominate over others. They viewed society as a hierarchical structure in which some men were endowed with greater talents than others and destined to rule. The social order, they believed, was held together by webs of influence that linked patrons and those dependent on them. Each place in the hierarchy carried with it different responsibilities, and one's status was revealed in dress, manners, and the splendor of one's home. "Superiority" and "dependence," as one colonial newspaper put it, were natural elements of any society. An image of refinement served to legitimate wealth and political power. Colonial elites prided themselves on developing aristocratic manners, cultivating the arts, and making productive use of leisure. Indeed, on both sides of the Atlantic, elites viewed work as something reserved for common folk and slaves. Freedom from labor was the mark of the gentleman.

POVERTY IN THE COLONIES

At the other end of the social scale, poverty emerged as a visible feature of eighteenth-century colonial life. Although not considered by most colonists part of their society, the growing number of slaves lived in impoverished conditions. Among free Americans, poverty was hardly as widespread as in Britain, where in the early part of the century between one-quarter and one-half of the people regularly required public assistance. But as the colonial population expanded, access to land diminished rapidly, especially in long-settled areas. In New England, which received few immigrants, the high birthrate fueled population growth. With the supply of land limited, sons who could not hope to inherit farms were forced to move to other colonies or to try their hand at a trade in the region's towns. By mid-century, tenants and wage laborers were a growing presence on farms in the Middle Colonies.

In colonial cities, the number of propertyless wage earners subsisting at the poverty line steadily increased. In Boston, one-third of the population in 1771 owned no property at all. In rural Augusta County, carved out of Virginia's Shenandoah River valley in 1738, land was quickly engrossed by planters and speculators. By the 1760s, two-thirds of the county's white men owned no land and had little prospect of obtaining it unless they migrated further west. Taking the colonies as a whole, half of the wealth at mid-century was concentrated in the hands of the richest 10 percent of the population.

Attitudes and policies toward poverty in colonial America mirrored British precedents. The better-off colonists generally viewed the poor as lazy, shiftless, and responsible for their own plight. Both rural communities and cities did accept responsibility for assisting their own. But to minimize the burden on taxpayers, poor persons were frequently set to labor in workhouses, where they produced goods that reimbursed authorities for part of their upkeep. Their children were sent to work as apprentices in local homes or workshops. And most communities adopted stringent measures to "warn out" unemployed and propertyless newcomers who might become dependent on local poor relief. This involved town authorities either expelling the unwanted poor from an area or formally declaring certain persons ineligible for assistance. In Essex County, Massachusetts, the number of poor persons warned out each year rose from 200 in the 1730s to 1,700 in the 1760s. Many were members of families headed by widowed or abandoned women.

THE MIDDLE RANKS

The large majority of free Americans lived between the extremes of wealth and poverty. Along with racial and ethnic diversity, what distinguished the mainland colonies from Europe was the wide distribution of land and the economic autonomy of most ordinary free families. The anonymous author of the book *American Husbandry*, published in 1775, reported that "little freeholders who live upon their own property" made up "the most considerable part" of the people, especially in the northern colonies and

The seven-foot-long Van Bergen Overmantel, *painted by John Heaten around 1733, was probably designed to hang above a wide fireplace in the home of Marten Van Bergen, a Dutch farmer in colonial New York. It offers a rare contemporary view of a prosperous colonial farm, with a full granary and livestock. Native Americans and African-American slaves are among the individuals depicted by the artist.*

the nonplantation parts of the South. Altogether, perhaps two-thirds of the free male population were farmers who owned their own land. England, to be sure, had no class of laborers as exploited as American slaves, but three-fifths of its people owned no property at all.

By the eighteenth century, colonial farm families viewed landownership almost as a right, the social precondition of freedom. They strongly resented efforts, whether by Native Americans, great landlords, or colonial governments, to limit their access to land. A dislike of personal dependence and an understanding of freedom as not relying on others for a livelihood sank deep roots in British North America. These beliefs, after all, accorded with social reality—a wide distribution of property that made economic independence part of the lived experience of large numbers of white colonists.

WOMEN AND THE HOUSEHOLD ECONOMY

In the household economy of eighteenth-century America, the family was the center of economic life. Most work revolved around the home, and all members—men, women, and children—contributed to the family's livelihood. The independence of the small farmer depended in considerable measure on the labor of dependent women and children. "He that hath an industrious family shall soon be rich," declared one colonial saying, and the high birthrate in part reflected the need for as many hands as possible on colonial farms. Most farmers concentrated first on growing food for their own consumption and acquiring enough land to pass it along to their sons. But the consumer revolution and expanding networks of Atlantic trade drew increasing numbers of farmers into production for the market as well.

As the population grew and the death rate declined, family life stabilized and more marriages became lifetime commitments. Free women were expected to devote their lives to being good wives and mothers. Already enshrined in law and property relations, male domination took on greater and greater social reality. In several colonies, the law mandated primogeniture— meaning that estates must be passed intact to the oldest son. As colonial society became more structured, opportunities that had existed for women in the early period receded. In Connecticut, for example, the courts were informal and unorganized in the seventeenth century, and women often represented themselves. In the eighteenth century, it became necessary to hire a lawyer as one's spokesman in court. Women, barred from practicing as attorneys, disappeared from judicial proceedings. Because of the desperate need for labor, men and women in the seventeenth century both did various kinds of work. In the eighteenth century, the division of labor along gender lines solidified. Women's work was clearly defined, including cooking, cleaning, sewing, making butter, and assisting with agricultural chores. The work of farmers' wives and daughters often spelled the difference between a family's self-sufficiency and poverty.

"Women's work is never done." This popular adage was literally true. Even as the consumer revolution reduced the demands on many women by making available store-bought goods previously produced at home, women's work seemed to increase. Lower infant mortality meant more time spent in child care and domestic chores. The demand for new goods increased the need for all family members to contribute to family income. For most women, work was incessant and exhausting. "I am dirty and distressed, almost wearied to death," wrote Mary Cooper, a Long Island woman, in her diary in 1769. "This day," she continued, "is forty years since I left my father's house and come here, and here have I seen little else but hard labor and sorrow."

NORTH AMERICA AT MID-CENTURY

By the mid-eighteenth century, the area that would become the United States was home to a remarkable diversity of peoples and different kinds of social organization, from Pueblo villages of the Southwest to tobacco plantations of the Chesapeake, towns and small farms of New England, landholdings in the Hudson Valley that resembled feudal estates, and fur trading outposts of the northern and western frontier. Elites tied to imperial centers of power dominated the political and economic life of nearly every colony. But large numbers of colonists enjoyed far greater opportunities for freedom—access to the vote, prospects of acquiring land, the right to worship as they pleased, and an escape from oppressive government—than existed in Europe. Free colonists probably enjoyed the highest per capita income in the world. The colonies' economic growth contributed to a high birthrate, long life expectancy, and expanding demand for consumer goods.

In the British colonies, writes one historian, lived "thousands of the freest individuals the Western world has ever known." Yet many others found themselves confined to the partial freedom of indentured servitude or to the complete absence of freedom in slavery. Both timeless longings for freedom and new and unprecedented forms of unfreedom had been essential to the North American colonies' remarkable development.

This portrait of the Cheney family by an unknown late eighteenth-century artist illustrates the high birthrate in colonial America, and suggests how many years of a woman's life were spent bearing and raising children.

SUGGESTED READING

Bailyn, Bernard. *The Peopling of British North America* (1986). A brief survey of the movement of peoples across the Atlantic.

Berlin, Ira. *Many Thousands Gone: The First Two Centuries of Slavery in North America* (1998). The most extensive study of the origins and development of colonial slavery.

Bushman, Richard. *The Refinement of America: Persons, Houses, Cities* (1992). A study of how a more "refined" lifestyle emerged in the eighteenth-century colonies.

Dayton, Cornelia H. *Women before the Bar: Gender, Law, and Society in Connecticut, 1639–1789* (1995). Examines the changing legal status of women in one American colony.

Fogleman, Aaron S. *Hopeful Journeys: German Immigration, Settlement, and Political Culture in Colonial America, 1717–1775* (1996). The most comprehensive study of German migration to eighteenth-century America.

Jordan, Winthrop D. *White over Black: American Attitudes toward the Negro, 1550–1812* (1968). A detailed look at how ideas about race developed over time in England and the American colonies.

Kulikoff, Allan. *Tobacco and Slaves: The Development of Southern Cultures in the Chesapeake, 1680–1800* (1986). Explores how the rise of slave-grown tobacco affected society in the Chesapeake.

Lemon, James T. *The Best Poor Man's Country: A Geographical Study of Early Southeastern Pennsylvania* (1972). A study of agriculture and the environment in one of the most successful farming areas of colonial America.

Lepore, Jill. *The Name of War: King Philip's War and the Origin of American Identity* (1998). An examination not only of the war itself but also of its long-term consequences for Indian-white relations.

Lovejoy, David S. *The Glorious Revolution in America* (1972). Explores how the revolution in England in 1689 affected the American colonies.

Mintz, Sidney. *Sweetness and Power: The Place of Sugar in Modern History* (1985). A global history of the significance of sugar in the making of the modern world.

Morgan, Edmund S. *American Slavery, American Freedom: The Ordeal of Colonial Virginia* (1975). An influential study of the slow development of slavery in seventeenth-century Virginia.

Norton, Mary Beth. *In the Devil's Snare: The Salem Witchcraft Crisis of 1692* (2002). The most recent study of the witch trials, placing them in the context of anxieties over Indian warfare on the Massachusetts frontier.

Saxton, Martha. *Being Good: Women's Moral Values in Early America* (2003). Examines social standards for women's behavior and how women tried to live up to them.

Washburn, Wilcomb E. *The Governor and the Rebel: A History of Bacon's Rebellion in Virginia* (1957). Explores the causes and consequences of the 1676 uprising in Virginia.

REVIEW QUESTIONS

1. Both the Puritans and William Penn viewed their colonies as "holy experiments." How did they differ?

2. Eric Foner writes, "prejudice by itself did not create North American slavery." Examine what did create slavery and the role racial prejudice played.

3. How were the actions of King James II toward New England perceived as threats to colonial liberty?

4. How did King Philip's War, Bacon's Rebellion, and the Salem witch trials illustrate a widespread crisis in British North America in the late seventeenth century?

5. The social structure of the eighteenth-century colonies was growing more dynamic for some but not for others. For whom was there more opportunity, and for whom not?

KEY TERMS

Navigation Acts (p. 94)

Yamasee Uprising (p. 97)

slave codes (p. 98)

sugar (p. 101)

slaves in Jamestown (p. 103)

Bacon's Rebellion (p. 104)

Anglicanism (p. 107)

Salem witch trials (p. 110)

redemptioners (p. 114)

REVIEW TABLE

Colonial Crisis in the Late Seventeenth Century

Crisis	Dates	Origins of Conflict	Action	Resolution
King Philip's War	1675–1676	White settlers' encroachment on Indian land	Philip's forces attack forty-five New England towns	Settlers counter-attack, breaking Indians' power
Bacon's Rebellion	1676	Corruption of Virginia's government	Bacon burns Jamestown and takes power	Virginia's ruling elite undertake reforms
Glorious Revolution	1688	James II threatens to restore Catholicism to England	A bloodless coup to overthrow James II; Colonists overthrow Dominion of New England	Protestants William and Mary of Orange are crowned
Salem Witch Trials	1691–1692	Amidst political and social tensions, young girls begin to experiment with magic	Hundreds accused of witchcraft and nineteen people are hanged	Governor dissolves the Salem court

CHAPTER 4

Slavery, Freedom, and the Struggle for Empire to 1763

The Old Plantation, *a late-eighteenth-century watercolor by an unknown artist, depicts slaves dancing in a plantation's slave quarters, perhaps at a wedding. The scene may take place in South Carolina, where the painting was found. The musical instruments and pottery are African in origin while much of the clothing is of European manufacture, indicating the mixing of African and white cultures among the era's slaves.*

FOCUS QUESTIONS

- What were the major varieties of African slavery in eighteenth-century America?

- How did African-American cultures begin to emerge in the eighteenth century?

- What were the meanings of British liberty in the eighteenth century?

- What were the characteristics of colonial politics in the eighteenth century?

- What was the significance of the Great Awakening?

- How did the Spanish and French empires in America develop in the eighteenth century?

- What was the impact of the Seven Years' War on imperial and Indian–white relations?

Sometime in the mid-1750s, Olaudah Equiano, the eleven-year-old son of a West African village chief, was kidnapped by slave traders. He soon found himself on a ship headed for Barbados. After a short stay on that Caribbean island, Equiano was sold to a plantation owner in Virginia and then purchased by a British sea captain, who renamed him Gustavus Vassa. He accompanied his owner on numerous voyages on Atlantic trading vessels. While still a slave, he enrolled in a school in England where he learned to read and write, and then enlisted in the Royal Navy. He fought in Canada under General James Wolfe in 1758 during the Seven Years' War. In 1763, however, Equiano was sold once again and returned to the Caribbean. Three years later, he was able to purchase his freedom. Equiano went on to live through shipwrecks, took part in an English colonizing venture in Central America, and even participated in an expedition to the Arctic Circle.

Equiano eventually settled in London, and in 1789 he published *The Interesting Narrative of the Life of Olaudah Equiano, or Gustavus Vassa, the African,* which he described as a "history of neither a saint, a hero, nor a tyrant," but of a victim of slavery who through luck or fate ended up more fortunate than most of his people. He condemned the idea that Africans were inferior to Europeans and therefore deserved to be slaves. He urged the European reader to recall that "his ancestors were once, like the Africans, uncivilized" and asked, "did nature make them inferior . . . and should they too have been made slaves?" Persons of all races, he insisted, were capable of intellectual improvement. The book became the era's most widely read account by a slave of his own experiences. Equiano died in 1797.

Recent scholars have suggested that Equiano may actually have been born in the New World rather than Africa. In either case, while his rich variety of experience was no doubt unusual, his life illuminates broad patterns of eighteenth-century American history. As noted in the previous chapter, this was a period of sustained development for British North America. Compared to England and Scotland—united to create Great Britain by the Act of Union of 1707—the colonies were growing much more rapidly. Some contemporaries spoke of British America as a "rising empire" that would one day eclipse the mother country in population and wealth.

It would be wrong, however, to see the first three-quarters of the eighteenth century simply as a prelude to American independence. As Equiano's life illustrates, the Atlantic was more a bridge than a barrier between the Old and New Worlds. Ideas, people, and goods flowed back and forth across the ocean. Even as the colonies' population became more diverse, they were increasingly integrated into the British empire. Their laws and political institutions were extensions of those of Britain,

The title page of Olaudah Equiano's account of his life, the best-known narrative by an eighteenth-century slave. The portrait of Equiano in European dress and holding a Bible challenges stereotypes of blacks as "savages" incapable of becoming civilized.

their ideas about society and culture reflected British values, their economies were geared to serving the empire's needs. As European powers jockeyed for advantage in North America, colonists were drawn into an almost continuous series of wars with France and its Indian allies, which reinforced their sense of identification with and dependence on Great Britain.

Equiano's life also underscores the greatest irony or contradiction in the history of the eighteenth century—the simultaneous expansion of freedom and slavery. This was the era when the idea of the "freeborn Englishman" became powerfully entrenched in the outlook of both colonists and Britons. More than any other principle, liberty was seen as what made the British empire distinct. Yet the eighteenth century was also the great era of the Atlantic slave trade, a commerce increasingly dominated by British merchants and ships. One of the most popular songs of the period included the refrain, "Britons never, never, never will be slaves." But during the eighteenth century, more than half the Africans shipped to the New World as slaves were carried on British vessels. Most were destined for the plantations of the West Indies and Brazil, but slaves also made up around 280,000 of the 585,000 persons who arrived in Britain's mainland colonies between 1700 and 1775. Although concentrated in the Chesapeake and areas further south, slavery existed in every colony of British North America. And unlike Equiano, very few slaves were fortunate enough to gain their freedom.

SLAVERY AND THE EMPIRE

Of the estimated 7.7 million Africans transported to the New World between 1492 and 1820, over half arrived between 1700 and 1800. The Atlantic slave trade would later be condemned by statesmen and general opinion as a crime against humanity. But in the eighteenth century, it was a regularized business in which European merchants, African traders, and American planters engaged in complex bargaining over human lives, all with the expectation of securing a profit. The slave trade was a vital part of world commerce. Every European empire in the New World utilized slave labor and battled for control of this lucrative trade. The *asiento*—an agreement whereby Spain subcontracted to a foreign power the right to provide slaves to Spanish America—was an important diplomatic prize. Britain's acquisition of the *asiento* from the Dutch in the Treaty of Utrecht of 1713 was a major step in its rise to commercial supremacy.

In the British empire of the eighteenth century, free laborers working for wages were atypical and slavery the norm. Slave plantations contributed mightily to English economic development. The first mass consumer goods in international trade were produced by slaves—sugar, rice, coffee, and tobacco. The rising demand for these products fueled the rapid growth of the Atlantic slave trade.

An early-eighteenth-century panorama of the slave trade on the western coast of Africa. In the foreground, canoes carry slaves to a waiting ship for transportation to the New World. In the background are noted some of the many slave-trading outposts established by European powers, including Elmina (Mina) castle, which the Dutch had seized from Portugal in 1637, and Cape Coast (Corso), the chief base of the Royal African Company of England.

THE TRIANGULAR TRADES

In the eighteenth century, the Caribbean remained the commercial focus of the British empire and the major producer of revenue for the crown. But slave-grown products from the mainland occupied a larger and larger part of Atlantic commerce. A series of triangular trading routes crisscrossed the Atlantic, carrying British manufactured goods to Africa and the colonies, colonial products including tobacco, indigo, sugar, and rice to Europe, and slaves from Africa to the New World. Areas where slavery was only a minor institution also profited from slave labor. Merchants in New York, Massachusetts, and Rhode Island participated actively in the slave trade, shipping slaves from Africa to the Caribbean or southern colonies. The slave

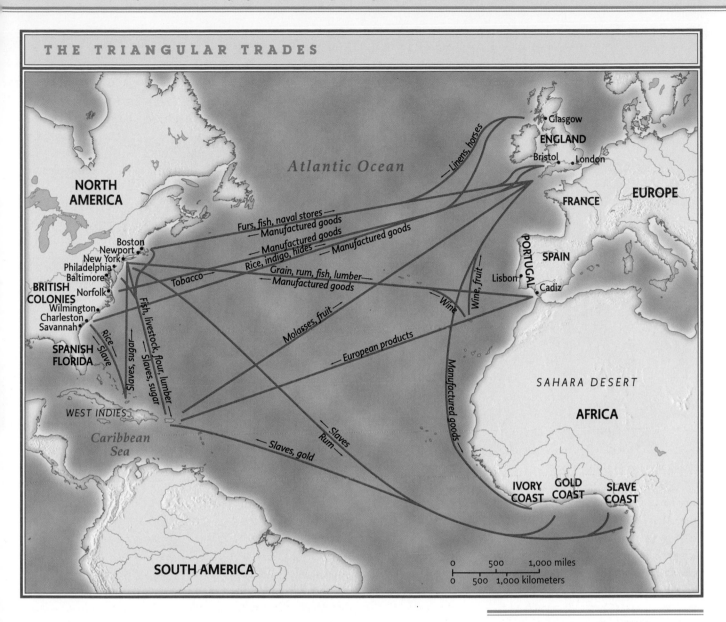

THE TRIANGULAR TRADES

A series of "triangular" trading routes crisscrossed the Atlantic, bringing manufactured goods to Africa and Britain's American colonies, slaves to the New World, and colonial products to Europe.

economies of the West Indies were the largest market for fish, grain, live-stock, and lumber exported from New England and the Middle Colonies. In 1720, half the ships entering or leaving New York Harbor were engaged in trade with the Caribbean. Indeed, one historian writes, "The growth and prosperity of the emerging society of free colonial British America . . . were achieved as a result of slave labor." In Britain itself, the profits from slavery and the slave trade stimulated the rise of ports like Liverpool and Bristol and the growth of banking, shipbuilding, and insurance. They also helped to finance the early industrial revolution.

Overall, in the eighteenth century, Atlantic commerce consisted pri-marily of slaves, crops produced by slaves, and goods destined for slave societies. It should not be surprising that for large numbers of free colonists and Europeans, freedom meant in part the power and right to enslave others. And as slavery became more and more entrenched, so too, as the Quaker abolitionist John Woolman commented in 1762, did "the

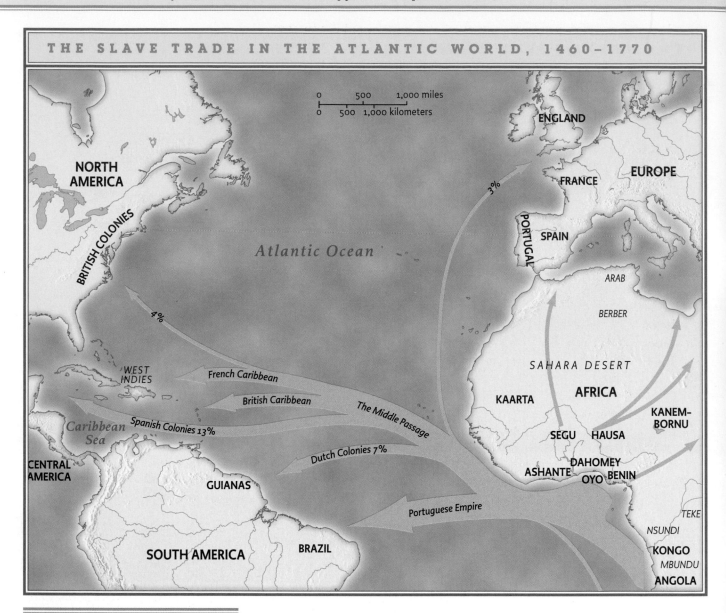

THE SLAVE TRADE IN THE ATLANTIC WORLD, 1460–1770

The Atlantic slave trade expanded rapidly in the eighteenth century. The mainland colonies received only a tiny proportion of the Africans brought to the New World, most of whom were transported to Brazil and the West Indies.

idea of slavery being connected with the black color, and liberty with the white."

AFRICA AND THE SLAVE TRADE

A few African societies, like Benin for a time, opted out of the Atlantic slave trade, hoping to avoid the disruptions it inevitably caused. But most African rulers took part, and they proved quite adept at playing the Europeans off against one another, collecting taxes from foreign merchants, and keeping the capture and sale of slaves under their own control. Few Europeans ventured inland from the coast. Traders remained in their "factories" and purchased slaves brought to them by African rulers and dealers.

The transatlantic slave trade made Africa a major market for European goods, especially textiles and guns. Both disrupted relationships within and among African societies. Cheap imported textiles undermined traditional craft production, while guns encouraged the further growth of slavery, since the only way to obtain European weapons was to supply slaves. By the eighteenth century, militarized states like Ashanti and Dahomey would arise in West Africa, with large armies using European firearms to prey on their neighbors in order to capture slaves. From a minor institution, slavery grew to become more and more central to West African society, a source of wealth for African merchants and of power for newly emerging African kingdoms. The loss every year of tens of thousands of men and women in the prime of their lives to the slave trade weakened and distorted West Africa's society and economy.

THE MIDDLE PASSAGE

For slaves, the voyage across the Atlantic—known as the Middle Passage because it was the second, or middle, leg in the triangular trading routes linking Europe, Africa, and America—was a harrowing experience. Since a slave could be sold in America for twenty to thirty times the price in Africa, men, women, and children were crammed aboard vessels as tightly as possible to maximize profits. "The height, sometimes, between decks," wrote one slave trader, "was only eighteen inches, so that the unfortunate human beings could not turn around, or even on their sides . . . and here they are usually chained to the decks by their necks and legs." Equiano, who later described "the shrieks of the women and the groans of the dying," survived the Middle Passage, but many Africans did not. Diseases like measles and smallpox spread rapidly, and about one slave in five perished before reaching the New World. Ship captains were known to throw the sick overboard in order to prevent the spread of epidemics. The crews on slave ships also suffered a high death rate.

Only a small proportion (perhaps 5 percent) of slaves carried to the New World were destined for mainland North America. The vast majority landed in Brazil or the West Indies, where the high death rate on the sugar plantations led to a constant demand for new slave imports. As late as 1700, only about 20,000 Africans had been landed in Britain's colonies there. In the eighteenth century, however, their numbers increased steadily. Overall, the area that was to become the United States imported between 400,000 and 600,000 slaves. By 1770, due to the natural reproduction of the slave population, around one-fifth of the estimated 2.3 million persons (not including Indians) living in the English colonies of North America were Africans and their descendants.

An architect's plan for a slave ship. These drawings illustrate the conditions under which slaves endured the Middle Passage across the Atlantic.

Benjamin Latrobe's watercolor, An Overseer Doing His Duty, *was sketched near Fredericksburg, Virginia, in 1798. The title is meant to be ironic: the well-dressed overseer relaxes while two female slaves work in the fields.*

CHESAPEAKE SLAVERY

By the mid-eighteenth century, three distinct slave systems were well entrenched in Britain's mainland colonies: tobacco-based plantation slavery in the Chesapeake, rice-based plantation slavery in South Carolina and Georgia, and nonplantation slavery in New England and the Middle Colonies. The largest and oldest of these was the tobacco plantation system of the Chesapeake, where more than 270,000 slaves resided in 1770, nearly half of the region's population. On the eve of the Revolution, Virginia and Maryland were as closely tied to Britain as any other colonies and their economies were models of mercantilist policy (described in Chapter 3). They supplied the mother country with a valuable raw material, imported large amounts of British goods, and were closely linked in culture and political values to the metropolis. As we have seen, the period after 1680 witnessed a rapid shift from indentured servitude to slavery on the region's tobacco plantations. In the eighteenth century, the growing world demand for tobacco encouraged continued slave imports. When tobacco prices fell in the early part of the century, some planters shifted to grain production. But tobacco remained their primary source of wealth.

A detail from a 1768 map of Virginia and Maryland illustrates a tobacco wharf. A planter negotiates with a merchant or sea captain, while slaves go about their work.

As Virginia expanded westward, so did slavery. By the eve of the American Revolution, the center of gravity of slavery in the colony had shifted from the Tidewater (the region along the coast) to the Piedmont farther inland. Most Chesapeake slaves, male and female, worked in the fields, but thousands labored as teamsters, as boatmen, and in skilled crafts. Numerous slave women became cooks, seamstresses, dairy maids, and personal servants. The son of George Mason, one of Virginia's leading planters and statesmen, recorded that his father's slaves included "coopers, sawyers, blacksmiths, tanners, shoemakers, spinners, weavers, knitters, and even a distiller." Slavery was common on small farms as well as plantations; nearly half of Virginia's white families owned at least one slave in 1770. Because there is little "economy of scale" in tobacco growing—that is, enlarging the size of the producing unit does not lower costs and maximize productivity—Chesapeake plantations tended to be smaller than in the Caribbean and daily interactions between masters and slaves were more extensive.

Slavery laid the foundation for the consolidation of the Chesapeake elite, a landed gentry that, in conjunction with merchants who handled the tobacco trade and lawyers who defended the interests of slaveholders, dominated the region's society and politics. Meanwhile, even as the consumer revolution improved the standard of living of lesser whites, their long-term economic prospects diminished. As slavery expanded, planters engrossed the best lands and wealth among the white population became more and more concentrated. Slavery transformed Chesapeake society into an elaborate hierarchy of degrees of freedom. At the top stood large planters, below them numerous lesser planters and landowning yeomen, and at the bottom a large population of convicts, indentured servants, tenant farmers (who made up half the white households in 1770), and, of course, the slaves.

FREEDOM AND SLAVERY IN THE CHESAPEAKE

With the consolidation of a slave society in the Chesapeake, planters filled the law books with measures enhancing the master's power over his human property and restricting blacks' access to freedom. Violence lay at the heart of the slave system. Even a planter like Landon Carter, who prided himself on his concern for the well-being of his slaves, noted casually in his diary, "they have been severely whipped day by day."

Race took on more and more importance as a line of social division. Whites increasingly considered free blacks dangerous and undesirable. Free blacks lost the right to employ white servants and to bear arms, were subjected to special taxes, and could be punished for striking a white person, regardless of the cause. In 1723, Virginia revoked the voting privileges of property-owning free blacks. When the Lords of Trade in London asked Virginia's governor to justify discriminating among "freemen, merely upon account of their complexion," he responded that "a distinction ought to be made between their offspring and the descendants of an Englishman, with whom they never were to be accounted equal." Because Virginia law required that freed slaves be sent out of the colony, free blacks remained only a tiny part of the population—less than 4 percent in 1750. "Free" and "white" had become virtually identical.

INDIAN SLAVERY IN EARLY CAROLINA

Farther south, a different slave system, based on rice production, emerged in South Carolina and Georgia. The Barbadians who initially settled South Carolina in the 1670s were quite familiar with African slavery, but their

Henry Darnall III, painted around 1710 by Justus Engelhardt Kühn, who produced numerous portraits of prominent Marylanders in the early eighteenth century. The boy, clearly the son of a member of the colony's wealthy gentry, stands next to a young slave, a symbol of his family's wealth. The background is an idealized European palace and formal garden.

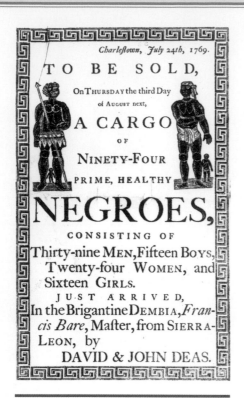

A 1769 broadside advertising the sale of ninety-four slaves who had just arrived at Charleston from West Africa.

first victims were members of the area's native population. The early Carolina economy focused on the export to the Caribbean of Indian slaves and to England of deerskins and furs obtained from Indians. The local Creek Indians initially welcomed the settlers and began selling them slaves, generally war captives and their families, most of whom were sold to the West Indies. They even launched wars against neighboring tribes specifically for the purpose of capturing and selling slaves. As the plantation system expanded, however, the Creeks became more and more concerned, not only because it led to encroachments on their land but also because they feared enslavement themselves. They were aware that only a handful of slaves worked in nearby Spanish Florida. The Creeks, one leader remarked in 1738, preferred to deal with the Spanish, who "enslave no one as the English do."

THE RICE KINGDOM

As in early Virginia, frontier conditions allowed leeway to South Carolina's small population of African-born slaves, who farmed, tended livestock, and were initially allowed to serve in the militia to fight the Spanish and Indians. And as in Virginia, the introduction of a marketable staple crop, in this case rice, led directly to economic development, the large-scale importation of slaves, and a growing divide between white and black. South Carolina was the first mainland colony to achieve a black majority. By the 1730s (by which time North Carolina had become a separate colony), two-thirds of its population was black. In the 1740s, another staple, indigo (a crop used in producing blue dye), was developed. Like rice, indigo required large-scale cultivation and was grown by slaves.

Ironically, it was Africans, familiar with the crop at home, who taught English settlers how to cultivate rice, which then became the foundation of South Carolina slavery and of the wealthiest slaveowning class on the North American mainland. Since rice production requires considerable capital investment to drain swamps and create irrigation systems, it is economically advantageous for rice plantations to be as large as possible. Thus, South Carolina planters owned far more land and slaves than their counterparts in Virginia. Moreover, since mosquitoes bearing malaria (a disease to which Africans had developed partial immunity) flourished in the watery rice fields, planters tended to leave plantations under the control of overseers and the slaves themselves.

In the Chesapeake, field slaves worked in groups under constant supervision. Under the "task" system that developed in eighteenth-century South Carolina, individual slaves were assigned daily jobs, the completion of which allowed them time for leisure or to cultivate crops of their own. In 1762, one rice district had a population of only 76 white males among 1,000 slaves. Fearful of the ever-increasing black population majority, South Carolina's legislature took steps to encourage the immigration of "poor Protestants," offering each newcomer a cash bounty and occasionally levying taxes on slave imports, only to see such restrictions overturned in London. By 1770, the number of South Carolina slaves had reached 100,000, well over half the colony's population.

THE GEORGIA EXPERIMENT

Rice cultivation also spread into Georgia in the mid-eighteenth century. The colony was founded in 1733 by a group of philanthropists led by James Oglethorpe, a wealthy reformer whose causes included improved conditions for imprisoned debtors and the abolition of slavery. Oglethorpe hoped to establish a haven where the "worthy poor" of England could enjoy economic opportunity. The government in London supported the creation of Georgia to protect South Carolina against the Spanish and their Indian allies in Florida.

Initially, the proprietors banned the introduction of both liquor and slaves, leading to continual battles with settlers, who desired both. By the 1740s, Georgia offered the spectacle of colonists pleading for the "English liberty" of self-government so that they could enact laws introducing slavery. In 1751, the proprietors surrendered the colony to the crown. The colonists quickly won the right to an elected assembly, which met in Savannah, Georgia's main settlement. It repealed the ban on slavery (and liquor), as well as an early measure that had limited land holdings to 500 acres. Georgia became a miniature version of South Carolina. By 1770, as many as 15,000 slaves labored on its coastal rice plantations.

SLAVERY IN THE NORTH

Compared to the plantation regions, slavery was far less central to the economies of New England and the Middle Colonies, where small farms predominated. Slaves represented only a minor part of these colonies' populations, and it was unusual for even rich families to own more than one slave. Sections of Rhode Island and Connecticut did develop large tobacco and livestock farms employing slave labor, but northern slaves were far more dispersed than in the South. Nonetheless, slavery was not entirely marginal to northern colonial life. Slaves worked as farm hands, in artisan shops, as stevedores loading and unloading ships, and as personal servants. In the early eighteenth century, about three-quarters of the urban elite owned at least one slave. But with slaves so

Slavery existed in the eighteenth century in all the colonies. In this 1741 painting of the Potter family of Matunuck, Rhode Island, a young African-American boy serves tea.

Table 4.1 SLAVE POPULATION AND PERCENTAGE OF TOTAL POPULATION OF ORIGINAL THIRTEEN COLONIES, 1770		
Colony	Slave Population	Percentage
New Hampshire	654	1%
Massachusetts	4,754	2
Connecticut	5,698	3
Rhode Island	3,761	6
New York	19,062	12
New Jersey	8,220	7
Pennsylvania	5,561	2
Delaware	1,836	5
Maryland	63,818	32
Virginia	187,600	42
North Carolina	69,600	35
South Carolina	75,168	61
Georgia	15,000	45

small a part of the population that they seemed to pose no threat to the white majority, laws were less harsh than in the South. In New England, where in 1770 the 17,000 slaves represented less than 3 percent of the region's population, slave marriages were recognized in law, the severe physical punishment of slaves was prohibited, and slaves could bring suits in court, testify against whites, and own property and pass it on to their children—rights unknown in the South.

Slavery had been present in New York from the earliest days of Dutch settlement. With white immigration lagging behind that of Pennsylvania, the colony's Hudson Valley landlords, small farmers, and craftsmen continued to employ considerable amounts of slave labor in the eighteenth century. As New York City's role in the slave trade expanded, so did slavery in the city. In 1746, its 2,440 slaves amounted to one-fifth of New York City's total population. Some 30 percent of its laborers were slaves, a proportion second only to Charleston among American cities. Most were domestic workers, but slaves worked in all sectors of the economy. In 1770, about 27,000 slaves lived in New York and New Jersey, 10 percent of their total population. Slavery was also a significant presence in Philadelphia, although the institution stagnated after 1750 as artisans and merchants relied increasingly on wage laborers, whose numbers were augmented by population growth and the completion of the terms of indentured servants. In an urban economy that expanded and contracted according to the ups and downs of international trade, many employers concluded that relying on wage labor, which could be hired and fired at will, made more economic sense than a long-term investment in slaves.

SLAVE CULTURES AND SLAVE RESISTANCE

BECOMING AFRICAN-AMERICAN

The nearly 300,000 Africans brought to the mainland colonies during the eighteenth century were not a single people. They came from different cultures, spoke different languages, and practiced many religions. Eventually, an African-American people would emerge from the diverse peoples transported to the British colonies in the Middle Passage. Slavery threw together individuals who would never otherwise have encountered one another and who had never considered their color or residence on a single continent a source of identity or unity. Their bond was not kinship, language, or even "race," but slavery itself. The process of creating a cohesive culture and community took many years, and it proceeded at different rates in different regions. But by the nineteenth century, slaves no longer identified themselves as Ibo, Ashanti, Yoruba, and so on, but as African-Americans. In music, art, folklore, language, and religion, their cultural expressions emerged as a synthesis of African traditions, European elements, and new conditions in America.

For most of the eighteenth century, the majority of American slaves were African by birth. For many years, they spoke African languages and practiced African religions. Advertisements seeking information about runaways often described them by African origin ("young Gambia Negro," "new Banbara Negro fellow") and spoke of their bearing on their bodies "country marks"—visible signs of ethnic identity in Africa. Indeed, during the eighteenth century, black life in the colonies was "re-Africanized" as the earlier Creoles (slaves born in the New World) came to be outnumbered by large-scale importations from Africa. Compared to the earliest generation of slaves, the newcomers worked harder, died earlier, and had less access to freedom. Charles Hansford, a white Virginia blacksmith, noted in a 1753 poem that he had frequently heard slaves speak of their desire to "reenjoy" life in Africa:

> I oft with pleasure have observ'd how they
> Their sultry country's worth strive to display
> In broken language, how they praise their case
> And happiness when in their native place ...
> How would they dangers court and pains endure
> If to their country they could get secure!

AFRICAN-AMERICAN CULTURES

By the mid-eighteenth century, the three slave systems in British North America had produced distinct African-American cultures. In the Chesapeake, because of a more healthful climate, the slave population began to reproduce itself by 1740, creating a more balanced sex ratio than in the seventeenth century and making possible the creation of family-centered slave communities. Because of the small size of most plantations and the large number of white yeoman farmers, slaves here were continuously exposed to white culture. They soon learned English, and many were swept up in the religious revivals known as the Great Awakening, discussed later in this chapter.

In South Carolina and Georgia, two very different black societies emerged. On the rice plantations, slaves lived in extremely harsh conditions and had a low birthrate throughout the eighteenth century, making rice production dependent on continued slave imports from Africa. The slaves seldom came into contact with whites and enjoyed far more autonomy than elsewhere in the colonies. The larger structures of their lives were established by slavery, but they were able to create an African-based culture. They constructed African-style houses, chose African names for their children, and spoke Gullah, a language that mixed various African roots and was unintelligible to most whites. Despite a continuing slave trade in which young, single males predominated, slaves slowly created families and communities that bridged generations. The experience of slaves who labored in Charleston and Savannah as servants and skilled workers was quite different. These assimilated more quickly into Euro-American culture, and sexual liaisons between white owners and slave women produced the beginnings of a class of free mulattos.

In the northern colonies, where slaves represented a smaller part of the population, dispersed in small holdings among the white population, a distinctive African-American culture developed more slowly. Living in close proximity to whites, they enjoyed more mobility and access to the mainstream of life than their counterparts further south. Slaves in cities like Philadelphia and New York gathered on holidays to perform African dances. But they had fewer opportunities to create stable family life or a cohesive community.

RESISTANCE TO SLAVERY

The common threads that linked these regional African-American cultures were the experience of slavery and the desire for freedom. Throughout the eighteenth century, blacks risked their lives in efforts to resist enslavement. Colonial newspapers, especially in the southern colonies, were filled with advertisements for runaway slaves. Most fugitives were young African men who had arrived recently. In South Carolina and Georgia, they fled to Florida, to uninhabited coastal and river swamps, or to Charleston and Savannah, where they could pass for free. In the Chesapeake and Middle Colonies, fugitive slaves tended to be familiar with white culture and therefore, as one advertisement put it, could "pretend to be free."

What Edward Trelawny, the colonial governor of Jamaica, called "a dangerous spirit of liberty" was widespread among the New World's slaves. The eighteenth century's first slave uprising occurred in New York City in 1712, when a group of slaves set fire to houses on the outskirts of the city and killed the first nine whites who arrived on the scene. Subsequently, eighteen conspirators were executed; some were tortured and burned alive in a public spectacle meant to intimidate the slave population. During the 1730s and 1740s, continuous warfare involving European empires and Indians opened the door to slave resistance. In 1731, a slave rebellion in Louisiana, where the French and Natchez Indians were at war, temporarily halted efforts to introduce the plantation system in that region. There were uprisings throughout the West Indies, including in the Virgin Islands, owned by Denmark, and the French island of Guadeloupe. On Jamaica, a major British center of sugar production, communities of fugitive slaves known as "maroons" waged outright warfare against British authorities until a treaty of 1739 recognized their freedom, in exchange for which they agreed to return future escapees.

An advertisement seeking the return of a runaway slave from Port Royal, in the Sea Islands of South Carolina. "Mustee" was a term for a person of mixed European and African ancestry. From the South Carolina Gazette, *June 11, 1747.*

THE CRISIS OF 1739–1741

On the mainland, slaves seized the opportunity for rebellion offered by the War of Jenkins' Ear, which pitted England against Spain. In September 1739, a group of South Carolina slaves, most of them recently arrived from Kongo where some, it appears, had been soldiers, seized a store containing numerous weapons at the town of Stono. Beating drums to attract followers, the armed band marched southward toward

Florida, burning houses and barns, killing whites they encountered, and shouting "Liberty." (Florida's Spanish rulers offered "Liberty and Protection" to fugitives from the British colonies.) The group eventually swelled to some 100 slaves. After a pitched battle with the colony's militia, the rebels were dispersed. Some forty were killed, but others managed to reach Florida, where in 1740 they were armed by the Spanish to help repel an attack on St. Augustine by a force from Georgia. The Stono Rebellion led to a severe tightening of the South Carolina slave code and the temporary imposition of a prohibitive tax on imported slaves.

In 1741, a panic (which some observers compared to the fear of witches in Salem in the 1690s), swept New York City. After a series of fires broke out, rumors spread that slaves, with some white allies, planned to burn part of the city, seize weapons, and either turn New York over to Spain or murder the white population. Over 150 blacks and 20 whites were arrested and 34 alleged conspirators, including 4 white persons, executed. Historians still disagree as to how extensive the plot was or whether it existed at all. But dramatic events like revolts, along with the constant stream of runaways, disproved the idea, voiced by the governor of South Carolina, that slaves had "no notion of liberty." In eighteenth-century America, dreams of freedom knew no racial boundary. When white colonists rose in rebellion against British rule, tens of thousands of slaves would seize the opportunity to strike for their own liberty.

AN EMPIRE OF FREEDOM

BRITISH PATRIOTISM

Despite the centrality of slavery to its empire, eighteenth-century Great Britain prided itself on being the world's most advanced and freest nation. It was not only the era's greatest naval and commercial power but also the home of a complex governmental system with a powerful Parliament representing the interests of a self-confident landed aristocracy and merchant class. In London, the largest city in Europe with a population approaching 1 million by the end of the eighteenth century, Britain possessed a single political-cultural-economic capital. It enjoyed a common law, common language, and, with the exception of a small number of Jews, Catholics, and Africans, common devotion to Protestantism. For much of the eighteenth century, Britain found itself at war with France, which had replaced Spain as its major continental rival. This situation led to the development of a large military establishment, high taxes, and the creation of the Bank of England to help finance European and imperial conflicts. For both Britons and colonists, war helped to sharpen a sense of national identity against foreign foes.

British patriotic sentiment became more and more assertive as the eighteenth century progressed. Symbols of British identity proliferated: the songs "God Save the King" and "Rule Britannia," and even the modern rules of cricket, the national sport. The rapidly expanding British economy formed another point of pride uniting Britons and colonists. Continental peoples, according to a popular saying, wore "wooden shoes"—that is, their standard of living was far below that of Britons. Writers hailed commerce as a progressive, civilizing force, a way for different peoples to interact for mutual benefit without domination or military conflict. Especially in contrast to France, Britain saw itself as a realm of widespread prosperity, individual liberty, the rule of law, and the Protestant faith. Wealth, religion, and freedom went together. "There is no Popish nation," wrote the Massachusetts theologian Cotton Mather in 1710, "but what by embracing the Protestant Religion would . . . not only assert themselves into a glorious liberty, but also double their wealth immediately."

THE BRITISH CONSTITUTION

Central to this sense of British identity was the concept of liberty. The fierce political struggles of the English Civil War and the Glorious Revolution bequeathed to eighteenth-century Britons an abiding conviction that liberty was their unique possession. They believed power and liberty to be natural antagonists. To mediate between them, advocates of British freedom celebrated the rule of law, the right to live under legislation to which one's representatives had consented, restraints on the arbitrary exercise of political authority, and rights like trial by jury enshrined in the common law. On both sides of the Atlantic, every political cause, it seemed, wrapped itself in the language of liberty and claimed to be defending the "rights of Englishmen." Continental writers dissatisfied with the lack of liberty in their own countries looked to Britain as a model. The House of Commons, House of Lords, and king each checked the power of the others. This structure, wrote the French political philosopher Baron Montesquieu, made Britain "the one nation in the world whose constitution has political liberty for its purpose." In its "balanced constitution" and the principle that no

Even though less than 5 percent of the British population enjoyed the right to vote, representative government was central to the eighteenth-century idea of British liberty. In this painting from 1793, Prime Minister William Pitt addresses the House of Commons.

man, even the king, is above the law, Britons claimed to have devised the best means of preventing political tyranny. Until the 1770s, most colonists believed themselves to be part of the freest political system mankind had ever known.

As the coexistence of slavery and liberty within the empire demonstrated, British freedom was anything but universal. It was closely identified with the Protestant religion and was invoked to contrast Britons with the "servile" subjects of Catholic countries, especially France, Britain's main rival in eighteenth-century Europe. It viewed nearly every other nation on earth as "enslaved"—to popery, tyranny, or barbarism. One German military officer commented in 1743 on the British "contempt" of foreigners: "They [pride] themselves not only upon their being free themselves, but being the bulwarks of liberty all over Europe; and they vilify most of the Nations on the continent . . . for being slaves, as they call us." British liberty was fully compatible with wide gradations in personal rights. Yet in the minds of the free residents of Great Britain and its North American colonies, liberty was the bond of empire.

A 1770 engraving from the Boston Gazette *by Paul Revere illustrates the association of British patriotism and liberty. Britannia sits with a liberty cap and her national shield, and releases a bird from a cage.*

THE LANGUAGE OF LIBERTY

These ideas sank deep roots not only within the "political nation"—those who voted, held office, and engaged in structured political debate—but also far more broadly in British and colonial society. Laborers, sailors, and artisans spoke the language of British freedom as insistently as pamphleteers and parliamentarians. Increasingly, the idea of liberty lost its traditional association with privileges derived from membership in a distinct social class and became more and more identified with a general right to resist arbitrary government.

On both sides of the Atlantic, liberty emerged as the battle cry of the rebellious. Frequent crowd actions protesting violations of traditional rights gave concrete expression to popular belief in the right to oppose tyranny. Ordinary persons thought nothing of taking to the streets to protest efforts by merchants to raise the cost of bread above the traditional "just price," or the Royal Navy's practice of "impressment"—kidnapping poor men on the streets for maritime service.

REPUBLICAN LIBERTY

Liberty was central to two sets of political ideas that flourished in the Anglo-American world. One is termed by scholars "republicanism" (although few in eighteenth-century England used the word, which literally meant a government without a king and conjured up memories of the beheading of Charles I). Republicanism celebrated active participation in public life by economically independent citizens as the essence of liberty. Republicans assumed that only property-owning citizens possessed "virtue"—defined in the eighteenth century not simply as a personal moral quality but as the willingness to subordinate self-interest to the pursuit of the public good. "Only a virtuous people are capable of freedom," wrote Benjamin Franklin.

In eighteenth-century Britain, this body of thought about freedom was most closely associated with a group of critics of the established political order known as the "Country Party" because much of their support arose from the landed gentry. They condemned what they considered the corruption of British politics, evidenced by the growing number of government appointees who sat in the House of Commons. They called for the election of men of "independence" who could not be controlled by the ministry, and they criticized the expansion of the national debt and the growing wealth of financial speculators in a commercializing economy. Britain, they claimed, was succumbing to luxury and political manipulation—in a word, a loss of virtue—thereby endangering the careful balance of its system of government and, indeed, liberty itself. In Britain, Country Party publicists like John Trenchard and Thomas Gordon, authors of *Cato's Letters*, published in the 1720s, had little impact. But their writings were eagerly devoured in the American colonies, whose elites found appealing Trenchard and Gordon's stress on the political role of the independent landowner and their warnings against the constant tendency of political power to infringe upon liberty.

LIBERAL FREEDOM

The second set of eighteenth-century political ideas celebrating freedom came to be known as "liberalism" (although its meaning was quite different

The Polling, *by the renowned eighteenth-century British artist William Hogarth, satirizes the idea that British elections are decided by the reasoned deliberations of upstanding property owners. Inspired by a corrupt election of 1754, Hogarth depicts an election scene in which the maimed and dying are brought to the polls to cast ballots. At the center, lawyers argue over whether a man who has a hook for a hand can swear on the Bible.*

from what the word suggests today). Whereas republican liberty had a public and social quality, liberalism was essentially individual and private. The leading philosopher of liberty was John Locke, whose *Two Treatises on Government*, written around 1680, had limited influence in his own lifetime but became extremely well known in the next century. Many previous writers had compared government to the family, assuming that in both, inequality was natural and power always emanated from the top. Locke held that the principles that governed the family were inappropriate for organizing public life. Government, he wrote, was formed by a mutual agreement among equals (the parties being male heads of households, not all persons). In this "social contract," men surrendered a part of their right to govern themselves in order to enjoy the benefits of the rule of law. They retained, however, their natural rights, whose existence predated the establishment of political authority. Protecting the security of life, liberty, and property required shielding a realm of private life and personal concerns—including family relations, religious preferences, and economic activity—from interference by the state. During the eighteenth century, Lockean ideas—individual rights, the consent of the governed, the right of rebellion against unjust or oppressive government—would become familiar on both sides of the Atlantic.

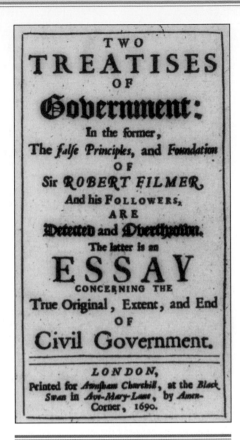

The title page of John Locke's Two Treatises of Government, *which traced the origins of government in an original state of nature and insisted that political authorities must not abridge mankind's natural rights.*

Like other Britons, Locke spoke of liberty as a universal right yet seemed to exclude many persons from its full benefits. Since the protection of property was one of government's main purposes, liberalism was compatible with substantial inequalities in wealth and well-being. Moreover, while Locke was one of the first theorists to defend the property rights of women and even their access to divorce, and condemned slavery as a "vile and miserable estate of man," the free individual in liberal thought was essentially the propertied white man. Locke himself had helped to draft the Fundamental Constitutions of Carolina, discussed in Chapter 3, which provided for slavery, and he was an investor in the Royal African Company, the slave-trading monopoly. Slaves, he wrote, "cannot be considered as any part of civil society." Nonetheless, by proclaiming that all individuals possess natural rights that no government may violate, Lockean liberalism opened the door to the poor, women, and even slaves to challenge limitations on their own freedom.

Republicanism and liberalism would eventually come to be seen as alternative understandings of freedom. In the eighteenth century, however, these systems of thought overlapped and often reinforced each other. Both political outlooks could inspire a commitment to constitutional government and restraints on despotic power. Both emphasized the security of property as a foundation of freedom. Both traditions were transported to eighteenth-century America. Ideas about liberty imported from Britain to the colonies would eventually help to divide the empire.

THE PUBLIC SPHERE

Colonial politics for most of the eighteenth century was considerably less tempestuous than in the seventeenth, with its bitter struggles for power and frequent armed uprisings. Political stability in Britain coupled with the maturation of local elites in America made for more tranquil government. New York stood apart from this development. With its diverse population and bitter memories of Leisler's rebellion (see Chapter 3, p. 109), New York continued to experience intense political strife among its many economic interests and ethnic groups. By the 1750s, semipermanent political parties competed vigorously for popular support in New York elections. But in most other colonies, while differences over policies of one kind or another were hardly absent, they rarely produced the civil disorder or political passions of the previous century.

THE RIGHT TO VOTE

In many respects, politics in eighteenth-century America had a more democratic quality than in Great Britain. Suffrage requirements varied from colony to colony, but as in Britain the linchpin of voting laws was the property qualification. Its purpose was to ensure that men who possessed an economic stake in society and the independence of judgment that went with it determined the policies of the government. The "foundation of liberty," the parliamentary leader Henry Ireton had declared during the English Civil War of the 1640s, "is that those who shall choose the lawmakers shall be men freed from dependence upon others." Slaves, servants, tenants, adult sons living in the homes of their parents, the poor, and women all lacked a "will of their own" and were therefore ineligible to vote. The wide distribution of property in the colonies, however, meant that a far higher percentage of the population enjoyed voting rights than in the Old World. It is estimated that between 50 and 80 percent of adult white men could vote in eighteenth-century colonial America, as opposed to less than 5 percent in Britain at the time.

Colonial politics, however, was hardly democratic in a modern sense. In a few instances—some towns in Massachusetts and on Long Island—propertied women, generally widows, cast ballots. But voting was almost everywhere considered a male prerogative. In some colonies, Jews, Catholics, and Protestant Dissenters like Baptists and Quakers could not vote. Propertied free blacks, who enjoyed the franchise in Virginia, North Carolina, South Carolina, and Georgia in the early days of settlement, lost that right during the eighteenth century (although North Carolina restored it in the 1730s). In the northern colonies, while the law did not bar blacks from voting, local custom did. Native Americans were generally prohibited from voting.

POLITICAL CULTURES

Despite the broad electorate among white men, "the people" existed only on election day. Between elections, mem-

This anonymous engraving depicting a 1764 Pennsylvania election suggests the intensity of political debate in the Middle Colonies.

bers of colonial assemblies remained out of touch with their constituents. Strongly competitive elections were the norm only in the Middle Colonies. Elsewhere, many elections went uncontested, either because only one candidate presented himself or because the local culture stressed community harmony, as in many New England towns. Considerable power in colonial politics rested with those who held appointive, not elective, office. Governors and councils were appointed by the crown in the nine royal colonies and by the proprietors of Pennsylvania and Maryland. Only in Rhode Island and Connecticut were these offices elective. Moreover, laws passed by colonial assemblies could be vetoed by governors or in London. Outside New England, where most town officers were elected, local officials were appointed by the governor or by powerful officials in London. The Duke of Newcastle alone could appoint eighty-three colonial officials.

Property qualifications for officeholding were far higher than for voting. In South Carolina, for example, nearly every adult male could meet the voting qualification of fifty acres of land or payment of twenty shillings in taxes, but to sit in the assembly one had to own 500 acres of land and ten slaves or town property worth £1,000. As a result, throughout the eighteenth century nearly all of South Carolina's legislators were planters or wealthy merchants. Despite its boisterous and competitive politics, New York's diminutive assembly, with fewer than thirty members, was dominated by relatives and allies of the great landed families, especially the Livingstons and DeLanceys. Of seventy-two men who sat in the New York Assembly between 1750 and 1776, fifty-two were related to the families who owned the great Hudson River estates.

In some colonies, a majority of free men possessed the right to vote, but an ingrained tradition of "deference"—the assumption among ordinary people that wealth, education, and social prominence carried a right to public office—sharply limited effective choice in elections. Virginia politics, for example, combined political democracy for white men with the tradition that voters should choose among candidates from the gentry. Aspirants for public office actively sought to ingratiate themselves with ordinary voters, distributing food and liquor freely at the courthouse where balloting took place. In Thomas Jefferson's first campaign for the House of Burgesses in 1768, his expenses included hiring two men "for bringing up rum" to the polling place. Even in New England, with its larger number of elective positions, town leaders were generally the largest property holders and offices frequently passed down from generation to generation of the same family. Few Americans vigorously pursued elective office or took an active role in public affairs. By the mid-eighteenth century, the typical officeholder was considerably richer than the norm when the century began.

COLONIAL GOVERNMENT

Preoccupied with events in Europe and imperial rivalries, successive British governments during the first half of the eighteenth century adopted a policy of "salutary neglect" toward the colonies, leaving them largely to govern themselves. With imperial authority so weak, the large landowners, merchants, and lawyers who dominated colonial assemblies increasingly claimed the right to control local politics.

Convinced that they represented the will of the people, elected colonial assemblies used their control of finance to exert influence over governors and appointed councils. While governors desired secure incomes for themselves and permanent revenue for their administrations (some, like Robert Hunter of New York, demanded a life salary), assemblies often authorized salaries only one year at a time and refused to levy taxes except in exchange for concessions on appointments, land policy, and other issues. Generally members of the British gentry who had suffered financial reversals and hoped to recoup their fortunes in America, governors learned that to rule effectively they would have to cooperate with the colonial elite.

THE RISE OF THE ASSEMBLIES

In the seventeenth century, the governor was the focal point of political authority, and colonial assemblies were weak bodies that met infrequently. But in the eighteenth, as economic development enhanced the power of American elites, the assemblies they dominated became more and more assertive. Their leaders insisted that assemblies possessed the same rights and powers in local affairs as the House of Commons enjoyed in Britain. The most successful governors were those who accommodated the rising power of the assemblies and used their appointive powers and control of land grants to win allies among assembly members.

The most powerful assembly was Pennsylvania's, where a new charter, adopted in 1701, eliminated the governor's council, establishing the only unicameral (one-house) legislature in the colonies. Controlled until mid-century by an elite of Quaker merchants, the assembly wrested control of finance, appointments, and the militia from a series of governors representing the Penn family. Close behind in terms of power and legislative independence were the assemblies of New York, Virginia, South Carolina, and, especially, Massachusetts, which successfully resisted governors' demands for permanent salaries for appointed officials. Many of the issues between governors and elected assemblies stemmed from the colonies' economic growth. To deal with the scarcity of gold and silver coins, the only legal form of currency, some colonies printed paper money, although this was strongly opposed by the governors, authorities in London, and British merchants who did not wish to be paid in what they considered worthless paper. Numerous battles also took place over land policy (sometimes involving divergent attitudes toward the remaining Indian population) and the level of rents charged to farmers on land owned by the crown or proprietors.

In their negotiations and conflicts with royal governors, leaders of the assemblies drew on the writings of the English Country Party, whose emphasis on the constant tension between liberty and political power and the dangers of executive influence over the legislature made sense of their own experience. Of the European settlements in North America, only the British colonies possessed any considerable degree of popular participation in government. This fact reinforced the assemblies' claim to embody the rights of Englishmen and the principle of popular consent to government. They were defenders of "the people's liberty," in the words of one New York legislator.

POLITICS IN PUBLIC

This language reverberated outside the relatively narrow world of elective and legislative politics. The "political nation" was dominated by the American gentry, whose members addressed each other in letters, speeches, newspaper articles, and pamphlets filled with Latin expressions and references to classical learning. But especially in colonial towns and cities, the eighteenth century witnessed a considerable expansion of the "public sphere"—the world of political organization and debate independent of the government, where an informed citizenry openly discussed questions that had previously been the preserve of officials.

In Boston, New York, and Philadelphia, clubs proliferated where literary, philosophical, scientific, and political issues were debated. Among the best known was the Junto, a "club for mutual improvement" founded by Benjamin Franklin in Philadelphia in 1727 for weekly discussion of political and economic questions. Beginning with only a dozen members, it eventually evolved into the much larger American Philosophical Society. Such groups were generally composed of men of property and commerce, but some drew ordinary citizens into discussions of public affairs. Colonial taverns and coffeehouses also became important sites not only for social conviviality but also for political debates. Philadelphia had a larger number of drinking establishments per capita than Paris. In Philadelphia, one clergyman commented, "the poorest laborer thinks himself entitled to deliver his sentiments in matters of religion or politics with as much freedom as the gentleman or scholar."

THE COLONIAL PRESS

Neither the Spanish possessions of Florida and New Mexico nor New France possessed a printing press, although missionaries had established one in Mexico City in the 1530s. In British North America, however, the press expanded rapidly during the eighteenth century. So did the number of political broadsides and pamphlets published, especially at election time. Widespread literacy created an expanding market for printed materials. By the eve of the American Revolution, some three-quarters of the free adult male population in the colonies (and over one-third of the women) could read and write, and a majority of American families owned at least one book. Philadelphia boasted no fewer than seventy-seven bookshops in the 1770s.

Circulating libraries appeared in many colonial cities and towns, making possible a wider dissemination of knowledge at a time when books were still expensive. The first, the Library Company of Philadelphia, was established by Benjamin Franklin in 1731. "So few were the readers at that time, and the majority of us so poor," Franklin recalled in his *Autobiography* (1791), that he could find only fifty persons, mostly "young tradesmen," anxious for self-improvement and willing to pay for the privilege of borrowing books. But reading, he added, soon "became fashionable." Libraries sprang up in other towns, and ordinary Americans came to be "better instructed and more intelligent than people of the same rank" abroad.

The first continuously published colonial newspaper, the *Boston News-Letter*, appeared in 1704 (a predecessor, *Publick Occurrences, Both Foreign and*

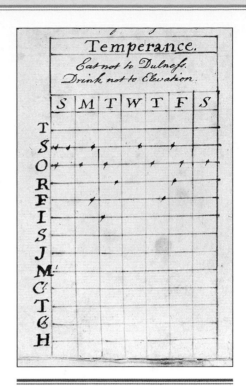

Benjamin Franklin's quest for self-improvement, or, as he put it in his autobiography, "moral perfection," is illustrated in this "Temperance diagram," which charts his behavior each day of the week with regard to thirteen virtues. They are listed on the left by their first letters: temperance, silence, order, resolution, frugality, industry, sincerity, justice, moderation, cleanliness, tranquility, chastity, and humility.

A portrait of Benjamin Franklin in fur hat and spectacles, dated 1777, depicts him as a symbol of America.

Domestick, established in Boston in 1690, had been suppressed by authorities after a single issue for criticizing military cooperation with the Iroquois). There were thirteen colonial newspapers by 1740 and twenty-five in 1765, mostly weeklies with small circulations—an average of 600 sales per issue. Probably the best-edited newspaper was the *Pennsylvania Gazette*, established in 1728 in Philadelphia and purchased the following year by Benjamin Franklin, who had earlier worked as an apprentice printer on his brother's Boston periodical, the *New England Courant*. At its peak, the *Gazette* attracted 2,000 subscribers. Newspapers initially devoted most of their space to advertisements, religious affairs, and reports on British society and government. But by the 1730s, political commentary was widespread in the American press.

FREEDOM OF EXPRESSION AND ITS LIMITS

The public sphere thrived on the free exchange of ideas. But free expression was not generally considered one of the ancient rights of Englishmen. The phrase "freedom of speech" originated in Britain during the sixteenth century in Parliament's struggle to achieve the privilege of unrestrained debate. A right of legislators, not ordinary citizens, it referred to the ability of members of Parliament to express their views without fear of reprisal, on the grounds that only in this way could they effectively represent the people. Outside of Parliament, free speech had no legal protection. A subject could be beheaded for accusing the king of failing to hold "true" religious beliefs, and language from swearing to criticism of the government exposed a person to criminal penalties.

As for freedom of the press, governments on both sides of the Atlantic viewed this as extremely dangerous, partly because they considered ordinary citizens as prone to be misled by inflammatory printed materials. During the English Civil War of the 1640s, the Levelers had called for the adoption of a written constitution, an Agreement of the People, containing guarantees of religious liberty and freedom of the press. But until 1695, when a British law requiring the licensing of printed works before publication lapsed, no newspaper, book, or pamphlet could legally be printed without a government license. The instructions of colonial governors included a warning about the "great inconveniences that may arise by the liberty of printing." After 1695, the government could not censor newspapers, books, and pamphlets before they appeared in print, although it continued to try to manage the press by direct payments to publishers and individual journalists. Authors and publishers could still be prosecuted for "seditious libel"—a crime that included defaming government officials—or punished for contempt.

Elected assemblies, not governors, most frequently violated freedom of the press in colonial America. Dozens of publishers were hauled before assemblies and forced to apologize for comments regarding one or another member. If they refused, they were jailed. James Franklin, Benjamin's older brother, spent a month in prison in 1722 after publishing a piece satirizing public authorities in Massachusetts. Colonial newspapers vigorously defended freedom of the press as a central component of liberty, insisting that the citizenry had a right to monitor the workings of government and subject public officials to criticism. Many newspapers reprinted passages from *Cato's Letters* in which Trenchard and Gordon strongly opposed prosecutions for libel. "Without freedom of thought," they declared, "there can be no such thing as wisdom, and no such thing as public liberty, without freedom of speech." But since government printing contracts were crucial for economic success, few newspapers attacked colonial governments unless financially supported by an opposition faction.

THE TRIAL OF ZENGER

The most famous colonial court case involving freedom of the press demonstrated that popular sentiment opposed prosecutions for criticism of public officials. This was the 1735 trial of John Peter Zenger, a German-born printer who had emigrated to New York as a youth. Financed by wealthy opponents of Governor William Cosby, Zenger's newspaper, the *Weekly Journal*, lambasted the governor for corruption, influence peddling, and "tyranny." New York's council ordered four issues burned and had Zenger himself arrested and tried for seditious libel. The judge instructed the jurors to consider only whether Zenger had actually published the offending words, not whether they were accurate. But Zenger's attorney, Andrew Hamilton, urged the jury to judge not the publisher but the governor. If they decided that Zenger's charges were correct, they must acquit him, and, Hamilton proclaimed, "every man who prefers freedom to a life of slavery will bless you."

Zenger was found not guilty. The case sent a warning to prosecutors that libel cases might be very difficult to win, especially in the superheated atmosphere of New York partisan politics. To be sure, had Zenger lambasted the assembly rather than the governor, he would in all likelihood have been lodged in jail without the benefit of a trial. The law of libel remained on the books. But the outcome helped to promote the idea that the publication of truth should always be permitted, and it demonstrated that the idea of free expression was becoming ingrained in the popular imagination.

THE AMERICAN ENLIGHTENMENT

During the eighteenth century, many educated Americans began to be influenced by the outlook of the European Enlightenment. This philosophical movement, which originated among French thinkers and soon spread to Britain, sought to apply to political and social life the scientific method of careful investigation based on research and experiment. Enlightenment ideas crisscrossed the Atlantic along with goods and people. Enlightenment thinkers insisted that every human institution, authority, and tradition be judged before the bar of reason. The self-educated Benjamin Franklin's wide range of activities—establishing a newspaper, debating club, and library; publishing the widely circulated *Poor Richard's Almanack*; and conducting experiments to demonstrate that lightning is a form of electricity—exemplified the Enlightenment spirit and made him probably the best-known American in the eighteenth-century world.

Ideas

The first page of the New York Weekly Journal, *edited by John Peter Zenger, one of four issues ordered to be burned by local authorities.*

One inspiration for the Enlightenment was a reaction against the bloody religious wars that racked Europe in the seventeenth century. Enlightenment thinkers hoped that "reason," not religious enthusiasm, could govern human life. The criticism of social and political institutions based on tradition and hereditary privilege rather than the dictates of reason could also be applied to established churches. John Locke himself had published *The Reasonableness of Christianity* in 1695, which insisted that religious belief should rest on scientific evidence. During the eighteenth century, many prominent Americans moved toward the position called Arminianism, which taught that reason alone was capable of establishing the essentials of religion. Others adopted Deism, a belief that God essentially withdrew after creating the world, leaving it to function according to scientific laws without divine intervention. Belief in miracles, in the revealed truth of the Bible, and in the innate sinfulness of mankind were viewed by Arminians, Deists, and others as outdated superstitions that should be abandoned in the modern age.

In the seventeenth century, the English scientist Isaac Newton had revealed the natural laws that governed the physical universe. Here, Deists believed, was the purest evidence of God's handiwork. Many Protestants of all denominations could accept Newton's findings while remaining devout churchgoers (as Newton himself had). But Deists concluded that the best form of religious devotion was to study the workings of nature, rather than to worship in organized churches or appeal to divine grace for salvation. By the late colonial era, a small but influential group of leading Americans, including Benjamin Franklin and Thomas Jefferson, could be classified as Deists.

THE GREAT AWAKENING

Like freedom of the press, religion was another realm where the actual experience of liberty outstripped its legal recognition. Religion remained central to eighteenth-century American life. Sermons, theological treatises, and copies of the Bible were by far the largest category of material produced by colonial printers. Religious disputes often generated more public attention than political issues. Yet many church leaders worried about lax religious observance as colonial economic growth led people to be more and more preoccupied with worldly affairs.

RELIGIOUS REVIVALS

Many ministers were concerned that westward expansion, commercial development, the growth of Enlightenment rationalism, and lack of individual engagement in church services were undermining religious devotion. These fears helped to inspire the revivals that swept through the colonies beginning in the 1730s. Known as the Great Awakening, the revivals were less a coordinated movement than a series of local events united by a commitment to a "religion of the heart," a more emotional and personal Christianity than that offered by existing churches. The revivals redrew the religious map of the colonies. Like other intellectual currents of the time, the Great Awakening was a transatlantic movement.

During the 1720s and 1730s, the New Jersey Dutch Reformed clergyman Theodore Frelinghuysen, his Presbyterian neighbors William and Gilbert Tennent, and the Massachusetts Congregationalist minister Jonathan

Edwards pioneered an intensely emotional style of preaching. Edwards's famous sermon *Sinners in the Hands of an Angry God* portrayed sinful man as a "loathsome insect" suspended over a bottomless pit of eternal fire by a slender thread that might break at any moment. Edwards's preaching, declared a member of his congregation, inspired worshipers to cry out, "What shall I do to be saved—oh, I am going to hell!" Only a "new birth"—immediately acknowledging one's sins and pleading for divine grace—could save men from eternal damnation. "It is the new birth that makes [sinners] free," declared the Reverend Joshua Tufts.

THE PREACHING OF WHITEFIELD

Religious emotionalism was not confined to the American colonies—it spread through much of mid-eighteenth-century Europe as well. More than any other individual, the English minister George Whitefield, who declared "the whole world his parish," sparked the Great Awakening. For two years after his arrival in America in 1739, Whitefield brought his highly emotional brand of preaching to colonies from Georgia to New England. God, Whitefield proclaimed, was merciful. Rather than being predestined for damnation, men and women could save themselves by repenting of their sins. Whitefield appealed to the passions of his listeners, powerfully sketching the boundless joy of salvation and the horrors of damnation. In every sermon, he asked his listeners to look into their own hearts and answer the question, "Are you saved?" If not, they must change their sinful ways and surrender their lives to Christ.

Tens of thousands of colonists flocked to Whitefield's sermons, which were widely reported in the American press, making him a celebrity and helping to establish the revivals as the first major intercolonial event in North American history. Although a Deist, Benjamin Franklin helped to publicize Whitefield's tour (and made a tidy profit) by publishing his sermons and journals. In Whitefield's footsteps, a host of traveling preachers or "evangelists" (meaning, literally, bearers of good news) held revivalist meetings, often to the alarm of established ministers.

Critics of the Great Awakening produced sermons, pamphlets, and newspaper articles condemning the revivalist preachers for lacking theological training, encouraging disrespect for "the established church and her ministers," and filling churches with "general disorder." Connecticut sought to stem the revivalist tide through laws punishing disruptive traveling preachers. By the time they subsided in the 1760s, the revivals had changed the religious configuration of the colonies and enlarged the boundaries of liberty. Whitefield had inspired the emergence of numerous Dissenting churches. Congregations split into factions headed by Old Lights (traditionalists) and New Lights (revivalists), and new churches proliferated—Baptist, Methodist, Presbyterian, and others. Many of these new churches began to criticize the colonial practice of levying taxes to support an established church; they defended religious freedom as one of the natural rights government must not restrict.

THE AWAKENING'S IMPACT

Although the revivals were primarily a spiritual matter, the Great Awakening reflected existing social tensions, threw into question many forms of

George Whitefield, the English evangelist who helped to spark the Great Awakening in the colonies. Painted around 1742 by John Wollaston, who had emigrated from England to the colonies, the work depicts Whitefield's powerful effect on male and female listeners. It also illustrates Whitefield's eye problem, which led critics to dub him "Dr. Squintum."

authority, and inspired criticism of aspects of colonial society. They attracted primarily men and women of modest means—"rude, ignorant, void of manners, education or good breeding," one Anglican minister complained. Revivalist preachers frequently criticized commercial society, insisting that believers should make salvation, not profit, "the one business of their lives." In New England, they condemned merchants who ensnared the unwary in debt as greedy and unchristian. Preaching to the small farmers of the southern backcountry, Baptist and Methodist revivalists criticized the worldliness of wealthy planters and attacked as sinful activities such as gambling, horse racing, and lavish entertainments on the Sabbath.

A few preachers explicitly condemned slavery. And a few converts, such as Robert Carter III, the grandson of the wealthy planter Robert "King" Carter, emancipated their slaves after concluding that black and white were brothers in Christ. Most masters managed to reconcile Christianity and slaveholding. But especially in the Chesapeake, the revivals brought numerous slaves into the Christian fold, an important step in their acculturation as African-Americans. And a few blacks, touched by the word of God, took up preaching themselves. The revivals also spawned a group of female exhorters, who for a time shattered the male monopoly on preaching.

The revivals broadened the range of religious alternatives available to Americans, thereby leaving them more divided than before and at the same time more fully integrated into transatlantic religious developments. But the impact of the Great Awakening spread beyond purely spiritual matters. The newspaper and pamphlet wars it inspired greatly expanded the circulation of printed material in the colonies. The revivals encouraged many colonists to trust their own views rather than those of established elites. In listening to the sermons of self-educated preachers, forming Bible study groups, and engaging in intense religious discussions, ordinary colonists asserted the right to independent judgment. "The common people," proclaimed Baptist minister Isaac Backus, "claim as good a right to judge and act for themselves in matters of religion as civil rulers or the learned clergy." The revivalists' aim was spiritual salvation, not social or political revolution. But the independent frame of mind they encouraged would have significant political consequences.

IMPERIAL RIVALRIES

SPANISH NORTH AMERICA

The rapid growth of Britain's North American colonies took place at a time of increased jockeying for power among European empires, involving much of the area today included in the United States. But the colonies of England's rivals, although covering immense territories, remained thinly populated and far weaker economically. The Spanish empire encompassed an area that stretched from the Pacific coast and New Mexico into the Great Plains and eastward through Texas and Florida. After 1763, it also included Louisiana, which Spain obtained from France. On paper a vast territorial empire, Spanish North America actually consisted of a few small and isolated urban clusters, most prominently St. Augustine in Florida, San Antonio in Texas, and Santa Fe and Albuquerque in New Mexico.

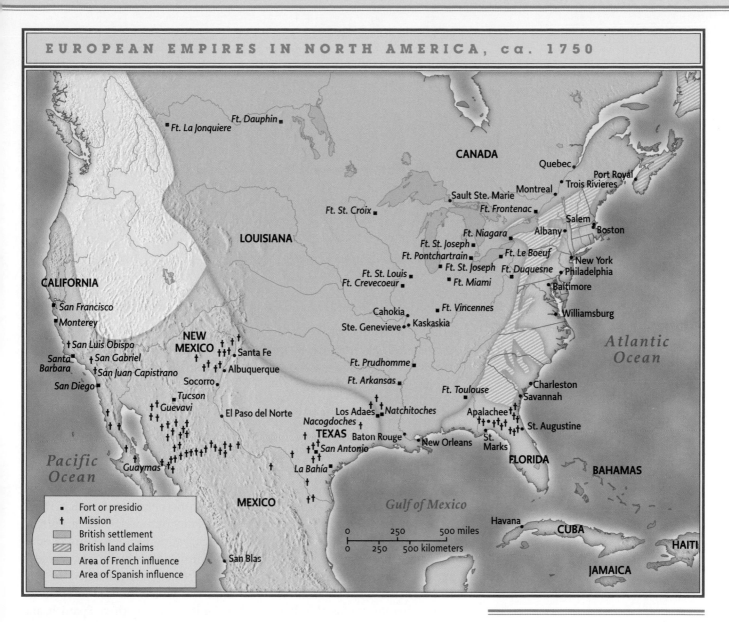

EUROPEAN EMPIRES IN NORTH AMERICA, ca. 1750

Ft. Dauphin

Ft. La Jonquiere

CANADA

Quebec
Port Royal
Trois Rivieres
Montreal
Sault Ste. Marie
Ft. Frontenac
Ft. St. Croix
Salem
LOUISIANA
Ft. Niagara
Albany
Boston
Ft. St. Joseph
Ft. Pontchartrain
Ft. Le Boeuf
Ft. St. Louis
Ft. St. Joseph
Ft. Duquesne
New York
Ft. Crevecoeur
Ft. Miami
Philadelphia
Baltimore

CALIFORNIA

Williamsburg

San Francisco
Cahokia
Ft. Vincennes
Monterey
Ste. Genevieve
Kaskaskia
Atlantic
Ocean
NEW
San Luis Obispo
MEXICO
Santa Fe
Santa
Barbara
San Gabriel
Ft. Prudhomme
San Juan Capistrano
Albuquerque
San Diego
Socorro
Ft. Arkansas
Charleston
Tucson
Savannah
Guevavi
El Paso del Norte
Los Adaes
Natchitoches
Ft. Toulouse
Apalachee
St. Augustine
Nacogdoches
Pacific
TEXAS
Baton Rouge
St.
Ocean
San Antonio
New Orleans
Marks
Guaymas
La Bahía
FLORIDA
BAHAMAS

MEXICO
Gulf of Mexico

Havana
CUBA
San Blas
HAITI
JAMAICA

- Fort or presidio
† Mission
British settlement
British land claims
Area of French influence
Area of Spanish influence

0   250   500 miles
0   250   500 kilometers

Three great empires—the British, French, and Spanish—competed for influence in North America for much of the eighteenth century.

In the second half of the century, the Spanish government made a concerted effort to reinvigorate its empire north of the Rio Grande. It stabilized relations with Indians, especially the nomadic Comanches and Apaches who had wreaked havoc in New Mexico. But although ranching expanded in New Mexico and Texas, the economy of the Spanish colonies essentially rested on trading with and extracting labor from the surviving Indian population. New Mexico's population in 1765 was only 20,000, equally divided between Spanish settlers and Pueblo Indians. Spain began the colonization of Texas at the beginning of the eighteenth century, partly as a buffer to prevent French commercial influence, then spreading in the Mississippi Valley, from intruding into New Mexico. The Spanish established complexes consisting of religious missions and *presidios* (military outposts) at Los Adaes, La Bahia, and San Antonio. But the region attracted few settlers. Texas had only 1,200 Spanish colonists in 1760. Florida stagnated as well, remaining an impoverished military outpost. Around 1770, its population

In this lithograph from 1816, Indians perform a dance-in at Mission San Francisco in California. Priests watch from the front of the mission church.

consisted of about 2,000 Spanish, 1,000 black slaves, and a few hundred Indians, survivors of many decades of war and disease.

THE SPANISH IN CALIFORNIA

On the Pacific coast, Russian fur traders in the eighteenth century established a series of forts and trading posts in Alaska. Although only a handful of Russian colonists lived in the region, Spain, alarmed by what it saw as a danger to its American empire, ordered the colonization of California. A string of Spanish missions and *presidios* soon dotted the California coastline, from San Diego to Los Angeles, Santa Barbara, Monterey, San Francisco, and Sonoma. Born on the Spanish Mediterranean island of Mallorca, Father Junípero Serra became one of the most controversial figures in California's early history. He founded the first California mission, in San Diego, in 1769 and administered the mission network until his death in 1784. Serra was widely praised in Spain for converting thousands of Indians to Christianity, teaching them Spanish, and working to transform their hunting-and-gathering economies by introducing settled agriculture and skilled crafts. Today, he is being considered by the Catholic Church for elevation to sainthood. But forced labor and disease took a heavy toll among Indians who lived at the missions Serra directed.

Present-day California was a densely populated area, with a native population of perhaps 250,000 when Spanish settlement began. But as in other regions, the coming of soldiers and missionaries proved a disaster for the Indians. More than any other Spanish colony, California was a mission frontier. These outposts served simultaneously as religious institutions and centers of government and labor. Their aim was to transform the culture of the local population and eventually assimilate it into Spanish civilization. Father Serra and other missionaries hoped to convert the natives to Christianity and settled farming. The missions also relied on forced Indian labor to grow grain, work in orchards and vineyards, and tend cattle. The combination of new diseases and the resettlement of thousands of Indians in villages around the missions devastated Indian society. By 1821, when Mexico won its independence from Spain, California's native population had declined by over one-third. But the area had not attracted Spanish settlers. In 1800, Los Angeles, with a population of 300, was the largest town. When Spanish rule came to an end in 1821, *Californios* (California residents of Spanish descent) numbered only 3,200.

THE FRENCH EMPIRE

Spain's North American colonies remained peripheral parts of its empire when compared with its possessions in Central and South America and the Caribbean. A greater rival to British power in North America—as well as in Europe and the Caribbean—was France. During the eighteenth century, the population and economy of Canada expanded. At the same time, French traders pushed into the Mississippi Valley southward from the Great Lakes and northward from Mobile, founded in 1702, and New Orleans, established in 1718. In the St. Lawrence Valley of French Canada, prosperous farming communities developed. By 1750, the area had a population of about 55,000 colonists. Another 10,000 (about half Europeans, half African-American slaves) resided in Louisiana, mostly concentrated on the lower Mississippi River and along the Gulf Coast. By mid-century, sugar plantations had sprung up in the area between New Orleans and Baton Rouge. New Orleans already had a vibrant social life as well as an established community with churches, schools, and governmental buildings.

Nonetheless, the population of French North America continued to be dwarfed by the British colonies. Prejudice against emigration to North America remained widespread in France. A French novel written in 1731, known today as the basis for the nineteenth-century opera *Manon*, told the story of a prostitute punished by being transported to Louisiana and of her noble lover who followed her there. It expressed the popular view of the colony as a place of cruel exile for criminals and social outcasts. Nonetheless, by claiming control of a large arc of territory and by establishing close trading and military relations with many Indian tribes, the French empire posed a real challenge to the British. French forts and trading posts ringed the British colonies. In present-day Mississippi and Alabama and in the western regions of Georgia and the Carolinas, French and British traders competed to form alliances with local Indians and control the trade in deerskins. The French were a presence on the New England and New York frontiers and in western Pennsylvania.

A sketch of New Orleans as it appeared in 1720.

BATTLE FOR THE CONTINENT

THE MIDDLE GROUND

For much of the eighteenth century, the western frontier of British North America was the flashpoint of imperial rivalries. The Ohio Valley became caught up in a complex struggle for power involving the French, British, rival Indian communities, and settlers and land companies pursuing their own interests. Here by mid-century resided numerous Indians, including Shawnees and Delawares who had been pushed out of Pennsylvania by advancing white settlement, Cherokees and Chickasaws from the southern colonies who looked to the region for new hunting grounds, and Iroquois seeking to exert control over the area's fur trade. On this "middle ground" between European empires and Indian sovereignty, villages sprang up where members of numerous tribes lived side by side, along with European traders and the occasional missionary.

By the mid-eighteenth century, Indians had learned that direct military confrontation with Europeans meant suicide, and that an alliance with a single European power exposed them to danger from others. The Indians of the Ohio Valley recognized that the imperial rivalry of Britain and France posed both threat and opportunity. As one Delaware spokesman remarked, it was impossible to know "where the Indians' land lay, for the French claimed all the land on one side of the Ohio River and the English on the other side." On the other hand, Indians sought (with some success) to play European empires off against one another and to control the lucrative commerce with whites. The Iroquois were masters of balance-of-power diplomacy. The British accepted their sovereignty in the Ohio Valley, but it was challenged by the French and their Indian allies.

In 1750, few white settlers inhabited the Ohio Valley. But already, Scotch-Irish and German immigrants, Virginia planters, and land speculators were eyeing the region's fertile soil. In 1749, the government of Virginia awarded an immense land grant—half a million acres—to the Ohio Company, an example of the huge domains being parceled out to those with political connections. The company's members included the colony's royal governor, Robert Dinwiddie, and the cream of Virginia society—Lees, Carters, and the young George Washington. The land grant threatened the region's Indians as well as Pennsylvania land speculators, who also had claims in the area. It sparked the French to bolster their presence in the region. It was the Ohio Company's demand for French recognition of its land claims that inaugurated the Seven Years' War (known in the colonies as the French and Indian War), the first of the century's imperial wars to begin in the colonies and the first to result in a decisive victory for one combatant. It permanently altered the global balance of power.

THE SEVEN YEARS' WAR

By the 1750s, British possessions and trade reached around the globe. "Every part of the world affects us, in some way or another," remarked the Duke of Newcastle. The existence of global empires implied that warfare among them would also be global. What became a worldwide struggle for

The cover of a magazine published in Pennsylvania in 1758 depicts English and French attempting to trade with an Indian. The Frenchman offers a tomahawk and musket, the Englishman a Bible and cloth.

imperial domination, which eventually spread to Europe, West Africa, and Asia, began in 1754 with British efforts to dislodge the French from forts they had constructed in western Pennsylvania. In the previous year, George Washington, then only twenty-one years old, had been dispatched by the colony's governor on an unsuccessful mission to persuade French soldiers to abandon a fort they were building on lands claimed by the Ohio Company. In 1754, Washington returned to the area with two companies of soldiers. He hastily constructed Fort Necessity. After an ill-considered attempt to defend it against a larger French and Indian force, resulting in the loss of one-third of his men, Washington was forced to surrender. Soon afterwards, an expedition led by General Edward Braddock against Fort Duquesne (today's Pittsburgh) was ambushed by French and Indian forces, leaving Braddock and two-thirds of his 3,000 soldiers dead or wounded.

For two years, the war went against the British. French and Indian forces captured British forts in northern New York. The southern backcountry was ablaze with fighting among British forces, colonists, and Indians. Inhumanity flourished on all sides. Indians killed hundreds of colonists in western Pennsylvania and pushed the line of settlement all the way back to Carlisle, only 100 miles west of Philadelphia. In Nova Scotia, the British rounded up around 5,000 local French residents, called Acadians, confiscated their land, and expelled them from the region, selling their farms to settlers from New England. Some of those expelled eventually returned to France; others ended up as far away as Louisiana, where their descendants came to be known as Cajuns.

As the British government under Prime Minister William Pitt, who took office in 1757, raised huge sums of money and poured men and naval forces into the war, the tide of battle turned. Pitt's strategy was to provide funds to Prussia and Austria to enable them to hold the line against France and its ally Spain in Europe, while the British struck at the French weak point, its colonies. By 1759, Britain—with colonial and Indian soldiers playing a major role—had captured the pivotal French outposts at Forts Duquesne, Ticonderoga (north of Albany), and Louisbourg on Cape Breton Island, which guarded the mouth of the St. Lawrence River. In September of that year, a French army was defeated on the Plains of Abraham near Quebec. In 1760, Montreal, the last outpost of New France, surrendered. British forces also seized nearly all the islands in the French Caribbean and established control of India. In Europe, meanwhile, Prussia and Austria managed to fend off the coalition of France, Russia, and Spain.

A WORLD TRANSFORMED

"As long as the world has stood there has not been such a war," declared a British emissary to the Delaware Indians. Britain's victory fundamentally reshaped the world balance of power. In the Peace of Paris in 1763, France ceded Canada to Britain, receiving back in return the sugar islands of Guadeloupe and Martinique (far more lucrative colonies from the point of view of French authorities). As part of the reshuffling of imperial possessions, Spain ceded Florida to Britain in exchange for the return of the Philippines and Cuba (seized by the British during the war). Spain also acquired from France the vast Louisiana colony. France's 200-year-old

North American empire had come to an end. With the exception of two tiny islands retained by France off the coast of Newfoundland, the entire continent east of the Mississippi River was now in British hands.

"Peace," remarked Prime Minister Pitt, "will be as hard to make as war." Eighteenth-century warfare, conducted on land and sea across the globe, was enormously expensive. The Seven Years' War put strains on all the participants. The war's cost produced a financial crisis in France that almost three decades later would help to spark the French Revolution. The British would try to recoup part of the cost of war by increasing taxes on their American colonies. "We no sooner leave fighting our neighbors, the French," commented the British writer Dr. Samuel Johnson, "but we must fall to quarreling among ourselves." In fact, the Peace of Paris was soon followed by open warfare in North America between the British and Native Americans.

PONTIAC'S REBELLION

Throughout eastern North America, the abrupt departure of the French in the aftermath of the Seven Years' War eliminated the balance-of-power diplomacy that had enabled groups like the Iroquois to maintain a significant degree of autonomy. Even as England and its colonies celebrated their victory as a triumph of liberty, Indians saw it as a threat to their own freedom. Indians had fought on both sides in the war, although mainly as allies of the French. Their primary aim, however, was to maintain their independence from both empires. Domination by any outside power, Indians feared, meant the loss of freedom. Without consulting them, the French had ceded land Indians claimed as their own, to British control. The Treaty of Paris left Indians more dependent than ever on the British and ushered in a period of confusion over land claims, control of the fur trade, and tribal relations in general. To Indians, it was clear that continued expansion of the British colonies posed a dire threat. One British army officer reported that Native Americans "say we mean to make slaves of them," by taking their land.

In 1763, in the wake of the French defeat, Indians of the Ohio Valley and Great Lakes launched a revolt against British rule. Although known as Pontiac's Rebellion after an Ottawa war leader, the rebellion owed at least as much to the teachings of Neolin, a Delaware religious prophet. During a religious vision, the Master of Life instructed Neolin that his people must reject European technology, free themselves from commercial ties with whites and dependence on alcohol, clothe themselves in the garb of their ancestors, and drive the British from their territory (although friendly French inhabitants could remain). Neolin combined this message with the relatively new idea of pan-Indian identity. All Indians, he preached, were a single people, and only through cooperation could they regain their lost independence. The common experience of dispossession, the intertribal communities that had developed in the Ohio country, and the mixing of Indian warriors in French armies had helped to inspire this sense of identity as Indians rather than members of individual tribes.

THE PROCLAMATION LINE

In the spring and summer of 1763, Ottawas, Hurons, and other Indians besieged Detroit, then a major British military outpost, seized nine other

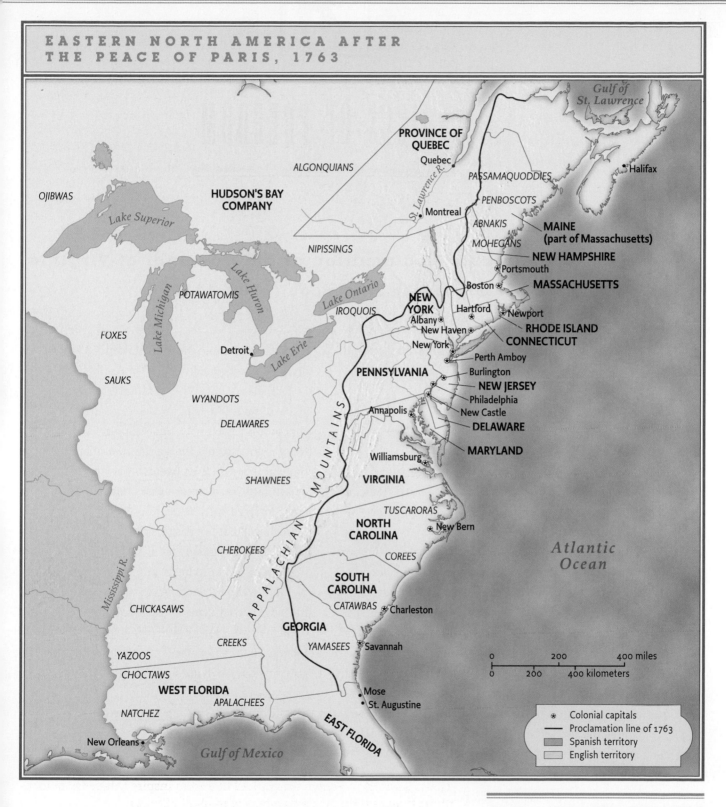

EASTERN NORTH AMERICA AFTER THE PEACE OF PARIS, 1763

Gulf of St. Lawrence

PROVINCE OF QUEBEC

ALGONQUIANS

Quebec

· Halifax

PASSAMAQUODDIES

OJIBWAS

HUDSON'S BAY COMPANY

PENBOSCOTS

Montreal

ABNAKIS

MAINE (part of Massachusetts)

NIPISSINGS

MOHEGANS

NEW HAMPSHIRE

Lake Superior

Portsmouth

Boston

MASSACHUSETTS

POTAWATOMIS

Lake Huron

Lake Michigan

Lake Ontario

NEW YORK

Hartford

Albany

New Haven

Newport

RHODE ISLAND

CONNECTICUT

IROQUOIS

FOXES

Detroit

Lake Erie

New York

Perth Amboy

PENNSYLVANIA

Burlington

NEW JERSEY

SAUKS

Philadelphia

New Castle

WYANDOTS

Annapolis

DELAWARE

DELAWARES

MARYLAND

Williamsburg

A
P
P
A
L
A
C
H
I
A
N

M
O
U
N
T
A
I
N
S

SHAWNEES

VIRGINIA

TUSCARORAS

NORTH CAROLINA

New Bern

CHEROKEES

Mississippi R.

COREES

Atlantic Ocean

SOUTH CAROLINA

CATAWBAS

Charleston

CHICKASAWS

GEORGIA

CREEKS

YAMASEES

Savannah

YAZOOS

0   200   400 miles
0   200   400 kilometers

CHOCTAWS

WEST FLORIDA

APALACHEES

Mose

NATCHEZ

St. Augustine

New Orleans

EAST FLORIDA

Gulf of Mexico

⊛ Colonial capitals
— Proclamation line of 1763
  Spanish territory
  English territory

The Peace of Paris, which ended the Seven Years' War, left all of North America east of the Mississippi in British hands, ending the French presence on the continent.

VOICES OF FREEDOM

From Speech and Proclamation of the Governor of Virginia, ALEXANDER SPOTSWOOD (1709–1710)

The early eighteenth century witnessed the rapid growth of Virginia's slave population, growing fears of slave unrest, and governmental efforts to prevent slave uprisings.

I would willingly whisper to you [the House of Burgesses] the strength of your country and the state of your militia, which . . . is so imaginary a defence, that we cannot too cautiously conceal it from our neighbors and our slaves, nor too earnestly pray that neither their lust of domination nor the desire of freedom may stir those people to any attempts. The latter sort (I mean our Negroes) by their daily increase seem to be the most dangerous. And . . . we are not to depend on either their stupidity, or that babel of languages among them; freedom wears a cap without a tongue. Call together all those who long to shake off the fetters of slavery and as such an

insurrection would surely be attended with most dreadful consequences.

A Proclamation. Whereas I have received intelligence of several illegal, unusual, and unwarrantable concourses, meetings, and assemblings together of Negro, Mulatto, and Indian slaves at quarters where there are no white or freemen overseers and more particularly of a notorious insurrection intended and contrived at such meetings by several slaves . . . I [proclaim] that no master, mistress, or overseer of a family shall knowingly permit any slave not belonging to him or her to be and remain upon his or her plantation above four hours at any one time without the leave of such slave's master, mistress, or overseer on penalty of one hundred and fifty pounds of tobacco to the informer . . . and also . . . that no slave go armed with gun, sword, club, staff, or other weapon nor go off the plantation . . . without a certificate of leave in writing for doing so from his master, mistress, or overseer.

From Pontiac,

Speeches (1762 and 1763)

Pontiac was a leader of the pan-Indian resistance to English rule known as Pontiac's Rebellion, which followed the end of the Seven Years' War. Neolin was a Delaware religious prophet who helped to inspire the rebellion.

———

Englishmen, although you have conquered the French, you have not yet conquered us! We are not your slaves. These lakes, these woods, and mountains were left to us by our ancestors. They are our inheritance; and we will part with them to none. Your nation supposes that we, like the white people, cannot live without bread and pork and beef! But you ought to know that He, the Great Spirit and Master of Life, has provided food for us in these spacious lakes, and on these woody mountains.

[The Master of Life has said to Neolin:]

I am the Maker of heaven and earth, the trees, lakes, rivers, and all else. I am the Maker of all mankind; and because I love you, you must do my will. The land on which you live I have made for you and not for others. Why do you suffer the white man to dwell among you? My children, you have forgotten the customs and traditions of your forefathers. Why do you not clothe yourselves in skins, as they did, use bows and arrows and the stone-pointed lances, which they used? You have bought guns, knives, kettles and blankets from the white man until you can no longer do without them; and what is worse, you have drunk the poison firewater, which turns you into fools. Fling all these things away; live as your wise forefathers did before you. And as for these English,—these dogs dressed in red, who have come to rob you of your hunting-grounds, and drive away the game,—you must lift the hatchet against them. Wipe them from the face of the earth, and then you will win my favor back again, and once more be happy and prosperous.

———

QUESTIONS

1. Based on Spotswood's "Speech and Proclamation," how do the laws of slavery limit the freedom of whites as well as slaves?

2. What elements of Indian life does Neolin criticize most strongly?

3. Compare how slaves and Native Americans understood freedom, as indicated by these documents.

forts, and killed hundreds of white settlers who had intruded onto Indian lands. British forces soon launched a counterattack, and over the next few years the tribes one by one made peace. But the uprising inspired the government in London to issue the Proclamation of 1763, prohibiting further colonial settlement west of the Appalachian Mountains. These lands were reserved exclusively for Indians. Moreover, the Proclamation banned the sale of Indian lands to private individuals. Henceforth, only colonial governments could arrange such purchases.

The British aim was less to protect the Indians than to stabilize the situation on the colonial frontier and to avoid being dragged into an endless series of border conflicts. But the Proclamation enraged both settlers and speculators hoping to take advantage of the expulsion of the French to consolidate their claims to western lands. They ignored the new policy. George Washington himself ordered his agents to buy up as much Indian land as possible, while keeping the transactions "a profound secret" because of their illegality. Failing to offer a viable solution to the question of westward expansion, the Proclamation of 1763 ended up further exacerbating settler-Indian relations.

PENNSYLVANIA AND THE INDIANS

The Seven Years' War not only redrew the map of the world but produced dramatic changes within the American colonies as well. Nowhere was this more evident than in Pennsylvania, where the conflict shattered the decades-old rule of the Quaker elite and dealt the final blow to the colony's policy of accommodation with the Indians. During the war, with the frontier ablaze with battles between settlers and French and Indian warriors, western Pennsylvanians demanded that colonial authorities adopt a more aggressive stance. When the governor declared war on hostile Delawares, raised a militia, and offered a bounty for Indian scalps, many of the assembly's pacifist Quakers resigned their seats, effectively ending their control of Pennsylvania politics. The war deepened the antagonism of western farmers toward Indians and witnessed numerous indiscriminate assaults on Indian communities, both allies and enemies.

In December 1763, while Pontiac's Rebellion still raged, a party of fifty armed men, mostly Scotch-Irish farmers from the vicinity of the Pennsylvania town of Paxton, destroyed the Indian village of Conestoga, massacring half a dozen men, women, and children who lived there under the protection of Pennsylvania's governor. They then marched on Lancaster, where they killed fourteen additional Indians. Like participants in Bacon's Rebellion nearly a century earlier, they accused colonial authorities of treating Indians too leniently. They petitioned the legislature to remove all Indians from the colony. The Indians' "claim to freedom and indepen-dency," they insisted, threatened Pennsylvania's stability. When the Paxton Boys marched on Philadelphia in February 1764, intending to attack Moravian Indians who resided near the city, the governor ordered the expulsion of much of the Indian population. By the 1760s, Pennsylvania's Holy Experiment was at an end and with it William Penn's promise of "true friendship and amity" between colonists and the native population. No other large colony had a smaller Indian population or a more remorseless determination on the part of settlers to eliminate those who remained.

COLONIAL IDENTITIES

Like the Indians, colonists emerged from the Seven Years' War with a heightened sense of collective identity. Before the war, the colonies had been largely isolated from one another. Outside of New England, more Americans probably traveled to England than from one colony to another. In 1751, Governor George Clinton of New York had called for a general conference on Indian relations, but only three colonies bothered to send delegates. The Albany Plan of Union of 1754, drafted by Benjamin Franklin at the outbreak of the Seven Years' War, envisioned the creation of a Grand Council composed of delegates from each colony, with the power to levy taxes and deal with Indian relations and the common defense. Rejected by the colonial assemblies, whose powers Franklin's proposal would curtail, the plan was never sent to London for approval.

Participation in the Seven Years' War created greater bonds among the colonies. But the war also strengthened colonists' pride in being members of the British empire. It has been said that the Americans were never more British than in 1763. Colonial militiamen and British regulars fought along side each other against the French. Tensions developed between the professional British military and the often undisciplined American citizen-soldiers, but the common experience of battle and victory also forged bonds between them. For much of the century, New Englanders had called for the conquest of Canada as a blow for "Protestant freedom" against "popish slavery." Now that this had been accomplished, British victory in the Seven Years' War seemed a triumph of liberty over tyranny. The defeat of the Catholic French reinforced the equation of British nationality, Protestantism, and freedom.

In fact, however, after 1763 Britain's global empire was neither predominantly Protestant nor British nor free. It now included tens of thousands of French Catholics and millions of persons in India governed as subjects rather than as citizens. The English statesman Edmund Burke wondered whether British liberty could be reconciled with rule over this "vast, heterogeneous, intricate mass of interests." Burke was almost alone in seeing the newly expanded empire as a challenge to the principles of British freedom. But soon, the American colonists would come to believe that membership in the empire jeopardized their liberty. When they did, they set out on a road that led to independence.

Benjamin Franklin produced this famous cartoon in 1754, calling on Britain's North American colonies to unite against the French.

SUGGESTED READING

Anderson, Fred. *Crucible of War: The Seven Years' War and the Fate of Empire in British North America, 1754–1766* (2000). The most recent general history of the Seven Years' War and its consequences.

Beeman, Richard R. *Varieties of Political Experience in Eighteenth-Century America* (2004). Explores how political life differed from colony to colony, and what characteristics they had in common.

Blackburn, Robin. *The Making of New World Slavery: From the Baroque to the Modern, 1492–1800* (1997). A comprehensive history of the rise of slavery in the Western Hemisphere and its centrality to European empires.

Calloway, Colin G. *The Scratch of a Pen: 1763 and the Transformation of North America* (2006). Examines the impact of the Peace of Paris on North America, especially the Native American population.

Clark, Charles E. *The Public Prints: The Newspaper in Anglo-American Culture, 1665–1740* (1994). Presents the early history of newspapers in colonial America.

Colley, Linda. *Britons: Forging the Nation, 1707–1837* (1992). An influential study of the rise of a sense of national identity in Great Britain, relevant also for the American colonies.

Faragher, John Mack. *A Great and Noble Scheme: The Tragic Story of the Expulsion of the French Acadians from their American Homeland* (2005). A detailed account of a notorious episode during the Seven Years' War.

Gomez, Michael A. *Exchanging Our Country Marks: The Transformation of African Identities in the Colonial and Antebellum South* (1998). The most detailed study of the process by which Africans became African-Americans.

Greene, Jack P. *The Quest for Power: The Lower Houses of Assembly in the Southern Royal Colonies, 1689–1776* (1963). A careful examination of how elected Assemblies expanded their authority in the eighteenth-century South.

Lepore, Jill. *New York Burning: Liberty, Slavery, and Conspiracy in Eighteenth-Century Manhattan* (2005). An investigation of the alleged slave conspiracy of 1741 and of black life in colonial New York.

Morgan, Philip D. *Slave Counterpoint: Black Culture in the Eighteenth-Century Chesapeake and Lowcountry* (1998). A detailed comparison of the nature of slave life in the two key slave systems of British North America.

Noll, Mark. *Rise of Evangelicism: The Age of Edwards, Whitefield, and the Wesleys* (2004). Explores the Great Awakening on both sides of the Atlantic and its impact on religious life.

Weber, David J. *The Spanish Frontier in North America* (1992). The most comprehensive account of Spanish settlement in what is now the United States.

White, Richard. *The Middle Ground: Indians, Empires, and Republics in the Great Lakes Region, 1650–1815* (1991). The book that developed the idea of a middle ground where Europeans and Indians both exercised authority.

Wood, Peter H. *Black Majority: Negroes in Colonial South Carolina from 1670 through the Stono Rebellion* (1974). Examines how the expansion of rice production affected the slave system and the lives of slaves in South Carolina.

CHAPTER REVIEW

REVIEW QUESTIONS

1. Why was Father Junípero Serra such a controversial and significant figure?

2. How did the ideas of republicanism and liberalism differ in eighteenth century British North America?

3. Three distinct slave systems were well entrenched in Britain's mainland colonies. Describe the main characteristics of each system.

4. What were the bases of the colonists' sense of a collective British identity in the eighteenth century?

5. What elements of the Great Awakening helped to inspire the enlargement of the public sphere?

KEY TERMS

Middle Passage (p. 137)

free blacks in the Chesapeake (p. 139)

disease and slavery in South Carolina (p. 140)

runaways (p. 144)

slavery in Louisiana (p. 144)

Great Awakening (p. 156)

California missions (p. 160)

Acadians (p. 163)

Albany Plan of Union (p. 169)

REVIEW TABLE

Major Slave Systems of the British Colonies

Region	Major Economy	Slave Environment
Chesapeake	Tobacco	Smaller plantations with substantial master-slave contact
South Carolina and Georgia	Rice and indigo	Large plantations requiring intensive labor
New England and Middle Colonies	Small family farms	Urban laborers

Part 2

A NEW NATION, 1763–1840

During the 1760s and 1770s, a dispute over taxation within the British empire escalated into a conflict that gave birth to a new nation, the United States of America. The American Revolution inaugurated an era of political upheaval throughout the Western world, known to historians ever since as the Age of Revolution. It helped to inspire popular uprisings in Europe, the Caribbean, and Latin America and forever changed the course of American development. Liberty emerged as the era's foremost rallying cry. The revolutionary generation insisted that the meaning of their struggle lay not only in political independence but also in the establishment of what the writer Thomas Paine called an asylum of liberty for all mankind.

The American Revolution not only broke the political bond with Great Britain but also inspired groups within American society to claim greater rights for themselves. Propertyless men demanded the right to vote. Women began to challenge their subordination to men. Indentured servants ran away from their masters. And slaves seized the opportunity to gain their freedom by fighting in the Continental army or by escaping to the British.

By the time it had run its course, the Revolution had greatly expanded some realms of American freedom. It severed the connection between church and state, promoted the emergence of a lively public sphere in which ordinary men and, sometimes, women participated in political debate, and it challenged the monopoly on political power by colonial elites. It set in motion the abolition of slavery in the northern states. On the other hand, for some Americans independence meant a loss of liberty. Many of those who had remained loyal to England suffered persecution and were forced to leave the country. The end of the British presence removed the last barrier to the westward expansion of the American population, making inevitable the dispossession of the remaining Indian population east of the Mississippi River. The formation of a national government in which slaveowners occupied the presidency for most of the half-century after independence, helped to consolidate the institution of slavery in the South.

Three processes that were set in motion by the Revolution and that gained strength in the early decades of the nineteenth century profoundly affected Americans' ideas about freedom. The first was the democratization of politics. Most members of the convention that drafted the nation's constitution in 1787 assumed that men of property and education would dominate the new American government. But the democratic upsurge inspired by the Revolution, coupled with the swift emergence of political parties offering radically different programs for national development, encouraged a broad popular participation in politics. By the 1830s, a flourishing democratic system was firmly in place. Property qualifications for voting had been eliminated in nearly every state, two parties competed throughout the country, and voter turnout stood at record levels. Political democracy had become a defining element of American freedom.

Second, the development of steamboats, canals, and railroads brought rapid improvements in transportation and communication and created a broad market for farm products and manufactured goods. The "market revolution" opened up vast areas of the American interior to commercial farming, and it stimulated the early development of factory production. It offered new opportunities for personal advancement to many Americans while reducing others to what seemed an "unfree" situation—working for wages under the constant supervision of an employer. The market revolution also made possible the third major development of this era, the population's westward movement and the rise of the West as a distinct social and political region. The market revolution and westward shift of population also helped to reshape the idea of freedom, identifying it more and more closely with economic opportunity, physical mobility, and individual self-definition and fulfillment.

Many of the founding fathers had feared that economic growth, rapid territorial expansion, and the development of political parties would endanger the unity of the new republic. And between the coming of independence and 1840, the new nation faced a series of crises, as Americans divided according to political and regional loyalties and battled for advantage in the expanding economy. Political conflict often revolved around the relationship between government and the economy. Should the national government seek to promote economic development and direct its course by enacting a system of tariffs, internal improvements, and a national bank? Or should it stand aside and allow Americans to pursue economic self-interest without governmental interference? In the 1790s, the former view was represented by the Federalist Party, the latter by the Jeffersonian Republicans. In the 1830s, a similar division emerged between Whigs and Democrats. Advocates of both visions of the role of the national government insisted that theirs was the best program to promote American liberty.

American freedom also continued to be shaped by the presence of slavery. Rather than dying out, as some of the founders had hoped, slavery expanded rapidly in territorial extent and economic importance. Slavery helped to define the boundaries of American freedom. The privileges of voting, officeholding, and access to economic opportunity were increasingly restricted to whites. Women, too, were barred from these elements of freedom. Their role, according to the prevailing social values, was to remain in the "private sphere" of the home.

The contradiction embedded in American life from the earliest days of settlement—expanding freedom for some coexisting with and, indeed, depending on lack of freedom for others—continued to bedevil the new nation.

Chapter 5

The American Revolution, 1763–1783

An engraving by Paul Revere depicts British troops landing from warships in Boston harbor in 1768 and marching into the city. The troops arrived as Americans were boycotting British goods to protest the Townshend Acts, (the taxes Parliament imposed on the colonies) one of many precipitants of the movement for greater American rights within the empire and, eventually, independence.

FOCUS QUESTIONS

- What were the roots and significance of the Stamp Act controversy?

- What key events sharpened the divisions between Britain and the colonists in the late 1760s and early 1770s?

- What were the key steps on the way to independence in the mid-1770s?

- How were American forces able to prevail in the Revolutionary War?

On the night of August 26, 1765, a violent crowd of Bostonians assaulted the elegant home of Thomas Hutchinson, chief justice and lieutenant governor of Massachusetts. Hutchinson and his family were eating dinner when the rioters arrived. They barely had time to escape before the crowd broke down the front door and proceeded to destroy or carry off most of their possessions, including paintings, furniture, silverware, and notes for a history of Massachusetts Hutchinson was writing. By the time they departed, only the outer walls of the home remained standing.

The immediate cause of the riot was the Stamp Act, a recently enacted British tax that many colonists felt violated their liberty. Critics of the measure had spread a rumor that Hutchinson had written to London encouraging its passage (in fact, he privately opposed it). Only a few days earlier, Hutchinson had helped to disperse a crowd attacking a building owned by his relative Andrew Oliver, a merchant who had been appointed to help administer the new law. Both crowds were led by Ebenezer Mackintosh, a shoemaker who had fought against the French during the Seven Years' War and enjoyed a wide following among Boston's working people. Arrested after the destruction of Hutchinson's home, Mackintosh was released after the intervention of the Loyal Nine, a group of merchants and craftsmen who had taken the lead in opposing the Stamp Act. The violence had gone far beyond what the Loyal Nine intended, and they promised authorities that resistance to the Stamp Act would henceforth be peaceful. The riot, nonetheless, convinced Hutchinson that for Britain to rule America effectively, "there must be an abridgement of what are called English liberties." Whether colonists would accept such an abridgement, however, was very much in doubt.

The riot of August 26 was one small episode in a series of events that launched a half-century of popular protest and political upheaval throughout the Western world. The momentous era that came to be called the Age of Revolution began in British North America, spread to Europe and the Caribbean, and culminated in the Latin American wars for independence. In all these struggles, liberty emerged as the foremost rallying cry for popular discontent. Rarely has the idea played so central a role in political debate and social upheaval.

If the attack on Hutchinson's home demonstrated the depths of feeling aroused by Britain's efforts to impose greater control over its empire, it also revealed that revolution is a dynamic process whose consequences no one can anticipate. The crowd's fury expressed resentments against the rich and powerful quite different from colonial leaders' objections to Parliament's attempt to tax the colonies. The Stamp Act crisis inaugurated not only a struggle for colonial liberty in relation to Great Britain but also a multi-sided battle to define and extend liberty within America.

THE CRISIS BEGINS

When George III assumed the throne of Great Britain in 1760, no one on either side of the Atlantic imagined that within two decades Britain's American colonies would separate from the empire. But the Seven Years' War, which left Britain with an enormous debt and vastly enlarged overseas possessions to defend, led successive governments in London to seek ways to make the colonies share the cost of empire. Having studied the writings of British opposition thinkers who insisted that power inevitably seeks to encroach upon liberty, colonial leaders came to see these measures as part of a British design to undermine their freedom. Having only recently gloried in their enjoyment of "British liberty," they came to conclude that membership in the empire was a threat to freedom, rather than its foundation. This conviction set the colonies on the road to independence.

CONSOLIDATING THE EMPIRE

The Seven Years' War, to which the colonists contributed soldiers and economic resources, underscored for rulers in London how important the empire was to Britain's well-being and its status as a great power. Now, they believed, new regulations were needed to help guarantee the empire's continued strength and prosperity. Before 1763, Parliament had occasionally acted to forbid the issuance of paper money in America and to restrict colonial economic activities that competed with businesses at home. The Wool Act of 1699, Hat Act of 1732, and Iron Act of 1750 forbade colonial manufacture of these items. The Molasses Act of 1733 sought to curtail trade between New England and the French Caribbean by imposing a prohibitive tax on French-produced molasses used to make rum in American distilleries. And the Navigation Acts, discussed in Chapter 3, sought to channel key American exports like tobacco through British ports. The colonists frequently ignored all these measures.

As to internal affairs within the colonies, the British government frequently seemed uninterested. There was no point, one official said, in worrying about the behavior of colonists who "plant tobacco and Puritanism only, like fools." Beginning in the late 1740s, the Board of Trade, which was responsible for overseeing colonial affairs, attempted to strengthen imperial authority. It demanded that colonial laws conform to royal instructions and encouraged colonial assemblies to grant permanent salaries to royal governors. But the outbreak of the Seven Years' War suspended this initiative.

Having treated the colonists as allies during the war, Britain reverted in the mid-1760s to seeing them as subordinates whose main role was to enrich the mother country. During this period, the government in London concerned itself with the colonies in unprecedented ways, hoping to make British rule more efficient and systematic and to raise funds to help pay for the war and to finance the empire. Nearly all British political leaders supported the new laws that so enraged the colonists. Americans, Britons felt, should be grateful to the empire. To fight the Seven Years' War, Britain had borrowed from banks and individual investors over £150 million (the equivalent of tens of trillions of dollars in today's money). Interest on the

An engraving from a Massachusetts almanac published in 1774 depicts the lieutenant governor Thomas Hutchinson, whose house had been destroyed by a mob nine years earlier. The devil carries a list of Hutchinson's "crimes."

According to the doctrine of "virtual representation," the House of Commons represented all residents of the British empire, whether or not they could vote for members. In this 1775 cartoon criticizing the idea, a blinded Britannia, on the far right, stumbles into a pit. Next to her, two colonists complain of being robbed by British taxation. In the background, according to an accompanying explanation of the cartoon, stand the "Catholic" city of Quebec and the "Protestant town of Boston," the latter in flames.

debt absorbed half the government's annual revenue. The tax burden in Britain had reached unprecedented heights. It seemed only reasonable that the colonies should help pay this national debt, foot part of the bill for continued British protection, and stop cheating the Treasury by violating the Navigation Acts.

Nearly all Britons, moreover, believed that Parliament represented the entire empire and had a right to legislate for it. Millions of Britons, including the residents of major cities like Manchester and Birmingham, had no representatives in Parliament. But according to the widely accepted theory of "virtual representation"—which held that each member represented the entire empire, not just his own district—the interests of all who lived under the British crown were supposedly taken into account. When Americans began to insist that because they were unrepresented in Parliament, the British government could not tax the colonies, they won little support in the mother country. To their surprise, however, British governments found that the effective working of the empire required the cooperation of local populations. Time and again, British officials backed down in the face of colonial resistance, only to return with new measures to centralize control of the empire that only stiffened colonial resolve.

The British government had already alarmed many colonists by issuing writs of assistance to combat smuggling. These were general search warrants that allowed customs officials to search anywhere they chose for smuggled goods. In a celebrated court case in Boston in 1761, the lawyer James Otis insisted that the writs were "an instrument of arbitrary power, destructive to English liberty, and the fundamental principles of the Constitution," and that Parliament therefore had no right to authorize them. ("American independence was then and there born," John Adams later remarked—a considerable exaggeration.) Many colonists were also outraged by the Proclamation of 1763 (mentioned in the previous chapter) barring further settlement on lands west of the Appalachian Mountains.

TAXING THE COLONIES   *Know details*

In 1764, the Sugar Act, introduced by Prime Minister George Grenville, reduced the existing tax on molasses imported into North America from the French West Indies from six pence to three pence per gallon. But the act also established a new machinery to end widespread smuggling by colonial merchants. And to counteract the tendency of colonial juries to acquit merchants charged with violating trade regulations, it strengthened the admiralty courts, where accused smugglers could be judged without benefit of a jury trial. Thus, colonists saw the measure not as a welcome reduction in taxation but as an attempt to get them to pay a levy they would otherwise have evaded.

At the same time, a Revenue Act placed goods such as wool and hides, which had previously been traded freely with Holland, France, and southern Europe, on the enumerated list, meaning they had to be shipped through England. Together, these measures threatened the profits of colonial merchants and seemed certain to aggravate an already serious economic recession resulting from the end of the Seven Years' War. They were accompanied by the Currency Act, which reaffirmed the earlier ban on colonial assemblies issuing paper as "legal tender"—that is, money that individuals are required to accept in payment of debts.

THE STAMP ACT CRISIS

The Sugar Act was an effort to strengthen the long-established (and long-evaded) Navigation Acts. The Stamp Act of 1765 represented a new departure in imperial policy. For the first time, Parliament attempted to raise money from direct taxes in the colonies rather than through the regulation of trade. The act required that all sorts of printed material produced in the colonies—newspapers, books, court documents, commercial papers, land deeds, almanacs, etc.—carry a stamp purchased from authorities. Its purpose was to help finance the operations of the empire, including the cost of stationing British troops in North America, without seeking revenue from colonial assemblies.

While the Sugar Act had mainly affected residents of colonial ports, the Stamp Act managed to offend virtually every free colonist—rich and poor, farmers, artisans, and merchants. It was especially resented by members of the public sphere who wrote, published, and read books and newspapers and followed political affairs. The prospect of a British army permanently stationed on American soil also alarmed many colonists. And by imposing the stamp tax without colonial consent, Parliament directly challenged the authority of local elites who, through the assemblies they controlled, had established their power over the raising and spending of money. They were ready to defend this authority in the name of liberty.

Opposition to the Stamp Act was the first great drama of the revolutionary era and the first major split between colonists and Great Britain over the meaning of freedom. Nearly all colonial political leaders opposed the act. In voicing their grievances, they invoked the rights of the freeborn Englishman, which, they insisted, colonists should also enjoy. Opponents of the act occasionally referred to the natural rights of all mankind. More frequently, however, they drew on time-honored British principles such as a community's right not to be taxed except by its elected representatives. Liberty, they insisted, could not be secure where property was "taken away without consent."

TAXATION AND REPRESENTATION

At stake were clashing ideas of the British empire itself. American leaders viewed the empire as an association of equals in which free settlers overseas enjoyed the same rights as Britons at home. Colonists in other outposts of the empire, such as India, the West Indies, and Canada, echoed this outlook. All, in the name of liberty, claimed the right to govern their own

This teapot protesting the Stamp Act was produced in England and marketed in colonial America, illustrating the close political and economic connections between the two.

A woodcut depicting a crowd attempting to intimidate a New Hampshire official charged with carrying out the Stamp Act. They throw stones at his effigy, while, to the left, a mock funeral begins.

affairs. British residents of Calcutta, India, demanded the "rights inherent in Englishmen." British merchants in Quebec said that to allow French laws to remain in force would reduce them to "slavery." The British government and its appointed representatives in America, by contrast, saw the empire as a system of unequal parts in which different principles governed different areas, and all were subject to the authority of Parliament. To surrender the right to tax the colonies would set a dangerous precedent for the empire as a whole. "In an empire, extended and diversified as that of Great Britain," declared Governor Francis Bernard of Massachusetts in 1765, "there must be a supreme legislature, to which all other powers must be subordinate." Parliament, Bernard continued, was the "sanctuary of liberty"—a description with which many Americans were beginning to disagree.

Some opponents of the Stamp Act distinguished between "internal" taxes like the stamp duty, which they claimed Parliament had no right to impose, and revenue legitimately raised through the regulation of trade. But more and more colonists insisted that Britain had no right to tax them at all, since Americans were unrepresented in the House of Commons. "No taxation without representation" became their rallying cry. Virginia's House of Burgesses approved four resolutions offered by the fiery orator Patrick Henry. They insisted that the colonists enjoyed the same "liberties, privileges, franchises, and immunities" as residents of the mother country and that the right to consent to taxation was a cornerstone of "British freedom." (The House of Burgesses rejected as too radical three other resolutions, including Henry's call for outright resistance to unlawful taxation, but these were also reprinted in colonial newspapers.)

In October 1765, the Stamp Act Congress, with twenty-seven delegates from nine colonies, including some of the most prominent men in America, met in New York and endorsed Virginia's position. Its resolutions began by affirming the "allegiance" of all colonists to the "Crown of Great Britain" and their "due subordination" to Parliament. But they went on to insist that the right to consent to taxation was "essential to the freedom of a people." Soon, merchants throughout the colonies agreed to boycott British goods until Parliament repealed the Stamp Act. This was the first major cooperative action among Britain's mainland colonies. In a sense, by seeking to impose uniformity on the colonies rather than dealing with them individually as in the past, Parliament had inadvertently united America.

LIBERTY AND RESISTANCE

No word was more frequently invoked by critics of the Stamp Act than "liberty." Throughout the colonies, opponents of the new tax staged mock funerals in which liberty's coffin was carried to a burial ground only to have the occupant miraculously revived at the last moment, whereupon the assembled crowd repaired to a tavern to celebrate. As the crisis continued, symbols of liberty proliferated. The large elm tree in Boston on which protesters had hanged an effigy of the stamp distributor Andrew Oliver to persuade him to resign his post came to be known as the Liberty Tree. Its image soon began to appear in prints and pamphlets throughout the colonies. Open-air meetings were held beneath the tree, and as a result the space came to be called Liberty Hall. In New York City, a pine mast erected in 1766 as a meeting place for opponents of the Stamp Act was called the Liberty Pole.

Colonial leaders resolved to prevent the new law's implementation, and by and large they succeeded. Even before the passage of the Stamp Act, a Committee of Correspondence in Boston communicated with other colonies to encourage opposition to the Sugar and Currency Acts. Now, such committees sprang up in other colonies, exchanging ideas and information about resistance. Initiated by colonial elites, the movement against the Stamp Act quickly drew in a far broader range of Americans. The act, wrote John Adams, a Boston lawyer who drafted a set of widely reprinted resolutions against the measure, had inspired "the people, even to the lowest ranks," to become "more attentive to their liberties, more inquisitive about them, and more determined to defend them, than they were ever before known." Political debate, Adams added, pervaded the colonies— "our presses have groaned, our pulpits have thundered, our legislatures have resolved, our towns have voted."

POLITICS IN THE STREETS

Opponents of the Stamp Act, however, did not rely solely on debate. Even before the law went into effect, crowds forced those chosen to administer it to resign and destroyed shipments of stamps. In New York City, processions involving hundreds of residents shouting "liberty" paraded through the streets nearly every night in late 1765. They were organized by the newly created Sons of Liberty, a body led by talented and ambitious lesser merchants like Alexander McDougall, Isaac Sears, and John Lamb. Fluent in Dutch, French, and German, Lamb became the Sons' liaison to the city's numerous ethnic groups. These self-made men had earned fortunes as privateers plundering French shipping during the Seven Years' War and, complained New York's lieutenant governor, opposed "every limitation of trade and duty on it." While they enjoyed no standing among the colony's wealthy elite and carried little weight in municipal affairs, they enjoyed a broad following among the city's craftsmen, laborers, and sailors.

The Sons posted notices reading "Liberty, Property, and No Stamps" and took the lead in enforcing the boycott of British imports. Their actions were viewed with increasing alarm by the aristocratic Livingston and De Lancey families, who dominated New York politics. As the assault on Thomas Hutchinson's house in Boston demonstrated, crowds could easily get out of hand. In

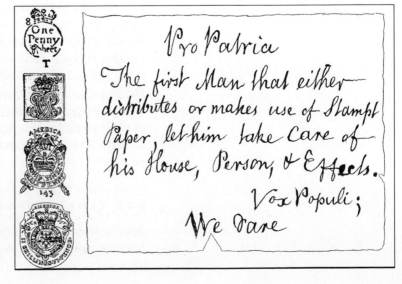

A warning by the Sons of Liberty against using the stamps required by the Stamp Act, which are shown on the left.

Pro Patria

The first Man that either distributes or makes use of Stampt Paper, let him take Care of his House, Person, & Effects.

Vox Populi;

We Dare

November 1765, a New York crowd reportedly composed of sailors, blacks, laborers, and youths hurled stones at Fort George at the tip of Manhattan Island. They then proceeded to destroy the home of Major Thomas James, a British officer who was said to have boasted that he would force the stamps down New Yorkers' throats.

Stunned by the ferocity of American resistance and pressured by London merchants and manufacturers who did not wish to lose their American markets, the British government retreated. In 1766, Parliament repealed the Stamp Act. But this concession was accompanied by the Declaratory Act, which rejected Americans' claims that only their elected representatives could levy taxes. Parliament, proclaimed this measure, possessed the power to pass laws for "the colonies and people of America . . . in all cases whatever." Since the debt-ridden British government continued to need money raised in the colonies, passage of the Declaratory Act promised further conflict.

THE REGULATORS

The Stamp Act crisis was not the only example of violent social turmoil during the 1760s. Many colonies experienced contentious internal divisions as well. As population moved westward, the conflicting land claims of settlers, speculators, colonial governments, and Indians sparked fierce disputes. Rural areas had a long tradition of resistance by settlers and small farmers against the claims of land speculators and large proprietors. As in the Stamp Act crisis, "liberty" was their rallying cry, but in this case liberty had less to do with imperial policy than secure possession of land.

Beginning in the mid-1760s, a group of wealthy residents of the South Carolina backcountry calling themselves Regulators protested the underrepresentation of western settlements in the colony's assembly and the legislators' failure to establish local governments that could regularize land titles and suppress bands of outlaws. The lack of courts in the area, they claimed, had led to a breakdown of law and order, allowing "an infernal gang of villains" to commit "shocking outrages" on persons and property. They added: "We are *Free-men*—British subjects—Not Born Slaves."

A parallel movement in North Carolina mobilized small farmers, who refused to pay taxes, kidnapped local officials, assaulted the homes of land speculators, merchants, and lawyers, and disrupted court proceedings. Here, the complaint was not a lack of government, but corrupt county authorities. These local officials, the Regulators claimed, threatened inexpensive access to land and the prosperity of ordinary settlers through high taxes and court fees. Demanding the democratization of local government, the Regulators condemned the "rich and powerful" (the colony's elite) who used their political authority to prosper at the expense of "poor industrious" farmers. At their peak, the Regulators numbered around 8,000 armed farmers. The region remained in turmoil until 1771, when, in the "battle of Alamance," the farmers were suppressed by the colony's militia.

THE TENANT UPRISING

Also in the mid-1760s, tenants on the Livingston, Philipse, and Cortland manors along the Hudson River north of New York City stopped paying rent and began seizing land. Like opponents of the Stamp Act, they called themselves the Sons of Liberty. The original Sons, however, opposed their uprising, and it was soon suppressed by British and colonial troops. Meanwhile, small farmers in the Green Mountains took up arms to protect their holdings against intrusions by New York landlords. The legal situation there was complex. The area was part of New York, but during the 1750s the governor of New Hampshire had issued land grants to New England families, pocketing a fortune in fees. When New Yorkers tried to enforce their own title to the area, the settlers' leader, Ethan Allen, insisted that land should belong to the person who worked it. Outsiders, he claimed, were trying to "enslave a free people." In the mid-1770s, Allen and his Green Mountain Boys would carve out the new state of Vermont.

The emerging rift between Britain and America eventually superimposed itself on conflicts within the colonies. But the social divisions revealed in the Stamp Act riots and backcountry uprisings made some members of the colonial elite fear that opposition to British measures might unleash turmoil at home. As a result, they were more reluctant to challenge British authority when the next imperial crisis arose.

THE ROAD TO REVOLUTION

THE TOWNSHEND CRISIS

In 1767, the government in London decided to impose a new set of taxes on Americans. They were devised by the chancellor of the Exchequer (the cabinet's chief financial minister), Charles Townshend. In opposing the Stamp Act, some colonists, including Benjamin Franklin (then representing the Pennsylvania assembly in London), had seemed to suggest that they would not object if Britain raised revenue by regulating trade. Taking them at their word, Townshend persuaded Parliament to impose new taxes on goods imported into the colonies and to create a new board of customs commissioners to collect them and suppress smuggling. He intended to use the new revenues to pay the salaries of American governors and judges, thus freeing them from dependence on colonial assemblies. Although many merchants objected to the new enforcement procedures, opposition to the Townshend duties developed more slowly than in the case of the Stamp Act. Leaders in several colonies nonetheless decided in 1768 to reimpose the ban on importing British goods.

HOMESPUN VIRTUE

The boycott began in Boston and soon spread to the southern colonies. Reliance on American rather than British goods, on homespun clothing rather than imported finery, became a symbol of American resistance. It also reflected, as the colonists saw it, a virtuous spirit of self-sacrifice as compared to the self-indulgence and luxury many Americans were coming to associate with Britain. Women who spun and wove at home so as not to purchase British goods were hailed as Daughters of Liberty.

The idea of using homemade rather than imported goods especially appealed to Chesapeake planters, who found themselves owing

The Boston Massacre, *a 1770 engraving by Paul Revere produced less than a month after the event in which five colonists died. Although quite inaccurate in depicting what was actually a disorganized brawl between residents of Boston and British soldiers, this image became one of the most influential pieces of political propaganda in the revolutionary era, helping to stir up resentment against Great Britain.*

increasing amounts of money to British merchants. Nonimportation, wrote George Washington, reflecting Virginia planters' concern about their growing burden of debt, gave "the extravagant man" an opportunity to "retrench his expenses" by reducing the purchase of British luxuries, without having to advertise to his neighbors that he might be in financial distress. In this way, Washington continued, Virginians could "maintain the liberty which we have derived from our ancestors," while reducing their "considerable" debts. Virginia's leaders also announced a temporary ban on the importation of slaves, but smaller planters in the Piedmont region away from the coast, where the institution was expanding, ignored this restriction.

Urban artisans, who welcomed an end to competition from imported British manufactured goods, strongly supported the boycott. Philadelphia and New York merchants at first were reluctant to take part, although they eventually agreed to go along. Nonimportation threatened their livelihoods and raised the prospect of unleashing further lower-class turmoil. As had happened during the Stamp Act crisis, the streets of American cities filled with popular protests against the new duties. Extralegal local committees attempted to enforce the boycott of British goods.

THE BOSTON MASSACRE

Boston once again became the focal point of conflict. Royal troops had been stationed in the city in 1768 after rioting that followed the British seizure of the ship *Liberty* for violating trade regulations. The sloop belonged to John Hancock, one of the city's most prominent merchants. The soldiers, who competed for jobs on Boston's waterfront with the city's laborers, became more and more unpopular. On March 5, 1770, a fight between a snowball-throwing crowd of Bostonians and British troops escalated into an armed confrontation that left five Bostonians dead. One of those who fell in what came to be called the Boston Massacre was Crispus Attucks, a sailor of mixed Indian-African-white ancestry. Attucks would later be remembered as the "first martyr of the American Revolution." The commanding officer and eight soldiers were put on trial in Massachusetts. Ably defended by John Adams, who viewed lower-class crowd actions as a dangerous method of opposing British policies, seven were found not guilty, while two were convicted of manslaughter. But Paul Revere, a member of the Boston Sons of Liberty and a silversmith and engraver, helped to stir up indignation against the British army by producing a widely circulated (and quite inaccurate) print of the Boston Massacre depicting a line of British soldiers firing into an unarmed crowd.

By 1770, as merchants' profits shriveled and many members of the colonial elite found they could not do without British goods, the nonimportation movement was collapsing. The value of British imports to the colonies declined by about one-third during 1769, but then rebounded to its former level. But British merchants, who wished to remove a possible source of future interruption of trade, pressed for repeal of the Townshend duties. When the British ministry agreed, leaving in place only a tax on tea, and agreed to remove troops from Boston, American merchants quickly abandoned the boycott.

WILKES AND LIBERTY

Once again, an immediate crisis had been resolved. Nonetheless, many Americans concluded that Britain was succumbing to the same pattern of political corruption and decline of liberty that afflicted other countries. The overlap of the Townshend crisis with a controversy in Britain over the treatment of John Wilkes reinforced this sentiment. A radical journalist known for scandalous writings about the king and ministry, Wilkes had been elected to Parliament from London but was expelled from his seat. "Wilkes and Liberty" became a popular rallying cry on both sides of the Atlantic. In addition, rumors circulated in the colonies that the Anglican Church in England planned to send bishops to America. Among members

The Liberty Bowl, *made in 1768 by Paul Revere, an accomplished silversmith, for the Boston Sons of Liberty. The bowl includes the names of Massachusetts legislators who protested parliamentary taxation. Beneath a liberty cap is engraved "No. 45, Wilkes and Liberty." Issue No. 45 of John Wilkes's publication* North Briton *bitterly attacked the king and prime minister, for which Wilkes was arrested, tried, and acquitted by a London jury. Flags celebrate the Magna Carta and the Bill of Rights, central documents of British freedom, while a general warrant authorizing the searching of private homes lies torn to pieces.*

The Bostonians Paying the Excise-Man, *a 1774 engraving, shows colonists pouring tea down the throat of a tax collector, who has been covered with tar and feathers. A noose hangs menacingly from the Liberty Tree. In the background is the Boston Tea Party.*

This 1774 cartoon shows the British prime minister Lord North (holding the Boston Port Bill in his pocket) forcing the Intolerable Acts down the throat of America, portrayed as a scantily dressed Native American woman. A Frenchman and a Spaniard look on in glee, while Britannia averts her eyes.

of other Protestant denominations, the rumors—strongly denied in London—sparked fears that bishops would establish religious courts like those that had once persecuted Dissenters. The conviction that the British government had set itself on a course dangerous to liberty underpinned colonial resistance when the next crisis arose.

THE TEA ACT

The next crisis underscored how powerfully events in other parts of Britain's global empire affected the American colonies. The East India Company, a giant trading monopoly, effectively governed recently acquired British possessions in India. Numerous British merchants, bankers, and other individuals had invested heavily in its stock. A classic speculative bubble ensued, with the price of stock in the company rising sharply and then collapsing. To rescue the company and its investors, the British government decided to help it market its enormous holdings of Chinese tea in North America.

Tea, once a preserve of the wealthy, had by now become a drink consumed by all social classes in England and the colonies. To further stimulate its sales and bail out the East India Company, the British government, now headed by Frederick Lord North, offered the company a series of rebates and tax exemptions. These enabled it to dump low-priced tea on the American market, undercutting both established merchants and smugglers. Money raised through taxing imported tea would be used to help defray the costs of colonial government, thus threatening, once again, the assemblies' control over finance.

The tax on tea was not new. But many colonists insisted that to pay it on this large new body of imports would acknowledge Britain's right to tax the colonies. As tea shipments arrived, resistance developed in the major ports. On December 16, 1773, a group of colonists disguised as Indians boarded three ships at anchor in Boston Harbor and threw more than 300 chests of tea into the water. Among the participants was Samuel Adams, a cousin of John Adams who had played a leading role in organizing the Sons of Liberty and Committee of Correspondence in Boston. The loss to the East India Company was around £10,000 (the equivalent of over $4 million today).

THE INTOLERABLE ACTS

The British government, declared Lord North, must now demonstrate "whether we have, or have not, any authority in that country." Its response to the Boston Tea Party was swift and decisive. Parliament closed the port of Boston to all trade until the tea was paid for. It radically altered the Massachusetts Charter of 1691 by curtailing town meetings and authorizing the governor to appoint previously elected members of the council. Parliament also empowered military commanders to lodge soldiers in private homes. These measures, called the Coercive or Intolerable Acts by Americans, united the colonies in opposition to what was widely seen as a direct threat to their political freedom.

At almost the same time, Parliament passed the Quebec Act. This extended the southern boundary of that Canadian province to the Ohio River and granted legal toleration to the Roman Catholic Church in Canada. With an eye to the growing tensions in colonies to the south, the act sought to secure the allegiance of Quebec's Catholics by offering rights denied to their coreligionists in Britain, including practicing their faith freely and holding positions in the civil service. The act not only threw into question land claims in the Ohio country but persuaded many colonists that the government in London was conspiring to strengthen Catholicism—dreaded by most Protestants—in its American empire. Fears of religious and political tyranny mingled in the minds of many colonists. Especially in New England, the cause of liberty became the cause of God. A gathering of 1,000 residents of Farmington, Connecticut, in May 1774 adopted resolutions proclaiming that as "the sons of freedom," they would resist every attempt "to take away our liberties and properties and to enslave us forever." They accused the British ministry of being "instigated by the devil."

The Mitred Minuet, *a British cartoon from 1774, shows four Roman Catholic bishops dancing around a copy of the Quebec Act. On the left, British officials Lord Bute, Lord North, and Lord Mansfield look on, while the devil oversees the proceedings.*

THE COMING OF INDEPENDENCE

THE CONTINENTAL CONGRESS

British actions had destroyed the legitimacy of the imperial government in the eyes of many colonists. Opposition to the Intolerable Acts now spread to small towns and rural areas that had not participated actively in previous resistance. In September 1774, a convention of delegates from Massachusetts towns approved a series of resolutions (called the Suffolk Resolves for the county in which Boston is located) that urged Americans to refuse obedience to the new laws, withhold taxes, and prepare for war.

To coordinate resistance to the Intolerable Acts, a Continental Congress convened in Philadelphia that month, bringing together the most prominent political leaders of twelve mainland colonies (Georgia did not take part). From Massachusetts came the "brace of Adamses"—John and his more radical cousin Samuel. Virginia's seven delegates included George Washington, Richard Henry Lee, and the renowned orator Patrick Henry. Henry's power as a speaker came from a unique style that combined moral appeals with blunt directness. His manner, one contemporary observed, "was vehement, without transporting him beyond the power of self-command. . . . His lightning consisted in quick successive flashes." "The distinctions between Virginians, Pennsylvanians, New Yorkers, and New Englanders," Henry declared, "are no more. I am not a Virginian, but an American." In March 1775, Henry concluded a speech urging a Virginia convention to begin military preparations with a legendary credo: "Give me liberty, or give me death!"

THE ASSOCIATION

Before it adjourned at the end of October 1774, with an agreement to reconvene the following May if colonial demands had not been met, the Congress endorsed the Suffolk Resolves and adopted the Continental Association, which called for an almost complete halt to trade with Great Britain and the West Indies (at South Carolina's insistence, exports of rice to Europe were exempted). The Association also encouraged domestic manufacturing and denounced "every species of extravagance and dissipation." Congress authorized local Committees of Safety to oversee its mandates and to take action against "enemies of American liberty," including businessmen who tried to profit from the sudden scarcity of goods.

The Committees of Safety began the process of transferring effective political power from established governments whose authority derived from Great Britain to extralegal grassroots bodies reflecting the will of the people. By early 1775, some 7,000 men were serving on local committees throughout the colonies, a vast expansion of the "political nation." The committees became training grounds where small farmers, city artisans, propertyless laborers, and others who had heretofore had little role in government discussed political issues and exercised political power. In Philadelphia, the extralegal committees of the 1760s that oversaw the boycott of British goods had been composed almost entirely of prominent lawyers and merchants. But younger merchants, shopkeepers, and artisans dominated the committee elected in November 1774 to enforce the Continental Association. They were determined that resistance to British measures not be dropped as it had been in 1770. When the New York assembly refused to endorse the Association, local committees continued to enforce it anyway. In North Carolina, local committees declared the cause of Boston to be that of all the colonies and called for all the friends of "American Liberty" to unite.

THE SWEETS OF LIBERTY

By 1775, talk of liberty pervaded the colonies. The past few years had witnessed an endless parade of pamphlets with titles like *A Chariot of Liberty* and *Oration on the Beauties of Liberty* (the latter, a sermon delivered in Boston by Joseph Allen in 1772, became the most popular public address of the years before independence). Sober men spoke longingly of the "sweets of liberty." While sleeping, Americans dreamed of liberty. One anonymous essayist reported a "night vision" of the word written in the sun's rays. Commented a British emigrant who arrived in Maryland early in 1775: "They are all liberty mad."

The right to resist oppressive authority and the identification of liberty with the cause of God, so deeply ingrained by the imperial struggles of the eighteenth century, were now invoked against Britain itself, by colonists of all backgrounds. The first mass meeting in the history of Northampton County, Pennsylvania, whose population was overwhelmingly of German ancestry, gathered in 1774. By the following year, a majority of the county's adult population had joined militia associations. Many German settlers, whose close-knit communities had earlier viewed with some suspicion "the famous English liberty" as a byword for selfish individualism, now claimed all the "rights and privileges of natural-born subjects of his majesty."

As the crisis deepened, Americans increasingly based their claims not simply on the historical rights of Englishmen but on the more abstract language of natural rights and universal freedom. The First Continental Congress defended its actions by appealing to the "principles of the English constitution," the "liberties of free and natural-born subjects within the realm of England," and the "immutable law of nature." John Locke's theory of natural rights that existed prior to the establishment of government offered a powerful justification for colonial resistance. Americans, declared Thomas Jefferson in *A Summary View of the Rights of British America* (written in 1774 to instruct Virginia's delegates to the Continental Congress), were "a free people claiming their rights, as derived from the laws of nature, and not as the gift of their chief magistrate." Americans, Jefferson insisted, still revered the king. But he demanded that empire henceforth be seen as a collection of equal parts held together by loyalty to a constitutional monarch, not a system in which one part ruled over the others.

THE OUTBREAK OF WAR

By the time the Second Continental Congress convened in May 1775, war had broken out between British soldiers and armed citizens of Massachusetts. On April 19, a force of British soldiers marched from Boston toward the nearby town of Concord seeking to seize arms being stockpiled there. Riders from Boston, among them Paul Revere, warned local leaders of the troops' approach. Militiamen took up arms and tried to resist the British advance. Skirmishes between Americans and British soldiers took place at Lexington and again at Concord. By the time the British retreated to the safety of Boston, some forty-nine Americans and seventy-three members of the Royal Army lay dead.

In March 1776, James Pike, a soldier in the Massachusetts militia, carved this scene on his powder horn to commemorate the battles of Lexington and Concord. At the center stands the Liberty Tree.

What the philosopher Ralph Waldo Emerson would later call "the shot heard 'round the world" began the American War of Independence. It reverberated throughout the colonies. When news of the skirmish reached Lemuel Roberts, a poor New York farmer, he felt his "bosom glow" with the "call of liberty." Roberts set off for Massachusetts to enlist in the army. In May 1775, Ethan Allen and the Green Mountain Boys, together with militiamen from Connecticut led by Benedict Arnold, surrounded Fort Ticonderoga in New York and forced it to surrender. The following winter, Henry Knox, George Washington's commander of artillery, arranged for some of the Ticonderoga cannon to be dragged hundreds of miles to the east to reinforce the siege of Boston, where British forces were ensconced. On June 17, 1775, two months after Lexington and Concord, the British had dislodged colonial militiamen from Breed's Hill, although only at a heavy cost in casualties. (The battle came to be named after the nearby Bunker Hill.) But the arrival of American cannon and their entrenchment above the city made the British position in Boston untenable. In March 1776, the British army under the command of Sir William Howe was forced to abandon the city. Before leaving, Howe's forces cut down the original Liberty Tree.

Meanwhile, the Second Continental Congress authorized the raising of an army, printed money to pay for it, and appointed George Washington its commander. Washington, who had gained considerable fighting experience during the Seven Years' War, was not only the colonies' best-known military officer but also a prominent Virginian. John Adams, who proposed his name, recognized that having a southerner lead American forces would reinforce colonial unity. In response, Britain declared the colonies in a state of rebellion, dispatched thousands of troops, and ordered the closing of all colonial ports.

INDEPENDENCE?

By the end of 1775, the breach with Britain seemed irreparable. But many colonists shied away from the idea of independence. Pride in membership in the British empire was still strong, and many political leaders, especially in colonies that had experienced internal turmoil, feared that a complete break with the mother country might unleash further conflict. Anarchy from below, in their view, was as much a danger as tyranny from above. Many advocates of independence, one opponent warned, would find it "very agreeable" to divide the property of the rich among the poor.

Such fears affected how colonial leaders responded to the idea of independence. The elites of Massachusetts and Virginia, who felt supremely confident of their ability to retain authority at home, tended to support a break with Britain. Massachusetts had borne the brunt of the Intolerable Acts. Southern leaders not only were highly protective of their political liberty but also were outraged by a proclamation issued in November 1775 by the earl of Dunmore, the British governor and military commander in Virginia, offering freedom to any slave who escaped to his lines and bore arms for the king.

In New York and Pennsylvania, however, the diversity of the population made it difficult to work out a consensus on how far to go in resisting British measures. Here opposition to previous British laws had unleashed demands by small farmers and urban artisans for a greater voice in political affairs. As a result, many established leaders drew back from further resistance. Joseph Galloway, a Pennsylvania leader and delegate to the Second Continental Congress who worked to devise a compromise between British and colonial positions, warned that independence would be accompanied by constant disputes within America. He even predicted a war between the northern and southern colonies. Americans, Galloway declared, could only enjoy "true liberty"—self-government and security for their persons and property—by remaining within the empire.

COMMON SENSE ✗ *Memorized Him*

As 1776 dawned, America presented the unusual spectacle of colonists at war against the British empire but still pleading for their rights within it. Even as fighting raged, Congress in July 1775 had addressed the Olive Branch Petition to George III, reaffirming Americans' loyalty to the crown and hoping for a "permanent reconciliation." Ironically, it was a recent emigrant from England, not a colonist from a family long-established on American soil, who grasped the inner logic of the situation and offered a vision of the broad significance of American independence. An English craftsman and minor government official, Thomas Paine had emigrated to Philadelphia late in 1774. He quickly became associated with a group of advocates of the American cause, including John Adams and Dr. Benjamin Rush, a leading Philadelphia physician. It was Rush who suggested to Paine that he write a pamphlet supporting American independence.

Its author listed only as "an Englishman," *Common Sense* appeared in January 1776. The pamphlet began not with a recital of colonial grievances but with an attack on the "so much boasted Constitution of England" and the principles of hereditary rule and monarchical government. Rather than being the most perfect system of government in the world, Paine wrote, the English monarchy was headed by "the royal brute of England," and the English constitution was composed in large part of "the base remains of two ancient tyrannies . . . monarchical tyranny in the person of the king [and] aristocratical tyranny in the persons of the peers." "Of more worth is one honest man to society, and in the sight of God," he continued, "than all the crowned ruffians that ever lived." Far preferable than monarchy would be a democratic system based on frequent elections, with citizens' rights protected by a written constitution.

Turning to independence, Paine drew on the colonists' experiences to make his case. "There is something absurd," he wrote, "in supposing a Continent to be perpetually governed by an island." Within the British empire, America's prospects were limited; liberated from the Navigation Acts and trading freely with the entire world, its "material eminence" was certain. Paine tied the economic hopes of the new nation to the idea of commercial freedom. With independence, moreover, the colonies could for the first time insulate themselves from involvement in the endless imperial wars of Europe. Britain had "dragged" its American colonies into conflicts with countries like Spain and France, which "never were . . . our enemies as *Americans*, but as our being the subjects of Great Britain." Membership in the British empire, Paine insisted, was a burden to the colonies, not a benefit.

Toward the close of the pamphlet, Paine moved beyond practical considerations to outline a breathtaking vision of the historical importance of the American Revolution. "The cause of America," he proclaimed in stirring language, "is in great measure, the cause of all mankind." The new nation would become the home of freedom, "an asylum for mankind."

Thomas Paine, advocate of American independence.

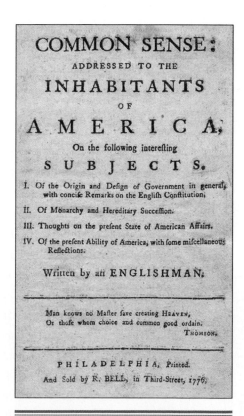

The cover of Common Sense, *Thomas Paine's influential pamphlet denouncing the idea of hereditary rule and calling for American independence.*

VOICES OF FREEDOM

From Thomas Paine, Common Sense (1776)

A recent emigrant from England, Thomas Paine in January 1776 published *Common Sense*, a highly influential pamphlet that in stirring language made the case for American independence.

In the following pages I offer nothing more than simple facts, plain arguments, and common sense....

Male and female are the distinctions of nature, good and bad the distinctions of heaven; but how a race of men came into the world so exalted above the rest, and distinguished like some new species, is worth enquiring into, and whether they are the means of happiness or of misery to mankind.... One of the strongest *natural* proofs of the folly of hereditary right in kings, is, that nature disapproves it, otherwise she would not so frequently turn it into ridicule, by giving mankind an *ass for a lion*....

The sun never shined on a cause of greater worth. 'Tis not the affair of a city, a country, a province, or a kingdom, but of a continent—of at least one eighth part of the habitable globe. 'Tis not the concern of a day, a year, or an age; posterity are virtually involved in the context, and will be more or less affected, even to the end of time, by the proceedings now. Now is the seed time of continental union, faith and honor....

I challenge the warmest advocate for reconciliation to show a single advantage that this continent can reap by being connected with Great Britain.... But the injuries and disadvantages which we sustain by that connection, are without number.... Any submission to, or dependence on, Great Britain, tends directly to involve this Continent in European wars and quarrels, and set us at variance with nations who would otherwise seek our friendship, and against whom we have neither anger nor complaint.

O ye that love mankind! Ye that dare oppose, not only the tyranny, but the tyrant, stand forth! Every spot of the old world is overrun with oppression. Freedom hath been hunted round the globe. Asia, and Africa, have long expelled her. Europe regards her like a stranger, and England hath given her warning to depart. O! Receive the fugitive, and prepare in time an asylum for mankind.

FROM JAMES CHALMERS,
Plain Truth, Addressed to the Inhabitants of America (1776)

Common Sense inspired a wide-ranging debate about whether American freedom would be more secure inside or outside the British empire. James Chalmers, a Maryland plantation owner, made the case for the Loyalists, as those who opposed American independence were called.

If indignant at the doctrine contained in the pamphlet entitled Common Sense I have expressed myself in the following observations with some ardor . . . [it is because] I adore my country. Passionately devoted to true liberty, I glow with the purest flame of patriotism [and have an] abhorrence of Independency, which if effected, would inevitably plunge our once preeminently envied country into ruin, horror, and desolation. . . .

Can a reasonable being for a moment believe that Great Britain, whose political existence depends on our constitutional obedience, who but yesterday made such prodigious efforts to save us from France, will not exert herself as powerfully to preserve us from our frantic schemes of Independency? . . . We remember with unfeigned gratitude, the many benefits derived through our connections with Great Britain, by whom but yesterday we were emancipated from slavery and death. . . . We venerate the constitution, which with all its imperfections (too often exaggerated) we apprehend almost approaches as near to perfection as human kind can bear. . . .

His scheme of independency would soon, very soon give way to a government imposed on us, by some Cromwell of our armies. . . . A failure of commerce [would] preclude the numerous tribe of planters, farmers and others, from paying their debts. . . . A war will ensue between the creditors and their debtors, which will eventually end in a general abolition of debts.

Volumes were insufficient to describe the horror, misery and desolation, awaiting the people at large in the form of American independence. In short, I affirm that it would be most excellent policy in those who wish for True Liberty to submit by an advantageous reconciliation to the authority of Great Britain. . . . Independence and Slavery are synonymous terms.

QUESTIONS

1. What does Paine see as the global significance of the American struggle for independence?

2. Why does Chalmers equate independence with slavery?

3. How does the language used by the two writers differ, and what does this tell us about their views of politics?

PAINE'S IMPACT

Most of Paine's ideas were not original. What made *Common Sense* unique was his mode of expressing them and the audience he addressed. Previous political writings had generally been directed toward the educated elite. "When I mention the public," declared John Randolph of Virginia in 1774, "I mean to include the rational part of it. The ignorant vulgar are unfit . . . to manage the reins of government." Just as evangelical ministers had shattered the trained clergy's monopoly on religious preaching, Paine pioneered a new style of political writing, one designed to expand dramatically the public sphere where political discussion took place. He wrote clearly and directly, and he avoided the complex language and Latin phrases common in pamphlets aimed at educated readers. *Common Sense* quickly became one of the most successful and influential pamphlets in the history of political writing, selling, by Paine's estimate, some 150,000 copies. Paine directed that his share of the profits be used to buy supplies for the Continental Army.

In February 1776, the Massachusetts political leader Joseph Hawley read *Common Sense* and remarked, "Every sentiment has sunk into my well prepared heart." The hearts of Hawley and thousands of other Americans had been prepared for Paine's arguments by the extended conflict over Britain's right to tax the colonies, the outbreak of war in 1775, and the growing conviction that Britain was a corrupt society where liberty was diminishing. The intensification of fighting in the winter of 1775–1776, when Americans unsuccessfully invaded Canada while the British burned Falmouth (now Portland), Maine, and bombarded Norfolk, Virginia, gave added weight to the movement for independence. In the spring of 1776, scores of American communities adopted resolutions calling for a separation from Britain. Only six months elapsed between the appearance of *Common Sense* and the decision by the Second Continental Congress to sever the colonies' ties with Great Britain.

THE DECLARATION OF INDEPENDENCE

On July 2, 1776, the Congress formally declared the United States an independent nation. Two days later, it approved the Declaration of Independence, written by Thomas Jefferson and revised by the Congress before approval (See the Appendix for the full text). Most of the Declaration consists of a lengthy list of grievances directed against King George III, ranging from quartering troops in colonial homes to imposing taxes without the colonists' consent. Britain's aim, it declared, was to establish "absolute tyranny" over the colonies. One clause in Jefferson's draft, which condemned the inhumanity of the slave trade and criticized the king for overturning colonial laws that sought to restrict the importation of slaves, was deleted by the Congress at the insistence of Georgia and South Carolina.

The Declaration's enduring impact came not from the complaints against George III but from Jefferson's preamble, especially the second paragraph, which begins, "We hold these truths to be self-evident, that all men are created equal, that they are endowed by their Creator with certain unalienable Rights, that among these are Life, Liberty, and the pursuit of Happiness." By "unalienable rights," Jefferson meant rights so basic, so rooted in human nature itself (or in what John Locke had called the state of nature), that no government could take them away.

Jefferson then went on to justify the breach with Britain. Government, he wrote, derives its powers from "the consent of the governed." When a government threatens its subjects' natural rights, the people have the authority "to alter or to abolish it." The Declaration of Independence is ultimately an assertion of the right of revolution. Its purpose is not simply to put forward a theory of government, but to justify rebellion. For more than two centuries, the Declaration has remained an inspiration to generations of Americans denied the enjoyment of their natural rights, as well as to colonial peoples throughout the world seeking independence and self-government. It quickly appeared in French and German translations, although not, at first, in Spanish, since the government feared it would inspire dangerous ideas among the peoples of Spain's American empire.

An early draft, with corrections, of the Declaration of Independence, in Thomas Jefferson's handwriting. Note how the elimination of unnecessary words added to the document's power—"all men are created equal and independent" became "all men are created equal," and "inherent and inalienable" rights became "inalienable" (in the final version, this would be changed to "unalienable").

THE DECLARATION AND AMERICAN FREEDOM

The Declaration of Independence changed forever the meaning of American freedom. It completed the shift from the rights of Englishmen to the rights of mankind as the object of American independence. In Jefferson's language, "the Laws of Nature and of Nature's God," not the British constitution or the heritage of the freeborn Englishman, justified independence. No longer a set of specific rights, no longer a privilege to be enjoyed by a corporate body or people in certain social circumstances, liberty had become a universal entitlement.

Jefferson's argument—natural rights, the right to resist arbitrary authority, etc.—drew on the writings of John Locke, who, as explained in the previous chapter, saw government as resting on a "social contract," violation of which destroyed the legitimacy of authority. But when Jefferson substituted the "pursuit of happiness" for property in the familiar Lockean triad that opens the Declaration, he tied the new nation's star to an open-ended, democratic process whereby individuals develop their own potential and seek to realize their own life goals. Individual self-fulfillment, unimpeded by government, would become a central element of American freedom. Tradition would no longer rule the present, and Americans could shape their society as they saw fit.

America as a symbol of liberty, a 1775 engraving from the cover of the Pennsylvania Magazine, *edited by Thomas Paine soon after his arrival in America. The shield displays the colony's coat of arms. The female figure holding a liberty cap is surrounded by weaponry of the patriotic struggle, including a cartridge box marked "liberty," hanging from a tree (right).*

AN ASYLUM FOR MANKIND

A distinctive definition of nationality resting on American freedom was born in the Revolution. From the beginning, the idea of "American exceptionalism"—the belief that the United States has a special mission to serve as a refuge from tyranny, a symbol of freedom, and a model for the rest of the world—has occupied a central place in American nationalism. The new nation declared itself, in the words of Virginia leader James Madison, the "workshop of liberty to the Civilized World." Paine's remark in *Common Sense*, "we have it in our power to begin the world over again," and his description of the new nation as an "asylum for mankind," expressed a sense that the Revolution was an event of global historical importance. Countless sermons, political tracts, and newspaper articles of the time repeated this idea. Unburdened by the institutions—monarchy, aristocracy, hereditary privilege—that oppressed the peoples of the Old World, America and America alone was the place where the principle of universal freedom could take root. This was why Jefferson addressed the Declaration to "the opinions of mankind," not just the colonists themselves or Great Britain.

First to add his name to the Declaration of Independence was the Massachusetts merchant John Hancock, with a signature so large, he declared, according to legend, that King George III could read it without his spectacles.

SECURING INDEPENDENCE

THE BALANCE OF POWER

Declaring Americans independent was one thing; winning independence another. The newly created American army confronted the greatest military power on earth. Viewing the Americans as traitors, Britain resolved to crush the rebellion. On the surface, the balance of power seemed heavily weighted in Britain's favor. It had a well-trained army (supplemented by hired soldiers from German states like Hesse), the world's most powerful navy, and experienced military commanders. The Americans had to rely on local militias and an inadequately equipped Continental army. Washington himself felt that militiamen were too "accustomed to unbounded freedom" to accept the "proper degree of subordination" necessary in soldiers. Moreover, many Americans were not enthusiastic about independence, and some actively supported the British.

On the other hand, many American soldiers did not lack military experience, having fought in the Seven Years' War or undergone intensive mili-

A French engraving depicts New Yorkers tearing down the statue of King George III in July 1776, after the approval of the Declaration of Independence. The statue was later melted down to make bullets for the Continental army.

tia training in the early 1770s. They were fighting on their own soil for a cause that inspired devotion and sacrifice. During the eight years of war from 1775 to 1783, some 200,000 men bore arms in the American army (whose soldiers were volunteers) and militias (where service was required of every able-bodied man unless he provided a substitute). As the war progressed, enlistment waned among propertied Americans and the Continental army increasingly drew on young men with limited economic prospects—landless sons of farmers, indentured servants, laborers, and African-Americans. The patriots suffered dearly for the cause. Of the colonies' free white male population aged sixteen to forty-five, one in twenty died in the War of Independence, the equivalent of nearly 3 million deaths in today's population. But so long as the Americans maintained an army in the field, the idea of independence remained alive no matter how much territory the British occupied.

Despite British power, to conquer the thirteen colonies would be an enormous and expensive task, and it was not at all certain that the public at home wished to pay the additional taxes that a lengthy war would require. The British, moreover, made a string of serious mistakes. Their soldiers sometimes plundered colonists' homes and committed sexual assaults against civilian women, alienating far more Americans than they intimidated. Most notably, from the outset the British misjudged the degree of support for independence among the American population, as well as the capacity of American citizen-soldiers. "These people," admitted the British general Thomas Gage, "show a spirit and conduct against us that they never showed against the French [in the Seven Years'

The Female Combatants, a 1776 cartoon depicting Great Britain and the colonies as women engaged in a fistfight. Portrayed as a lady of fashion, Britain demands obedience, while America, as an Indian princess, calls for liberty.

War], and everybody has judged them from their former appearance and behavior, which has led many into great mistakes." Moreover, European rivals, notably France, welcomed the prospect of a British defeat. If the Americans could forge an alliance with France, a world power second only to Britain, it would go a long way toward equalizing the balance of forces.

BLACKS IN THE REVOLUTION

At the war's outset, George Washington refused to accept black recruits. But he changed his mind after Lord Dunmore's 1775 proclamation, mentioned above, which offered freedom to slaves who joined the British cause. Some 5,000 blacks enlisted in state militias and the Continental army and navy. Since individuals drafted into the militia were allowed to provide a substitute, slaves suddenly gained considerable bargaining power. Not a few acquired their freedom by agreeing to serve in place of an owner or his son. In 1778, Rhode Island, with a higher proportion of slaves in its population than any other New England state, formed a black regiment and promised freedom to slaves who enlisted, while compensating the owners for their loss of property. Blacks who fought under George Washington and in other state militias did so in racially integrated companies (although invariably under white officers). They were the last black American soldiers to do so officially until the Korean War (except for the few black and white soldiers who fought alongside each other in irregular units at the end of World War II).

Except for South Carolina and Georgia, the southern colonies also enrolled free blacks and slaves to fight. They were not explicitly promised freedom, but many received it individually after the war ended. And in 1783, the Virginia legislature emancipated slaves who had "contributed towards the establishment of American liberty and independence" by serving in the army.

Fighting on the side of the British also offered opportunities for freedom. Before his forces were expelled from Virginia, 800 or more slaves had escaped from their owners to join Lord Dunmore's Ethiopian Regiment, wearing uniforms that bore the motto "Liberty to Slaves." During the war, blacks fought with the British in campaigns in New York, New Jersey, and South Carolina. Other escaped slaves served the Royal Army as spies, guided their troops through swamps, and worked as military cooks, laundresses, and construction workers. George Washington himself saw seventeen of his slaves flee to the British, some of whom signed up to fight the colonists. "There is not a man of them, but would leave us, if they believed they could make their escape," his cousin Lund Washington reported. "Liberty is sweet."

American Foot Soldiers, Yorktown Campaign, a 1781 watercolor by a French officer, includes a black soldier from the First Rhode Island Regiment, an all-black unit of 250 men.

Triumphant Entry of the Royal Troops into New York, *an engraving showing the army of Sir William Howe occupying the city in 1776. New York City would remain in British hands for the duration of the War of Independence.*

THE FIRST YEARS OF THE WAR

Had the British commander, Sir William Howe, prosecuted the war more vigorously at the outset, he might have nipped the rebellion in the bud by destroying Washington's army. But while he suffered numerous defeats in the first years of the war, Washington generally avoided direct confrontations with the British and managed to keep his army intact. Having abandoned Boston, Howe attacked New York City in the summer of 1776. Washington's army had likewise moved from Massachusetts to Brooklyn to defend the city. Howe pushed American forces back and almost cut off Washington's retreat across the East River. Washington managed to escape to Manhattan and then north to Peekskill, where he crossed the Hudson River to New Jersey. But the 3,000 men he had left behind at Fort Washington on Manhattan Island were captured by Howe.

Howe pursued the American army but never managed to inflict a decisive defeat. Demoralized by successive failures, however, many American soldiers simply went home. Once 28,000 men, Washington's army dwindled to fewer than 3,000. Indeed, Washington feared that without a decisive victory, it would melt away entirely. To restore morale and regain the initiative, he launched successful surprise attacks on Hessian soldiers at Trenton, New Jersey, on December 26, 1776, and on a British force at Princeton on January 3, 1777. Shortly before crossing the Delaware River to attack the Hessians, Washington had Thomas Paine's

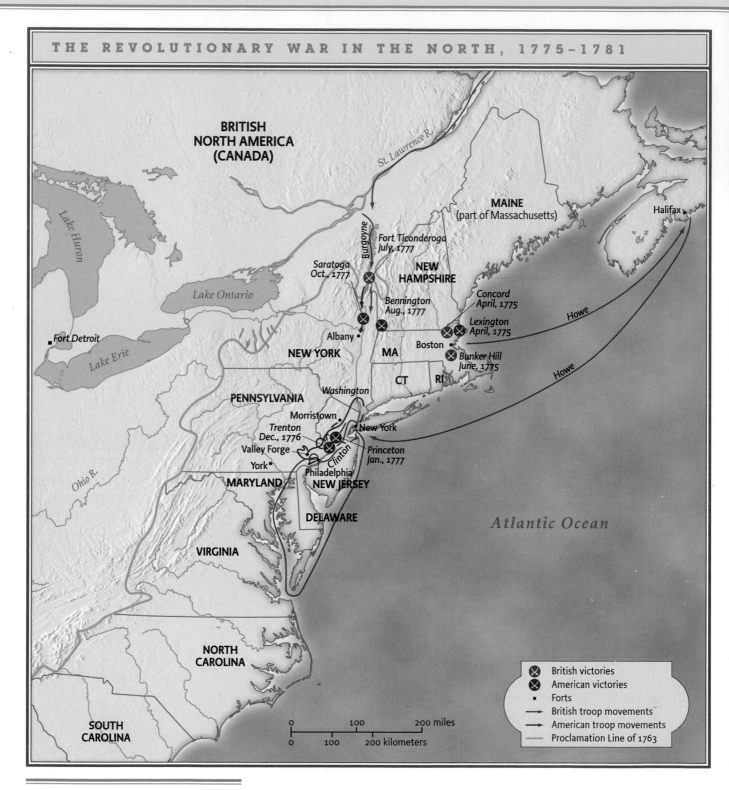

THE REVOLUTIONARY WAR IN THE NORTH, 1775–1781

BRITISH NORTH AMERICA (CANADA)

St. Lawrence R.

Lake Huron

Lake Ontario

Fort Detroit

Lake Erie

MAINE
(part of Massachusetts)

Halifax

Burgoyne

Fort Ticonderoga
July, 1777

Saratoga
Oct., 1777

NEW HAMPSHIRE

Concord
April, 1775

Bennington
Aug., 1777

Lexington
April, 1775

Howe

Albany

NEW YORK

MA

Boston

Howe

Bunker Hill
June, 1775

CT   **RI**

Washington

PENNSYLVANIA

Morristown

New York

Trenton
Dec., 1776

Valley Forge

Clinton

Princeton
Jan., 1777

Ohio R.

York

Philadelphia

MARYLAND

NEW JERSEY

DELAWARE

Atlantic Ocean

VIRGINIA

NORTH CAROLINA

SOUTH CAROLINA

| 0 | 100 | 200 miles |
| 0 | 100 | 200 kilometers |

Legend:
- British victories
- American victories
- Forts
- British troop movements
- American troop movements
- Proclamation Line of 1763

Key battles in the North during the War of Independence included Lexington and Concord, which began the armed conflict; the campaign in New York and New Jersey; and Saratoga, sometimes called the turning point of the war.

inspiring essay *The American Crisis* read to his troops. "These are the times that try men's souls," Paine wrote. "The summer soldier and the sunshine patriot will, in this crisis, shrink from the service of their country; but he that stands it *now*, deserves the love and thanks of man and woman."

THE BATTLE OF SARATOGA

In the summer of 1777, a second British army, led by General John Burgoyne, advanced south from Canada hoping to link up with Howe and isolate New England. But in July, Howe instead moved his forces from New York City to attack Philadelphia. In September, Congress fled to Lancaster, in central Pennsylvania, and Howe occupied the City of Brotherly Love. Not having been informed of Burgoyne's plans, Howe had unintentionally abandoned him. American forces blocked Burgoyne's way, surrounded his army, and on October 17, 1777, forced him to surrender at Saratoga. The victory provided a significant boost to American morale.

During the winter of 1777–1778, the British army, now commanded by Sir Henry Clinton, was quartered in Philadelphia. (In the Revolution, as in most eighteenth-century wars, fighting came to a halt during the winter.) British officers took part in an elegant social life complete with balls and parties. Most notable was the great *Meschianza*, an extravaganza that included a regatta, a procession of medieval knights, and a jousting tournament. Meanwhile, Washington's army remained encamped at Valley Forge, where they suffered terribly from the frigid weather.

But Saratoga helped to persuade the French that American victory was possible. In 1778, American diplomats led by Benjamin Franklin concluded a Treaty of Amity and Commerce in which France recognized the United States and agreed to supply military assistance. Still smarting from their defeat in the Seven Years' War, the French hoped to weaken Britain, their main European rival, and perhaps regain some of their lost influence and territory in the Western Hemisphere. Soon afterwards, Spain also joined the war on the American side. French assistance would play a decisive part in the war's end. At the outset, however, the French fleet showed more interest in attacking British outposts in the West Indies than directly aiding the Americans. And the Spanish confined themselves to regaining control of Florida, which they had lost to the British in the Seven Years' War. Nonetheless, French and Spanish entry transformed the War for Independence into a global conflict. By putting the British on the defensive in places ranging from Gibraltar to the West Indies, it greatly complicated their military prospects.

THE WAR IN THE SOUTH

In 1778, the focus of the war shifted to the South. Here the British hoped to exploit the social tensions between backcountry farmers and wealthy planters that had surfaced in the Regulator movements, to enlist the support of the numerous colonists in the region who remained loyal to the crown, and to disrupt the economy by encouraging slaves to escape. In December 1778, British forces occupied Savannah, Georgia. In May 1780, Clinton captured Charleston, South Carolina, and with it an American army of 5,000 men.

The year 1780 was arguably the low point of the struggle for independence. Congress was essentially bankrupt, and the army went months without being paid. The British seemed successful in playing upon social conflicts within the colonies, as thousands of southern Loyalists joined up

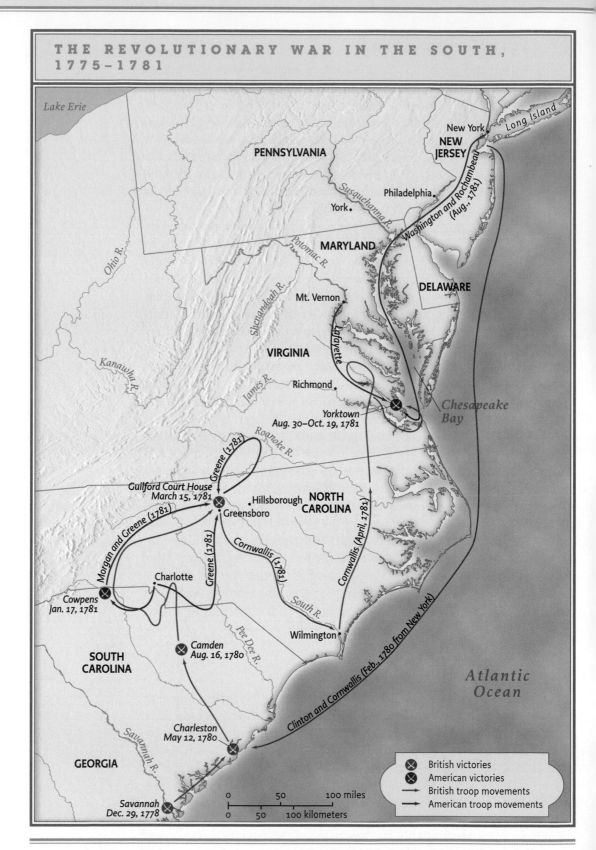

THE REVOLUTIONARY WAR IN THE SOUTH, 1775–1781

After 1777, the focus of the War of Independence shifted to the South, where it culminated in 1781 with the British defeat at Yorktown.

with British forces (fourteen regiments from Savannah alone) and tens of thousands of slaves sought freedom by fleeing to British lines. In August, Lord Charles Cornwallis routed an American army at Camden, South Carolina. The following month one of Washington's ablest commanders, Benedict Arnold, defected and almost succeeded in turning over to the British the important fort at West Point on the Hudson River. On January 1, 1781, 1,500 disgruntled Pennsylvania soldiers stationed near Morristown, New Jersey, killed three officers and marched toward Philadelphia, where Congress was meeting. Their mutiny ended when the soldiers were promised discharges or bounties for reenlistment. Harsher treatment awaited a group of New Jersey soldiers who also mutinied. On Washington's orders, two of their leaders were executed.

But the British failed to turn these advantages into victory. British commanders were unable to consolidate their hold on the South. Wherever their forces went, American militias harassed them. Hit-and-run attacks by militiamen under Francis Marion, called the "swamp fox" because his men emerged from hiding places in swamps to strike swiftly and then disappear, eroded the British position in South Carolina. A bloody civil war engulfed North and South Carolina and Georgia, with patriot and Loyalist militias inflicting retribution on each other and plundering the farms of their opponents' supporters. The brutal treatment of civilians by British forces under Colonel Banastre Tarleton persuaded many Americans to join the patriot cause.

VICTORY AT LAST

In January 1781, American forces under Daniel Morgan dealt a crushing defeat to Tarleton at Cowpens, South Carolina. Two months later, at Guilford Courthouse, North Carolina, General Nathanael Greene, while conducting a campaign of strategic retreats, inflicted heavy losses on Lord Charles Cornwallis, the British commander in the South. Cornwallis moved into Virginia and encamped at Yorktown, located on a peninsula

A 1781 French engraving showing the surrender of Lord Charles Cornwallis's army at Yorktown, ending the War of Independence. The French fleet sits just offshore.

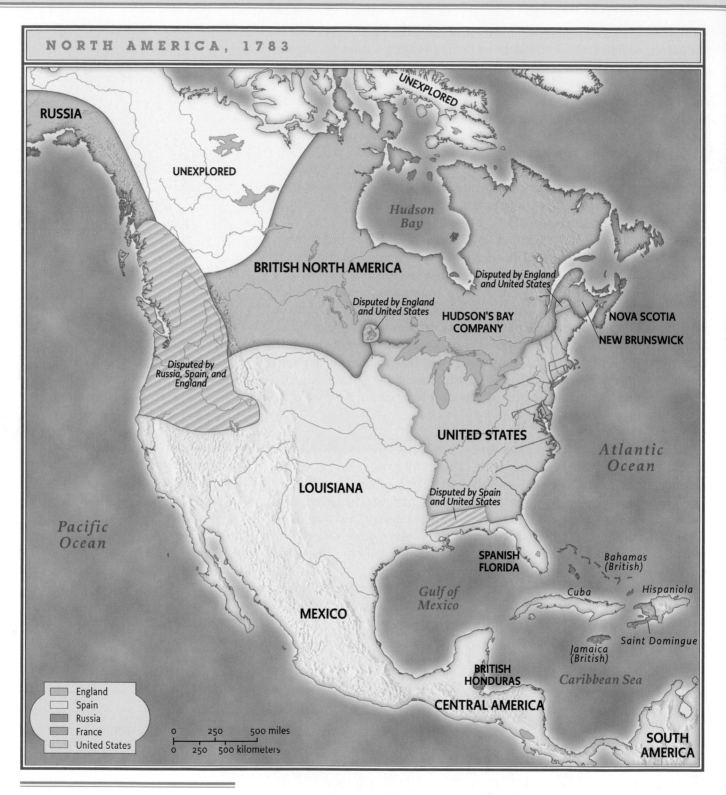

NORTH AMERICA, 1783

RUSSIA

UNEXPLORED

UNEXPLORED

Hudson Bay

BRITISH NORTH AMERICA

Disputed by England and United States

Disputed by England and United States

HUDSON'S BAY COMPANY

NOVA SCOTIA

NEW BRUNSWICK

Disputed by Russia, Spain, and England

UNITED STATES

Atlantic Ocean

LOUISIANA

Disputed by Spain and United States

Pacific Ocean

SPANISH FLORIDA

Bahamas (British)

Cuba

Hispaniola

MEXICO

Gulf of Mexico

Saint Domingue

Jamaica (British)

BRITISH HONDURAS

Caribbean Sea

CENTRAL AMERICA

SOUTH AMERICA

England
Spain
Russia
France
United States

0   250   500 miles
0   250   500 kilometers

The newly independent United States occupied only a small part of the North American continent in 1783.

that juts into Chesapeake Bay. Brilliantly recognizing the opportunity to surround Cornwallis, Washington rushed his forces, augmented by French troops under the Marquis de Lafayette, to block a British escape by land. Meanwhile, a French fleet controlled the mouth of the Chesapeake, preventing supplies and reinforcements from reaching Cornwallis's army.

Imperial rivalries had helped to create the American colonies. Now, the rivalry of European empires helped to secure American independence. Taking land and sea forces together, more Frenchmen than Americans participated in the decisive Yorktown campaign. On October 18, 1781, Cornwallis surrendered his army of 8,000 men. When the news reached London, public support for the war evaporated and peace negotiations soon began.

Two years later, in September 1783, American and British negotiators concluded the Treaty of Paris. The American delegation—John Adams, Benjamin Franklin, and John Jay—achieved one of the greatest diplomatic triumphs in the country's history. They not only won recognition of American independence but also gained control of the entire region between Canada and Florida east of the Mississippi River, and the right of Americans to fish in Atlantic waters off of Canada (a matter of considerable importance to New Englanders). At British insistence, the Americans agreed that colonists who had remained loyal to the mother country would not suffer persecution and that Loyalists' property that had been seized by local and state governments would be restored.

The Apotheosis of Benjamin Franklin and George Washington, *a printed cotton fabric produced in Great Britain soon after the end of the American War of Independence and used as a bedcover. Franklin, accompanied by a goddess of liberty with her liberty cap, carries a banner reading, "where liberty dwells there is my country," while angels display a map of the United States.*

Until independence, the thirteen colonies had formed parts of Britain's American empire, along with Canada and the West Indies. But Canada rebuffed repeated calls to join the War of Independence, and leaders of the West Indies, fearful of slave uprisings, also remained loyal to the crown. With the Treaty of Paris, the United States of America became the Western Hemisphere's first independent nation. Its boundaries reflected not so much the long-standing unity of a geographical region, but the specific circumstances of its birth.

SUGGESTED READING

Bailyn, Bernard. *The Ideological Origins of the American Revolution* (1967). A classic study of the ideas that shaped the movement for independence.

Bloch, Ruth. *Visionary Republic: Millennial Themes in American Thought, 1756–1800* (1988). Explores how the religious vision of a more perfect society contributed to the coming of the Revolution.

Breen, T. H. *Marketplace of Revolution: How Consumer Politics Shaped American Independence* (2004). An examination of how the colonists' very dependence on British consumer goods led them to resent interference with trade.

Countryman, Edward. *The American Revolution* (rev. ed., 2002). A brief summary of the Revolution's causes, conduct, and consequences.

Fischer, David H. *Washington's Crossing* (2004). A detailed study of Washington's 1776 victory at Trenton and of the nature of his military leadership.

Foner, Eric. *Tom Paine and Revolutionary America* (1976). Examines the ideas of the era's greatest pamphleteer of revolution and how they contributed to the struggle for independence.

Gross, Robert. *The Minutemen and Their World* (1976). A social history of the militia of Concord, Massachusetts, where the War of Independence began.

Maier, Pauline. *American Scripture: Making the Declaration of Independence* (1997). The most detailed study of the writing of the Declaration and of previous calls for independence within the colonies.

Middlekauff, Robert. *The Glorious Cause: The American Revolution, 1763–1789* (1982). A comprehensive history of the Revolution.

Morgan, Edmund S., and Helen M. Morgan. *The Stamp Act Crisis: Prologue to Revolution* (1953). An influential study of the first crisis over British taxation of the colonies.

Nash, Gary. *The Urban Crucible: Social Change, Political Consciousness, and the Origins of the American Revolution* (1979). Explores how the social history of American cities contributed to the coming of the Revolution.

Raphael, Ray. *The First American Revolution: Before Lexington and Concord* (2002). A study of grassroots resistance to British measures before the outbreak of war.

Royster, Charles. *A Revolutionary People at War: The Continental Army and American Character* (1979). A social history of the army and the impact of military service on American soldiers.

Shy, John. *A People Numerous and Armed: Reflections on the Military Struggle for American Independence* (1976). A study of military strategy and the conduct of the war.

Withington, Anne. *Toward a More Perfect Union: Virtue and the Formation of American Republics* (1991). Considers how the boycotts of British goods promoted the idea of America's superior virtue, contributing to the movement for independence.

REVIEW QUESTIONS

1. Explain what "homespun virtue" meant and how it set the colonists apart from the British.

2. Patrick Henry proclaimed that he was not a Virginian, but rather an American. What unified the colonists and what divided them at the time of the Revolution?

3. Discuss the ramifications of using slaves in the British and Continental Armies. Why did the British authorize the use of slaves? Why did the Americans? How did the slaves benefit?

4. Why did the colonists increasingly believe that British rule threatened their liberty?

5. Describe how *Common Sense* and the Declaration of Independence reflected the idea put forth by philosophers such as John Locke that liberty was a natural right.

KEY TERMS

Sugar Act (p. 180)

Daughters of Liberty (p. 185)

Boston Massacre (p. 186)

tea imports (p. 188)

Quebec Act (p. 189)

Lord Dunmore's Proclamation (p. 192)

Declaration of Independence (p. 196)

Valley Forge (p. 203)

REVIEW TABLE

British Acts Imposed on the Colonies

Act	Date	Function
Proclamation of 1763	1763	To halve colonial settlement west of the Appalachian mountains and prevent warfare with Indians
Sugar Act	1764	To collect revenue by reducing the tax on molasses and discouraging smuggling
Stamp Act	1765	To directly tax all printed materials
Declaratory Act	1766	To declare that the British Parliament made laws for its colonies
Townshend Act	1767	To tax imported goods such as paper, glass, paint, lead, and tea
Tea Act	1773	To tax tea as part of an effort to help the failing East India Company
Intolerable Acts	1774	To close the port of Boston and restrict the colony's political autonomy
Quebec Act	1774	To grant religious toleration for Catholics in Canada

Chapter 6

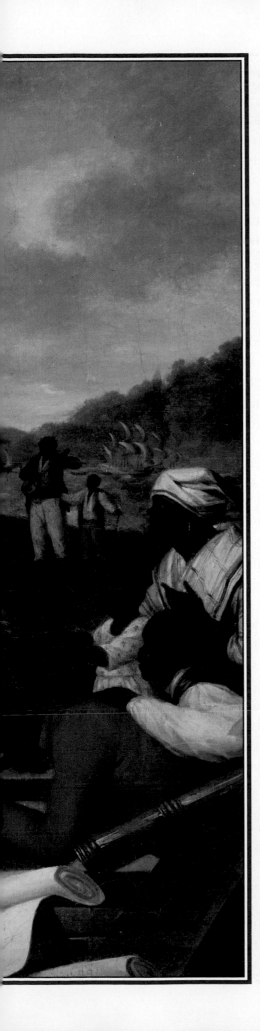

The Revolution Within

Liberty Displaying the Arts and Sciences. *This 1792 painting by Samuel Jennings, commissioned by the Library Company of Philadelphia, is one of the few visual images of the early republic explicitly to link slavery with tyranny and liberty with abolition. The female figure of Liberty offers books to newly freed slaves; beneath her left foot lies a broken chain.*

- How did equality become a stronger component of American freedom after the Revolution?

- How did religious liberty expand after the Revolution?

- How did economic freedom change after the Revolution?

- How did the Revolution bring a loss of freedom for Indians?

- What was the impact of the Revolution on slavery?

- How did the Revolution affect the status of women?

Born in Massachusetts in 1744, Abigail Adams became one of the revolutionary era's most articulate and influential women. At a time when educational opportunities for girls were extremely limited, she taught herself by reading books in the library of her father, a Congregational minister. In 1764, she married John Adams, a young lawyer about to emerge as a leading advocate of resistance to British taxation and, eventually, of American independence. During the War of Independence, with her husband away in Philadelphia and Europe serving the American cause, she stayed behind at their Massachusetts home, raising their four children and managing the family's farm. The letters they exchanged form one of the most remarkable correspondences in American history. She addressed John as "Dear friend," and signed her letters "Portia"—after Brutus's devoted wife in Shakespeare's play *Julius Caesar*. Though denied an official role in politics, Abigail Adams was a keen observer of public affairs. She kept her husband informed of events in Massachusetts and offered opinions on political matters. Later, when Adams served as president, he relied on her advice more than on members of his cabinet.

In March 1776, a few months before the Second Continental Congress declared American independence, Abigail Adams wrote her best-known letter to her husband. She began by commenting indirectly on the evils of slavery. How strong, she wondered, could the "passion for Liberty" be among those "accustomed to deprive their fellow citizens of theirs." She went on to urge Congress, when it drew up a "Code of Laws" for the new republic, to "remember the ladies." All men, she warned, "would be tyrants if they could." Women, she playfully suggested, "will not hold ourselves bound by any laws in which we have no voice or representation."

It was the leaders of colonial society who initiated resistance to British taxation. But, as Abigail Adams's letter illustrates, the struggle for American liberty emboldened other colonists to demand more liberty for themselves. All revolutions enlarge the public sphere, inspiring previously marginalized groups to express their own dreams of freedom. At a time when so many Americans—slaves, indentured servants, women, Indians, apprentices, propertyless men—were denied full freedom, the struggle against Britain threw into question many forms of authority and inequality.

Abigail Adams did not believe in female equality in a modern sense. She accepted the prevailing belief that a woman's primary responsibility was to her family. But she resented the "absolute power" husbands exercised over their wives. "Put it out of the power of husbands," she wrote, "to use us as they will"—a discreet reference to men's legal control over the bodies of their wives, and their right to inflict physical punishment on them. Her letter is widely remembered today. Less familiar is John Adams's response, which illuminated how the Revolution had unleashed challenges to all sorts of inherited ideas of deference and authority: "We have been told that our struggle has loosened the bands of government everywhere; that children and apprentices were disobedient; that schools and colleges were grown turbulent; that Indians slighted their guardians, and negroes grew insolent to their masters." To John Adams, this upheaval, including his wife's claim to greater freedom, was an affront to the natural order of things. To others, it formed the essence of the American Revolution.

Abigail Adams, *a portrait by Gilbert Stuart, painted over several years beginning in 1800. Stuart told a friend that as a young woman, Adams must have been a "perfect Venus."*

DEMOCRATIZING FREEDOM

THE DREAM OF EQUALITY

The American Revolution took place at three levels simultaneously. It was a struggle for national independence, a phase in a century-long global battle among European empires, and a conflict over what kind of nation an independent America should be.

With its wide distribution of property, lack of a legally established hereditary aristocracy, and established churches far less powerful than in Britain, colonial America was a society with deep democratic potential. But it took the struggle for independence to transform it into a nation that celebrated equality and opportunity. The Revolution unleashed public debates and political and social struggles that enlarged the scope of freedom and challenged inherited structures of power within America. In rejecting the crown and the principle of hereditary aristocracy, many Americans also rejected the society of privilege, patronage, and fixed status that these institutions embodied. To be sure, the men who led the Revolution from start to finish were by and large members of the American elite. The lower classes did not rise to power as a result of independence. Nonetheless, the idea of liberty became a revolutionary rallying cry, a standard by which to judge and challenge home-grown institutions as well as imperial ones.

Jefferson's seemingly straightforward assertion in the Declaration of Independence that "all men are created equal" announced a radical principle whose full implications no one could anticipate. In both Britain and its colonies, a well-ordered society was widely thought to depend on obedience to authority—the power of rulers over their subjects, husbands over wives, parents over children, employers over servants and apprentices, slaveholders over slaves. Inequality had been fundamental to the colonial social order; the Revolution challenged it in many ways. Henceforth, American freedom would be forever linked with the idea of equality—equality before the law, equality in political rights, equality of economic opportunity, and, for some, equality of condition. "Whenever I use the words *freedom* or *rights*," wrote Thomas Paine, "I desire to be understood to mean a perfect equality of them. . . . The floor of Freedom is as level as water."

CÉRÉMONIE DU SACRE DE LOUIS XVI

The Coronation of Louis XVI of France, 1774, *an engraving that reveals the splendor of the royal court. Even though France became an ally of the United States in the War of Independence, this image illustrates the Old World society of fixed, unequal classes and social privilege repudiated by American revolutionaries.*

EXPANDING THE POLITICAL NATION

With liberty and equality as their rallying cries, previously marginalized groups advanced their demands. Long-accepted relations of dependency and restrictions on freedom suddenly appeared illegitimate—a process not intended by most of the leading patriots. In political, social, and religious life, Americans challenged the previous domination by a privileged few. In the end, the Revolution did not undo the obedience to which male heads of household were entitled from their wives and children, and, at least in the southern states, their slaves. For free men, however, the democratization of freedom was dramatic. Nowhere was this more evident than in challenges to the traditional limitation of political participation to those who owned property.

"We are all, from the cobbler up to the senator, become politicians," declared a Boston letter writer in 1774. Throughout the colonies, election campaigns became freewheeling debates on the fundamentals of government. Universal male suffrage, religious toleration, and even the abolition of slavery were discussed not only by the educated elite but by artisans, small farmers, and laborers, now emerging as a self-conscious element in politics. In many colonies-turned-states, the militia, composed largely of members of the "lower orders," became a "school of political democracy." Its members demanded the right to elect all their officers and to vote for public officials whether or not they met age and property qualifications. They thereby established the tradition that service in the army enabled excluded groups to stake a claim to full citizenship.

THE REVOLUTION IN PENNSYLVANIA

The Revolution's radical potential was more evident in Pennsylvania than in any other state. Elsewhere, the established leadership either embraced independence by the spring of 1776 or split into pro-British and pro-independence factions (in New York, for example, the Livingstons and their supporters ended up as patriots, the De Lanceys as Loyalists). But in Pennsylvania nearly the entire prewar elite opposed independence, fearing that severing the tie with Britain would lead to rule by the "rabble" and attacks on property.

The vacuum of political leadership opened the door for the rise of a new pro-independence grouping, based on the artisan and lower-class communities of Philadelphia, and organized in extralegal committees and the local militia. Their leaders included Thomas Paine (the author of *Common Sense*), Benjamin Rush (a local physician), Timothy Matlack (the son of a local brewer), and Thomas Young (who had already been involved in the Sons of Liberty in Albany and Boston). As a group, these were men of modest wealth who stood outside the merchant elite, had little political influence before 1776, and believed strongly in democratic reform. Paine and Young had only recently arrived in Philadelphia. They formed a temporary alliance with supporters of independence in the Second Continental Congress (then meeting in Philadelphia), who disapproved of their strong belief in equality but hoped to move Pennsylvania toward a break with Britain.

As the public sphere expanded far beyond its previous boundaries, equality became the rallying cry of Pennsylvania's radicals. They particularly attacked property qualifications for voting. "God gave mankind freedom by nature," declared the anonymous author of the pamphlet *The People the Best Governors*, "and made every man equal to his neighbors." The people, therefore, were "the best guardians of their own liberties," and every free man should be eligible to vote and hold office. In June 1776, a broadside (a printed sheet posted in public places) warned citizens to distrust "great and over-grown rich men" who were inclined "to be framing distinctions in society." Three months after independence, Pennsylvania adopted a new state constitution that sought to institutionalize democracy by concentrating power in a one-house legislature elected annually by all men over age twenty-one who paid taxes. It abolished the office of governor, dispensed with property qualifications for officeholding, and provided that schools with low fees be established in every county. It also included clauses guaranteeing "freedom of speech, and of writing," and religious liberty.

THE NEW CONSTITUTIONS

Like Pennsylvania, every state adopted a new constitution in the aftermath of independence. Nearly all Americans now agreed that their governments must be republics, meaning that their authority rested on the consent of the governed, and that there would be no king or hereditary aristocracy. The essence of a republic, Paine wrote, was not the "particular form" of government, but its object: the "public good." But as to how a republican

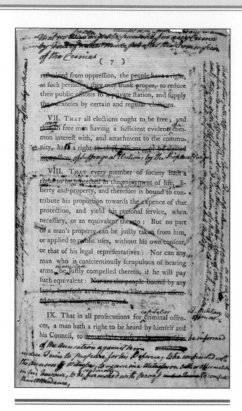

John Dickinson's copy of the Pennsylvania constitution of 1776, with handwritten proposals for changes. Dickinson, one of the more conservative advocates of independence, felt the new state constitution was far too democratic. He crossed out a provision that all "free men" should be eligible to hold office, and another declaring the people not bound by laws that did not promote "the common good."

government should be structured so as to promote the public good, there was much disagreement.

Pennsylvania's new constitution reflected the belief that since the people had a single set of interests, a single legislative house was sufficient to represent it. In part to counteract what he saw as Pennsylvania's excessive radicalism, John Adams in 1776 published *Thoughts on Government*, which insisted that the new constitutions should create "balanced governments" whose structure would reflect the division of society between the wealthy (represented in the upper house) and ordinary men (who would control the lower). A powerful governor and judiciary would ensure that neither class infringed on the liberty of the other. Adams's call for two-house legislatures was followed by every state except Pennsylvania, Georgia, and Vermont. But only his own state, Massachusetts, gave the governor an effective veto over laws passed by the legislature. Americans had come to believe that excessive royal authority had undermined British liberty. They had long resented efforts by appointed governors to challenge the power of colonial assemblies. They preferred power to rest with the legislature.

THE RIGHT TO VOTE

The issue of requirements for voting and officeholding proved far more contentious. Conservative patriots struggled valiantly to reassert the rationale for the old voting restrictions. It was ridiculous, wrote one pamphleteer, to think that "every silly clown and illiterate mechanic [artisan]" deserved a voice in government. To John Adams, as conservative on the internal affairs of America as he had been radical on independence, freedom and equality were opposites. Men without property, he believed, had no "judgment of their own," and the removal of property qualifications, therefore, would "confound and destroy all distinctions, and prostrate all ranks to one common level." Eliminating traditional social ranks, however, was precisely the aim of the era's radical democrats, including the most influential promoter of independence, Thomas Paine.

The provisions of the new state constitutions reflected the balance of power between advocates of internal change and those who feared excessive democracy. The least democratization occurred in the southern states, whose highly deferential political traditions enabled the landed gentry to retain their control of political affairs. In Virginia and South Carolina, the new constitutions retained property qualifications for voting and authorized the gentry-dominated legislature to choose the governor. Maryland combined a low property qualification for voting with high requirements for officeholding, including £5,000—a veritable fortune—for the governor.

The most democratic new constitutions moved much of the way toward the idea of voting as an entitlement rather than a privilege, but they generally stopped short of universal suffrage, even for free men. Vermont's constitution of 1777 was the only one to sever voting completely from financial considerations, eliminating not only property qualifications but the requirement that voters pay taxes. Pennsylvania's constitution no longer required ownership of property, but it retained the taxpaying qualification. As a result, it enfranchised nearly all of the state's free male population but left a small number, mainly paupers and domestic servants, still barred from voting. Nonetheless, even with the taxpaying requirement it represented a dramatic departure from the colonial practice of restricting the suffrage to those who could claim to be economically independent. It elevated "personal liberty," in the words of one essayist, to a position more important than property ownership in defining the boundaries of the political nation.

DEMOCRATIZING GOVERNMENT

Overall, the Revolution led to a great expansion of the right to vote. By the 1780s, with the exceptions of Virginia, Maryland, and New York, a large majority of the adult white male population could meet voting requirements. New Jersey's new state constitution, of 1776, granted suffrage to all "inhabitants" who met a property qualification. Until the state added the word "male" (along with "white") in 1807, property-owning women, mostly widows, did cast ballots. The new constitutions also expanded the number of legislative seats, with the result that numerous men of lesser property assumed political offices. The debate over the suffrage would, of course, continue for many decades. For white men, the process of democratization did not run its course until the Age of Jackson; for women and non-whites, it would take much longer.

Even during the Revolution, however, in the popular language of politics if not in law, freedom and an individual's right to vote had become interchangeable. "The suffrage," declared a 1776 petition of disenfranchised North Carolinians, was "a right essential to and inseparable from freedom." Without it, Americans could not enjoy "equal liberty." A proposed new constitution for Massachusetts was rejected by a majority of the towns in 1778, partly because it contained a property qualification for voting. "All men were born equally free and independent," declared the town of Lenox. How could they defend their "life and liberty and property" without a voice in electing public officials? A new draft, which retained a substantial requirement for voting in state elections but allowed virtually all men to vote for town officers, was approved in 1780. And every state except South Carolina provided for annual legislative elections, to ensure that representatives remained closely accountable to the people. Henceforth, political freedom would mean not only, as in the past, a people's right to be ruled by their chosen representatives but also an individual's right to political participation.

TOWARD RELIGIOUS TOLERATION

As remarkable as the expansion of political freedom was the Revolution's impact on American religion. Religious toleration, declared one Virginia patriot, was part of "the common cause of Freedom." In Britain, Dissenters—Protestants who belonged to other denominations than the Anglican Church—had long invoked the language of liberty in seeking repeal of the laws that imposed various disabilities on non-Anglicans. (Few, however, included Catholics in their ringing calls for religious freedom.) We have already seen that some colonies, like Rhode Island and Pennsylvania, had

Prospect of the City of NEW-YORK

1 Fort George	6 The Prison.	11 Old Dutch Church	16 Quaker's Meeting
2 Trinity Church	7 New Brick Meeting	12 Jew's Synagogue	17 Calvinist Church
3 Presbyter. Meeting	8 King's College	13 Lutheran Church	18 Anabaptist Meeting
4 North D. Church	9 St. Paul's Church	14 The French Church	19 Moravian Meeting
5 St. George's Chapel	10 N.Dutch Cal.Church	15 New Scot's Meeting	20 N. Lutheran Church
			21 Methodist Meeting

A 1771 image of New York City lists some of the numerous churches visible from the New Jersey shore, illustrating the diversity of religions practiced in the city.

long made a practice of toleration. But freedom of worship before the Revolution arose more from the reality of religious pluralism than from a well-developed theory of religious liberty. Apart from Rhode Island, New England had little homegrown experience of religious pluralism. Indeed, authorities in England had occasionally pressed the region's rulers to become more tolerant. Before the Revolution, most colonies supported religious institutions with public funds and discriminated in voting and officeholding against Catholics, Jews, and even dissenting Protestants. On the very eve of independence, Baptists who refused to pay taxes to support local Congregational ministers were still being jailed in Massachusetts. "While our country are pleading so high for liberty," the victims complained, "yet they are denying of it to their neighbors."

CATHOLIC AMERICANS

The War of Independence weakened the deep tradition of American anti-Catholicism. The First Continental Congress denounced the Quebec Act of 1774, which, as noted in the previous chapter, allowed Canadian Catholics to worship freely, as part of a plot to establish "popery" in North America. But a year later, when the Second Continental Congress decided on an ill-fated invasion of Canada, it invited the inhabitants of Quebec to join in the struggle against Britain, assuring them that Protestants and Catholics could readily cooperate. However, predominantly Catholic Quebec preferred being ruled from distant London rather than from Boston or Philadelphia. In 1778, the United States formed an alliance with France, a Catholic nation. Benedict Arnold justified his treason, in part, by saying that an alliance with "the enemy of the protestant faith" was too much for him to bear. But the indispensable assistance provided by France to American victory strengthened the idea that Catholics had a role to play in the newly independent nation. In fact, this represented a marked departure from the traditional notion that the full rights of Englishmen only applied to Protestants. When America's first Roman Catholic bishop, James Carroll of Maryland, visited Boston in 1791, he received a cordial welcome.

THE FOUNDERS AND RELIGION

The end of British rule immediately threw into question the privileged position enjoyed by the Anglican Church in many colonies. In Virginia, for example, backcountry Scotch-Irish Presbyterian farmers demanded relief from taxes supporting the official Anglican Church. "The free exercise of our rights of conscience," one patriotic meeting resolved, formed an essential part of "our liberties."

Many of the leaders of the Revolution considered it essential for the new nation to shield itself from the unruly passions and violent conflicts that religious differences had inspired during the past three centuries. Men like Thomas Jefferson, John Adams, James Madison, and Alexander Hamilton believed religion necessary as a foundation of public morality. But they viewed religious doctrines through the Enlightenment lens of rationalism and skepticism. They believed in a benevolent Creator but not in supernatural interventions into the affairs of men. Jefferson wrote a version of the Bible and a life of Jesus that insisted that while Jesus had lived a deeply moral life, he was not divine and performed no miracles. In discussing the natural history of the Blue Ridge Mountains in his book *Notes on the State of Virginia*, he rejected the biblical account of creation in favor of a prolonged process of geological change.

SEPARATING CHURCH AND STATE

The drive to separate church and state brought together Deists like Jefferson, who hoped to erect a "wall of separation" that would free politics and the exercise of the intellect from religious control, with members of evangelical sects, who sought to protect religion from the corrupting embrace of government. Religious leaders continued to adhere to the traditional definition of Christian liberty—submitting to God's will and leading a moral life—but increasingly felt this could be achieved without the support of government. Christ's kingdom, as Isaac Backus, the Baptist leader, put it, was "not of this world."

The movement toward religious freedom received a major impetus during the revolutionary era. Throughout the new nation, states disestablished their established churches—that is, deprived them of public funding and special legal privileges—although in some cases they appropriated money for the general support of Protestant denominations. The seven state constitutions that began with declarations of rights all declared a commitment to "the free exercise of religion."

To be sure, every state but New York—whose constitution of 1777 established complete religious liberty—kept intact colonial provisions barring Jews from voting and holding public office. Seven states limited officeholding to Protestants. Massachusetts retained its Congregationalist establishment well into the nineteenth century. Its new constitution declared church attendance compulsory while guaranteeing freedom of individual worship. It would not end public financial support for religious institutions until 1833. Throughout the colonies, however, Catholics gained the right to worship without persecution. Maryland's constitution of 1776 restored to the large Catholic population the civil and political rights that had been denied them for nearly a century.

In Side of the Old Lutheran Church in 1800, York, Pa. A watercolor by a local artist depicts the interior of one of the numerous churches that flourished after independence. While the choir sings, a man chases a dog out of the building while another man stokes the stove.

JEFFERSON AND RELIGIOUS LIBERTY

In Virginia, Thomas Jefferson drew up a Bill for Establishing Religious Freedom, introduced in the House of Burgesses in 1779 and adopted, after considerable controversy, in 1786. "I have sworn eternal opposition," he would later write, "to every form of tyranny over the mind of man," and he viewed established churches as a major example of such despotism. Jefferson's bill, whose preamble declared that God "hath created the mind free," eliminated religious requirements for voting and officeholding and government financial support for churches, and barred the state from "forcing" individuals to adopt one or another religious outlook. Late in life, Jefferson would list this measure, along with the Declaration of Independence and the founding of the University of Virginia, as the three accomplishments (leaving out his two terms as president) for which he wished to be remembered.

Religious liberty became the model for the revolutionary generation's definition of "rights" as private matters that must be protected from governmental interference. In an overwhelmingly Christian (though not necessarily churchgoing) nation, the separation of church and state drew a sharp line between public authority and a realm defined as "private," reinforcing the idea that rights exist as restraints on the power of government. It also offered a new justification for the idea of the United States as a beacon of liberty. In successfully opposing a Virginia tax for the general support of Christian churches, James Madison insisted that one reason for the complete separation of church and state was to reinforce the principle that the new nation offered "asylum to the persecuted and oppressed of every nation and religion."

THE REVOLUTION AND THE CHURCHES

Thus, the Revolution enhanced the diversity of American Christianity and expanded the idea of religious liberty. But even as the separation of church and state created the social and political space that allowed all kinds of religious institutions to flourish, the culture of individual rights of which that separation was a part threatened to undermine church authority.

One example was the experience of the Moravian Brethren, who had emigrated from Germany to North Carolina on the eve of independence. To the dismay of the Moravian elders, younger members of the community, like so many other Americans of the revolutionary generation, insisted on asserting "their alleged freedom and human rights." Some became unruly and refused to obey the orders of town leaders. Many rejected the community's tradition of arranged marriages, insisting on choosing their own husbands and

Ezra Stiles, the president of Yale College, drew this sketch of a flag in his diary on April 24, 1783, shortly after Congress ratified the Treaty of Paris. Thirteen stars surround the coat of arms of Pennsylvania. The text illustrates the linkage among virtue, liberty, and American independence.

wives. To the elders, the idea of individual liberty—which they called, disparagingly, "the American freedom"—was little more than "an opportunity for temptation," a threat to the spirit of self-sacrifice and communal loyalty essential to Christian liberty.

But despite such fears, the Revolution did not end the influence of religion on American society—quite the reverse. American churches, in the words of one Presbyterian leader, learned to adapt to living at a time when "a spirit of liberty prevails." Thanks to religious freedom, the early republic witnessed an amazing proliferation of religious denominations. The most well-established churches—Anglican, Presbyterian, and Congregationalist—found themselves constantly challenged by upstarts like Free-Will Baptists and Universalists. Today, even as debate continues over the proper relationship between spiritual and political authority, more than 1,300 religions are practiced in the United States.

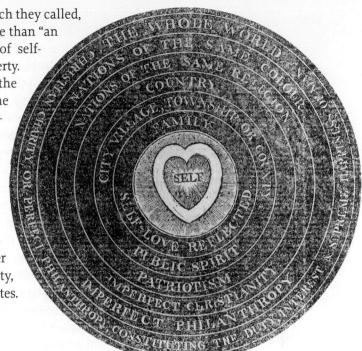

The Self, *an engraving in* The Columbian Magazine, *1789, illustrates various admirable qualities radiating outward from the virtuous citizen, including love for one's family, community, and nation.*

A VIRTUOUS CITIZENRY

Despite the separation of church and state, colonial leaders were not hostile to religion. Most were devout Christians, and even Deists who attended no organized church believed religious values reinforced the moral qualities necessary for a republic to prosper. Public authority continued to support religious values, in laws barring non-Christians from office and in the continued prosecution of blasphemy and breaches of the Sabbath. Pennsylvania's new democratic constitution required citizens to acknowledge the existence of God, and it directed the legislature to enact "laws for the prevention of vice and immorality." In the nineteenth century, Pennsylvania's lawmakers took this mandate so seriously that the state became as famous for its laws against swearing and desecrating the Sabbath as it had been in colonial times for religious freedom.

Patriot leaders worried about the character of future citizens, especially how to encourage the quality of "virtue," the ability to sacrifice self-interest for the public good. Some, like Jefferson, John Adams, and Benjamin Rush, put forward plans for the establishment of free, state-supported public schools. These would instruct future citizens in what Adams called "the principles of freedom," equipping them for participation in the now-expanded public sphere and for the wise election of representatives. A broad diffusion of knowledge was essential for a government based on the will of the people to survive and for America to avoid the fixed class structure of Europe. No nation, Jefferson wrote, could "expect to be ignorant and free."

DEFINING ECONOMIC FREEDOM

TOWARD FREE LABOR

In economic as well as political and religious affairs, the Revolution rewrote the definition of freedom. In colonial America, slavery was one part of a broad spectrum of kinds of unfree labor. In the generation after independence, with the rapid decline of indentured servitude and apprenticeship and the transformation of paid domestic service into an occupation for blacks and white females, the halfway houses between slavery and freedom disappeared, at least for white men. The decline of these forms of labor had many causes. Wage workers became more available as indentured servants completed their terms of required labor, and considerable numbers of servants and apprentices took advantage of the turmoil of the Revolution to escape from their masters.

The democratization of freedom contributed to these changes. The lack of freedom inherent in apprenticeship and servitude increasingly came to be seen as incompatible with republican citizenship. Ebenezer Fox, a young apprentice on a Massachusetts farm, later recalled how he and other youths "made a direct application of the doctrines we heard daily, in relation to the oppression of the mother country, to our own circumstance. . . . I thought that I was doing myself a great injustice by remaining in bondage, when I ought to go free." Fox became one of many apprentices during the Revolution who decided to run away—or, as he put it, to "liberate myself." On the eve of the battles of Lexington and Concord in 1775, Fox and a friend set off for Rhode Island. After briefly working as a sailor, Fox, still a teenager, joined the Continental army.

In 1784, a group of "respectable" New Yorkers released a newly arrived shipload of indentured servants on the grounds that their status was "contrary to . . . the idea of liberty this country has so happily established." By 1800, indentured servitude had all but disappeared from the United States. This development sharpened the distinction between freedom and slavery and between a northern economy relying on what would come to be called "free labor" (that is, working for wages or owning a farm or shop) and a southern economy ever more heavily dependent on the labor of slaves.

THE SOUL OF A REPUBLIC

Americans of the revolutionary generation were preoccupied with the social conditions of freedom. Could a republic survive with a sizable dependent class of citizens? "A general and tolerably equal distribution of landed property," proclaimed the educator and newspaper editor Noah Webster, "is the whole basis of national freedom." "Equality," he added, was "the very soul of a republic." It outstripped in importance liberty of the press, trial by jury, and other "palladia of freedom." Even a conservative like John Adams, who distrusted the era's democratic upsurge, hoped that every member of society could acquire land, "so that the multitude may be possessed of small estates" and the new nation could avoid the emergence of fixed and unequal social classes. At the Revolution's radical edge, some patriots believed that government had a responsibility to limit accumulations of property in the name of equality. To most free Americans, however, "equality" meant equal opportunity, rather than equality of condition. Many leaders of the Revolution nevertheless assumed that in the exceptional circumstances of the New World, with its vast areas of available land and large population of independent farmers and artisans, the natural workings of society would produce justice, liberty, and equality.

Like many other Americans of his generation, Thomas Jefferson believed that to lack economic resources was to lack freedom. Jefferson favored a limited state, but he also believed that government could help create freedom's institutional framework. His proudest achievements included laws passed by Virginia abolishing entail (the limitation of inheritance to a specified line of heirs to keep an estate within a family) and primogeniture (the practice of passing a family's land entirely to the eldest son). These measures, he believed, would help to prevent the rise of a "future aristocracy." To the same end, Jefferson proposed to award fifty acres of land to "every person of full age" who did not already possess it, another way government could enhance the liberty of its subjects. Of course, the land Jefferson hoped would secure American liberty would have to come from Indians.

THE POLITICS OF INFLATION

The Revolution thrust to the forefront of politics debates over whether local or national authorities should take steps to bolster household independence and protect Americans' livelihoods by limiting price increases. Economic dislocations sharpened the controversy. To finance the war, Congress issued hundreds of millions of dollars in paper money. Coupled with wartime disruption of agriculture and trade and the hoarding of goods by some Americans hoping to profit from shortages, this produced an enormous increase in prices. The country, charged a letter to a Philadelphia newspaper in 1778, had been "reduced to the brink of ruin by the infamous practices of monopolizers." "Hunger," the writer warned, "will break through stone walls."

Between 1776 and 1779, more than thirty incidents took place in which crowds confronted merchants accused of holding scarce goods off the market. Often, they seized stocks of food and sold them at the traditional "just price," a form of protest common in eighteenth-century England. In one such incident, a crowd of 100 Massachusetts women accused an "eminent, wealthy, stingy merchant" of hoarding coffee, opened his warehouse, and carted off the goods. "A large concourse of men," wrote Abigail Adams, "stood amazed, silent spectators of the whole transaction."

THE DEBATE OVER FREE TRADE

In 1779, with inflation totally out of control (in one month, prices in Philadelphia jumped 45 percent), Congress urged states to adopt measures to fix wages and prices. The policy embodied the belief that the task of republican government was to promote the public good, not individuals' self-interest. Bitter comments appeared in the Philadelphia press about the city's elite expending huge sums on "public dinners and other extravaganzas" while many in the city were "destitute of the necessities of life." But when a Committee of Safety tried to enforce price controls, it met spirited opposition from merchants and other advocates of a free market.

In opposition to the traditional view that men should sacrifice for the public good, believers in freedom of trade argued that economic development arose from economic self-interest. Just as Newton had revealed the inner workings of the natural universe, so the social world also followed unchanging natural laws, among them that supply and demand regulated

A broadside printed by the extralegal Philadelphia price-control committee, setting the retail prices of various goods such as coffee, sugar, and rum. Advocates of a free market strongly opposed the committee's efforts.

the prices of goods. Adam Smith's great treatise on economics, *The Wealth of Nations*, published in England in 1776, was beginning to become known in the United States. Smith's argument that the "invisible hand" of the free market directed economic life more effectively and fairly than governmental intervention offered intellectual justification for those who believed that the economy should be left to regulate itself.

Advocates of independence had envisioned America, released from the British Navigation Acts, trading freely with all the world. Opponents of price controls advocated free trade at home as well. "Let trade be as free as air," wrote one merchant. "Natural liberty" would regulate prices. Here were two competing conceptions of economic freedom—one based on the traditional view that the interests of the community took precedence over the property rights of individuals, the other that unregulated economic freedom would produce social harmony and public gain. After 1779, the latter view gained ascendancy. In 1780, Robert Morris, a Philadelphia merchant and banker, became director of congressional fiscal policy. State and federal efforts to regulate prices ceased. But the clash between these two visions of economic freedom would continue long after independence had been achieved.

"Yield to the mighty current of American freedom." So a member of the South Carolina legislature implored his colleagues in 1777. The current of freedom swept away not only British authority but also the principle of hereditary rule, the privileges of established churches, long-standing habits of deference and hierarchy, and old limits on the political nation. Yet in other areas, the tide of freedom encountered obstacles that did not yield as easily to its powerful flow.

THE LIMITS OF LIBERTY

COLONIAL LOYALISTS

Not all Americans shared in the democratization of freedom brought on by the American Revolution. Loyalists—those who retained their allegiance to the crown—experienced the conflict and its aftermath as a loss of liberty. Many leading Loyalists had supported American resistance in the 1760s but drew back at the prospect of independence and war. Loyalists included some of the most prominent Americans and some of the most humble. Altogether, an estimated 20 to 25 percent of free Americans remained loyal to the British, and nearly 20,000 fought on their side. At some points in the war, Loyalists serving with the British outnumbered Washington's army.

There were Loyalists in every colony, but they were most numerous in New York, Pennsylvania, and the backcountry of the Carolinas and Georgia. Some were wealthy men whose livelihoods depended on close working relationships with Britain—lawyers, merchants, Anglican ministers, and imperial officials. Many feared anarchy in the event of an American victory. "Liberty," one wrote, "can have no existence without obedience to the laws."

The struggle for independence heightened existing tensions between ethnic groups and social classes within the colonies. Some Loyalist ethnic minorities, like Highland Scots in North Carolina, feared that local majorities would infringe on their freedom to enjoy cultural autonomy. In the South, many backcountry farmers who had long resented the domination of public affairs by wealthy planters sided with the British. So did tenants on the New York estates of patriot landlords like the Livingston family. Robert Livingston had signed the Declaration of Independence. When the army of General Burgoyne approached Livingston's manor in 1777, tenants rose in revolt, hoping the British would confiscate his land and distribute it among themselves. Their hopes were dashed by Burgoyne's defeat at Saratoga. In the South, numerous slaves sided with the British, hoping an American defeat would bring them freedom.

THE LOYALISTS' PLIGHT

The War of Independence was in some respects a civil war among Americans. "This country," wrote a German colonel fighting with the British, "is the scene of the most cruel events. Neighbors are on opposite sides, children are against their fathers." Freedom of expression is often a casualty of war, and many Americans were deprived of basic rights in the name of liberty. After Dr. Abner Beebe, of East Haddam, Connecticut, spoke "very freely" in favor of the British, a mob attacked his house and destroyed his gristmill. Beebe himself was "assaulted, stripped naked, and hot pitch [tar] was poured upon him." The new state governments, or in other instances crowds of patriots, suppressed newspapers thought to be loyal to Britain.

Pennsylvania arrested and seized the property of Quakers, Mennonites, and Moravians—pacifist denominations who refused to bear arms because of their religious beliefs. With the approval of Congress, many states required residents to take oaths of allegiance to the new nation. Those who refused were denied the right to vote and in many cases forced into exile. "The flames of discord," wrote one British observer, "are sprouting from the seeds of liberty." Some wealthy Loyalists saw their land confiscated and sold at auction. Twenty-eight estates belonging to New Hampshire governor John Wentworth and his family were seized, as were the holdings of great New York Loyalist landlords like the De Lancey and Philipse families. Most of the buyers of this land were merchants, lawyers, and established landowners. Unable to afford the purchase price, tenants had no choice but to continue to labor for the new owners.

When the war ended, as many as 100,000 Loyalists (including 20,000 slaves) were banished from the United States or emigrated voluntarily—mostly to Britain, Canada, or the West Indies— rather than live in an independent United States. But for those who remained, hostility proved to be short-lived. In the Treaty of Paris of 1783, as noted in Chapter 5, Americans pledged to end the persecution of Loyalists by state and local governments and to restore property seized during the war. American leaders believed the new nation needed to establish an international reputation for

A 1780 British cartoon commenting on the "cruel fate" of American Loyalists. Pro-independence colonists are likened to savage Indians.

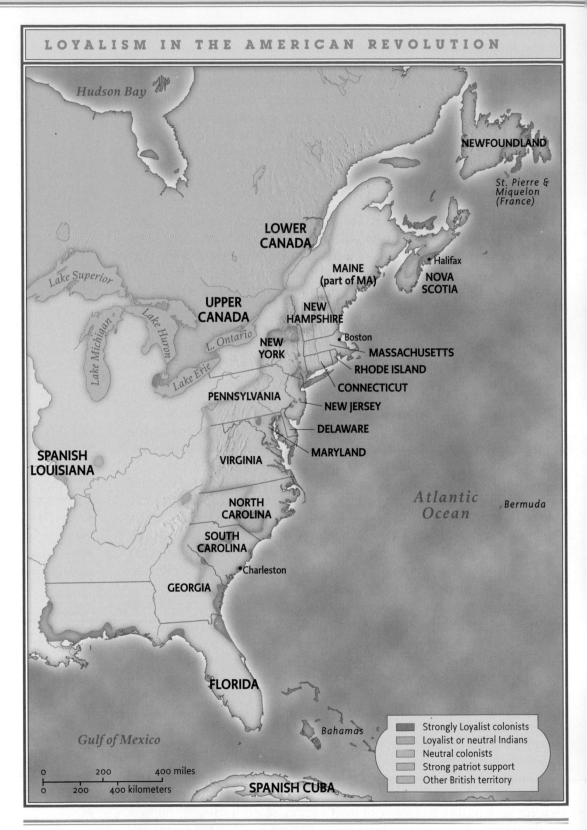

LOYALISM IN THE AMERICAN REVOLUTION

Strongly Loyalist colonists
Loyalist or neutral Indians
Neutral colonists
Strong patriot support
Other British territory

The Revolutionary War was, in some ways, a civil war within the colonies. There were Loyalists in every colony; they were most numerous in New York and North and South Carolina.

fairness and civility. States soon repealed their test oaths for voting and officeholding. Loyalists who did not leave the country were quickly reintegrated into American society, although despite the promise of the Treaty of Paris, confiscated Loyalist property was not returned.

THE INDIANS' REVOLUTION

Another group for whom American independence spelled a loss of freedom—the Indians—was less fortunate. Despite the Proclamation of 1763, discussed in Chapter 4, colonists had continued to move westward during the 1760s and early 1770s, leading Indian tribes to complain of intrusions on their land. Lord Dunmore, Virginia's royal governor, observed in 1772 that he had found it impossible "to restrain the Americans. . . . They do not conceive that government has any right to forbid their taking possession of a vast tract of country" or to force them to honor treaties with Indians.

Kentucky, the principal hunting ground of southern Cherokees and numerous Ohio Valley Indians, became a flash point of conflict among settlers, land speculators, and Native Americans, with the faraway British government seeking in vain to impose order. Many patriot leaders, including George Washington, Patrick Henry, and Thomas Jefferson, were deeply involved in western land speculation. Washington himself had acquired over 60,000 acres of land in western Pennsylvania after the Seven Years' War by purchasing land vouchers (a form of soldiers' wages) from his men at discount rates. Indeed, British efforts to restrain land speculation west of the line specified by the Proclamation of 1763 had been one of the many grievances of Virginia's revolutionary generation.

About 200,000 Native Americans lived east of the Mississippi River in 1790. Like white Americans, Indians divided in allegiance during the War of Independence. Some, like the Stockbridge tribe in Massachusetts, suffered heavy losses fighting the British. Many tribes tried to maintain neutrality, only to see themselves break into pro-American and pro-British factions. Most of the Iroquois nations sided with the British, but the Oneida joined the Americans. Despite strenuous efforts to avoid conflict, members of the Iroquois Confederacy for the first time faced each other in battle. (After the war, the Oneida submitted to Congress claims for losses suffered during the war, including sheep, hogs, kettles, frying pans, plows, and pewter plates—evidence of how fully they had been integrated into the market economy.) In the South, younger Cherokee leaders joined the British while older chiefs tended to favor the Americans. Other southern tribes like the Choctaw and Creek remained loyal to the crown.

Among the grievances listed by Jefferson in the Declaration of Independence was Britain's enlisting "savages" to fight on its side. But in the war that raged throughout the western frontier, savagery was not confined to either combatant. In the Ohio country, the British encouraged Indian allies to burn frontier farms and settlements. For their part, otherwise humane patriot leaders ignored the traditional rules of warfare when it came to Indians. William Henry Drayton, a leader of the patriot cause in South Carolina and the state's chief justice in 1776, advised officers marching against the Cherokees to "cut up every Indian cornfield, burn every Indian town," and enslave all Indian captives. Three years later, Washington dispatched an expedition,

A cartoon depicting a British officer buying the scalps of patriots from Indians. Jefferson listed British incitement of Indians against the colonists as one of Americans' grievances in the Declaration of Independence.

led by General John Sullivan, against hostile Iroquois, with the aim of "the total destruction and devastation of their settlements and the capture of as many prisoners of every age and sex as possible." After his campaign ended, Sullivan reported that he had burned forty Indian towns, destroyed thousands of bushels of corn, and uprooted a vast number of fruit trees and vegetable gardens. Many Iroquois communities faced starvation. In the Ohio Valley, as we will see in Chapter 7, fighting did not end until the 1790s.

WHITE FREEDOM, INDIAN FREEDOM

Independence created governments democratically accountable to voters who coveted Indian land. Indeed, to many patriots, access to Indian land was one of the fruits of American victory. Driving the Indians from the Ohio Valley, wrote Jefferson, would "add to the Empire of Liberty an extensive and fertile country." But liberty for whites meant loss of liberty for Indians. "The whites were no sooner free themselves," a Pequot, William Apess, would later write, than they turned on "the poor Indians." Independence offered the opportunity to complete the process of dispossessing Indians of their rich lands in upstate New York, the Ohio Valley, and the southern backcountry. The only hope for the Indians, Jefferson wrote, lay in their "removal beyond the Mississippi." Even as the war raged, Americans forced defeated tribes like the Cherokee to cede most of their land. By the time peace arrived, the Shawnees had been driven from Ohio to Missouri.

American independence, a group of visiting Indians told the Spanish governor at St. Louis, was "the greatest blow that could have been dealt us." The Treaty of Paris marked the culmination of a century in which the balance of power in eastern North America shifted away from the Indians and toward white Americans. The displacement of British power to Canada, coming twenty years after the departure of the French, left Indians with seriously diminished white support. Some Indian leaders, like Joseph Brant, a young Mohawk in upstate New York, hoped to create an Indian confederacy lying between Canada and the new United States. He sided with the British to try to achieve this goal. But in the Treaty of Paris, the British abandoned their Indian allies, agreeing to recognize American sovereignty over the entire region east of the Mississippi River, completely ignoring the Indian presence.

To Indians, freedom meant defending their own independence and retaining possession of their land. Like other Americans, they appropriated the language of the Revolution and interpreted it according to their own experiences and for their own purposes. The Iroquois, declared one spokesman, were "a free people subject to no power on earth." Creeks and Choctaws denied having done anything to forfeit their "independence and natural rights." When Massachusetts established a system of state "guardianship" over previously self-governing tribes, a group of Mashpees petitioned the legislature claiming for themselves "the rights of man" and complaining of this "infringement of freedom."

"Freedom" had not played a major part in Indians' vocabulary before the Revolution. By the early nineteenth century, dictionaries of Indian languages for the first time began to include the word. In a sense, Indians' definition of their rights was becoming Americanized. But there seemed to be no permanent place for the descendants of the continent's native population in a new nation bent on creating an empire in the West.

SLAVERY AND THE REVOLUTION

While Indians experienced American independence as a real threat to their own liberty, African-Americans saw in the ideals of the Revolution and the reality of war an opportunity to claim freedom. When the United States declared its independence in 1776, the slave population had grown to 500,000, about one-fifth of the new nation's inhabitants. Slaveowning and slave trading were accepted routines of colonial life. Advertisements announcing the sale of slaves and seeking the return of runaways filled colonial newspapers. Sometimes, the same issues of patriotic newspapers that published accounts of the activities of the Sons of Liberty or arguments against the Stamp Act also contained slave sale notices.

THE LANGUAGE OF SLAVERY AND FREEDOM

Slavery played a central part in the language of revolution. Apart from "liberty," it was the word most frequently invoked in the era's legal and political literature. Eighteenth-century writers frequently juxtaposed freedom and slavery as "the two extremes of happiness and misery in society." Yet in the era's debates over British rule, slavery was primarily a political category, shorthand for the denial of one's personal and political rights by arbitrary government. Those who lacked a voice in public affairs, declared a 1769 petition demanding an expansion of the right to vote in Britain, were "enslaved." By the eve of independence, the contrast between Britain, "a kingdom of slaves," and America, a "country of free men," had become a standard part of the language of resistance. Such language was employed

Advertisement for newly arrived slaves, in a Savannah newspaper, 1774. Even as colonists defended their own liberty against the British, the buying and selling of slaves continued.

without irony even in areas where nearly half the population in fact consisted of slaves. South Carolina, one writer declared in 1774, was a "sacred land" of freedom, where it was impossible to believe that "slavery shall soon be permitted to erect her throne."

Colonial writers of the 1760s occasionally made a direct connection between slavery as a reality and slavery as a metaphor. Few were as forthright as James Otis of Massachusetts, whose pamphlets did much to popularize the idea that Parliament lacked the authority to tax the colonies and regulate their commerce. Freedom, Otis insisted, must be universal: "What man is or ever was born free if every man is not?" Otis wrote of blacks not as examples of the loss of rights awaiting free Americans, but as flesh and blood British subjects "entitled to all the civil rights of such."

Otis was hardly typical of patriot leaders. But the presence of hundreds of thousands of slaves powerfully affected the meaning of freedom for the leaders of the American Revolution. In a famous speech to Parliament warning against attempts to intimidate the colonies, the British statesman Edmund Burke suggested that familiarity with slavery made colonial leaders unusually sensitive to threats to their own liberties. Where freedom was a privilege, not a common right, he observed, "those who are free are by far the most proud and jealous of their freedom." On the other hand, many British observers could not resist pointing out the colonists' apparent hypocrisy. "How is it," asked Dr. Samuel Johnson, "that we hear the loudest yelps for liberty from the drivers of negroes?"

OBSTACLES TO ABOLITION

The contradiction between freedom and slavery seems so self-evident that it is difficult today to appreciate the power of the obstacles to abolition. At the time of the Revolution, slavery was already an old institution in America. It existed in every colony and formed the basis of the economy and social structure from Maryland southward. At least 40 percent of Virginia's population and even higher proportions in Georgia and South Carolina were slaves.

Virtually every founding father owned slaves at one point in his life, including not only southern planters but northern merchants, lawyers, and farmers. (John Adams and Tom Paine were notable exceptions.) Thomas Jefferson owned over 100 slaves when he wrote of mankind's unalienable right to liberty, and everything he cherished in his own manner of life, from lavish entertainments to the leisure that made possible the pursuit of arts and sciences, ultimately rested on slave labor.

Some patriots, in fact, argued that slavery for blacks made freedom possible for whites. Eliminating the great bulk of the dependent poor from the political nation left the public arena to men of propertied independence. Owning slaves offered a route to the economic autonomy widely deemed necessary for genuine freedom, a point driven home by a 1780 Virginia law that rewarded veterans of the War of Independence with 300 acres of land—and a slave. South Carolina and Georgia promised every white military volunteer a slave at the war's end.

So, too, the Lockean vision of the political community as a group of individuals contracting together to secure their natural rights could readily be invoked to defend bondage. Nothing was more essential to freedom, in this view, than the right of self-government and the protection of property against outside interference. These principles suggested that for the government to seize property—including slave property—against the owner's will would be an infringement on liberty. If government by the consent of the governed formed the essence of political freedom, then to require owners to give up their slave property would reduce *them* to slavery.

THE CAUSE OF GENERAL LIBERTY

Nonetheless, by imparting so absolute a value to liberty and defining freedom as a universal entitlement rather than a set of rights specific to a particular place or people, the Revolution inevitably raised questions about the status of slavery in the new nation. Before independence, there had been little public discussion of the institution, even though enlightened opinion in the Atlantic world had come to view slavery as morally wrong and economically inefficient, a relic of a barbarous past.

As early as 1688, a group of German Quakers issued a "protest" regarding the rights of blacks, declaring it as unjust "to have them slaves, as it is to have other white ones." Samuel Sewall, a Boston merchant, published *The Selling of Joseph* in 1700, the first antislavery tract printed in America. All "the sons of Adam," Sewall insisted, were entitled to "have equal right unto liberty." Slavery, as noted in Chapter 4, had initially been banned in Georgia (although it later came to sustain the rice-based plantation economy in that colony). During the course of the eighteenth century, antislavery sentiments had spread among Pennsylvania's Quakers, whose belief that all persons possessed the divine "inner light" made them particularly receptive.

But it was during the revolutionary era that slavery for the first time became a focus of public debate. The Pennsylvania patriot Benjamin Rush in 1773 called upon "advocates for American liberty" to "espouse the cause of . . . general liberty" and warned that slavery was one of those "national crimes" that one day would bring "national punishment." Jefferson, as mentioned in the previous chapter, unsuccessfully tried to include criticism of slavery in the Declaration of Independence. Although a slaveholder himself, in private he condemned slavery as a system that every day imposed on its victims "more misery, than ages of that which [the colonists] rose in rebellion to oppose."

A 1775 notice in The Massachusetts Spy *reporting a resolution of the Committees of Correspondence of Worcester County, advocating the abolition of slavery.*

PETITIONS FOR FREEDOM

The Revolution inspired widespread hopes that slavery could be removed from American life. Most dramatically, slaves themselves appreciated that by defining freedom as a universal right, the leaders of the Revolution had

WHEREAS the NEGROES in the counties of Briftol and Worcefter, the 24th of March laft, petitioned the Committees of Correfpondence for the county of Worcefter (then convened in Worcefter) to affift them in obtaining their freedom.   THEREFORE,

In County Convention, June 14th, 1775.

RESOLVED, That we abhor the enflaving of any of the human race, and particularly of the NEGROES in this country. And that whenever there fhall be a door opened, or opportunity prefent, for any thing to be done toward the emancipating the NEGROES; we will ufe our influence and endeavour that fuch a thing may be effected.   *Atteft.* WILLIAM HENSHAW, Clerk.

devised a weapon that could be used against their own bondage. The language of liberty echoed in slave communities, North and South. Living amid freedom but denied its benefits, slaves appropriated the patriotic ideology for their own purposes. The most insistent advocates of freedom as a universal entitlement were African-Americans, who demanded that the leaders of the struggle for independence live up to their self-proclaimed creed. As early as 1766, white Charlestonians had been shocked when their opposition to the Stamp Act inspired a group of blacks to parade about the city crying "Liberty." Nine years later, the Provincial Congress of South Carolina felt compelled to investigate the "high notions of liberty" the struggle against Britain had inspired among the slaves.

The first concrete steps toward emancipation in revolutionary America were "freedom petitions"—arguments for liberty presented to New England's courts and legislatures in the early 1770s by enslaved African-Americans. How, one such petition asked, could America "seek release from English tyranny and not seek the same for disadvantaged Africans in her midst?" Some slaves sued in court for being "illegally detained in slavery." The turmoil of war offered other avenues to freedom. Many slaves ran away from their masters and tried to pass as freeborn. The number of fugitive slave advertisements in colonial newspapers rose dramatically in the 1770s and 1780s. As one owner put it in accounting for his slave Jim's escape, "I believe he has nothing in view but freedom."

In 1776, the year of American independence, Lemuel Haynes, a black member of the Massachusetts militia and later a celebrated minister, urged that Americans "extend" their conception of freedom. If liberty were truly "an innate principle" for all mankind, Haynes insisted, "even an African [had] as equally good a right to his liberty in common with Englishmen." Throughout the revolutionary period, petitions, pamphlets, and sermons by blacks expressed "astonishment" that white patriots failed to realize that "every principle from which America has acted" demanded emancipation. Blacks sought to make white Americans understand slavery as a concrete reality—the denial of all the essential elements of freedom—not merely as a metaphor for the loss of political self-determination. Petitioning for their freedom in 1773, a group of New England slaves exclaimed, "We have no property! We have no wives! No children! We have no city! No country!"

Most slaves of the revolutionary era were only one or two generations removed from Africa. They did not need the ideology of the Revolution to persuade them that freedom was a birthright—the experience of their parents and grandparents suggested as much. "My love of freedom," wrote the black poet Phillis Wheatley in 1783, arose from the "cruel fate" of being "snatch'd from Afric's" shore. Brought as a slave to Boston in 1761, Wheatley learned to read and published her first poem in a New England newspaper in 1765, when she was around twelve years old. The fact that a volume of her poems had to be printed with a testimonial from prominent citizens, including patriot leader John Hancock, affirming that she was in fact the author, illustrates that many whites found it difficult to accept the idea of blacks' intellectual ability. Yet by invoking the Revolution's ideology of liberty to demand their own rights and by defining freedom as a universal entitlement, blacks demonstrated how American they had become, even as they sought to redefine what American freedom in fact represented.

A portrait of the poet Phillis Wheatley (1753–1784).

BRITISH EMANCIPATORS

As noted in the previous chapter, some 5,000 slaves fought for American independence and many thereby gained their freedom. Yet far more slaves obtained liberty from the British. Lord Dunmore's proclamation of 1775, and the Phillipsburgh Proclamation of General Henry Clinton issued four years later, offered sanctuary to slaves who escaped to British lines. Numerous signers of the Declaration of Independence lost slaves as a result. Thirty of Thomas Jefferson's slaves ran away to the British, as did slaves owned by Patrick Henry and James Madison. All told, nearly 100,000 slaves, including one-quarter of all the slaves in South Carolina and one-third of those in Georgia, deserted their owners and fled to British lines. This was by far the largest exodus from the plantations until the outbreak of the Civil War.

Some of these escaped slaves were recaptured as the tide of battle turned in the patriots' favor. But at the war's end, some 20,000 were living in three enclaves of British control—New York, Charleston, and Savannah. George Washington insisted they must be returned. Sir Guy Carleton, the British commander in New York, replied that to do so would be "a dishonorable violation of the public faith," since they had been promised their freedom. In the end, over 15,000 black men, women, and children accompanied the British out of the country. They ended up in Nova Scotia, England, and Sierra Leone, a settlement for former slaves from the United States established by the British on the coast of West Africa. Some were re-enslaved in the West Indies. A number of their stories were indeed remarkable. Harry Washington, an African-born slave of George Washington, had run away from Mount Vernon in 1771 but was recaptured. In 1775, he fled to join Lord Dunmore and eventually became a corporal in a black British regiment, the Black Pioneers. He eventually ended up in Sierra Leone, where in 1800 he took part in an unsuccessful uprising by black settlers against the British-appointed government.

The issue of compensation for the slaves who departed with the British poisoned relations between Britain and the new United States for decades to come. Finally, in 1827, Britain agreed to make payments to 1,100 Americans who claimed they had been improperly deprived of their slave property.

VOLUNTARY EMANCIPATIONS

For a brief moment, the revolutionary upheaval appeared to threaten the continued existence of slavery. During the War of Independence, nearly every state prohibited or discouraged the further importation of slaves from Africa. The war left much of the plantation South in ruins. During the 1780s, a considerable number of slaveholders, especially in Virginia and Maryland, voluntarily emancipated their slaves. In 1796, Robert Carter III, a member of one of Virginia's wealthiest families, provided for the gradual emancipation of the over 400 slaves he owned. In the same year, Richard Randolph, a member of another prominent Virginia family, drafted a will that condemned slavery as an "infamous practice," provided for the freedom of about 90 slaves, and set aside part of his land for them to own.

Farther south, however, the abolition process never got under way. When the British invaded South Carolina during the war, John Laurens,

VOICES OF FREEDOM

From their home in Massachusetts, Abigail Adams maintained a lively correspondence with her husband while he was in Philadelphia serving in the Continental Congress. In this letter, she suggests some of the limits of the patriots' commitment to liberty.

I wish you would write me a letter half as long as I write you, and tell me if you may where your fleet have gone? What sort of defense Virginia can make against our common enemy? Whether it is so situated as to make an able defense? . . . I have sometimes been ready to think that the passion for Liberty cannot be equally strong in the breasts of those who have been accustomed to deprive their fellow creatures of theirs. Of this I am certain, that it is not founded upon that generous and Christian principle of doing to others as we would that others should do unto us. . . .

I long to hear that you have declared an independency, and by the way in the new Code of Laws which I suppose it will be necessary for you to make I desire you would Remember the Ladies, and be more generous and favorable to them than your ancestors. Do not put such unlimited power into the hands of the husbands. Remember all men would be tyrants if they could. If particular care and attention is not paid to the Ladies we are determined to foment a Rebellion, and will not hold ourselves bound by any such laws in which we have no voice, or representation.

That your sex are naturally tyrannical is a truth so thoroughly established as to admit of no dispute, but such of you as wish to be happy willingly give up the harsh title of Master for the more tender and endearing one of Friend. Why then, not put it out of the power of the vicious and the lawless to use us with cruelty and indignity with impunity? Men of sense in all ages abhor those customs which treat us only as the vassals of your sex. Regard us then as beings placed by providence under your protection and in imitation of the Supreme Being make use of that power only for our happiness.

From Petitions of Slaves to the Massachusetts Legislature (1773 and 1777)

Numerous slaves saw the struggle for independence as an opportunity to assert their own claims to freedom. Among the first efforts toward abolition were petitions by Massachusetts slaves to their legislature.

The efforts made by the legislative of this province in their last sessions to free themselves from slavery, gave us, who are in that deplorable state, a high degree of satisfaction. We expect great things from men who have made such a noble stand against the designs of their *fellow-men* to enslave them. We cannot but wish and hope Sir, that you will have the same grand object, we mean civil and religious liberty, in view in your next session. The divine spirit of *freedom*, seems to fire every breast on this continent. . . .

* * *

Your petitioners apprehend that they have in common with all other men a natural and unalienable right to that freedom which the great parent of the universe hath bestowed equally on all mankind and which they have never forfeited by any compact or agreement whatever but [they] were unjustly dragged by the hand of cruel power from their dearest friends and . . . from a populous, pleasant, and plentiful country and in violation of laws of nature and of nations and in defiance of all the tender feelings of humanity brought here . . . to be sold like beast[s] of burden . . . among a people professing the mild religion of Jesus. . . .

In imitation of the laudable example of the good people of these states your petitioners have long and patiently waited the event of petition after petition by them presented to the legislative body. . . . They cannot but express their astonishment that it has never been considered that every principle from which America has acted in the course of their unhappy difficulties with Great Britain pleads stronger than a thousand arguments in favor of your petitioners [and their desire] to be restored to the enjoyment of that which is the natural right of all men.

QUESTIONS

1. What does Abigail Adams have in mind when she refers to the "unlimited power" husbands exercise over their wives?

2. How do the slaves employ the principles of the Revolution for their own aims?

3. What do these documents suggest about the boundaries of freedom in the era of the American Revolution?

whose father Henry was Charleston's leading merchant and revolutionary-era statesman, proposed to "lead a corps of emancipated blacks in the defense of liberty." South Carolina's leaders rejected the idea. They would rather lose the war than lose their slaves. (However, black soldiers from the colony of Saint Domingue, some free and some slave, fought on the American side as part of a French contingent in the unsuccessful defense of Savannah, Georgia, in 1778.)

ABOLITION IN THE NORTH

Between 1777 (when Vermont drew up a constitution that banned slavery) and 1804 (when New Jersey acted), every state north of Maryland took steps toward emancipation, the first time in recorded history that legislative power had been invoked to eradicate slavery. But even here, where slavery was peripheral to the economy, the method of abolition reflected how property rights impeded emancipation. Generally, abolition laws did not free living slaves. Instead, they provided for the liberty of any child born in the future to a slave mother, but only after he or she had served the mother's master until adulthood as compensation for the owner's future economic loss. Children born to slave mothers in Pennsylvania after passage of the state's emancipation act of 1780 had to serve the owner for twenty-eight years, far longer than had been customary for white indentured servants. These laws gave indentured servitude, rapidly declining among whites, a new lease on life in the case of northern blacks.

Abolition in the North was a slow, drawn-out process. For slaves alive when the northern laws were passed, hopes for freedom rested on their own ability to escape and the voluntary actions of their owners. And many northern slaveholders proved reluctant indeed when it came to liberating their slaves. New York City, where one-fifth of the white families owned at least one slave in 1790, recorded only seventy-six such voluntary acts between 1783 and 1800. The first national census, in 1790, recorded 21,000 slaves still living in New York and 11,000 in New Jersey. New Yorker John Jay, chief justice of the United States, owned five slaves in 1800. As late as 1830, the census revealed that there were still 3,500 slaves in the North. The last slaves in Connecticut did not become free until 1848. In 1860, eighteen elderly slaves still resided in New Jersey.

An engraving from a commemorative pitcher presented to the abolitionist Joseph Curtis by the New York Manumission Society in 1819 depicts Liberty releasing slaves from bondage. Curtis holds aloft a mirror reflecting the rising sun. Founded in 1785 by Alexander Hamilton, John Jay, and others, the Society was instrumental in the passage of New York's 1799 law providing for the gradual abolition of slavery.

FREE BLACK COMMUNITIES

All in all, the Revolution had a contradictory impact on American slavery and, therefore, on American freedom. Gradual as it was, the abolition of slavery in the North drew a line across the new nation, creating the dangerous division between free and slave states. Abolition in the North, voluntary emancipation in the Upper South, and the escape of thousands from bondage created, for the first time in American history, a sizable free black population (many of whose members took new family names like Freeman or Freeland).

On the eve of independence, virtually every black person in America had been a slave. Now, free communities, with their own churches, schools, and leaders, came into existence. They formed a standing challenge to the logic of slavery, a haven for fugitives, and a springboard for further efforts at abolition. In 1776, fewer than 10,000 free blacks resided in the United States. By

1810, their numbers had grown to nearly 200,000, most of them living in Maryland and Virginia. In all the states except Virginia, South Carolina, and Georgia, free black men who met tax-paying or property qualifications enjoyed the right to vote under new state constitutions. As the widespread use of the term "citizens of color" suggests, the first generation of free blacks, at least in the North, formed part of the political nation.

For many Americans, white as well as black, the existence of slavery would henceforth be recognized as a standing affront to the ideal of American freedom, a "disgrace to a free government," as a group of New Yorkers put it. In 1792, when Samuel Jennings of Philadelphia painted *Liberty Displaying the Arts and Sciences*, he included among the symbols of freedom a slave's broken chain, graphically illustrating how freedom had become identified not simply with political independence, but with emancipation. Nonetheless, the stark fact is that slavery survived the War of Independence and, thanks to the natural increase of the slave population, continued to grow. The national census of 1790 revealed that despite all those who had become free through state laws, voluntary emancipation, and escape, the number of slaves in the United States had grown to 700,000—200,000 more than in 1776.

A tray painted by an unknown artist in the early nineteenth century portrays Lemuel Haynes, a celebrated black preacher and critic of slavery.

DAUGHTERS OF LIBERTY

REVOLUTIONARY WOMEN

The revolutionary generation included numerous women who contributed to the struggle for independence. Deborah Sampson, the daughter of a poor Massachusetts farmer, disguised herself as a man and in 1782, at age 21, enlisted in the Continental Army. Sampson displayed remarkable courage, participating in several battles and extracting a bullet from her own leg so as not to have a doctor discover her identity. Ultimately, her commanding officer discovered her secret but kept it to himself, and she was honorably discharged at the end of the war. Years later, Congress awarded her a soldier's pension. Other patriotic women participated in crowd actions against merchants accused of seeking profits by holding goods off the market until their prices rose, contributed homespun goods to the army, and passed along information about British army movements.

In Philadelphia, Esther Reed, the wife of patriot leader Joseph Reed, and Sarah Franklin Bache, the daughter of Benjamin Franklin, organized a Ladies' Association to raise funds to assist American soldiers. They issued public broadsides calling for the "women of America" to name a "Treasuress" in each county in the United States, who would collect funds and forward them to the governor's wife or, if he were unmarried, to "Mistress Washington." Referring to themselves as "brave Americans" who had been

In this painting from 1797, Deborah Sampson, who donned men's clothes to fight in the War of Independence, is portrayed in genteel female attire.

"born for liberty," the Ladies' Association illustrated how the Revolution was propelling women into new forms of public activism.

Within American households, women participated in the political discussions unleashed by independence. "Was not every fireside," John Adams later recalled, "a theater of politics?" Adams's own wife, Abigail Adams, as has been mentioned, was a shrewd analyst of public affairs. Mercy Otis Warren—the sister of James Otis and husband of James Warren, a founder of the Boston Committee of Correspondence—was another commentator on politics. She promoted the revolutionary cause in poems and dramas and later published a history of the struggle for independence.

GENDER AND POLITICS

Gender, nonetheless, formed a boundary limiting those entitled to the full blessings of American freedom. Lucy Knox, the wife of General Henry Knox, wrote her husband during the war that when he returned home he should not consider himself "commander in chief of your own house, but be convinced that there is such a thing as equal command." But the winning of independence did not alter the family law inherited from Britain. The principle of "coverture" (described in Chapter 1) remained intact in the new nation. The husband still held legal authority over the person, property, and choices of his wife. The words "to have and to hold" appeared in deeds conveying land from one owner to another, and in common marriage vows. Despite the expansion of democracy, politics remained overwhelmingly a male realm.

For men, political freedom meant the right to self-government, the power to consent to the individuals and political arrangements that ruled over them. For women, however, the marriage contract superseded the social contract. A woman's relationship to the larger society was mediated through her relationship with her husband. In both law and social reality, women lacked the essential qualification of political participation—the

The 1781 cipher book (a notebook for mathematics exercises) of Martha Ryan, a North Carolina girl, contains images of ships and a port town and the patriotic slogan "Liberty or Death," illustrating how women shared in the political culture of the revolutionary era.

opportunity for autonomy based on ownership of property or control of one's own person. Since the common law included women within the legal status of their husbands, women could not be said to have property in themselves in the same sense as men.

Men took pride in qualities like independence and masculinity that distinguished them from women and still considered control over their families an element of freedom. Among the deprivations of slavery cited by a group of black male petitioners in 1774 was that it prevented their wives from "submitting themselves to husbands in all things," as the natural order of the universe required. Many women who entered public debate felt the need to apologize for their forthrightness. A group of Quaker women who petitioned Congress during the War of Independence protesting the mistreatment of men who would not take an oath of loyalty hoped the lawmakers would "take no offense at the freedom of women."

Most men considered women to be naturally submissive and irrational, and therefore unfit for citizenship. While public debate in the revolutionary era viewed men's rights as natural entitlements, discussions of women's roles emphasized duty and obligations, not individual liberty. Their rights were nonpolitical, deriving from their roles as wives and mothers.

Overall, however, the republican citizen was, by definition, male. In a notable case, a Massachusetts court returned to James Martin confiscated property previously owned by his mother, who had fled the state during the Revolution with her Loyalist husband. Like other states, Massachusetts seized the land of those who had supported the British. But, the court ruled, it was unreasonable to expect a wife to exercise independent political judgment. To rebel against the king was one thing, but one could hardly ask Mrs. Martin to rebel against her husband. Therefore, the court reasoned, she should not have been punished for taking the British side.

REPUBLICAN MOTHERHOOD

The Revolution nonetheless did produce an improvement in status for many women. According to the ideology of "republican motherhood" that emerged as a result of independence, women played an indispensable role by training future citizens. The "foundation of national morality," wrote John Adams, "must be laid in private families." Even though republican motherhood ruled out direct female involvement in politics, it encouraged the expansion of educational opportunities for women, so that they could impart political wisdom to their children. Women, wrote Benjamin Rush, needed to have a "suitable education," to enable them to "instruct their sons in the principles of liberty and government."

The idea of republican motherhood reinforced the trend, already evident in the eighteenth century, toward the idea of "companionate" marriage, a voluntary union held together by affection and mutual dependency rather than male authority. In her letter to John Adams quoted above, Abigail Adams recommended that men should willingly give up "the harsh title of Master for the more tender and endearing one of Friend."

The structure of family life itself was altered by the Revolution. In colonial America, those living within the household often included indentured servants, apprentices, and slaves. After independence, southern slaves remained, rhetorically at least, members of the owner's "family." In the

Portrait of John and Elizabeth Lloyd Cadwalader and Their Daughter Anne. *This 1772 portrait of a prominent Philadelphia businessman and his family by the American artist Charles Willson Peale illustrates the emerging ideal of the "companionate" marriage, which is based on affection rather than male authority.*

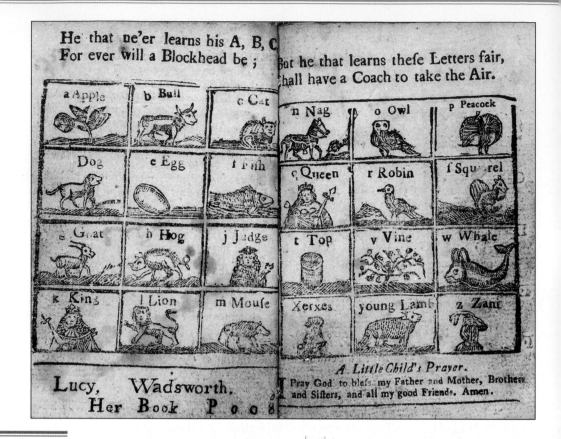

He that ne'er learns his A, B, C
For ever will a Blockhead be ;

But he that learns thefe Letters fair,
Shall have a Coach to take the Air.

a Apple   b Bull   c Cat

Dog   e Egg   f Fish

g Goat   h Hog   j Judge

k King   l Lion   m Moufe

n Nag   o Owl   p Peacock

q Queen   r Robin   f Squirrel

t Top   v Vine   w Whale

Xerxes   young Lamb   z Zani

Lucy,   Wadsworth.
Her Book   P o o

A Little Child's Prayer.
Pray God to blefs my Father and Mother, Brothers
and Sifters, and all my good Friends. Amen.

Two pages from the New England Primer Enlarged *(1779), teaching the alphabet to young children while warning of the consequences of illiteracy. Schoolbooks of the era emphasized both learning and virtuous behavior.*

Creating virtuous children

North, however, with the rapid decline of various forms of indentured servitude and apprenticeship, a more modern definition of the household as consisting of parents and their children took hold. Hired workers, whether domestic servants or farm laborers, were not considered parts of the family.

Like slaves, some free women adapted the rhetoric of the Revolution to their own situation. Ann Baker Carson later recalled how she became estranged from the tyrannical husband she had married at age sixteen. "I was an American," she wrote. "A land of liberty had given me birth. I felt myself his equal." She left the marriage rather than continue as a "female slave." But unlike the case of actual slaves, the subordination of women did not become a major source of public debate until long after American independence.

THE ARDUOUS STRUGGLE FOR LIBERTY

The Revolution changed the lives of virtually every American. As a result of the long struggle against British rule, the public sphere, and with it the right to vote, expanded markedly. Bound labor among whites declined dramatically, religious groups enjoyed greater liberty, blacks mounted a challenge to slavery in which many won their freedom, and women in some ways enjoyed a higher status. On the other hand, for Indians, many Loyalists, and the majority of slaves, American independence meant a deprivation of freedom.

In the words of one British admirer, "the genuine liberty on which America is founded is totally and entirely a new system of things and men." A new nation, which defined itself as an embodiment of freedom, had taken its place on the world stage. "Not only Britain, but all Europe are spectators

America Triumphant and Britannia in Distress. *An elaborate allegory representing American independence as a triumph of liberty, from an almanac published in Boston in 1781. An accompanying key explains the symbolism: (1) America [on the right] holds an olive branch of peace and invites all nations to trade with her. (2) News of America's triumph is broadcast around the world. (3) Britain, seated next to the devil, laments the loss of trade with America. (4) The British flag falls from a fortress. (5) European ships in American waters. (6) Benedict Arnold, the traitor, hangs himself in New York City [in fact, Arnold died of natural causes in London in 1801].*

of the conflict, the arduous struggle for liberty," wrote Ezra Stiles, a future president of Yale College, in 1775. "We consider ourselves as laying the foundation of a glorious future empire, and acting a part for the contemplation of the ages."

Like Stiles, many other Americans were convinced that their struggle for independence had worldwide significance. American independence, indeed, formed part of a larger set of movements that transformed the Atlantic world. The year 1776 saw not only Paine's *Common Sense* and Jefferson's Declaration but also the publication in England of Adam Smith's *The Wealth of Nations*, which attacked the British policy of closely regulating trade, and Jeremy Bentham's *Fragment on Government*, which criticized the nature of British government.

The winds of change were sweeping across the Atlantic world. In 1780, even as the American War for Independence raged, a Jesuit-educated Indian of Peru took the name of the last Inca ruler, Túpac Amaru, and led an uprising against Spanish rule. By the time it was suppressed in 1783, some 10,000 Spanish and 100,000 Indians had perished. In the Dutch, French, and Spanish empires, local elites demanded greater autonomy, often drawing on the constitutional arguments of American patriots. The idea that "the people" possessed rights was quickly internationalized. Slaves in the Caribbean, colonial subjects in India, indigenous inhabitants of Latin America could speak this language. The ideals of the American Revolution helped to inspire countless subsequent struggles for social equality and national independence, from the French Revolution, which exploded in 1789, to the uprising that overthrew the slave system in Haiti in the 1790s, to the Latin American wars for independence in the early nineteenth century, and numerous struggles of colonial peoples for nationhood in the twentieth. But within the new republic, the debate over who should enjoy the blessings of liberty would continue long after indepen-dence had been achieved.

SUGGESTED READING

Berkin, Carol. *Revolutionary Mothers: Women in the Struggle for American Independence* (2005). Presents profiles of women who took part in the movement for independence.

Brown, Wallace. *The Good Americans: The Loyalists in the American Revolution* (1969). A study of Americans who remained loyal to Great Britain during the War of Independence.

Calloway, Colin. *The American Revolution in Indian Country* (1995). Examines how the Revolution affected Indians in each region of the United States.

Davis, David Brion. *The Problem of Slavery in the Age of Revolution* (1975). An influential study of the emergence of slavery as a major public issue in the Atlantic world.

Doerflinger, Thomas M. *A Vigorous Spirit of Enterprise: Merchants and Economic Development in Revolutionary Philadelphia* (1986). Explores how Philadelphia merchants participated in and reacted to the upheavals of the revolutionary era.

Frey, Sylvia R. *Water from the Rock: Black Resistance in a Revolutionary Age* (1991). A study of the many ways blacks sought to gain freedom for themselves during the Revolution.

Hatch, Nathan O. *The Democratization of American Christianity* (1989). A comprehensive account of the impact on religion of the Revolution and its aftermath.

Holton, Woody. *Forced Founders: Indians, Debtors, Slaves and the Making of the American Revolution in Virginia* (1999). Explores how the struggles of those outside Virginia's elite contributed to the movement for independence.

Kruman, Marc. *Between Authority and Liberty: State Constitution Making in Revolutionary America* (1997). The most detailed account of how state constitutions were changed during the era.

Main, Jackson T. *The Social Structure of Revolutionary America* (1965). A careful analysis of American society in the revolutionary era.

Nash, Gary. *The Unknown American Revolution: The Unruly Birth of Democracy and the Struggle to Create America* (2005). Emphasizes the role of ordinary Americans in the struggle for independence.

Norton, Mary Beth. *Liberty's Daughters: The Revolutionary Experience of American Women, 1750–1800* (1980). A pioneering study of women's lives in the era of the Revolution.

Schama, Simon. *Rough Crossing: Britain, the Slaves and the American Revolution* (2006). A detailed look at the experience of the thousands of slaves who escaped to British lines and their fate after the end of the War of Independence.

Taylor, Alan. *The Divided Ground: Indians, Settlers, and the Northern Borderland of the American Revolution* (2006). Examines the Revolution and its consequence in the Iroquois region of upstate New York.

Wood, Gordon. *The Radicalism of the American Revolution* (1992). An influential work that sees the Revolution as transforming a hierarchical society into a democratic one.

REVIEW QUESTIONS

1. Why did the Revolution have more radical effects in Pennsylvania than elsewhere?

2. What role did the founders see for religion in the state?

3. What was the impact of the Revolution on Native Americans?

4. What were the most important features of the new state constitutions?

5. What was "republican motherhood" and why was it significant?

KEY TERMS

unicameral legislatures (p. 215)

woman's suffrage (p. 217)

free labor (p. 222)

inflation (p. 223)

Stockbridge Indians (p. 227)

gradual emancipation (p. 236)

free blacks (p. 236)

women's education (p. 239)

REVIEW TABLE

Freedom and the State Constitutions

Provision	States
Eliminated property qualification for voting	All states except Virginia, Maryland, South Carolina
Eliminated all property and tax qualifications for voting	Vermont
Granted vote to free blacks who met qualifications	All states except Virginia, South Carolina, Georgia
One-house state government	Pennsylvania, Georgia, Vermont
Two-house state government	All states except Pennsylvania, Georgia, Vermont
Guaranteed complete religious liberty	New York

CHAPTER 7

Founding a Nation, 1783–1789

The Signing of the Constitution, *by the mid-nineteenth century American artist Thomas Pritchard Rossiter, depicts the conclusion of the Constitutional Convention of 1787. Among the founding fathers depicted are James Wilson, signing the document at the table in the center, and George Washington, presiding from the dais with an image of the sun behind him.*

FOCUS QUESTIONS

- What were the achievements and problems of the Confederation government?

- What were the major debates that gave shape to the Constitution?

- What were the purpose and meaning of the Bill of Rights as it emerged from the ratification process?

- What did "We the People" mean in the new nation for Indians and African-Americans?

During June and July of 1788, civic leaders in cities up and down the Atlantic coast organized colorful pageants to celebrate the ratification of the United States Constitution. For one day, Benjamin Rush commented of Philadelphia's parade, social class "forgot its claims," as thousands of marchers—rich and poor, businessman and apprentice—joined in a common public ceremony. New York's Grand Federal Procession was led by farmers, followed by the members of every craft in the city from butchers and coopers (makers of wooden barrels) to bricklayers, blacksmiths, and printers. Lawyers, merchants, and clergymen brought up the rear. The parades testified to the strong popular support for the Constitution in the nation's cities. And the prominent role of skilled artisans reflected how the Revolution had secured their place in the American public sphere. Elaborate banners and floats gave voice to the hopes inspired by the new structure of government. "May commerce flourish and industry be rewarded," declared Philadelphia's mariners and shipbuilders.

Throughout the era of the Revolution, Americans spoke of their nation as a "rising empire," destined to populate and control the entire North American continent. While Europe's empires were governed by force, America's would be different. In Jefferson's phrase, it would be "an empire of liberty," bound together by a common devotion to the principles of the Declaration of Independence. Already, the United States exceeded in size Great Britain, Spain, and France combined. As a new nation, it possessed many advantages, including physical isolation from the Old World (a significant asset between 1789 and 1815, when European powers were almost constantly at war), a youthful population certain to grow much larger, and a broad distribution of property ownership and literacy among white citizens.

On the other hand, while Americans dreamed of economic prosperity and continental empire, the nation's prospects when it became independent were not entirely promising. Control of its vast territory was by no means secure. Nearly all of the 3.9 million Americans recorded in the first national census of 1790 lived near the Atlantic coast. Large areas west of the Appalachian Mountains remained in Indian hands. The British retained military posts on American territory near the Great Lakes, and there were fears that Spain might close the port of New Orleans to American commerce on the Mississippi River.

Away from navigable waterways, communication and transportation were primitive. The country was overwhelmingly rural—fewer than one American in thirty lived in a place with 8,000 inhabitants or more. The population consisted of numerous ethnic and religious groups and some 700,000 slaves, making unity difficult to achieve. No republican government had ever been established over so vast a territory or with so diverse a population. Local loyalties outweighed national patriotism. "We have no Americans in America," commented John Adams. It would take time for consciousness of a common nationality to sink deep roots.

Today, with the United States the most powerful country on earth, it is difficult to recall that in 1783 the future seemed precarious indeed for the fragile nation seeking to make its way in a world of hostile great powers. Profound questions needed to be answered. What course of development should the United States follow? How could the competing claims of local self-government, sectional interests, and national authority be balanced? Who should be considered full-fledged members of the American people, entitled to the blessings of liberty? These issues became the focus of heated debate as the first generation of Americans sought to consolidate their new republic.

AMERICA UNDER THE CONFEDERATION

THE ARTICLES OF CONFEDERATION

The first written constitution of the United States was the Articles of Confederation, drafted by Congress in 1777 and ratified by the states four years later. The Articles sought to balance the need for national coordination of the War of Independence with widespread fear that centralized political power posed a danger to liberty. It explicitly declared the new national government to be a "perpetual union." But it resembled less a blueprint for a common government than a treaty for mutual defense—in its own words, a "firm league of friendship" among the states. Under the Articles, the thirteen states retained their individual "sovereignty, freedom, and independence." The national government consisted of a one-house Congress, in which each state, no matter how large or populous, cast a single vote. There was no president to enforce the laws and no judiciary to interpret them. Major decisions required the approval of nine states rather than a simple majority.

The only powers specifically granted to the national government by the Articles of Confederation were those essential to the struggle for independence—declaring war, conducting foreign affairs, and making treaties with other governments. Congress had no real financial resources. It could coin money but lacked the power to levy taxes or regulate commerce. Its revenue came mainly from contributions by the individual states. To amend the Articles required the unanimous consent of the states, a formidable obstacle to change. Various amendments to strengthen the national government were proposed during the seven years (1781–1788) when the Articles of Confederation were in effect, but none received the approval of all the states.

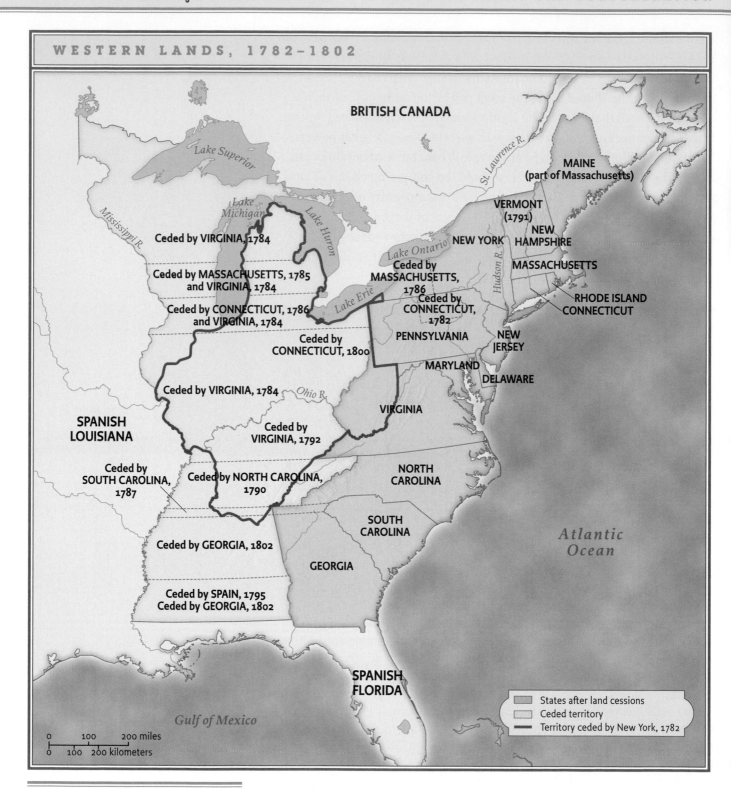

WESTERN LANDS, 1782–1802

BRITISH CANADA

Lake Superior

Mississippi R.

Lake Michigan

Lake Huron

Ceded by VIRGINIA, 1784

Ceded by MASSACHUSETTS, 1785 and VIRGINIA, 1784

Ceded by CONNECTICUT, 1786 and VIRGINIA, 1784

Lake Erie

Ceded by CONNECTICUT, 1800

Ceded by VIRGINIA, 1784

Ohio R.

Ceded by VIRGINIA, 1792

SPANISH LOUISIANA

Ceded by SOUTH CAROLINA, 1787

Ceded by NORTH CAROLINA, 1790

Ceded by GEORGIA, 1802

Ceded by SPAIN, 1795
Ceded by GEORGIA, 1802

MAINE
(part of Massachusetts)

St. Lawrence R.

VERMONT
(1791)

NEW YORK

NEW HAMPSHIRE

Lake Ontario

Ceded by MASSACHUSETTS, 1786

Hudson R.

MASSACHUSETTS

Ceded by CONNECTICUT, 1782

RHODE ISLAND
CONNECTICUT

PENNSYLVANIA

NEW JERSEY

MARYLAND

DELAWARE

VIRGINIA

NORTH CAROLINA

SOUTH CAROLINA

GEORGIA

Atlantic Ocean

SPANISH FLORIDA

Gulf of Mexico

	States after land cessions
	Ceded territory
	Territory ceded by New York, 1782

0   100   200 miles
0   100   200 kilometers

The creation of a nationally controlled public domain from western land ceded by the states was one of the main achievements of the federal government under the Articles of Confederation.

The Articles made energetic national government impossible. But Congress in the 1780s did not lack for accomplishments. The most important was establishing national control over land to the west of the thirteen states and devising rules for its settlement. Disputes over access to western land almost prevented ratification of the Articles in the first place. Citing their original royal charters, which granted territory running all the way to the "South Sea" (the Pacific Ocean), states like Virginia, the Carolinas, and Connecticut claimed immense tracts of western land. Land speculators, politicians, and prospective settlers from states with clearly defined boundaries insisted that such land must belong to the nation at large. Only after the land-rich states, in the interest of national unity, ceded their western claims to the central government did the Articles win ratification.

CONGRESS AND THE WEST

Establishing rules for the settlement of this national domain—the area controlled by the federal government, stretching from the western boundaries of existing states to the Mississippi River—was by no means easy. Although some Americans spoke of it as if it were empty, some 100,000 Indians in fact inhabited the region. In the immediate aftermath of independence, Congress took the position that by aiding the British, Indians had forfeited the right to their lands. It made little distinction among tribes that had sided with the enemy, those that had aided the patriots, and those in the interior that had played no part in the war at all. At peace conferences at Fort Stanwix, New York, in 1784 and Fort McIntosh near Pittsburgh the following year, American representatives demanded and received large surrenders of Indian land north of the Ohio River. Similar treaties soon followed with the Cherokee, Choctaw, and Chickasaw tribes in the South, although here Congress guaranteed the permanency of the Indians' remaining, much-reduced holdings. The treaties secured national control of a large part of the country's western territory.

When it came to disposing of western land and regulating its settlement, the Confederation government faced conflicting pressures. Many leaders believed that the economic health of the new republic required that farmers have access to land in the West. But they also saw land sales as a potential source of revenue and worried that unregulated settlement would produce endless conflicts with the Indians. Land companies, which lobbied Congress vigorously, hoped to profit by purchasing real estate and reselling it to settlers. The government, they insisted, should step aside and allow private groups to take control of the West's economic development.

SETTLERS AND THE WEST

The arrival of peace meanwhile triggered a large population movement from settled parts of the original states into frontier areas like upstate New York and across the Appalachian Mountains into Kentucky and Tennessee. To settlers, the right to take possession of western lands and use them as they saw fit was an essential element of American freedom. When a group

An engraving from The Farmer's and Mechanics Almanac *shows farm families moving west along a primitive road through the wilderness.*

of Ohioans petitioned Congress in 1785, assailing landlords and speculators who monopolized available acreage and asking that preference in land ownership be given to "actual settlements," their motto was "Grant us Liberty." Indeed, settlers paid no heed to Indian land titles and urged the government to set a low price on public land or give it away. They frequently occupied land to which they had no legal title. By the 1790s, Kentucky courts were filled with lawsuits over land claims and many settlers lost land they thought they had owned. Eventually, disputes over land forced many early settlers (including the parents of Abraham Lincoln) to leave Kentucky for opportunities in other states.

At the same time, however, like British colonial officials before them, many leaders of the new nation feared that an unregulated flow of population across the Appalachian Mountains would provoke constant warfare with Indians. Moreover, they viewed frontier settlers as disorderly and lacking in proper respect for authority—"our debtors, loose English people, our German servants, and slaves," Benjamin Franklin had once called them. Establishing law and order in the West and strict rules for the occupation of land there seemed essential to attracting a better class of settlers to the West and avoiding discord between the settled and frontier parts of the new nation.

THE LAND ORDINANCES

A series of measures approved by Congress during the 1780s defined the terms by which western land would be marketed and settled. Drafted by Thomas Jefferson, the Ordinance of 1784 established stages of self-government for the West. The region would be divided into districts initially governed by Congress and eventually admitted to the Union as member states. By a single vote, Congress rejected a clause that would have prohibited slavery throughout the West. A second ordinance, in 1785, regulated land sales in the region north of the Ohio River, which came to be known as the Old Northwest. Land would be surveyed by the government and then sold in "sections" of a square mile (640 acres) at $1 per acre. In each township, one section would be set aside to provide funds for public education. The system promised to control and concentrate settlement and raise money for Congress. But settlers violated the rules by pressing westward before the surveys had been completed.

Like the British before them, American officials found it difficult to regulate the thirst for new land. The minimum purchase price of $640, however, put public land out of the financial reach of most settlers. They generally ended up buying smaller parcels from speculators and land companies. In 1787, Congress decided to sell off large tracts to private groups, including 1.5 million acres to the Ohio Company, organized by New England land speculators and army officers. (This was a different organization from the Ohio Company of the 1750s, mentioned in Chapter 4.) For many years, national land policy benefited private land companies and large buyers more than individual settlers. And for many decades, actual and prospective settlers pressed for a reduction in the price of government-owned land, a movement that did not end until the Homestead Act of 1862 offered free land on the public domain.

A final measure, the Northwest Ordinance of 1787, called for the eventual establishment of from three to five states north of the Ohio River and east of the Mississippi. Thus was enacted the basic principle of what Jefferson called the "empire of liberty"—rather than ruling over the West as a colonial power, the United States would admit the area's population as equal members of the political system. Territorial expansion and self-government would grow together.

The Northwest Ordinance pledged that "the utmost good faith" would be observed toward local Indians and that their land would not be taken without consent. This was the first official recognition that Indians continued to own their land. Congress realized that allowing settlers and state government simply to seize Indian lands would produce endless, expensive military conflicts on the frontier. "It will cost much less," one congressman noted, "to conciliate the good opinion of the Indians than to pay men for destroying them." But national land policy assumed that whether through purchase, treaties, or voluntary removal, the Indian presence would soon disappear. The Ordinance also prohibited slavery in the Old Northwest, a provision that would have far-reaching consequences when the sectional conflict between North and South developed. But for years, owners brought slaves into the area, claiming that they had voluntarily signed long-term labor contracts.

THE CONFEDERATION'S WEAKNESSES

Whatever the achievements of the Confederation government, in the eyes of many influential Americans they were outweighed by its failings. Both the national government and the country at large faced

WESTERN ORDINANCES, 1785–1787

BRITISH
NORTH AMERICA
(CANADA)

Lake Superior

St. Lawrence R.

MAINE
(part of Massachusetts)

Point-
au-Fer   Dutchman's
Point

Fort
Michilimackinac

WISCONSIN
(1848)

Lake Michigan

Lake Huron

NEW
HAMPSHIRE

Mississippi R.

Oswego

Lake Ontario

Fort
Niagara

MASSACHUSETTS

NEW YORK

Hudson R.

SPANISH
LOUISIANA

MICHIGAN
(1837)

Fort
Detroit

Lake Erie

RHODE ISLAND

CONNECTICUT

ILLINOIS
(1818)

INDIANA
(1816)

OHIO
(1803)

PENNSYLVANIA

NEW
JERSEY

MARYLAND

DELAWARE

Atlantic
Ocean

Ohio R.

VIRGINIA

KENTUCKY
(1792)

■ Forts
--- Disputed boundaries
▨ Northwest Territory

TENNESSEE (1796)

NORTH CAROLINA

0   100   200 miles
0   100   200 kilometers

THE SEVEN RANGES
First Area Survey

7th Range
6th Range
5th Range
4th Range
3rd Range
2nd Range
1st Range

VIRGINIA
PENNSYLVANIA

6 miles
6 miles

DETAIL OF TOWNSHIP
36 square miles

6	5	4	3	2	1
7	8	9	10	11	12
18	17	16	15	14	13
19	20	21	22	23	24
30	29	28	27	26	25
31	32	33	34	35	36

Income from section 16
reserved for school support

DETAIL OF SECTION
1 square mile (640 acres)

Half-section
(320 acres)

Half-quarter-section
(80 acres)

Quarter-quarter-section
(40 acres each)

Quarter
-section
(160 acres)

1 mile

1 mile

A series of ordinances in the 1780s provided for both the surveying and sale of lands in the public domain north of the Ohio River and the eventual admission of states carved from the area as equal members of the Union.

worsening economic problems. To finance the War of Independence, Congress had borrowed large sums of money by selling interest-bearing bonds and paying soldiers and suppliers in notes to be redeemed in the future. Lacking a secure source of revenue, it found itself unable to pay either interest or the debts themselves. With the United States now outside the British empire, American ships were barred from trading with the West Indies. Imported goods, however, flooded the market, undercutting the business of many craftsmen, driving down wages, and draining money out of the country.

With Congress unable to act, the states adopted their own economic policies. Several imposed tariff duties on goods imported from abroad. Indebted farmers, threatened with the loss of land because of failure to meet tax or mortgage payments, pressed state governments for relief, as did urban craftsmen who owed money to local merchants. In order to increase the amount of currency in circulation and make it easier for individuals to pay their debts, several states printed large sums of paper money. Others enacted laws postponing debt collection. Creditors considered such measures attacks on their property rights. In a number of states, legislative elections produced boisterous campaigns in which candidates for office denounced creditors for oppressing the poor and importers of luxury goods for undermining republican virtue.

SHAYS'S REBELLION

In late 1786 and early 1787, crowds of debt-ridden farmers led by Daniel Shays, a veteran of the War of Independence, closed the courts in western Massachusetts to prevent the seizure of their land for failure to pay debts and state taxes. Massachusetts had firmly resisted pressure to issue paper money or in other ways assist needy debtors. The participants in Shays's Rebellion believed they were acting in the spirit of the Revolution. They modeled their tactics on the crowd activities of the 1760s and 1770s and employed liberty trees and liberty poles as symbols of their cause. They received no sympathy from Governor James Bowdoin, who dispatched an army headed by former revolutionary war general Benjamin Lincoln. The rebels were dispersed in January 1787, and over 1,000 were arrested. Without adherence to the rule of law, Bowdoin declared, Americans would descend into "a state of anarchy, confusion and slavery."

Observing Shays's Rebellion from Paris where he was serving as ambassador, Thomas Jefferson refused to be alarmed. "A little rebellion now and then is a good thing," he wrote to a friend. "The tree of liberty must be refreshed from time to time with the blood of patriots and tyrants." But the uprising was the culmination of a series of events of the 1780s that persuaded an influential group of Americans that the national government must be strengthened so that it could develop uniform economic policies and protect property owners from infringements on their rights by local majorities. The actions of state legislatures (most of them elected annually by an expanded voting population), followed by Shays's Rebellion, produced fears that the Revolution's democratic impulse had gotten out of hand.

A Bankruptcy Scene. *Creditors repossess the belongings of a family unable to pay its debts, while a woman weeps in the background. Popular fears of bankruptcy led several states during the 1780s to pass laws postponing the collection of debts.*

James Madison, "father of the Constitution," a miniature portrait by Charles Willson Peale, painted in 1783. Madison was only thirty-six years old when the Constitutional Convention met.

Alexander Hamilton, another youthful leader of the nationalists of the 1780s, was born in the West Indies in 1755. This portrait was painted by Charles Willson Peale in the early 1790s.

"Our government," Samuel Adams wrote in 1785, "at present has liberty for its object." But among proponents of stronger national authority, liberty had lost some of its luster. The danger to individual rights, they came to believe, now arose not from a tyrannical central government, but from the people themselves. "Liberty," declared James Madison, "may be endangered by the abuses of liberty as well as the abuses of power." To put it another way, private liberty, especially the secure enjoyment of property rights, could be endangered by public liberty—unchecked power in the hands of the people.

NATIONALISTS OF THE 1780S

Madison, a diminutive, colorless Virginian and the lifelong disciple and ally of Thomas Jefferson, thought deeply and creatively about the nature of political freedom. He was among the group of talented and well-organized men who spearheaded the movement for a stronger national government. Another was Alexander Hamilton, who had come to North America as a youth from the West Indies, served at the precocious age of twenty as an army officer during the War of Independence, and married into a prominent New York family. Hamilton was perhaps the most vigorous proponent of an "energetic" government that would enable the new nation to become a powerful commercial and diplomatic presence in world affairs. Genuine liberty, he insisted, required "a proper degree of authority, to make and exercise the laws." Men like Madison and Hamilton were nation-builders. They came to believe during the 1780s that Americans were squandering the fruits of independence and that the country's future greatness depended on enhancing national authority.

The concerns voiced by critics of the Articles found a sympathetic hearing among men who had developed a national consciousness during the Revolution. Nationalists included army officers, members of Congress accustomed to working with individuals from different states, and diplomats who represented the country abroad. In the army, John Marshall (later a chief justice of the Supreme Court) developed "the habit of considering America as my country, and Congress as my government." Influential economic interests also desired a stronger national government. Among these were bondholders who despaired of being paid so long as Congress lacked a source of revenue, urban artisans seeking tariff protection from foreign imports, merchants desiring access to British markets, and all those who feared that the states were seriously interfering with property rights. While these groups did not agree on many issues, they all believed in the need for a stronger national government.

In September 1786, delegates from six states met at Annapolis, Maryland, to consider ways for better regulating interstate and international commerce. The delegates proposed another gathering, in Philadelphia, to amend the Articles of Confederation. Shays's Rebellion greatly strengthened the nationalists' cause. "The late turbulent scenes in Massachusetts," wrote Madison, underscored the need for a new constitution. "No respect," he complained, "is paid to the federal authority." Without a change in the structure of government, either anarchy or monarchy was the likely outcome, bringing to an end the experiment in republican government. Every state except Rhode Island, which had gone the furthest in developing its own debtor relief and trade policies, decided to send delegates to the Philadelphia convention. When they assembled in May 1787, they decided to scrap the Articles of Confederation entirely and draft a new constitution for the United States.

A NEW CONSTITUTION

The fifty-five men who gathered for the Constitutional Convention included some of the most prominent Americans. Thomas Jefferson and John Adams, serving as diplomats in Europe, did not take part. But among the delegates were George Washington (whose willingness to lend his prestige to the gathering and to serve as presiding officer was an enormous asset), George Mason (author of Virginia's Declaration of Rights of 1776), and Benjamin Franklin (who had returned to Philadelphia after helping to negotiate the Treaty of Paris of 1783, and was now eighty-one years old). John Adams described the convention as a gathering of men of "ability, weight, and experience." He might have added, "and wealth." Few men of ordinary means attended. Although a few, like Alexander Hamilton, had risen from humble origins, most had been born into propertied families. They earned their livings as lawyers, merchants, planters, and large farmers. Nearly all were quite prosperous by the standards of the day.

At a time when fewer than one-tenth of 1 percent of Americans attended college, more than half the delegates had college educations. A majority had participated in interstate meetings of the 1760s and 1770s, and twenty-two had served in the army during the Revolution. Their shared social status and political experiences bolstered their common belief in the need to strengthen national authority and curb what one called "the excesses of democracy." To ensure free and candid debate, the deliberations took place in private. Madison, who believed the outcome would have great consequences for "the cause of liberty throughout the world," took careful notes. They were not published, however, until 1840, four years after he became the last delegate to pass away.

THE STRUCTURE OF GOVERNMENT

It quickly became apparent that the delegates agreed on many points. The new Constitution would create a legislature, an executive, and a national judiciary. Congress would have the power to raise money without relying on the states. States would be prohibited from infringing on the rights of property. And the government would represent the people. Hamilton's proposal for a president and

A fifty-dollar note issued by the Continental Congress during the War of Independence. Congress's inability to raise funds to repay such paper money in gold or silver was a major reason why nationalists desired a stronger federal government.

The Philadelphia State House (now called Independence Hall), where the Declaration of Independence was signed in 1776 and the Constitutional Convention took place in 1787.

Senate serving life terms, like the king and House of Lords of England, received virtually no support. The "rich and well-born," Hamilton told the convention, must rule, for the masses "seldom judge or determine right." Most delegates, however, hoped to find a middle ground between the despotism of monarchy and aristocracy and what they considered the excesses of popular self-government. "We had been too democratic," observed George Mason, but he warned against the danger of going to "the opposite extreme." The key to stable, effective republican government was finding a way to balance the competing claims of liberty and power.

Differences quickly emerged over the proper balance between the federal and state governments and between the interests of large and small states. Early in the proceedings, Madison presented what came to be called the Virginia Plan. It proposed the creation of a two-house legislature with a state's population determining its representation in each. Smaller states, fearing that populous Virginia, Massachusetts, and Pennsylvania would dominate the new government, rallied behind the New Jersey Plan. This called for a single-house Congress in which each state cast one vote, as under the Articles of Confederation. In the end, a compromise was reached—a two-house Congress consisting of a Senate in which each state had two members, and a House of Representatives apportioned according to population. Senators would be chosen by state legislatures for six-year terms. They were thus insulated from sudden shifts in public opinion. Representatives were to be elected every two years directly by the people.

THE LIMITS OF DEMOCRACY

Under the Articles of Confederation, no national official had been chosen by popular vote. Thus, the mode of choosing the House of Representatives represented an expansion of democracy. Popular election of at least one part of the political regime, Madison declared, was "essential to every plan of free government." The Constitution, moreover, imposed neither property nor religious qualifications for voting, leaving it to the states to set voting rules.

Overall, however, the new structure of government was less than democratic. The delegates sought to shield the national government from the popular enthusiasms that had alarmed them during the 1780s and to ensure that the right kind of men held office. The people would remain sovereign, but they would choose among the elite to staff the new government. The delegates assumed that the Senate would be composed of each state's most distinguished citizens. They made the House of Representatives quite small (initially 65 members, at a time when the Massachusetts assembly had 200), on the assumption that only prominent individuals could win election in large districts.

Nor did the delegates provide for direct election of either federal judges or the president. Members of the Supreme Court would be appointed by the president for life terms. The president would be chosen either by members of an electoral college or by the House of Representatives. The number of electors for each state was determined by adding together its allocation of senators and representatives. A state's electors would be chosen either by its legislature or by popular vote. In either case, the delegates assumed, electors would be prominent, well-educated individuals better qualified than ordinary voters to choose the head of state.

The actual system of election seemed a recipe for confusion. Each elector was to cast votes for two candidates for president, with the second-place finisher becoming vice president. If no candidate received a majority of the electoral ballots—as the delegates seem to have assumed would normally be the case—the president would be chosen from among the top three finishers by the House of Representatives, with each state casting one vote. The Senate would then elect the vice president. The delegates devised this extremely cumbersome system of indirect election because they did not trust ordinary voters to choose the president and vice president directly.

THE DIVISION AND SEPARATION OF POWERS

Hammered out in four months of discussion and compromise, the Constitution is a spare document of only 4,000 words that provides only the briefest outline of the new structure of government (See the Appendix for the full text). It embodies two basic political principles—federalism, sometimes called the "division of powers," and the system of "checks and balances" between the different branches of the national government, also known as the "separation of powers."

Federalism refers to the relationship between the national government and the states. Compared to the Articles of Confederation, the Constitution significantly strengthened national authority. It charged the president with enforcing the law and commanding the military. It empowered Congress to levy taxes, borrow money, regulate commerce, declare war, deal with foreign nations and Indians, and promote the "general welfare." Madison proposed to allow Congress to veto state laws, but this proved too far-reaching for most delegates. The Constitution did, however, declare

This advertisement for the sale of one hundred slaves from Virginia to states further south appeared in a Richmond newspaper only a few months after the signing of the Constitution. Slavery was a major subject of debate at the Constitutional Convention.

national legislation the "supreme Law of the Land." And it included strong provisions to prevent the states from infringing on property rights. They were barred from issuing paper money, impairing contracts, interfering with interstate commerce, and levying their own import or export duties. On the other hand, most day-to-day affairs of government, from education to law enforcement, remained in the hands of the states. This principle of divided sovereignty was a recipe for debate, which continues to this day, over the balance of power between the national government and the states.

The "separation of powers," or the system of "checks and balances," refers to the way the Constitution seeks to prevent any branch of the national government from dominating the other two. To prevent an accumulation of power dangerous to liberty, authority within the government is diffused and balanced against itself. Congress enacts laws, but the president can veto them, and a two-thirds majority is required to pass legislation over his objection. Federal judges are nominated by the president and approved by Congress, but to ensure their independence, the judges then serve for life. The president can be impeached by the House and removed from office by the Senate for "high crimes and misdemeanors."

THE DEBATE OVER SLAVERY

The structure of government was not the only source of debate at the Constitutional Convention. As Madison recorded, "the institution of slavery and its implications" divided the delegates at many sessions. Those who gathered in Philadelphia included numerous slaveholders, as well as some dedicated advocates of abolition. Madison, like Jefferson a Virginia slaveholder who detested slavery, told the convention that the "distinction of color" had become the basis for "the most oppressive dominion ever exercised by man over man." Yet he later assured the Virginia ratifying convention that the Constitution offered slavery "better security than any that now exists."

The words "slave" and "slavery" did not appear in the Constitution—a concession to the sensibilities of delegates who feared they would "contaminate the glorious fabric of American liberty." As Luther Martin of Maryland wrote, his fellow delegates "anxiously sought to avoid the admission of expressions which might be odious to the ears of Americans." But, he continued, they were "willing to admit into their system those *things* which the *expressions signified.*" The document prohibited Congress from abolishing the African slave trade for twenty years. It required states to return to their owners fugitives from bondage. And it provided that three-fifths of the slave population would be counted in determining each state's representation in the House of Representatives and its electoral votes for president.

South Carolina's delegates had come to Philadelphia determined to defend slavery, and they had a powerful impact on the final document. They originated the fugitive slave clause, the three-fifths clause, and the electoral college. They insisted on strict limits on the power of Congress to levy taxes within the states, fearing future efforts to raise revenue by taxing slave property. They threatened disunion if the Atlantic slave trade were prohibited immediately, as the New England states and Virginia, with its abundance of native-born slaves, demanded. Their threats swayed many delegates. Gouverneur Morris, one of Pennsylvania's delegates, declared that he was being forced to decide between offending the southern states or doing injustice to "human nature." For the sake of national unity, he said, he would choose the latter.

SLAVERY IN THE CONSTITUTION

The Constitution's slavery clauses were compromises, efforts to find a middle ground between the institution's critics and defenders. Taken together, however, they embedded slavery more deeply than ever in American life and politics. The slave trade clause allowed a commerce condemned by civilized society—one that had been suspended during the War of Independence—to continue until 1808. On January 1, 1808, the first day that Congress was allowed under the Constitution, it prohibited the further importation of slaves. But in the interim, partly to replace slaves who had escaped to the British and partly to provide labor for the expansion of slavery to fertile land away from the coast, some 170,000 Africans were brought to the new nation as slaves. South Carolina and Georgia imported 100,000. This represented more than one-quarter of all the slaves brought to mainland North America after 1700.

The fugitive slave clause accorded slave laws "extraterritoriality"—that is, the condition of bondage remained attached to a person even if he or she escaped to a state where slavery had been abolished. John Jay, while serving in Spain on a diplomatic mission, once wrote of how he missed the "free air" of America. Jay was probably unaware of the phrase's full implications. In the famous *Somerset* case of 1772, the lawyer for a West Indian slave brought to Britain had obtained his client's freedom by invoking the memorable words, "the air of England is too pure for a slave to breathe" (that is, the moment any person sets foot on British soil, he or she becomes free). Yet the new federal Constitution required all the states, North and South, to recognize and help police the institution of slavery. For slaves, there was no "free air" in America.

The Constitution gave the national government no power to interfere with slavery in the states. And the three-fifths clause allowed the white South to exercise far greater power in national affairs than the size of its free population warranted. It greatly enhanced the number of southern votes in the House of Representatives and therefore in the electoral college (where, as noted above, the number of electors for each state was determined by adding its number of senators and representatives). Of the first sixteen presidential elections, between 1788 and 1848, all but four placed a southern slaveholder in the White House.

Even the initial failure to include a Bill of Rights resulted, in part, from the presence of slavery. As South Carolina delegate Charles C. Pinckney explained, "such bills generally begin with declaring that all men are by nature born free," a declaration that would come "with a very bad grace, when a large part of our property consists in men who are actually born slaves."

But buried in the Constitution, some slaveholders detected a potential threat. Patrick Henry, who condemned slavery but feared abolition, warned that in time of war, the new government might take steps to arm and liberate the slaves. "May Congress not say," he asked, "that every black man must fight? Did we not see a little of this [in the] last war?" What Henry could not anticipate was that the war that eventually destroyed slavery would be launched by the South itself to protect the institution.

In this engraving, Americans celebrate the signing of the Constitution beneath a temple of liberty.

The preamble to the Constitution, as printed in a Pennsylvania newspaper two days after the Constitutional Convention adjourned.

THE FINAL DOCUMENT

Gouverneur Morris put the finishing touches on the final draft of the new Constitution, trying to make it, he explained, "as clear as our language would permit." For the original preamble, which began, "We the people of the States of New Hampshire, Massachusetts," etc., he substituted the far more powerful, "We the people of the United States." He added a statement of the Constitution's purposes, including to "establish justice," promote "the general welfare," and "secure the blessings of liberty"—things the Articles of Confederation, in the eyes of most of the delegates, had failed to accomplish.

The last session of the Constitutional Convention took place on September 17, 1787. Benjamin Franklin urged the delegates to put aside individual objections and approve the document, whatever its imperfections. "The older I grow," he remarked, "the more apt I am to . . . pay more respect to the judgment of others." Of the forty-five delegates who remained in Philadelphia, thirty-nine signed the Constitution. It was then sent to the states for ratification.

The Constitution created a new framework for American development. By assigning to Congress power over tariffs, interstate commerce, the coining of money, patents, rules for bankruptcy, and weights and measures, and by prohibiting states from interfering with property rights, it made possible a national economic market. It created national political institutions, reduced the powers of the states, and sought to place limits on popular democracy. "The same enthusiasm, *now* pervades all classes in favor of *government*," observed Benjamin Rush, "that actuated us in favor of *liberty* in the years 1774 and 1775." Whether "all classes" truly agreed may be doubted, for the ratification process unleashed a nationwide debate over the best means of preserving American freedom.

THE RATIFICATION DEBATE AND THE ORIGIN OF THE BILL OF RIGHTS

THE FEDERALIST

Even though the Constitution provided that it would go into effect when nine states, not all thirteen as required by the Articles of Confederation, had given their approval, ratification was by no means certain. Each state held an election for delegates to a special ratifying convention. A fierce public battle ensued, producing hundreds of pamphlets and newspaper articles and spirited campaigns to elect delegates. To generate support, Hamilton, Madison, and Jay composed a series of eighty-five essays that appeared in newspapers under the pen name Publius and were gathered as a book, *The Federalist*, in 1788. Hamilton wrote fifty, Madison thirty, and Jay the remainder. Today, the essays are regarded as among the most important American contributions to political thought.

Again and again, Hamilton and Madison repeated that rather than posing a danger to Americans' liberties, the Constitution in fact protected them. Hamilton's essays sought to disabuse Americans of their fear of political power. Government, he insisted, was an expression of freedom, not its enemy. Any government could become oppressive, but with its checks and balances and division of power, the Constitution made political tyranny almost impossible. Hamilton insisted that he was "as zealous an advocate for liberty as any man whatever." But "want of power" had been the fatal flaw of the Articles. At the New York ratifying convention, Hamilton assured the delegates that the Constitution had created "the perfect balance between liberty and power."

"EXTEND THE SPHERE"

Madison, too, emphasized how the Constitution was structured to prevent abuses of authority. But in several essays, especially *Federalist* nos. 10 and 51, he moved beyond such assurances to develop a strikingly new vision of the relationship between government and society in the United States. Madison identified the essential dilemma, as he saw it, of the new republic—government must be based on the will of the people, yet the people had shown themselves susceptible to dangerous enthusiasms. Most worrisome, they had threatened property rights, whose protection was the "first object of government." The problem of balancing democracy and respect for property would only grow in the years ahead since, he warned, economic development would inevitably increase the numbers of poor. What was to prevent them from using their political power to secure "a more equal distribution" of wealth?

The answer, Madison explained, lay not simply in the way power balanced power in the structure of government, but in the nation's size and diversity. Previous republics had existed only in small territories—the Dutch republic, or Italian city-states of the Renaissance. But, argued Madison, the very size of the United States was a source of stability, not, as many feared, weakness. "Extend the sphere," he wrote. The multiplicity of religious denominations, he argued, offered the best security for religious liberty. Likewise, in a nation as large as the United States, so many distinct interests—economic, regional, and political—would arise, that no single one would ever be able to take over the government and oppress the rest. Every majority would be a coalition of minorities, and thus "the rights of individuals" would be secure.

Madison's writings did much to shape the early nation's understanding of its new political institutions. In arguing that the size of the republic helped to secure Americans' rights, they reinforced the tradition that saw continuous westward expansion as essential to freedom. And in basing the preservation of freedom on the structure of government and size of the republic, not the character of the people, his essays represented a major shift away from the "republican" emphasis on a virtuous citizenry devoted to the common good as the foundation of proper government. Madison helped to popularize the "liberal" idea that men are generally motivated by self-interest, and that the good of society arises from the clash of these private interests.

THE ANTI-FEDERALISTS

Opponents of ratification, called Anti-Federalists, insisted that the Constitution shifted the balance between liberty and power too far in the direction of the latter. Anti-Federalists lacked the coherent leadership of the Constitution's defenders. They included state politicians fearful of seeing their influence diminish, among them such revolutionary heroes as Samuel Adams, John Hancock, and Patrick Henry. Small farmers, many of whom supported the state debtor-relief measures of the 1780s that the Constitution's supporters deplored, also saw no need for a stronger central government. Some opponents of the Constitution denounced the document's protections for slavery; others warned that the powers of Congress were so broad that it might enact a law for abolition.

Anti-Federalists repeatedly predicted that the new government would fall under the sway of merchants, creditors, and others hostile to the interests of ordinary Americans. Repudiating Madison's arguments in *Federalist* nos. 10 and 51, Anti-Federalists insisted that "a very extensive territory cannot be governed on the principles of freedom." Popular self-government, they claimed, flourished best in small communities, where rulers and ruled interacted daily. Only men of wealth, "ignorant of the sentiments of the middling and lower class of citizens," would have the resources to win election to a national government. The result of the Constitution, warned Melancton Smith of New York, a member of Congress under the Articles of Confederation, would be domination of the "common people" by the "wellborn." "This," Smith predicted, "will be a government of oppression."

Liberty was the Anti-Federalists' watchword. America's happiness, they insisted, "arises from the freedom of our institutions and the limited nature of our government," both threatened by the new Constitution. Maryland Anti-Federalists had caps manufactured bearing the word "Liberty," to wear to the polls when members of the state's ratification convention were elected. To the vision of the United States as an energetic great power, Anti-Federalists counterposed a way of life grounded in local, democratic institutions. "What is Liberty?" asked James Lincoln of South Carolina. "The power of governing yourselves. If you adopt this constitution, have you this power? No."

Anti-Federalists also pointed to the Constitution's lack of a Bill of Rights, which left unprotected rights such as trial by jury and freedom of speech and the press. The absence of a Bill of Rights, declared Patrick Henry, was "the most absurd thing to mankind that ever the world saw." State constitutions had bills of rights, yet the states, Henry claimed, were now being asked to surrender most of their powers to the federal government, with no requirement that it respect Americans' basic liberties.

In general, pro-Constitution sentiment flourished in the nation's cities and in rural areas closely tied to the commercial marketplace. The Constitution's most energetic supporters were men of substantial property. But what George Bryan of Pennsylvania, a supporter of ratification, called the "golden phantom" of prosperity also swung urban artisans, laborers, and sailors behind the movement for a government that would use its "energy and power" to revive the depressed economy. Anti-Federalism drew its support from small farmers in more isolated rural areas such as the Hudson Valley of New York, western Massachusetts, and the southern backcountry.

In the end, the supporters' energy and organization, coupled with their domination of the colonial press, carried the day. Ninety-two newspapers and magazines existed in the United States in 1787. Of these, only twelve published a significant number of Anti-Federalist pieces. Madison also won support for the new Constitution by promising that the first Congress would enact a Bill of Rights. By mid-1788, the required nine states had ratified. Although there was strong dissent in Massachusetts, New York, and Virginia, only Rhode Island and North Carolina voted against ratification, and they subsequently had little choice but to join the new government. Anti-Federalism died. But as with other movements in American history that did not immediately achieve their goals—for example, the Populists of the late nineteenth century—some of the Anti-Federalists' ideas eventually entered the political mainstream. To this day, their belief that a too-powerful central government is a threat to liberty continues to influence American political culture.

THE BILL OF RIGHTS

Among the Anti-Federalists' enduring legacies is the Bill of Rights, the ten constitutional amendments approved by the first Congress and ratified by the states in 1791. Madison was so convinced that the balances of the Constitution would protect liberty that he believed a Bill of Rights "redundant or pointless." Amendments restraining federal power, he believed, would have no effect on the danger to liberty posed by unchecked majorities in the states, and no list of rights could ever anticipate the numerous ways that Congress might operate in the future. "Parchment barriers" to the abuse of authority, he observed, would prove least effective when most needed. Madison's prediction would be amply borne out at future times of popular hysteria, such as the Red Scare following World War I and the McCarthy era of the 1950s, when all branches of government joined in trampling on freedom of expression, and during World War II, when hatred of a foreign enemy led to the internment of over 100,000 Japanese-Americans, most of them citizens of the United States.

Nonetheless, in order to satisfy the Constitution's critics, Madison presented to Congress a series of amendments that became known as the Bill of Rights. The First Amendment prohibited Congress from legislating with regard to religion or infringing on freedom of speech, freedom of the press, or the right of assembly. The Second upheld the people's right to "keep and bear arms" in conjunction with "a well-regulated militia." Others prohibited abuses such as arrests without warrants and forcing a person accused of a crime to testify against himself, and reaffirmed the right to trial by jury.

In a sense, the Bill of Rights offered a definition of the "unalienable rights" Jefferson had mentioned in the Declaration

Banner of the Society of Pewterers, one of many artisan groups that took part in New York City's Grand Federal Procession of 1788 celebrating the ratification of the Constitution. The banner depicts the interior of an artisan shop, and the inscription hails the Constitution as a solid foundation for Americans' prosperity and freedom.

of Independence—rights inherent in the human condition. Not having been granted by government in the first place, they could not be rescinded by government. In case any had been accidentally omitted, the Ninth Amendment declared that rights not specifically mentioned in the Constitution were "retained by the people." Its suggestion that the Constitution was not meant to be complete opened the door to future legal recognition of rights not grounded in the actual text (such as the right to privacy). The Tenth Amendment, meant to answer fears that the federal government would ride roughshod over the states, affirmed that powers not delegated to the national government or prohibited to the states continued to reside with the states.

The roots and even the specific language of some parts of the Bill of Rights lay far back in English history. The Eighth Amendment, prohibiting excessive bail and cruel and unusual punishments, incorporates language that originated in a declaration by the House of Lords in 1316 and was repeated centuries later in the English Bill of Rights and the constitutions of a number of American states.

Other provisions reflected the changes in American life brought about by the Revolution. The most remarkable of these was constitutional recognition of religious freedom. Unlike the Declaration of Independence, which invokes the blessing of divine providence, the Constitution is a purely secular document that contains no reference to God and bars religious tests for federal officeholders. The First Amendment prohibits the federal government from legislating on the subject of religion—a complete departure from British and colonial precedent. Under the Constitution it was and remains possible, as one critic complained, for "a papist, a Mohomatan, a deist, yea an atheist" to become president of the United States. Madison was so adamant about separating church and state that he even opposed the appointment of chaplains to serve Congress and the military.

Today, when Americans are asked to define freedom, they instinctively turn to the Bill of Rights and especially the First Amendment, with its guarantees of freedom of speech, the press, and religion. Yet the Bill of Rights aroused little enthusiasm on ratification and for decades was all but ignored. Not until the twentieth century would it come to be revered as an indispensable expression of American freedom. Nonetheless, the Bill of Rights subtly affected the language of liberty. Applying only to the federal government, not the states, it reinforced the idea that concentrated national power posed the greatest threat to freedom. And it contributed to the long process whereby freedom came to be discussed in the vocabulary of rights.

Among the most important rights were freedom of speech and the press, vital building blocks of a democratic public sphere. Once an entitlement of

An engraving and poem, published in 1788 in an American newspaper, after New York became the eleventh state to ratify the new Constitution. North Carolina would ratify in 1789 and Rhode Island in 1790.

What were the purpose and meaning of the Bill of Rights as it emerged from the ratification process?

265

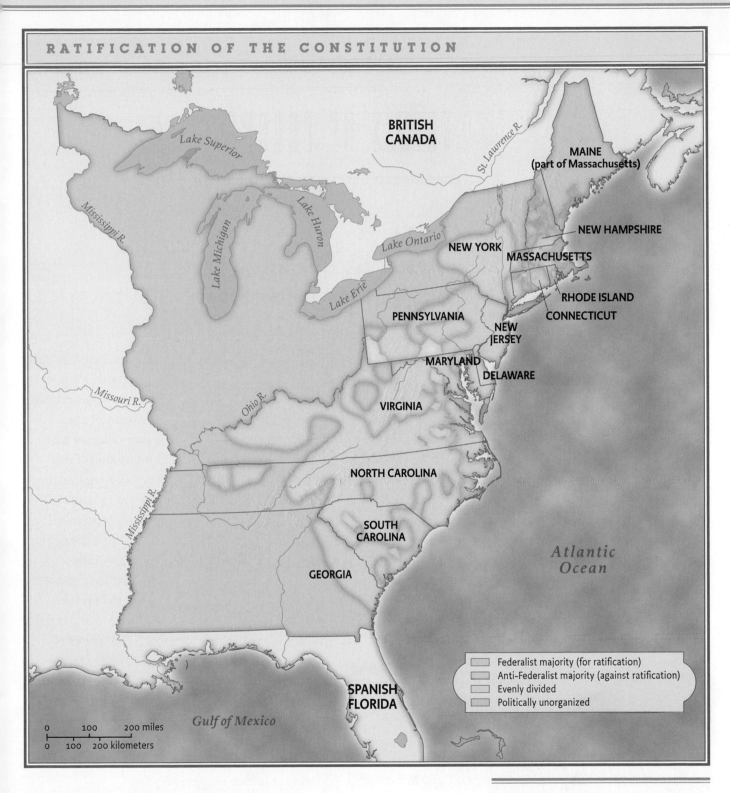

RATIFICATION OF THE CONSTITUTION

BRITISH CANADA

MAINE (part of Massachusetts)

NEW HAMPSHIRE

NEW YORK

MASSACHUSETTS

RHODE ISLAND

CONNECTICUT

PENNSYLVANIA

NEW JERSEY

MARYLAND

DELAWARE

VIRGINIA

NORTH CAROLINA

SOUTH CAROLINA

GEORGIA

SPANISH FLORIDA

Atlantic Ocean

Gulf of Mexico

Lake Superior

Lake Michigan

Lake Huron

Lake Ontario

Lake Erie

Mississippi R.

Missouri R.

Ohio R.

Mississippi R.

St. Lawrence R.

Federalist majority (for ratification)
Anti-Federalist majority (against ratification)
Evenly divided
Politically unorganized

0   100   200 miles
0   100   200 kilometers

members of Parliament and colonial assemblies, free speech came to be seen as a basic right of citizenship. Although the legal implementation remained to be worked out, and serious infringements would occur at many points in American history, the Bill of Rights did much to establish freedom of expression as a cornerstone of the popular understanding of American freedom.

Federalists—those who supported the new Constitution—tended to be concentrated in cities and nearby rural areas, while backcountry farmers were more likely to oppose the new frame of government.

VOICES OF FREEDOM

FROM JAMES MADISON,
The Federalist no. 51 (1787)

Written by James Madison, Alexander Hamilton, and John Jay, *The Federalist* was a series of articles making the case for ratification of the new Constitution. *Federalist* no. 51 was a classic statement of Madison's belief that the structure of government must be arranged so as to protect liberty by dividing political power.

To what expedient, then, shall we finally resort, for maintaining in practice the necessary partition of power among the several [branches of government]? . . . Ambition must be made to counteract ambition. The interest of the man must be connected with the constitutional rights of the place. It may be a reflection on human nature, that such devices should be necessary to control the abuses of government. But what is government itself, but the greatest of all reflections on human nature? If men were angels, no government would be necessary. . . . In framing a government which is to be administered by men over men, the great difficulty lies in this: you must first enable the government to control the governed; and in the next place oblige it to control itself.

It is of great importance in a republic not only to guard the society against the oppression of its rulers, but to guard one part of society against the injustice of the other part. Different interests necessarily exist in different classes of citizens. If a majority be united by common interest, the rights of the minority will be insecure. . . . In a free government the security for civil rights might be the same as for religious rights. It consists in the one case in the multiplicity of interests, and in the other in the multiplicity of sects. The degree of security in both cases will depend on the number of interests and sects. . . . In the extended republic of the United States, and among the great variety of interests, parties, and sects which it embraces, a coalition of the majority of the whole society could seldom take place on any other principles than those of justice and general good.

From James Winthrop,

Anti-Federalist Essay Signed "Agrippa" (1787)

A local official in Middlesex, Massachusetts, James Winthrop published sixteen public letters between November 1787 and February 1788 opposing ratification of the Constitution.

———————

It is the opinion of the ablest writers on the subject, that no extensive empire can be governed upon republican principles, and that such a government will degenerate into a despotism, unless it be made up of a confederacy of smaller states, each having the full powers of internal regulation. This is precisely the principle which has hitherto preserved our freedom. No instance can be found of any free government of considerable extent which has been supported upon any other plan. Large and consolidated empires may indeed dazzle the eyes of a distant spectator with their splendor, but if examined more nearly are always found to be full of misery.... It is under such tyranny that the Spanish provinces languish, and such would be our misfortune and degradation, if we should submit to have the concerns of the whole empire managed by one empire. To promote the happiness of the people it is necessary that there should be local laws; and it is necessary that those laws should be made by the representatives of those who are immediately subject to [them]....

It is impossible for one code of laws to suit Georgia and Massachusetts. They must, therefore, legislate for themselves. Yet there is, I believe, not one point of legislation that is not surrendered in the proposed plan. Questions of every kind respecting property are determinable in a continental court, and so are all kinds of criminal causes. The continental legislature has, therefore, a right to make rules in all cases.... No rights are reserved to the citizens.... This new system is, therefore, a consolidation of all the states into one large mass, however diverse the parts may be of which it is composed....

A bill of rights . . . serves to secure the minority against the usurpation and tyranny of the majority. . . . The experience of all mankind has proved the prevalence of a disposition to use power wantonly. It is therefore as necessary to defend an individual against the majority in a republic as against the king in a monarchy.

═══════════════════

QUESTIONS

1. Why does Madison make an analogy between the security of civil and religious rights?

2. Why does Winthrop believe that a bill of rights is essential in the Constitution?

3. How do Madison and Winthrop differ concerning the political implications of the large geographical size of the American republic?

"WE THE PEOPLE"

NATIONAL IDENTITY

The colonial population had been divided by ethnicity, religion, class, and status and united largely by virtue of their allegiance to Britain. The Revolution created not only a new nation but also a new collective body, the American people, whose members were to enjoy freedom as citizens in a new political community. Since government in the United States rested on the will of the people, it was all the more important to identify who the people were.

The Constitution opens with the words, "We the People," describing those who, among other things, are to possess "the Blessings of Liberty" as a birthright and pass them on to "Posterity." (Abraham Lincoln would later cite these words to argue that since the nation had been created by the people, not the states, the states could not dissolve it.) Although one might assume that the "people" of the United States included all those living within the nation's borders, the text made clear that this was not the case. The Constitution identifies three populations inhabiting the United States: Indians, treated as members of independent tribes and not part of the American body politic; "other persons"—that is, slaves; and the "people." Only the third were entitled to American freedom.

Every nation confronts the task of defining its identity. Historians have traditionally distinguished between "civic nationalism," which envisions the nation as a community open to all those devoted to its political institutions and social values, and "ethnic nationalism," which defines the nation as a community of descent based on a shared ethnic heritage, language, and culture. At first glance, the United States appears to conform to the civic model. It lacked a clear ethnic identity or long-established national boundaries—the political principles of the Revolution held Americans together. To be an American, all one had to do was commit oneself to an ideology of liberty, equality, and democracy. From the outset, however, American nationality combined both civic and ethnic definitions. For most of our history, American citizenship has been defined by blood as well as by political allegiance.

INDIANS IN THE NEW NATION

The early republic's policies toward Indians and African-Americans illustrate the conflicting principles that shaped American nationality. American leaders agreed that the West should not be left in Indian hands, but they disagreed about the Indians' ultimate fate. The government hoped to encourage the westward expansion of white settlement, which implied one of three things: the removal of the Indian population to lands even farther west, their total disappearance, or their incorporation into white "civilization" with the expectation that they might one day become part of American society.

Many white Americans, probably most, deemed Indians savages unfit for citizenship. Indian tribes had no representation in the new government, and the Constitution excluded Indians "not taxed" from being counted in determining each state's number of congressmen. The treaty system gave them a unique status within the American political system. But despite this recognition of their sovereignty, treaties were essentially ways of trans-

A painting depicting the signing of the Treaty of Greenville of 1795, by an unknown member of General Anthony Wayne's staff. In the treaty, a group of tribes ceded most of the area of the current state of Ohio, along with the site that became the city of Chicago, to the United States.

ferring land from Indians to the federal government or the states. Often, a treaty was agreed to by only a small portion of a tribe, but the whole tribe was then forced to accept its legitimacy.

During Washington's administration, Secretary of War Henry Knox hoped to deal with Indians with a minimum of warfare and without undermining the new nation's honor. He recognized, he said in 1794, that American treatment of the continent's native inhabitants had been even "more destructive to the Indian" than Spain's conduct in Mexico and Peru. His conciliatory policy had mixed results. Congress forbade the transfer of Indian land without federal approval. But several states ignored this directive and continued to negotiate their own agreements.

Open warfare continued in the Ohio Valley. In 1791, Little Turtle, leader of the Miami Confederacy, inflicted a humiliating defeat on American forces led by Arthur St. Clair, the American governor of the Northwest Territory. With 630 dead, this was the costliest loss ever suffered by the United States Army at the hands of Indians. In 1794, 3,000 American troops under Anthony Wayne defeated Little Turtle's forces at the Battle of Fallen Timbers. This led directly to the Treaty of Greenville of 1795, in which twelve Indian tribes ceded most of Ohio and Indiana to the federal government. The treaty also established the "annuity" system—yearly grants of federal money to Indian tribes that institutionalized continuing government influence in tribal affairs and gave outsiders considerable control over Indian life.

INDIAN TRIBES, 1790

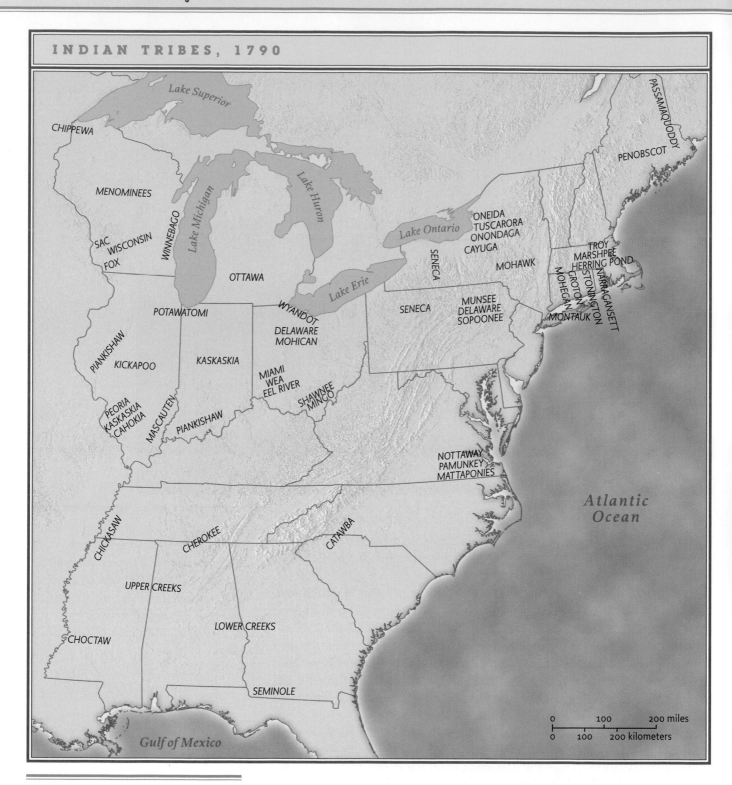

By 1790, the Indian population had declined significantly from the early colonial era, but the area west of the Appalachian Mountains was still known as "Indian country."

Many prominent figures, however, rejected the idea that Indians were innately inferior to white Americans. Thomas Jefferson believed that Indians merely lived at a less advanced stage of civilization. Indians could become full-fledged members of the republic by abandoning communal landholding and hunting in favor of small-scale farming. Once they "possessed property," Jefferson told one Indian group, they could "join us in our government" and, indeed, "mix your blood with ours."

To pursue the goal of assimilation, Congress in the 1790s authorized President Washington to distribute agricultural tools and livestock to Indian men and spinning wheels and looms to Indian women. To whites, the adoption of American gender norms, with men working the land and women tending to their homes, would be a crucial sign that the Indians were becoming "civilized." But the American notion of civilization required so great a transformation of Indian life that most tribes rejected it. One missionary was told, "If we want to work, we know how to do it according to our own way and as it pleases us." To Indians, freedom meant retaining tribal autonomy and identity, including the ability to travel widely in search of game. "Since our acquaintance with our brother white people," declared a Mohawk speaker at a 1796 treaty council, "that which we call freedom and liberty, becomes an entire stranger to us." There was no room for Indians who desired to retain their traditional way of life in the American empire of liberty.

BLACKS AND THE REPUBLIC

By 1790, the number of African-Americans far exceeded the Indian population within the United States. The status of free blacks was somewhat indeterminate. Nowhere does the original Constitution define who in fact are citizens of the United States. The individual states were left free to determine the boundaries of liberty. The North's gradual emancipation acts assumed that former slaves would remain in the country, not be colonized abroad. Northern statesmen like Hamilton, Jay, and Franklin worked for abolition, and some helped to establish schools for black children. During the era of the Revolution, free blacks enjoyed at least some of the legal rights, including, in most states, the right to vote, accorded to whites. Some cast ballots in the election of delegates to conventions that ratified the Constitution. The large majority of blacks, of course, were slaves, and slavery rendered them all but invisible to those imagining the American community. Slaves, as Edmund Randolph, the nation's first attorney general, put it, were "not . . . constituent members of our society," and the language of liberty did not apply to them.

One of the era's most widely read books, *Letters from an American Farmer*, published in France in 1782 by Hector St. John Crèvecoeur, strikingly illustrated this process of exclusion. Born in France, Crèvecoeur had taken part in the unsuccessful defense of Quebec during the Seven Years' War. Instead of returning home, he came to New York City in 1759. As a trader and explorer, he visited most of the British mainland colonies, as well as the Ohio and Mississippi Valleys. Crèvecoeur eventually married the daughter of a prominent New York landowner and lived with his own family on a farm in Orange County. Seeking to remain neutral during the War of Independence, he suffered persecution by both patriots and the British, and eventually returned to France.

In *Letters from an American Farmer*, Crèvecoeur popularized the idea, which would become so common in the twentieth century, of the United States as a melting pot. "Here," he wrote, "individuals of all nations are melted into a new one." The American left behind "all his ancient prejudices and manners [and received] new ones from the new mode of life he has embraced." Crèvecoeur was well aware of what he called "the horrors

Table 7.1 TOTAL POPULATION AND BLACK POPULATION OF THE UNITED STATES, 1790

State	Total Population	Slaves	Free Blacks
New England:			
New Hampshire	141,899	158	630
Vermont*	85,341	0	271
Massachusetts	378,556	0	5,369
Connecticut	237,655	2,764	2,771
Rhode Island	69,112	948	3,484
Maine**	96,643	0	536
Middle States:			
New York	340,241	21,324	4,682
New Jersey	184,139	11,423	2,762
Pennsylvania	433,611	3,737	6,531
South:			
Delaware	59,096	8,887	3,899
Maryland	319,728	103,036	8,043
Virginia	747,610	292,627	12,866
North Carolina	395,005	100,572	5,041
South Carolina	249,073	107,094	1,801
Georgia	82,548	29,264	398
Kentucky*	73,677	12,430	114
Tennessee*	35,691	3,417	361
Total	3,929,625	697,624	59,557

*Vermont, Kentucky, and Tennessee were territories that had not yet been admitted as states.
**Maine was part of Massachusetts in 1790.

of slavery." But when he posed the famous question, "What then is the American, this new man?" he answered, "a mixture of English, Scotch, Irish, French, Dutch, Germans, and Swedes. . . . He is either a European, or the descendant of a European." This at a time when fully one-fifth of the population (the highest proportion in U.S. history) consisted of Africans and their descendants.

Like Crèvecoeur, many white Americans excluded blacks from their conception of the American people. The Constitution empowered Congress to create a uniform system by which immigrants became citizens, and the Naturalization Act of 1790 offered the first legislative definition of American nationality. With no debate, Congress restricted the process of becoming a citizen from abroad to "free white persons."

The law initiated a policy that some historians, with only partial accuracy, call "open immigration." For Europeans, the process was indeed open. Only in the last quarter of the nineteenth century were groups of whites, beginning with prostitutes, convicted felons, lunatics, and persons likely to become a "public charge," barred from entering the country. For the first century of the republic, virtually the only white persons in the entire world ineligible to claim American citizenship were those unwilling to renounce hereditary titles of nobility, as required in an act of 1795. And yet, the word "white" in the Naturalization Act excluded a large majority of the world's population from emigrating to the "asylum for mankind" and partaking in the blessings of American freedom. For eighty years, no non-white immigrant could become a naturalized citizen. Africans were allowed to do so in 1870, but not until the 1940s did persons of Asian origin become eligible. (Native Americans were granted American citizenship in 1924.)

JEFFERSON, SLAVERY, AND RACE

Man's liberty, John Locke had written, flowed from "his having reason." To deny liberty to those who were not considered rational beings did not seem to be a contradiction. White Americans increasingly viewed blacks as permanently deficient in the qualities that made freedom possible—the capacity for self-control, reason, and devotion to the larger community. These were the characteristics that Jefferson, in a famous comparison of the races in his book *Notes on the State of Virginia*, published in 1785, claimed blacks lacked, partly due to natural incapacity and partly because the bitter experience of slavery had (quite understandably, he felt) rendered them disloyal to the nation. Jefferson was reluctant to "degrade a whole race of men from the rank in the scale of beings which their Creator may perhaps have given them." He therefore voiced the idea "as a suspicion only," that blacks "are inferior to the whites in the endowments both of body and mind." Yet this "unfortunate" circumstance, he went on, "is a powerful obstacle to the emancipation of these people."

Jefferson was obsessed with the connection between heredity and environment, race and intelligence. His belief that individuals' abilities and achievements are shaped by social conditions inclined him to hope that no group was fixed permanently in a status of inferiority. He applied this principle, as has been noted, to Indians, whom he believed naturally the equal of whites in intelligence. In the case of blacks, however, he could not avoid the "suspicion" that nature had permanently deprived them of the qualities that made republican citizenship possible. Benjamin Banneker, a free African-American from Maryland who had taught himself the principles of mathematics, sent Jefferson a copy of an astronomical almanac he had published, along with a plea for the abolition of slavery. Jefferson replied, "Nobody wishes more than I do to see such proofs as you exhibit, that nature has given to our black brethren, talents equal to the other colors of men." To his friend Joel Barlow, however, Jefferson suggested that a white person must have helped Banneker with his calculations.

"Nothing is more certainly written in the book of fate," wrote Jefferson, "than that these people are to be free." Yet he felt that America should have a homogeneous citizenry with common experiences, values, and inborn abilities. Americans' essential sameness would underpin the ideal of equal rights for all, making it possible to realize the idea of the public good. Black Americans, Jefferson affirmed, should eventually enjoy the natural rights enumerated in the Declaration of Independence, but in Africa or the Caribbean, not in the United States. He foresaw Indians merging with whites into a single people, but he was horrified by the idea of miscegenation between blacks and whites. Unlike Indians, blacks, he believed, were unfit for economic independence and political self-government. Freeing the slaves without removing them from the country would endanger the nation's freedom.

Jefferson reflected the divided mind of his generation. Some prominent Virginians assumed that blacks could become part of the American nation. Edward Coles, an early governor of Illinois, brought his slaves from Virginia, freed them, and settled them on farms. Washington, who died in 1799, provided in his will that his 277 slaves would become free after the death of his wife, Martha. (Feeling uncomfortable living among men and women who looked forward to her death, she emancipated them the following year.) Jefferson thought of himself as a humane owner. The slave cabins at his estate, Monticello, one visitor wrote, "are all much better than I have seen on any other plantation," although he could not help adding that "their cabins form a most unpleasant contrast with the palace that rises so near them." Believing the slave trade immoral, Jefferson tried to avoid selling slaves to pay off his mounting debts. But his will provided for the freedom of only five, all relatives of his slave Sally Hemings, with whom he appears to have had fathered one or more children. When he died in 1826, Jefferson owed so much money that his property, including the majority of his more than 200 slaves, was sold at auction, thus destroying the slave community he had tried to keep intact.

This painting by the artist Gilbert Stuart, best known for his portraits of George Washington, is thought to depict Hercules, Washington's slave and the chief cook at his estate at Mount Vernon. As president, Washington brought Hercules to Philadelphia, then the nation's capital, in violation of the state's 1780 emancipation law that freed any slave who resided in the state for six months. In 1797, as Washington and his family were preparing to return home at the end of his term in office, Hercules escaped. Washington died two years later. His will freed his slaves, including Hercules.

PRINCIPLES OF FREEDOM

Even as the decline of apprenticeship and indentured servitude narrowed the gradations of freedom among the white population, the Revolution widened the divide between free Americans and those who remained in slavery. Race, one among many kinds of legal and social inequality in colonial America, now emerged as a convenient justification for the existence of slavery in a land that claimed to be committed to freedom. Blacks' "natural faculties," Alexander Hamilton noted in 1779, were "probably as good as ours." But the existence of slavery, he added, "makes us fancy many things that are founded neither in reason or experience."

"We the people" increasingly meant only white Americans. "Principles of freedom, which embrace only half mankind, are only half systems," declared the anonymous author of a Fourth of July speech in Hartford, Connecticut, in 1800. "Declaration of Independence," he wondered, "where art thou now?" The answer came from a Richmond newspaper: "Tell us not of principles. Those principles have been annihilated by the existence of slavery among us."

SUGGESTED READING

Amar, Akhil Reed. *Bill of Rights: Creation and Reconstruction* (1998). Presents the history of the Bill of Rights from its ratification through the Reconstruction era.

Aron, Stephen. *How the West Was Lost: The Transformation of Kentucky from Daniel Boone to Henry Clay* (1996). Relates the evolution of Kentucky from a pioneer society to one dominated by slaveowners.

Berkin, Carol. *A Brilliant Solution: Inventing the American Constitution* (2002). A lively account of the proceedings of the Constitutional Convention.

Cornell, Saul. *The Other Founders: Anti-Federalism and the Dissenting Tradition in America, 1788–1828* (1999). A careful examination of the ideas of those who opposed ratification of the Constitution.

Dowd, Gregory E. *A Spirited Resistance: The North American Indian Struggle for Unity, 1745–1815* (1992). Contains an important discussion of the place of Indians in the new American nation.

Einhorn, Robin. *American Taxation, American Slavery* (2006). Explores how the existence of slavery inspired a hostility to taxation that has survived to the present.

Kettner, James T. *The Development of American Citizenship, 1608–1870* (1978). Traces the development of the definition of American citizenship from early colonization to the aftermath of the Civil War.

Levy, Leonard. *The Establishment Clause: Religion and the First Amendment* (1994). A historical account of one of the key components of the Bill of Rights.

MacLeod, Duncan J. *Slavery, Race, and the American Revolution* (1974). A British scholar's interpretation of the role of race and slavery in the revolutionary era.

McMillin, James A. *The Final Victims: Foreign Slave Trade to North America, 1783–1810* (2004). A study of the last phase of the American slave trade, as made possible by the new Constitution.

Morris, Richard B. *The Forging of the Union, 1781–1789* (1987). A comprehensive account of the nation's history under the Articles of Confederation.

Nedelsky, Jennifer. *Private Property and the Limits of American Constitutionalism* (1990). Analyzes how the protection of private property shaped the writing of the Constitution.

Rakove, Jack. *Original Meanings: Politics and Ideas in the Making of the Constitution* (1996). An influential interpretation of the ideas that went into the drafting of the Constitution.

Richards, Leonard L. *Shays's Rebellion: The American Revolution's Final Battle* (2002). The most recent study of the uprising that helped to produce the Constitution.

Wood, Gordon S. *The Creation of the American Republic, 1776–1789* (1969). Presents the evolution of American political ideas and institutions from the Declaration of Independence to the ratification of the Constitution.

REVIEW QUESTIONS

1. How did Shays's Rebellion highlight the ineffectiveness of the Articles of Confederation?

2. The Constitution is a document of many compromises. Identify which compromises you believe to be most significant to the success of the new nation and explain why.

3. How accurate was Hector St. John Crèvecoeur in his description of America in 1782 as a melting pot?

4. Why was a new constitution needed, according to nationalists such as James Madison and Alexander Hamilton?

5. What were the major arguments put forth by the Anti-Federalists?

KEY TERMS

Northwest Ordinance and slavery (p. 251)

Shays's Rebellion (p. 253)

international trade (p. 254)

three-fifths clause (p. 258)

Anti-Federalism (p. 262)

Bill of Rights (p. 263)

Battle of Fallen Timbers (p. 269)

REVIEW TABLE

Debates Surrounding the Constitutional Convention

Interests at Stake	Issue	Resolution
Big v. small states	Representation in Congress • Virginia plan • New Jersey plan	• Proportional representation in House • Equal representation in Senate
Slave v. non-slave states	• Size of population in determining proportional representation • When to stop the slave trade	• Three-fifths clause • Twenty years after ratification Congress could ban the slave trade
Advocates of strong v. weak central government	• Preventing one branch of the government from dominating the others • Preventing the federal government from dominating state governments	• Separation of powers • Division of powers

CHAPTER 8

Securing the Republic, 1790–1815

This colorful image from around the time of the War of 1812 contains numerous symbols of freedom, among them the goddess of liberty with her liberty cap, a broken chain at the sailor's feet, the fallen crown (under his left foot), a broken royal scepter, and the sailor himself, since English interference with American shipping was one of the war's causes.

☞ FOCUS QUESTIONS

• Why were the politics of the 1790s so divisive?

• In what ways was freedom at issue in the political divisions of the 1790s?

• What were the achievements and failures of Jefferson's presidency?

• What was the larger significance of the War of 1812?

An early American coin, bearing an image of liberty and the word itself, as directed by Congress in a 1792 law.

On April 30, 1789, in New York City, the nation's temporary capital, George Washington became the first president under the new Constitution. All sixty-nine electors had awarded him their votes. Dressed in a plain suit of "superfine American broad cloth" rather than European finery, Washington took the oath of office on the balcony of Federal Hall before a large crowd that reacted with "loud and repeated shouts" of approval. He then retreated inside to deliver his inaugural address before members of Congress and other dignitaries.

Washington's speech expressed the revolutionary generation's conviction that it had embarked on an experiment of enormous historical importance, whose outcome was by no means certain. "The preservation of the sacred fire of liberty and the destiny of the republican model of government," Washington proclaimed, depended on the success of the American experiment in self-government. Most Americans seemed to agree that freedom was the special genius of American institutions. In a resolution congratulating Washington on his inauguration, the House of Representatives observed that he had been chosen by "the freest people on the face of the earth." When the time came to issue the nation's first coins, Congress directed that they bear the image not of the head of state (as would be the case in a monarchy) but "an impression emblematic of liberty," with the word itself prominently displayed.

American leaders believed that the success of the new government depended, above all, on maintaining political harmony. They were especially anxious to avoid the emergence of organized political parties, which had already appeared in several states. Parties were considered divisive and disloyal. "They serve to organize faction," Washington would later declare, and to substitute the aims of "a small but artful" minority for the "will of the nation." The Constitution makes no mention of political parties, and the original method of electing the president assumes that candidates will run as individuals, not on a party ticket (otherwise, the second-place finisher would not have become vice president). Nonetheless, national political parties quickly arose. Originating in Congress, they soon spread to the general populace. Instead of harmony, the 1790s became, in the words of one historian, an "age of passion," with each party questioning the loyalty of the other and lambasting its opponent in the most extreme terms. Political rhetoric became inflamed because the stakes seemed so high—nothing less than the legacy of the Revolution, the new nation's future, and the survival of American freedom.

POLITICS IN AN AGE OF PASSION

President Washington provided a much-needed symbol of national unity. Having retired to private life after the War of Independence (despite some army officers' suggestion that he set himself up as a dictator), he was a model of self-sacrificing republican virtue. His vice president, John Adams, was widely respected as one of the main leaders in the drive for independence. Washington brought into his cabinet some of the new nation's most prominent political leaders, including Thomas Jefferson as secretary of state and Alexander Hamilton to head the Treasury Department. He also appointed a Supreme Court of six members, headed by John Jay of New York. But harmonious government proved short-lived.

HAMILTON'S PROGRAM

Political divisions first surfaced over the financial plan developed by Secretary of the Treasury Hamilton in 1790 and 1791. Hamilton's immediate aims were to establish the nation's financial stability, bring to the government's support the country's most powerful financial interests, and encourage economic development. His long-term goal was to make the United States a major commercial and military power. Hamilton's model was Great Britain. The goal of national greatness, he believed, could never be realized if the government suffered from the same weaknesses as under the Articles of Confederation.

Hamilton's program had five parts. The first step was to establish the new nation's credit-worthiness—that is, to create conditions under which persons would loan money to the government by purchasing its bonds, confident that they would be repaid. Hamilton proposed that the federal government assume responsibility for paying off at its full face value the national debt inherited from the War of Independence, as well as outstanding debts of the states. Second, he called for the creation of a new national debt. The old debts would be replaced by new interest-bearing bonds issued to the government's creditors. This would give men of economic substance a stake in promoting the new nation's stability, since the stronger and more economically secure the federal government, the more likely it would be to pay its debts.

The third part of Hamilton's program called for the creation of a Bank of the United States, modeled on the Bank of England, to serve as the nation's main financial agent. A private corporation rather than a branch of the government,

The Washington Family. *This painting by Edward Savage, begun in 1789 and completed in 1796, became one of the most popular representations of national pride in the early republic. Widely reproduced in engravings and embroidery, it shows the president, his wife, her two children by a previous marriage, and a black slave in a room at the Washington estate at Mt. Vernon, Virginia. On the table is Pierre Charles L'Enfant's plan for the city of Washington.*

The Bank of Pennsylvania, Philadelphia. Designed by the architect Benjamin Latrobe and built between 1798 and 1801, this elegant structure with Greek columns housed one of the country's first banks. Hamilton's program was intended to give the country's financial leaders a stake in the stability of the federal government.

it would hold public funds, issue bank notes that would serve as currency, and make loans to the government when necessary, all the while returning a tidy profit to its stockholders. Fourth, to raise revenue, Hamilton proposed a tax on producers of whiskey. Finally, in a Report on Manufactures delivered to Congress in December 1791, Hamilton called for the imposition of a tariff (a tax on imported foreign goods) and government subsidies to encourage the development of factories that could manufacture products currently purchased from abroad. Privately, Hamilton promoted an unsuccessful effort to build an industrial city at present-day Paterson, New Jersey. He also proposed the creation of a national army to deal with uprisings like Shays's Rebellion.

THE EMERGENCE OF OPPOSITION

Hamilton's vision of a powerful commercial republic won strong support from American financiers, manufacturers, and merchants. But it alarmed those who believed the new nation's destiny lay in charting a different path of development. Hamilton's plans hinged on close ties with Britain, America's main trading partner. To James Madison and Thomas Jefferson, the future lay in westward expansion, not connections with Europe. They had little desire to promote manufacturing or urban growth or to see economic policy shaped in the interests of bankers and business leaders. Their goal was a republic of independent farmers marketing grain, tobacco, and other products freely to the entire world. Free trade, they believed, not a system of government favoritism through tariffs and subsidies, would promote American prosperity while fostering greater social equality. Jefferson and Madison quickly concluded that the greatest threat to American freedom lay in the alliance of a powerful central government with an emerging class of commercial capitalists, such as Hamilton appeared to envision.

To Jefferson, Hamilton's system "flowed from principles adverse to liberty, and was calculated to undermine and demolish the republic." Hamilton's plans for a standing army seemed to his critics a bold threat to freedom. The national bank and assumption of state debts, they feared, would introduce into American politics the same corruption that had undermined British liberty, and enrich those already wealthy at the expense of ordinary Americans. During the 1780s, speculators had bought up at great discounts (often only a few cents on the dollar) government bonds and paper notes that had been used to pay those who fought in the Revolution or supplied the army. Under Hamilton's plan, speculators would reap a windfall by being paid at face value while the original holders received nothing. Because transportation was so poor, moreover, many backcountry farmers were used to distilling their grain harvest into whiskey, which could then be carried more easily to market. Hamilton's whiskey tax seemed to single them out unfairly in order to enrich bondholders.

THE JEFFERSON-HAMILTON BARGAIN

At first, opposition to Hamilton's program arose almost entirely from the South, the region that had the least interest in manufacturing development and the least diversified economy. It also had fewer holders of federal bonds than the Middle States and New England. (Virginia had pretty much paid off its war debt; it did not see why it should be taxed to benefit states like Massachusetts that had failed to do so.) Hamilton insisted that all his plans were authorized by the Constitution's ambiguous clause empowering Congress to enact laws for the "general welfare." As a result, many southerners who had supported the new Constitution now became "strict constructionists," who insisted that the federal government could only exercise powers specifically listed in the document. Jefferson, for example, believed the new national bank unconstitutional, since the right of Congress to create a bank was not mentioned in the Constitution.

Opposition in Congress threatened the enactment of Hamilton's plans. Behind-the-scenes negotiations followed. They culminated at a famous dinner in 1790 at which Jefferson brokered an agreement whereby southerners accepted Hamilton's fiscal program (with the exception of subsidies to manufacturers) in exchange for the establishment of the permanent national capital on the Potomac River between Maryland and Virginia. Southerners hoped that the location would enhance their own power in the government while removing it from the influence of the northern financiers and merchants with whom Hamilton seemed to be allied. Major Pierre-Charles L'Enfant, a French-born veteran of the War of Independence, designed a grandiose plan for the "federal city" modeled on the great urban centers of Europe, with wide boulevards, parks, and fountains. The job of surveying was done, in part, by Benjamin Banneker, the free African-American scientist mentioned in the previous chapter. When it came to constructing public buildings in the nation's new capital, most of the labor was done by slaves.

THE IMPACT OF THE FRENCH REVOLUTION

Political divisions began over Hamilton's fiscal program, but they deepened in response to events in Europe. When it began in 1789, nearly all Americans

Venerate the Plough, *a medal of the Philadelphia Society for the Promotion of Agriculture, 1786. Americans like Jefferson and Madison believed that agriculture must remain the foundation of American life.*

Pierre Charles L'Enfant's 1791 plan for Washington, D.C., includes broad avenues that crisscross the city and that are named for the thirteen states, and a long mall stretching from the Potomac River to the Capitol building, slightly to the right of center.

welcomed the French Revolution, inspired in part by the example of their own rebellion. John Marshall, a Virginian who would become chief justice of the Supreme Court, later recalled, "I sincerely believed human liberty to depend in a great measure on the success of the French Revolution." But in 1793, the Revolution took a more radical turn with the execution of King Louis XVI along with numerous aristocrats and other foes of the new government, and war broke out between France and Great Britain.

Events in France became a source of bitter conflict in America. Jefferson and his followers believed that despite its excesses the Revolution marked a historic victory for the idea of popular self-government, which must be defended at all costs. Enthusiasm for France inspired a rebirth of symbols of liberty. Liberty poles and caps reappeared on the streets of American towns and cities. To Washington, Hamilton, and their supporters, however, the Revolution raised the specter of anarchy. America, they believed, had no choice but to draw closer to Britain.

American leaders feared being divided into parties "swayed by rival European powers," in the words of John Quincy Adams. But the rivalry between Britain and France did much to shape early American politics. The "permanent" alliance between France and the United States, which dated to 1778, complicated the situation. No one advocated that the United States should become involved in the European war, and Washington in April 1793 issued a proclamation of American neutrality. But that spring the French Revolution's American admirers organized tumultuous welcomes for Edmond Genet, a French envoy seeking to arouse support for his beleaguered government. When Genet began commissioning American ships to attack British vessels under the French flag, the Washington administration asked for his recall. (Deeming the situation in France too dangerous, he decided to remain in America and married the daughter of George Clinton, the governor of New York.)

Meanwhile, the British seized hundreds of American ships trading with the French West Indies and resumed the hated practice of impressment—kidnapping sailors, including American citizens of British origin, to serve in their navy. Sent to London to present objections, while still serving as chief justice, John Jay negotiated an agreement in 1794 that produced the greatest public controversy of Washington's presidency. Jay's Treaty contained no British concessions on impressment or the rights of American shipping. Britain did agree to abandon outposts on the western frontier, which it was supposed to have done in 1783. In return, the United States guaranteed favored treatment to British imported goods. In effect, the treaty canceled the American-French alliance and recognized British economic and naval supremacy as unavoidable facts of life. Critics of the administration charged that it aligned the United States with monarchical Britain in its conflict with republican France. Ultimately, Jay's Treaty sharpened political divisions in the United States and led directly to the formation of an organized opposition party.

POLITICAL PARTIES

By the mid-1790s, two increasingly coherent parties had appeared in Congress, calling themselves Federalists and Republicans. (The latter had no connection with today's Republican Party, which was founded in the 1850s.) Both parties laid claim to the language of liberty, and each accused its opponent of engaging in a conspiracy to destroy it.

The Federalists, supporters of the Washington administration, favored Hamilton's economic program and close ties with Britain. Prosperous merchants, farmers, lawyers, and established political leaders (especially outside

Infant Liberty Nursed by Mother Mob, a Federalist cartoon from 1807, illustrates the party's fear that the spirit of liberty was degenerating into anarchy. In the background, a mob assaults a building, while in the foreground a pile of books burn.

Infant Liberty nursed by Mother Mob.

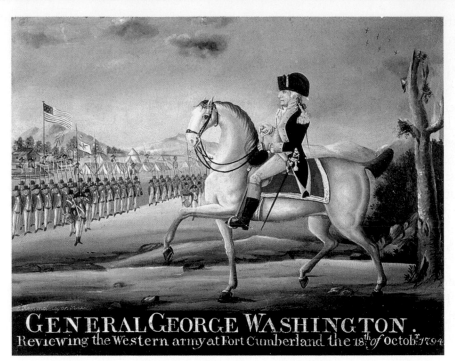

GENERAL GEORGE WASHINGTON.
Reviewing the Western army at Fort Cumberland the 18ᵗʰ of octobᵣ 1794

*A 1794 painting by the Baltimore artist
and sign painter Frederick Kemmelmayer
depicting President Washington as
commander in chief of the army
dispatched to put down the Whiskey
Rebellion.*

the South) tended to support the Federalists. Their outlook was generally elitist, reflecting the traditional eighteenth-century view of society as a fixed hierarchy and of public office as reserved for men of economic substance—the "rich, the able, and the well-born," as Hamilton put it. Freedom, Federalists insisted, rested on deference to authority. It did not mean the right to stand up in opposition to government. Federalists feared that the "spirit of liberty" unleashed by the Revolution was degenerating into anarchy and "licentiousness." When the New York Federalist leader Rufus King wrote an essay on the "words . . . with wrong meaning" that had "done great harm" to American society, his first example was "Liberty."

THE WHISKEY REBELLION

The Federalists may have been the only major party in American history forthrightly to proclaim democracy and freedom dangerous in the hands of ordinary citizens. The Whiskey Rebellion of 1794, when backcountry Pennsylvania farmers sought to block collection of the new tax on distilled spirits, reinforced this conviction. The "rebels" invoked the symbols of 1776, displaying liberty poles and banners reading "Liberty or Death." "The citizens of the western country," one group wrote to the president, "consider [the tax] as repugnant to liberty, [and] an invasion of those privileges which the revolution bestowed upon them." But Washington dispatched 13,000 militiamen to western Pennsylvania (a larger force than he had commanded during the Revolution). He accompanied them part of the way to the scene of the disturbances, the only time in American history that the president has actually commanded an army in the field. The "rebels" offered no resistance. His vigorous response, Washington wrote, was motivated in part by concern for "the impression" the restoration of public order "will make on others"—the "others" being Europeans who did not believe the American experiment in self-government could survive.

THE REPUBLICAN PARTY

Republicans, led by Madison and Jefferson, were more sympathetic to France than the Federalists and had more faith in democratic self-government. They drew their support from an unusual alliance of wealthy southern planters and ordinary farmers throughout the country. Enthusiasm for the French Revolution increasingly drew urban artisans into Republican ranks as well. Republicans preferred what a New Hampshire editor called the "boisterous sea of liberty" to the "calm of despotism." They were far more critical than the Federalists of social and economic inequality, more accepting of broad democratic participation as essential to freedom.

Each emerging party considered itself the representative of the nation and the other an illegitimate "faction." As early as 1792, Madison composed an imaginary dialogue between spokesmen for the two groups. The Federalist described ordinary people as "stupid, suspicious, licentious" and accused the Republican of being "an accomplice of atheism and anarchy." The latter called the Federalist an opponent of liberty and "an idolater of tyranny."

In real life, too, political language became more and more heated. Federalists denounced Republicans as French agents, anarchists, and traitors. Republicans called their opponents monarchists intent on transforming the new national government into a corrupt, British-style aristocracy. Each charged the other with betraying the principles of the Revolution and of American freedom. Washington himself received mounting abuse. When he left office, a Republican newspaper declared that his name had become synonymous with "political iniquity" and "legalized corruption." One contemporary complained that the American press, "one of the great safeguards of free government," had become "the most scurrilous in the civilized world."

A Peep into the Antifederal Club. *This 1793 cartoon illustrates the heated nature of political debate. Thomas Jefferson presides over a rowdy gathering that includes blacks and a drunken pirate. Seated on the left is the devil. On the floor on the right is a figure resembling Thomas Paine. The text repeats Federalist charges against their opponents—that they oppose all government and define liberty as "the power of doing anything we like."*

AN EXPANDING PUBLIC SPHERE

The debates of the 1790s produced not only one of the most intense periods of partisan warfare in American history but also an enduring expansion of the public sphere, and with it the democratic content of American freedom. More and more citizens attended political meetings and became avid readers of pamphlets and newspapers. The establishment of nearly 1,000 post offices made possible the wider circulation of personal letters and printed materials. The era witnessed the rapid growth of the American press—the number of newspapers rose from around 100 to 260 during the 1790s, and reached nearly 400 by 1810.

Hundreds of "obscure men" wrote pamphlets and newspaper essays and formed political organizations. The decade's democratic ferment was reflected in writings like *The Key of Liberty* by William Manning, a self-educated Massachusetts farmer who had fought at the battle of Concord that began the War of Independence. Although not published until many years later, Manning's work, addressed to "friends to liberty and free government," reflected the era's popular political thought. The most important division in society, Manning declared, was between the "few" and the "many." He called for the latter to form a national political association to prevent the "few" from destroying "free government" and "tyrannizing over" the people.

VOICES OF FREEDOM

From Address of the Democratic-Republican Society of Pennsylvania (December 18, 1794)

The creation of around fifty Democratic-Republican societies in 1793 and 1794 reflected the expansion of the public sphere. The Pennsylvania society issued an address defending itself against critics who questioned its right to criticize the administration of George Washington.

The principles and proceedings of our Association have lately been caluminated [tarred by malicious falsehoods]. We should think ourselves unworthy to be ranked as Freemen, if awed by the name of any man, however he may command the public gratitude for past services, we could suffer in silence so sacred a right, so important a principle, as the freedom of opinion to be infringed, by attack on Societies which stand on that constitutional basis.

Freedom of thought, and a free communication of opinions by speech through the medium of the press, are the safeguards of our Liberties. . . . By the freedom of opinion, cannot be meant the right of thinking merely; for of this right the greatest Tyrant cannot deprive his meanest slave; but, it is freedom in the communication of sentiments [by] speech or through the press. This liberty is an imprescriptable [unlimitable] right, independent of any Constitution or social compact; it is as complete a right as that which any man has to the enjoyment of his life. These principles are eternal—they are recognized by our Constitution; and that nation is already enslaved that does not acknowledge their truth. . . .

If freedom of opinion, in the sense we understand it, is the right of every Citizen, by what mode of reasoning can that right be denied to an assemblage of Citizens? . . . The Society are free to declare that they never were more strongly impressed with . . . the importance of associations . . . than at the present time. The germ of an odious Aristocracy is planted among us—it has taken root. . . . Let us remain firm in attachment to principles. . . . Let us be particularly watchful to preserve inviolate the freedom of opinion, assured that it is the most effectual weapon for the protection of our liberty.

From Judith Sargent Murray,
"On the Equality of the Sexes" (1790)

A prominent writer of plays, novels, and poetry, Judith Sargent Murray of Massachusetts was one of the first women to demand equal educational opportunities for women.

Is it upon mature consideration we adopt the idea, that nature is thus partial in her distributions? Is it indeed a fact, that she hath yielded to one half of the human species so unquestionable a mental superiority? I know that to both sexes elevated understandings, and the reverse, are common. But, suffer me to ask, in what the minds of females are so notoriously deficient, or unequal....

Are we deficient in reason? We can only reason from what we know, and if an opportunity of acquiring knowledge hath been denied us, the inferiority of our sex cannot fairly be deduced from thence.... Will it be said that the judgment of a male of two years old, is more sage than that of a female's of the same age? I believe the reverse is generally observed to be true. But from that period what partiality! How is the one exalted, and the other depressed, by the contrary modes of education which are adopted! The one is taught to aspire, and the other is early confined and limited. As their years increase, the sister must be wholly domesticated, while the brother is led by the hand through all the flowery paths of science. Grant that their minds are by nature equal, yet who shall wonder at the *apparent* superiority.... At length arrived at womanhood, the uncultivated fair one feels a void, which the employments allotted her are by no means capable of filling.... She herself is most unhappy; she feels the want of a cultivated mind.... Should it ... be vociferated, 'Your domestic employments are sufficient'—I would calmly ask, is it reasonable, that a candidate for immortality, for the joys of heaven, an intelligent being, who is to spend an eternity in contemplating the works of Deity, should at present be so degraded, as to be allowed no other ideas, than those which are suggested by the mechanism of a pudding, or the sewing the seams of a garment? ...

Yes, ye lordly, ye haughty sex, our souls are by nature *equal* to yours.

QUESTIONS

1. Why does the Democratic-Republican society insist on the centrality of "free communication of opinions" in preserving American liberty?

2. How does Murray answer the argument that offering education to women will lead them to neglect their "domestic employments"?

3. How do these documents reflect expanding ideas about who should enjoy the freedom to express one's ideas in the early republic?

A print shop in the early republic. The increasing number of newspapers played a major role in the expansion of the public sphere.

THE DEMOCRATIC-REPUBLICAN SOCIETIES

Inspired by the Jacobin clubs of Paris, supporters of the French Revolution and critics of the Washington administration in 1793 and 1794 formed nearly fifty Democratic-Republican societies. The Republican press publicized their meetings, replete with toasts to French and American liberty. The declaration of the Democratic Society of Addison County, Vermont, was typical: "That all men are naturally free, and possess equal rights. That all legitimate government originates in the voluntary social compact of the people."

Federalists saw the societies as another example of how liberty was getting out of hand. The government, not "self-created societies," declared the president, was the authentic voice of the American people. Forced to justify their existence, the societies developed a defense of the right of the people to debate political issues and organize to affect public policy. To the societies, "free inquiry" and "free communication" formed the first line of defense of "the unalienable rights of free men." Political liberty meant not simply voting at elections but constant involvement in public affairs. "We make no apology for thus associating ourselves," declared the Addison County society. "Political freedom" included the right to "exercise watchfulness and inspection, upon the conduct of public officers." Blamed by Federalists for helping to inspire the Whiskey Rebellion, the societies disappeared by the end of 1795. But much of their organization and outlook was absorbed into the emerging Republican Party. They helped to legitimize the right of "any portion of the people," regardless of station in life, to express political opinions and take an active role in public life.

The Republicans also gained support from immigrants from the British Isles, where war with France inspired a severe crackdown on dissent. Thomas Paine had returned to Britain in 1787. Five years later, after publishing *The Rights of Man*, a defense of the French Revolution and a stirring call for democratic change at home, he was forced to flee to France one step ahead of the law. But his writings inspired the emergence of a mass movement for political and social change, which authorities brutally suppressed. Threatened with arrest for treason, a number of British and Irish radicals emigrated to America. They included journalists like Joseph Gales and John D. Burk, who soon found themselves editing Republican newspapers that condemned social privilege on both sides of the Atlantic and charged the Federalists with attempting to introduce European tyranny in America.

THE RIGHTS OF WOMEN

The democratic ferment of the 1790s inspired renewed discussion about women's rights. In 1792, Mary Wollstonecraft published in England her extraordinary pamphlet, *A Vindication of the Rights of Woman.* Inspired by Paine's *Rights of Man,* she asserted that the "rights of humanity" should not be "confined to the male line." Wollstonecraft did not directly challenge traditional gender roles. Her call for greater access to education and to paid employment for women rested on the idea that this would enable single women to support themselves and married women to perform more capably as wives and mothers. But she did "drop a hint," as she put it, that women "ought to have representation" in government. Within two years, American editions of Wollstonecraft's work had appeared, along with pamphlets defending and attacking her arguments. A short-lived women's rights magazine was published in 1795 in New York City.

The expansion of the public sphere offered new opportunities to women. Increasing numbers began expressing their thoughts in print. Hannah Adams of Massachusetts became the first American woman to support herself as an author, publishing works on religious history and the history of New England. Other women took part in political discussions, read newspapers, and listened to orations, even though outside of New Jersey none could vote. In 1792, Sarah W. Morton of Boston published *The African Chief,* a lengthy poem recounting the enslavement of an African.

Judith Sargent Murray, one of the era's most accomplished American women, wrote essays for the *Massachusetts Magazine* under the pen name "The Gleaner." Murray's father, a prosperous Massachusetts merchant, had taken an enlightened view of his daughter's education. Although Judith could not attend college because of her sex, she studied alongside her brother with a tutor preparing the young man for admission to Harvard. In her essay "On the Equality of the Sexes," written in 1779 and published in 1790, Murray insisted that women had as much right as men to exercise all their talents and should be allowed equal educational opportunities to enable them to do so. Women's apparent mental inferiority to men, she insisted, simply reflected the fact that they had been denied "the opportunity of acquiring knowledge." "The idea of the incapability of women," she maintained, was "totally inadmissable in this enlightened age."

WOMEN AND THE REPUBLIC

Were women part of the new body politic? Until after the Civil War, the word "male" did not appear in the Constitution. Women were counted fully in determining representation in Congress, and there was nothing explicitly limiting the rights outlined in the Constitution to men. A few

An engraving from The Lady's Magazine and Repository of Entertaining Knowledge, *published in Philadelphia in 1792. A woman identified as the "Genius of the Ladies Magazine" kneels before Liberty, presenting a petition for the "Rights of Women." In the foreground are symbols of the arts, science, and literature—knowledge that should be available to women as well as men.*

An engraving of Hannah Adams, the first American woman to support herself as an author. Her published books included An Alphabetical Compendium of the Various Sects Which Have Appeared in the World from the Beginning of the Christian Era to the Present Day *(1784) and* A Summary History of New England *(1799). The engraving is based on a portrait painted in 1827, the year Adams became the first woman permitted to use the library of the Boston Athanaeum.*

contributors to the pamphlet debate on women's rights admitted that, according to the logic of democracy, women ought to have a voice in government. The Constitution's use of the word "he" to describe officeholders, however, reflected an assumption so widespread that it scarcely required explicit defense: politics was a realm for men. The time had not yet arrived for a broad assault on gender inequality. But like the activities of the Democratic-Republican societies, the discussion of women's status helped to popularize the language of rights in the new republic.

The men who wrote the Constitution did not envision the active and continuing involvement of ordinary citizens in affairs of state. But the rise of political parties seeking to mobilize voters in hotly contested elections, the emergence of the "self-created societies," the stirrings of women's political consciousness, and even armed uprisings like the Whiskey Rebellion broadened and deepened the democratization of public life set in motion by the American Revolution.

THE ADAMS PRESIDENCY

In 1792, Washington won unanimous reelection. Four years later, he decided to retire from public life, in part to establish the precedent that the presidency is not a life office. In his Farewell Address (mostly drafted by Hamilton and published in the newspapers rather than delivered orally; see the Appendix for excerpts from the speech), Washington defended his administration against criticism, warned against the party spirit, and advised his countrymen to steer clear of international power politics by avoiding "permanent alliances with any portion of the foreign world."

THE ELECTION OF 1796

George Washington's departure unleashed fierce party competition over the choice of his successor. In this, the first contested presidential election, two tickets presented themselves: John Adams, with Thomas Pinckney of South Carolina for vice president, representing the Federalists, and Thomas Jefferson, with Aaron Burr of New York, for the Republicans. In a majority of the sixteen states (Vermont, Kentucky, and Tennessee had been added to the original thirteen during Washington's presidency), the legislature still chose presidential electors. But in the six states where the people voted for electors directly, intense campaigning took place. Adams received seventy-one electoral votes to Jefferson's sixty-eight. Because of factionalism among the Federalists, Pinckney received only fifty-nine votes, so Jefferson, the leader of the opposition party, became vice president. Voting fell almost entirely along sectional lines: Adams carried New England, New York, and New Jersey, while Jefferson swept the South, along with Pennsylvania.

In 1797, John Adams assumed leadership of a divided nation. Brilliant but austere, stubborn, and self-important, he was disliked even by those who honored his long career of service to the cause of independence. His presidency was beset by crises.

On the international front, the country was nearly dragged into the ongoing European war. As a neutral nation, the United States claimed the right to trade nonmilitary goods with both Britain and France, but both countries seized American ships with impunity. In 1797, American diplomats were sent to Paris to negotiate a treaty to replace the old alliance of 1778. French officials presented them with a demand for bribes before negotiations could proceed. When Adams made public the envoys' dispatches, the French officials were designated by the last three letters of the alphabet. This "XYZ affair" poisoned America's relations with its former ally. By 1798, the United States and France were engaged in a "quasi-war" at sea, with French ships seizing American vessels in the Caribbean and a newly enlarged American navy harassing the French. In effect, the United States had become a military ally of Great Britain. Despite pressure from Hamilton, who desired a declaration of war, however, Adams in 1800 negotiated peace with France.

Adams was less cautious in domestic affairs. Unrest continued in many rural areas. In 1799, farmers in southeastern Pennsylvania obstructed the assessment of a tax on land and houses that Congress had imposed to help fund an expanded army and navy. A crowd led by John Fries, a local militia leader and auctioneer, released arrested men from prison. No shots were fired in what came to be called Fries's Rebellion, but Adams dispatched units of the federal army to the area. The army arrested Fries for treason and proceeded to terrorize his supporters, tear down liberty poles, and whip Republican newspaper editors. Adams pardoned Fries in 1800, but the area, which had supported his election in 1796, never again voted Federalist.

THE "REIGN OF WITCHES"

But the greatest crisis of the Adams administration arose over the Alien and Sedition Acts of 1798. Confronted with mounting opposition, some of it voiced by immigrant pamphleteers and editors, Federalists moved to silence their critics. A new Naturalization Act extended from five to fourteen years the residency requirement for immigrants seeking American citizenship. The Alien Act allowed the deportation of persons from abroad deemed "dangerous" by federal authorities. The Sedition Act (which was set to expire in 1801, by which time Adams hoped to have been reelected) authorized the prosecution of virtually any public assembly or publication critical of the government. While more lenient than many such measures in Europe (it did not authorize legal action before publication and allowed for trials by jury), the new law meant that opposition editors could be prosecuted for almost any

Congressional Pugilists, *a 1798 cartoon depicting a fight on the floor of Congress between Connecticut Federalist Roger Griswold and Matthew Lyon, a Republican from Vermont. Lyon would soon be jailed under the Sedition Act for criticizing the Adams administration in his newspaper.*

political comment they printed. The main target was the Republican press, seen by Federalists as a group of upstart workingmen (most editors had started out as printers) whose persistent criticism of the administration fomented popular rebelliousness and endangered "genuine liberty."

The passage of these measures launched what Jefferson, recalling events in Salem, Massachusetts, a century earlier, termed a "reign of witches." Eighteen individuals, including several Republican newspaper editors, were charged under the Sedition Act. Ten were convicted for spreading "false, scandalous, and malicious" information about the government. Matthew Lyon, a member of Congress from Vermont and editor of a Republican newspaper, *The Scourge of Aristocracy*, received a sentence of four months in prison and a fine of $1,000. (Lyon had been the first former printer and most likely the first former indentured servant elected to Congress.) The government also imprisoned Thomas Cooper, a lawyer and physician in Pennsylvania who had emigrated from England in 1794, for writings accusing the Adams administration of pro-British bias. In Massachusetts, authorities indicted several men for erecting a liberty pole bearing the inscription, "No Stamp Act, no Sedition, no Alien Bill, no Land Tax; Downfall to the Tyrants of America."

THE VIRGINIA AND KENTUCKY RESOLUTIONS

The Alien and Sedition Acts failed to silence the Republican press. Some newspapers ceased publication, but new ones, with names like *Sun of Liberty* and *Tree of Liberty*, entered the field. The Sedition Act thrust freedom of expression to the center of discussions of American liberty. Madison and Jefferson mobilized opposition, drafting resolutions adopted by the Virginia and Kentucky legislatures. Both resolutions attacked the Sedition Act as an unconstitutional violation of the First Amendment. Virginia's, written by Madison, called on the federal courts to protect free speech. The original version of Jefferson's Kentucky resolution went further, asserting that states could nullify laws of Congress that violated the Constitution—that is, states could unilaterally prevent the enforcement of such laws within their borders. The legislature prudently deleted this passage. The resolutions were directed against assaults on freedom of expression by the federal government, not the states. Jefferson took care to insist that the states "fully possessed" the authority to punish "seditious" speech, even if the national government did not. Indeed, state-level prosecutions of newspapers for seditious libel did not end when the Sedition Act expired in 1801.

An 1800 campaign banner, with a portrait of Thomas Jefferson and the words, "John Adams is no more."

No other state endorsed the Virginia and Kentucky resolutions. Many Americans, including many Republicans, were horrified by the idea of state action that might endanger the Union. But the "crisis of freedom" of the late 1790s strongly reinforced the idea that "freedom of discussion" was an indispensable attribute of American liberty and of democratic government. Free speech, as Massachusetts Federalist Harrison Gray Otis noted, had become the people's "darling privilege." The broad revulsion against the Alien and Sedition Acts contributed greatly to Jefferson's election as president in 1800.

THE "REVOLUTION OF 1800"

"Jefferson and Liberty" became the watchword of the Republican campaign. By this time, Republicans had developed effective techniques for mobilizing voters, such as printing pamphlets, handbills, and newspapers and holding mass meetings to promote their cause. The Federalists, who viewed politics as an activity for a small group of elite men, found it difficult to match their opponents' mobilization. Nonetheless, they still dominated New England and enjoyed considerable support in the Middle Atlantic states. Jefferson triumphed, with seventy-three electoral votes to Adams's sixty-five.

Before assuming office, Jefferson was forced to weather an unusual constitutional crisis. Each party arranged to have an elector throw away one of his two votes for president, so that its presidential candidate would come out a vote ahead of the vice presidential. But the designated Republican elector failed to do so. As a result, both Jefferson and his running mate, Aaron Burr, received seventy-three electoral votes. With no candidate having a majority, the election was thrown into the House of Representatives that had been elected in 1798, where the Federalists enjoyed a slight majority. For thirty-five ballots, neither man received a majority of the votes. Finally, Hamilton intervened. He disliked Jefferson but believed him enough of a statesman to recognize that the Federalist financial system could not be dismantled. Burr, he warned, was obsessed with power, "an embryo Caesar."

Hamilton's support for Jefferson tipped the balance. To avoid a repetition of the crisis, Congress and the states soon adopted the Twelfth Amendment to the Constitution, requiring electors to cast separate votes for president and vice president. The election of 1800 also set in motion a chain of events that culminated four years later when Burr killed Hamilton in a duel. Burr appears to have subsequently engaged in a plot to form a new nation in the West from land detached from the United States and the Spanish empire. Acquitted of treason in 1807, he went into exile in Europe, eventually returning to New York, where he practiced law until his death in 1836.

The events of the 1790s demonstrated that a majority of Americans believed ordinary people had a right to play an active role in politics, express their opinions freely, and contest the policies of their government. His party, wrote Samuel Goodrich, a prominent Connecticut Federalist, was overthrown because democracy had become "the watchword of popular liberty." To their credit, Federalists never considered resistance to the election result. Adams's acceptance of defeat established the vital precedent of a peaceful transfer of power from a defeated party to its successor.

The Providential Detection, *a Federalist political cartoon from 1800 attacking Thomas Jefferson. An eagle rescues the Constitution and Declaration of Independence before Jefferson can burn them on an "altar to Gallic [French] despotism." Feeding the flames are writings despised by Federalists, including Thomas Paine's* The Age of Reason, *which attacked organized religion, and the* Aurora, *a Jeffersonian newspaper. Jefferson drops a 1796 letter to his Italian friend Philip Mazzei that criticized President Washington.*

THE PROVIDENTIAL DETECTION

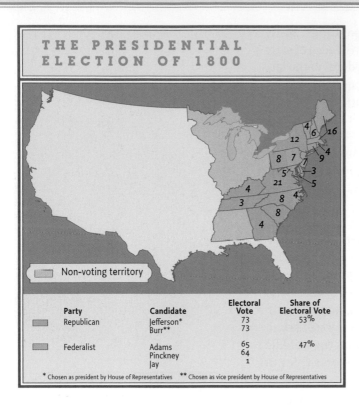

THE PRESIDENTIAL ELECTION OF 1800

Non-voting territory

Party	Candidate	Electoral Vote	Share of Electoral Vote
Republican	Jefferson*	73	53%
	Burr**	73	
Federalist	Adams	65	47%
	Pinckney	64	
	Jay	1	

* Chosen as president by House of Representatives   ** Chosen as vice president by House of Representatives

SLAVERY AND POLITICS — *origins of civil war pt. 1*

Lurking behind the political battles of the 1790s lay the potentially divisive issue of slavery. Jefferson, after all, received every one of the South's forty-one electoral votes. He always referred to his victory as the "Revolution of 1800" and saw it not simply as a party success but as a vindication of American freedom, securing for posterity the fruits of independence. Yet the triumph of "Jefferson and Liberty" would not have been possible without slavery. Had three-fifths of the slaves not been counted in apportionment, John Adams would have been reelected in 1800.

The issue of slavery would not disappear. The very first Congress under the new Constitution received petitions calling for emancipation. One bore the weighty signature of Benjamin Franklin, who in 1787 had agreed to serve as president of the Pennsylvania Abolition Society. The blessings of liberty, Franklin's petition insisted, should be available "without distinction of color to all descriptions of people."

A long debate followed, in which speakers from Georgia and South Carolina vigorously defended the institution and warned that behind northern criticism of slavery they heard "the trumpets of civil war." Madison found their forthright defense of slavery an embarrassment. But he concluded that the slavery question was so divisive that it must be kept out of national politics. He opposed Congress's even receiving a petition from North Carolina slaves on the grounds that they were not part of the American people and had "no claim" on the lawmakers' "attention." In 1793, to implement the Constitution's fugitive slave clause, Congress enacted a law providing for federal and state judges and local officials to facilitate the return of escaped slaves.

THE HAITIAN REVOLUTION

Events during the 1790s underscored how powerfully slavery defined and distorted American freedom. The same Jeffersonians who hailed the French Revolution as a step in the universal progress of liberty reacted in horror against the slave revolution that began in 1791 in Saint Domingue, the jewel of the French overseas empire situated not far from the southern coast of the United States. Toussaint L'Ouverture, an educated slave on a sugar plantation, forged the rebellious slaves into an army able to defeat British forces seeking to seize the island and then an expedition hoping to reestablish French authority. The slave uprising led to the establishment of Haiti as an independent nation in 1804.

Although much of the country was left in ruins by years of warfare, the Haitian Revolution affirmed the universality of the revolutionary era's creed of liberty. It inspired hopes for freedom among slaves in the United States. But to most whites, the rebellious slaves seemed not men and women seeking liberty in the tradition of 1776, but a danger to American institutions. Their resort to violence was widely taken to illustrate blacks' unfitness for republican freedom. Ironically, the Adams administration, which hoped that American merchants could replace their French counterparts in the island's lucrative sugar trade, encouraged the independence of black Haiti. Jefferson as president, on the other hand, sought to quarantine and destroy the hemisphere's second independent republic.

GABRIEL'S REBELLION

The momentous year 1800 witnessed not only the "revolution" of Jefferson's election but an attempted real one, a plot by slaves in Virginia itself to gain their freedom. It was organized by a Richmond blacksmith, Gabriel, and his brothers Solomon, also a blacksmith, and Martin, a slave preacher. The conspirators planned to march on the city, which had recently become the state capital, from surrounding plantations. They would kill some white inhabitants and hold the rest, including Governor James Monroe, hostage until their demand for the abolition of slavery was met. Gabriel hoped that "poor white people" would join the insurrection, and he ordered that Quakers and Methodists (many of whom were critics of slavery) and "French people" (whose country was engaged in the "quasi-war" with the United States described earlier) be spared. On the night when the slaves were to gather, a storm washed out the roads to Richmond. The plot was soon discovered and the leaders arrested. Twenty-six slaves, including Gabriel, were hanged and dozens more transported out of the state.

Blacks in 1800 made up half of Richmond's population. One-fifth were free. A black community had emerged in the 1780s and 1790s, and the conspiracy was rooted in its institutions. Gabriel gathered recruits at black Baptist churches, funerals, barbecues, and other gatherings. In cities like Richmond, many skilled slave craftsmen, including Gabriel himself, could read and write and enjoyed the privilege of hiring themselves out to employers—that is, negotiating their own labor arrangements, with their owner receiving their "wages." Their relative autonomy helps account for slave artisans' prominent role in the conspiracy.

Gabriel's Rebellion was a product of its age. Gabriel himself had been born in 1776. Like other Virginians, the participants in the conspiracy spoke the language of liberty forged in the American Revolution and reinvigorated during the 1790s. The rebels even planned to carry a banner emblazoned with the slogan, reminiscent of Patrick Henry, "Death or Liberty." "We have as much right," one conspirator declared, "to fight for our liberty as any men." Another likened himself to George Washington, who had rebelled against established authority to "obtain the liberty of [his] countrymen." (This analogy carried the disturbing implication that Virginia officials had now replaced the British as enemies of freedom.)

If Gabriel's conspiracy demonstrated anything, commented the prominent Virginian George Tucker, it was that slaves possessed "the love of freedom" as fully as other men. Gabriel's words, he added, reflected "the advance of knowledge" among Virginia's slaves, including knowledge of the American language of liberty. When slaves escaped to join Lord Dunmore during the War of Independence, he wrote, "they sought freedom merely as a good; now they also claim it as a right." Tucker believed Virginians should emancipate their slaves and settle them outside of the state. The legislature,

Toussaint L'Ouverture, leader of the slave revolution in Saint Domingue, in a portrait from a history of the island published in 1805.

however, moved in the opposite direction. It tightened controls over the black population—making it illegal for them to congregate on Sundays without white supervision—and severely restricted the possibility of masters voluntarily freeing their slaves. Any slave freed after 1806 was required to leave Virginia or be sold back into slavery. The door to emancipation, thrown open during the American Revolution, had been slammed shut.

JEFFERSON IN POWER

The first president to begin his term in Washington, D.C., Jefferson assumed office on March 4, 1801. The city, with its unpaved streets, impoverished residents, and unfinished public buildings, scarcely resembled L'Enfant's grand plan. At one point, part of the roof of the Capitol collapsed, narrowly missing the vice president. The capital's condition seemed to symbolize Jefferson's intention to reduce the importance of the national government in American life.

Jefferson's inaugural address was conciliatory toward his opponents. "Every difference of opinion," he declared, "is not a difference of principle. . . . We are all Republicans, we are all Federalists." He went on to expound the policies his administration would follow—economy in government, unrestricted trade, freedom of religion and the press, friendship to all nations but "entangling alliances" with none. America, "the world's best hope," would flourish if a limited government allowed men "free to regulate their own pursuits."

Jefferson hoped to dismantle as much of the Federalist system as possible. Among his first acts as president was to pardon all those imprisoned under the Sedition Act. During his eight years as president, he reduced the number of government employees and slashed the army and navy. He abolished all taxes except the tariff, including the hated tax on whiskey, and paid off part of the national debt. He aimed to minimize federal power and eliminate government oversight of the economy. His policies ensured that the United States would not become a centralized state on a European model, as Hamilton had envisioned.

JUDICIAL REVIEW

Nonetheless, as Hamilton predicted, it proved impossible to uproot national authority entirely. Jefferson distrusted the unelected judiciary and always believed in the primacy of local self-government. But during his presidency, and for many years thereafter, Federalist John Marshall headed the Supreme Court. Marshall had served John Adams as secretary of state and was appointed by the president to the Court shortly before Jefferson took office. A strong believer in national supremacy, Marshall established the Court's power to review laws of Congress and the states.

The first landmark decision of the Marshall Court came in 1803, in the case of *Marbury v. Madison*. On the eve of leaving office, Adams had appointed a number of justices of the peace for the District of Columbia. Madison, Jefferson's secretary of state, refused to issue commissions (the official documents entitling them to assume their posts) to these "midnight judges." Four, including William Marbury, sued for their offices. Marshall's decision declared unconstitutional the section of the Judiciary Act of 1789 that allowed the courts to order executive officials to deliver judges' commissions. It exceeded the power of Congress as outlined in the Constitution and was therefore void. Marbury, in other words, may have been entitled to his commission, but the Court had no power under the Constitution to order Madison to deliver it. On the immediate issue, therefore, the administration got its way. But the cost, as Jefferson saw it, was high. The Supreme Court had assumed the right to determine whether an act of Congress violates the Constitution—a power known as "judicial review."

A watercolor by the artist William Russell Birch depicts the Capitol in 1800, the year Congress first occupied the building. Washington, D. C. was clearly a small community at the time.

Seven years later, in *Fletcher v. Peck*, the Court extended judicial review to state laws. In 1794, four land companies had paid nearly every member of the state legislature, Georgia's two U.S. senators, and a number of federal judges, to secure their right to purchase land in present-day Alabama and Mississippi claimed by Georgia. They then sold the land to individual buyers at a large profit. Two years later, many of the corrupt lawmakers were defeated for reelection and the new legislature rescinded the land grant and subsequent sales. Whatever the circumstances of the legislature's initial action, Marshall declared, the Constitution forbade Georgia from taking any action that impaired a contract. Therefore, the individual purchasers could keep their land and the legislature could not repeal the original grant.

THE LOUISIANA PURCHASE

But the greatest irony of Jefferson's presidency involved his greatest achievement, the Louisiana Purchase. This resulted not from astute American diplomacy but because the rebellious slaves of Saint Domingue defeated forces sent by the ruler of France, Napoleon Bonaparte, to reconquer the island. Moreover, to take advantage of the sudden opportunity to purchase Louisiana, Jefferson had to abandon his conviction that the federal government was limited to powers specifically mentioned in the Constitution, since the document said nothing about buying territory from a foreign power.

This vast Louisiana Territory, which stretched from the Gulf of Mexico to Canada and from the Mississippi River to the Rocky Mountains, had been ceded by France to Spain in 1762 as part of the reshuffling of colonial

THE LOUISIANA PURCHASE

Legend:
— Lewis and Clark's expedition, 1804–1806
Louisiana Purchase, 1803
United States, 1803

The Louisiana Purchase of 1803 doubled the land area of the United States.

possessions at the end of the Seven Years' War. France secretly reacquired it in 1800. Soon after taking office, Jefferson learned of the arrangement. He had long been concerned about American access to the port of New Orleans, which lay within Louisiana at the mouth of the Mississippi River. The right to trade through New Orleans, essential to western farmers, had been acknowledged in the Treaty of San Lorenzo (also known as Pinckney's Treaty) of 1795 between the United States and Spain. But Jefferson feared that the far more powerful French might try to interfere with American commerce. He dispatched envoys to France offering to purchase the city. Needing money for military campaigns in Europe and with his dreams of American empire in ruins because of his inability to reestablish control over Saint Domingue, Napoleon offered to sell the entire Louisiana Territory. The cost, $15 million (the equivalent of perhaps $250 million in today's money), made the Louisiana Purchase one of history's greatest real-estate bargains.

In a stroke, Jefferson had doubled the size of the United States and ended the French presence in North America. Federalists were appalled. "We are to give money, of which we have too little," one declared, "for land, of which we already have too much." Jefferson admitted that he had "done an act beyond the Constitution." But he believed the benefits justified his transgression. Farmers, Jefferson had written, were "the chosen people of God," and the country would remain "virtuous" as long as it was "chiefly agricultural." Madison, in *Federalist* no. 10, had explained that the large size of the republic made self-government possible—"extend the sphere," he had proclaimed. Now, Jefferson believed, he had ensured the agrarian character of the United States and its political stability for centuries to come.

LEWIS AND CLARK

Within a year of the purchase, Jefferson dispatched an expedition led by Meriwether Lewis and William Clark, two Virginia-born veterans of Indian wars in the Ohio Valley, to explore the new territory. Their objects were both scientific and commercial—to study the area's plants, animal life, and geography, and to discover how the region could be exploited economically. Jefferson hoped the explorers would establish trading relations with western Indians and locate a water route to the Pacific Ocean—an updated version of the old dream of a Northwest Passage that could facilitate commerce with Asia.

In the spring of 1804, Lewis and Clark's fifty-member "corps of discovery" set out from St. Louis on the most famous exploring party in American history. They spent the winter in the area of present-day North Dakota and then resumed their journey in April 1805. They were now accompanied by a fifteen-year-old Shoshone Indian woman, Sacajawea, the slave wife of a French fur trader, who served as their interpreter. After crossing the Rocky Mountains, the expedition reached the Pacific Ocean in the area of present-day Oregon (which lay beyond the nation's new boundaries) in November 1805. They returned in 1806, bringing with them an immense amount of information about the region as well as numerous plant and animal specimens. Reports about geography, plant and animal life, and Indian cultures filled their daily journals. Although Lewis and Clark failed to find a commercial route to Asia, they demonstrated the possibility of overland travel to the Pacific coast. They found Indians in the trans-Mississippi West accustomed to dealing with European traders and already connected to global markets. The success of their journey helped to strengthen the idea that American territory was destined to reach all the way to the Pacific.

INCORPORATING LOUISIANA

The only part of the Louisiana Purchase with a significant non-Indian population in 1803 was the region around New Orleans. When the United States took control, the city had around 8,000 inhabitants, including nearly 3,000 slaves and 1,300 free persons of color. Incorporating this diverse population into the United States was by no means easy. French and Spanish law accorded free blacks, many of whom were the offspring of unions between white military officers and slave women, nearly all the rights of white citizens. Slaves in Louisiana, as in Florida and Texas under Spanish rule, enjoyed legal protections unknown in the United States. Spain made it easy for slaves to obtain their freedom through purchase or voluntary emancipation by the owners. Slave women had the right to go to court for protection against cruelty or rape by their owners.

A page from William Clark's journal of the Lewis and Clark expedition, depicting a salmon. Among their tasks was to record information about the West's plants, animal life, and geography.

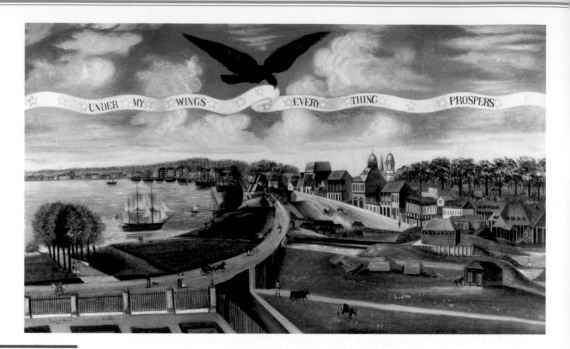

New Orleans in 1803, at the time of the Louisiana Purchase. The painting shows a view of the city from a nearby plantation. The town houses of merchants and plantation owners line the broad promenade along the waterfront. At the lower center, a slave goes about his work. An eagle holds aloft a banner that suggests the heady optimism of the young republic: Under My Wings Every Thing Prospers.

The treaty that transferred Louisiana to the United States promised that all free inhabitants would enjoy "the rights, advantages, and immunities of citizens." Spanish and French civil codes, unlike British and American law, recognized women as co-owners of family property. Under American rule, Louisiana retained this principle of "community property" within marriage. But free blacks suffered a steady decline in status. And the local legislature soon adopted one of the most sweeping slave codes in the South, forbidding blacks to "ever consider themselves the equal of whites" and limiting the practice of manumission and access to the courts. Louisiana's slaves had enjoyed far more freedom under the rule of tyrannical Spain than as part of the liberty-loving United States.

FOREIGN ENTANGLEMENTS

Among other things, the Louisiana Purchase demonstrated that despite its vaunted isolation from the Old World, the United States continued to be deeply affected by events throughout the Atlantic world. At a time when Americans still relied on British markets for their farm produce and British suppliers for manufactured goods, European wars directly influenced the livelihood of American farmers, merchants, and artisans. Jefferson hoped to avoid foreign entanglements, but he found it impossible as president to avoid being drawn into the continuing wars of Europe. Even as he sought to limit the power of the national government, foreign relations compelled him to expand it. The first war fought by the United States was to protect American commerce in a dangerous world.

Only a few months after taking office, Jefferson employed the very navy whose expansion by John Adams he had strongly criticized. The Barbary states on the northern coast of Africa had long preyed on shipping in the Mediterranean and Atlantic, receiving tribute from several countries, including the United States, to protect their vessels. In 1801, Jefferson refused demands for increased payments, and the pasha of Tripoli declared war on the United States. The naval conflict lasted until 1804, when an American squadron won a victory at Tripoli Harbor.

THE EMBARGO

Far more serious in its impact on the United States was warfare between Britain and France, which resumed in 1803 after a brief lull. According to international law, neutral nations had a right to trade nonmilitary goods with countries at war. By 1806, however, each combatant had declared the other under blockade, seeking to deny trade with America to its rival. The Royal Navy resumed the practice of impressment. By the end of 1807, it had seized over 6,000 American sailors (claiming they were British citizens and deserters), including men from the U.S. warship *Chesapeake*, which the British frigate *Leopard* bombarded and boarded in American waters off the coast of Maryland.

To Jefferson, the economic health of the United States required freedom of trade with which no foreign government had a right to interfere. American farmers needed access to markets in Europe and the Caribbean. As colonial patriots had done in the 1760s and 1770s, he decided to use trade as weapon. In December 1807, he persuaded Congress to enact the Embargo, a ban on all American vessels sailing for foreign ports. For a believer in limited government, this was an amazing exercise of federal power.

Enforcement of the Embargo brought back memories of the Intolerable Acts of 1774, with the navy sealing off ports and seizing goods without warrants and the army arresting accused smugglers. Jefferson hoped it would lead Europeans to stop their interference with American shipping and also reduce the occasion for impressment. In 1808, American exports plummeted by 80 percent. Unfortunately, neither Britain nor France, locked in a death struggle, took much notice. But the Embargo devastated the economies of American port cities. Just before his term ended, in March 1809, Jefferson signed the Non-Intercourse Act, banning trade only with Britain and France but providing that if either side rescinded its edicts against American shipping, commerce with that country would resume.

O-Grab-Me, or, the American Snapping-Turtle, *a cartoon criticizing Jefferson's Embargo (spelled backward as o-grab-me), which banned all American shipping to foreign ports.*

MADISON AND PRESSURE FOR WAR

Jefferson left office at the lowest point of his career. He had won a sweeping reelection in 1804, receiving 162 electoral votes to only 14 for the Federalist candidate, Charles C. Pinckney. With the exception of Connecticut, he even carried the Federalist stronghold of New England. Four years later, his handpicked successor, James Madison, also won an easy victory. The Embargo, however, had failed to achieve its diplomatic aims and was increasingly violated by American shippers and resented by persons whose livelihoods depended on trade. In 1810, Madison adopted a new policy. Congress enacted a measure known as Macon's Bill No. 2, which allowed trade to resume but provided that if either France or Britain ceased interfering with American rights, the president could reimpose an embargo on the other. With little to lose, since Britain controlled the seas, the French emperor Napoleon announced that he had repealed his decrees against neutral shipping. But the British continued to attack American vessels and, with their navy hard-pressed for manpower, stepped up the impressment of American sailors. In the spring of 1812, Madison reimposed the embargo on trade with Britain.

Meanwhile, a group of younger congressmen, mostly from the West, were calling for war with Britain. Known as the War Hawks, this new generation of political leaders had come of age after the winning of independence and were ardent nationalists. Their leaders included Henry Clay of Kentucky, elected Speaker of the House of Representatives in 1810, and John C. Calhoun of South Carolina. The War Hawks spoke passionately of defending the national honor against British insults, but they also had more practical goals in mind, notably the annexation of Canada. "Agrarian cupidity [greed], not maritime rights," declared Congressman John Randolph of Virginia, "urges the war. We have heard but one word . . . Canada! Canada! Canada!" Randolph exaggerated, for many southern War Hawks also pressed for the conquest of Florida, a haven for fugitive slaves owned by Britain's ally Spain. Members of Congress also spoke of the necessity of upholding the principle of free trade and liberating the United States once and for all from European infringements on its independence. Unimpeded access to overseas markets was essential if the agrarian republic were to prosper.

THE "SECOND WAR OF INDEPENDENCE"

The growing crisis between the United States and Britain took place against the background of deteriorating Indian relations in the West, which also helped propel the United States down the road to war. Jefferson had long favored the removal beyond the Mississippi River of Indian tribes who refused to cooperate in "civilizing" themselves. The Louisiana Purchase made this policy more feasible. "The acquisition of Louisiana," he wrote, "will, it is hoped, put in our power the means of inducing all the Indians on this side [of the Mississippi River] to transplant themselves to the other side." Jefferson enthusiastically pursued efforts to purchase Indian lands west of the Appalachian Mountains. He encouraged traders to lend money to Indians, in the hope that accumulating debt would force them to sell some of their holdings, thus freeing up more land for "our increasing numbers." On the other hand, the government continued Washington's policy of promoting settled farming among the Indians. Benjamin Hawkins, a friend of Jefferson who served as American agent for Indian affairs south of the Ohio River, also encouraged the expansion of African-American slavery among the tribes as one of the elements of advancing civilization.

THE INDIAN RESPONSE

By 1800, nearly 400,000 American settlers lived west of the Appalachian Mountains. They far outnumbered remaining Indians. Their seemingly irreversible decline in power led some Indians to rethink their opposition to assimilation. Among the Creek and Cherokee, a group led by men of mixed Indian-white ancestry like Major Ridge and John Ross enthusiastically endorsed the federal policy of promoting "civilization." Many had established businesses as traders and slaveowning farmers with the help of their white fathers. Their views, in turn, infuriated "nativists," who wished to root out European influences and resist further white encroachment on Indian lands.

The period from 1800 to 1812 was an "age of prophecy" among the Indians. Movements for the revitalization of Indian life arose among the Creeks, Cherokees, Shawnees, Iroquois, and other tribes. Handsome Lake of the Seneca, who had overcome an earlier addiction to alcohol, preached that Indians must refrain from fighting, gambling, drinking, and sexual promiscuity. He believed Indians could regain their autonomy without directly challenging whites or repudiating all white ways, and he urged his people to take up farming and attend school.

TECUMSEH'S VISION

A more militant message was expounded by two Shawnee brothers, Tecumseh, a chief who had refused to sign the Treaty of Greenville in 1795, and Tenskwatawa, a religious prophet who called for complete separation from whites, the revival of traditional Indian culture, and resistance to federal policies. White people, Tenskwatawa preached, were the source of all evil in the world, and Indians should abandon American alcohol, clothing, food, and manufactured goods. His followers gathered at Prophetstown, located on the Wabash River in Indiana.

Tecumseh meanwhile traversed the Mississippi Valley, seeking to revive Neolin's pan-Indian alliance of the 1760s (discussed in Chapter 4). The alternative to resistance was extermination. "Where today are the Pequot?"

Benjamin Hawkins Trading with the Creek Indians, *a painting depicting the federal government's agent to southern Indians, encouraging settled agriculture as part of a plan to promote "civilization." Two Indians hold a plow, while farm animals graze in the background.*

he asked. "Where are the Narragansett, the Mohican, the Pocanet, and other powerful tribes of our people? They have vanished before the avarice [greed] and oppression of the white man, as snow before the summer sun." Indians, he proclaimed, must recognize that they were a single people and unite in claiming "a common and equal right in the land." He repudiated chiefs who had sold land to the federal government: "Sell a country! Why not sell the air, the great sea, as well as the earth? Did not the Great Spirit make them all for the use of his children?" In 1810, Tecumseh called for attacks on American frontier settlements. In November 1811, while he was absent, American forces under William Henry Harrison destroyed Prophetstown in the Battle of Tippecanoe.

THE WAR OF 1812

Reports that the British were encouraging Tecumseh's efforts contributed to the coming of the War of 1812. In June 1812, with assaults on American shipping continuing, Madison asked Congress for a declaration of war. American nationality, the president declared, was at stake—would Americans remain "an independent people" or become "colonists and vassals" of Great Britain? The vote revealed a deeply divided country. Both Federalists and Republicans representing the states from New Jersey northward, where most of the mercantile and financial resources of the country were concentrated, voted against war. The South and West were strongly in favor.

In retrospect, it seems remarkably foolhardy for a disunited and militarily unprepared nation to go to war with one of the world's two major powers. And with the expiration in 1811 of the charter of the Bank of the United States and the refusal of northern merchants and bankers to loan money, the federal government found it increasingly difficult to finance the war. Before the conflict ended, it was essentially bankrupt. Fortunately for the United States, Great Britain at the outset was preoccupied with the struggle in Europe. But it easily repelled two feeble American invasions of Canada and imposed a blockade that all but destroyed American commerce. In 1814, having finally defeated Napoleon, Britain invaded the United States. Its forces seized Washington, D.C., and burned the White House, while the government fled for safety.

Americans did enjoy a few military successes. In August 1812, the American frigate *Constitution* defeated the British warship *Guerriere*. Commodore Oliver H. Perry defeated a British naval force in September 1813 on Lake Erie (a startling result considering that Britain prided itself on having the world's most powerful navy—although the Americans outgunned them on the Great Lakes). In the following year, a British assault on Baltimore was repulsed when Fort McHenry at the entrance to the harbor withstood a British bombardment. This was the occasion when Francis Scott Key composed "The Star-Spangled Banner," an ode to the "land of the free and home of the brave" that became the national anthem during the 1930s.

The lid of a chest decorated with scenes from the War of 1812. Images of Hope, on the left, and Liberty flank a picture of the naval battle in which the USS Constitution *defeated a British warship. Liberty holds a paper that reads, "Free Trade and Sailors Rights," two of the issues that drew the United States into the war.*

THE WAR OF 1812

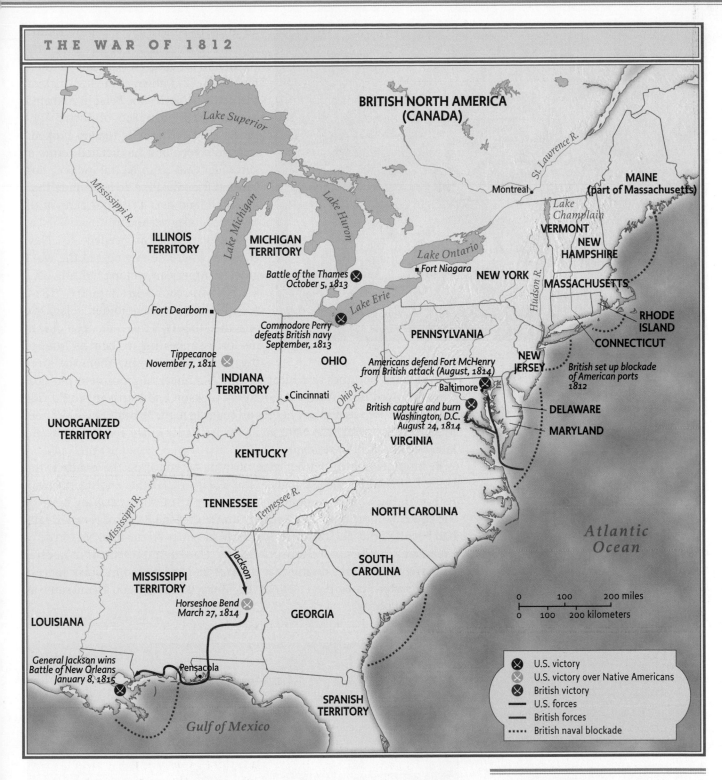

Like the War of Independence, the War of 1812 was a two-front struggle—against the British and against the Indians. The war produced significant victories over western Indians who sided with the British. In 1813, pan-Indian forces led by Tecumseh (who had been commissioned a general in the British army) were defeated and he himself killed at the Battle of the Thames, near Detroit, by an American force led by William Henry Harrison. In March 1814,

Although the British burned the nation's capital, the War of 1812 essentially was a military draw.

The Taking of the City of Washington, *an 1814 engraving produced in London, portrays the assault during which British forces captured the undefended city and burned the White House, the Capitol, and several warships.*

an army of Americans and pro-assimilation Cherokees and Creeks under the command of Andrew Jackson defeated hostile Creeks known as the Red Sticks at the Battle of Horseshoe Bend in Alabama, killing more than 800 of them. "The power of the Creeks is forever broken," Jackson wrote, and he dictated terms of surrender that required the Indians, hostile and friendly alike, to cede more than half their land, over 23 million acres in all, to the federal government.

Jackson then proceeded to New Orleans, where he engineered the war's greatest American victory, fighting off a British invasion in January 1815. Although a slaveholder, Jackson recruited the city's free men of color into his forces, appealing to them as "sons of freedom" and promising them the same pay and land bounties as white recruits. A number of prominent political careers flowed from American victories. Jackson and Harrison would ride their reputations as military heroes all the way to the White House. Colonel Richard M. Johnson, who claimed to have actually killed Tecumseh, would later be elected vice president.

By this time, with neither side wishing to continue the conflict, the United States and Britain signed the Treaty of Ghent, ending the war. Although the treaty was signed in December 1814, ships carrying news of the agreement did not reach America until after the Battle of New Orleans had been fought. The treaty restored the previous status quo. No territory exchanged hands, nor did any provisions relate to impressment or neutral shipping rights. Considering that the war had not been a military success for the United States, the Treaty of Ghent was about as good an outcome as could be expected.

The bombardment of Fort McHenry in Baltimore Harbor in September 1814 was of minor military importance, but it is remembered as the inspiration for Francis Scott Key's poem "The Star-Spangled Banner."

THE WAR'S AFTERMATH

A number of contemporaries called the War of 1812 the Second War of Independence. Despite widespread opposition to the conflict, it confirmed the ability of a republican government to conduct a war without surrendering its institutions. Jackson's victory at New Orleans not only made him a national hero but also became a celebrated example of the ability of virtuous citizens of a republic to defeat the forces of despotic Europe.

Moreover, the war completed the conquest of the area east of the Mississippi River, which had begun during the Revolution. Never again would the British or Indians pose a threat to American control of this vast region. The war also broke the remaining power of Indians in the Old Northwest and significantly reduced their holdings in the South, opening rich new lands to American settlers. In its aftermath, white settlers poured into Indiana, Michigan, Alabama, and Mississippi, bringing with them their distinctive forms of social organization. "I have no doubt," Jackson wrote to his wife, "but in a few years the banks of the Alabama will present a beautiful view of elegant mansions and extensive rich and productive farms." He did not mention that those mansions would be built and the farms worked by slaves.

Britain's defeat of Napoleon inaugurated a long period of peace in Europe. With diplomatic affairs playing less and less of a role in American public life, Americans' sense of separateness from the Old World grew ever stronger. The war also strengthened a growing sense of nationalism in Canada, based in part on separateness from the United States. As in 1775, Canadians did not rise up to welcome an invading army from the south, to the puzzlement of Americans who could not understand why they did not wish to become part of the empire of liberty.

THE END OF THE FEDERALIST PARTY

Jefferson and Madison succeeded in one major political aim—the elimination of the Federalist Party. At first, the war led to a revival of Federalist fortunes. With antiwar sentiment at its peak in 1812, Madison had been reelected by the relatively narrow margin of 128 electoral votes to 89 over his Federalist opponent, DeWitt Clinton of New York. But then came a self-inflicted blow. In December 1814, a group of New England Federalists gathered at Hartford, Connecticut, to give voice to their party's long-standing grievances, especially the domination of the federal government by Virginia presidents and their own region's declining influence as new western states entered the Union. They called for amending the Constitution to eliminate the three-fifths clause that strengthened southern political power, and to require a two-thirds vote of Congress for the admission of new states, declarations of war, and laws restricting trade. Contrary to later myth, the Hartford Convention did not call for secession or disunion. But it affirmed the right of a state to "interpose" its authority if the federal government violated the Constitution.

The Hartford Convention had barely adjourned before Jackson electrified the nation with his victory at New Orleans. "Rising Glory of the American Republic," one newspaper exulted. In speeches and sermons, political and religious leaders alike proclaimed that Jackson's triumph revealed, once again, that a divine hand oversaw America's destiny. The Federalists could not free themselves from the charge of lacking patriotism. Within a few years, their party no longer existed. Its stance on the war was only one cause of the party's demise. The urban commercial and financial interests it championed represented a small minority in an expanding agricultural nation. Their elitism and distrust of popular self-government placed Federalists more and more at odds with the new nation's democratic ethos. Yet in their dying moments Federalists had raised an issue—southern domination of the national government—that would long outlive their political party. And the country stood on the verge of a profound economic and social transformation that strengthened the very forces of commercial development that Federalists had welcomed and many Republicans feared.

SUGGESTED READING

Appleby, Joyce. *Capitalism and a New Social Order: The Republican Vision of the 1790s* (1984). Explores how the Jeffersonians sought simultaneously to expand economic enterprise and equality of opportunity.

Banning, Lance. *The Jeffersonian Persuasion: Evolution of a Party Ideology* (1978). A careful examination of Jeffersonian ideas, relating them to the ideological origins of the American Revolution.

Egerton, Douglas R. *Gabriel's Rebellion: The Virginia Slave Conspiracies of 1800 and 1802* (1993). The most comprehensive account of one the most important slave conspiracies in American history.

Elkins, Stanley, and Eric L. McKitrick. *The Age of Federalism* (1993). A detailed account of the politics of the 1790s.

Hofstadter, Richard. *The Idea of a Party System: The Rise of Legitimate Opposition in the United States, 1780–1840* (1969). Considers how Americans began by rejecting the idea of organized political parties and ended up accepting their legitimacy.

Kerber, Linda K. *Women of the Republic: Intellect and Ideology in Revolutionary America* (1980). A study of prevailing ideas about women's place in the new republic.

McCoy, Drew. *The Elusive Republic: Political Economy in Jeffersonian America* (1980). An influential study of the economic and political outlooks and policies of Federalists and Jeffersonians.

Miller, John C. *Crisis in Freedom: The Alien and Sedition Acts* (1952). Examines how the Adams administration sought to use the power of the federal government to stifle dissent and the free press.

Ronda, James P. *Lewis and Clark among the Indians* (1984). An account of the most famous exploring party in American history.

Rothman, Adam. *Slave Country: American Expansion and the Origins of the Deep South* (2005). A pioneering study of how the United States secured control of what are now the Gulf states, opening the door for the expansion of slavery.

Shankman, Andrew. *Crucible of American Democracy: The Struggle to Fuse Egalitarianism and Capitalism in Jeffersonian Pennsylvania* (2004). Explores the experience of Jeffersonian democracy in one pivotal state.

Smelser, Marshall. *The Democratic Republic, 1801–1815* (1968). Still the best narrative history of the presidencies of Jefferson and Madison.

Sugden, John. *Tecumseh's Last Stand* (1985). Relates the rise and fall of the era's most prominent Indian leader.

Waldstreicher, David. *In the Midst of Perpetual Fetes: The Making of American Nationalism, 1776–1820* (1997). Explores how Americans celebrated and thought about their nation's independence in the years of the early republic.

Watts, Steven. *The Republic Reborn: War and the Making of Liberal America, 1790–1820* (1987). An examination of the causes and consequences of the War of 1812.

REVIEW QUESTIONS

1. Describe how the rivalry between Britain and France did much to shape early American politics.

2. How did the expansion of the public sphere offer new opportunities to women?

3. Analyze why contemporaries referred to the War of 1812 as the Second War for Independence.

4. In what ways was liberty restricted during the Adams presidency?

5. Thomas Jefferson spoke of creating an "empire of liberty." What actions did he take toward that goal?

KEY TERMS

Report on the National Bank (p. 281)

The Genet affair (p. 282)

Whiskey Rebellion (p. 284)

XYZ affair (p. 291)

Lyon versus Griswold (p. 292)

Embargo Act (p. 301)

Battle of New Orleans (p. 306)

REVIEW TABLE

Road to War

Issue	Action	Date	Purpose
Impressment of American sailors by the British	Embargo Act	1807	To ban all American exports
Crippling of American economy by the Embargo	Non-Intercourse Act	1809	To restrict the embargo to only Britain and France
The need to trade with British or French to revive economy	Macon's Bill No. 2	1810	To lift the embargo with provisions to reestablish it if needed
Increased British interference with American trade and continued impressments	Reestablishment of embargo against Britain	1812	Last resort before declaration of war in June

CHAPTER 9

The Market Revolution, 1800–1840

Mill on the Brandywine, *an 1830 watercolor of a Pennsylvania paper mill. Because it relied on water power, much early manufacturing took place in the countryside.*

👉 FOCUS QUESTIONS

- What were the main features of the new economy taking shape in the early nineteenth century?

- What were the effects of the market revolution in early nineteenth-century America?

- How did economic and social change recast American freedom in this period?

- How did the market revolution affect the lives of women and African-Americans?

In 1824, the Marquis de Lafayette visited the United States. Nearly fifty years had passed since, as a youth of twenty, the French nobleman fought at Washington's side in the War of Independence. Now, his thirteen-month tour became a triumphant Jubilee of Liberty. Americans had good reason to celebrate Lafayette's visit and their own freedom. Since 1784, when he had last journeyed to the United States, the nation's population had tripled to nearly 12 million, its size had more than doubled, and its political institutions had thrived. Lafayette's tour demonstrated how profoundly the nation had changed. The thirteen states of 1784 had grown to twenty-four, and he visited every one—a journey that would have been almost impossible forty years earlier. Lafayette traveled up the Mississippi and Ohio Rivers by steamboat, a recent invention that was helping to bring economic development to the trans-Appalachian West, and crossed upstate New York via the Erie Canal, the world's longest man-made waterway, which linked the region around the Great Lakes with the Atlantic coast via the Hudson River.

Americans in the first half of the nineteenth century were fond of describing liberty as the defining quality of their new nation, the unique genius of its institutions. The poet Walt Whitman wrote of his countrymen's "deathless attachment to freedom." Likenesses of the Goddess of Liberty, a familiar figure in eighteenth-century British visual imagery, became even more common in the United States, appearing in paintings and sculpture and on folk art from weather vanes to quilts and tavern signs. Never, declared President Andrew Jackson in his farewell address in 1837, had any population "enjoyed so much freedom and happiness as the people of these United States." The celebration of freedom could be found in sermons, newspaper editorials, and political pronouncements in every region of the country. In *Democracy in America*, the French historian and politician Alexis de Tocqueville wrote of the "holy cult of freedom" he encountered on his own visit to the United States during the early 1830s. "For fifty years," he wrote, "the inhabitants of the United States have been repeatedly and constantly told that they are the only religious, enlightened, and free people. They . . . have an immensely high opinion of them-

An 1804 embroidery by sixteen-year-old Mary Green of Worcester, Massachusetts, based on Liberty in the Form of the Goddess of Youth, *a widely reprinted engraving linking liberty and nationhood. Atop the American flag sits a liberty cap. At the goddess's feet lie symbols of Old World monarchy, including the key to the Bastille (the Paris prison stormed by a crowd at the outset of the French Revolution) and a broken royal scepter.*

selves and are not far from believing that they form a species apart from the rest of the human race."

Even as Lafayette, Tocqueville, and numerous other visitors from abroad toured the United States, however, Americans' understandings of freedom were changing. Three historical processes unleashed by the Revolution accelerated after the War of 1812: the spread of market relations, the westward movement of the population, and the rise of a vigorous political democracy. (The first two will be discussed in this chapter, the third in Chapter 10.) All powerfully affected the development of American society. They also helped to reshape the idea of freedom, identifying it ever more closely with economic opportunity, physical mobility, and participation in a vibrantly democratic political system.

But American freedom also continued to be shaped by the presence of slavery. Lafayette, who had purchased a plantation in the West Indies and freed its slaves, once wrote, "I would never have drawn my sword in the cause of America if I could have conceived that thereby I was founding a land of slavery." Yet slavery was moving westward with the young republic. The same steamboats and canals that enabled millions of farm families to send their goods to market also facilitated the growth of slave-based cotton plantations in the South. And slavery drew a strict racial boundary around American democracy, making voting, officeholding, and participation in the public sphere privileges for whites alone. In several southern cities, public notices warned "persons of color" to stay away from the ceremonies honoring Lafayette. Half a century after the winning of independence, the coexistence of liberty and slavery, and their simultaneous expansion, remained the central contradiction of American life.

A NEW ECONOMY

In the first half of the nineteenth century, an economic transformation known to historians as the market revolution swept over the United States. Its catalyst was a series of innovations in transportation and communication. American technology had hardly changed during the colonial era. No important alterations were made in sailing ships, no major canals were built, and manufacturing continued to be done by hand, with skills passed on from artisan to journeyman and apprentice. At the dawn of the nineteenth century, most roads were little more than rutted paths through the woods. Apart from sailing ships plying the Atlantic coast and flatboats floating downstream on major rivers, trade within the new nation faced insuperable barriers. Transporting goods thirty miles inland by road cost as much as shipping the same cargo from England. In 1800, it took fifty days to move goods from Cincinnati to New York City, via a flatboat ride down

An 1810 advertisement for a stagecoach route linking Boston and Sandwich, Massachusetts, reveals the slow speed and high cost of land transportation in the early nineteenth century. It took the entire day (beginning at 5 A.M.), and cost around fifty dollars in today's money to travel the fifty-seven miles between the towns, with stops along the way for breakfast and lunch.

the Mississippi River to New Orleans and then a journey by sail along the Gulf and Atlantic coasts.

The market revolution represented an acceleration of developments already under way in the colonial era. As noted in previous chapters, southern planters were marketing the products of slave labor in the international market as early as the seventeenth century. By the eighteenth, many colonists had been drawn into Britain's commercial empire. Consumer goods like sugar and tea, and market-oriented tactics like the boycott of British goods, had been central to the political battles leading up to independence.

Nonetheless, as Americans moved across the Appalachian Mountains, and into interior regions of the states along the Atlantic coast, they found themselves more and more isolated from markets. In 1800, American farm families produced at home most of what they needed, from clothing to farm implements. What they could not make themselves, they obtained by bartering with their neighbors or purchasing from local stores and from rural craftsmen like blacksmiths and shoemakers. Those farmers not located near cities or navigable waterways found it almost impossible to market their produce.

The early life of Abraham Lincoln was typical of those who grew up in the pre-market world. Lincoln was born in Kentucky in 1809 and seven years later moved with his family to Indiana, where he lived until 1831. His father occasionally took pork down the Ohio and Mississippi Rivers to market in New Orleans, and Lincoln himself at age nineteen traveled by flatboat to that city to sell the goods of a local merchant. But essentially, the Lincoln family was self-sufficient. They hunted game for much of their food and sewed most of their clothing at home. They relied little on cash; Lincoln's father sometimes sent young Abraham to work for neighbors as a way of settling debts. As an adult, however, Lincoln embraced the market revolution. In the Illinois legislature in the

An 1837 copy of a color drawing that accompanied a patent application for a type of raft designed in 1818. For many years, rafts like this were used to transport goods to market on western rivers.

1830s, he would eagerly promote the improvement of rivers to facilitate access to markets. As a lawyer he would eventually come to represent the Illinois Central Railroad, which opened large areas of Illinois to commercial farming.

Many Americans devoted their energies to solving the technological problems that inhibited commerce within the country. Thomas Paine spent the 1780s and 1790s not only promoting democracy in America and Europe but also developing a design for an iron bridge, so that rivers could be crossed in all seasons of the year without impeding river traffic.

ROADS AND STEAMBOATS

In the first half of the nineteenth century, in rapid succession, the steamboat, canal, railroad, and telegraph wrenched America out of its economic past. These innovations opened new land to settlement, lowered transportation costs, and made it far easier for economic enterprises to sell their products. They linked farmers to national and world markets and made them major consumers of manufactured goods. Americans, wrote Tocqueville, had "annihilated space and time."

The first advance in overland transportation came through the construction of toll roads, or "turnpikes," by localities, states, and private companies. Between 1800 and 1830, the New England and Middle Atlantic states alone chartered over 900 companies to build new roads. In 1806, Congress authorized the construction of the paved National Road from Cumberland, Maryland, to the Old Northwest. It reached Wheeling, on the Ohio River, in 1818 and by 1838 extended to Illinois, where it ended.

Because maintenance costs were higher than expected and many towns built "shunpikes"—short detours that enabled residents to avoid tollgates, most private toll roads never turned a profit. Even on the new roads, horse-drawn wagons remained an inefficient mode of getting goods to market, except over short distances. It was improved water

RATES OF TOLL.

IN BALTIMORE COUNTY COURT,
September Term, 1817.

License is granted to Dennis A. Smith, proprietor of a Bridge over Patapsco River, at the place where Norwood's Ferry was heretofore established, to keep the said Bridge as a Toll Bridge, with proper gates and bars to secure the same, and to ask, demand and receive as toll for passage of said Bridge the following sums of money, to wit:

For all **four-wheel Carriages, driver included,**	**25 cts.**
For all **two-wheel Carriages, driver included,**	**20 cts.**
For **Man and Horse,**	**6¼ cts.**
For each **Stage Passenger,**	**3 cts.**
For each **Foot Passenger,**	**3 cts.**
For each **Horse without a rider,**	**6 cts.**
For **Cattle, each,**	**3 cts.**
For **Sheep and Hogs, each,**	**1 ct.**

Test: WM. GIBSON, Clerk.

A sign from a Maryland toll road lists rates for the passage of various livestock and modes of transportation.

A view of New York City, in 1849, by the noted lithographer Nathaniel Currier. Steamships and sailing vessels of various sizes crowd the harbor of the nation's largest city and busiest port.

Rochester, New York, one of the many cities that sprang up along the Erie Canal, shown in the foreground. This engraving shows the city in 1853.

transportation that most dramatically increased the speed and lowered the expense of commerce.

Robert Fulton, a Pennsylvania-born artist and engineer, had experimented with steamboat designs while living in France during the 1790s. He even launched a steamboat on the Seine River in Paris in 1803. But not until 1807, when Fulton's ship, the *Clermont*, navigated the Hudson River from New York City to Albany, was the steamboat's technological and commercial feasibility demonstrated. The invention made possible upstream commerce (that is, travel against the current) on the country's major rivers as well as rapid transport across the Great Lakes and, eventually, the Atlantic Ocean. By 1811, the first steamboat had been introduced on the Mississippi River; twenty years later some 200 plied its waters.

THE ERIE CANAL

The completion in 1825 of the 363-mile Erie Canal across upstate New York (a remarkable feat of engineering at a time when America's next largest canal was only twenty-eight miles long) allowed goods to flow between the Great Lakes and New York City. Almost instantaneously, the canal attracted an influx of farmers migrating from New England, giving birth to cities like Buffalo, Rochester, and Syracuse along its path. Its water, wrote the novelist Nathaniel Hawthorne after a trip on the canal, served as a miraculous "fertilizer," for "it causes towns with their masses of brick and stone, their churches and theaters, their business . . . to spring up."

New York governor DeWitt Clinton, who oversaw the construction of the state-financed canal, predicted that it would make New York City "the granary of the world, the emporium of commerce, the seat of manufactures, the focus of great moneyed operations." And, indeed, the canal gave New York primacy over competing ports in access to trade with the Northwest. In its financing by the state government, the Erie Canal typified the developing transportation infrastructure. With the federal government generally under the control of political leaders hostile to federal funding for internal improvements, the burden fell on the states. Between 1787 and 1860, the federal government spent about $60 million building roads and canals and improving harbors; the states spent nearly ten times that sum.

The completion of the Erie Canal set off a scramble among other states to match New York's success. Several borrowed so much money to finance elaborate programs of canal construction that they went bankrupt during the economic depression that began in 1837. By then, however, over 3,000 miles of canals had been built, creating a network linking the Atlantic states with the Ohio and Mississippi Valleys and drastically reducing the cost of transportation.

An 1827 engraving designed to show the feasibility of railroads driven by steam-powered locomotives, and dedicated to the president of the Baltimore and Ohio Railroad, which began construction in the following year. The engraver placed passengers as far from the locomotive as possible to ensure their safety in case of an explosion.

RAILROADS AND THE TELEGRAPH

Canals connected existing waterways. The railroad opened vast new areas of the American interior to settlement, while stimulating the mining of coal for fuel and the manufacture of iron for locomotives and rails. Work on the Baltimore and Ohio, the nation's first commercial railroad, began in 1828. Five years later, the South Carolina Canal and Railroad, which stretched from Charleston across the state to Hamburg, became the first long-distance line to begin operation. By 1860, the railroad network had grown to 30,000 miles, more than the total in the rest of the world combined.

At the same time, the telegraph made possible instantaneous communication throughout the nation. The device was invented during the 1830s by Samuel F. B. Morse, an artist and amateur scientist living in New York City, and it was put into commercial operation in 1844. Using Morse code, messages could be sent over electric wires, with each letter and number represented by its own pattern of electrical pulses. Within sixteen years, some 50,000 miles of telegraph wire had been strung. Initially, the telegraph was a service for businesses, and especially newspapers, rather than individuals. It helped speed the flow of information and brought uniformity to prices throughout the country.

THE RISE OF THE WEST

Improvements in transportation and communication made possible the rise of the West as a powerful, self-conscious region of the new nation. Between 1790 and 1840, some 4.5 million people crossed the Appalachian Mountains—more than the entire U.S. population at the time of Washington's first inauguration. Most of this migration took place after the end of the War of 1812, which unleashed a flood of land-hungry settlers moving from eastern states. In the six years following the end of the war in 1815, six new states entered the Union (Indiana, Illinois, Missouri, Alabama, Mississippi, and Maine—the last an eastern frontier for New England).

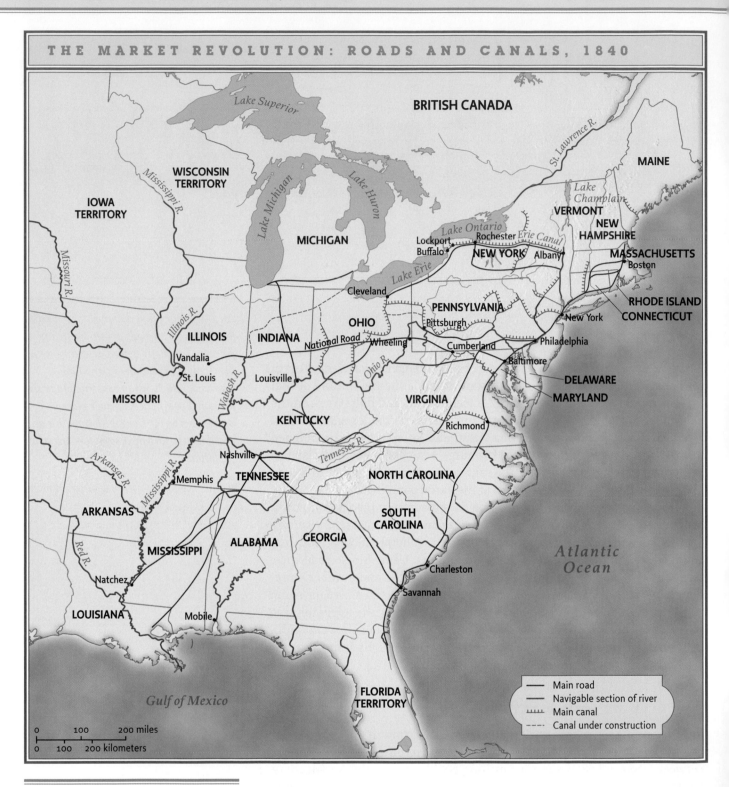

THE MARKET REVOLUTION: ROADS AND CANALS, 1840

Legend:
- Main road
- Navigable section of river
- Main canal
- Canal under construction

The improvement of existing roads and building of new roads and canals sharply reduced transportation times and costs and stimulated the growth of the market economy.

Few Americans moved west as lone pioneers. More frequently, people traveled in groups and, once they arrived in the West, cooperated with each other to clear land, build houses and barns, and establish communities. One stream of migration, including both small farmers and planters with their slaves, flowed out of the South to create the new Cotton Kingdom of Alabama, Mississippi, Louisiana, and Arkansas. Many farm families from the Upper South crossed into southern Ohio, Indiana, and Illinois. A third population stream moved from New England across New York to the Upper Northwest—northern Ohio, Indiana, and Illinois, and Michigan and Wisconsin.

Some western migrants became "squatters," setting up farms on unoccupied land without a clear legal title. Those who purchased land acquired it either from the federal government, at the price, after 1820, of $1.25 per acre payable in cash, or from land speculators on long-term credit. By 1840, settlement had reached the Mississippi River and two large new regions—the Old Northwest and Old Southwest—had entered the Union. The West became the home of regional cultures very much like those the migrants had left behind. Upstate New York and the Upper Northwest resembled New England, with its small towns, churches, and schools, while the Lower South replicated the plantation-based society of the South Atlantic states.

As population moved west, the nation's borders expanded. National boundaries made little difference to territorial expansion—in Florida, and later in Texas and Oregon, American settlers rushed in to claim land under the jurisdiction of foreign countries (Spain, Mexico, and Britain) or Indian tribes, confident that American sovereignty would soon follow in their wake. Nor did the desire of local inhabitants to remain outside the American republic deter the nation's expansion. Florida, for example, fell into American hands despite the resistance of local Indians and Spain's rejection of American offers to buy the area. In 1810, American residents of West Florida rebelled and seized Baton Rouge, and the United States soon annexed the area. The drive for the acquisition of East Florida was spurred by Georgia and Alabama planters who wished to eliminate a refuge for fugitive slaves and hostile Seminole Indians. Andrew Jackson led troops into the area in 1818. While on foreign soil, he created an international crisis by executing two British traders and a number of

A watercolor by the artist Edwin Whitefield depicts a squatter's cabin in the Minnesota woods.

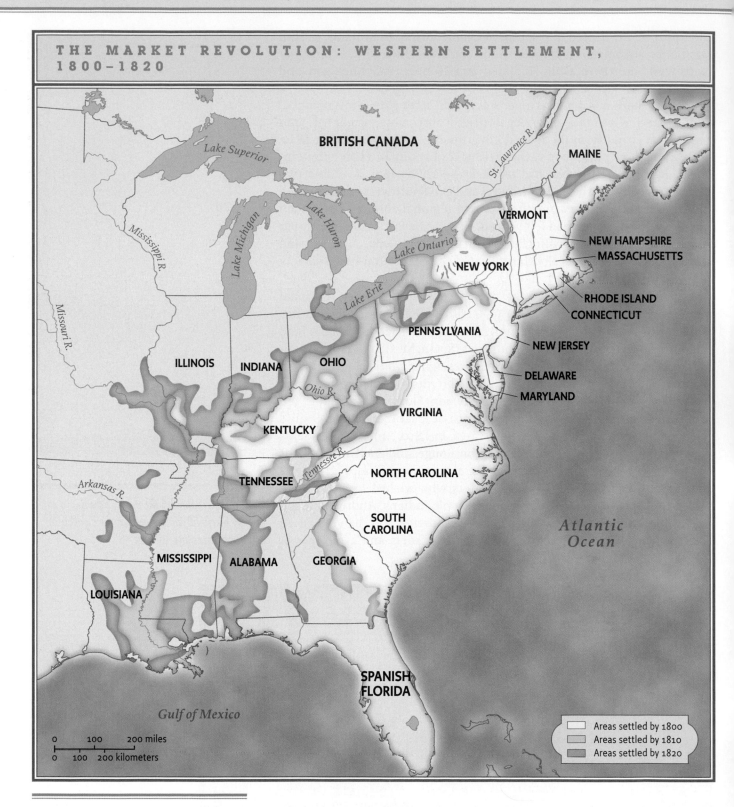

THE MARKET REVOLUTION: WESTERN SETTLEMENT, 1800–1820

BRITISH CANADA

Lake Superior

MAINE

St. Lawrence R.

Mississippi R.

Lake Michigan

Lake Huron

VERMONT

NEW HAMPSHIRE
MASSACHUSETTS

Missouri R.

Lake Ontario

NEW YORK

RHODE ISLAND
CONNECTICUT

Lake Erie

PENNSYLVANIA

NEW JERSEY

ILLINOIS   INDIANA   OHIO

DELAWARE
MARYLAND

Ohio R.

VIRGINIA

KENTUCKY

Tennessee R.

Arkansas R.

TENNESSEE

NORTH CAROLINA

SOUTH
CAROLINA

*Atlantic
Ocean*

MISSISSIPPI   ALABAMA   GEORGIA

LOUISIANA

SPANISH
FLORIDA

Gulf of Mexico

	Areas settled by 1800
	Areas settled by 1810
	Areas settled by 1820

0   100   200 miles
0   100   200 kilometers

In the first two decades of the nineteenth century, the westward movement of the population brought settlement to and across the Mississippi River.

Indian chiefs. Although Jackson withdrew, Spain, aware that it could not defend the territory, sold it to the United States in the Adams-Onís Treaty of 1819.

Successive censuses told the remarkable story of western growth. In 1840, by which time the government had sold to settlers and land compa-

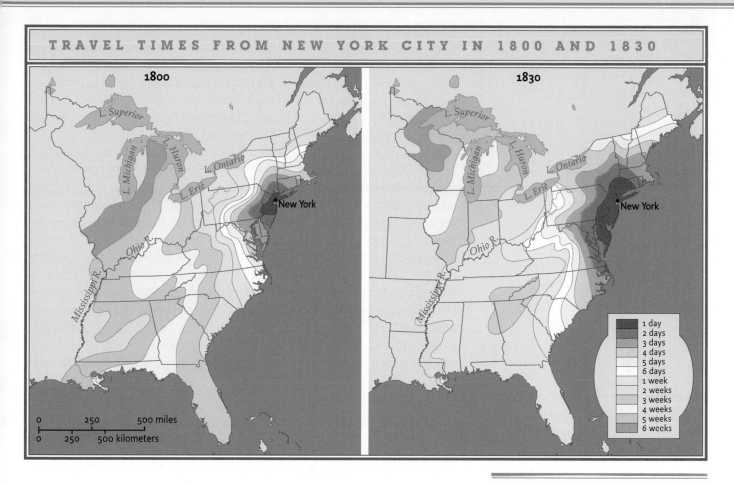

TRAVEL TIMES FROM NEW YORK CITY IN 1800 AND 1830

These maps illustrate how the transportation revolution of the early nineteenth century made possible much more rapid travel within the United States.

nies nearly 43 million acres of land, 7 million Americans—two-fifths of the total population—lived beyond the Appalachian Mountains. Between 1810 and 1830, Ohio's population grew from 231,000 to over 900,000. It reached nearly 2 million in 1850, when it ranked third among all the states. The careers of the era's leading public figures reflected the westward movement. Andrew Jackson, Henry Clay, and many other statesmen had been born in states along the Atlantic coast but made their mark in politics after moving west.

THE COTTON KINGDOM

Although the market revolution and westward expansion occurred simultaneously in the North and the South, their combined effects heightened the nation's sectional divisions. In some ways, the most dynamic feature of the American economy in the first thirty years of the nineteenth century was the rise of the Cotton Kingdom. The early industrial revolution, which began in England and soon spread to parts of the North, centered on factories producing cotton textiles with water-powered spinning and weaving machinery. These factories generated an immense demand for cotton, a crop the Deep South was particularly suited to growing because of its climate and soil fertility. Until 1793, the marketing of cotton had been slowed by the laborious task of removing seeds from the plant itself. But in that year, Eli Whitney, a Yale graduate working in Georgia as a private tutor, invented the cotton gin.

Table 9.1 POPULATION GROWTH OF SELECTED WESTERN STATES, 1800–1850 (EXCLUDING INDIANS)

State	*1810*	*1830*	*1850*
Alabama	9,000	310,000	772,000
Illinois	12,000	157,000	851,000
Indiana	25,000	343,000	988,000
Louisiana	77,000	216,000	518,000
Mississippi	31,000	137,000	607,000
Missouri	20,000	140,000	682,000
Ohio	231,000	938,000	1,980,000

A fairly simple device consisting of rollers and brushes, the gin quickly separated the seed from the cotton. It made possible the growing and selling of cotton on a large scale.

Coupled with rising demand for cotton and the opening of new lands in the West to settlement, Whitney's invention revolutionized American slavery. An institution that many Americans had expected to die out because its major crop, tobacco, exhausted the soil, now embarked on a period of unprecedented expansion. In the first decade of the nineteenth century, cotton plantations spread into the South Carolina upcountry (the region inland from the Atlantic coast previously dominated by small farms), a major reason why the state reopened the African slave trade between 1803 and 1808. After the War of 1812, the federal government moved to consolidate American control over the Deep South, forcing defeated Indians to cede land, encouraging white settlement, and acquiring Florida. With American sovereignty came the expansion of slavery. Settlers from the older southern states flooded into the region. Planters monopolized the most fertile land, while poorer farmers were generally confined to less productive and less accessible areas in the "hill country" and piney woods. After Congress prohibited the Atlantic slave trade in 1808, a massive trade in slaves developed within the United States, supplying the labor force required by the new Cotton Kingdom.

THE UNFREE WESTWARD MOVEMENT

Historians estimate that around 1 million slaves were shifted from the older slave states to the Deep South between 1800 and 1860. Some traveled with their owners to newly established plantations, but the majority were transported by slave traders to be sold at auction for work in the cotton fields. Slave trading became a well-organized business, with firms gathering slaves in Maryland, Virginia, and South Carolina and shipping them to markets in Mobile, Natchez, and New Orleans. Slave coffles—groups chained to one another on forced marches to the Deep South—became a common sight. A British visitor to the United States in the 1840s encountered what he called a "disgusting and hideous spectacle," a file of "about two hundred slaves, manacled and chained together," being marched from Virginia to Louisiana. A source of greater freedom for many whites, the westward movement meant to African Americans the destruction of family ties, the breakup of long-standing communities, and receding opportunities for liberty.

In 1793, when Whitney designed his invention, the United States produced 5 million pounds of cotton. By 1820, the crop had grown to nearly 170 million

Slave Trader, Sold to Tennessee, *a watercolor sketch by the artist Lewis Miller from the mid-1850s. Miller depicts a group of slaves being marched from Virginia to Tennessee.*

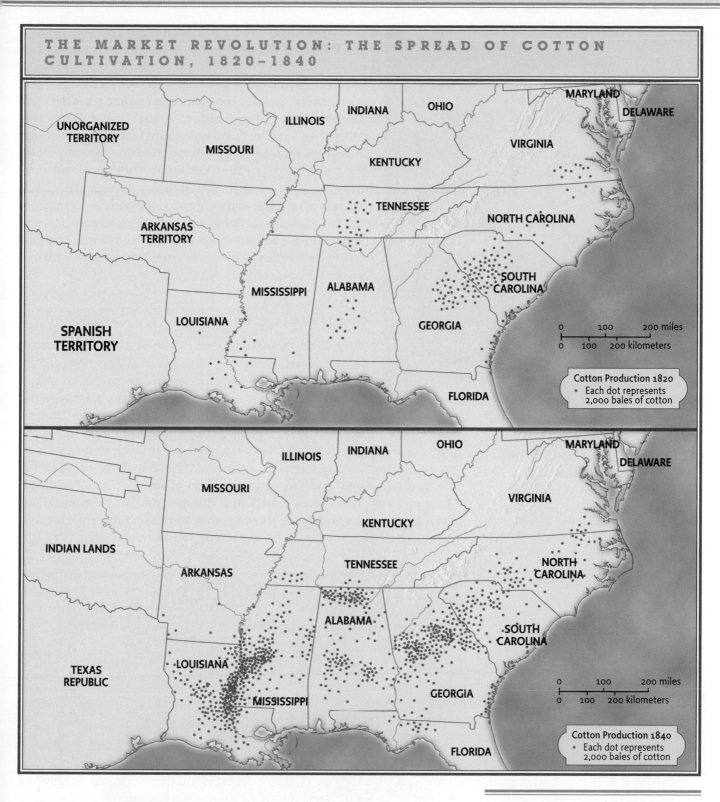

THE MARKET REVOLUTION: THE SPREAD OF COTTON CULTIVATION, 1820–1840

Maps of cotton production graphically illustrate the rise of the Cotton Kingdom stretching from South Carolina to Louisiana.

pounds. Thomas Jefferson had believed that European demand for American grain would underpin the nation's economic growth and the small farmer's independence. But as the southern economy expanded westward, it was cotton produced on slave plantations, not grain grown by sturdy yeomen, that became the linchpin of southern development and by far the most important export of the empire of liberty.

A photograph from around 1850 of a peddler with cases containing his wares. Peddlers were pioneers of the market revolution, carrying goods into areas remote from transportation.

MARKET SOCIETY

Since cotton was produced solely for sale in national and international markets, the South was in some ways the most commercially oriented region of the United States. Yet rather than spurring economic change, the South's expansion westward simply reproduced the same agrarian, slave-based social order of the older states. The region remained overwhelmingly rural. In 1860, roughly 80 percent of southerners worked the land—the same proportion as in 1800. The South's transportation and banking systems remained adjuncts of the plantation economy, geared largely to transporting cotton and other staple crops to market and financing the purchase of land and slaves.

COMMERCIAL FARMERS

In the North, however, the market revolution and westward expansion set in motion changes that transformed the region into an integrated economy of commercial farms and manufacturing cities. As in the case of Lincoln's family, the initial pioneer stage of settlement reinforced the farmer's self-sufficiency, for the tasks of felling trees, building cabins, breaking the soil, and feeding the family left little time for agriculture geared to the market. But as the Northwest became a more settled society, bound by a web of transportation and credit to eastern centers of commerce and banking, farmers found themselves drawn into the new market economy. They increasingly concentrated on growing crops and raising livestock for sale, while purchasing at stores goods previously produced at home.

Lagonda Agricultural Works, a color lithograph from 1859 advertising an Ohio manufacturer of agricultural machinery, in this case a horse-drawn reaper.

Western farmers found in the growing cities of the East a market for their produce and a source of credit. Loans originating with eastern banks and insurance companies financed the acquisition of land and supplies and, in the 1840s and 1850s, the purchase of fertilizer and new agricultural machinery to expand production. The steel plow, invented by John Deere in 1837 and mass-produced by the 1850s, made possible the rapid subduing of the western prairies. The reaper, a horse-drawn machine that greatly increased the amount of wheat a farmer could harvest, was invented by Cyrus McCormick in 1831 and produced in large quantities soon afterwards. Tens of thousands were in use on the eve of the Civil War. Between 1840 and 1860, America's output of wheat nearly tripled. Unlike cotton, however, the bulk of the crop was consumed within the country. Eastern farmers, unable to grow wheat and corn as cheaply as their western counterparts, increasingly concentrated on producing dairy products, fruits, and vegetables for nearby urban centers.

THE GROWTH OF CITIES

From the beginning, cities formed part of the western frontier. Western cities like Cincinnati and St. Louis that stood at the crossroads of interregional trade experienced extraordinary growth. Cincinnati was known as "porkopolis," after its slaughterhouses where hundreds of thousands of pigs were butchered each year and processed for shipment to eastern consumers of meat. The greatest of all the western cities was Chicago. In the early 1830s, it was a tiny settlement on the shore of Lake Michigan. By 1860, thanks to the railroad, Chicago had become the nation's fourth largest city, where farm products from throughout the Northwest were gathered to be sent east.

A view of Cincinnati, self-styled Queen City of the West, in a photograph from 1848. Steamboats line the Ohio River waterfront.

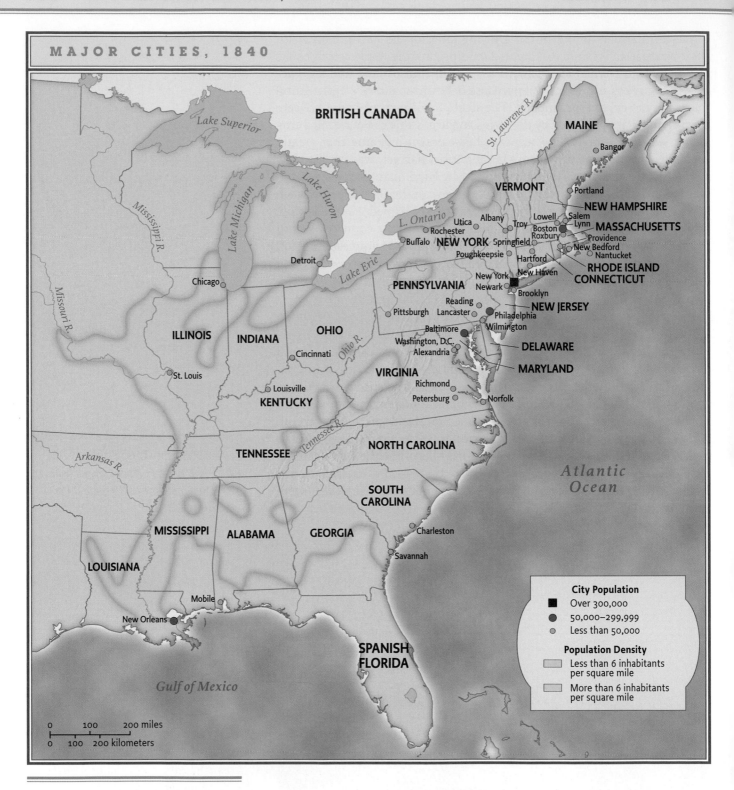

MAJOR CITIES, 1840

City Population
■ Over 300,000
● 50,000–299,999
○ Less than 50,000

Population Density
Less than 6 inhabitants per square mile
More than 6 inhabitants per square mile

Although the United States was still predominantly agricultural, by 1840 major cities had arisen in the northern and northwestern states. The South lagged far behind in urban growth.

Like rural areas, urban centers witnessed dramatic changes due to the market revolution. The number of cities with populations exceeding 5,000 rose from 12 in 1820 to nearly 150 three decades later, by which time the urban population numbered over 6 million. Urban merchants, bankers, and master craftsmen took advantage of the economic opportunities created by the expanding market among commercial farmers. The drive among these businessmen to increase production and reduce labor costs fundamentally altered the nature of work. Traditionally, skilled artisans had manufactured goods at home, where they controlled the pace and intensity of their own labor. Now, entrepreneurs gathered artisans into large workshops in order to oversee their work and subdivide their tasks. Craftsmen who traditionally produced an entire pair of shoes or piece of furniture saw the labor process broken down into numerous steps requiring far less skill and training. They found themselves subjected to constant supervision by their employers and relentless pressure for greater output and lower wages.

THE FACTORY SYSTEM

In some industries, most notably textiles, the factory superceded traditional craft production altogether. Factories gathered large groups of workers under central supervision and replaced hand tools with power-driven machinery. Samuel Slater, an immigrant from England, established America's first factory in 1790 at Pawtucket, Rhode Island. Since British law made it illegal to export the plans for industrial machinery, Slater, a skilled mechanic, built from memory a power-driven spinning jenny, one of the key inventions of the early industrial revolution.

Spinning factories such as Slater's produced yarn, which was then sent to traditional hand-loom weavers and farm families to be woven into cloth. This "outwork" system, in which rural men and women earned money by taking in jobs from factories, typified early industrialization. Before shoe production was fully mechanized, for example, various parts of the shoe were produced in factories, then stitched together in nearby homes, and then returned to the factories for finishing. Eventually, however, the entire manufacturing process in textiles, shoes, and many other products was brought under a single factory roof.

A tinsmith with his tools and wares, in a photograph from around 1850. Despite the emergence of factories, artisan production survived in many crafts.

Mill Pond and Mills, Lowell, Massachusetts. *This painting from the early 1830s shows the most famous of the early factory towns. The artist's prominent depiction of trees surrounding the factory, and their reflection in the river water where a man maneuvers his small boat, suggests that nature and industry can coexist harmoniously.*

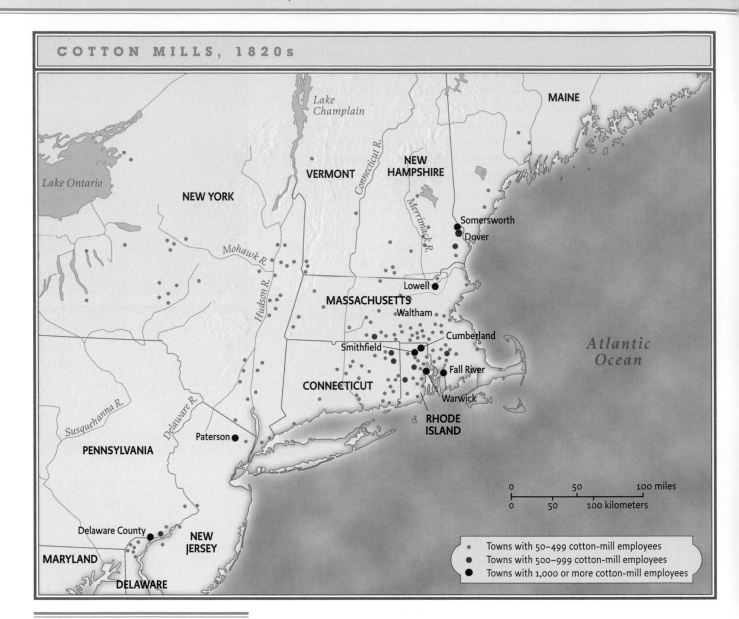

COTTON MILLS, 1820s

Towns with 50–499 cotton-mill employees
Towns with 500–999 cotton-mill employees
Towns with 1,000 or more cotton-mill employees

The early industrial revolution was concentrated in New England, where factories producing textiles from raw cotton sprang up along the region's many rivers, taking advantage of water power to drive their machinery.

The cutoff of British imports because of the Embargo of 1807 and the War of 1812 stimulated the establishment of the first large-scale American factory utilizing power looms for weaving cotton cloth. This was constructed in 1814 at Waltham, Massachusetts, by a group of merchants who came to be called the Boston Associates. In the 1820s, they expanded their enterprise by creating an entirely new factory town (incorporated as the city of Lowell in 1836) on the Merrimack River, twenty-seven miles from Boston. Here they built a group of modern textile factories that brought together all phases of production from the spinning of thread to the weaving and finishing of cloth. By 1850, Lowell's fifty-two mills employed more than 10,000 workers. Across New England, small industrial cities sprang up patterned on Waltham and Lowell. Massachusetts soon became the second most industrialized region of the world, after Great Britain.

The earliest factories, including those at Pawtucket, Waltham, and Lowell, were located along the "fall line" where waterfalls and river rapids could be harnessed to provide power for spinning and weaving machinery. By the 1840s, steam power made it possible for factory owners to locate in towns like New Bedford nearer to the coast, and in large cities like Philadelphia and Chicago with their immense local markets. In 1850, manufacturers produced in factories not only textiles but also a wide variety of other goods, including tools, firearms, shoes, clocks, ironware, and agricultural machinery. What came to be called the "American system of manufactures" relied on the mass production of interchangeable parts that could be rapidly assembled into standardized finished products. This technique was first perfected in the manufacture of clocks by Eli Terry, a Connecticut craftsman, and in small-arms production by Eli Whitney, who had previously invented the cotton gin. More impressive, in a way, than factory production was the wide dispersion of mechanical skills throughout northern society. Every town, it seemed, had its sawmill, paper mill, iron works, shoemaker, hatmaker, tailor, and a host of other such small enterprises.

The early industrial revolution was largely confined to New England and a few cities outside it. Lacking a strong internal market, and with its slave holding class generally opposed to industrial development, the South lagged in factory production. And outside New England, most northern manufacturing was still done in small-scale establishments employing a handful of workers, not in factories. In Cincinnati, for example, most workers in 1850 still labored in small unmechanized workshops.

A broadside from 1853, illustrating the long hours of work (twelve hours per day, with thirty minutes for lunch) in the Lowell mills and the way factory labor was strictly regulated by the clock.

THE INDUSTRIAL WORKER

The market revolution helped to change Americans' conception of time itself. Farm life continued to be regulated by the rhythms of the seasons. But in cities, clocks became part of daily life, and work time and leisure time came to be clearly marked off from one another. In artisan workshops of the colonial and early national eras, bouts of intense work alternated with periods of leisure. Artisans would set down their tools to enjoy a drink at a tavern or attend a political discussion. As the market revolution accelerated, work in factories, workshops, and even for servants in Americans' homes, took place for a specified number of hours per day. In colonial America, an artisan's pay was known as his "price," since it was linked to the goods he produced. In the nineteenth century, pay increasingly became a "wage," paid according to an hourly or daily rate. The increasing reliance on railroads, which operated according to fixed schedules, also made Americans more conscious of arranging their lives according to "clock time."

Closely supervised work tending a machine for a period determined by a clock seemed to violate the independence Americans considered an essential element of freedom. Consequently, few native-born men could be attracted to work in the early factories. Employers turned instead to those who lacked other ways of earning a living.

THE "MILL GIRLS"

While some factories employed entire families, the early New England textile mills relied largely on female and child labor. At Lowell, the most

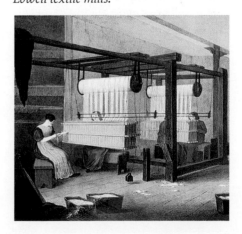

Women at work tending machines in the Lowell textile mills.

A photograph from around 1860 of four anonymous working women. Their stance and gaze suggest a spirit of independence.

famous center of early textile manufacturing, young unmarried women from Yankee farm families dominated the workforce that tended the spinning machines. To persuade parents to allow their daughters to leave home to work in the mills, Lowell owners set up boarding houses with strict rules regulating personal behavior. They also established lecture halls, churches, and even a periodical edited by factory workers, the *Lowell Offering*, to occupy the women's free time.

The constant supervision of the workers' private lives seems impossibly restrictive from a modern point of view. But this was the first time in history that large numbers of women left their homes to participate in the public world. Most valued the opportunity to earn money independently at a time when few other jobs were open to women. Home life, Lucy Larcom later recalled, was narrow and confining, while living and working at Lowell gave the "mill girls" a "larger, firmer idea of womanhood," teaching them "to go out of themselves and enter into the lives of others. . . . It was like a young man's pleasure in entering upon business for himself." But women like Larcom did not become a permanent class of factory workers. They typically remained in the factories for only a few years, after which they left to return home, marry, or move west. Larcom herself migrated to Illinois, where she became a teacher and writer. The shortage of industrial labor continued, easing only when large-scale immigration began in the 1840s and 1850s.

THE GROWTH OF IMMIGRATION

Economic expansion fueled a demand for labor, which was met, in part, by increased immigration from abroad. Between 1790 and 1830, immigrants contributed only marginally to American population growth. But between 1840 and 1860, over 4 million people (more than the entire population of 1790) entered the United States, the majority from Ireland and Germany. About 90 percent headed for the northern states, where job opportunities were most abundant and the new arrivals would not have to compete with slave labor. Immigrants were virtually unknown in the slave states, except in cities on the periphery of the South, such as New Orleans, St. Louis, and Baltimore. In the North, however, they became a visible presence in both urban and rural areas. In 1860, the 814,000 residents of New York City, the major port of entry, included over 384,000 immigrants, and one-third of the population of Wisconsin was foreign-born.

Numerous factors inspired this massive flow of population across the Atlantic. In Europe, the modernization of agriculture and the industrial revolution disrupted centuries-old patterns of life, pushing peasants off the land and eliminating the jobs of traditional craft workers. The introduction of the ocean-going steamship and the railroad made long-distance travel more practical. The Cunard Line began regular sailings with inexpensive fares from Britain to Boston and New York City in the 1840s. Beginning

Table 9.2 TOTAL NUMBER OF IMMIGRANTS BY FIVE-YEAR PERIOD	
Years	*Number of Immigrants*
1841–1845	430,000
1846–1850	1,283,000
1851–1855	1,748,000
1856–1860	850,000

around 1840, emigration from Europe accelerated, not only to the United States but to Canada and Australia as well. Frequently, a male family member emigrated first; he would later send back money for the rest of the family to follow.

IRISH AND GERMAN NEWCOMERS

To everyone discontented in Europe, commented the *New York Times*, "thoughts come of the New Free World." America's political and religious freedoms attracted Europeans who chafed under the continent's repressive governments and rigid social hierarchies, including political refugees from the failed revolutions of 1848. "In America," wrote a German newcomer, "there aren't any masters, here everyone is a free agent."

The largest number of immigrants, however, were refugees from disaster—Irish men and women fleeing the Great Famine of 1845–1851, when a blight destroyed the potato crop on which the island's diet rested. An estimated 1 million persons starved to death and another million emigrated in those years, most of them to the United States. Lacking industrial skills and capital, these impoverished agricultural laborers and small farmers ended up filling the low-wage unskilled jobs native-born Americans sought to avoid. Male Irish immigrants built America's railroads, dug canals, and worked as common laborers, servants, longshoremen, and factory operatives. Irish women frequently went to work as servants in the homes of native-born Americans, although some preferred factory work to domestic service. "It's the freedom that we want when the day's work is done," one Irish woman explained. Servants were on call at any time; "our day is ten hours long, but when it's done it's done." By the end of the 1850s, the Lowell textile mills had largely replaced Yankee farm women with immigrant Irish families. Four-fifths of Irish immigrants remained in the Northeast. In

Although our image of the West emphasizes the lone pioneer, many migrants settled in tightly knit communities and worked cooperatively. This painting by Olof Krans, who came to the United States from Sweden with his family in 1850 at the age of twelve, shows a group of women preparing to plant corn at the immigrant settlement of Bishop Hill, Illinois.

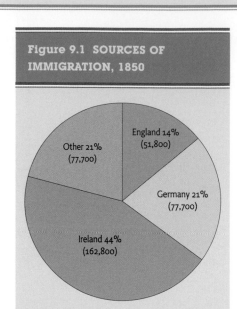

Figure 9.1 SOURCES OF IMMIGRATION, 1850

Other 21% (77,700)

England 14% (51,800)

Germany 21% (77,700)

Ireland 44% (162,800)

Boston, New York, and smaller industrial cities, they congregated in overcrowded urban ghettos notorious for poverty, crime, and disease.

The second-largest group of immigrants, Germans, included a considerably larger number of skilled craftsmen than the Irish. Germans also settled in tightly knit neighborhoods in eastern cities, but many were able to move to the West, where they established themselves as craftsmen, shopkeepers, and farmers. The "German triangle," as the cities of Cincinnati, St. Louis, and Milwaukee were sometimes called, all attracted large German populations. A vibrant German-language culture, with its own schools, newspapers, associations, and churches, developed wherever large numbers of Germans settled. "As one passes along the Bowery," one observer noted of a part of New York City known as Kleindeutschland (little Germany), "almost everything is German."

Some 40,000 Scandinavians also emigrated to the United States in these years, most of whom settled on farms in the Old Northwest. The continuing expansion of industry and the failure of the Chartist movement of the 1840s, which sought to democratize the system of government in Britain, also inspired many English workers to emigrate to the United States.

THE RISE OF NATIVISM

Immigrants from England (whose ranks included the actor Junius Brutus Booth, father of John Wilkes Booth) were easily absorbed, but those from Ireland encountered intense hostility. As Roman Catholics, they faced discrimination in a largely Protestant society in which the tradition of "antipopery" still ran deep. The Irish influx greatly enhanced the visibility and power of the Catholic Church, previously a minor presence in most parts of the country. During the 1840s and 1850s, Archbishop John Hughes of New York City made the church a more assertive institution. Hughes pressed Catholic parents to send their children to an expanding network of parochial schools, and he sought government funding to pay for them. He aggressively attempted to win converts from Protestantism.

The idea of the United States as a refuge for those seeking economic opportunity or escape from oppression has always coexisted with suspicion of and hostility to foreign newcomers. American history has witnessed periods of intense anxiety over immigration. The Alien Act of 1798 reflected fear of immigrants with radical political views. During the early twentieth century, as will be discussed below, there was widespread hostility to the "new immigration" from southern and eastern Europe. In the early twenty-first century, the question of how many persons should be allowed to enter the United States, and under what circumstances, remains a volatile political issue.

The Irish influx of the 1840s and 1850s thoroughly alarmed many native-born Americans. Those who feared the impact of immigration on American political and social life were called "nativists." They blamed immigrants for urban crime, political corruption, and a fondness for intoxicating liquor, and they accused them of undercutting native-born skilled laborers by working for starvation wages. The Irish were quickly brought into the urban political machines of the Democratic Party, whose local bosses provided jobs and poor relief to struggling newcomers. Nativists contended that the Irish, supposedly unfamiliar with American conceptions of liberty and subservient to the Catholic Church, posed a threat to democratic institutions, social reform, and public education. Stereotypes similar to those directed at blacks flourished regarding the Irish as well—childlike, lazy, and slaves of their passions, they were said to be unsuited for republican freedom.

Nativism would not become a national political movement until the 1850s, as we will see in Chapter 13. But in the 1840s, New York City and Philadelphia witnessed violent anti-immigrant riots. Appealing mainly to skilled native-born workers who feared that immigrants were taking their jobs and undercutting their wages, a nativist candidate was elected New York's mayor in 1844.

THE TRANSFORMATION OF LAW

American law increasingly supported the efforts of entrepreneurs to participate in the market revolution, while shielding them from interference by local governments and liability for some of the less desirable results of economic growth. The corporate form of business organization became central to the new market economy. A corporate firm enjoys special privileges and powers granted in a charter from the government, among them that investors and directors are not personally liable for the company's debts. Unlike companies owned by an individual, family, or limited partnership, in other words, a corporation can fail without ruining its directors and stockholders. Corporations were therefore able to raise far more capital than these traditional forms of enterprise. By the 1830s, many states had replaced the granting of charters through specific acts of legislation with "general incorporation laws," allowing any company to obtain a corporate charter if it paid a specified fee.

Many Americans distrusted corporate charters as a form of government-granted special privilege. But the courts upheld their validity, while opposing efforts by established firms to limit competition from newcomers. In *Dartmouth College v. Woodward* (1819), John Marshall's Supreme Court defined corporate charters issued by state legislatures as contracts, which future lawmakers could not alter or rescind. Five years later, in *Gibbons v. Ogden*, the Court struck down a monopoly the New York legislature had granted for steamboat navigation. And in 1837, with Roger B. Taney now the chief justice, the Court ruled that the Massachusetts legislature did not infringe the charter of an existing company that had constructed a bridge over the Charles River when it empowered a second company to build a competing bridge. The community, Taney declared, had a legitimate interest in promoting transportation and prosperity.

Local judges, meanwhile, held businessmen blameless for property damage done by factory construction (such as the flooding of upstream farmlands and the disruption of fishing when dams were built to harness water power). Numerous court decisions also affirmed employers' full authority over the workplace and invoked the old common law of conspiracy to punish workers who sought to strike for higher wages. Not until 1842, in *Commonwealth v. Hunt*, did Massachusetts chief justice Lemuel Shaw decree that there was nothing inherently illegal in workers organizing a union or a strike. Like changes in work and time, changes in the law illustrated the comment of Horace Bushnell, a Connecticut minister, that the market economy had produced a "complete revolution" in Americans' "life and manners."

THE FREE INDIVIDUAL

By the 1830s, the market revolution and westward expansion had produced a society that amazed European visitors: energetic, materialistic, and seemingly in constant motion. Arriving in Chicago in 1835, the British writer Harriet Martineau found the streets "crowded with land speculators, hurrying from one sale to another. . . . As the gentlemen of our party walked the streets, store-keepers hailed them from their doors, with offers of farms, and all manner of land-lots, advising them to speculate before the price of land rose higher." Alexis de Tocqueville was struck by Americans' restless energy and apparent lack of attachment to place. "No sooner do you set foot on American soil," he observed, "than you find yourself in a sort of tumult. All around you, everything is on the move." Westward migration and urban development created a large mobile population no longer tied to local communities who sought to seize the opportunities offered by economic change. "In the United States," wrote Tocqueville, "a man builds a house in which to spend his old age, and sells it before the roof is on; he plants a garden and [rents] it just as the trees are coming into bearing; he brings a field into tillage and leaves other men to gather the crops."

THE WEST AND FREEDOM

Westward expansion and the market revolution profoundly affected the lives of all Americans. They reinforced some older ideas of freedom and helped to create new ones. American freedom, for example, had long been linked with the availability of land in the West. A New York journalist, John L. O'Sullivan, first employed the phrase "manifest destiny," meaning that the United States had a divinely appointed mission, so obvious as to be beyond dispute, to occupy all of North America. Americans, he proclaimed, had a far better title to western lands than could be provided by any international treaty, right of discovery, or long-term settlement. Their right to the continent was provided by the nation's mission to extend the area of freedom. Other peoples' claims, O'Sullivan wrote, must give way to "our manifest destiny to overspread and to possess the whole of the continent which providence has given us for the development of the great experiment in liberty." Those who stood in the way of expansion—European powers like Great Britain and Spain, Native Americans, Mexicans—were by definition obstacles to the progress of freedom.

O'Sullivan wrote these words in 1845, but the essential idea was familiar much earlier. As the population moved across the Appalachian Mountains, so did the linkage between westward expansion and freedom. "The Goddess of Liberty," declared Senator John Breckinridge of Kentucky, was not "governed by geographical limits." A sense of spatial openness, of the constant opportunity to pick up and move when the pursuit of happiness seemed to demand it, became a more and more central component of American freedom. Like its predecessors, this generation of Americans believed that the United States had been selected by God for the greatest experiment in human history, the achievement of liberty, and that westward expansion was part and parcel of this destiny. Freedom in the United States, wrote the French historian Michel Chevalier, one of the many Europeans who visited the country in the 1830s, was a "practical idea" as much as a "mystical one"—it meant "a liberty of action and motion which the American uses to expand over the vast territory that Providence has given him and to subdue it to his uses."

In national myth and ideology, the West would long remain, as the writer Wallace Stegner would later put it, "the last home of the freeborn American." The settlement and economic exploitation of the West promised to prevent the United States from following down the path of Europe and becoming a society with fixed social classes and a large group of wage-earning poor. In the West, land was more readily available and oppressive factory labor far less common. With population and the price of land rising dramatically in the older states and young men's prospects for acquiring a farm or setting up an independent artisan shop declining, the West still held out the chance to achieve economic independence, the social condition of freedom.

THE TRANSCENDENTALISTS

The restless, competitive world of the market revolution strongly encouraged the identification of American freedom with the absence of restraints on self-directed individuals seeking economic advancement and personal development. The "one important revolution" of the day, the philosopher Ralph Waldo Emerson wrote in the 1830s, was "the new value of the private man." The opportunity for personal growth offered a new definition of Jefferson's pursuit of happiness, one well suited to a world in which territorial expansion and the market revolution had shattered traditional spatial and social boundaries and made moving from place to place and status to status common features of American life.

In a widely reprinted 1837 address, "The American Scholar," Emerson called on the person engaged in writing and thinking to "feel all confidence in himself, . . . to never defer to the popular cry," and to find and trust his own "definition of freedom." In Emerson's definition, rather than a pre-existing set of rights or privileges, freedom was an open-ended process of self-realization by which individuals could remake themselves and their own lives. The keynote of the times, he declared, was "the new importance given to the single person" and the "emancipation" of the individual, the "American idea."

Emerson was perhaps the most prominent member of a group of New England intellectuals known as the transcendentalists, who insisted on the primacy of individual judgment over existing social traditions and institutions. Emerson's Concord, Massachusetts, neighbor, the writer Henry David Thoreau, echoed his call for individual self-reliance. "Any man more right than his neighbors," Thoreau wrote, "is a majority of one."

The daguerreotype, an early form of photography, required the sitter to remain perfectly still for twenty seconds or longer. The philosopher Ralph Waldo Emerson, depicted here, did not like the result. He complained in his journal that in his "zeal not to blur the image," every muscle had become "rigid" and his face was fixed in a frown as "in madness, or in death."

VOICES OF FREEDOM

FROM RALPH WALDO EMERSON, "The American Scholar" (1837)

Ralph Waldo Emerson was perhaps the most prominent intellectual in mid-nineteenth-century America. In this famous address, delivered at Harvard College, he insisted on the primacy of individual judgment over existing social traditions as the essence of freedom.

Perhaps the time is already come, when . . . the sluggard intellect of this continent will look from under its iron lids and fill the postponed expectation of the world with something better than the exertions of mechanical skill. Our day of dependence, our long apprenticeship to the learning of other lands, draws to a close. . . .

In self-trust, all the virtues are comprehended. Free should the scholar be,–free and brave. Free even to the definition of freedom. . . . Not he is great who can alter matter, but he who can alter my state of mind. They are the kings of the world who give the color of their present thought to all nature and all art. . . .

[A] sign of the times . . . is the new importance given to the single individual. Every thing that tends to insulate the individual,–to surround him with barriers of natural respect, so that each man shall feel the world is his, and man shall treat with man as a sovereign state with a sovereign state:–tends to true union as well as greatness. 'I learned,' said the melancholy Pestalozzi [a Swiss educator], "that no man in God's wide earth is either willing or able to help any other man." Help must come from his bosom alone. . . .

We have listened too long to the courtly muses of Europe. The spirit of the American freeman is already suspected to be timid, imitative, tame. . . . The scholar is decent, indolent, complaisant. See already the tragic consequence. The mind of this country taught to aim at low objects, eats upon itself. Young men . . . do not yet see, that if the single man [should] plant himself indomitably on his instincts, and there abide, the huge world will come round to him. . . . We will walk on our own feet; we will work with our own hands; we will speak our own minds.

FROM ORESTES BROWNSON,
"The Laboring Classes" (1840)

Like Emerson a member of the New England movement known as transcendentalism, Orestes Brownson came to believe that individual self-realization was not an adequate solution to the social problems of a market society. "The Laboring Classes," published during a serious economic depression, called for a change in the prevailing system of wage labor.

No one can observe the signs of the times with much care, without perceiving that a crisis as to the relation of wealth and labor is approaching. . . . We or our children will have to meet this crisis. The old war between the King and the Barons is well nigh ended, and so is that between the Barons and the Merchants and Manufacturers,–landed capital and commercial capital. And now commences the new struggle between the operative and the employer, between wealth and labor. . . .

All over the world this facts stares us in the face, the workingman is poor and depressed, while a large portion of the non-workingmen, in the sense we now use the term, are wealthy. It may be laid down as a general rule, with but few exceptions, that men are rewarded in an inverse ratio to the amount of actual service they perform. . . .

Now the great work for this age and the coming, is to raise up the laborer, and to realize in our own social arrangements and in the actual condition of all men, that equality between man and man, which God has established between the rights of one and those of another. In other words, our business is to emancipate the proletariat, as the past has emancipated the slaves. This is our work. There must be no class of our fellow men doomed to toil through life as mere workmen at wages. . . .

The truth is, the evil we have pointed out is not merely individual in its character. It is not, in the case of any single individual, of any one man's procuring, nor can the efforts of any one man, directed solely to his own moral and religious perfection, do aught to remove it. What is purely individual in its nature, efforts of individuals to perfect themselves, may remove. But the evil we speak of is inherent in all our social arrangements, and cannot be cured without a radical change of those arrangements. Could we convert all men to Christianity in both theory and practice . . . the evils of the social state would remain untouched. Continue our present system of trade, and all its present evil consequences will follow, whether it be carried on by your best men or your worst. . . . The only way to get rid of its evils is to change the system, not its managers.

QUESTIONS

1. How does Emerson define the freedom of what he calls "the single individual"?

2. How does Brownson define economic freedom for workers?

3. What does the contrast between these two documents suggest about the impact of the market revolution on American thought?

INDIVIDUALISM

Ironies abounded in the era's "individualism" (a term that first entered the language in the 1820s). For even as the market revolution promoted commercial connections between far-flung people, the idea of the "sovereign individual" proclaimed that Americans should depend on no one but themselves. Of course, personal independence had long been associated with American freedom. But eighteenth-century thinkers generally saw no contradiction between private happiness and self-sacrificing public virtue, defined as devotion to the common good. Now, Tocqueville observed, individualism led "each member of the community to sever himself from the mass of his fellows and to draw apart with his family and his friends . . . [leaving] society at large to itself." Americans increasingly understood the realm of the self—which came to be called "privacy"—as one with which neither other individuals nor government had a right to interfere. As will be discussed in the next chapter, individualism also helped to inspire the expansion of democracy. Ownership of one's self rather than ownership of property now made a person capable of exercising the right to vote.

Looking back from the 1880s, Emerson would recall the era before the Civil War as a time when "social existence" gave way to "the enlargement and independency of the individual, . . . driven to find all his resources, hopes, rewards, society, and deity within himself." In his own life, Thoreau illustrated Emerson's point about the primacy of individual conscience in matters political, social, and personal, and the need to find one's own way rather than following the crowd. Like other transcendentalists, he did not approve of the way individuals in a market economy engaged in this pursuit of happiness. Thoreau became persuaded that modern society stifled individual judgment by making men "tools of their tools," trapped in stultifying jobs by their obsession with acquiring wealth. Even in "this comparatively free country," he wrote, most persons were so preoccupied with material things that they had no time to contemplate the beauties of nature.

To escape this fate, Thoreau retreated for two years to a cabin on Walden Pond near Concord, where he could enjoy the freedom of isolation from the "economical and moral tyranny" he believed ruled American society. He subsequently published *Walden* (1854), an account of his experiences and a critique of how the market revolution was, in his opinion, degrading both Americans' values and the natural environment. An area that had been covered with dense forest in his youth, he observed, had been so transformed by woodcutters and farmers that it had become almost completely devoid of trees and wild animals. In one famous passage, Thoreau noted how his enjoyment of nature was disturbed by the distant sound of a locomotive whistle—a symbol of how it seemed impossible to escape the market revolution. Thoreau appealed to Americans to "simplify" their lives rather than become obsessed with the accumulation of wealth. Genuine freedom, he insisted, lay within.

In part as a reaction against the expansion of cities and factories, a group of artists known as the Hudson River school devoted themselves to portraying the glories of nature. Thomas Cole's The Falls of the Kaaterskill *(1826) depicts a spectacular site in the Catskill mountains of New York state. Apart from a lone figure overlooking the falls, no human being intrudes into the landscape. Cole chose not to include in his painting a house that had been built at the falls a few years earlier.*

THE SECOND GREAT AWAKENING

The popular religious revivals that swept over the country during the Second Great Awakening added a religious underpinning to the celebration of personal self-improvement, self-reliance, and self-determination. These revivals, which began at the turn of the century, were originally organized by established religious leaders alarmed by low levels of church attendance in the young republic (perhaps as few as 10 percent of white Americans regularly attended church during the 1790s). But they quickly expanded far beyond existing churches. They reached a crescendo in the 1820s and early 1830s, when the Reverend Charles Grandison Finney held months-long revival meetings in upstate New York and New York City.

Religious Camp Meeting, *a watercolor from the late 1830s depicting an evangelical preacher at a revival meeting. Some of the audience members seem inattentive, while others are moved by his fiery sermon.*

The son of Connecticut farmers, Finney had been inspired to preach after attending a religious revival in 1821. Like the evangelists (traveling preachers) of the first Great Awakening of the mid-eighteenth century, discussed in Chapter 4, Finney warned of hell in vivid language while offering the promise of salvation to converts who abandoned their sinful ways. He became a national celebrity after his success in Oneida County in upstate New York. After Finney's preaching, according to one report, the area had been "completely overthrown by the Holy Ghost" so that "the theater has been deserted, the tavern sanctified . . . and far higher and purer enjoyment has been found in exercises of devotion."

The Second Great Awakening democratized American Christianity, making it a truly mass enterprise. At the time of independence, fewer than 2,000 Christian ministers preached in the United States. In 1845, they numbered 40,000. Evangelical denominations like the Methodists and Baptists enjoyed explosive growth in membership, and smaller sects proliferated. By the 1840s, Methodism, with over 1 million members, had become the country's largest denomination. Deism, a form of religious belief hostile to organized churches, had been prominent among the generation of the founding fathers. It now waned, and Christianity became even more central to American culture. Americans, wrote Tocqueville, "combine the notions of Christianity and of liberty so intimately in their minds that it is impossible to make them conceive the one without the other."

New religious prophets seemed to appear regularly in early-nineteenth-century America, determined, in novelist Herman Melville's phrase, to "gospelize the world anew." At great camp meetings, especially prominent on the frontier, fiery revivalist preachers rejected the idea that man is a sinful

Das neue Jerusalem (*The New Jerusalem*), an early nineteenth-century watercolor, in German, illustrates the narrow gateway to heaven and the fate awaiting sinners in hell. These were common themes of preachers in the Second Great Awakening.

creature with a preordained fate, promoting instead the doctrine of human free will. At these gatherings, rich and poor, male and female, and in some instances whites and blacks worshiped alongside one another and pledged to abandon worldly sins in favor of the godly life.

THE AWAKENING'S IMPACT

Even more than its predecessor of several decades earlier, the Second Great Awakening stressed the right of private judgment in spiritual matters and the possibility of universal salvation through faith and good works. Every person, Finney insisted, was a "moral free agent," that is, a person free to choose between a Christian life and sin. Sinners could experience a "change of heart" and embrace spiritual freedom, defined, in the words of evangelical minister Jonathan Blanchard, as "Christ ruling in and over rational creatures who are obeying him freely and from choice."

Revivalist ministers seized the opportunities offered by the market revolution to spread their message. They raised funds, embarked on lengthy preaching tours by canal, steamboat, and railroad, and flooded the country with mass-produced, inexpensive religious tracts. The revivals' opening of religion to mass participation and their message that ordinary Americans could shape their own spiritual destinies resonated with the spread of market values.

To be sure, evangelical preachers can hardly be described as cheerleaders for a market society. They regularly railed against greed and indifference to the welfare of others as sins. Finney called selfishness—an extreme form of individualism encouraged by the scramble for wealth produced by the market revolution—"the law of Satan's empire," not God's. Yet the revivals thrived in areas caught up in the rapid expansion of the market economy, such as the region of upstate New York along the path of the Erie Canal.

Most of Finney's converts here came from the commercial and professional classes. Evangelical ministers promoted what might be called a controlled individualism as the essence of freedom. In stressing the importance of industry, sobriety, and self-discipline as examples of freely chosen moral behavior, evangelical preachers promoted the very qualities necessary for success in a market culture.

THE LIMITS OF PROSPERITY

LIBERTY AND PROSPERITY

As the market revolution progressed, the right to compete for economic advancement became a touchstone of American freedom. "The whole question of freedom or slavery for man," argued Henry C. Carey, perhaps the era's most prominent economist, was bound up with economic achievement. Official imagery linked the goddess of liberty ever more closely to emblems of material wealth. New Jersey, whose official seal, adopted in 1776, had paired liberty with Ceres, the Roman goddess of agriculture, in 1821 added the motto "Liberty and Prosperity." The state seal of Arkansas, admitted to the Union in 1836, pictured liberty atop an image of a steamboat and two overflowing horns of plenty.

Many enterprising Americans seized the opportunities offered by the market revolution to enrich themselves. John Jacob Astor, the son of a poor German butcher who emigrated to the United States at the end of the War of Independence, earned large profits in the early nineteenth century by shipping furs to China and importing teas and silk. Astor invested his wealth in Manhattan real estate, which was rapidly rising in value, and built Astor House, which quickly became the nation's most famous hotel. He died in 1848 the richest man in the United States, leaving a fortune of perhaps $10 million, the equivalent of hundreds of millions of dollars today.

Astor's story seemed to exemplify the opportunities open to the "self-made man," a term that came into use during his lifetime. According to this idea, those who achieved success in America did so not as a result of hereditary privilege or government favoritism as in Europe, but through their own intelligence and hard work. In the extent of his wealth, of course, Astor was hardly typical. But the market revolution and the quickening of commercial life enriched numerous bankers, merchants, industrialists, and planters. It produced a new middle class—an army of clerks, accountants, and other office employees who staffed businesses in Boston, New York, and elsewhere. It created new opportunities for farmers who profited from the growing demand at home and abroad for American agricultural products, and for skilled craftsmen like Thomas Rodgers, a machine builder who established a successful locomotive factory in Paterson, New Jersey. New opportunities for talented men opened in professions like law, medicine, and teaching. By the early 1820s, there were an estimated 10,000 physicians in the United States.

RACE AND OPPORTUNITY

The market revolution affected the lives of all Americans. But not all were positioned to take advantage of its benefits. Most blacks, of course, were

The official seal of Arkansas (1836) reflects the widespread identification of freedom with technological progress (a steamboat) and material prosperity (the two horns of plenty at bottom).

Pat Lyon at the Forge, *an 1826–1827 painting of a prosperous blacksmith. Proud of his accomplishments as a self-made man who had achieved success through hard work and skill rather than inheritance, Lyon asked the artist to paint him in his shop wearing his work clothes.*

slaves, but even free blacks found themselves excluded from the new economic opportunities. The 220,000 blacks living in the free states on the eve of the Civil War (less than 2 percent of the North's population) suffered discrimination in every phase of their lives. Although virtually every northern county east of the Mississippi River reported some black residents, the majority of blacks lived in the poorest, unhealthiest sections of cities like New York, Philadelphia, and Cincinnati. And even these neighborhoods were subjected to occasional violent assault by white mobs, like the armed bands that attacked blacks and destroyed their homes and businesses in Cincinnati in 1829.

Barred from schools and other public facilities, free blacks laboriously constructed their own institutional life, centered on mutual aid and educational societies, as well as independent churches, most notably the African Methodist Episcopal Church. Richard Allen of Philadelphia, a Methodist preacher, had been spurred to found the church after being forcibly removed from his former church for praying at the altar rail, a place reserved for whites.

While many white Americans could look forward to a life of economic accumulation and individual advancement, large numbers of free blacks experienced downward mobility. As noted in Chapter 6, northern free blacks were the last large group to experience indentured servitude, since the terms of emancipation generally required children of slave mothers to work for their owners before being freed. At the time of abolition, because of widespread slave ownership among eighteenth-century artisans, a considerable number of northern blacks possessed craft skills. But it became more and more difficult for blacks to utilize these skills once they became free. Although many white artisans criticized slavery, most viewed the freed slaves as low-wage competitors and sought to bar them from skilled employment. "They are leaders in the cause of equal rights for themselves," a black editor commented of New York City's artisans in the 1830s.

Hostility from white craftsmen, however, was only one of many obstacles that kept blacks confined to the lowest ranks of the labor market. White employers refused to hire them in anything but menial positions, and white customers did not wish to be served by them. The result was a rapid decline in economic status, until by mid-century, the vast majority of northern blacks labored for wages in unskilled jobs and as domestic servants. The state census of 1855 revealed 122 black barbers and 808 black servants in New York City, but only 1 lawyer and 6 doctors. Nor could free blacks take advantage of the opening of the West to improve their economic status, a central component of American freedom. Federal law barred them from access to public land, and by 1860 four states—Indiana, Illinois, Iowa, and Oregon—prohibited them from entering their territory altogether.

THE CULT OF DOMESTICITY

Women, too, found many of the opportunities opened by the market revolution closed to them. As the household declined as a center of economic production, many women saw their traditional roles undermined by the availability of mass-produced goods previously made at home. Some women, as noted above, followed work as it moved from household to fac-

Juliann Jane Tillman, a preacher in the African Methodist Episcopal Church, in an 1844 engraving. Many Protestant denominations allowed women to preach, although their presence also aroused much criticism.

tory. Others embraced a new definition of femininity, which glorified not a woman's contribution to the family's economic well-being, but her ability to create a private environment shielded from the competitive tensions of the market economy. Woman's "place" was in the home, a site increasingly emptied of economically productive functions as work moved from the household to workshops and factories. Her role was to sustain nonmarket values like love, friendship, and mutual obligation, providing men with a shelter from the competitive marketplace.

The earlier ideology of "republican motherhood," which allowed women a kind of public role as mothers of future citizens, subtly evolved into the mid-nineteenth-century "cult of domesticity." "Virtue," which in the eighteenth century was a political characteristic of men essential to the success of republican government, came to be redefined as a personal moral quality associated more and more closely with women. "Virtue" for a woman meant not only sexual innocence but beauty, frailty, and depen-dence on men. "In whatever situation of life a woman is placed from her cradle to her grave," declared *The Young Lady's Book*, one of numerous popular magazines addressed to female audiences of the 1820s and 1830s, "a spirit of obedience and submission, pliability of temper, and humility of mind, are required from her." These magazines carried articles such as "Woman, a Source of Comfort," "Woman, a Being to Come Home To," and "Woman—Man's Best Friend."

With more and more men leaving the home for work, women did exercise considerable power over personal affairs within the family. The rapid decline in the American birthrate during the nineteenth century (from an average of seven children per woman in 1800 to four in 1900) cannot be explained except by the conscious decision of millions of women to limit the number of children they bore. But the idea of domesticity minimized even women's indirect participation in the outside world. For both sexes, freedom meant fulfilling their respective "inborn" qualities. Men were rational, aggressive, and domineering, while women were nurturing, selfless, ruled by the emotions, and thus less fitted for public life. If submission to the will of another increasingly seemed inadmissible for free men, it remained a condition natural to women and expected of them. Men moved freely between the public and private "spheres"; women were supposed to remain cloistered in the private realm of the family.

A page from the drawing book of Lewis Miller, a Pennsylvania-German folk artist, reflects the nineteenth-century cult of domesticity, which stressed women's moral influence within the home. On the left, a woman prays that God will make her children "do thy will." On the right, a mother exclaims, "Happy world, if all were Christians!"

WOMEN AND WORK

Prevailing ideas concerning gender bore little relation to the experience of those women who worked for wages at least some time in their lives.

They did so despite severe disadvantages. Women could not compete freely for employment, since only low-paying jobs were available to them. Married women still could not sign independent contracts or sue in their own name, and not until after the Civil War did they, not their husbands, control the wages they earned. Nonetheless, for poor city dwellers and farm families, the labor of all family members was essential to economic survival. Thousands of poor women found jobs as domestic servants, factory workers, and seamstresses. Early industrialization enhanced the availability of paid work for northern women, as the spread of the putting-out system in such industries as shoemaking, hatmaking, and clothing manufacture allowed women laboring at home to contribute to family income even as they retained responsibility for domestic chores.

For the expanding middle class, however, it became a badge of respectability for wives to remain at home, outside the disorderly new market economy, while husbands conducted business in their offices, shops, and factories. In larger cities, where families of different social classes had previously lived alongside one another, fashionable middle-class neighborhoods populated by merchants, factory owners, and professionals like lawyers and doctors began to develop. Work in middle-class homes was done by domestic servants, the largest employment category for women in nineteenth-century America. The freedom of the middle-class woman—defined in part as freedom from labor—rested on the employment of other women within her household.

Even though most women were anything but idle, in a market economy where labor increasingly meant work that created monetary value, it became more and more difficult to think of labor as encompassing anyone but men. Lydia Maria Child wrote a popular book, *The Frugal Housewife*, published in 1829, that sought to prepare women for the ups and downs of the market revolution (one chapter was entitled "How to Endure Poverty"). Child supported her family by her writing and became a prominent advocate of antislavery and of greater rights for women. Her diary reveals that in a single year she also sewed thirty-six pieces of clothing, prepared over 700 meals, and spent much time supervising household help.

By any reasonable definition, Child worked—at home and as a writer. But discussions of labor rarely mentioned housewives, domestic servants, and female outworkers, except as an indication of how the spread of capitalism was degrading men. The idea that the male

An image from a female infant's 1830 birth and baptismal certificate depicts a domestic scene, with women at work while men relax.

head of household should command a "family wage" that enabled him to support his wife and children became a popular definition of social justice. It sank deep roots not only among middle-class Americans but among working-class men as well. Capitalism, said the newspaper *Workingman's Advocate*, tore women from their role as "happy and independent mistresses" of the domestic sphere and forced them into the labor market, thereby undermining the natural order of the household and the authority of its male head.

THE EARLY LABOR MOVEMENT

As this complaint suggests, although many Americans welcomed the market revolution, others felt threatened by its consequences. Surviving members of the revolutionary generation feared that the obsession with personal economic gain was undermining devotion to the public good. "Commerce, luxury, and avarice," warned John Adams, "have destroyed every republican government." In the 1820s, as he neared the end of his life, Jefferson was denouncing "stockjobbers," financiers, speculators, and others for leading the nation away from his idealized virtuous agrarian republic.

Many Americans experienced the market revolution not as an enhancement of the power to shape their own lives, but as a loss of freedom. The period between the War of 1812 and 1840 witnessed a sharp economic downturn in 1819, a full-fledged depression starting in 1837, and numerous ups and downs in between, during which employment was irregular and numerous businesses failed. For every aspiring American who rode the tide of economic progress, another seemed to sink beneath the waves. The economic transformation produced an explosive growth in the nation's output and trade and a rise in the general standard of living. But especially in the growing cities of the Northeast, it significantly widened the gap between wealthy merchants and industrialists on the one hand and impoverished factory workers, unskilled dockworkers, and seamstresses laboring at home on the other. In Massachusetts, the most industrialized state in the country, the richest 5 percent of the population owned over half the wealth. Inequality was even more pronounced in Philadelphia, where the top 1 percent possessed more wealth than the rest of the population combined. Bankruptcy was a common fact of life, and men unable to pay their debts filled the prisons of major cities.

Alarmed at the erosion of traditional skills and the threat of being reduced to the status of dependent wage earners, skilled craftsmen in the late 1820s created the world's first Workingmen's Parties, short-lived

No More Grinding the Poor—But Liberty and the Rights of Man, *a labor movement cartoon of the 1830s. The devil and a millionaire conspire to buy an election with money (in the box at the lower left), while an honest workingman hands his ballot to a female figure of liberty. The worker's motto is "Liberty, Equity, Justice, and The Rights of Man."*

political organizations that sought to mobilize lower-class support for candidates who would press for free public education, an end to imprisonment for debt, and legislation limiting work to ten hours per day. In the 1830s, a time of rapidly rising prices, union organization spread and strikes became commonplace. Along with demands for higher wages and shorter hours, the early labor movement called for free homesteads for settlers on public land and an end to the imprisonment of union leaders for conspiracy.

THE "LIBERTY OF LIVING"

But over and above these specific issues, workers' language of protest drew on older ideas of freedom linked to economic autonomy, public-spirited virtue, and social equality. The conviction of twenty New York tailors in 1835 under the common law of conspiracy for combining to seek higher wages inspired a public procession marking the "burial of liberty." Such actions and language were not confined to male workers. The young mill women of Lowell walked off their jobs in 1834 to protest a reduction in wages and again two years later when employers raised rents at their boardinghouses. They carried banners affirming their rights as "daughters of free men," and, addressing the factory owners, they charged, "the oppressive hand of avarice [greed] would enslave us." Freedom, Noah Webster's *American Dictionary* declared in 1828, was "a state of exemption from the power or control of another." The labor movement asked how many wage earners truly enjoyed such "exemption."

Some labor spokesmen, like Langdon Byllesby of Philadelphia, went so far as to describe wage labor itself as the "very essence of slavery," since dependence on another person for one's economic livelihood was incompatible with freedom. The idea that permanent wage work bore some resemblance to slavery was not confined to labor radicals. In Herman Melville's short story *The Tartarus of Maids*, workers in a New England paper mill stand by their machines "mutely and cringingly as the slave."

Rooted in the traditions of the small producer and the identification of freedom with economic independence, labor's critique of the market economy directly challenged the idea that individual improvement—Emerson's "self-trust, self-reliance, self-control, self-culture"—offered an adequate response to social inequality. "Wealth and labor," wrote Orestes Brownson in his influential essay "The Laboring Classes" (1840), were at war. Workers' problems, he went on, must be understood as institutional, not individual. They had their root in "the constitution of society," and their solu-

Certificate of the New York Mechanick's Society, 1795. The central image and motto, "By Hammer and Hand, all Arts do Stand," illustrate the pride in the dignity of labor shared by the artisans who formed the society.

tion required not a more complete individualism, but a "radical change [in] existing social arrangements" so as to produce "equality between man and man."

"We are free," wrote Peter Rödel, an immigrant German shoemaker, "but not free enough. . . . We want the liberty of living." Here lay the origins of the idea, which would become far more prominent in the late nineteenth and twentieth centuries, that economic security—a standard of life below which no person would fall—formed an essential part of American freedom.

Thus, the market revolution transformed and divided American society and its conceptions of freedom. It encouraged a new emphasis on individualism and physical mobility among white men, while severely limiting the options available to women and African-Americans. It opened new opportunities for economic freedom for many Americans, while leading others to fear that their traditional economic independence was being eroded. In a democratic society, it was inevitable that the debate over the market revolution and its consequences for freedom would be reflected in American politics.

The Shoemakers' Strike in Lynn—Procession in the Midst of a Snow-Storm, of Eight Hundred Women Operatives, *an engraving from* Frank Leslie's Illustrated Newspaper, *March 17, 1860. The striking women workers carry a banner comparing their condition to that of slaves.*

SUGGESTED READING

Arieli, Yehoshua. *Individualism and Nationalism in American Ideology* (1964). A study of the rise of individualism and other key ideas in American thought.

Boydston, Jeanne. *Home and Work: Housework, Wages, and the Ideology of Work in the Early Republic* (1990). Examines how the market revolution affected ideas relating to women's work.

Butler, Jon. *Awash in a Sea of Faith: Christianizing the American People* (1990). A history of American religion with emphasis on evangelical movements, including the Second Great Awakening.

Clark, Christopher. *The Roots of Rural Capitalism: Western Massachusetts, 1780–1860* (1990). Considers how the market revolution transformed economic and social life in one region of the North.

Deyle, Steven. *Carry Me Back: The Domestic Slave Trade in American Life* (2005). The most comprehensive history of the internal slave trade, by which millions of slaves were transported to the Deep South.

Dublin, Thomas. *Women at Work: The Transformation of Work in Lowell, Massachusetts, 1826–1860* (1975). A pioneering study of the working and nonworking lives of Lowell "factory girls."

Faragher, John M. *Sugar Creek: Life on the Illinois Prairie* (1986). Traces the growth of a frontier community from early settlement to market society.

Harris, Leslie. *In the Shadow of Slavery: African-Americans in New York City, 1626–1863* (2003). A study that emphasizes the exclusion of African-Americans from the economic opportunities offered by the market revolution.

Horwitz, Morton J. *The Transformation of American Law, 1780–1860* (1977). Analyzes how changes in American law facilitated the market revolution.

Johnson, Paul E. *A Shopkeeper's Millennium: Society and Revivals in Rochester, New York, 1815–1837* (1978). Explores the impact of religious revivals on a key city of upstate New York.

Miller, Kerby A. *Exiles and Emigrants: Ireland and the Irish Exodus to North America* (1985). An examination of Irish immigration over the course of American history.

Ryan, Mary P. *Cradle of the Middle Class: The Family in Oneida County, New York, 1790–1865* (1981). Examines how economic change helped to produce a new kind of middle-class family structure centered on women's dominance of the household.

Sellers, Charles G. *The Market Revolution: Jacksonian America, 1815–1846* (1991). The most comprehensive study of the market revolution and its consequences.

Stansell, Christine. *City of Women: Sex and Class in New York, 1789–1860* (1986). Considers how gender conventions and economic change shaped the lives of working-class women.

Wilentz, Sean. *Chants Democratic: New York City and the Rise of the American Working Class, 1788–1850* (1984). A study of the early labor movement in one of its key centers in antebellum America.

REVIEW QUESTIONS

1. What were the major social effects of the market revolution?

2. How did ideas of American freedom change in this period?

3. What revolutionary changes did American slavery undergo in this period?

4. What role did immigration play in the market revolution?

5. The Second Great Awakening both took advantage of the market revolution and criticized its excesses. Explain this statement.

KEY TERMS

Erie Canal (p. 316)

cotton gin (p. 321)

slave coffles (p. 322)

Deere plow (p. 325)

Charles River Bridge v. Warren Bridge (p. 333)

workers and unions (p. 333)

camp meetings (p. 340)

working-class women (p. 344)

REVIEW TABLE

Landmarks of the Market Revolution

Event	Date	Accomplishment
Congress approves funds for a National Road	1806	Cumberland Road reaches Ohio River in 1818 and Illinois in 1838
Robert Fulton's steamboat *The Clermont* navigates the Hudson River	1807	Makes possible upstream commerce of the country's major rivers
Waltham textile mills open	1814	By 1850, the area's 52 mills employ 10,000 workers
Dartmouth College case	1819	Court defines corporate charters issued by states as contracts
Erie Canal completed	1825	Connects New York City to the Great Lakes
Work begun on B&O railroad, the nation's first commercial railroad	1828	National railroad network grows to 30,000 miles by 1860
Telegraph put into commercial operation	1844	50,000 miles of telegraph wire is strung by 1860

CHAPTER 10

Democracy in America, 1815–1840

Stump Speaking. *In this painting from the 1850s, George Caleb Bingham depicts a candidate in a county election addressing a group of voters, an illustration of grassroots democracy in action. One of the listeners appears about to question or challenge the speaker. A founder of the Whig Party in Missouri, Bingham himself ran for office several times and was elected to the Missouri legislature in 1848.*

- What were the social bases for the flourishing democracy of the early mid-nineteenth century?

- What efforts were made in this period to strengthen the economic integration of the nation?

- What were the major expressions of nationalism and sectionalism in this period?

- In what ways did Andrew Jackson embody the democratic nationalism of this period?

- Why was the Bank War so central to the Jacksonian period?

The inauguration of Andrew Jackson on March 4, 1829, made it clear that something had changed in American politics. The swearing-in of the president had previously been a small, dignified event. Jackson's inauguration attracted a crowd of some 20,000 people who poured into the White House after the ceremony, ruining furniture and breaking china and glassware in the crush. It was "the reign of King Mob," lamented Justice Joseph Story of the Supreme Court.

Jackson aroused powerful feelings, pro and con. His supporters viewed his election as the advent of genuine democracy, the coming to power of the "common man." Philip Hone, a New York political leader who kept a detailed diary for more than thirty years, recorded that Jackson was "the most popular man we have ever known." Hone had voted for President John Quincy Adams in 1828, but he recognized that Jackson's democratic bearing and beliefs "suit [the people] exactly." Jackson's critics, on the other hand, considered him a tyrant. They called him King Andrew I, and when they organized politically they borrowed their name, the Whig Party, from the opponents of royal power in eighteenth-century England.

Andrew Jackson's career embodied the major developments of his era—the market revolution, the westward movement, the expansion of slavery, and the growth of democracy. He was a symbol of the self-made man. Unlike previous presidents, Jackson rose to prominence from a humble background, reflecting his era's democratic opportunities. Born in 1767 on the South Carolina frontier, he had been orphaned during the American Revolution. Early on, Jackson displayed the courage and impetuousness for which he would later become famous. While still a youth, he served as a courier for patriotic forces during the War of Independence. Captured and imprisoned, he was almost killed when a British officer struck him with a sword after Jackson refused an order to polish the officer's boots.

As a young man, Jackson moved to Tennessee, where he studied law, became involved in local politics, and in the 1790s won election to the House of Representatives and the Senate, and became a judge on the state supreme court. His military campaigns against the British and Indians helped to consolidate American control over the Deep South, making possible the rise of the Cotton Kingdom. He himself acquired a large plantation in Tennessee. But more than anything else, to this generation of Americans Andrew Jackson symbolized one of the most crucial features of national life—the triumph of political democracy.

THE TRIUMPH OF DEMOCRACY

PROPERTY AND DEMOCRACY

The market revolution and territorial expansion were intimately connected with a third central element of American freedom—political democracy. The challenge to property qualifications for voting, begun during the American Revolution, reached its culmination in the early nineteenth century. Not a single state that entered the Union after the original thirteen required ownership of property to vote. In the older states, constitutional conventions during the 1820s and 1830s reconsidered democracy's economic basis. Even as the expansion of industry and commercial agriculture increased the number of wage earners in cities and older rural areas, men who could not meet property requirements insisted that they were as fit as others to exercise the rights of citizens. Their insistent pressure did much to democratize American politics.

Owning property, declared a petition by "Non-Freeholders" [landless men] of Richmond to the Virginia constitutional convention of 1829, did not necessarily mean the possession of "moral or intellectual endowments" superior to those of the poor. "They alone deserve to be called free," they continued, "who participate in the formation of their political institutions." By this time, only North Carolina, Rhode Island, and Virginia still retained property requirements. The large slaveholders who dominated Virginia politics successfully resisted demands for changes in voting qualifications in 1829, but a subsequent constitutional convention, in 1850, eliminated the property requirement. Although the speed of the process varied from state to state, by 1860 all but one had ended property requirements for voting (although several continued to bar persons accepting poor relief on the grounds that they lacked genuine independence). The personal independence necessary in the citizen now rested not on ownership of property, but on ownership of one's self—a reflection of the era's individualism.

THE DORR WAR

The lone exception to the trend toward democratization was Rhode Island, which required voters to own real estate valued at $134 or rent property for at least $7 per year. A center of factory production, Rhode Island had a steadily growing population of propertyless wage earners unable to vote. Leaders of the state's labor movement complained repeatedly about the absence of "free suffrage." In October 1841, proponents of democratic reform organized a People's Convention, which drafted a new state constitution. It enfranchised all adult white men while eliminating entirely blacks, who previously could vote if they owned the required amount of property (another illustration of how the expansion of white freedom sometimes went hand in hand with restrictions on the freedom of nonwhites). When the reformers ratified their constitution in an extralegal referendum and proceeded to inaugurate Thomas Dorr, a prominent Rhode Island lawyer, as governor, President John Tyler dispatched federal troops to the state. The movement collapsed, and Dorr subsequently served nearly

An anti-Jackson cartoon from 1832 portrays Andrew Jackson as an aspiring monarch, wielding the veto power while trampling on the Constitution.

VOICES OF FREEDOM

From "The Memorial of the Non-Freeholders of the City of Richmond" (1829)

By 1829, only Virginia, North Carolina, and Rhode Island still retained property qualifications for voting. When Virginia held a convention to draft a new state constitution, "non-freeholders" (men who did not own enough land to enable them to vote) submitted a memorial claiming that right. They were not successful, and the property qualification was not abolished there until 1850.

Your memorialists ... belong to that class of citizens, who, not having the good fortune to possess a certain portion of land, are, for that cause only, debarred from the enjoyment of the right of suffrage.... Comprising a very large part, probably a majority of male citizens of mature age, they have been passed by, like aliens or slaves, as if ... unworthy of a voice, in the measures involving their future political destiny.... whilst the freeholders, sole possessors, under the existing Constitution, of the elective franchise, have, upon the strength of that possession alone, asserted and maintained in themselves, the exclusive power of new-modelling the fundamental laws of the State: in other words, have seized upon the sovereign authority.

It cannot be necessary, in addressing the Convention now assembled, to expatiate on the momentous importance of the right of suffrage, or to enumerate the evils consequent upon its unjust limitation.... To that privilege they respectfully contend, they are entitled equally with its present possessors ... [We] appeal to the heart, as well as the understanding, of all who comprehend and duly appreciate the principles of free Government....

The existing regulation of the suffrage ... creates an odious distinction between members of the same community; robs of all share, in the enactment of the laws, a large portion of the citizens, ... and vests in a favored class, not in consideration of their public services, but of their private possessions, the highest of all privileges.... [We] cannot discern in the possession of land any evidence of peculiar merit, or superior title [to] moral or intellectual endowments. ... Such possession no more proves him who has it, wiser or better, than it proves him taller or stronger, than him who has it not....

Let us concede that the right of suffrage is a social right; that it must of necessity be regulated by society.... For obvious reasons, by almost universal consent, women and children, aliens and slaves, are excluded.... But the exclusion of these classes for reasons peculiarly applicable to them, is no argument for excluding others....

They alone deserve to be called free, or have a guarantee for their rights, who participate in the formation of their political institutions, and in control of those who make and administer the law.

FROM JOHN C. CALHOUN,
"A Disquisition on Government" (ca. 1845)

The most prominent political philosopher in the pre–Civil War South, John C. Calhoun sought to devise ways that the South could retain the power to protect its interests within the Union (especially the institution of slavery) as it fell behind the North in population and political power.

There are two different modes in which the sense of the community may be taken; one, simply by the right of suffrage, unaided; the other, by the right through a proper organism. Each collects the sense of the majority. But one regards numbers only, and considers the whole community as a unit, having but one common interest throughout; and collects the sense of the greater number of the whole, as that of the community. The other, on the contrary, regards interests as well as numbers;–considering the community as made up of different and conflicting interests, as far as the action of the government is concerned; and takes the sense of each, through its majority or appropriate organ, and the united sense of all, as the sense of the entire community. The former of these I shall call the numerical, or absolute majority; and the latter, the concurrent, or constitutional majority. I call it the constitutional majority, because it is an essential element in every constitutional government,–be whatever form it takes. So great is the difference, politically speaking, between the two majorities, that they cannot be confounded, without leading to great and fatal errors; and yet the distinction between them has been so entirely over-looked, that when the term *majority* is used in political discussions, it is applied exclusively to designate the numerical,–as if there were no other. . . .

The first and leading error which naturally arises from overlooking the distinction referred to, is, to confound the numerical majority with the people, and this is so completely as to regard them as identical. This is a consequence that necessarily results from considering the numerical as the only majority. All admit, that a popular government, or democracy, is the government of the people. . . . Those who regard the numerical as the only majority . . . [are] forced to regard the numerical majority as, in effect, the entire people. . . .

The necessary consequence of taking the sense of the community by the concurrent majority is . . . to give to each interest or portion of the community a negative on the others. It is this mutual negative among its various conflicting interests, which invests each with the power of protecting itself; . . . Without this, there can be no constitution.

QUESTIONS

1. Why do the non-freeholders consider the right to vote essential to the enjoyment of freedom?

2. Which Americans would be most likely to object to Calhoun's political system?

3. How do the two documents differ in their understanding of democracy?

Dorr Liberation Stock, *a certificate indicating that a person has helped to finance Thomas Dorr's appeal to the U.S. Supreme Court of his conviction for treason against the state of Rhode Island because of his role in the Dorr War. The Court ruled against him, and Dorr served two years in prison.*

two years in prison for treason. The Dorr War demonstrated the passions aroused by the continuing exclusion of any group of white men from voting. And the legislature soon eliminated the property qualification for native-born men, black as well as white, although it retained it for immigrants until 1888.

TOCQUEVILLE ON DEMOCRACY

By 1840, more than 90 percent of adult white men were eligible to vote. A flourishing democratic system had been consolidated. American politics was boisterous, highly partisan, and sometimes violent, and it engaged the energies of massive numbers of citizens. In a country that lacked more traditional bases of nationality—a powerful and menacing neighbor, historic ethnic, religious, and cultural unity—democratic political institutions came to define the nation's sense of its own identity.

Alexis de Tocqueville, the French writer who visited the United States in the early 1830s, returned home to produce *Democracy in America*, a classic account of a society in the midst of a political transformation. Tocqueville had come to the United States to study prisons. But he soon realized that to understand America, one must understand democracy (which as a person of aristocratic background he rather disliked). His key insight was that democracy by this time meant far more than either the right to vote or a particular set of political institutions. It was what scholars call a "habit of the heart," a culture that encouraged individual initiative, belief in equality, and an active public sphere populated by numerous voluntary organizations that sought to improve society. Democracy, Tocqueville saw, had become an essential attribute of American freedom.

As Tocqueville recognized, the rise of democracy represented a profound political transformation. The idea that sovereignty belongs to the mass of ordinary citizens was a new departure in Western thought. As long ago as Aristotle, political philosophers had warned that democracy inevitably degenerated into anarchy and tyranny. For centuries, doctrines of divine right and hierarchical authority had dominated political thought. The founders of the republic, who believed that government must rest on the consent of the governed, also sought to shield political authority from excessive influence by ordinary people (hence the Electoral College, Supreme Court, and other undemocratic features of the Constitution). Nonetheless, thanks to persistent pressure from those originally excluded from political participation, democracy—for white males—had triumphed by the Age of Jackson.

Democracy reinforced a sense of equality among those who belonged to the political nation, and it deepened the divide separating them from those who did not. Participation in elections and the pageantry surrounding them—parades, bonfires, mass meetings, party conventions—helped to define the "people" of the United States. The right to vote increasingly became the emblem of American citizenship. In law, voting was still, strictly speaking, a privilege rather than a right, subject to regulation by the individual states. But Noah Webster's *American Dictionary* noted that according to common usage and understanding in America (but not in Europe), the term "citizen" had become synonymous with the right to vote. The suffrage, said one advocate of democratic reform, was "the first mark of liberty, the only true badge of the freeman."

THE LIMITS OF DEMOCRACY

By the 1830s, the time of Andrew Jackson's presidency, the axiom that "the people" ruled had become a universally accepted part of American politics. Those who opposed this principle, wrote Tocqueville, "hide their heads." But the very centrality of democracy to the definition of both freedom and nationality made it all the more necessary to define the boundaries of the political nation. As older economic exclusions fell away, others survived and new ones were added. The vigorous public life of antebellum America was simultaneously expansive and exclusive, and its limits were as essential to its nature as its broad scope. Democracy in America could absorb native-born poor white men as well as waves of immigrants, yet it erected impenetrable barriers to the participation of women and non-white men—groups also excluded, as noted in the previous chapter, from full participation in the market revolution.

The "principle of universal suffrage," declared the *United States Magazine and Democratic Review* in 1851, meant that "white males of age constituted the political nation." How could the word "universal" be reconciled with barring blacks and women from political participation? As democracy triumphed, the intellectual grounds for exclusion shifted from economic dependency to natural incapacity. Gender and racial differences were widely understood as part of a single, natural hierarchy of innate endowments. A boundary drawn by nature itself was not really exclusion at all. "How did woman first become subject to man, as she now is all over the world?" asked the *New York Herald* in 1852. "By her nature, her sex, just as the negro is and always will be, to the end of time, inferior to the white race, and, therefore, doomed to subjection." Paradoxically, therefore, while freedom for white men involved an open-ended process of personal transformation, developing to the fullest the potential inherent within each human being, the limits of American democracy rested on the belief that the character and abilities of non-whites and women were forever fixed by nature.

THE INFORMATION REVOLUTION

The market revolution and political democracy produced a large expansion of the public sphere and an explosion in printing sometimes called the "information revolution." The application of steam power to newspaper printing led to a great increase in output and the rise of the mass-circulation "penny press," priced at one cent per issue instead of the traditional six. Newspapers like the *New York Sun* and *New York Herald*

The American Woman's Home, *a guide to domestic life by the sisters Catharine Beecher and Harriet Beecher Stowe. Even though works like this were meant to instruct middle-class women on how to meet their domestic responsibilities, their popularity allowed talented women to take on a new public role as writers.*

introduced a new style of journalism, appealing to a mass audience by emphasizing sensationalism, crime stories, and exposés of official misconduct. By 1840, according to one estimate, the total weekly circulation of newspapers in the United States, whose population was 17 million, exceeded that of Europe, with 233 million people.

Thanks to low postal rates, many newspapers circulated far beyond their places of publication. Indeed, by the 1830s, newspapers accounted for most postal traffic, outstripping private letters. The emergence of organized political parties also spurred newspaper publication. Each major party needed to have newspapers supporting its views in every part of the country, and government printing contracts were essential to most newspapers' survival. The publication of all sorts of magazines, travel guides, advice manuals, religious titles, and other reading materials rose dramatically.

The reduction in the cost of printing also made possible the appearance of "alternative" newspapers in the late 1820s and early 1830s, including *Freedom's Journal* (the first black newspaper), *Philadelphia Mechanic's Advocate* and other labor publications, the abolitionist weekly *The Liberator*, and *Cherokee Phoenix*, the first Native American newspaper.

WOMEN AND THE PUBLIC SPHERE

The growth of the reading public, yet another facet of the democratization of American life, opened the door for the rise of a new generation of women writers. Lydia Maria Child, Catharine Maria Sedgwick, Catharine Beecher, and others published stories, poetry, essays, and guides to domestic life. By the 1830s, moreover, through participation in religious and reform movements, thousands of women would establish a public presence, as will be described in Chapter 12. Nonetheless, once New Jersey added the word "male" to its voting requirements in 1807, women everywhere, whether married or single, propertied or dependent, were denied the right to vote. The Creator, said a delegate to Virginia's 1829 constitutional convention, had rendered woman "weak and timid, in comparison with man, and had thus placed her under his *control*, as well as under his protection." Since the right of suffrage "necessarily implied *free-agency* [that is, the right and ability to make decisions for one's self] and *intelligence*," nature had decreed women's "incapacity to exercise political power."

The political world of the nineteenth century, so crucial an arena for the exercise of American freedom, was in part defined in contrast to the feminine sphere of the home. Freedom in the public realm in no way implied freedom in private life. The "most rabid Radical," Ralph Waldo Emerson remarked in his journal in 1841, was likely to be conservative "in relation to the theory of Marriage." Beyond the right to "decent treatment" by her husband and to whatever property the law allowed her to control, declared the *New York Herald*, a woman had "no rights . . . with which the public have any concern."

A RACIAL DEMOCRACY

If the exclusion of women from political freedom continued a longstanding practice, the increasing identification of democracy and whiteness marked something of a departure. Tocqueville noted that by the 1830s, "equality" had become an American obsession. In contrast to the highly stratified societies of Europe, white Americans of all social classes dressed the same, traveled in the same stagecoaches and railroad cars, and stayed in the same hotels. Yet at the same time, blacks were increasingly considered a group apart.

Racist imagery became the stock-in-trade of popular theatrical presentations like minstrel shows, in which white actors in blackface entertained the audience by portraying African-Americans as stupid, dishonest, and altogether ridiculous. With the exception of Herman Melville, who portrayed complex, sometimes heroic black characters in works like *Moby Dick* and *Benito Cereno* (the latter a fictionalized account of a shipboard slave rebellion), American authors either ignored blacks entirely or presented them as stereotypes—happy slaves prone to superstition or long-suffering but devout Christians. Meanwhile, the somewhat tentative thinking of the revolutionary era about the status of non-whites flowered into an elaborate ideology of racial superiority and inferiority, complete with "scientific" underpinnings. These developments affected the boundaries of the political nation.

In the revolutionary era, only Virginia, South Carolina, and Georgia explicitly confined the vote to whites, although elsewhere, custom often made it difficult for free blacks to exercise the franchise. As late as 1800, no northern state barred blacks from voting. But every state that entered the Union after that year, with the single exception of Maine, limited the right to vote to white males. And, beginning with Kentucky in 1799 and Maryland two years later, states that had allowed blacks to vote rescinded the privilege.

Jim Crow, *a piece of sheet music from 1829. Minstrel shows were a form of nineteenth-century entertainment in which white actors impersonated blacks. One of the most popular characters was Jim Crow, the happy, childlike plantation slave created by Thomas D. Rice. Years later, "Jim Crow" would come to mean the laws and customs of segregation.*

RACE AND CLASS

In 1821, the same New York constitutional convention that removed property qualifications for white voters raised the requirement for blacks to $250, a sum beyond the reach of nearly all of the state's black residents. North Carolina disenfranchised free blacks in 1835, and Pennsylvania, home of an articulate, economically successful black community in Philadelphia, did the same three years later. One delegate to the Pennsylvania constitutional convention refused to sign the completed document because of its provision limiting suffrage to whites. This was Thaddeus Stevens, who would later become a leader in the drive for equal rights for African-Americans after the Civil War. By 1860, blacks could vote on the same basis as whites only in five New England states, which contained only 4 percent of the nation's free black population. A delegate to the Pennsylvania convention of 1837 described the United States as "a political community of white persons."

Despite racial inequalities, many whites of the revolutionary generation had thought of African-Americans as "citizens of color," potential members of the body politic. But in the nineteenth century, the definition of the political nation became more and more associated with race. The federal government barred free blacks from service in state militias and the army (although the navy did enroll some black sailors). No state accorded free blacks what today would be considered full equality before the law. In

Illinois, for example, blacks could not vote, testify or sue in court, serve in the militia, or attend public schools. Blacks were aliens, not Americans, "intruders among us," declared a political leader in Minnesota.

In effect, race had replaced class as the boundary between those American men who were entitled to enjoy political freedom and those who were not. Even as this focus on race limited America's political community as a whole, it helped to solidify a sense of national identity among the diverse groups of European origin. In a country where the right to vote had become central to the meaning of freedom, it is difficult to overstate the importance of the fact that white male immigrants could vote in some states almost from the moment they landed in America, while nearly all free blacks (and, of course, slaves), whose ancestors had lived in the country for centuries, could not vote at all.

NATIONALISM AND ITS DISCONTENTS

THE AMERICAN SYSTEM

The War of 1812, which the United States and Great Britain—the world's foremost military power—fought to a draw, inspired an outburst of nationalist pride. But the war also revealed how far the United States still was from being a truly integrated nation. With the Bank of the United States having gone out of existence when its charter expired in 1811, the country lacked a uniform currency and found it almost impossible to raise funds for the war effort. Given the primitive state of transportation, it proved very difficult to move men and goods around the country. One shipment of supplies from New England had taken seventy-five days to reach New Orleans. With the coming of peace, the manufacturing enterprises that sprang up while trade with Britain had been suspended faced intense competition from low-cost imported goods. A younger generation of Republicans, led by Henry Clay and John C. Calhoun, believed these "infant industries" deserved national protection. While retaining their Jeffersonian belief in an agrarian republic, they insisted that agriculture must be complemented by a manufacturing sector if the country were to become economically independent of Britain.

In 1806, Congress, as noted in the previous chapter, had approved using public funds to build a paved National Road from Cumberland, Maryland, to the Ohio Valley. Two years later, Albert Gallatin, Jefferson's secretary of the treasury, outlined a plan for the federal government to tie the vast nation together by constructing roads and canals up and down the eastern seaboard, and by connecting the Atlantic coast with the Great Lakes and Ohio and Mississippi Rivers. Gallatin's proposal fell victim to regional rivalries and fears of excessive national power. But the idea revived after the War of 1812.

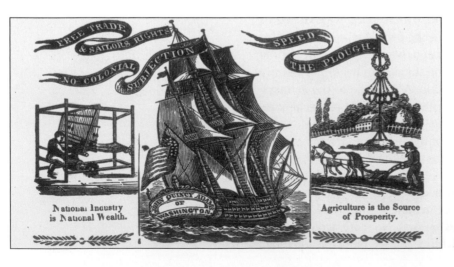

An image from a broadside from the campaign of 1824, promoting the American System of government-sponsored economic development. The illustrations represent industry, commerce, and agriculture. The ship at the center is named the John Quincy Adams. *Its flag, "No Colonial Subjection," suggests that without a balanced economy, the United States will remain economically dependent on Great Britain.*

In his annual message (now known as the State of the Union address) to Congress in December 1815, President James Madison put forward a blueprint for government-promoted economic development that came to be known as the American System, a label coined by Henry Clay. (It should not be confused with the "American system of manufactures" mentioned in the previous chapter, which referred to a way of mass-producing goods with interchangeable parts, not a political program for economic growth.) The plan rested on three pillars: a new national bank, a tariff on imported manufactured goods to protect American industry, and federal financing of improved roads and canals. The last was particularly important to those worried about the dangers of disunity. "Let us bind the nation together, with a perfect system of roads and canals," John C. Calhoun implored Congress in 1815. "Let us conquer space." When believers in strict construction of the Constitution objected, Calhoun replied: "If we are restricted in the use of money to the enumerated powers, on what principle can the purchase of Louisiana be justified?"

Government-sponsored "internal improvements," as the construction of roads and canals was called, proved to be the most controversial part of the plan. Congress enacted an internal-improvements program drafted by Calhoun only to be astonished when the president, on the eve of his retirement from office in March 1817, vetoed the bill. Since calling for its enactment, Madison had become convinced that allowing the national government to exercise powers not mentioned in the Constitution would prove dangerous to individual liberty and southern interests. A constitutional amendment would be necessary, he declared, before the federal government could build roads and canals. The other two parts of his plan, however, became law. The tariff of 1816 offered protection to goods that could be produced in the United States, especially cheap cotton textiles, while admitting tax-free those that could not be manufactured at home. Many southerners supported the tariff, believing that it would enable their region to develop a manufacturing base to rival New England's. And in 1816, a new Bank of the United States was created, with a twenty-year charter from Congress.

John C. Calhoun in an 1822 portrait by the artist Charles Bird King. Calhoun would evolve from a nationalist into the most prominent spokesman for state sovereignty and the right of nullification.

BANKS AND MONEY

The Second Bank of the United States soon became the focus of public resentment. Like its predecessor, it was a private, profit-making corporation that served as the government's financial agent, issuing paper money, collecting taxes, and paying the government's debts. It was also charged with ensuring that paper money issued by local banks had real value. The number of local banks had risen to over 200—a sign of the accelerating market revolution. They promoted economic growth by helping to finance manufacturing and commerce and extending loans to farmers for the purchase of land, tools, consumer goods, and, in the South, slaves. They also printed paper money.

Today, only the federal government issues paper money, and the amount is determined by the Federal Reserve Bank, not the amount of gold held at the repository at Fort Knox. But in the nineteenth century, paper money consisted of notes promising to pay the bearer on demand a specified amount of "specie" (gold or silver). The value of the currency issued by individual banks depended on their reputation for stability. Since banks often printed far more money than the specie in their vaults, the value of paper currency fluctuated wildly. The Bank of the United States was supposed to prevent the overissuance of money. Because it held all the funds of the federal government, it accumulated a large amount of paper money issued by local banks, which had been used to purchase public land. The Bank of the United States could demand payment in gold and silver from a local bank in exchange for that bank's paper money. This prospect was supposed to prevent local banks from acting improperly, for if it could not provide the specie when asked, it would have to suspend operations.

THE PANIC OF 1819

But instead of effectively regulating the currency and loans issued by local banks, the Bank of the United States participated in a speculative fever that swept the country after the end of the War of 1812. The resumption of trade with Europe created a huge overseas market for American cotton and grain. Coupled with the rapid expansion of settlement into the West, this stimulated demand for loans to purchase land, which local banks and branches of the Bank of the United States were only too happy to meet by printing more money. The land boom was especially acute in the South, where the Cotton Kingdom was expanding.

Early in 1819, as European demand for American farm products returned to normal levels, the economic bubble burst. The demand for land plummeted, and speculators lost millions as the price of western land fell. At this time, loans tended to be for short duration and banks could demand repayment at any time. The Bank of the United States, followed by state banks, began asking for payments from those to whom it had loaned money. Farmers and businessmen who could not do so declared bankruptcy, and unemployment rose in eastern cities.

THE POLITICS OF THE PANIC

The Panic of 1819 lasted little more than a year, but it severely disrupted the political harmony of the previous years. Those suffering from the economic downturn pressed the state and national governments for assistance. To the consternation of creditors, many states, especially in the West, responded by suspending the collection of debts. Kentucky went even further, establishing a state bank that flooded the state with paper money that creditors were required to accept in repayment of loans. This eased the burden on indebted farmers, but injured those who had loaned them the money. Overall, the Panic deepened many Americans' traditional distrust of banks. It undermined the reputation of the Second Bank of the United States, which was widely blamed for causing the Panic. Several states retaliated against the national bank by taxing its local branches.

These tax laws produced another of John Marshall's landmark Supreme Court decisions, in the case of *McCulloch v. Maryland* (1819). Reasserting his broad interpretation of governmental powers, Marshall declared the Bank a legitimate exercise of congressional authority under the Constitution's clause that allowed Congress to pass "necessary and proper" laws. Marshall's interpretation of the Constitution directly contradicted the "strict construction" view that limited Congress to powers specifically granted in the Constitution. Marshall acknowledged that the Constitution nowhere mentions the right of lawmakers to issue corporate charters. But, he wrote, where the aim of legislation—in this case to promote the "general welfare"—was legitimate, "all means which are . . . not prohibited . . . are constitutional." Maryland, the chief justice continued, could not tax the Bank. "The power to tax," Marshall remarked, "involves the power to destroy," and the states lacked the authority to destroy an agency created by the national government.

THE MISSOURI CONTROVERSY ✗ ✗ ✗ ✗ — leds to the civil war

In 1816, James Monroe handily defeated Federalist candidate Rufus King, becoming the last of the Virginia presidents. By 1820, the Federalists fielded electoral tickets in only two states, and Monroe carried the entire country. (One elector, William Plumer of New Hampshire, however, cast his vote for John Quincy Adams, whom he deemed more qualified than Monroe to be president. The legend later arose that Plumer voted as he did because he wished George Washington to remain the only president elected unanimously.) Monroe's two terms in office were years of one-party government, sometimes called the Era of Good Feelings. Plenty of bad feelings, however, surfaced during his presidency. In the absence of two-party competition, politics was organized along lines of competing sectional interests.

Even as political party divisions faded and John Marshall aligned the Supreme Court with the aggressive nationalism of Clay, Calhoun, and others, the troublesome issue of slavery again threatened to disrupt the nation's unity. In 1819, Congress considered a request from Missouri, an area carved out of the Louisiana Purchase, to form a constitution in preparation for admission to the Union as a state. Missouri's slave population already exceeded 10,000. James Tallmadge, a Republican congressman from New York, moved that the introduction of further slaves be prohibited and that children of those already in Missouri be freed at age twenty-five.

Tallmadge's proposal sparked two years of controversy, during which Republican unity shattered along sectional lines. His restriction passed the House, where most northern congressmen supported it over the objections of southern representatives. It died in the Senate, however. When Congress reconvened in 1820, Senator Jesse Thomas of Illinois proposed a compromise with three parts. Missouri would be authorized to draft a constitution without Tallmadge's restriction. Maine, which prohibited slavery, would be admitted to the Union to maintain the sectional balance between free and slave states. And slavery would be prohibited in all remaining territory within the Louisiana Purchase north of latitude 36°30' (Missouri's southern boundary). Congress adopted Thomas's plan as the Missouri Compromise.

A year later, Missouri presented to Congress its new constitution, which not only protected slavery but prohibited free blacks from entering the

THE MISSOURI COMPROMISE, 1820

OREGON
TERRITORY
(Joint U.S.-British
occupation of
disputed territory)

BRITISH
NORTH AMERICA

Missouri R.

L. Superior

ME
(Admitted as a
free state, 1820)

Snake R.

UNORGANIZED
TERRITORY

MICHIGAN
TERRITORY

L. Michigan *L. Huron*

St. Lawrence R.

VT
NH
MA
CT
RI

Mississippi R.

L. Ontario
L. Erie

NY

Colorado R.

IL

IN

OH
Washington, D.C.

PA

DE
MD

Arkansas R.

MO
(Admitted as a
slave state, 1821)

Ohio R.

KY

VA

Missouri
Compromise line
36°30'

*Pacific
Ocean*

NEW SPAIN
(Independent Mexico, 1821)

Red R.

ARKANSAS
TERRITORY

TN

NC

SC

*Atlantic
Ocean*

Rio Grande

MI

AL

GA

LA

Gulf of Mexico

FLORIDA
TERRITORY

Territory closed to slavery by the Missouri Compromise
Free states and territories
Territory opened to slavery by the Missouri Compromise
Slave states and territories

0   250   500 miles
0   250   500 kilometers

The Missouri Compromise temporarily settled the question of the expansion of slavery by dividing the Louisiana Purchase into free and slave areas.

state. Since some northern states still considered blacks citizens, this seemed to violate the federal Constitution's "comity" clause, which requires each state to recognize the rights of citizens of other states. Henry Clay engineered a second Missouri Compromise, according to which Congress accepted the state's constitution as written, but instructed Missouri that it could not deprive the citizens of any states of their rights under the U.S. Constitution. Missouri, however, largely ignored this provision.

THE SLAVERY QUESTION

Thomas Jefferson, who had drafted the clause of the Northwest Ordinance of 1787 prohibiting slavery north of the Ohio River, strenuously opposed efforts to keep the institution out of Missouri. He saw the entire controversy as an attempt by Federalists to revive their party by setting northern and southern Republicans against each other. Jefferson was correct that political power, not moral scruples, motivated most northern congressmen. But Republicans, not the few remaining Federalists, provided the bulk of the votes against slavery in Missouri. By 1820, New York had surpassed Virginia in population, and New York Republicans were among the leading advocates of emancipation in Missouri. Twenty-eight years of Virginia presidents, interrupted only by the single term of John Adams of Massachusetts, had persuaded many northerners that the South exercised undue influence in Washington. More slave states meant more southern congressmen and electoral votes.

The Missouri controversy raised for the first time what would prove to be a fatal issue—the westward expansion of slavery. The sectional division it revealed aroused widespread feelings of dismay. "This momentous question," wrote Jefferson, "like a fire bell in the night, awakened and filled me with terror. I considered it at once as the knell of the union." John Quincy Adams wrote of the debate in his diary:

> [It] disclosed a secret: it revealed the basis for a new organization of parties.... Here was a new party really formed ... terrible to the whole Union, but portentously terrible to the South—threatening in its progress the emancipation of all their slaves, threatening in its immediate effect that southern domination which has swayed the Union for the last twenty years.

The "dissolution of the Union" over the issue of slavery, Adams mused, disastrous as that might be, would result in civil war and the "extirpation of slavery from this whole continent." It would take more than forty years for Adams's prediction to be fulfilled. For the moment, the slavery issue faded once again from national debate.

NATION, SECTION, AND PARTY

THE MONROE DOCTRINE

In a way, it is remarkable that John Quincy Adams, who was serving as James Monroe's secretary of state, even contemplated the breakup of the Union. For his long public career was devoted to consolidating the power of the national government at home and abroad. Soon after the resolution of the Missouri controversy, Adams seized upon an opportunity to enhance America's role in the world. Between 1810 and 1822, Spain's Latin American colonies rose in rebellion and established a series of independent nations, including Mexico, Venezuela, Ecuador, and Peru. The uprisings, which appeared to Americans to be implementing the principles of 1776, inspired a wave of sympathy in the United States. In 1822, the Monroe administration became the first government to extend diplomatic recognition to the new Latin American republics.

Adams feared that Spain would try to regain its colonies. In 1823, he drafted a section of the president's annual message to Congress that became known as the Monroe Doctrine. It expressed three principles. First, the United States would oppose any further efforts at colonization by European powers in the Americas (a statement aimed not only against Spain but also at France, which had designs on Cuba, and at Russia, which was seeking to expand its holdings on the Pacific coast). Second, the United States would abstain from involvement in the wars of Europe. Finally, Monroe warned European powers not to interfere with the newly independent states of Latin America.

The Monroe Doctrine is sometimes called America's diplomatic declaration of independence. For many decades, it remained a cornerstone of

THE AMERICAS, 1830

BRITISH NORTH AMERICA

(disputed)

UNITED STATES

Atlantic Ocean

MEXICO
1821

*Gulf of
Mexico*

Lucayas/Bahama
Islands
(Br.)

Cuba
(Sp.)

HAITI
1804

Puerto Rico
(Sp.)

Mexico

Veracruz

BRITISH
HONDURAS

Jamaica (Br.)

*Caribbean
Sea*

Trinidad
(Br.)

Windward Islands
(British, French, Dutch,
and Danish Possessions)

UNITED PROVINCES OF
CENTRAL AMERICA
1821

Caracas

BRITISH GUIANA
DUTCH GUIANA
FRENCH GUIANA

Pacific Ocean

Bogotá

VENEZUELA
1830

COLOMBIA
1821

Quito

*Galapagos
Islands*

ECUADOR
1830

BRAZIL
1822

PERU
1821

Salvador

Lima

La Paz

BOLIVIA
1825

0   500   1000 miles
0   500   1000 kilometers

PARAGUAY
1811

Sao
Paulo

Rio de Janeiro

Asunción

URUGUAY
1828

CHILE
1818

Buenos Aires

Montevideo

UNITED PROVINCES
RIO DEL LA PLATA
1816

PATAGONIA

ARGENTINE
CONFEDERATION
1825

Colonies and other dependent areas

*Falkland Islands
(Br.)*

This map depicts the Western Hemisphere after Spain's colonies achieved their independence.

American foreign policy. Based on the assumption that the Old and New Worlds formed separate political and diplomatic systems, it claimed for the United States the role of dominant power in the Western Hemisphere. For Adams, the commercial implications were as important as the political ones. In 1823, Latin America was a major market for British goods, and British citizens were heavily involved in mining, banking, and commercial enterprises there. Adams hoped that the United States could eventually assume Britain's economic role.

THE ELECTION OF 1824

The Monroe Doctrine reflected a rising sense of American nationalism. But sectionalism seemed to rule domestic politics. As the election of 1824 approached, only Andrew Jackson could claim truly national support. Jackson's popularity rested not on any specific public policy—few voters knew his views—but on military victories over the British at the Battle of New Orleans, and over the Creek and Seminole Indians. Other candidates included John Quincy Adams, Secretary of the Treasury William H. Crawford of Georgia, and Henry Clay of Kentucky. Adams's support was concentrated in New England and, more generally, in the North, where Republican leaders insisted the time had come for the South to relinquish the presidency. Crawford represented the South's Old Republicans, who wanted the party to reaffirm the principles of states' rights and limited government. Clay was one of the era's most popular politicians, but his support in 1824 lay primarily in the West. A caucus of Republican congressmen traditionally chose the party's nominee for president. The caucus selected Crawford, but this did not deter the other candidates, a sign that at a time of expanding democracy a small group of officials could no longer determine who ran for office.

Jackson received 153,544 votes and carried states in all the regions outside of New England. But with four candidates in the field, none received a majority of the electoral votes. As required by the Constitution, Clay, who finished fourth, was eliminated, and the choice among the other three fell to the House of Representatives. Sincerely believing Adams to be the most qualified candidate and the one most likely to promote the American System, and probably calculating that the election of Jackson, a westerner, would impede his own presidential ambitions, Clay gave his support to Adams, helping to elect him. He soon became secretary of state in Adams's cabinet. The charge that he had made a "corrupt bargain"—bartering critical votes in the presidential contest for a public office—clung to Clay for the rest of his career, making it all but impossible for him to reach the White House. The election of 1824 laid the groundwork for a new system of political parties. Supporters of Jackson and Crawford would soon unite in a new organization, the Democratic Party, determined to place Jackson in the White House in 1828. The alliance of Clay and Adams became the basis for the Whig Party of the 1830s.

THE NATIONALISM OF JOHN QUINCY ADAMS

John Quincy Adams enjoyed one of the most distinguished pre-presidential careers of any American president. The son

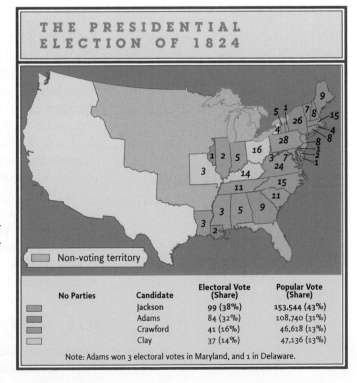

THE PRESIDENTIAL ELECTION OF 1824

Non-voting territory

No Parties	Candidate	Electoral Vote (Share)	Popular Vote (Share)
	Jackson	99 (38%)	153,544 (43%)
	Adams	84 (32%)	108,740 (31%)
	Crawford	41 (16%)	46,618 (13%)
	Clay	37 (14%)	47,136 (13%)

Note: Adams won 3 electoral votes in Maryland, and 1 in Delaware.

John Quincy Adams in an 1843 daguerreotype.

of John Adams, he had witnessed the Battle of Bunker Hill at age eight and at fourteen had worked as private secretary and French interpreter for an American envoy in Europe. He had gone on to serve as ambassador to Prussia, the Netherlands, Britain, and Russia, and as senator from Massachusetts. Although elected as a Federalist, Adams cast one of New England's few votes in favor of Jefferson's embargo policy, arguing that his region must rise above sectional self-interest to defend the national good. Given the intense political passions of the time, he had been forced to resign his seat as a result of his vote, and he soon abandoned the Federalist Party.

Adams was not an engaging figure. He described himself as "a man of cold, austere, and foreboding manners." But he had a clear vision of national greatness. At home, he strongly supported the American System of government-sponsored economic development. Abroad, he hoped to encourage American commerce throughout the world and, as illustrated by his authorship of the Monroe Doctrine, enhance American influence in the Western Hemisphere. As Monroe's secretary of state, he had been the only cabinet member to oppose reprimanding Andrew Jackson for his violent incursion into Florida. In 1819, as noted in the previous chapter, Adams negotiated a treaty by which the United States acquired Florida from Spain. He also concluded an agreement with Great Britain fixing the Canadian-American border at the northern boundary of the Louisiana Purchase.

"LIBERTY IS POWER"

Adams held a view of federal power far more expansive than most of his contemporaries. In his first message to Congress, in December 1825, he set forth a comprehensive program for an activist national state. "The spirit of improvement is abroad in the land," Adams announced, and the federal government should be its patron. He called for legislation promoting agriculture, commerce, manufacturing, and "the mechanical and elegant arts." His plans included the establishment of a national university, an astronomical observatory, and a naval academy. At a time when many Americans felt that governmental authority posed the greatest threat to freedom, Adams astonished many listeners with the bold statement "liberty is power." The United States, the freest nation on earth, would also, he predicted, become the mightiest.

Adams's proposals alarmed all believers in strict construction of the Constitution. His administration spent more on internal improvements than his five predecessors combined, and it enacted a steep increase in tariff rates in 1828. But the rest of Adams's ambitious ideas received little support in Congress. Not until the twentieth century would the kind of national economic and educational planning envisioned by Adams be realized. Some of his proposals, like the adoption by the United States of the metric system of weights and measures used by nearly every other nation in the world, and the building of a national university, have yet to be implemented.

MARTIN VAN BUREN AND THE DEMOCRATIC PARTY

Adams's program handed his political rivals a powerful weapon. With individual liberty, states' rights, and limited government as their rallying cries,

Jackson's supporters began to organize for the election of 1828 almost as soon as Adams assumed office. Martin Van Buren, a senator from New York, oversaw the task. The clash between Adams and Van Buren demonstrated how democracy was changing the nature of American politics. Adams typified the old politics—he was the son of a president and, like Jefferson and Madison, a man of sterling intellectual accomplishments. Van Buren represented the new political era. The son of a tavern keeper, he was a talented party manager, not a person of great vision or intellect.

But Van Buren did have a compelling idea. Rather than being dangerous and divisive, as the founding generation had believed, political parties, he insisted, were a necessary and indeed desirable element of political life. Party competition provided a check on those in power and offered voters a real choice in elections. And by bringing together political leaders from different regions in support of common candidates and principles, national parties could counteract the sectionalism that had reared its head during the 1820s. Like many of his contemporaries, Van Buren had been alarmed when politics divided along sectional lines in the Missouri debates and again in the election of 1824. He attributed this in part to a loss of discipline within the ruling Republican Party. "Party attachment," Van Buren wrote to Virginia editor Thomas Ritchie, "in former times furnished a complete antidote for sectional prejudices by producing counteracting feelings. It was not until that defense had been broken down that the clamor against southern influence and African slavery could be made effectual in the North." National political parties, Van Buren realized, formed a bond of unity in a divided nation. He set out to reconstruct the Jeffersonian political alliance between "the planters of the South and the plain republicans [the farmers and urban workers] of the North."

THE ELECTION OF 1828

By 1828, Van Buren had established the political apparatus of the Democratic Party, complete with local and state party units overseen by a national committee and a network of local newspapers devoted to the party. Adams, for his part, disdained political organization. Despite Clay's urging, he refused to dismiss federal officeholders who campaigned for Jackson and did little to promote his own reelection.

Apart from a general commitment to limited government, Jackson's supporters made few campaign promises, relying on their candidate's popularity and the workings of party machinery to get out the vote. The 1828 election campaign was scurrilous. Jackson's supporters accused Adams of having had a series of mistresses while serving as a diplomat in Europe. They praised their candidate's frontier manliness and ridiculed Adams's intellectual attainments. ("Vote for Andrew Jackson who can fight, not John Quincy Adams who can write," declared one campaign slogan.) Jackson's opponents condemned him as a murderer for having executed army deserters and killing men in duels. They questioned the morality of his wife, Rachel, because she had married Jackson before her divorce from her first husband had become final. Jackson always believed his opponents' slanders had contributed to his wife's death shortly after the election.

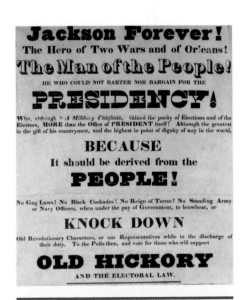

A broadside from the 1828 campaign illustrates how Andrew Jackson's supporters promoted him as a military hero and "man of the people."

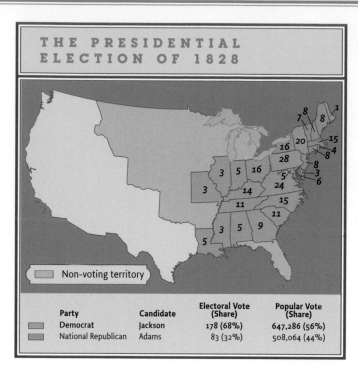

THE PRESIDENTIAL ELECTION OF 1828

Non-voting territory

Party	Candidate	Electoral Vote (Share)	Popular Vote (Share)
Democrat	Jackson	178 (68%)	647,286 (56%)
National Republican	Adams	83 (32%)	508,064 (44%)

By 1828, voters, not the legislature, chose presidential electors in every state except South Carolina, a fact that helped to encourage vigorous campaigning and high turnout. Nearly 57 percent of the eligible electorate cast ballots, more than double the percentage four years earlier. Jackson won a resounding victory, with around 650,000 votes to 500,000 for Adams. He carried the entire South and West, along with Pennsylvania. Jackson's election was the first to demonstrate how the advent of universal white male voting, organized by national political parties, had transformed American politics. For better or worse, the United States had entered the Age of Jackson.

THE AGE OF JACKSON

Andrew Jackson was a man of many contradictions. Although he had little formal education (Adams called him "a barbarian who could not write a sentence of grammar"), Jackson was capable of genuine eloquence in his public statements. A self-proclaimed champion of the common man, his vision of democracy excluded any role for Indians, who he believed should be pushed west of the Mississippi River, and African-Americans, who should remain as slaves or be freed and sent abroad. Although he rose from modest beginnings on the South Carolina frontier to become one of the richest men in Tennessee, he had an abiding suspicion of banks and paper money, and he shared the fears of many Americans that the market revolution was a source of moral decay rather than progress. A strong nationalist, Jackson nonetheless believed that the states, not Washington, D.C., should be the focal point of governmental activity. He opposed federal efforts to shape the economy or interfere in individuals' private lives.

THE PARTY SYSTEM

By the time of Jackson's presidency, politics had become more than a series of political contests—it was a spectacle, a form of mass entertainment, a part of Americans' daily lives. Every year witnessed elections to some office—local, state, or national—and millions took part in the parades and rallies organized by the parties. Politicians were popular heroes with mass followings and popular nicknames. Jackson was Old Hickory, Clay Harry of the West, and Van Buren the Little Magician (or, to his critics, the Sly Fox). Thousands of Americans willingly attended lengthy political orations and debates. An audience of 100,000 was said to have gathered on a Massachusetts hillside to hear a speech by the great Whig orator Daniel Webster.

"Politics," one newspaper editor remarked, "seems to enter into everything." Indeed, party machines, headed by professional politicians, reached into every neighborhood, especially in cities. They provided benefits like jobs to constituents and ensured that voters went to the polls on election day. Party functionaries were rewarded with political offices. Government posts,

Jackson declared, should be open to the people, not reserved for a privileged class of permanent bureaucrats. He introduced the principle of rotation in office (called the "spoils system" by opponents) into national government, making loyalty to the party the main qualification for jobs like postmaster and customs official.

Large national conventions where state leaders gathered to hammer out a platform now chose national candidates. Newspapers played a greater and greater role in politics. Nearly 400 were published in 1830, compared to 90 in 1790. Every significant town, it seemed, had its Democratic and Whig papers whose job was not so much to report the news as to present the party's position on issues of the day. Jackson's Kitchen Cabinet—an informal group of advisers who helped to write his speeches and supervise communication between the White House and local party officials—mostly consisted of newspaper editors.

County Election, a painting by George Caleb Bingham depicting American democracy in action. In this 1852 work, a voter takes an oath while party workers dispense liquor, seek to persuade voters, and keep track of who has cast ballots. The banner reads, "The Will of the People the Supreme Law." The slogan is meant to be ironic. Bingham includes a number of Democratic politicians he accused of cheating him in a recent election.

DEMOCRATS AND WHIGS

There was more to party politics, however, than spectacle and organization. Jacksonian politics revolved around issues spawned by the market revolution and the continuing tension between national and sectional loyalties. The central elements of political debate were the government's stance toward banks, tariffs, currency, and internal improvements, and the balance of power between national and local authority. Although both parties were coalitions of groups with varied, sometimes contradictory approaches to the issues of the day, the market revolution did much to determine their views and makeup. Democrats tended to be alarmed by the widening gap between social classes. They warned that "nonproducers"— bankers, merchants, and speculators—were seeking to use connections with government to enhance their wealth to the disadvantage of the "producing classes" of farmers, artisans, and laborers. They believed the government should adopt a hands-off attitude toward the economy and not award special favors to entrenched economic interests.

"All bank charters, all acts of incorporation," declared a Democratic newspaper, "are calculated to enhance the power of wealth, produce inequalities among the people and to subvert liberty." If the national government removed itself from the economy, ordinary Americans could test their abilities in the fair competition of the self-regulating market. The Democratic Party attracted aspiring entrepreneurs who resented government aid to established businessmen, as well as large numbers of farmers and city workingmen suspicious of new corporate enterprises. Poorer farming regions isolated from markets, like the lower Northwest and the southern backcountry, tended to vote Democratic.

Whigs united behind the American System, believing that via a protective tariff, a national bank, and aid to internal improvements, the federal

Procession of Victuallers, *a lithograph commemorating a parade of butchers through the streets of Philadelphia in 1821. Their banner, "We Feed the Hungry," illustrates the belief among members of the "producing classes" that their work led to practical benefits for society, unlike the activities of "nonproducers" like bankers.*

government could guide economic development. They were strongest in the Northeast, the most rapidly modernizing region of the country. Most established businessmen and bankers supported their program of government-promoted economic growth, as did farmers in regions near rivers, canals, and the Great Lakes, who benefited from economic changes or hoped to do so. The counties of upstate New York along the Erie Canal, for example, became a Whig stronghold, while more isolated rural communities tended to vote Democratic. Many slaveholders supported the Democrats, believing states' rights to be slavery's first line of defense. But like well-to-do merchants and industrialists in the North, the largest southern planters generally voted Whig.

PUBLIC AND PRIVATE FREEDOM

The party battles of the Jacksonian era reflected the clash between "public" and "private" definitions of American freedom and their relationship to governmental power, a persistent tension in the nation's history. For Democrats, liberty was a private entitlement best secured by local governments and endangered by powerful national authority. "The limitation of power, in every branch of our government," wrote a Democratic newspaper in 1842, "is the only safeguard of liberty." A "splendid" government was always "built upon the ruins of popular rights."

Under Jackson, even as democracy expanded, the power of the national government waned. Weak national authority, in the Democratic view, was essential to both private freedom and states' rights—"the freedom of the individual in the social union, [and] the freedom of the State in the Federative Union." Ralph Waldo Emerson called antebellum Americans "fanatics in freedom," whose obsession expressed itself in hatred of "tolls, taxes, turnpikes, banks, hierarchies, governors, yea, almost laws." Democrats regularly condemned the faraway federal government as the greatest "danger to liberty" in America and identified government-granted privilege as the root cause of social inequality. During Jackson's presidency, Democrats reduced expenditures, lowered the tariff, killed the national bank, and refused pleas for federal aid to internal improvements. By 1835, Jackson had even managed to pay off the national debt. As a result, states replaced the federal government as the country's main economic actors, planning systems of canals and roads and chartering banks and other corporations.

POLITICS AND MORALITY

Democrats, moreover, considered individual morality a private matter, not a public concern. They opposed attempts to impose a unified moral vision on society, such as "temperance" legislation, which restricted or outlawed the production and sale of liquor, and laws prohibiting various kinds of entertainment on Sundays. As noted in Chapter 9, Catholic Irish and German immigrants who began arriving in significant numbers in the 1830s flocked to the Democratic Party. One reason was that they did not wish to have Protestant moral standards enforced by the government. "In this country," declared the New York *Journal of Commerce* in 1848, "liberty is understood to be the *absence* of government from private affairs." The test of public policies was not whether they enhanced the common good, but the extent to which they allowed scope for "free agency"—that is, for individuals to make decisions, pursue their interests, and cultivate their unique talents without outside interference.

Whigs, for their part, insisted that liberty and power reinforced each other. "A weak government," wrote Francis Lieber, the founding father of American political science, was "a negation of liberty." An activist national government, on the other hand, could enhance the realm of freedom. Liberty, Whigs believed, required a prosperous and moral America. The government should create the conditions for balanced and regulated economic development, thereby promoting a prosperity in which all classes and regions would share. Like the Federalists before them, wealthy Whigs tended to view society as a hierarchy of social classes, in contrast to the disorderly world of unrestrained individual competition embraced by many Democrats. But unlike most Federalists, they insisted that in the United States class status was not fixed, since any individual could achieve upward mobility.

Whigs, moreover, rejected the premise that the government must not interfere in private life. To function as free—that is, self-directed and self-disciplined—moral agents, individuals required certain character traits, which government could help to instill. The role of government, declared one New York Whig, was not simply to stand aside but actively to "promote the welfare of the people." Many evangelical Protestants supported the Whigs, convinced that via public education, the building of schools and asylums, temperance legislation, and the like, democratic governments could inculcate the "principles of morality." And during the Jacksonian era, popularly elected local authorities enacted numerous laws, ordinances, and regulations that tried to shape public morals by banning prostitution and the consumption of alcohol, and regulating other kinds of personal behavior. Pennsylvania was as renowned in the nineteenth century for its stringent laws against profanity and desecrating the Sabbath as it had been in the colonial era for its commitment to religious liberty.

SOUTH CAROLINA AND NULLIFICATION

Andrew Jackson, it has been said, left office with many more principles than he came in with. Elected as a military hero backed by an efficient party machinery, he was soon forced to define his stance on public issues.

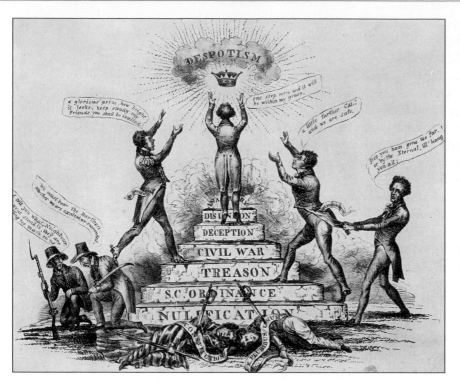

A cartoon published in 1833, at the height of the nullification controversy, shows John C. Calhoun climbing steps, including those marked "nullification," "treason," and "civil war," toward the goal of "despotism." He is flanked by James H. Hammond and Robert Y. Hayne, two of South Carolina's political leaders. On the right, President Jackson threatens to hang them.

Despite his commitment to states' rights, Jackson's first term was dominated by a battle to uphold the supremacy of federal over state law. The tariff of 1828, which raised taxes on imported manufactured goods made of wool as well as on raw materials like iron, had aroused considerable opposition in the South, nowhere more than in South Carolina, where it was called the "tariff of abominations." The state's leaders no longer believed it possible or desirable to compete with the North in industrial development. Insisting that the tariff on imported manufactured goods raised the prices paid by southern consumers to benefit the North, the legislature threatened to "nullify" it—that is, declare it null and void within their state.

The state with the largest proportion of slaves in its population (55 percent in 1830), South Carolina was controlled by a tightly knit group of large planters. They maintained their grip on power by a state constitution that gave plantation counties far greater representation in the legislature than their population warranted, as well as through high property qualifications for officeholders. They had been thoroughly alarmed by the Missouri crisis and by the steady strengthening of national authority by John Marshall's Supreme Court. Behind their economic complaints against the tariff lay the conviction that the federal government must be weakened lest it one day take action against slavery.

CALHOUN'S POLITICAL THEORY

John C. Calhoun soon emerged as the leading theorist of nullification. As the South began to fall behind the rest of the country in population, Calhoun had evolved from the nationalist of 1812 into a powerful defender of southern sectionalism. Having been elected vice president in 1828, Calhoun at first remained behind the scenes, secretly drafting the *Exposition and Protest* in which the South Carolina legislature justified nullification. The document drew on the arguments in the Virginia and Kentucky resolutions of 1798 (discussed in Chapter 8). The national government, Calhoun insisted, had been created by an agreement among sovereign states, each of which retained the right to prevent the enforcement within its borders of acts of Congress that exceeded the powers specifically spelled out in the Constitution.

Almost from the beginning of Jackson's first term, Calhoun's influence in the administration waned, while Secretary of State Martin Van Buren emerged as the president's closest adviser. One incident that helped set Jackson against Calhoun occurred a few weeks after the inauguration. Led by Calhoun's wife, Floride, Washington society women ostracized Peggy Eaton, the wife of Jackson's secretary of war, because she was the daughter of a Washington tavern keeper and, allegedly, a woman of "easy virtue." Van Buren, a widower, stood by her, as did Jackson, who identified criticism of Peggy Eaton with the abuse his own wife had suffered during the campaign of 1828.

Far weightier matters soon divided Jackson and Calhoun. Debate over nullification raged in Washington. In a memorable exchange in the Senate in January 1830, Daniel Webster responded to South Carolina senator Robert Y. Hayne, a disciple of Calhoun. The people, not the states, declared Webster, created the Constitution, making the federal government sovereign. He called nullification illegal, unconstitutional, and treasonous. Webster's ending was widely hailed throughout the country—"Liberty *and* Union, now and forever, one and inseparable." A few weeks later, at a White House dinner, Jackson delivered a toast while fixing his gaze on Calhoun: "Our Federal Union—it must be preserved." Calhoun's reply came immediately: "The Union—next to our liberty most dear." By 1831, Calhoun had publicly emerged as the leading theorist of states' rights.

THE NULLIFICATION CRISIS

Nullification was not a purely sectional issue. South Carolina stood alone during the crisis, and several southern states passed resolutions condemning its action. Nonetheless, the elaboration of the compact theory of the Constitution gave the South a well-developed political philosophy to which it would turn when sectional conflict became more intense. Calhoun denied that nullification was a step toward disunion. On the contrary, the only way to ensure the stability of a large, diverse nation was for each state to be assured that national actions would never trample on its rights or vital interests. According to Calhoun's theory of the "concurrent majority," each major interest, including slaveholders, should have a veto over all measures that affected it.

To Jackson, however, nullification amounted to nothing less than disunion. He dismissed Calhoun's constitutional arguments out of hand: "Can anyone of common sense believe the absurdity, that a faction of any state, or a state, has a right to secede and destroy this union, and the liberty of the country with it?" The issue came to a head in 1832, when a new tariff was enacted. Despite a reduction in tariff rates, South Carolina declared the tax on imported goods null and void in the state after the following February. In response, Jackson persuaded Congress to enact a Force Bill authorizing him to use the army and navy to collect customs duties.

To avert a confrontation, Henry Clay, with Calhoun's assistance, engineered the passage of a new tariff, in 1833, further reducing duties. South Carolina then rescinded the ordinance of nullification, although it proceeded to "nullify" the Force Act. Calhoun abandoned the Democratic Party for the Whigs, where, with Clay and Webster, he became part of a formidable trio of political leaders (even though the three agreed on virtually

An 1834 print portrays the United States as a Temple of Liberty. At the center, a figure of liberty rises from the flames, holding the Bill of Rights and a staff with a liberty cap. Justice and Minerva (Roman goddess of war and wisdom) flank the temple, above which flies a banner, "The Union Must and Shall Be Preserved."

Black Hawk and His Son, Whirling Thunder, *painted in 1833 by the artist John Wesley Jarvis shortly after the Black Hawk War. Jarvis hoped that traditional Indian ways, symbolized by the son's dress, would be replaced by Black Hawk's "civilized" appearance.*

A lithograph from 1836 depicts Scquoia, with the alphabet of the Cherokee language that he developed. Because of their written language and constitution, the Cherokee were considered by many white Americans to be a "civilized tribe."

nothing except hostility to Jackson). It is perhaps ironic that Andrew Jackson, a firm believer in states' rights and limited government, did more than any other individual to give an emotional aura to the idea of Union and to offer an example of willingness to go to war, if necessary, to preserve what he considered the national government's legitimate powers.

INDIAN REMOVAL

The nullification crisis underscored Jackson's commitment to the sovereignty of the nation. His exclusion of Indians from the era's assertive democratic nationalism led to the final act in the centuries-long conflict between white Americans and Indians east of the Mississippi River. The last Indian resistance to the advance of white settlement in the Old Northwest came in 1832, when federal troops and local militiamen routed the Sauk leader Black Hawk, who, with about 1,000 followers, attempted to reclaim ancestral land in Illinois. One of the Illinois militiamen was the young Abraham Lincoln, although, as he later remarked, he saw no action, except against mosquitoes.

In the slave states, the onward march of cotton cultivation placed enormous pressure on remaining Indian holdings. "Extending the area of slavery," proclaimed Thomas Hart Benton, who represented Missouri in the Senate for thirty years, required "converting Indian soil into slave soil." During the 1820s, Missouri forced its Indian population to leave the state. Soon, the policy of expulsion was enacted in the older slave states. One of the early laws of Jackson's administration, the Indian Removal Act of 1830, provided funds for uprooting the so-called Five Civilized Tribes—the Cherokee, Chickasaw, Choctaw, Creek, and Seminole—with a population of around 60,000 living in North Carolina, Georgia, Florida, Alabama, and Mississippi.

The law marked a repudiation of the Jeffersonian idea that "civilized" Indians could be assimilated into the American population. These tribes had made great efforts to become everything republican citizens should be. The Cherokee had taken the lead, establishing schools, adopting written laws and a constitution modeled on that of the United States, and becoming successful farmers, many of whom owned slaves. But in his messages to Congress, Jackson repeatedly referred to them as "savages" and supported Georgia's effort to seize Cherokee land and nullify the tribe's laws.

"Free citizens of the Cherokee nation" petitioned Congress for aid in remaining "in peace and quietude upon their ancient territory." In good American fashion, Cherokee leaders also went to court to protect their rights, guaranteed in treaties with the federal government. Their appeals forced the Supreme Court to clarify the unique status of American Indians.

THE SUPREME COURT AND THE INDIANS

In a crucial case involving Indians in 1823, *Johnson v. M'Intosh*, the Court had proclaimed that Indians were not in fact owners of their land, but merely had a "right of occupancy." Chief Justice John Marshall, himself a speculator in western lands, claimed that from the early colonial era, Indians had lived as nomads and hunters, not farmers. Entirely inaccurate as history, the decision struck a serious blow against Indian efforts to retain their lands. In *Cherokee Nation v. Georgia* (1831), Marshall described Indians as "wards" of the federal government. They deserved paternal regard and

INDIAN REMOVALS, 1830–1840

The removal of the so-called Five Civilized Tribes from the Southeast all but ended the Indian presence east of the Mississippi River.

protection, but they lacked the standing as citizens that would allow the Supreme Court to enforce their rights. The justices could not, therefore, block Georgia's effort to extend its jurisdiction over the tribe.

Marshall, however, believed strongly in the supremacy of the federal government over the states. In 1832, in *Worcester v. Georgia*, the Court seemed to change its mind, holding that Indian nations were a distinct people with the right to maintain a separate political identity. They must be dealt with by the federal government, not the states, and Georgia's actions violated the Cherokees' treaties with Washington. But despite his strong assertion of national supremacy in the nullification crisis, Jackson refused to recognize the validity of the *Worcester* ruling. "John Marshall has made his decision," he supposedly declared, "now let him enforce it."

With legal appeals exhausted, one faction of the tribe agreed to cede their lands, but the majority, led by John Ross, who had been elected "principal chief" under the Cherokee constitution, adopted a policy of passive resistance. Federal soldiers forcibly removed them during the presidency of Jackson's successor, Martin Van Buren. The army herded 18,000 men, women, and children into stockades and then forced them to move west. At least one-quarter perished during the winter of 1838–1839 on the Trail of Tears, as the removal route from Georgia to the area of present-day

Oklahoma came to be called. (In the Cherokee language, it literally meant "the trail on which we cried.")

During the 1830s, most of the other southern tribes bowed to the inevitable and departed peacefully. But the Seminoles of sparsely settled Florida resisted. Osceola, one of the leaders of Seminole resistance to removal, was a Red Stick who had survived Andrew Jackson's assault on hostile Creeks during the War of 1812. The Indians were assisted by escaped slaves. As early as colonial times, Florida had been a refuge for fugitive slaves from South Carolina and Georgia, to whom Spanish officials offered freedom. The administration of George Washington attempted to persuade the Seminoles to expel the fugitives, but they refused. Georgia sent the militia into Florida to recapture them, but it was driven out by Seminole and African-American fighters. In the Second Seminole War, which lasted from 1835 to 1842 (the first had followed American acquisition of Florida in 1819), some 1,500 American soldiers and the same number of Seminoles were killed, and perhaps 3,000 Indians and 500 blacks were forced to move to the West. A small number of Seminoles managed to remain in Florida, a tiny remnant of the once sizable Indian population east of the Mississippi River.

In 1831, William Apess, a descendant of Metacom, or King Philip, who had battled New England colonists in the 1670s, published *A Son of the Forest*, the first significant autobiography by a Native American. The son of a white man and an Indian woman, Apess had served with American forces in an unsuccessful attack on Canada during the War of 1812. He later converted to Methodism and became a revivalist preacher. His book appealed for harmony between white Americans and Indians. "How much better it would be if the whites would act like civilized people [and] give every one his due," Apess wrote. "What do they, the Indians, want? You have only to look at the unjust laws made for them and say, 'They want what I want.'"

Removal was the alternative to the coexistence championed by Apess. It powerfully reinforced the racial definition of American nationhood and

The Trapper and His Family *(1845), by the artist Charles Deas, depicts a white pioneer who married an Indian woman.*

Buffalo Hunt, *an 1844 painting by George Caitlin, who created dozens of works depicting Native Americans in the Trans-Mississippi West in the 1830s and 1840s. Caitlin saw himself as recording for posterity a vanishing way of life.*

freedom. At the time of independence, Indians had been a familiar presence in many parts of the United States. John Adams once recalled how, when he was young, local Indians "were frequent visitors in my father's house," and how he would visit a nearby Indian family, "where I never failed to be treated with whortleberries, blackberries, strawberries or apples, plums, peaches, etc." By 1840, in the eyes of most whites east of the Mississippi River, they were simply a curiosity, a relic of an earlier period of American history. Although Indians still dominated the trans-Mississippi West, as American settlement pushed relentlessly westward it was clear that their days of freedom there were also numbered.

THE BANK WAR AND AFTER

BIDDLE'S BANK

The central political struggle of the Age of Jackson was the president's war on the Bank of the United States. The Bank symbolized the hopes and fears inspired by the market revolution. The expansion of banking helped to finance the nation's economic development. But many Americans, including Jackson, distrusted bankers as "nonproducers" who contributed nothing to the nation's wealth but profited from the labor of others. The tendency of banks to overissue paper money, whose deterioration in value reduced the real income of wage earners, reinforced this conviction. Jackson himself had long believed that "hard money"—gold and silver—was the only honest currency. Nonetheless, when he assumed office there was little reason to believe that the Bank War would become the major event of his presidency.

Heading the Bank was Nicholas Biddle of Pennsylvania, who during the 1820s had effectively used the institution's power, discussed earlier in this chapter, to curb the overissuing of money by local banks and to create a stable currency throughout the nation. A snobbish, aristocratic Philadelphian, Biddle was as strong-willed as Jackson and as unwilling to back down in a fight. In 1832, he told a congressional committee that his Bank had the ability to "destroy" any state bank. He hastened to add that he had never "injured" any of them. But Democrats wondered whether any institution, public or private, ought to possess such power. Many called it the Monster Bank, an illegitimate union of political authority and entrenched economic privilege. The issue of the Bank's future came to a head in 1832. Although the institution's charter would not expire until 1836, Biddle's allies persuaded Congress to approve a bill extending it for another twenty years. Jackson saw the tactic as a form of blackmail—if he did not sign the bill, the Bank would use its considerable resources to oppose his reelection. "The Bank," he told Van Buren, "is trying to destroy me, but I will kill it."

Jackson's veto message is perhaps the central document of his presidency. Its argument resonated with popular values. In a democratic government, Jackson insisted, it was unacceptable for Congress to create a source of concentrated power and economic privilege unaccountable to the people. "It is to be regretted," he declared, "that the rich and powerful too often bend the acts of government to their selfish purposes." Exclusive privileges like the Bank's charter widened the gap between the wealthy and "the humble members of society—the farmers, mechanics, and laborers." Jackson presented himself as the defender of these "humble" Americans.

The Bank War reflected how Jackson enhanced the power of the presidency during his eight years in office, proclaiming himself the symbolic representative of all the people. He was the first president to use the veto power as a major weapon and to appeal directly to the public for political support, over the head of Congress. Whigs denounced him for usurping the power of the legislature. They insisted that Congress, not the president, represented the will of the people and that the veto power, while created by the Constitution, should only be used in extraordinary circumstances. But Jackson's effective appeal to democratic popular sentiments helped him win a sweeping reelection victory in 1832 over the Whig candidate, Henry Clay. His victory ensured the death of the Bank of the United States.

THE PET BANKS AND THE ECONOMY

What, however, would take the Bank's place? Two very different groups applauded Jackson's veto—state bankers who wished to free themselves from Biddle's regulations and issue more paper currency (called "soft money"), and "hard money" advocates who opposed all banks, whether chartered by the states or the federal government, and believed that gold and silver formed the only reliable currency.

During Jackson's second term, state bankers were in the ascendancy. Not content to wait for the charter of the Bank of the United States to expire in 1836, Jackson authorized the removal of federal funds from its vaults and their deposit in local banks. Not surprisingly, political and personal connections often determined the choice of these "pet banks." The director of the Maine Bank of Portland, for example, was the brother-in-law of Levi Woodbury, a member of Jackson's cabinet. A justice of the Supreme Court recommended the Planters Bank of Savannah. Two secretaries of the treasury refused to transfer federal money to the pet banks, since the law creating the Bank had specified that government funds could not be removed except for a good cause, communicated to Congress. Jackson finally appointed Attorney General Roger B. Taney, a loyal Maryland Democrat, to the treasury post, and he carried out the order. When John Marshall died in 1835, Jackson rewarded Taney by appointing him chief justice.

Without government deposits, the Bank of the United States lost its ability to regulate the activities of state banks. They issued more and more paper money, partly to help finance the rapid expansion of industrial development in New England, agriculture in the South and West, and canal and railroad systems projected by many states. The value of bank notes in circulation rose from $10 million in 1833 to $149 million in 1837.

Prices rose dramatically, and even though wages also increased, they failed to keep pace. As a result, workers' "real wages"—the actual value of their pay—declined. Numerous labor unions emerged, which attempted to protect the earnings of urban workers. Speculators hastened to cash in on rising land prices. Using paper money, they bought up huge blocks of public land, which they resold to farmers or to eastern purchasers of lots in entirely nonexistent western towns. States projected tens of millions of dollars in internal improvements.

The Downfall of Mother Bank, *a Democratic cartoon celebrating the destruction of the Second Bank of the United States. President Jackson topples the building by brandishing his order removing federal funds from the Bank. Led by Nicholas Biddle, with the head of a demon, the Bank's corrupt supporters flee, among them Henry Clay, Daniel Webster, and newspaper editors allegedly paid by the institution.*

THE PANIC OF 1837

Inevitably, the speculative boom collapsed. The government sold 20 million acres of federal land in 1836, ten times the amount sold in 1830, nearly all of it paid for in paper money, often of questionable value. In July 1836, the Jackson administration issued the Specie Circular, declaring that henceforth it would only accept gold and silver as payment for public land. At the same time, the Bank of England, increasingly suspicious about the value of American bank notes, demanded that American merchants pay their creditors in London in gold or silver. Then, an economic downturn in Britain dampened demand for American cotton, the country's major export.

Taken together, these events triggered an economic collapse in the United States, the Panic of 1837, followed by a depression that lasted to 1843. Prices fell by 25 percent in the first year of the downturn. Businesses throughout the country failed, and many farmers, unable to meet mortgage payments because of declining income, lost their land. Tens of thousands of urban workers saw their jobs disappear. The fledgling labor movement collapsed as strikes became impossible given the surplus of unemployed labor. By 1842, nine states had defaulted on their debts, mostly incurred to finance ambitious internal improvement projects. During the 1840s, states amended their constitutions to prohibit legislatures from borrowing money, issuing corporate charters, and buying stock in private enterprises. For the time being, the Jacksonians had succeeded in separating government—both federal and state—from the economy.

The Times, *an 1837 engraving that blames Andrew Jackson's policies for the economic depression. The Custom House is idle, while next door a bank is mobbed by worried depositors. Beneath Jackson's hat, spectacles, and clay pipe (with the ironic word "glory"), images of hardship abound.*

VAN BUREN IN OFFICE

The president forced to deal with the depression was Martin Van Buren, who had been elected in 1836 over three regional candidates put forward by the Whigs in an attempt to maximize the party's electoral vote and throw the election into the House of Representatives. Under Van Buren, the hard money, anti-bank wing of the Democratic Party came to power. In 1837, the administration announced its intention to remove federal funds from the pet banks and hold them in the Treasury Department in Washington, under the control of government officials. Not until 1840 did Congress approve the new policy, known as the Independent Treasury, which completely separated the federal government from the nation's banking system. It would be repealed in 1841 when the Whigs returned to power, but it was reinstated under President James K. Polk in 1846. Making federal funds unavailable for banks to use for investment would have dampened future economic growth had not the discovery of gold in California in 1848 poured new money into the economy.

The Independent Treasury split the Democratic Party. Business-oriented Democrats, often connected with the state banks, strongly opposed Van Buren's policy and shifted wholesale to the Whigs. Meanwhile, the party's "agrarian" wing—small farmers and urban laborers opposed to all banking and paper money and uncomfortable with the market revolution in general, rallied to Van Buren. Many advocates of state sovereignty who had joined the Whigs after the nullification crisis now returned to the Democratic fold, including Van Buren's old nemesis, John C. Calhoun.

THE ELECTION OF 1840

Despite his reputation as a political magician, Van Buren found that without Jackson's personal popularity he could not hold the Democratic coalition together. In 1840, he also discovered that his Whig opponents had mastered the political techniques he had helped to pioneer. Confronting an unprecedented opportunity for victory because of the continuing economic depression, the Whigs abandoned their most prominent leader, Henry Clay, and nominated William Henry Harrison. Like Jackson when he first sought the presidency, Harrison's main claim to fame was military success against the British and Indians during the War of 1812.

The party nominated Harrison without a platform. In a flood of publications, banners, parades, and mass meetings, they promoted him as the "log cabin" candidate, the champion of the common man. This tactic proved enormously effective, even though it bore little relationship to the actual life of the wealthy Harrison. The Whigs also denounced Van Buren as an aristocrat who had squandered the people's hard-earned money on "expensive furniture, china, glassware, and gold spoons" for the White House. Harrison's running mate was John Tyler, a states'-rights Democrat from Virginia who had joined the Whigs after the nullification crisis and did not follow Calhoun back to the Democrats. On almost every issue of political significance, Tyler held views totally opposed to those of other Whigs. But party leaders hoped he could expand their base in the South.

By 1840, the mass democratic politics of the Age of Jackson had absorbed the logic of the marketplace. Selling candidates and their images was as important as the positions for which they stood. With two highly organized parties competing throughout the country, voter turnout soared to 80 percent of those eligible, a level at which it remained for the rest of the nineteenth century. Harrison won a sweeping victory. "We have taught them how to conquer us," lamented a Democratic newspaper.

A Whig campaign publication illustrates the way the party promoted its 1840 presidential candidate, William Henry Harrison, as a humble, cider-drinking common man—an image far removed from the wealthy Harrison's actual social status.

HIS ACCIDENCY

Whig success proved short-lived. Immediately upon assuming office, Harrison contracted pneumonia. He died a month later, and John Tyler succeeded him. When the Whig majority in Congress tried to enact the American System into law, Tyler vetoed nearly every measure, including a new national bank and higher tariff. Most of the cabinet resigned, and his party repudiated him. Whig newspapers were soon calling the president His Accidency and The Executive Ass.

Tyler's four years in office were nearly devoid of accomplishment. If the campaign that resulted in the election of Harrison and Tyler demonstrated how a flourishing system of democratic politics had come into existence, Tyler's lack of success showed that political parties had become central to American government. Without a party behind him, a president could not govern. But a storm was now gathering that would test the stability of American democracy and the statesmanship of its political leaders.

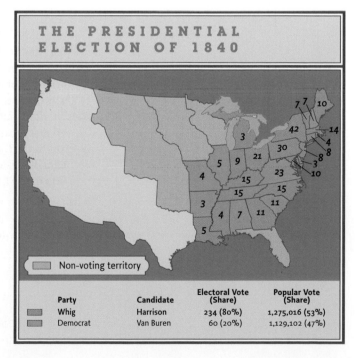

THE PRESIDENTIAL ELECTION OF 1840

Non-voting territory

Party	Candidate	Electoral Vote (Share)	Popular Vote (Share)
Whig	Harrison	234 (80%)	1,275,016 (53%)
Democrat	Van Buren	60 (20%)	1,129,102 (47%)

SUGGESTED READING

Ashworth, John. *"Agrarians" and "Aristocrats": Party Ideology in the United States, 1837–1846* (1983). A careful study of political ideas in the last years of Jacksonian politics, stressing increasing class divisions between the parties.

Cott, Nancy. *The Bonds of Womanhood: "Woman's Sphere" in New England, 1780–1835* (1977). A pioneering study of the emergence of the ideological separation between gender-defined "public" and "private" spheres.

Dangerfield, George. *The Awakening of American Nationalism, 1815–1828* (1965). A narrative of events during the presidencies of James Monroe and John Quincy Adams.

Formisano, Ronald P. *The Transformation of Political Culture: Massachusetts Parties, 1790–1840s* (1983). A study of politics in one key state, stressing the importance of ethnocultural divisions in shaping political alignments.

Freehling, William G. *Prelude to Civil War: The Nullification Controversy in South Carolina, 1816–1836* (1966). Still the standard account of the nullification crisis during Jackson's presidency.

Holt, Michael. *The Rise and Fall of the American Whig Party* (1999). A comprehensive history of the second major party of the Jacksonian era.

Howe, Daniel W. *The Political Culture of the American Whigs* (1979). Illuminates the key ideas that held the Whig Party together.

Keyssar, Alexander. *The Right to Vote: The Contested History of Democracy in the United States* (2000). The most up-to-date history of the right to vote in America from the colonial era to the present.

McFaul, James. *The Politics of Jacksonian Finance* (1972). A careful examination of party differences on currency and banking questions.

Remini, Robert. *Martin Van Buren and the Making of the Democratic Party* (1959). Examines how Van Buren created the structure of party organization that elected Andrew Jackson in 1828.

Schlesinger, Arthur M., Jr. *The Age of Jackson* (1945). An influential account of Jacksonian ideas and politics, which shaped debate among a generation of historians.

Starr, Paul. *Creation of the Media: Political Origins of Modern Communications* (2004). Contains an illuminating account of the "information revolution" in Jacksonian America.

Wallace, Anthony. *The Long, Bitter Trail: Andrew Jackson and the Indians* (1993). A brief history of Jackson's Indian policies, especially Indian Removal in the southern states.

Watson, Harry. *Liberty and Power: The Politics of Jacksonian America* (1990). A valuable brief account of the politics of the 1820s and 1830s.

Wilentz, Sean. *The Rise of American Democracy: Jefferson to Lincoln* (2005). A comprehensive history of democratic ideas and politics from the American Revolution to the Civil War.

REVIEW QUESTIONS

1. How did John Quincy Adams envision the United States' becoming the "freest and mightiest nation in the world"?

2. How did Democrats and Whigs differ in their understanding of American freedom and its relationship to governmental power?

3. What were the main characteristics of "The American System"?

4. What were the main arguments for and against Indian removal?

5. How did the Missouri Compromise and the nullification crisis demonstrate increasing sectional differences in antebellum America?

KEY TERMS

The Dorr War (p. 353)

McCulloch v. Maryland (p. 362)

Missouri Compromise (p. 363)

"corrupt bargain" (p. 367)

Eaton affair (p. 374)

Tariff of 1832 (p. 375)

Worcester v. Georgia (p. 377)

"hard money" advocates (p. 379)

Jackson and the veto (p. 380)

REVIEW TABLE

Major Events of the Jackson Administration, 1829–1836			
Event	**Dates**	**Origin of Crisis**	**Resolution**
Nullification crisis	1830–1833	South Carolina's opposition to a tariff becomes a battle to uphold the supremacy of federal over state law	Force Bill authorizes Jackson to use the military to collect customs duties after South Carolina nullifies the tariff
Bank War	1833–1836	Jackson opposes attempt of Congress to extend the Bank of the United States's charter another twenty years	Jackson vetoes Congress's resolution to grant the extension, effectively killing the Bank
Indian removal	1830–1838	Georgians want Cherokee land for expansion of cotton agriculture	Indian Removal Act of 1830, calls for the relocation of 46,000 Southeastern Indians to west of the Mississippi

Part 3

SLAVERY, FREEDOM, AND THE CRISIS OF THE UNION, 1840–1877

During the middle part of the nineteenth century, the United States confronted its greatest crisis, as the division between slave and free societies tore the country apart. A new nation emerged from the Civil War, with slavery abolished and the meaning of freedom transformed for all Americans.

Despite the hope of some of the founders that slavery might die out, the institution grew in size and economic importance as the nineteenth century progressed. Slavery expanded westward with the young republic, and the slave population grew to nearly 4 million by 1860. After the northern states abolished slavery, it became the "peculiar institution" of the South, the basis of a society growing ever more different from the rest of the country in economic structure and social values. Planters who dominated southern life also exerted enormous influence in national affairs. They developed a defense of slavery that insisted that the institution was the foundation of genuine freedom for white citizens. Slaves, meanwhile, created their own semiautonomous culture that nurtured from one generation to the next their hope for liberation from bondage. Nonetheless, slavery was in some ways a national institution. Slave-grown cotton, a source of wealth to slaveowners, also provided the raw material for the North's growing textile industry and became the country's most important export.

During the 1820s and 1830s, numerous social movements arose that worked to reform American society. Their inspiration lay primarily in the Second Great Awakening, the religious revivals that swept both North and South and offered salvation to sinners and improvement to society at large. While some reform movements were national in scope, others existed only in the North. Most notable among the latter was a new, militant movement demanding the immediate abolition of slavery and the incorporation of blacks as equal citizens of the republic. The abolitionists helped to focus discussions of freedom on the sharp contradiction between liberty and slavery. They promoted an understanding of freedom as control over one's self and participation as an equal member in social and political life. They not only helped to place the issue of slavery squarely on the national agenda but also inspired the stirrings of protest among a number of northern women, whose work in the antislavery movement led them to resent their own lack of legal rights and educational and economic opportunities.

In the 1840s, the conflict between free and slave societies moved to the center stage of American politics. It did so as a result of the nation's territorial expansion. The acquisition of a vast new area of land as the result of the Mexican War raised the question of whether slavery would be able to expand further westward. By the 1850s, this issue had destroyed the Whig Party, weakened the Democrats, and led to the creation of an entirely new party, the Republicans, dedicated to confining slavery to the states where it already existed. Exalting the superiority of northern society, based on "free labor," to southern society, based on slavery, Republicans elected Abraham Lincoln as president in 1860, even though he did not receive a single vote in most of the southern states. In response, seven slave states seceded from the Union and formed a new nation, the Confederate States of America. When southern forces fired on Fort Sumter, an enclave of Union control in Charleston Harbor, they inaugurated the Civil War, by far the bloodiest conflict in American history.

Begun as a struggle to preserve the Union, the Civil War eventually became a crusade for emancipation, which brought the nation what President Lincoln called "a new birth of freedom." The North's failure to achieve military victory in the first two years of the war, coupled with the actions of slaves who by the thousands abandoned the plantations to flee to Union lines, propelled the Lincoln administration down the road to emancipation. Although it freed few slaves on the day it was issued, January 1, 1863, Lincoln's Emancipation Proclamation proved to be the turning point of the Civil War for it announced that, henceforth, the Union army would serve as an agent of freedom. And by authorizing, for the first time, the enlistment of black men into the Union army, the Proclamation raised the question of black citizenship in the postwar world.

The era of Reconstruction that followed the Civil War was a time of intense political and social conflict, in which the definition of freedom and the question of who was entitled to enjoy it played a central role. Former slaves claimed that freedom meant full incorporation into American society, with the same rights and opportunities whites enjoyed. They also demanded that the government guarantee them access to land, to provide an economic foundation for their freedom. Most southern whites believed that blacks should go back to work on the plantations, enjoying very few political and civil rights. Andrew Johnson, who succeeded Lincoln as president, shared their view. But the majority of northern Republicans came to believe that the emancipated slaves should enjoy the same legal rights as whites. In 1867, they granted black men in the South the right to vote. During Reconstruction, northern Republicans rewrote the laws and Constitution to incorporate the ideal of equal citizenship for all Americans, regardless of race. This was a dramatic expansion of the meaning of freedom.

In the South, Reconstruction witnessed a short-lived period in which former slaves voted and held office alongside whites, a remarkable experiment in interracial democracy. On the other hand, the former slaves failed to achieve the economic freedom they desired, since the North proved unwilling to distribute land. As a result, most former slaves, and increasing numbers of whites in the war-devastated South, found themselves confined to working as sharecroppers on land owned by others. But the genuine advances achieved during Reconstruction, such as improved access to education, exercise of political rights, and the creation of new black institutions like independent churches, produced a violent reaction by upholders of white supremacy. During the 1870s, the North retreated from its commitment to equality. In 1877, Reconstruction came to an end. Many of the rights guaranteed to the former slaves were violated in the years that followed.

Although Reconstruction only lasted from 1865 to 1877, the issues debated then forecast many of the controversies that would envelop American society in the decades that followed. The definition of American citizenship, the power of the federal government and its relationship to the states, the future of political democracy in a society marked by increasing economic inequality—all these were Reconstruction issues, and all reverberated in the Gilded Age and Progressive era that followed.

The Civil War era resolved the contradiction of the existence of slavery in a land that celebrated freedom. But just as the American Revolution left to nineteenth-century Americans the problem of slavery, the Civil War and Reconstruction left to future generations the challenge of bringing genuine freedom to the descendants of slavery.

CHAPTER 11

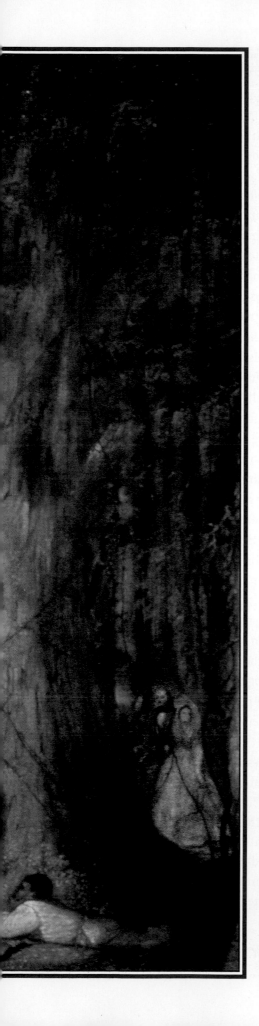

The Peculiar Institution

Plantation Burial, *a painting from around 1860 by John Antrobus, an English artist who emigrated to New Orleans in 1850 and later married the daughter of a plantation owner. A slave preacher conducts a funeral service while black men, women, and children look on. The well-dressed white man and woman on the far right are, presumably, the plantation owner and his wife. This is a rare eyewitness depiction of black culture under slavery.*

FOCUS QUESTIONS

- How did slavery shape social and economic relations in the Old South?

- What were the material and legal conditions in which slaves lived and worked?

- What were the foundations of the culture the slaves themselves forged?

- What were the major forms of resistance to slavery?

A photograph of Frederick Douglass, the fugitive slave who became a prominent abolitionist, taken between 1847 and 1852. As a fellow abolitionist noted at the time, "The very look and bearing of Douglass are an irresistible logic against the oppression of his race."

In an age of "self-made" men, no American rose more dramatically from humble origins to national and international distinction than Frederick Douglass. Born into slavery in 1818, he became a major figure in the crusade for abolition, the drama of emancipation, and the effort during Reconstruction to give meaning to black freedom.

Douglass was the son of a slave mother and an unidentified white man, possibly his owner. As a youth in Maryland, he gazed out at the ships in Chesapeake Bay, seeing them as "freedom's swift-winged angels." He secretly taught himself to read and write. "From that moment," he later wrote, he understood that knowledge was "the pathway from slavery to freedom." Douglass experienced slavery in all its variety, from work as a house servant and as a skilled craftsman in a Baltimore shipyard to labor as a plantation field hand. When he was fifteen, Douglass's owner sent him to a "slave breaker" to curb his independent spirit. After numerous whippings, Douglass defiantly refused to allow himself to be disciplined again. This confrontation, he recalled, was "the turning-point in my career as a slave." It rekindled his desire for freedom. In 1838, having borrowed the free papers of a black sailor, he escaped to the North.

Frederick Douglass went on to become the most influential African-American of the nineteenth century and the nation's preeminent advocate of racial equality. "He who has endured the cruel pangs of slavery," he wrote, "is the man to advocate liberty." Douglass lectured against slavery throughout the North and the British Isles, and he edited a succession of anti-slavery publications. He published a widely read autobiography that offered an eloquent condemnation of slavery and racism. Indeed, his own accomplishments testified to the incorrectness of prevailing ideas about blacks' inborn inferiority. Douglass was also active in other reform movements, including the campaign for women's rights. During the Civil War, he advised Abraham Lincoln on the employment of black soldiers and became an early advocate of giving the right to vote to the emancipated slaves. Douglass died in 1895, as a new system of white supremacy based on segregation and disenfranchisement was being fastened upon the South.

Throughout his career, Douglass insisted that slavery could only be overthrown by continuous resistance. "Those who profess to favor freedom, and yet deprecate agitation," he declared, "are men who want crops without plowing up the ground, they want rain without thunder and lightning, they want the ocean without the awful roar of its many waters." In effect, Douglass argued that in their desire for freedom, the slaves were truer to the nation's underlying principles than the white Americans who annually celebrated the Fourth of July while allowing the continued existence of slavery.

THE OLD SOUTH

When Frederick Douglass was born, slavery was already an old institution in America. Two centuries had passed since the first twenty Africans were landed in Virginia from a Dutch ship. After abolition in the North, slavery had become the "peculiar institution" of the South—that is, an institution unique to southern society. The Mason-Dixon Line, drawn by two surveyors in the eighteenth century to settle a boundary dispute between Maryland and Pennsylvania, eventually became the dividing line between slavery and freedom.

Despite the hope of some of the founders that slavery might die out, in fact the institution survived the crisis of the American Revolution and rapidly expanded westward. During the first thirty years of Douglass's life, the number of slaves and the economic and political importance of slavery continued to grow. On the eve of the Civil War, the slave population had risen to nearly 4 million, its high rate of natural increase more than making up for the prohibition in 1808 of further slave imports from Africa. In the South as a whole, slaves made up one-third of the total population and in the cotton-producing states of the Deep South, around half. By the 1850s, slavery had crossed the Mississippi River and was expanding rapidly in Arkansas, Louisiana, and eastern Texas. In 1860, one-third of the nation's cotton crop was grown west of the Mississippi.

COTTON IS KING

In the nineteenth century, cotton replaced sugar as the world's major crop produced by slave labor. And although slavery survived in Brazil and the Spanish and French Caribbean, its abolition in the British empire in 1833 made the United States indisputably the center of New World slavery.

Table 11.1 GROWTH OF THE SLAVE POPULATION	
Year	*Slave Population*
1790	697,624
1800	893,602
1810	1,191,362
1820	1,538,022
1830	2,009,043
1840	2,487,355
1850	3,204,313
1860	3,953,760

Cotton Pressing in Louisiana, *an engraving from* Ballou's Magazine, *1856. The process of compressing cotton into bales for shipment was only partially mechanized; on the right, slaves provide the power.*

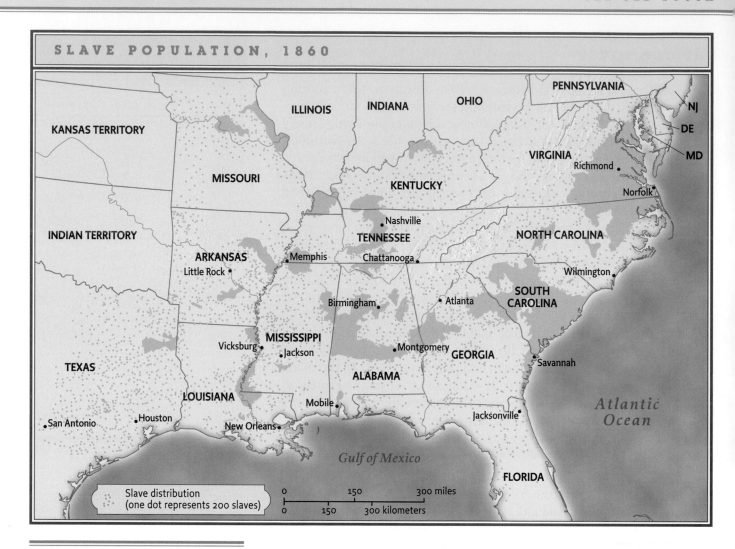

SLAVE POPULATION, 1860

Slave distribution
(one dot represents 200 slaves)

0   150   300 miles
0   150   300 kilometers

Rather than being evenly distributed throughout the South, the slave population was concentrated in areas with the most fertile soil and easiest access to national and international markets.

When measured by slavery's geographic extent, the numbers held in bondage, and the institution's economic importance both regionally and nationally, the Old South was the largest and most powerful slave society the modern world has known. Its strength rested on a virtual monopoly of cotton, the South's "white gold." Cotton had been grown for thousands of years in many parts of the globe. The conquistador Hernán Cortés was impressed by the high quality of woven cotton clothing worn by the Aztecs. But in the nineteenth century, cotton assumed an unprecedented role in the world economy.

Because the early industrial revolution centered on factories using cotton as the raw material to manufacture cloth, cotton had become by far the most important commodity in international trade. And three-fourths of the world's cotton supply came from the southern United States. Throughout the world, hundreds of thousands of workers loaded, unloaded, spun, and wove cotton, and thousands of manufacturers and merchants owed their wealth to the cotton trade. Textile manufacturers in places as far-flung as Massachusetts, Lancashire in Great Britain, Normandy in France, and the suburbs of Moscow depended on a regular supply of American cotton.

As early as 1803, cotton had become the most important American export. Cotton sales earned the money from abroad that allowed the

An American Slave Market, *painted in 1852 by the unknown artist Taylor, depicts the sale of slaves, including one who had attempted to run away.*

United States to pay for imported manufactured goods. On the eve of the Civil War, it represented well over half of the total value of American exports. In 1860, the economic investment represented by the slave population exceeded the value of the nation's factories, railroads, and banks combined.

THE SECOND MIDDLE PASSAGE

As noted in Chapter 9, to replace the slave trade from Africa, prohibited by Congress in 1808, a massive trade in slaves developed within the United States. Over 2 million slaves were sold between 1820 and 1860, a majority to local buyers but hundreds of thousands from older states to "importing" states of the Lower South. Slave trading was a visible, established business. The main business districts of southern cities contained the offices of slave traders, complete with signs reading "Negro Sales" or "Negroes Bought Here." Auctions of slaves took place at public slave markets, as in New Orleans, or at courthouses. Southern newspapers carried advertisements for slave sales, southern banks financed slave trading, southern ships and railroads carried slaves from buyers to sellers, and southern states and municipalities earned revenue by taxing the sale of slaves. Virtually every slaveowner at one time or another bought and sold slaves. The Cotton Kingdom could not have arisen without the internal slave trade, and the economies of older states like Virginia came increasingly to rely on the sale of slaves.

SLAVERY AND THE NATION

Slavery, Henry Clay proclaimed in 1816, "forms an exception . . . to the general liberty prevailing in the United States." But Clay, like many of his contemporaries, underestimated slavery's impact on the entire nation. The "free

This 1860 view of New Orleans captures the size and scale of the cotton trade in the South's largest city. More than 3,500 steamboats arrived in New Orleans in 1860.

states" had ended slavery, but they were hardly unaffected by it. The Constitution, as we have seen, enhanced the power of the South in the House of Representatives and electoral college and required all states to return fugitives from bondage. Slavery shaped the lives of all Americans, white as well as black. It helped to determine where they lived, how they worked, and under what conditions they could exercise their freedom of speech, assembly, and the press.

Northern merchants and manufacturers participated in the slave economy and shared in its profits. Money earned in the cotton trade helped to finance industrial development and internal improvements in the North. Northern ships carried cotton to New York and Europe, northern bankers financed cotton plantations, northern companies insured slave property, and northern factories turned cotton into cloth. New York City's rise to commercial prominence depended as much on the establishment of shipping lines that gathered the South's cotton and transported it to Europe, as on the Erie Canal. The Lords of the Loom (New England's early factory owners) relied on cotton supplied by the Lords of the Lash (southern slaveowners). Northern manufacturers like Brooks Brothers supplied cheap fabrics (called "Negro cloth") to clothe the South's slaves.

THE SOUTHERN ECONOMY

Slavery led the South down a very different path of economic development than the North's, limiting the growth of industry, discouraging immigrants from entering the region, and inhibiting technological progress. The South did not share in the urban growth experienced by the rest of the country. Most southern cities were located on the region's periphery and served mainly as centers for gathering and shipping cotton. Southern banks existed primarily to help finance the plantations. They loaned money for the purchase of land and slaves, not manufacturing development. Southern railroads mostly consisted of short lines that brought cotton from the interior to coastal ports.

In the Cotton Kingdom, the only city of significant size was New Orleans. With a population of 168,000 in 1860, New Orleans ranked as the nation's sixth-largest city. As the gathering point for cotton grown along the Mississippi River and sugar from the plantations of southeastern Louisiana, it was the world's leading exporter of slave-grown crops. Unlike other cities with slavery (apart from St. Louis and Baltimore, on the periphery of the South), New Orleans also attracted large numbers of European immigrants. In 1860, 40 percent of its population was foreign-born. And New Orleans's rich French heritage and close connections with the Caribbean produced a local culture quite different from that of the rest of the United States, reflected in the city's distinctive music, dance, religion, and cuisine.

In 1860, the South produced less than 10 percent of the nation's manufactured goods. Many northerners viewed slavery as an obstacle to American economic progress. But as New Orleans showed, slavery and economic growth could go hand in hand. In general, the southern economy was hardly stagnant, and slavery proved very profitable for most owners. The profits produced by slavery for the South and the nation as a whole formed a powerful obstacle to abolition. Speaking of cotton, Senator James Henry Hammond of South Carolina declared, "No power on earth dares to make war upon it. Cotton is king."

PLAIN FOLK OF THE OLD SOUTH

The foundation of the Old South's economy, slavery powerfully shaped race relations, politics, religion, and the law. Its influence was pervasive: "Nothing escaped," writes one historian, "nothing and no one." This was true despite the fact that the majority of white southerners—three out of four white families—owned no slaves. Since planters monopolized the best land, most small white farmers lived outside the plantation belt in hilly areas unsuitable for cotton production. They worked the land using family labor rather than slaves or hired workers.

Many southern farmers lived lives of economic self-sufficiency remote from the market revolution. They raised livestock and grew food for their families, purchasing relatively few goods at local stores. Those residing on marginal land in isolated hill areas and the Appalachian Mountains were often desperately poor and, since nearly all the southern states lacked systems of free public education, were more often illiterate than their northern counterparts. Not

An upcountry family, dressed in homespun, in Cedar Mountain, Virginia. Many white families in the pre–Civil War South were largely isolated from the market economy.

until the arrival of railroads and coal mining later in the nineteenth century would such areas become integrated into the market economy. Most yeoman farmers enjoyed a comfortable standard of living, and many owned a slave or two. But even successful small farmers relied heavily on home production to supply their basic needs. Unlike northern farmers, therefore, they did not provide a market for manufactured goods. This was one of the main reasons why the South did not develop an industrial base.

Some poorer whites resented the power and privileges of the great planters. Politicians like Andrew Johnson of Tennessee and Joseph Brown of Georgia rose to power as self-proclaimed spokesmen of the common man against the "slaveocracy." But most poor whites made their peace with the planters in whose hands economic and social power was concentrated. Racism, kinship ties, common participation in a democratic political culture, and regional loyalty in the face of outside criticism all served to cement bonds between planters and the South's "plain folk." In the plantation regions, moreover, small farmers manned the slave patrols that kept a lookout for runaway slaves and those on the roads without permission. Non-slaveholders frequently rented slaves from planters and regularly elected slaveowners to public offices in the South. Like other white southerners, most small farmers believed their economic and personal freedom rested on slavery. Not until the Civil War would class tensions among the white population threaten the planters' domination.

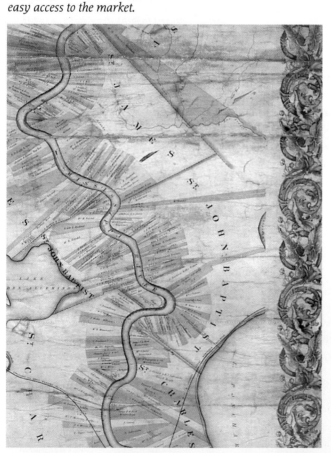

A detail from Norman's Chart of the Lower Mississppi River *(1858) shows slave plantations laid out so that each fronted on the river and, therefore, had easy access to the market.*

THE PLANTER CLASS

Even among slaveholders, the planter was far from typical. In 1850, a majority of slaveholding families owned five or fewer slaves. Less than 40,000 families possessed the twenty or more slaves that qualified them as planters. Fewer than 2,000 families owned a hundred slaves or more. Nonetheless, even though the planter was not the typical slaveholder or white southerner, his values and aspirations dominated southern life. The plantation, wrote Frederick Douglass, was "a little nation by itself, with its own language, its own rules, regulations, and customs." These rules and customs set the tone for southern society.

Ownership of slaves provided the route to wealth, status, and influence. Planters not only held the majority of slaves, but they controlled the most fertile land, enjoyed the highest incomes, and dominated state and local offices and the leadership of both political parties. Small slaveholders aspired to move up into the ranks of the planter class. Those who acquired wealth almost always invested it in land and slaves. But as the price of a "prime field hand" rose from $1,000 in 1840 to $1,800 in 1860 (the latter figure equivalent to around $40,000 today), it became more and more difficult for poorer white southerners to become slaveholders.

Slavery, of course, was a profit-making system, and slaveowners kept close watch on world prices for their products, invested in enterprises such as railroads and canals, and carefully supervised their plantations. Their wives—the "plantation mistresses" idealized in southern lore for femininity, beauty, and dependence on men—were hardly idle. They cared for sick slaves, directed the domestic servants, and supervised the entire plantation when their husbands were away. The wealthiest Americans before the Civil War were planters in the South Carolina low country and the cotton region around Natchez, Mississippi. Frederick Stanton, a cotton broker turned planter in the Natchez area, owned 444 slaves and over 15,000 acres of land in Mississippi and Louisiana.

Nonetheless, Alexis de Tocqueville observed that "the northerner loves to make money, the southerner to spend it." Many of the richest planters squandered their wealth in a lifestyle complete with lavish entertainments and summer vacations in Newport and Saratoga. House slaves were so numerous in Charleston, wrote one visitor to the city, that "the Charlestonians are obliged to exercise their wits to devise sufficient variety to keep them employed." On the cotton frontier, many planters lived in rude log homes. But in the older slave states, and as settled society developed in the Deep South, they constructed elegant mansions adorned with white columns in the Greek Revival style of architecture. Planters discouraged their sons from entering "lowly" trades like commerce and manufacturing, one reason why the South remained overwhelmingly agricultural.

not just hypothetical, they believed it

THE PATERNALIST ETHOS

The slave plantation was deeply embedded in the world market, and planters sought to accumulate land, slaves, and profits. Many invested in railroads and banks as well as slaves. But planters' values glorified not the competitive capitalist marketplace, but a hierarchical, agrarian society in which slaveholding gentlemen took personal responsibility for the physical and moral well-being of their dependents—women, children, and slaves. "The master," wrote one planter, "as the head of the system, has a right to the obedience and labor of the slave, but the slave has also his mutual rights in the master; the right of protection, the right of counsel and guidance, the right of subsistence, the right of care and attention in sickness and old age."

This outlook, known as "paternalism" (from the Latin word for "father"), had been a feature of American slavery even in the eighteenth century. But it became more ingrained after the closing of the African slave trade in 1808, which narrowed the cultural gap between master and slave and gave owners an economic interest in the survival of their human property. Unlike the absentee planters of the West Indies, many of whom resided in Great Britain, southern slaveholders lived on their plantations and thus had year-round contact with their slaves.

The paternalist outlook both masked and justified the brutal reality of slavery. It enabled slaveowners to think of themselves as kind, responsible masters even as they bought and sold their human property—a practice at odds with the claim that slaves formed part of the master's "family." Some

Table 11.2 SLAVEHOLDING, 1850 (IN ROUND NUMBERS)	
Number of Slaves Owned	*Slaveholders*
1	68,000
2–4	105,000
5–9	80,000
10–19	55,000
20–49	30,000
50–99	6,000
100–199	1,500
200+	250

A pre–Civil War engraving depicting the paternalist ideal. The old slave in the foreground says, "God Bless you massa! you feed and clothe us, . . . and when too old to work, you provide for us!" The master replies, "These poor creatures are a sacred legacy from my ancestors and while a dollar is left me, nothing shall be spared to increase their comfort and happiness."

Average number of slaves
per slaveholding, 1860

- 20+
- 15–20
- 10–15
- 5–10
- 0–5

Most southern slaveholders owned fewer than five slaves. The largest plantations were concentrated in coastal South Carolina and along the Mississippi River.

slaveowners tried to reform the system to eliminate its most oppressive features. The Reverend Charles C. Jones, a wealthy planter of Liberty County, Georgia, organized his neighbors to promote the religious instruction of slaves, improve slave housing, diet, and medical care, and discourage severe punishments. But even Jones believed his slaves so "degraded" and lacking in moral self-discipline that he could not contemplate an end to slavery.

THE CODE OF HONOR

As time went on, the dominant southern conception of the good society diverged more and more sharply from that of the egalitarian, competitive, individualistic North. In the South, for example, both upper- and lower-class whites adhered to a code of personal honor, in which men were expected to defend, with violence if necessary, their own reputation and that of their families. Although dueling was illegal, many prominent southerners took part in duels to avenge supposed insults. In 1826, Henry Clay and John Randolph, two of the most important southern political leaders, fought a duel with pistols after Clay took exception to criticisms by Randolph on the floor of Congress. Fortunately, each missed the other.

Twenty years later, however, John H. Pleasants, editor of the *Richmond Whig*, died in a duel with the son of a rival newspaperman.

Just as southern men had a heightened sense of their own honor and masculinity, white southern women, even more than in the North, were confined within the "domestic circle." "A man loves his children," wrote George Fitzhugh, a Virginia lawyer and author of numerous books and articles on social issues, "because they are weak, helpless, and dependent. He loves his wife for similar reasons." As will be discussed in the next chapter, many northern women before the Civil War became part of a thriving female culture centered on voluntary religious and reform organizations. Few parallels existed in the South, and plantation mistresses often complained of loneliness and isolation.

THE PROSLAVERY ARGUMENT

Some southerners worried about their standing in the eyes of the world, especially how others viewed the intellectual life of their region. "We of the South," one wrote, "must, to Europe, continue to appear inferior to the North in intellectual cultivation." The free states outstripped the slave states in public education, the number of colleges, and in newspapers, literary journals, and other publications. Nonetheless, the life of the mind flourished in the Old South, and the region did not lack for novelists, political philosophers, scientists, and the like.

In the thirty years before the outbreak of the Civil War, however, even as northern criticism of the "peculiar institution" began to deepen, proslavery thought came to dominate southern public life. Fewer and fewer white southerners shared the view, common among the founding fathers, that slavery was, at best, a "necessary evil." "Many in the South," John C. Calhoun proclaimed in 1837, "once believed that [slavery] was a moral and political evil. . . . That folly and delusion are gone; we see it now in its true light, and regard it as the most safe and stable basis for free institutions in the world."

Even those who had no direct stake in slavery shared with planters a deep commitment to white supremacy. Indeed, racism—the belief that blacks were innately inferior to whites and unsuited for life in any condition other than slavery—formed one pillar of the proslavery ideology. Most slaveholders also found legitimation for slavery in biblical passages such as the injunction that servants should obey their masters. Others argued that slavery was essential to human progress. Had not the ancient republics of Greece and Rome and the great European empires of the seventeenth and eighteenth centuries rested on slave labor? Without slavery, planters would be unable to cultivate the arts, sciences, and other civilized pursuits.

Model Plantation, *an engraving from* Frank Leslie's Illustrated Newspaper, *February 6, 1864. This portrait of Oak Lawn, a Louisiana sugar plantation, depicts the variety of buildings that could be found on the largest southern estates, including the planter's residence, the slave quarters, the sugar and saw mill, and even a hospital and church.*

Slavery as It Exists in America; Slavery as It Exists in England, *a lithograph published in Boston in 1850. Illustrating one aspect of proslavery thought, the artist depicts southern slaves as happy and carefree, while English workers, including children, are victims of the oppressive system of "factory slavery." At the bottom is George Thompson, the English abolitionist who traveled to the United States to lecture against slavery.*

Still other defenders of slavery insisted that the institution guaranteed equality for whites by preventing the growth of a class doomed to a life of unskilled labor. Like northerners, they claimed to be committed to the ideal of freedom. Slavery for blacks, they declared, was the surest guarantee of "perfect equality" among whites, liberating them from the "low, menial" jobs like factory labor and domestic service performed by wage laborers in the North. Slavery made possible the considerable degree of economic autonomy (the social condition of freedom) enjoyed not only by planters but by nonslaveholding whites. Because of slavery, claimed one congressman, white southerners were as "independent as the bird which cleaves the air." And because independence was necessary for citizenship, slavery was the "cornerstone of our republican edifice."

SLAVERY AND LIBERTY

Many white southerners declared themselves the true heirs of the American Revolution. They claimed to be inspired by "the same spirit of freedom and independence" that motivated the founding generation. Like their ancestors of the 1760s and 1770s, their political language was filled with contrasts between liberty and slavery and complaints that outsiders proposed to reduce them to "slaves" by interfering with their local institutions. Southern state constitutions enshrined the idea of equal rights for free men, and the South participated fully in the movement toward political democracy for whites.

Beginning in the 1830s, however, proslavery writers began to question the ideals of liberty, equality, and democracy so widely shared elsewhere in the nation. South Carolina, the only southern state where a majority of white families owned slaves, became the home of an aggressive defense of slavery that repudiated the idea that freedom and equality were universal entitlements. The language of the Declaration of Independence—that all men were created equal and entitled to liberty—was "the most false and dangerous of all political errors," insisted John C. Calhoun. Proslavery spokesmen returned to the older definition of freedom as a privilege rather than a universal entitlement, a "reward to be earned, not a blessing to be gratuitously lavished on all alike."

As the sectional controversy intensified after 1830, a number of southern writers and politicians came to defend slavery less as the basis of equality for whites than as the foundation of an organic, hierarchical society. Many southern clergymen, in the course of offering a religious defense of slavery, argued that inequality and hence the submission of inferior to superior—black to white, female to male, lower classes to upper classes—was a "fundamental law" of human existence. A hierarchy of "ranks and orders in human society," insisted John B. Alger, a Presbyterian minister in South Carolina, formed part of the "divine arrangement" of the world.

SLAVERY AND CIVILIZATION *defense*

The Virginia writer George Fitzhugh took the argument to its most radical conclusion, repudiating not only Jeffersonian ideals but the notion of America's special mission in the world. Far from being the natural condition of mankind, Fitzhugh wrote, "universal liberty" was the exception, an experiment carried on "for a little while" in "a corner of Europe" and the northern United States. Taking the world and its history as a whole, slavery, "without regard to race and color," was "the general, . . . normal, natural" basis of "civilized society." Indeed, wrote Fitzhugh, slaveowners and slaves shared a "community of interest" unknown in "free society." Since they lacked economic cares, he contended, "the Negro slaves of the South are the happiest, and, in some degree, the freest people in the world." White workers in both the North and South, according to Fitzhugh, would fare better having individual owners, rather than living as "slaves" of the economic marketplace.

It seems safe to assume that few non-slaveholding white southerners agreed that enslavement would offer them greater freedom than they already enjoyed. Nor was Fitzhugh entirely consistent. Sometimes, he argued that all free laborers would be better off as slaves. On other occasions, he spoke of slavery only for blacks—perpetual "children" for whom liberty would be "a curse."

Abraham Lincoln would later observe that the essential function of the proslavery argument was to serve the interests of those who benefited from a system of extreme inequality. He imagined Dr. Frederick A. Ross, a leading proslavery clergyman, considering whether he should free his slave Sambo. God's view of the subject, Lincoln noted, was not entirely clear, and "no one thinks of asking Sambo's opinion." Therefore, it fell to Dr. Ross to decide the question. "If he decides that God wills Sambo to continue a slave," Lincoln wrote, "he thereby retains his own comfortable position; but if he decides that God wills Sambo to be free, he thereby has to walk out of the shade, take off his gloves, and [work] for his own bread." Under these circumstances, it was hardly surprising that Dr. Ross found the argument that Sambo should remain a slave very persuasive.

After 1830, southern writers, newspaper editors, politicians, and clergymen increasingly devoted themselves to spreading the defense of slavery. The majority of white southerners came to believe that freedom for whites rested on the power to command the labor of blacks. In the words of the Richmond *Enquirer*, "freedom is not possible without slavery."

LIFE UNDER SLAVERY

SLAVES AND THE LAW

For slaves, the "peculiar institution" meant a life of incessant toil, brutal punishment, and the constant fear that their families would be destroyed by sale. Before the law, slaves were property. Although they had a few legal

VOICES OF FREEDOM

FROM SOLOMON NORTHUP, *Twelve Years a Slave* (1853)

A free black resident of New York state, Solomon Northup was kidnapped in 1841 while in Washington, D.C., and sold as a slave. After twelve years, during which he labored on plantations in Louisiana, he managed to contact friends in the North who arranged for his release. His memoir, published in 1853, became one of the most widely read accounts of slavery by someone who had experienced it. In this passage, Northup describes a sale at the New Orleans slave market, a focal point of the nation's internal slave trade.

Mr. Theophilus Freeman, a partner of consignee of James H. Burch, and keeper of the slave pen in New Orleans [got] his property ready for the sales-room. . . . Many customers called to examine Freeman's "new lot." . . . He would make us hold up our heads, walk briskly back and forth, while customers would feel of our hands and arms and bodies, turn us about, ask us what we could do, make us open our mouths and show our teeth, precisely as a jockey examines a horse which he is about to barter for or purchase. Sometimes a man or woman was taken into the small house in the yard, stripped, and inspected more minutely. . . .

Lethe was sold to a planter of Baton Rouge, her eyes flashing with anger as she was led away. The same man also purchased Randall. The little fellow was made to jump, and run across the floor, and perform many other feats, exhibiting his activity and condition. All the time the trade was going on, Eliza was crying aloud, and wringing her hands. She besought the man not to buy him, unless he also bought herself and Emily. She promised, in that case, to be the most faithful slave that ever lived. The man answered that he could not afford it, and then Eliza burst into a paroxysm of grief, weeping plaintively. Freeman turned round to her, savagely, with his whip in his uplifted hand, ordering her to stop her noise, or he would flog her. . . . Eliza shrunk before him, and tried to wipe away her tears, but it was all in vain. She wanted to be with her children, she said, the little time she had to live. . . . She kept on begging and beseeching them, most piteously, not to separate the three. Over and over again she told them how she loved her boy. . . . But it was of no avail; the man could not afford it. The bargain was agreed upon, and Randall must go alone. Then Eliza ran to him; embraced him passionately; kissed him again and again; told him to remember her—all the while her tears falling in the boy's face like rain. . . .

The planter from Baton Rouge, with his new purchases, was ready to depart.

"Don't cry, mama. I will be a good boy. Don't cry," said Randall, looking back, as they passed out of the door.

What has become of the lad, God knows. It was a mournful scene indeed. I would have cried myself if I had dared.

From J. D. B. De Bow, "The Non-Slaveholders of the South" (1861)

J. D. B. De Bow, a prominent southern editor, wrote this essay on the eve of the Civil War to convince non-slaveholders that they benefited from the existence of slavery and that their interests were the same as those of the slaveowners.

The non-slaveholder of the South is assured that the remuneration afforded by this labor, over and above the expense of living, is larger than that which is afforded by the same labor in the free States. . . . They have but to compare their condition, in this particular, with the mining and manufacturing operatives of the North and Europe, to be thankful that God has reserved them for a better fate. . . .

The non-slaveholder is not subjected to that competition with foreign pauper labor which has degraded the free labor of the North, and demoralized it to an extent which perhaps can never be estimated. . . .

The non-slaveholder of the South preserves the status of the white man, and is not regarded as an inferior or dependent. He is not told that the Declaration of Independence, when it says that all men are born free and equal, refers to the negro equally with himself. It is not proposed to him that the free negro's vote shall weigh equally with his own at the ballot-box. . . . No white man at the South serves another as a body-servant, to clean his boots, wait on his table, and perform the menial services of his household! . . . He is a companion and an equal. . . . The poor white laborer at the North is at the bottom of the social ladder, while his brother here has ascended several steps, and can look down upon those who are beneath him at an infinite remove! . . .

Without the institution of slavery the great staple products of the South would cease to be grown, and the immense annual results which are distributed among every class of the community, and which give life to every branch of industry, would cease. The world furnishes no instances of these products being grown upon a large scale by free labor. . . .

If emancipation be brought about . . . the slaveholders, in the main, will escape the degrading equality which must result, by emigration, for which they have the means, by disposing of their personal chattels, while the non-slaveholders, without these resources, would be compelled to remain and endure the degradation. . . . Low as would [freed slaves] sink by emancipation in idleness, superstition, and vice, the white man compelled to live among them would, by the power exerted over him, sink even lower.

QUESTIONS

1. What aspects of the buying and selling of slaves does Northup single out for condemnation?

2. How does De Bow argue that the condition of non-slaveholders in the South is improved by the existence of slavery?

3. These pieces attempt to convince readers of the desirability or evil of slavery. What are the similarities and differences between the ways De Bow and Northup appeal to their respective audiences?

Metal shackles, from around 1850. Slaves were shackled as a form of punishment, or to prevent escape when being transported from one place to another.

rights (all states made it illegal to kill a slave except in self-defense, and slaves accused of serious crimes were entitled to their day in court, before all-white judges and juries), these were haphazardly enforced. Slaves could be sold or leased by their owners at will and lacked any voice in the governments that ruled over them. They could not testify in court against a white person, sign contracts or acquire property, own firearms, hold meetings unless a white person was present, or leave the farm or plantation without the permission of their owner. By the 1830s, it was against the law to teach a slave to read or write.

Not all of these laws were rigorously enforced. Some members of slave-holding families taught slave children to read (although rather few, since well over 90 percent of the slave population was illiterate in 1860). In the South Carolina rice fields, owners allowed some slaves to carry shotguns, in defiance of the law, to scare off birds feasting on rice seeds. It was quite common throughout the South for slaves to gather without white supervision at crossroads villages and country stores on Sunday, their day of rest. But the extent to which authorities enforced or bent the law depended on the decisions of the individual owners.

The slave, declared a Louisiana law, "owes to his master . . . a respect without bounds, and an absolute obedience." Not only did the owner have the legal right to what Alabama's legal code called the "time, labor, and services" of his slaves, but no aspect of their lives, from the choice of marriage partners to how they spent their free time, was immune from his interference. The entire system of southern justice, from the state militia and courts down to armed patrols in each locality, was designed to enforce the master's control over the person and labor of his slaves.

In one famous case, a Missouri court considered the "crime" of Celia, a slave who had killed her master while resisting a sexual assault. State law deemed "any woman" in such circumstances to be acting in self-defense. But Celia, the court ruled, was not a "woman" in the eyes of the law. She was a slave, whose master had complete power over her person. The court sentenced her to death. However, since Celia was pregnant, her execution was postponed until the child had been born, so as not to deprive her owners' heirs of their property rights.

CONDITIONS OF SLAVE LIFE

As the nineteenth century progressed, some southern states enacted laws to prevent the mistreatment of slaves, and their material living conditions improved. Food supplies and wild game were abundant in the South, and many slaves supplemented the food provided by their owners (primarily cornmeal and pork or bacon) with chickens and vegetables they raised themselves, animals they hunted in the forests, and, not infrequently, items they stole from the plantation smokehouse. Compared with their counterparts in the West Indies and Brazil, American slaves enjoyed better diets, lower rates of infant mortality, and longer life expectancies. Many factors contributed to improving material conditions. One was the growing strength of the planters' paternalist outlook. Douglass himself noted that "not to give a slave enough to eat, is regarded as the most aggravated development of meanness, even among slaveholders." Most of the South, moreover, lies outside the geographical area where tropical diseases like malaria, yellow fever, and typhoid fever flourish, so health among all southerners was better than in the Caribbean. Moreover, with the price of slaves rising dramatically after the closing of the African slave trade, it made economic sense for owners to become concerned with the health and living conditions of their human property.

Improvements in the slaves' living conditions were meant to strengthen slavery, not undermine it. Even as the material lives of the majority of slaves improved, the South drew tighter and tighter the chains of bondage. If slaves in the United States enjoyed better health and diets than elsewhere in the Western Hemisphere, they had far less access to freedom. In Brazil, it was not uncommon for an owner to free slaves as a form of celebration— on the occasion of a wedding in the owner's family, for example—or to allow slaves to purchase their freedom. Although slavery in Brazil lasted until 1888, over half the population of African descent was already free in 1850. (The comparable figure in the American South was well below 10 percent.) In the nineteenth-century South, more and more states set limits on voluntary manumission, requiring that such acts be approved by the legislature. "All the powers of earth," declared Abraham Lincoln in 1857, seemed to be "rapidly combining" to fasten bondage ever more securely upon American slaves. Few slave societies in history have so systematically closed off all avenues to freedom as the Old South.

FREE BLACKS IN THE OLD SOUTH

The existence of slavery helped to define the status of those blacks who did enjoy freedom. On the eve of the Civil War, nearly half a million free blacks lived in the United States, a majority in the South. Most were the descendants of slaves freed by southern owners in the aftermath of the Revolution or by the gradual emancipation laws of the northern states. Their numbers were supplemented by slaves who had been voluntarily liberated by their masters, who had been allowed to purchase their freedom, or who succeeded in running away.

When followed by "black" or "Negro," the word "free" took on an entirely new meaning. Whites defined their freedom, in part, by their distance from slavery. But among blacks, wrote Douglass, "the distinction between the slave and the free is not great." Northern free blacks, as noted in Chapter 10, generally could not vote and enjoyed few economic opportunities. Free blacks in the South could legally own property and marry and, of course, could not be bought and sold. But many

Table 11.3 FREE BLACK POPULATION, 1860		
Region	Free Black Population	Percentage of Total Black Population
North	226,152	100%
South	261,918	6.2
Upper South	224,963	12.8
Lower South	36,955	1.5
Delaware	19,829	91.7
Washington, D.C.	11,131	77.8
Kentucky	10,684	4.5
Maryland	83,942	49.1
Missouri	3,572	3.0
North Carolina	30,463	8.4
Tennessee	7,300	2.6
Virginia	58,042	10.6
Alabama	2,690	0.6
Arkansas	144	0.1
Florida	932	1.5
Georgia	3,500	0.8
Louisiana	18,647	5.3
Mississippi	773	0.2
South Carolina	9,914	2.4
Texas	355	0.2

regulations restricting the lives of slaves also applied to them. Free blacks had no voice in selecting public officials. Like slaves, they were prohibited from owning dogs, firearms, or liquor, and they could not strike a white person, even in self-defense. They were not allowed to testify in court or serve on juries, and they had to carry at all times a certificate of freedom. Poor free blacks who required public assistance could be bound out to labor alongside slaves. "Free negroes," declared a South Carolina judge in 1848, "belong to a degraded caste of society" and should learn to conduct themselves "as inferiors."

As noted above, nineteenth-century Brazil had a large free black population. In the West Indies, many children of white owners and female slaves gained their freedom, becoming part of a "free colored" population sharply distinguished from both whites above them and slaves below. In the absence of a white lower middle class, free blacks in Jamaica and other Caribbean islands operated shops and worked as clerks in government offices.

In the United States, a society that equated "black" and "slave" and left little room for a mulatto group between them, free blacks were increasingly considered an undesirable group, a potential danger to the slave system. By the 1850s, most southern states prohibited free blacks from entering their territory and a few states even moved to expel them altogether, offering the choice of enslavement or departure. Nonetheless, a few free blacks managed to prosper within slave society. William Johnson, a Natchez barber, acquired enough money to purchase a plantation with fifteen slaves; he hunted with upper-class whites and loaned them money. But he suffered from the legal disadvantages common to his race. He could not, for example, testify against his debtors in court when they failed to pay. In Virginia, the slaves freed and given land by the will of Richard Randolph (noted in Chapter 6) established a vibrant community they called Israel Hill. Despite the legal restrictions on free blacks in the state, they prospered as farmers and skilled craftsmen, and they learned to defend their rights in court, even winning lawsuits against whites who owed them money.

A portrait of a father, his daughters, and an elderly female slave, by the photographer Thomas Easterly, taken around 1850. It is unknown whether the man's wife had died or was simply not photographed.

THE UPPER AND LOWER SOUTH

Very few free blacks (around 37,000 persons, or less than 2 percent of the area's black population) lived in the Lower South in 1860. Like William Johnson, a majority of them resided in cities. Mississippi, an overwhelmingly rural state with no real urban centers, had fewer than 800 free blacks on the eve of the Civil War. In New Orleans and Charleston, on the other hand, relatively prosperous free black communities developed, mostly composed of mixed-race descendants of unions between

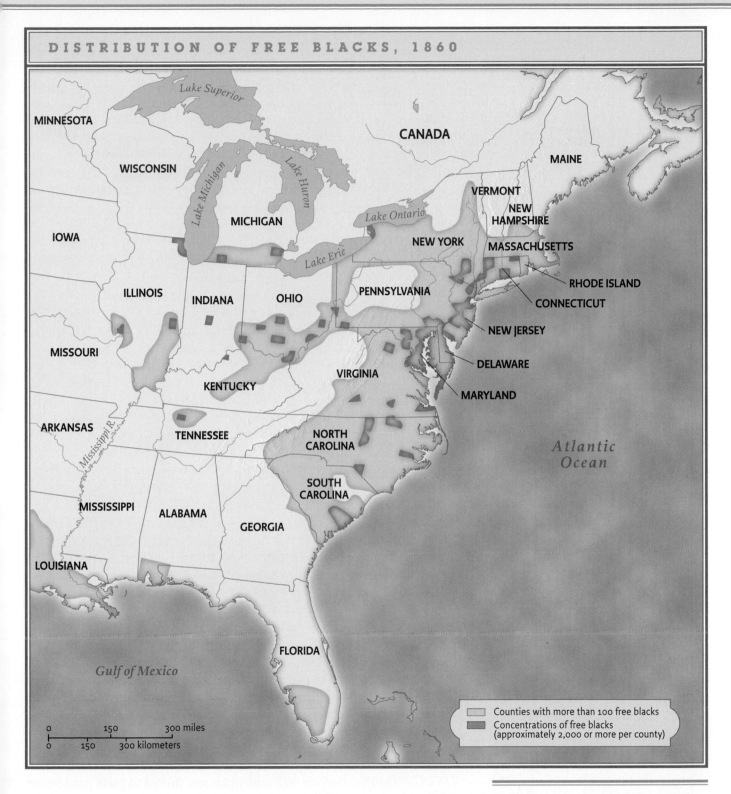

DISTRIBUTION OF FREE BLACKS, 1860

Counts with more than 100 free blacks
Concentrations of free blacks
(approximately 2,000 or more per county)

white men and slave women. Some became truly wealthy—Antoine Dubuclet of Louisiana, for example, owned 100 slaves. Many free blacks in these cities acquired an education and worked as skilled craftsmen such as tailors, carpenters, and mechanics. They established churches for their communities and schools for their children. Some New Orleans free blacks

The nation's population in 1860 included nearly 500,000 free blacks. The majority lived in the slave states, especially Maryland and Virginia.

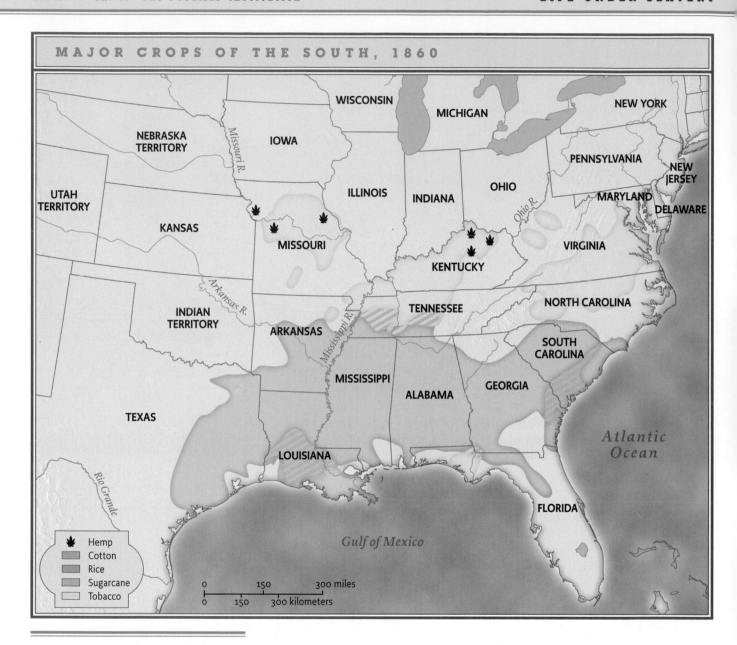

MAJOR CROPS OF THE SOUTH, 1860

Legend:
- Hemp
- Cotton
- Rice
- Sugarcane
- Tobacco

Cotton was the major agricultural crop of the South, and, indeed, the nation, but slaves also grew rice, sugarcane, tobacco, and hemp.

sent their children to France for an education. These elite free blacks did everything they could to maintain a separation from the slave population. The Brown Fellowship Society of Charleston, for example, would not even allow dark-skinned free men to join. Even in these cities, however, most free blacks were poor unskilled laborers.

In the Upper South, where the large majority of southern free blacks lived, they generally worked for wages as farm laborers. Here, where tobacco had exhausted the soil, many planters shifted to grain production, which required less year-round labor. They sold off many slaves to the Lower South and freed others. By 1860, half the African-American population of Maryland was free. Planters hired local free blacks to work alongside their slaves at harvest time. Free blacks in Virginia and Maryland were closely tied to the slave community and often had relatives in bondage.

Some owned slaves, but usually these were free men who had purchased their slave wives and children but could not liberate them because the law required any slave who became free to leave the state. Overall, in the words of Willis A. Hodges, a member of a free Virginia family that helped runaways to reach the North, free blacks and slaves were "one man of sorrow."

SLAVE LABOR

First and foremost, slavery was a system of labor; "from sunup to first dark," with only brief interruptions for meals, work occupied most of the slaves' time. Large plantations were diversified communities, where slaves performed all kinds of work. The 125 slaves on one plantation, for instance, included a butler, two waitresses, a nurse, a dairymaid, a gardener, ten carpenters, and two shoemakers. Other plantations counted among their slaves engineers, blacksmiths, and weavers, as well as domestic workers from cooks to coachmen.

Slaves cut wood to provide fuel for steamboats, worked in iron and coal mines, manned the docks in southern seaports, and laid railroad track. They were set to work by local authorities to construct and repair bridges, roads, and other facilities and by the federal government to build forts and other public buildings in the South. Businessmen, merchants, lawyers, and civil servants owned slaves, and by 1860 some 200,000 worked in industry, especially in the ironworks and tobacco factories of the Upper South. In southern cities, thousands were employed as unskilled laborers and skilled artisans. Reliance on unfree labor, moreover, extended well beyond the ranks of slaveholders, for, as noted earlier, many small farmers and manufacturers rented slaves from plantation owners. A few owners gave trusted slaves extensive responsibilities. Simon Gray's owner made him the head of a riverboat crew on the Mississippi. Gray supervised both white and slave workers, sold his owner's lumber at urban markets, and handled large sums of money.

GANG LABOR AND TASK LABOR

Gray's experience, of course, was hardly typical. The large majority of slaves—75 percent of women and nearly 90 percent of men, according to one study—worked in the fields. The precise organization of their labor varied according to the crop and the size of the holding. On small farms, the owner often toiled side-by-side with his slaves. The largest concentration of slaves, however, lived and worked on plantations in the Cotton Belt, where men, women, and children labored in gangs, often under the

A female slave drying cotton on a plantation in the South Carolina Sea Islands, 1862. Slave men, women, and children all worked in the cotton fields.

In this undated photograph, men, women, and children pick cotton under the watchful eye of an overseer. Unlike sugar cane, cotton does not grow to a great height, allowing an overseer to supervise a large number of slaves.

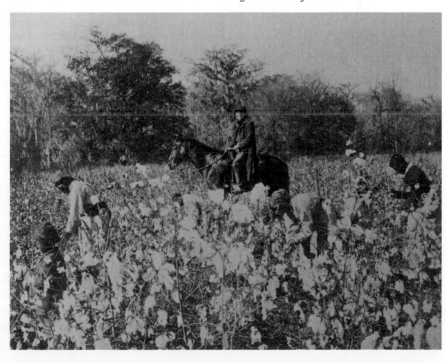

direction of an overseer and perhaps a slave "driver" who assisted him. Among slaves, overseers had a reputation for meting out harsh treatment. "The requisite qualifications for an overseer," wrote Solomon Northup, a free black who spent twelve years in slavery after being kidnapped from the North, "are utter heartlessness, brutality, and cruelty. It is his business to produce large crops, no matter [what the] cost."

The 150,000 slaves who worked in the sugar fields of southern Louisiana also labored in large gangs. Conditions here were among the harshest in the South, for the late fall harvest season required round-the-clock labor to cut and process the sugarcane before it spoiled. On the rice plantations of South Carolina and Georgia, the system of task labor, which had originated in the colonial era, prevailed. With few whites willing to venture into the malaria-infested swamps, slaves were assigned daily tasks and allowed to set their own pace of work. Once a slave's task had been completed, he or she could spend the rest of the day hunting, fishing, or cultivating garden crops.

SLAVERY IN THE CITIES

From the slaves' point of view, slavery in the different regions of the South could be "worse" in some respects and "better" in others. Slaves in the rice fields, for example, endured harsh working conditions but enjoyed more independence than other rural slaves because of the task system of labor and the absence of a large resident white population. Skilled urban craftsmen also enjoyed considerable autonomy. Most city slaves were servants, cooks, and other domestic laborers. But owners sometimes allowed those with craft skills to "hire their own time." This meant that they could make work arrangements individually with employers, with most of the wages going to the slave's owner. Many urban slaves even lived on their own. But slaveholders increasingly became convinced that, as one wrote, the growing independence of skilled urban slaves "exerts a most injurious influence upon the relation of master and servant." For this reason, many owners in the 1850s sold city slaves to the countryside and sought replacements among skilled white labor.

During his time in Baltimore, Frederick Douglass "sought my own employment, made my own contracts, and collected my own earnings." Compared to conditions on the plantation, he concluded, "I was really well off." Douglass hastened to add, however, that his favored treatment in no way lessened his desire for freedom—"it was *slavery*, not its mere incidents, that I hated."

MAINTAINING ORDER

Slaveowners employed a variety of means in their attempt to maintain order and discipline among their human property and persuade them to labor productively. At base, the system rested on force. Masters had almost complete discretion in inflicting punishment, and rare was the slave who went through his or her life without experiencing a whipping. Josiah Henson, who escaped to the North and published an autobiography, wrote that he could never erase from his memory the traumatic experience of seeing his father brutally whipped for striking a white man. Any infraction of plantation rules, no matter how minor, could be punished by the lash. One Georgia planter recorded in his journal that he had whipped a slave "for not bringing over milk for my coffee, being compelled to take it without."

Subtler means of control supplemented violence. Owners encouraged and exploited divisions among the slaves, especially between field hands and house servants. They created systems of incentives that rewarded good work with time off or even money payments. One Virginia slaveholder gave his slaves ten cents per day for good work and reported that this made them labor "with as much steadiness and cheerfulness as whites," thereby "saving all the expense of overseers." Probably the most powerful weapon wielded by slaveowners was the threat of sale, which separated slaves from their immediate families and from the communities that, despite overwhelming odds, African-Americans created on plantations throughout the South.

A Public Whipping of Slaves in Lexington, Missouri, in 1856, *an illustration from the abolitionist publication* The Suppressed Book about Slavery. *Whipping was a common form of punishment for slaves.*

SLAVE CULTURE

Slaves never abandoned their desire for freedom or their determination to resist total white control over their lives. In the face of grim realities, they succeeded in forging a semi-independent culture, centered on the family and church. This enabled them to survive the experience of bondage without surrendering their self-esteem and to pass from generation to generation a set of ideas and values fundamentally at odds with those of their masters.

Slave culture drew on the African heritage. African influences were evident in the slaves' music and dances, style of religious worship, and the use of herbs by slave healers to combat disease. (Given the primitive nature of professional medical treatment, some whites sought out slave healers instead of trained physicians.) Unlike the plantation regions of the Caribbean and Brazil, where the African slave trade continued into the

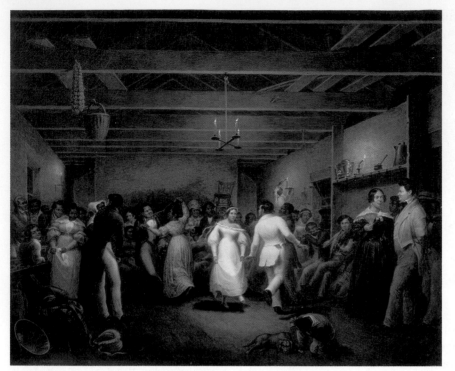

Kitchen Ball at White Sulphur Springs, Virginia, *an 1838 painting by the German-born American artist Christian Mayr. Fashionably dressed domestic slaves celebrate the wedding of a couple, dressed in white at the center.*

nineteenth century and the black population far outnumbered the white, most slaves in the United States were American-born and lived amidst a white majority. Slave culture was a new creation, shaped by African traditions and American values and experiences.

THE SLAVE FAMILY

At the center of the slave community stood the family. On the sugar plantations of the West Indies, the number of males far exceeded that of females, the workers lived in barracks-type buildings, and settled family life was nearly impossible. The United States, where the slave population grew from natural increase rather than continued importation from Africa, had an even male-female ratio, making the creation of families far more possible. To be sure, the law did not recognize the legality of slave marriages. The master had to consent before a man and woman could "jump over the broomstick" (the slaves' marriage ceremony), and families stood in constant danger of being broken up by sale.

Nonetheless, most adult slaves married, and their unions, when not disrupted by sale, typically lasted for a lifetime. To solidify a sense of family continuity, slaves frequently named children after cousins, uncles, grandparents, and other relatives. Nor did the slave family simply mirror kinship patterns among whites. Slaves, for example, did not marry first cousins, a practice common among white southerners. Most slaves lived in two-parent families. But because of constant sales, the slave community had a significantly higher number of female-headed households than among whites, as well as families in which grand-parents, other relatives, or even non-kin assumed responsibility for raising children.

THE THREAT OF SALE

As noted above, the threat of sale, which disrupted family ties, was perhaps the most powerful disciplinary weapon slaveholders possessed. As the domestic slave trade expanded with the rise of the Cotton Kingdom, about one slave marriage in three in slave-selling states like Virginia was broken by sale. Many children were separated from their parents by sale. According to one estimate, at least 10 percent of the teenage slaves in the Upper South were sold in the interstate slave trade. Fear of sale permeated slave life, especially in the Upper South. "Mother, is Massa going to sell us tomorrow?" ran a line in a popular slave song. As a reflection of their paternalist responsibilities, some owners encouraged slaves to marry. Others, however, remained unaware of their slaves' family connections, and their interest in slave children was generally limited to the childrens' ability to work in the fields. The federal census broke down the white population by five-year age categories, but it divided slaves only once, at age ten, the point at which they became old enough to enter the plantation labor force.

Slave traders gave little attention to preserving family ties. A public notice, "Sale of Slaves and Stock," announced the 1852 auction of property belonging to a recently deceased Georgia planter. It listed thirty-six individuals ranging from an infant to a sixty-nine-year old woman and ended with the proviso: "Slaves will be sold separate, or in lots, as best suits the purchaser." Sales like this were a human tragedy. "My dear wife," a Georgia slave wrote in 1858, "I take the pleasure of writing you these few [lines] with much regret to inform you that I am sold. . . . Give my love to my father and mother and tell them good bye for me, and if we shall not meet in this world I hope to meet in heaven. My dear wife for you and my children my pen cannot express the grief I feel to be parted from you all."

GENDER ROLES AMONG SLAVES

In some ways, gender roles under slavery differed markedly from those in the larger society. Slave men and women experienced, in a sense, the equality of powerlessness. The nineteenth century's "cult of domesticity," which defined the home as a woman's proper sphere, did not apply to slave women, who regularly worked in the fields. Slave men could not act as the economic providers for their families. Nor could they protect their wives from physical or sexual abuse by owners and overseers (a frequent occurrence on many plantations) or determine when and under what conditions their children worked.

Sale of Slaves and Stock.

The Negroes and Stock listed below, are a Prime Lot, and belong to the ESTATE OF THE LATE LUTHER McGOWAN, and will be sold on Monday, Sept. 22nd, 1852, at the Fair Grounds, in Savannah, Georgia, at 1:00 P. M. The Negroes will be taken to the grounds two days previous to the Sale, so that they may be inspected by prospective buyers.

On account of the low prices listed below, they will be sold for cash only, and must be taken into custody within two hours after sale.

No.	Name.	Age.	Remarks.	Price.
1	Lunesta	27	Prime Rice Planter,	$1,275.00
2	Violet	16	Housework and Nursemaid,	900.00
3	Lizzie	30	Rice, Unsound,	300.00
4	Minda	27	Cotton, Prime Woman,	1,200.00
5	Adam	28	Cotton, Prime Young Man,	1,100.00
6	Abel	41	Rice Hand, Eyesight Poor,	675.00
7	Tanney	22	Prime Cotton Hand,	950.00
8	Flementina	39	Good Cook, Stiff Knee,	400.00
9	Lanney	34	Prime Cottom Man,	1,000.00
10	Sally	10	Handy in Kitchen,	675.00
11	Maccabey	35	Prime Man, Fair Carpenter,	980.00
12	Dorcas Judy	25	Seamstress, Handy in House,	800.00
13	Happy	60	Blacksmith,	575.00
14	Mowden	15	Prime Cotton Boy,	700.00
15	Bills	21	Handy with Mules,	900.00
16	Theopolis	39	Rice Hand, Gets Fits,	575.00
17	Coolidge	29	Rice Hand and Blacksmith,	1,275.00
18	Bessie	69	Infirm, Sews,	250.00
19	Infant	1	Strong Likely Boy	400.00
20	Samson	41	Prime Man, Good with Stock,	975.00
21	Callie May	27	Prime Woman, Rice,	1,000.00
22	Honey	14	Prime Girl, Hearing Poor,	850.00
23	Angelina	16	Prime Girl, House or Field,	1,000.00
24	Virgil	21	Prime Field Hand,	1,100.00
25	Tom	40	Rice Hand, Lame Leg,	750.00
26	Noble	11	Handy Boy,	900.00
27	Judge Lesh	55	Prime Blacksmith,	800.00
28	Booster	43	Fair Mason, Unsound,	600.00
29	Big Kate	37	Housekeeper and Nurse,	950.00
30	Melie Ann	19	Housework, Smart Yellow Girl,	1,250.00
31	Deacon	26	Prime Rice Hand,	1,000.00
32	Coming	19	Prime Cotton Hand,	1,000.00
33	Mabel	47	Prime Cotton Hand,	800.00
34	Uncle Tim	60	Fair Hand with Mules,	600.00
35	Abe	27	Prime Cotton Hand,	1,000.00
36	Tennes	29	Prime Rice Hand and Cocahman,	1,250.00

There will also be offered at this sale, twenty head of Horses and Mules with harness, along with thirty head of Prime Cattle. Slaves will be sold separate, or in lots, as best suits the purchaser. Sale will be held rain or shine.

A broadside advertising the public sale of slaves, along with horses, mules, and cattle, after the death of their owner. The advertisement notes that the slaves will be sold individually or in groups "as best suits the purchaser," an indication that families were likely to be broken up. The prices are based on each slave's sex, age, and skill.

Virginian Luxuries. *Originally painted on the back panel of a formal portrait, this image illustrates two "luxuries" of a Virginia slaveowner—the power to sexually abuse slave women and to whip slaves.*

When slaves worked "on their own time," however, more conventional gender roles prevailed. Slave men chopped wood, hunted, and fished, while women washed, sewed, and assumed primary responsibility for the care of children. Some planters allowed their slaves small plots of land on which to grow food to supplement the rations provided by the owner; women usually took charge of these "garden plots." But whatever its internal arrangements, the family was central to the slave community, allowing for the transmission of values, traditions, and survival strategies—in a word, of slave culture—from one generation to the next.

SLAVE RELIGION

A distinctive version of Christianity also offered solace to slaves in the face of hardship and hope for liberation from bondage. Some blacks, free and slave, had taken part in the Great Awakening of the colonial era, and even more were swept into the South's Baptist and Methodist churches during the religious revivals of the late eighteenth and early nineteenth centuries. As one preacher recalled of the great camp meeting that drew thousands of worshipers to Cane Ridge, Kentucky, in 1801, no distinctions were made "as to age, sex, color, or anything of a temporary nature; old and young, male and female, black and white, had equal privilege to minister the light which they received, in whatever way the Spirit directed."

Even though the law prohibited slaves from gathering without a white person present, every plantation, it seemed, had its own black preacher. Usually the preacher was a "self-called" slave who possessed little or no formal education but whose rhetorical abilities and familiarity with the Bible made him one of the most respected members of the slave community. Especially in southern cities, slaves also worshiped in biracial congregations with white ministers, where they generally were required to sit in the back pews or in the balcony. Urban free blacks established their own churches, sometimes attended by slaves.

A black preacher, as portrayed in Harper's Weekly, *February 2, 1867. Although engraved after the Civil War, the scene is the same as religious services under slavery.*

PRAYER MEETING

To masters, Christianity offered another means of social control. Many required slaves to attend services conducted by white ministers, who preached that theft was immoral and that the Bible required servants to obey their masters. One slave later recalled being told in a white minister's sermon "how good God was in bringing us over to this country from dark and benighted Africa, and permitting us to listen to the sound of the gospel." Several slaves walked out of the service during a sermon by Charles C. Jones stressing that God had commanded servants to obey their masters and that they should not try to run away. One man came up to Jones at the end and said, "the doctrine is *one-sided.*"

THE GOSPEL OF FREEDOM

The slaves transformed the Christianity they had embraced, turning it to their own purposes. A blend of African traditions and Christian belief, slave religion was practiced in secret nighttime gatherings on plantations and in "praise meetings" replete with shouts, dances, and frequent emotional interchanges between the preacher and the congregation. One former slave later recalled typical secret religious gatherings: "We used to slip off into the woods in the old slave days on Sunday evening way down in the swamps to sing and pray to our own liking. We prayed for this day of freedom."

The biblical story of Exodus, in which God chose Moses to lead the enslaved Jews of Egypt into a promised land of freedom, played a central role in black Christianity. Slaves identified themselves as a chosen people, whom God in the fullness of time would deliver from bondage. At the same time, the figure of Jesus Christ represented to slaves a personal redeemer, one who truly cared for the oppressed. Slaves found other heroes and symbols in the Bible as well: Jonah, who overcame hard luck and escaped from the belly of a whale; David, who vanquished the more powerful Goliath; and Daniel, who escaped from the lion's den. And the Christian message of brotherhood and the equality of all souls before the Creator, in the slaves' eyes, offered an irrefutable indictment of the institution of slavery.

THE DESIRE FOR LIBERTY

If their masters developed an elaborate ideology defending the South's "peculiar institution," slave culture rested on a conviction of the unjustness of bondage and the desire for freedom. "Nobody," the British political philosopher Edmund Burke had written during the American Revolution, "will be argued into slavery." Frederick Douglass called the proslavery argument "flimsy nonsense," which men would be "ashamed to remember" once slavery had been abolished. Whatever proslavery writers asserted and ministers preached, blacks thought of themselves as a working people unjustly deprived of the fruits of their labor by idle planters who lived in luxury. "We bake the bread / they give us the crust," said a line from one slave song.

Most slaves fully understood the impossibility of directly confronting the system. Their folk tales had no figures equivalent to Paul Bunyan, the powerful, larger-than-life backwoodsman popular in white folklore. Slaves' folklore, such as the Brer Rabbit stories, glorified the weak hare who out-witted stronger foes like the bear and fox, rather than challenging them directly. Their religious songs, or spirituals, spoke of lives of sorrow ("I've been 'buked and I've been scorned"), while holding out hope for ultimate liberation ("Didn't my Lord deliver Daniel?"). When they sang, "I'm bound for the land of Canaan," slaves meant not only relief from worldly woes in an afterlife but also escaping to the North or, in God's good time, witnessing the breaking of slavery's chains.

"Freedom," declared a black minister after emancipation, "burned in the black heart long before freedom was born." A fugitive who reached the North later recalled that the "desire for freedom" was the "constant theme" of conversations in the slave quarters. Even the most ignorant slave, observed Solomon Northup, could not "fail to observe the difference between their own condition and the meanest white man's, and to realize the injustice of laws which place it within [the owner's] power not only to appropriate the profits of their industry, but to subject them to unmediated and unprovoked punishment without remedy."

The world of most rural slaves was bounded by their local communities and kin. They became extremely familiar with the local landscape, crops, and population, but had little knowledge of the larger world. Nonetheless, slaves could not remain indifferent to the currents of thought unleashed by the American Revolution or to the language of freedom in the society around them. "I am in a land of liberty," wrote Joseph Taper, a Virginia slave who escaped to Canada around 1840. "Here man is as God intended he should be . . . not like the southern laws which put man, made in the image of God, on level with brutes." The social and political agenda African-Americans would put forward in the Reconstruction era that followed emancipation—stressing civil and political equality, the strengthening of the black community, and autonomy in their working lives—flowed directly out of their experience in slavery.

RESISTANCE TO SLAVERY

Confronted with federal, state, and local authorities committed to preserving slavery, and outnumbered within the South as a whole by the white population, slaves could only rarely express their desire for freedom by outright rebellion. Compared to Brazil and the West Indies, which experienced numerous uprisings, involving hundreds or even thousands of slaves, revolts in the United States were smaller and less frequent. There was no parallel, of course, to the successful slave revolution in Haiti discussed in Chapter 8 or to the unsuccessful 1831 rebellion in Jamaica that appears to have involved as many as 20,000 slaves. This does not, however, mean that slaves in the United States placidly accepted the system under which they were compelled to live. Resistance to slavery took many forms in the Old South, from individual acts of defiance to occasional uprisings. These actions posed a constant challenge to the slaveholders' self-image as benign paternalists and their belief that slaves were obedient subjects grateful for their owners' care.

FORMS OF RESISTANCE

The most widespread expression of hostility to slavery was "day-to-day resistance" or "silent sabotage"—doing poor work, breaking tools, abusing animals, and in other ways disrupting the plantation routine. Frederick Law Olmsted, a northerner who toured the South in the 1850s, took note of "gates left open, rails removed from fences by the negroes, mules lamed and implements broken, a flat boat set adrift in the river, men ordered to cart rails for a new fence, depositing them so that a double expense of labor would be required to lay them." Many slaves made believe that they were ill to avoid work (although almost no slaves reported themselves sick on Sunday, their only day of rest). Then there was the theft of food, a form of resistance so common that one southern physician diagnosed it as a hereditary disease unique to blacks. Less frequent, but more dangerous, were serious crimes committed by slaves, including arson, poisoning, and armed assaults against individual whites.

FUGITIVE SLAVES

Even more threatening to the stability of the slave system was running away. Formidable obstacles confronted the prospective fugitive. As Solomon Northup recalled, "Every white man's hand is raised against him, the patrollers are watching for him, the hounds are ready to follow in his track." Slaves had little or no knowledge of geography, apart from understanding that following the north star led to freedom. No one knows how many slaves succeeded in reaching the North or Canada—the most common rough estimate is around 1,000 per year. Not surprisingly, most of those who succeeded lived, like Frederick Douglass, in the Upper South, especially Maryland, Virginia, and Kentucky, which bordered on the free states. Douglass, who escaped at age twenty, was also typical in that the large majority of fugitives were young men. Most slave women were not willing to leave children behind, and to take them along on the arduous escape journey was nearly impossible.

In the Deep South, fugitives tended to head for cities like New Orleans or Charleston, where they hoped to lose themselves in the free black community. Other escapees fled to remote areas like the Great Dismal Swamp of Virginia or the Florida Everglades, where the Seminole Indians offered refuge before they were forced to move west. Even in Tennessee, a study of newspaper advertisements for runaways finds that around 40 percent were thought to have remained in the local neighborhood, 30 percent to have headed to other locations in the South, while only 25 percent tried to reach the North.

The Underground Railroad, a loose organization of sympathetic abolitionists who hid fugitives in their homes and sent them on to the next "station," assisted some runaway slaves. A few courageous individuals made forays into the South to liberate slaves. The best known was Harriet Tubman. Born in Maryland in 1820, Tubman escaped to Philadelphia in 1849 and during the next decade risked her life by making some twenty trips back to her state of birth to lead relatives and other slaves to freedom. But

100 DOLLARS
REWARD.

Ranaway from the subscriber, on Monday June 15, a negro woman NELLY FORREST. She is about 45 years old, chunky built, large pouting mouth, good teeth, high cheek bones, walks pigeon-toed. She is slow in giving a direct answer when questioned; her manner of speaking is rather grum.

She has a free husband living on Capitol Hill, Washington City, near Sims' old rope walk, named Henson Forrest. I will give the above reward no matter where taken, so I get her again.

F. M. BOWIE,
Long Old Fields,
Prince George's County, Md.
July 6, 1857.

A typical broadside offering a reward for the capture of a runaway slave.

most who managed to reach the North did so on their own initiative, sometimes showing remarkable ingenuity. William and Ellen Craft impersonated a sickly owner traveling with her slave. Henry "Box" Brown packed himself inside a crate and literally had himself shipped from Georgia to freedom in the North.

THE *AMISTAD*

In a few instances, large groups of slaves collectively seized their freedom. The most celebrated instance involved fifty-three slaves who in 1839 took control of the *Amistad*, a ship transporting them from one port in Cuba to another, and tried to force the navigator to steer it to Africa. The *Amistad* wended its way up the Atlantic coast, until an American vessel seized it off the coast of Long Island. President Martin Van Buren favored returning the slaves to Cuba. But abolitionists brought their case to the Supreme Court, where former president John Quincy Adams argued that since they had been recently brought from Africa in violation of international treaties banning the slave trade, the captives should be freed. The Court accepted Adams's reasoning, and most of the captives made their way back to Africa.

The *Amistad* case had no legal bearing on slaves within the United States. But it may well have inspired a similar uprising in 1841, when 135 slaves being transported by sea from Norfolk, Virginia, to New Orleans seized control of the ship *Creole* and sailed for Nassau in the British Bahamas. Their leader had the evocative name Madison Washington. To the dismay of the Tyler administration, the British gave refuge to the *Creole* slaves.

SLAVE REVOLTS

Resistance to slavery occasionally moved beyond such individual and group acts of defiance to outright rebellion. The four largest conspiracies in American history occurred within the space of thirty-one years in the early nineteenth century. The first, organized by the Virginia slave Gabriel in 1800, was discussed in Chapter 8. It was followed eleven years later by an uprising on sugar plantations upriver from New Orleans. Somewhere between 200 and 500 men and women, armed with sugarcane knives, axes, clubs, and a few guns, marched toward the city, destroying property as they proceeded. The white population along the route fled in panic to New Orleans. Within two days, the militia and regular army troops met the rebels and dispersed them in a pitched battle, killing sixty-six. Soon afterwards, the principal leaders were executed. Captured

A lithograph depicting Joseph Cinqué, leader of the slave revolt on the Spanish ship Amistad *off the coast of Cuba in 1839. The ship was eventually seized near Long Island. After a long legal battle, the Supreme Court allowed the slaves to return to Africa.*

rebels offered little explanation for their revolt other than the desire, as one put it, "to kill the white." But they seem to have been inspired by the recent success of the slave revolution in Haiti.

The next major conspiracy was organized in 1822 by Denmark Vesey, a slave carpenter in Charleston, South Carolina, who had purchased his freedom after winning a local lottery. An outspoken, charismatic leader, Vesey rebuked blacks who stepped off the city's sidewalks to allow whites to pass and took a leading role in the local African Methodist Church. His conspiracy reflected the combination of American and African influences then circulating in the Atlantic world and coming together in black culture. "He studied the Bible a great deal," recalled one of his followers, "and tried to prove from it that slavery and bondage is against the Bible." Vesey also quoted the Declaration of Independence, pored over newspaper reports of the debates in Congress regarding the Missouri Compromise, and made pronouncements like "all men had equal rights, blacks as well as whites." And he read to his co-conspirators accounts of the successful slave revolution in Haiti. The African heritage was present in the person of Vesey's lieutenant Gullah Jack, a religious "conjurer" from Angola who claimed to be able to protect the rebels against injury or death. The plot was discovered before it could reach fruition.

As in the case of many slave conspiracies, evidence about the Vesey plot is contradictory and disputed. Much of it comes from a series of trials in which the court operated in secret and failed to allow the accused to confront those who testified against them. South Carolina's governor, Thomas Bennett Jr., a number of whose slaves were among the accused, complained to Robert Y. Hayne, the state's attorney general, that the court proceedings violated "the rules which universally obtain among civilized nations." Hayne replied that to try a "free white man" under such circumstances would clearly violate his fundamental rights. But, he added, "slaves are not entitled to these rights," since "all the provisions of our constitution in favor of liberty are intended for freemen only." In the end, thirty-five slaves and free blacks, among them Vesey and three slaves belonging to the governor, were executed and an equal number banished from the state.

NAT TURNER'S REBELLION

The best known of all slave rebels was Nat Turner, a slave preacher and religious mystic in Southampton County, Virginia, who came to believe that God had chosen him to lead a black uprising. Turner traveled widely in the county conducting religious services. He told of seeing black and white angels fighting in the sky and the heavens running red with blood. Perhaps from a sense of irony, Turner initially chose July 4, 1831, for his rebellion only to fall ill on the appointed day. On August 22, he and a handful of followers marched from farm to farm assaulting the white inhabitants. Most of their victims were women and children, for many of the area's men were attending a religious revival across the border in North Carolina. By the time the militia put down the uprising, about eighty slaves had joined Turner's band, and some sixty whites had been killed. Turner was subsequently captured and, with seventeen other rebels, condemned to die. Asked before his execution whether he regretted what he had done, Turner responded, "Was not Christ crucified?"

An engraving depicting Nat Turner's slave rebellion of 1831, from a book published soon after the revolt.

Nat Turner's was the last large-scale rebellion in southern history. Like Gabriel's and Vesey's conspiracies, Turner's took place outside the heart of the plantation South, where slavery was most rigidly policed. Because Turner began with only a handful of followers, he faced less chance of discovery or betrayal than Gabriel or Vesey. Nonetheless, his revolt demonstrated conclusively that in a region where whites outnumbered blacks and the white community was armed and united, slaves stood at a fatal disadvantage in any violent encounter. Only an outside force could alter the balance of power within the South. Slave resistance, however, hardly disappeared. Turner's uprising, in fact, demonstrated the connection between outright rebellion and less dramatic forms of resistance. For in its aftermath, numerous reports circulated of "insubordinate" behavior by slaves on Virginia's farms and plantations.

Turner's rebellion sent shock waves through the entire South. "A Nat Turner," one white Virginian warned, "might be in any family." In the panic that followed the revolt, hundreds of innocent slaves were whipped and scores executed. For one last time, Virginia's leaders openly debated whether steps ought to be taken to do away with the "peculiar institution." "The blood of Turner and his innocent victims," declared a Richmond newspaper, "has opened the doors which have been shut for fifty years." But a proposal to commit the state to gradual emancipation and the removal of the black population from the state failed to win legislative approval. The measure gained overwhelming support in the western part of Virginia, where slaves represented less than 10 percent of the population, but it failed to win sufficient votes in the eastern counties where slavery was centered.

Instead of moving toward emancipation, the Virginia legislature of 1832 decided to fasten even more tightly the chains of bondage. New laws prohibited blacks, free or slave, from acting as preachers (a measure that proved impossible to enforce), strengthened the militia and patrol systems, banned free blacks from owning firearms, and prohibited teaching slaves to read. Other southern states followed suit. In the debate's aftermath, Thomas R. Dew, a professor at the College of William and Mary in Virginia, published an influential pamphlet pointing to the absurdity of deporting the bulk of the state's labor force. The state, he insisted, faced a stark choice—retain slavery, or free the slaves and absorb them into Virginia society. Few critics of slavery were willing to accept the latter alternative.

In some ways, 1831 marked a turning point for the Old South. In that year, Parliament launched a program for abolishing slavery throughout the British empire (a process completed in 1838), underscoring the South's growing isolation in the Western world. Turner's rebellion, following only a few months after the appearance in Boston of William Lloyd Garrison's abolitionist journal, *The Liberator* (discussed in the next chapter), suggested that American slavery faced enemies both within and outside the South. The proslavery argument increasingly permeated southern intellectual and political life, while dissenting opinions were suppressed. Some states made membership in an abolitionist society a criminal offense, while mobs drove critics of slavery from their homes. The South's "great reaction" produced one of the most thoroughgoing suppressions of freedom of speech in American history. Even as reform movements arose in the North that condemned slavery as contrary to Christianity and to basic American values, and national debate over the peculiar institution intensified, southern society closed in defense of slavery.

SUGGESTED READING

Aptheker, Herbert. *American Negro Slave Revolts* (1943). Still the fullest account of slave rebellions in the United States.

Berlin, Ira. *Slaves without Masters: The Free Negro in the Antebellum South* (1974). A careful study of the status of free blacks, stressing differences between the Upper and Lower South.

Clarke, Erskine. *Dwelling Place: A Plantation Epic* (2005). A detailed account of the lives of masters and slaves on the Jones family plantations in Georgia.

Clinton, Catherine. *The Plantation Mistress: Woman's World in the Old South* (1982). Explores how the institution of slavery affected the lives of planters' wives and daughters.

Ely, Melvin P. *Israel on the Appomattox: A Southern Experiment in Black Freedom from 1790s through the Civil War* (2004). Relates the experience of free blacks freed by Richard Randolph in Virginia and the community they created.

Genovese, Eugene D. *Roll, Jordan, Roll: The World the Slaves Made* (1974). A classic study of the paternalist ethos and the culture that developed under slavery.

Gutman, Herbert G. *The Black Family in Slavery and Freedom* (1976). A pioneering examination of how slaves created and sustained families under the harsh conditions of slavery.

Johnson, Walter. *Soul by Soul: Life inside the Antebellum Slave Market* (1999). Considers the operations of the New Orleans slave market as a window into slavery as a whole.

Joyner, Charles D. *Down by the Riverside: A South Carolina Slave Community* (1984). Studies slave communities in coastal South Carolina, emphasizing the blend of African and American influences.

Kolchin, Peter. *American Slavery, 1619–1877* (rev. ed., 2003). A careful, up-to-date survey of the history of slavery in North America from its beginning through emancipation.

McCurry, Stephanie. *Masters of Small Worlds: Yeoman Households, Gender Relations, and the Political Culture of Antebellum South Carolina* (1995). Studies the lives of men and women in non-slaveholding families, to explore their links with the planter class.

O'Brien, Michael. *Conjectures of Order: Intellectual Life and the American South* (2004). A comprehensive study of intellectual life in the Old South.

Stevenson, Brenda. *Life in Black and White: Family and Community in the Slave South* (1996). Focusing on Virginia, an examination of how slaves adapted to the rise of the interstate slave trade.

Wade, Richard. *Slavery in the Cities: The South, 1820–1860* (1964). An examination of slavery in southern cities, and growing white fears of lack of control of the urban slave population.

Wright, Gavin. *The Political Economy of the Cotton South: Households, Markets, and Wealth in the Nineteenth Century* (1978). Presents the economic development and structure of the cotton South, by a prominent economic historian.

CHAPTER REVIEW

 Study and Review at wwnorton.com/studyspace

REVIEW QUESTIONS

1. Given that by 1860 the economic investment represented by the slave population exceeded the value of the nation's factories, railroads, and banks combined, explain how important slavery was to the national economy and the emergence of the United States as a great power.

2. Describe slave culture, explaining the similarities and differences among various regions.

3. Why did many white southerners support slavery even when they did not actually own any slaves?

4. What meanings of freedom were most important to the slaves?

5. What forms of slave resistance were practiced in the American South?

KEY TERMS

slavery and the economy (p. 396)

cost of slaves (p. 398)

proslavery argument (p. 401)

free black slaveowners (p. 407)

slaves in industry (p. 411)

African religious beliefs (p. 417)

runaways (p. 419)

REVIEW TABLE

Slave Rebellions

Rebellion	Date	Result
Gabriel's Rebellion	1800	Virginia prohibits blacks from congregating on Sundays without white supervision and restricts masters voluntarily freeing their slaves
Denmark Vesey's conspiracy	1822	Vesey is executed in South Carolina
Nat Turner's Rebellion	1831	The only large-scale rebellion in the South, it causes Virginia to further tighten its grip on slavery
Amistad	1839	Slaves aboard the ship win their freedom

Chapter 12

An Age of Reform, 1820–1840

Made only a few years after the Seneca Falls Convention of 1848, this quilt includes scenes illustrating some of the demands of the early women's rights movement. The individual images include a woman driving her own buggy with a banner advocating "woman rights," another dressing to go out while her husband remains at home wearing an apron, and a third addressing a public meeting.

• What were the major expressions of the antebellum reform impulse?

• What were the sources and significance of abolitionism?

• How did abolitionism challenge barriers to racial equality and free speech?

• What were the sources and significance of the antebellum women's rights movement?

Among the many Americans who devoted their lives to the crusade against slavery, few were as selfless or courageous as Abby Kelley. Born in Massachusetts in 1811, she was educated at a Quaker boarding school in Rhode Island. As a teacher in Lynn, Massachusetts, she joined the Female Anti-Slavery Society and, like thousands of other northern women, threw herself into the abolitionist movement. In 1838, Kelley began to give public speeches about slavery. Her first lecture outside of Lynn was literally a baptism of fire. Enraged by reports that abolitionists favored "amalgamation" of the races—that is, sexual relations between whites and blacks—residents of Philadelphia stormed the meeting hall and burned it to the ground.

For two decades, Kelley traveled throughout the North, speaking almost daily in churches, public halls, and antislavery homes on "the holy cause of human rights." Her career illustrated the interconnections of the era's reform movements. In addition to abolitionism, she was active in pacifist organizations—which opposed the use of force, including war, to settle disputes—and was a pioneer in the early struggle for women's rights. "In striving to strike [the slave's] irons off," she wrote, women "found most surely that we were manacled ourselves." Kelley was not the first American woman to speak in public. But she covered more miles and gave more speeches than any other female orator. She forthrightly challenged her era's assumption that woman's "place" was in the home. More than any other individual, remarked Lucy Stone, another women's rights advocate, Kelley "earned for us all the right of free speech."

Abby Kelley's private life was as unconventional as her public career. She enjoyed a long and happy marriage to Stephen S. Foster, a strong-willed abolitionist given to interrupting Sunday sermons to denounce ministers who failed to condemn slavery. She gave birth to a daughter in 1847 but soon returned to lecturing. When criticized for not devoting herself to the care of her infant, Kelley replied: "I have done it for the sake of the mothers whose babies are sold away from them. The most precious legacy I can leave my child is a free country."

THE REFORM IMPULSE

In the history of the world," wrote Ralph Waldo Emerson in 1841, "the doctrine of reform has never such hope as at the present hour." Abolitionism was only one of the era's numerous efforts to improve American society. During his visit in the early 1830s, Alexis de Tocqueville noted how in the absence of a powerful national government, Americans' political and social activities were organized through voluntary associations—

churches, fraternal orders, political clubs, and the like. The reform impulse was part of this proliferation of voluntary groups. Americans established organizations that worked to prevent the manufacture and sale of liquor, end public entertainments and the delivery of the mail on Sunday, improve conditions in prisons, expand public education, uplift the condition of wage laborers, and reorganize society on the basis of cooperation rather than competitive individualism.

Nearly all these groups worked to convert public opinion to their cause. They sent out speakers, gathered signatures on petitions, and published pamphlets. Like Abby Kelley, many reformers were active in more than one crusade. Some reform movements, like restraining the consumption of liquor and alleviating the plight of the blind and insane, flourished throughout the nation. Others, including women's rights, labor unionism, and educational reform, were weak or nonexistent in the South, where they were widely associated with antislavery sentiment. Reform was an international crusade. Peace, temperance, women's rights, and antislavery advocates regularly crisscrossed the Atlantic to promote their cause.

A rare photograph of an abolitionist meeting in New York State around 1850. The woman at the center wearing a bonnet may be Abby Kelley. Frederick Douglass sits immediately to her right.

Reformers adopted a wide variety of tactics to bring about social change. Some relied on "moral suasion" to convert people to their cause. Others, like opponents of the "demon rum," sought to use the power of the government to force sinners to change their ways. Some reformers decided to withdraw altogether from the larger society and establish their own cooperative settlements. They hoped to change American life by creating "heavens on earth," where they could demonstrate by example the superiority of a collective way of life. Reformers never amounted to anything like a majority of the population, even in the North, but they had a profound impact on both politics and society.

UTOPIAN COMMUNITIES

About 100 reform communities were established in the decades before the Civil War. Historians call them "utopian" after Thomas More's sixteenth-century novel *Utopia*, an outline of a perfect society. (The word has also come to imply that such plans are impractical and impossible to realize.) These communities differed greatly in structure and motivation. Some were subject to the iron discipline of a single leader, while others operated in a democratic fashion. Most arose from religious conviction, but others were inspired by the secular desire to counteract the social and economic changes set in motion by the market revolution.

Nearly all the communities set out to reorganize society on a cooperative basis, hoping to restore social harmony to a world of excessive individualism and to narrow the widening gap between rich and poor. Through their efforts, the words "socialism" and "communism," meaning a social organization in which productive property is owned by the community rather

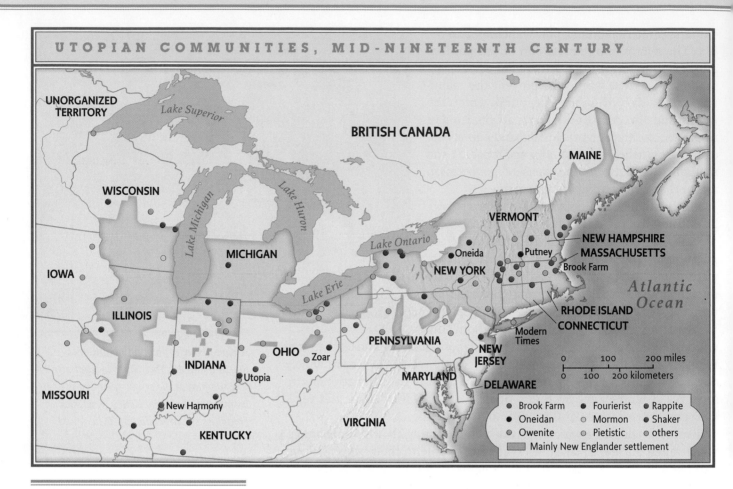

UTOPIAN COMMUNITIES, MID-NINETEENTH CENTURY

In the first half of the nineteenth century, dozens of utopian communities were established in the United States, where small groups of men and women attempted to establish a more perfect social order within the larger society.

than private individuals, entered the language of politics. Most utopian communities also tried to find substitutes for conventional gender relations and marriage patterns. Some prohibited sexual relations between men and women altogether; others allowed them to change partners at will. But nearly all insisted that the abolition of private property must be accompanied by an end to men's "property" in women.

THE SHAKERS

Religious communities attracted those who sought to find a retreat from a society permeated by sin, "a refuge from the evils of this Sodom," as the founders of Zoar, in Ohio, put it. But the Shakers, the most successful of the religious communities, also had a significant impact on the outside world. At their peak during the 1840s, cooperative Shaker settlements, which stretched from Maine to Kentucky, included over 5,000 members. The Shakers were founded in the late eighteenth century by Mother Ann Lee, the daughter of an English blacksmith who became a religious exhorter and claimed that Christ had directed her to emigrate with her followers to America. The first Shaker community was established in upstate New York in 1787.

God, the Shakers believed, had a "dual" personality, both male and female, and thus the two sexes were spiritually equal. Their work was deemed equally important (although each man was assigned a "sister" to take care of his washing and sewing). "Virgin purity" formed a pillar of the Shakers' faith. They completely abandoned traditional family life. Men and women lived separately in large dormitory-like structures and ate in communal dining rooms. Their numbers grew by attracting converts and adopting children from orphanages, rather than through natural increase. Numerous outsiders visited Shaker communities to observe the religious services that gave the group its name, in which men and women, separated by sex, engaged in frenzied dancing. Although they rejected the individual accumulation of private property, the Shakers proved remarkably successful economically. They were among the first to market vegetable and flower seeds and herbal medicines commercially and to breed cattle for profit. Their beautifully crafted furniture is still widely admired today.

This watercolor depicting a Shaker dance was drawn by Benson Lossing, an artist who visited a Shaker community and reported on life there for Harper's Magazine *in 1857.*

ONEIDA

Another influential community was Oneida, founded in 1848 in upstate New York by John Humphrey Noyes, the Vermont-born son of a U.S. congressman. After graduating from Dartmouth College, Noyes briefly studied law but soon experienced a conversion at a religious revival and decided to become a minister. Noyes took the revivalists' message that man could achieve moral perfection to an atypical extreme. He preached that he and his followers had become so perfect that they had achieved a state of complete "purity of heart," or sinlessness.

In 1836, Noyes and his followers formed a small community in Putney, Vermont. Like the Shakers, Noyes did away with private property and abandoned traditional marriage. But in contrast to Shaker celibacy, he taught that all members of his community formed a single "holy family" of equals. His community became notorious for what Noyes called "complex marriage," whereby any man could propose sexual relations to any woman, who had the right to reject or accept his invitation, which would then be registered in a public record book. The great danger was "exclusive affections," which, Noyes felt, destroyed the harmony of the community.

After being indicted for adultery by local officials, Noyes in 1848 moved his community to Oneida, where it survived until 1881. Oneida was an extremely dictatorial environment. To become a member of the community, one had to demonstrate command of Noyes's religious teachings and live according to his rules. Members carefully observed each other's conduct and publicly criticized those who violated Noyes's regulations. By the 1860s, a committee was even determining which couples would be permitted to have children—an early example of "eugenics," as the effort to improve the human race by regulating reproduction came to be known.

The Crisis, *a publication by the communitarian Robert Owen and his son, Robert Dale Owen. The cover depicts Owen's vision of a planned socialist community.*

WORLDLY COMMUNITIES

To outside observers, utopian communities like Oneida seemed a case of "voluntary slavery." But because of their members' selfless devotion to the teachings and rules laid down by their leader, spiritually oriented communities often achieved remarkable longevity. The Shakers survived well into the twentieth century. Communities with a more worldly orientation tended to be beset by internal divisions and therefore lasted for much shorter periods.

In 1841, New England transcendentalists established Brook Farm not far from Boston, where they hoped to demonstrate that manual and intellectual labor could coexist harmoniously. They modeled the community in part on the ideas of the French social reformer Charles Fourier, who envisioned communal living and working arrangements, while retaining private property. Fourier's blueprint for "phalanxes," as he called his settlements, planned everything to the last detail, from the number of residents (2,000) to how much income would be generated by charging admission to sightseers. With leisure time devoted to music, dancing, dramatic readings, and intellectual discussion, Brook Farm was like an exciting miniature university. But it attracted mostly writers, teachers, and ministers, some of whom disliked farm labor. The novelist Nathaniel Hawthorne, a resident for a time, complained about having to shovel manure. Brook Farm disbanded after a few years, and Hawthorne offered a skeptical view of life there in his 1852 novel *The Blithedale Romance.*

THE OWENITES

The most important secular communitarian (meaning a person who plans or lives in a cooperative community) was Robert Owen, a British factory owner. Appalled by the degradation of workers in the early industrial revolution, Owen created a model factory village at New Lanark, Scotland, which combined strict rules of work discipline with comfortable housing and free public education. Around 1815, its 1,500 employees made New Lanark the largest center of cotton manufacturing in the world. Convinced that the "rich and the poor, the governors and the governed, have really but one interest," Owen promoted communitarianism as a peaceful means of ensuring that workers received the full value of their labor. In 1824, he purchased the Harmony community in Indiana—originally founded by the German Protestant religious leader George Rapp, who had emigrated to America with his followers at the beginning of the nineteenth century. Here, Owen established New Harmony, where he hoped to create a "new moral world."

"The character of man is, without a single exception, always formed for him," Owen declared. Individuals could be transformed by changing the circumstances in which they lived. In Owen's scheme, children would be removed at an early age from the care of their parents to be educated in schools where they would be trained to subordinate individual ambition to the common good. Owen also defended women's rights, especially access to education and the right to divorce. At New Harmony, he promised, women would no longer be "enslaved" to their husbands, and "false notions" about innate differences between the sexes would be abandoned.

Harmony eluded the residents of New Harmony. They squabbled about everything from the community's constitution to the distribution of property. Owen's settlement survived for only a few years, but it strongly influenced the labor movement, educational reformers, and women's rights advocates. Owen's vision resonated with the widely held American belief that a community of equals could be created in the New World.

Quite different from Owen's planned system were the short-lived secular communities founded by Josiah Warren, an early American anarchist (one who believes that all institutions that exercise power over individuals, including government, are illegitimate). At Utopia, Ohio, and Modern Times, New York, Warren established totally unregulated voluntary settlements. Like other communitarians, Warren tried to address the sources of labor unrest and women's inequality. In an attempt to solve the labor problem, he created stores where goods were exchanged according to the amount of work that had gone into producing them, thus preventing middlemen like bankers and merchants from sharing in the hard-earned income of farmers, laborers, and manufacturers. Marriage in Warren's communities was a purely voluntary arrangement, since no laws regulated personal behavior. In effect, Warren took American individualism to its logical extreme. Freedom, he declared, meant "allowing each individual to be absolute despot or sovereign" over himself.

RELIGION AND REFORM

Most Americans saw the ownership of property as the key to economic independence—and, therefore, to freedom—and marriage as the foundation of the social order. Few were likely to join communities that required them to surrender both. Far more typical of the reform impulse were movements that aimed at liberating men and women either from restraints external to themselves, such as slavery and war, or from forms of internal "servitude" like drinking, illiteracy, and a tendency toward criminality. Drinkers, proclaimed one reformer, could not be considered free: they were "chained to alcohol, bound to the demon rum." Many of these reform movements drew their inspiration from the religious revivalism of the Second Great Awakening, discussed in Chapter 9. If, as the revivalist preachers maintained, God had created man as a "free moral agent," sinners could not only reform themselves but could also remake the world.

The revivals popularized the outlook known as "perfectionism," which saw both individuals and society at large as capable of indefinite improvement. Regions like upstate New York and northern Ohio became known as "burned-over districts" because of the intense revivals they experienced in the 1820s and 1830s. Such areas became fertile soil for the era's reform movements and their vision of a society freed from sin. Under the impact of the revivals, older reform efforts moved in a new, radical direction. Temperance (which literally means moderation in the consumption of liquor) was transformed into a crusade to eliminate drinking entirely. Criticism of war became outright pacifism. And, as will be related below, critics of slavery now demanded not gradual emancipation but immediate and total abolition.

The Drunkard's Progress, *an 1826 anti-liquor broadside illustrating how drinking leads a respectable man and his family to ruin.*

THE TEMPERANCE MOVEMENT

To members of the North's emerging middle-class culture, reform became a badge of respectability, an indication that individuals had taken control of their own lives and had become morally accountable human beings. The American Temperance Society, founded in 1826, directed its efforts to redeeming not only habitual drunkards but also the occasional drinker. It claimed by the 1830s to have persuaded hundreds of thousands of Americans to renounce liquor. By 1840, the consumption of alcohol per person had fallen to less than half the level of a decade earlier. (It had peaked in 1830 at seven gallons per person per year, compared to around two gallons today.) During the 1840s, the Washingtonian Society gathered reformed drinkers in "experience meetings" where they offered public testimony about their previous sins.

The temperance crusade and other reform movements aroused considerable hostility. One person's sin is another's pleasure or cherished custom. Those Americans who enjoyed Sunday recreation or a stiff drink from time to time did not think they were any less moral than those who had been reborn at a religious camp meeting, abandoned drinking, and devoted the Sabbath to religious observances.

CRITICS OF REFORM

Many Americans saw the reform impulse as an attack on their own freedom. Drinking was a prominent feature of festive celebrations and events like militia gatherings. As in the colonial era, taverns were popular meeting places for workingmen in early-nineteenth-century towns and cities, sites not only of drinking but also of political discussions, organizational meetings, and popular recreations. A "Liberty Loving Citizen" of Worcester, Massachusetts, wondered what gave one group of citizens the right to dictate to others how to conduct their personal lives.

American Catholics, their numbers growing because of Irish and German immigration, proved hostile to the reform impulse. Catholics understood freedom in ways quite different from Protestant reformers. They viewed sin as an inescapable burden of individuals and society. The perfectionist idea that evil could be banished from the world struck them as an affront to genuine religion, and they bitterly opposed what they saw as reformers' efforts to impose their own version of Protestant morality on their neighbors. While reformers spoke of man as a free moral agent, Catholics tended to place less emphasis on individual independence and more on the importance of communities centered on family and church. "Man," declared Archbishop John Hughes of New York, the nation's most prominent Catholic leader, was not an autonomous creature but "by his nature, a being of society."

REFORMERS AND FREEDOM

Reformers had to reconcile their desire to create moral order and their quest to enhance personal freedom. They did this through a vision of freedom that was liberating and controlling at the same time. On the one hand, reformers insisted that their goal was to enable Americans to enjoy genuine liberty. In a world in which personal freedom increasingly meant the opportunity to compete for economic gain and individual self-improvement, they spoke of liberating Americans from various forms of "slavery" that made it impossible to succeed—slavery to drink, to poverty, to sin.

On the other hand, reformers insisted that self-fulfillment came through self-discipline. Their definition of the free individual was the

A temperance banner from around 1850 depicts a young man torn between a woman in white, who illustrates female purity, and a temptress, who offers him a drink of liquor.

A German Beer Garden on Sunday Evening, *an engraving from* Harper's Weekly, *October 15, 1858. German and Irish immigrants resented efforts of temperance reformers to prohibit the sale of alcoholic beverages.*

person who internalized the practice of self-control. Philip Schaff, a German minister who emigrated to Pennsylvania in 1843, wrote that "true national freedom, in the American view," was "anything but an absence of restraint." Rather, it "rests upon a moral groundwork, upon the virtue of self-possession and self-control in individual citizens." In some ways, reformers believed, American society suffered from an excess of liberty—the anarchic "natural liberty" John Winthrop had warned against in the early days of Puritan Massachusetts, as opposed to the "Christian liberty" of the morally upright citizen.

Many religious groups in the East worried that settlers in the West and immigrants from abroad lacked self-control and led lives of vice, exhibited by drinking, violations of the Sabbath, and lack of Protestant devotion. They formed the American Tract Society, the American Bible Society, and other groups that flooded eastern cities and the western frontier with copies of the gospel and pamphlets promoting religious virtue. Between 1825 and 1835, the pamphlets distributed by the Tract Society amounted to over 500 million pages. Both their understanding of freedom and their ability to take advantage of the new printing technologies influenced the era's reform movements.

THE INVENTION OF THE ASYLUM

The tension between liberation and control in the era's reform movements was vividly evident in the proliferation of new institutions that reformers hoped could remake human beings into free, morally upright citizens. In colonial America, crime had mostly been punished by whipping, fines, or banishment. The poor received relief in their own homes, orphans lived with neighbors, and families took care of mentally ill members.

During the 1830s and 1840s, Americans embarked on a program of institution building—jails for criminals, poorhouses for the destitute, asylums for the insane, and orphanages for children without families. These institutions differed in many respects, but they shared with communitarians and religious believers in "perfectionism" the idea that social ills once considered incurable could in fact be eliminated. The way to "cure" undesirable elements of society was to place afflicted persons and impressionable youths in an environment where their character could be transformed. Prisons and asylums would eventually become overcrowded places where rehabilitating the inmates seemed less important than simply holding them at bay, away from society. At the outset, however, these institutions were inspired by the conviction that those who passed through their doors

The New York House of Refuge, one of many institutions established in the 1820s and 1830s to address social ills by assisting and reforming criminals and the poor. Young boys and girls convicted of petty theft were assigned to the House of Refuge, where they performed supervised labor and received some educational instruction.

could eventually be released to become productive, self-disciplined citizens.

THE COMMON SCHOOL

The largest effort at institution building before the Civil War came in the movement to establish common schools, that is, tax-supported state school systems open to all children. In the early nineteenth century, most children were educated in locally supported schools, private academies, charity schools, or at home, and many had no access to learning at all. School reform reflected the numerous purposes that came together in the era's reform impulse. Horace Mann, a Massachusetts lawyer and Whig politician who served as director of the state's board of education, was the era's leading educational reformer. His annual reports, widely read throughout the country, combined conservatism and radicalism, liberation and social control.

This daguerreotype from around 1850 depicts a classroom in a school for girls presided over by a male teacher.

Mann embraced the new industrial order of his state. But he hoped that universal public education could restore equality to a fractured society by bringing the children of all classes together in a common learning experience and equipping the less fortunate to advance in the social scale. Education would "equalize the conditions of men"—in effect, it would serve as industrial society's alternative to moving west to acquire a farm. This view of free public education as an avenue to social advancement was also shared by the early labor movement, which made the establishment of common schools one of its goals. At the same time, Mann argued that the schools would reinforce social stability by rescuing students from the influence of parents who failed to instill the proper discipline. Character building was as important a function of education as reading, writing, and arithmetic. To some extent, the schools' "silent curriculum"—obedience to authority, promptness in attendance, organizing one's day according to predetermined time periods that changed at the ringing of a bell—helped to prepare students for work in the new industrial economy.

The schools, Mann believed, were training free individuals—meaning persons who internalized self-discipline. But he encountered persistent opposition from parents who did not wish to surrender the moral education of their children to teachers and bureaucrats. Nonetheless, with labor organizations, factory owners, and middle-class reformers all supporting the idea, every northern state by 1860 had established tax-supported school systems for its children. The common school movement created the first real career opportunity for women, who quickly came to dominate the ranks of teachers. The South, where literate blacks were increasingly viewed as a danger to social order and planters had no desire to tax themselves to pay for education for poor white children, lagged far behind in public education. This was one of many ways in which North and South seemed to be growing apart.

THE CRUSADE AGAINST SLAVERY

Compared with drinking, Sabbath-breaking, and illiteracy, the greatest evil in American society at first appeared to attract the least attention from reformers. For many years, it seemed that the only Americans willing to challenge the existence of slavery were Quakers, slaves, and free blacks. After the antislavery impulse spawned by the Revolution died out, the slavery question faded from national life, with occasional eruptions like the Missouri controversy of 1819–1821.

COLONIZATION

Before the 1830s, those white Americans willing to contemplate an end to bondage almost always coupled calls for abolition with the "colonization" of freed slaves—their deportation to Africa, the Caribbean, or Central America. In 1816, proponents of this idea founded the American Colonization Society, which promoted the gradual abolition of slavery and the settlement of black Americans in Africa. It soon established Liberia on the coast of West Africa, an outpost of American influence whose capital, Monrovia, was named for President James Monroe.

Colonization struck many observers as totally impractical. When the English writer Harriet Martineau visited the United States in the 1830s, she was amazed that former president James Madison endorsed the idea. "How such a mind as his" could be convinced that slavery would not end unless blacks were deported from the country she could not understand. In her account of her travels, *Society in America* (1837), she called colonization a way in which "slave-owners who had scruples about holding men as property might, by sending their slaves away over sea, relieve their consciences without annoying their neighbors."

Nonetheless, numerous prominent political leaders of the Jacksonian era—including Henry Clay, John Marshall, Daniel Webster, and Jackson himself—supported the Colonization Society. Many northerners saw colonization as the only way to rid the nation of slavery. Southern supporters of colonization devoted most of their energy to persuading those African-Americans who were already free to leave the United States. Free blacks, they insisted, were a "degraded" group whose presence posed a danger to white society. Other colonizationists believed that slavery and racism were so deeply embedded in American life, that blacks could never achieve equality if freed and allowed to remain in the country. Like Indian removal, colonization rested on the premise that America is fundamentally a white society.

BLACKS AND COLONIZATION

In the decades before the Civil War, several thousand black Americans did emigrate to Liberia with the aid of the Colonization Society. Some were slaves emancipated by their owners on the condition that they depart, while others left voluntarily, motivated by a desire to spread Christianity in Africa or to enjoy rights denied them in the United States. Having experienced "the legal slavery of the South and the social slavery of the North," wrote one emigrant on leaving for Liberia, he knew he could "never be a free man in this country."

But most African-Americans adamantly opposed the idea of colonization. In fact, the formation of the American Colonization Society galvanized free blacks to claim their rights as Americans. Early in 1817, some 3,000 free blacks assembled in Philadelphia for the first national black convention. Their resolutions insisted that blacks were Americans, entitled to the same freedom and rights enjoyed by whites. "We have no wish to separate from our present homes," they declared. In the years that followed, a number of black organizations removed the word "African" from their names to eliminate a possible reason for being deported from the land of their birth.

MILITANT ABOLITIONISM

The abolitionist movement that arose in the 1830s differed profoundly from its genteel, conservative predecessor. Drawing on the religious conviction that slavery was an unparalleled sin and the secular one that it contradicted the values enshrined in the Declaration of Independence, a new generation of reformers rejected the traditional approach of gradual emancipation and demanded immediate abolition. Also unlike their predecessors, they directed explosive language against slavery and slaveholders and insisted that blacks, once free, should be incorporated as equal citizens of the republic rather than being deported. Perfecting American society, they insisted, meant rooting out not just slavery, but racism in all its forms.

The first indication of the new spirit of abolitionism came in 1829 with the appearance of *An Appeal to the Coloured Citizens of the World* by David Walker, a free black who had been born in North Carolina and now operated a used-clothing store in Boston. A passionate indictment of slavery and racial prejudice, the *Appeal* called on black Americans to mobilize for abolition—by force if necessary—and warned whites that the nation faced divine punishment if it did not mend its sinful ways. Walker invoked the Bible and the Declaration of Independence, but he went beyond these familiar arguments to call on blacks to take pride in the achievements of ancient African civilizations and to claim all their rights as Americans. "Tell us no more about colonization," Walker wrote, addressing white readers, "for America is as much our country as it is yours."

THE EMERGENCE OF GARRISON

Walker's language alarmed both slaveholders and many white critics of slavery. When free black sailors secretly distributed the pamphlet in the South, some southern states put a price on Walker's head. Walker, however, did not create an abolitionist organization, and he died in mysterious circumstances in 1830. Not until the appearance in 1831 of *The Liberator*, William Lloyd Garrison's weekly journal published in Boston, did the new breed of abolitionism find a permanent voice. "I will be as harsh as truth," Garrison announced, "and as uncompromising as justice. On this subject, I do not wish to think, or speak, or write, with moderation. . . . I will not

William Lloyd Garrison, editor of The Liberator *and probably the nation's most prominent abolitionist, in a daguerreotype from around 1850.*

The masthead of William Lloyd Garrison's The Liberator, *with engravings of scenes of slavery and freedom.*

equivocate—I will not excuse—I will not retreat a single inch—and I will be heard."

And heard he was, partly because southerners, outraged by his inflammatory rhetoric (one editorial called slaveowners "an adulterous and perverse generation, a brood of vipers"), reprinted Garrison's editorials in their own newspapers in order to condemn them, thus providing him with instant notoriety. Some of Garrison's ideas, such as his suggestion that the North abrogate the Constitution and dissolve the Union to end its complicity in the evil of slavery, were rejected by many abolitionists. But his call for the immediate abolition of slavery echoed throughout antislavery circles. Garrison's pamphlet, *Thoughts on African Colonization*, persuaded many foes of slavery that blacks must be recognized as part of American society, not viewed as aliens to be shipped overseas. Other antislavery publications soon emerged, but *The Liberator* remained the preeminent abolitionist journal.

SPREADING THE ABOLITIONIST MESSAGE

Beginning with a handful of activists, the abolitionist movement expanded rapidly throughout the North. Antislavery leaders took advantage of the rapid development of print technology and the expansion of literacy thanks to common school education to spread their message. Like radical pamphleteers of the American Revolution and evangelical ministers of the Second Great Awakening, they recognized the democratic potential in the production of printed material. Abolitionists seized upon the recently invented steam press to produce millions of copies of pamphlets, newspapers, petitions, novels, and broadsides. Between the formation of the American Anti-Slavery Society in 1833 and the end of the decade, some 100,000 northerners joined local groups devoted to abolition. Most were ordinary citizens—farmers, shopkeepers, craftsmen, laborers, along with a few prominent businessmen like the merchants Arthur and Lewis Tappan of New York.

If Garrison was the movement's most notable propagandist, Theodore Weld, a young minister who had been converted by the evangelical preacher Charles G. Finney, helped to create its mass constituency. A brilliant orator, Weld trained a band of speakers who brought the abolitionist message into the heart of the rural and small-town North. Their methods

A is an Abolitionist—
A man who wants to free
The wretched slave—and give to all
An equal liberty.

B is a Brother with a skin
Of somewhat darker hue,
But in our Heavenly Father's sight,
He is as dear as you.

C is the Cotton-field, to which
This injured brother's driven,
When, as the white man's *slave*, he toils
From early morn till even.

D is the Driver, cold and stern,
Who follows, whip in hand,
To punish those who dare to rest,
Or disobey command.

Pages from an abolitionist book for children. Abolitionists sought to convince young and old of the evils of slavery.

were those of the revivals—fervent preaching, lengthy meetings, calls for individuals to renounce their immoral ways—and their message was a simple one: slavery was a sin. "In discussing the subject of slavery," wrote Weld, "I have always presented it as preeminently a moral question, arresting the conscience of the nation. As a question of politics and national economy, I have passed it with scarce a look or a word."

There was far more to Weld's moralistic approach than a concern for religious righteousness. Identifying slavery as a sin was essential to replacing the traditional strategies of gradual emancipation and colonization with immediate abolition. The only proper response to the sin of slavery, abolitionist speakers proclaimed, was the institution's immediate elimination. Weld also supervised the publication of abolitionist pamphlets including his own *Slavery As It Is* (1839), a compilation of accounts of the maltreatment of slaves. Since Weld took all his examples from the southern press, they could not be dismissed as figments of the northern imagination.

SLAVERY AND MORAL SUASION

Many southerners feared that the abolitionists intended to spark a slave insurrection, a belief strengthened by the outbreak of Nat Turner's rebellion a few months after *The Liberator* made its appearance. Yet not only was Garrison completely unknown to Turner, but nearly all abolitionists, despite their militant language, rejected violence as a means of ending slavery. Many were pacifists or "non-resistants," who believed that coercion should be eliminated from all human relationships and institutions. Their strategy was "moral suasion" and their arena the public sphere. Slaveholders must be convinced of the sinfulness of their ways, and the North of its complicity in the peculiar institution. (Some critics charged that this approach left nothing for the slaves to do in seeking their own liberation but await the nation's moral regeneration.)

Standing outside established institutions, abolitionists adopted the role of radical social critics. Among the first to appreciate the key role of public opinion in a mass democracy, they focused their efforts not on infiltrating the existing political parties, but on awakening the nation to the moral evil of slavery. Their language was deliberately provocative, calculated to seize public attention. "Slavery," said Garrison, "will not be overthrown without excitement, without a most tremendous excitement."

ABOLITIONISTS AND THE IDEA OF FREEDOM

The abolitionist crusade both reinforced and challenged common understandings of freedom in Jacksonian America. Abolitionists helped to popularize the concept, fortified by the market revolution, that personal freedom derived not from the ownership of productive property such as land but from ownership of one's self and the ability to enjoy the fruits of one's labor. Abolitionists repudiated the idea of "wage slavery," which had been popularized by the era's labor movement. Compared with the slave, the person working for wages, they insisted, was an embodiment of freedom: the free laborer could change jobs if he wished, accumulate property, and enjoy a stable family life. Only slavery, wrote the abolitionist William Goodell, deprived human beings of their "grand central right—the inherent right of self-ownership."

On the other hand, abolitionists argued that slavery was so deeply embedded in American life that its destruction would require fundamental changes in the North as well as the South. They insisted that the inherent, natural, and absolute right to personal liberty, regardless of race, took precedence over other forms of freedom, such as the right of citizens to accumulate and hold property or self-government by local political communities.

A NEW VISION OF AMERICA

In a society in which the rights of citizenship had become more and more closely associated with whiteness, the antislavery movement sought to reinvigorate the idea of freedom as a truly universal entitlement. The origins of the idea of an American people unbounded by race lies not with the founders, who by and large made their peace with slavery, but with the abolitionists. The antislavery crusade viewed slaves and free blacks as members of the national community, a position summarized in the title of Lydia Maria Child's popular treatise of 1833, *An Appeal in Favor of That Class of Americans Called Africans.* Child's text insisted that blacks were fellow countrymen, not foreigners or a permanently inferior caste. They should no more be considered Africans than whites were Englishmen. The idea that birthplace alone, not race, should determine who was an American, later enshrined in the Fourteenth Amendment, represented a radical departure from the traditions of American life. "We do not admit," declared the *New England Magazine* in 1832, "that America is as much the country of the blacks, bound and free, as it is ours." But abolitionists maintained that

An abolitionist banner. Antislavery organizations adopted the Liberty Bell as a symbol of their campaign to extend freedom to black Americans. Previously, the bell, forged in Philadelphia in the eighteenth century, had simply been known as the Old State House Bell.

Slave Market of America, an engraving produced by the American Anti-Slavery Society in 1836, illustrates how abolitionists sought to identify their cause with American traditions, even as they mocked the nation's claim to be a "land of the free."

the slaves, once freed, should be empowered to participate fully in the public life of the United States.

The crusade against slavery, wrote Angelina Grimké, who became a leading abolitionist speaker, was the nation's preeminent "school in which human rights are . . . investigated." Abolitionists debated the Constitution's relationship to slavery. William Lloyd Garrison burned the document, calling it a covenant with the devil; Frederick Douglass came to believe that it offered no national protection to slavery. But despite this difference of opinion, abolitionists developed an alternative, rights-oriented view of constitutional law, grounded in their universalistic understanding of liberty. Seeking to define the core rights to which all Americans were entitled—the meaning of freedom in concrete legal terms—abolitionists invented the concept of equality before the law regardless of race, one all but unknown in American life before the Civil War. Abolitionist literature also helped to expand the definition of cruelty. The graphic descriptions of the beatings, brandings, and other physical sufferings of the slaves helped to popularize the idea of bodily integrity as a basic right that slavery violated.

Despite being denounced by their opponents as enemies of American principles, abolitionists consciously identified their movement with the revolutionary heritage. The Declaration of Independence was not as fundamental to public oratory in the early republic as it would later become. Abolitionists seized upon it, interpreting the document's preamble as a condemnation of slavery. The Liberty Bell, later one of the nation's most venerated emblems of freedom, did not achieve that status until abolitionists adopted it as a symbol and gave it its name, as part of an effort to identify their principles with those of the founders. (Prior to the 1830s, it was simply the Old State House Bell, used at various times to mark the death of prominent citizens, summon students at the University of Pennsylvania to their classes, and celebrate patriotic holidays.) Of course, Americans of all regions and political beliefs claimed the Revolution's legacy. Mobs that disrupted abolitionist meetings invoked the "spirit of '76," as did southern defenders of slavery. Abolitionists never represented more than a small

PERILOUS ESCAPE OF ELIZA AND CHILD.

One of many popular lithographs illustrating scenes from Harriet Beecher Stowe's novel Uncle Tom's Cabin, *the most widely read of all antislavery writings. This depicts the slave Eliza escaping with her child across the ice floes of the Ohio River.*

part of the North's population. But as the slavery controversy intensified, the belief spread far beyond abolitionist circles that slavery contradicted the nation's heritage of freedom.

BLACK AND WHITE ABOLITIONISM

BLACK ABOLITIONISTS

Blacks played a leading role in the antislavery movement. Even before the appearance of *The Liberator*, as we have seen, northern free blacks had organized in opposition to the Colonization Society. James Forten, a successful black sailmaker in Philadelphia, helped to finance *The Liberator* in its early years. As late as 1834, northern blacks, attracted by Garrison's rejection of colonization and his demand for equal rights for black Americans, made up a majority of the journal's subscribers. Several blacks served on the board of directors of the American Anti-Slavery Society, and northern-born blacks and fugitive slaves quickly emerged as major organizers and speakers.

Frederick Douglass was only one among many former slaves who published accounts of their lives in bondage; these accounts convinced thousands of northerners of the evils of slavery. Indeed, the most effective piece of antislavery literature of the entire period, Harriet Beecher Stowe's novel *Uncle Tom's Cabin*, was to some extent modeled on the autobiography of fugitive slave Josiah Henson. Serialized in 1851 in a Washington antislavery newspaper and published as a book the following year, *Uncle Tom's Cabin* sold over 1 million copies by 1854, and it also inspired numerous stage versions. By portraying slaves as sympathetic men and women, Christians at the mercy of slaveholders who split up families and set bloodhounds on innocent mothers and children, Stowe's melodrama gave the abolitionist message a powerful human appeal.

ABOLITIONISM AND RACE

The first racially integrated social movement in American history and the first to give equal rights for blacks a central place in its political agenda, abolitionism was nonetheless a product of its time and place. Racism, as we have seen, was pervasive in nineteenth-century America, North as well as South. White abolitionists could not free themselves entirely from this prejudice. They monopolized the key decision-making posts, charged black spokesman Martin R. Delany, relegating blacks to "a mere secondary, underling position." By the 1840s, black abolitionists sought an independent role within the movement, regularly holding their own conventions. The black abolitionist Henry Highland Garnet, who as a child had escaped from slavery in Maryland with his father, proclaimed at one such gathering in 1843 that slaves should rise in rebellion to throw off their shackles. His position was so at odds with the prevailing belief in moral suasion that the published proceedings entirely omitted the speech. Not until 1848 did Garnet's speech appear in print, along with David Walker's *Appeal*, in a pamphlet partially financed by a then-obscure abolitionist named John Brown.

The frontispiece of the 1848 edition of David Walker's Appeal *and Henry Highland Garnet's* Address to the Slaves *depicts a black figure receiving "liberty" and "justice" from heaven.*

What is remarkable, however, is not that white abolitionists reflected the prejudices of their society, but the extent to which they managed to rise above them. "While the word 'white' is on the statute-book of Massachusetts," declared Edmund Quincy, an active associate of William Lloyd Garrison, "Massachusetts is a slave state." Defying overwhelming odds, abolitionists launched legal and political battles against racial discrimination in the North. They achieved occasional victories, such as the end of school segregation in Massachusetts in 1855. Not only did abolitionists struggle to overturn northern laws discriminating against blacks but they refused to compromise the principle that the slave was a moral being, created in the image of God. The abolitionist emblem—a portrait of a slave in chains coupled with the motto, "Am I Not a Man and a Brother?"—challenged white Americans to face up to the reality that men and women no different from themselves were being held in bondage.

Most adamant in contending that the struggle against slavery required a redefinition of both freedom and Americanness were black members of the abolitionist crusade. Black abolitionists developed an understanding of freedom that went well beyond the usage of most of their white contemporaries. They worked to attack the intellectual foundations of racism, seeking to disprove pseudoscientific arguments for black inferiority. They challenged the prevailing image of Africa as a continent without civilization. Many black abolitionists called on free blacks to seek out skilled and dignified employment, to demonstrate the race's capacity for advancement.

An illustration from Types of Mankind, *an 1854 book by the physicians and racial theorists Josiah C. Nott and George R. Gliddon, who argued that blacks formed a separate species, midway between whites and chimpanzees. Abolitionists sought to counter the pseudoscientific defenses of slavery and racism.*

SLAVERY AND AMERICAN FREEDOM

At every opportunity, black abolitionists rejected the nation's pretensions as a land of liberty. Many free blacks dramatically reversed the common

Am I Not a Man and a Brother? *The most common abolitionist depiction of a slave, this image not only presents African-Americans as unthreatening individuals seeking white assistance but also calls upon white Americans to recognize blacks as fellow men unjustly held in bondage.*

association of the United States with the progress of freedom. Black communities in the North devised an alternative calendar of "freedom celebrations" centered on January 1, the date in 1808 on which the slave trade became illegal, and August 1, the anniversary of West Indian emancipation, rather than July 4. (Many localities forcibly barred them from Independence Day festivities.) In doing so, they offered a stinging rebuke to white Americans' claims to live in a land of freedom. Thanks to its embrace of emancipation in the 1830s, declared a group of black abolitionists in Philadelphia, Britain had become a model of liberty and justice, while the United States remained a land of tyranny.

Even more persistently than their white counterparts, black abolitionists articulated the ideal of color-blind citizenship. "The real battleground between liberty and slavery," wrote Samuel Cornish, "is prejudice against color." (Cornish, a Presbyterian minister, had helped to establish the nation's first black newspaper, *Freedom's Journal*, in New York City in 1827. The first editor, John B. Russwurm, closed the paper after two years and moved to Liberia, explaining, "we consider it a waste of mere words to talk of ever enjoying citizenship in this country.") Black abolitionists also identified the widespread poverty of the free black population as a consequence of slavery and insisted that freedom possessed an economic dimension. It must be part of the "great work" of the antislavery crusade, insisted Charles L. Reason, "to abolish not only chattel slavery, but that other kind of slavery, which, for generation after generation, dooms an oppressed people to a condition of dependence and pauperism."

The greatest oration on American slavery and American freedom was delivered in Rochester in 1852 by Frederick Douglass. Speaking just after the annual Independence Day celebration, Douglass posed the question, "What, to the Slave, is the Fourth of July?" (see the Voices of Freedom box, p. 453, for excerpts from the speech). He answered that Fourth of July festivities revealed the hypocrisy of a nation that proclaimed its belief in liberty yet daily committed "practices more shocking and bloody" than any other country on earth. Like other abolitionists, however, Douglass also laid claim to the founders' legacy. The Revolution had left a "rich inheritance of justice, liberty, prosperity, and independence," from which subsequent generations had tragically strayed. Only by abolishing slavery and freeing the "great doctrines" of the Declaration of Independence from the "narrow bounds" of race could the United States recapture its original mission.

GENTLEMEN OF PROPERTY AND STANDING

At first, abolitionism aroused violent hostility from northerners who feared that the movement threatened to disrupt the Union, interfere with profits wrested from slave labor, and overturn white supremacy. Led by "gentlemen of property and standing" (often merchants with close commercial ties to the South), mobs disrupted abolitionist meetings in northern cities. In 1835, a Boston crowd led William Lloyd Garrison through the streets with a rope around his neck. The editor barely escaped with his life. In the following year, a Cincinnati mob destroyed the printing press of James G. Birney, a former slaveholder who had been converted to abolitionism by Theodore Weld and had been forced to flee Kentucky for the North.

In 1837, antislavery editor Elijah P. Lovejoy became the movement's first martyr when he was killed by a mob in Alton, Illinois, while defending his press. A native of Maine and a Presbyterian minister, Lovejoy had begun his editorial career in the slave state of Missouri but had been soon forced to move to Illinois. His message, that "the system of Negro slavery is an awful evil and sin," won few converts in Alton, then the state's largest city, which enjoyed a flourishing trade with the South. Four times, mobs destroyed his printing press, only to see Lovejoy resume publication. The fifth attack ended in his death.

Elsewhere, crowds of southerners, with the unspoken approval of Andrew Jackson's postmaster general, Amos Kendall, burned abolitionist literature that they had removed from the mails. In 1836, when abolitionists began to flood Washington with petitions calling for emancipation in the nation's capital, the House of Representatives adopted the notorious "gag rule," which prohibited their consideration. The rule was repealed in 1844, thanks largely to the tireless opposition of former president John Quincy Adams, who since 1831 had represented Massachusetts in the House.

SLAVERY AND CIVIL LIBERTIES

Far from stemming the movement's growth, however, mob attacks and attempts to limit abolitionists' freedom of speech convinced many northerners that slavery was incompatible with the democratic liberties of white Americans. In a speech after Lovejoy's murder, Theodore Weld commented on the contrast between Americans' self-confident claims to freedom and the reality of anti-abolitionist violence: "The empty name is everywhere—*free* government, *free* men, *free* speech, *free* schools, and *free* churches. Hollow counterfeits all! . . . The substance has gone." It was the murder of

whites are killing whites

A broadside calling on "fellow citizens" to disrupt an 1837 lecture by "an abolitionist of the most revolting character."

A lithograph from an 1881 biography of Elijah P. Lovejoy shows the mob attack on the office of his newspaper, The Alton Observer, in 1837, which resulted in Lovejoy's death.

Lovejoy that led Wendell Phillips, who became one of the movement's greatest orators, to associate himself with the abolitionist cause. "We commenced the present struggle," announced abolitionist William Jay, "to obtain the freedom of the slave; we are compelled to continue it to preserve our own. We are now contending . . . for the liberty of speech, of the press, and of conscience."

The abolitionist movement now broadened its appeal so as to win the support of northerners who cared little about the rights of blacks but could be convinced that slavery endangered their own cherished freedoms. The gag rule aroused considerable resentment in the North. "If the government once begins to discriminate as to what is orthodox and what heterodox in opinion," wrote the *New York Evening Post*, hardly a supporter of abolitionism, "farewell, a long farewell to our freedom."

For many years, the American public sphere excluded discussion of slavery. Tocqueville had noted that in a democracy, individual dissenters found it difficult to stand up against the overwhelming power of majority opinion. Americans valued free speech, he wrote, but he did "not know any country where, in general, less independence of mind and genuine freedom of discussion reign than in America." The fight for the right to debate slavery openly and without reprisal led abolitionists to elevate "free opinion"—freedom of speech and of the press and the right of petition—to a central place in what Garrison called the "gospel of freedom." In defending free speech, abolitionists claimed to have become custodians of the "rights of every freeman."

THE ORIGINS OF FEMINISM

THE RISE OF THE PUBLIC WOMAN

"When the true history of the antislavery cause shall be written," Frederick Douglass later recalled, "women will occupy a large space in its pages." Much of the movement's grassroots strength derived from northern women, who joined by the thousands. Most were evangelical Protestants, New England Congregationalists, or Quakers convinced, as Martha Higginson of Vermont wrote, that slavery was "a disgrace in this land of Christian light and liberty." A few became famous, but most antislavery women remain virtually unknown to history. One such activist was Lucy Colman, whose mother sang her antislavery songs when she was a child. Colman's career illustrated how the era's reform movements often overlapped. She became an abolitionist lecturer, a teacher at a school for blacks in upstate New York, an advocate of women's rights, and an opponent of capital punishment.

The public sphere was open to women in ways government and party politics were not. Long before they could vote, women circulated petitions, attended meetings, marched in parades, and delivered public lectures. They became active in the temperance movement, the building of asylums, and other reform activities. Dorothea Dix, a Massachusetts schoolteacher, for example, was the leading advocate of more humane treatment of the insane, at the time generally placed in jails alongside debtors and hardened criminals. Thanks to her efforts, twenty-eight states constructed mental hospitals before the Civil War. In 1834, middle-class women in New York

City organized the Female Moral Reform Society, which sought to redeem prostitutes from lives of sin and to protect the morality of single women. They attacked the era's sexual double standard by publishing lists of men who frequented prostitutes or abused women. By 1840, the society had been replicated in hundreds of American communities.

WOMEN AND FREE SPEECH

All these activities enabled women to carve out a place in the public sphere. But it was participation in abolitionism that inspired the early movement for women's rights. In working for the rights of the slave, not a few women developed a new understanding of their own subordinate social and legal status. The daughters of a prominent South Carolina slave-holder, Angelina and Sarah Grimké had been converted first to Quakerism and then abolitionism while visiting Philadelphia. During the 1830s, they began to deliver popular lectures that offered a scathing condemnation of slavery from the perspective of those who had witnessed its evils firsthand.

The Grimké sisters were neither the first women to lecture in public nor the first to be feverishly condemned by self-proclaimed guardians of female modesty. Frances Wright, a Scottish-born follower of reformer Robert Owen, spoke at New York's Hall of Science in the late 1820s and early 1830s, on subjects ranging from communitarianism to slavery, women's rights, and the plight of northern laborers. One New York newspaper called Wright a "female monster" for "shamefully obtruding herself upon the public." Maria Stewart, a black Bostonian, in 1832 became the first American woman to lecture to mixed male and female audiences. She, too, received intense criticism. "I have made myself contemptible in the eyes of many," Stewart wrote. "This is the land of freedom," she added, "and we claim our rights," including the right to speak in public.

The May Session of the Woman's Rights Convention, *a cartoon published in* Harper's Weekly, *June 11, 1859. A female orator addresses the audience of men and women, while hecklers in the balcony disrupt the proceedings.*

Stewart left Boston in 1833 and rarely lectured again. The Grimké sisters, however, used the controversy over their speeches as a springboard for a vigorous argument against the idea that taking part in assemblies, demonstrations, and lectures was unfeminine. Outraged by the sight of females sacrificing all "modesty and delicacy" by appearing on the public lecture platform, a group of Massachusetts clergymen denounced the sisters. In reply, they forthrightly defended not only the right of women to take part in political debate but also their right to share the social and educational privileges enjoyed by men. "Since I engaged in the investigation of the rights of the slave," declared Angelina Grimké, I have necessarily been led to a better understanding of my own." Her sister Sarah proceeded to publish *Letters on the Equality of the Sexes* (1838), a powerful call for equal rights for women and a critique of the notion of separate spheres. The book raised numerous issues familiar even today, including what later generations would call "equal pay for equal work." Why, Sarah Grimké wondered, did male teachers invariably receive higher wages than women, and a male tailor earn "two or three times as much" as a female counterpart "although the work done by each may be equally good?"

WOMEN'S RIGHTS

The Grimkés were the first to apply the abolitionist doctrine of universal freedom and equality to the status of women. When the prominent writer Catharine Beecher reprimanded the sisters for stepping outside "the domestic and social sphere," urging them to accept the fact that "heaven" had designated man "the superior" and woman "the subordinate," Angelina Grimké issued a stinging answer. "I know nothing," she wrote, "of men's rights and women's rights. My doctrine, then is, that whatever it is morally right for man to do, it is morally right for woman to do." Like their predecessors Frances Wright and Maria Stewart, the Grimké sisters soon retired from the fray, after Angelina married Theodore Weld. But their writings helped to spark the movement for women's rights, which arose in the 1840s.

Elizabeth Cady Stanton and Lucretia Mott, the key organizers of the Seneca Falls Convention of 1848, were veterans of the antislavery crusade. In 1840, they had traveled to London as delegates to the World Anti-Slavery Convention, only to be barred from participating because of their sex. The Seneca Falls Convention, a gathering on behalf of women's rights held in the upstate-New York town where Stanton lived, raised the issue of women's suffrage for the first time. Stanton, the principal author, modeled the Seneca Falls Declaration of Sentiments on the Declaration of Independence (see the Appendix for the full text). But the document added "women" to Jefferson's axiom "all men are created equal," and in place of a list of injustices committed by George III, it condemned the "injuries and usurpations on the part of man toward woman." The first to be listed was denying her the right to vote. As Stanton told the convention, only the vote would make woman "free as man is free," since in a democratic society, freedom was impossible without access to the ballot. The argument was simple and irrefutable: in the words of Lydia Maria Child, "either the theory of our government [the democratic principle that government rests on the will of the people] is *false*, or women have a right to vote."

Seneca Falls marked the beginning of the seventy-year struggle for women's suffrage. The vote, however, was hardly the only issue raised at the convention. The Declaration of Sentiments condemned the entire structure of inequality that denied women access to education and employment, gave husbands control over the property and wages of their wives and custody of children in the event of divorce, deprived women of independent legal status after they married, and restricted them to the home as their "sphere of action." Equal rights became the rallying cry of the early movement for women's rights, and equal rights meant claiming access to all the prevailing definitions of freedom.

FEMINISM AND FREEDOM

Like abolitionism, temperance, and other reforms, women's rights was an international movement. Lacking broad backing at home, early feminists found allies abroad. "Women alone will say what freedom they want," declared an article in *The Free Woman*, a journal established in Paris in 1832. With their household chores diminished because of the availability of manufactured goods and domestic servants, many middle-class women chafed at the restrictions that made it impossible for them to gain an education, enter the professions, and in other ways exercise their talents. Whether married or not, early feminists insisted, women deserved the range of individual choices—the possibility of self-realization—that constituted the essence of freedom.

Women, wrote Margaret Fuller, had the same right as men to develop their talents, to "grow . . . to live freely and unimpeded." The daughter of a Jeffersonian congressman, Fuller was educated at home, at first under her father's supervision (she learned Latin before the age of six) and later on her own. She became part of New England's transcendentalist circle (discussed in Chapter 9) and from 1840 to 1842 edited *The Dial*, a magazine that reflected the group's views. In 1844, Fuller became literary editor of the *New York Tribune*, the first woman to achieve so important a position in American journalism.

In *Woman in the Nineteenth Century*, published in 1845, Fuller sought to apply to women the transcendentalist idea that freedom meant a quest for personal development. "Every path" to self-fulfillment, she insisted, should be "open to woman as freely as to man." Fuller singled out Abby Kelley as a "gentle hero" for continuing to speak in public despite being denounced by men for venturing "out of her sphere." Fearing that marriage to an American would inevitably mean subordination to male dictation, Fuller traveled to Europe as a correspondent for the *Tribune*. There she married an Italian patriot. Along with her husband and baby, she died in a shipwreck in 1850 while returning to the United States.

WOMEN AND WORK

Women also demanded the right to participate in the market revolution. At an 1851 women's rights convention, the black abolitionist Sojourner Truth insisted that the movement devote attention to the plight of poor and working-class women and repudiate the idea that women were too delicate

Portrait of feminist Margaret Fuller (1810–1850) from an undated daguerreotype.

VOICES OF FREEDOM

From Angelina Grimké,
Letter in *The Liberator* (August 2, 1837)

The daughters of a prominent South Carolina slaveholder, Angelina and Sarah Grimké became abolitionists after being sent to Philadelphia for education. In this article, Angelina Grimké explains how participation in the movement against slavery led her to a greater recognition of women's lack of basic freedoms.

Since I engaged in the investigation of the rights of the slave, I have necessarily been led to a better understanding of my own; for I have found the Anti-Slavery cause to be . . . the school in which human rights are more fully investigated, and better understood and taught, than in any other [reform] enterprise. . . . Here we are led to examine why human beings have any rights. It is because they are moral beings. . . . Now it naturally occurred to me, that if rights were founded in moral being, then the circumstance of sex could not give to man higher rights and responsibilities, than to woman. . . .

When I look at human brings as moral beings, all distinction in sex sinks to insignificance and nothingness; for I believe it regulates rights and responsibilities no more than the color of the skin or the eyes. My doctrine, then is, that whatever it is morally right for man to do, it is morally right for woman to do. . . . This regulation of duty by the mere circumstance of sex . . . has led to all that [numerous] train of evils flowing out of the anti-christian doctrine of masculine and feminine virtues. By this doctrine, man has been converted into the warrior, and clothed in sternness . . . whilst woman has been taught to lean upon an arm of flesh, to . . . be admired for her personal charms, and caressed and humored like a spoiled child, or converted into a mere drudge to suit the convenience of her lord and master. . . . It has robbed woman of . . . the right to think and speak and act on all great moral questions, just as men think and speak and act. . . .

The discussion of the wrongs of slavery has opened the way for the discussion of other rights, and the ultimate result will most certainly be . . . the letting of the oppressed of every grade and description go free.

From Frederick Douglass,
Speech on July 5, 1852, Rochester, New York

One of the most prominent reform leaders of his era, Frederick Douglass escaped from slavery in 1838 and soon became an internationally known writer and orator against slavery. His speech of July 1852 condemned the hypocrisy of a nation that proclaimed its devotion to freedom while practicing slavery. It was reprinted in 1855 in his autobiography, *My Bondage and My Freedom.*

Fellow-citizens, pardon me, allow me to ask, why am I called upon to speak here to-day? What have I, or those I represent, to do with your national independence? Are the great principles of political freedom and of natural justice, embodied in that Declaration of Independence, extended to us? . . . Such is not the case. I say it with a sad sense of the disparity between us. I am not included within the pale of this glorious anniversary! Your high independence only reveals the immeasurable distance between us. . . . The rich inheritance of justice, liberty, prosperity and independence, bequeathed by your fathers, is shared by you, not by me. . . .

For the present, it is enough to affirm the equal manhood of the negro race. Is it not astonishing that, while we are ploughing, planting and reaping, using all kinds of mechanical tools, erecting houses, constructing bridges, building ships, . . . acting as clerks, merchants and secretaries . . . confessing and worshiping the Christian's God, and looking hopefully for life and immortality beyond the grave, we are called upon to prove that we are men! . . .

Would you have me argue that man is entitled to liberty? That he is the rightful owner of his body? You have already declared it. Must I argue the wrongfulness of slavery? . . . that men have a natural right to freedom? . . . To do so, would be to make myself ridiculous, and to offer an insult to your understanding. There is not a man beneath the canopy of heaven, that does not know that slavery is wrong *for him.* . . .

What, to the American slave, is your 4th of July? I answer: a day that reveals to him, more than all other days in the year, the gross injustice and cruelty to which he is the constant victim. To him, your celebration is a sham; your boasted liberty, an unholy license; your national greatness, swelling vanity; your sounds of rejoicing are empty and heartless; your denunciations of tyrants, brass fronted impudence; your shouts of liberty and equality, hollow mockery—a thin veil to cover up crimes that would disgrace a nation of savages. There is not a nation on the earth guilty of practices, more shocking and bloody, than are the people of these United States, at this very hour.

QUESTIONS

1. What consequences does Grimké believe follow from the idea of rights being founded in the individual's "moral being"?

2. How does Douglass turn the ideals proclaimed by white Americans into weapons against slavery?

3. What do these documents suggest about the language and arguments employed by abolitionists?

to engage in work outside the home. Born a slave in New York State around 1799, Truth did not obtain her freedom until the state's emancipation law of 1827. A listener at her 1851 speech (which was not recorded at the time) later recalled that Truth had spoken of her years of hard physical labor, had flexed her arm to show her strength, and exclaimed, "and aren't I a woman?"

Although those who convened at Seneca Falls were predominantly from the middle class—no representatives of the growing number of "factory girls" and domestic servants took part—the participants rejected the identification of the home as the women's "sphere." Women, wrote Pauline Davis in 1853, "must go *to work*" to emancipate themselves from "bondage." During the 1850s, some feminists tried to popularize a new style of dress, devised by Amelia Bloomer, consisting of a loose-fitting tunic and trousers. In her autobiography, published in 1898, Elizabeth Cady Stanton recalled that women who adopted Bloomer's attire were ridiculed by the press and insulted by "crowds of boys in the streets." They found that "the physical freedom enjoyed did not compensate for the persistent persecution and petty annoyances suffered at every turn." The target of innumerable male jokes, the "bloomer" costume attempted to make a serious point—that the long dresses, tight corsets, and numerous petticoats considered to be appropriate female attire were so confining that they made it almost impossible for women to claim a place in the public sphere or to work outside the home.

In one sense, feminism demanded an expansion of the boundaries of freedom rather than a redefinition of the idea. Women, in the words of one reformer, should enjoy "the rights and liberties that every 'free white male citizen' takes to himself as God-given." But even as it sought to apply prevailing notions of freedom to women, the movement posed a fundamental challenge to some of society's central beliefs—that the capacity for independence and rationality were male traits, that the world was properly divided into public and private realms, and that issues of justice and freedom did not apply to relations within the family. In every realm of life,

Woman's Emancipation, a satirical engraving from Harper's Monthly, *August 1851, illustrating the much-ridiculed "Bloomer" costume.*

including the inner workings of the family, declared Elizabeth Cady Stanton, there could be "no happiness without freedom."

THE SLAVERY OF SEX

The dichotomy between freedom and slavery powerfully shaped early feminists' political language. Just as the idea of "wage slavery" enabled northern workers to challenge the inequalities inherent in market definitions of freedom, the concept of the "slavery of sex" empowered the women's movement to develop an all-encompassing critique of male authority and their own subordination. Feminists of the 1840s and 1850s pointed out that the law of marriage made nonsense of the description of the family as a "private" institution independent of public authority. When the abolitionists and women's rights activitists Lucy Stone and Henry Blackwell married, they felt obliged to repudiate New York's laws that clothed the husband "with legal powers which . . . no man should possess."

Feminist abolitionists did not invent the analogy between marriage and slavery. The English writer Mary Wollstonecraft had invoked it as early as the 1790s in *A Vindication of the Rights of Woman* (discussed in Chapter 8). But the analogy between free women and slaves gained prominence as it was swept up in the accelerating debate over slavery. "Woman is a slave, from the cradle to the grave," asserted Ernestine Rose. "Father, guardian, husband—master still. One conveys her, like a piece of property, over to the other." For their part, southern defenders of slavery frequently linked slavery and marriage as natural and just forms of inequality. Eliminating the former institution, they charged, would threaten the latter.

Marriage was not, literally speaking, equivalent to slavery. The married woman, however, did not enjoy the fruits of her own labor—a central element of freedom. Beginning with Mississippi in 1839, numerous states enacted married women's property laws, shielding from a husband's creditors property brought into a marriage by his wife. Such laws initially aimed not to expand women's rights as much as to prevent families from losing their property during the depression that began in 1837. But in 1860, New York enacted a more far-reaching measure, allowing married women to sign contracts, buy and sell property, and keep their own wages. In most states, however, property accumulated after marriage, as well as wages earned by the wife, still belonged to the husband.

"SOCIAL FREEDOM"

Influenced by abolitionism, women's rights advocates turned another popular understanding of freedom—self-ownership, or control over one's own person—in an entirely new direction. The emphasis in abolitionist literature on the violation of the slave woman's body by her master helped to give the idea of self-ownership a concrete reality that encouraged application to free women as well. The law of domestic relations presupposed the husband's right of sexual access to his wife and to inflict corporal punishment on her. Courts proved reluctant to intervene in cases of physical abuse so long as it was not "extreme" or "intolerable." "Women's Rights,"

Am I Not a Woman and a Sister?, *an illustration from* The Liberator, *1849. Identifying with the plight of the female slave enabled free women to see more clearly the inequalities they themselves faced.*

declared a Boston meeting in 1859, included "freedom and equal rights in the family." The demand that women should enjoy the rights to regulate their own sexual activity and procreation and to be protected by the state against violence at the hands of their husbands challenged the notion that claims for justice, freedom, and individual rights should stop at the household's door.

The issue of women's private freedom revealed underlying differences within the movement for women's rights. Belief in equality between the sexes and in the sexes' natural differences coexisted in antebellum feminist thought. Even as they entered the public sphere and thereby challenged some aspects of the era's "cult of domesticity" (discussed in Chapter 9), many early feminists accepted other elements. Allowing women a greater role in the public sphere, many female reformers argued, would bring their "inborn" maternal instincts to bear on public life, to the benefit of the entire society.

Even feminists critical of the existing institution of marriage generally refrained from raising in public the explosive issue of women's "private" freedom. The question frequently arose, however, in the correspondence of feminist leaders. "Social Freedom," Susan B. Anthony observed to Lucy Stone, "lies at the bottom of all—and until woman gets that, she must continue the slave of men in all other things." Women like Anthony, who never married, and Stone, who with her husband created their own definition of marriage, reflected the same dissatisfactions with traditional family life as the women who joined communitarian experiments. Not until the twentieth century would the demand that freedom be extended to intimate aspects of life inspire a mass movement. But the dramatic fall in the birthrate over the course of the nineteenth century suggests that many women were quietly exercising "personal freedom" in their most intimate relationships.

This image appeared on the cover of the sheet music for "Get Off the Track!" a song popularized by the Hutchinson singers, who performed antislavery songs. The trains Immediate Emancipation *(with* The Liberator *as its front wheel) and* Liberty Party *pull into a railroad station.* The Herald of Freedom *and* American Standard *were antislavery newspapers. The song's lyrics praised William Lloyd Garrison and criticized various politicians, among them Henry Clay. The chorus went: "Roll it along! Through the nation/Freedom's car, Emancipation."*

THE ABOLITIONIST SCHISM

Even in reform circles, the demand for a greater public role for women remained extremely controversial. Massachusetts physician Samuel Gridley Howe pioneered humane treatment of the blind and educational reform, and he was an ardent abolitionist. But Howe did not support his wife's participation in the movement for female suffrage, which, he complained, caused her to "neglect domestic relations." When organized abolitionism split into two wings in 1840, the immediate cause was a dispute over the proper role of women in antislavery work. Abby Kelley's appointment to the business committee of the American Anti-Slavery Society sparked the formation of a rival abolitionist organization, the American and Foreign Anti-Slavery Society, which believed it wrong for a woman to occupy so prominent a position. The antislavery poet John Greenleaf Whittier compared Kelley to Eve, Delilah, and Helen of Troy, women who had sown the seeds of male destruction.

Behind the split lay the fear among some abolitionists that Garrison's radicalism on issues like women's rights, as well as his refusal to support the idea of abolitionists voting or running for public office, impeded the movement's growth. Determined to make abolitionism a political movement, the seceders formed the Liberty Party, which nominated James G. Birney as its candidate for president. He received only 7,000 votes (about one-third of 1 percent of the total). In 1840, antislavery northerners saw little wisdom in "throwing away" their ballots on a third-party candidate.

While the achievement of most of their demands lay far in the future, the women's rights movement succeeded in making "the woman question" a permanent part of the transatlantic discussion of social reform. As for abolitionism, while it remained a significant presence in northern public life until emancipation had been achieved, by 1840 the movement had accomplished its most important work. Over 1,000 local antislavery societies were now scattered throughout the North, representing a broad constituency awakened to the moral issue of slavery. The "great duty of freedom," Ralph Waldo Emerson had declared in 1837, was "to open our halls to discussion of this question." The abolitionists' greatest achievement lay in shattering the conspiracy of silence that had sought to preserve national unity by suppressing public debate over slavery.

SUGGESTED READING

Bestor, Arthur E. *Backwoods Utopias: The Sectarian and Owenite Phases of Communitarian Socialism in America* (1948). An account of some of the numerous communitarian experiments in pre–Civil War America.

Boylan, Anne M. *The Origins of Women's Activism: New York and Boston, 1797–1840* (2002). Consider how middle-class urban women organized numerous associations for social improvement and thereby gained a place in the public sphere.

Burin, Eric. *Slavery and the Peculiar Solution: A History of the American Colonization Society* (2005). The most recent history of the movement to send black Americans, free and slave, to Africa.

Goodman, Paul. *Of One Blood: Abolitionists and the Origins of Racial Equality* (1998). Explores the origins of racial egalitarianism in the movement against slavery.

Harding, Vincent. *There Is a River: The Black Struggle for Freedom in America* (1981). A study that links slave resistance and black abolitionism as phases of a common struggle for freedom.

Hersh, Blanche G. *The Slavery of Sex: Feminist Abolitionists in America* (1978). Examines how the abolitionist movement gave rise to early feminism.

Jeffrey, Julie R. *The Great Silent Army of Abolitionism: Ordinary Women in the Antislavery Movement* (1998). The role of women as the grassroots foot soldiers of the abolitionist movement.

Kaestle, Carl F. *Pillars of the Republic: Common Schools and American Society, 1780–1860* (1983). Surveys the movement to introduce free public education in the United States.

Kraditor, Aileen S. *Means and Ends in American Abolitionism* (1969). An influential discussion of the political strategies of Garrisonian abolitionists.

McGreevy, John T. *Catholicism and American Freedom* (2003). Contains an illuminating discussion of how Catholics responded to Protestant-based reform movements.

Nye, Russell B. *Fettered Freedom: Civil Liberties and the Slavery Controversy, 1830–1860* (1949). Examines the impact of mob activities and other violations of civil liberties on the growth of abolitionism.

Richards, Leonard L. *Gentlemen of Property and Standing: Anti-Abolition Mobs in Jacksonian America* (1970). An examination of several anti-abolitionist mobs led by prominent residents of northern cities.

Rothman, David J. *The Discovery of the Asylum: Social Order and Disorder in the New Republic* (1971). Relates the rise of prisons, orphanages, and asylums and their common characteristics.

Stewart, James B. *Holy Warriors: The Abolitionists and American Slavery* (rev. ed., 1996). A recent survey of the history of the antislavery movement.

Tyrrell, Ian. *Sobering Up: From Temperance to Prohibition in Antebellum America, 1800–1860* (1979). Traces the movement against the sale and use of liquor and how it changed in the first part of the nineteenth century.

REVIEW QUESTIONS

1. Explore why Americans had an impulse to improve American society in the first half of the nineteenth century.

2. Explain the significance of the abolitionist movement to the idea of American freedom.

3. Analyze the pros and cons of the colonization movement and why many blacks were opposed to it.

4. Why was this a period of institution building?

5. How did the abolitionist movement and the women's movement influence each other?

KEY TERMS

Shakers (p. 430)

temperance movement (p. 434)

public education (p. 437)

British abolitionism (p. 446)

the gag rule (p. 447)

woman's suffrage (p. 450)

Liberty Party (p. 457)

REVIEW TABLE

Reform Organizations

Society	Date	Purpose
American Colonization Society	1816	To promote the gradual abolition of slavery and the settlement of black Americans in Africa
American Temperance Society	1826	To redeem all drinkers
American Anti-Slavery Society	1833	To abolish slavery immediately
Female Moral Reform Society	1834	To redeem prostitutes from lives of sin and protect the morality of single women

CHAPTER 13

A House Divided, 1840–1861

John Gast's 1872 painting American Progress, *commissioned by the author of a travel guide to the Pacific coast, reflects the ebullient spirit of manifest destiny. A female figure descended from earlier representations of Liberty wears the Star of Empire and leads the march of pioneers, enlightenment, and technological progress westward, while Indians retreat before her.*

☞

FOCUS QUESTIONS

- What were the major thrusts of territorial expansion west in the 1840s?

- Why did the expansion of slavery become such a divisive political issue in the 1840s?

- How did the Republican Party emerge from the social and political divisions of this period?

- How did Lincoln emerge as president from the divided politics of the 1850s?

- What were the final steps on the road to secession?

In 1855, Thomas Crawford, one of the era's most prominent American sculptors, was asked to design a statue to adorn the Capitol's dome, still under construction in Washington, D.C. He proposed a Statue of Freedom, a female figure wearing a liberty cap. Secretary of War Jefferson Davis of Mississippi, one of the country's largest slaveholders, objected to Crawford's plan. A familiar symbol in the colonial era, the liberty cap had fallen into disfavor among some Americans after becoming closely identified with the French Revolution. Davis's disapproval, however, rested on other grounds. Ancient Romans, he noted, regarded the cap as "the badge of the freed slave." Its use, he feared, might suggest that there was a connection between the slaves' longing for freedom and the liberty of free-born Americans. Davis ordered the liberty cap replaced with a less controversial military symbol, a feathered helmet.

Crawford died in Italy, where he had spent most of his career, in 1857. Two years later, the colossal Statue of Freedom, which weighed 15,000 pounds, was transported to the United States in several pieces and assembled at a Maryland foundry under the direction of Philip Reed, a slave craftsman. In 1863, it was installed atop the Capitol, where it can still be seen today. By the time it was put in place, the country was immersed in the Civil War and Jefferson Davis had become president of the Confederate States of America. The dispute over the Statue of Freedom offered a

The original and final designs for Thomas Crawford's Statue of Freedom *for the dome of the Capitol building. Secretary of War Jefferson Davis of Mississippi insisted that the liberty cap in the first design, a symbol of the emancipated slave in ancient Rome, be replaced.*

small illustration of how, by the mid-1850s, nearly every public question was being swept up into the gathering storm over slavery.

FRUITS OF MANIFEST DESTINY

CONTINENTAL EXPANSION

In the 1840s, slavery moved to the center stage of American politics. It did so not in the moral language or with the immediatist program of abolitionism, but as a result of the nation's territorial expansion. By 1840, with the completion of Indian removal, virtually all the land east of the Mississippi River was in white hands. The depression that began in 1837 sparked a large migration of settlers further west. Some headed to Oregon, whose Willamette Valley was reputed to be one of the continent's most beautiful and fertile regions. Until the 1840s, the American presence in the area had been limited to a few fur traders and explorers. But between 1840 and 1845, some 5,000 emigrants made the difficult 2,000-mile journey by wagon train to Oregon from jumping-off places on the banks of the Missouri River. By 1860, nearly 300,000 men, women, and children had braved disease, starvation, the natural barrier of the Rocky Mountains, and occasional Indian attacks to travel overland to Oregon and California.

THE MORMONS' TREK

Another migration brought thousands of members of the Church of Jesus Christ of Latter-day Saints, or Mormons, to modern-day Utah. One of the era's numerous religious sects that hoped to create a Kingdom of God on earth, the Mormons had been founded in the 1820s by Joseph Smith, a young farmer in upstate New York. Smith claimed to have been led by an angel to a set of golden plates covered with strange writing, which he translated as the Book of Mormon. He claimed that his church descended from the lost tribes of ancient Israel.

The absolute authority Smith exercised over his followers, as well as the refusal of the Mormons to separate church and state, alarmed many neighbors. Even more outrageous to the general community was the Mormon practice of polygamy, which allows one man to have several wives, a repudiation of traditional Christian teaching and nineteenth-century morality. Mobs drove Smith and his followers out of New York, Ohio, and Missouri before they settled in 1839 in Nauvoo, Illinois, where they hoped to await the Second Coming of Christ. There, five years later, Smith was arrested on the charge of inciting a riot that destroyed an anti-Mormon newspaper. While in jail awaiting trial, Smith was murdered by a group of intruders. His successor as Mormon leader, Brigham Young, led over 10,000 followers across the Great Plains and Rocky Mountains to the shores of the Great Salt Lake in present-day Utah, seeking a refuge where they could practice their faith undisturbed. The Mormons' plight revealed the limits of religious toleration in nineteenth-century America.

During most of the 1840s, the United States and Great Britain jointly administered Oregon, and Utah was part of Mexico. This did not stop Americans from settling in either region. National boundaries meant little to those who moved west. The 1840s witnessed an intensification of the old belief that God intended the American nation to reach all the way to the Pacific Ocean. As noted in Chapter 9, the term that became a shorthand for this expansionist spirit was "manifest destiny."

THE MEXICAN FRONTIER: NEW MEXICO AND CALIFORNIA

Settlement of Oregon did not directly raise the issue of slavery. But the nation's acquisition of part of Mexico did. When Mexico achieved its independence from Spain in 1821 it was nearly as large as the United States and its population of 6.5 million was about two-thirds that of its northern neighbor. Mexico's northern provinces—California, New Mexico, and Texas—however, were isolated and sparsely settled outposts surrounded by Indian country. New Mexico's population at the time of Mexican independence consisted of around 30,000 persons of Spanish origin, 10,000 Pueblo Indians, and an indeterminate number of "wild" Indians—nomadic bands of Apaches, Comanches, Navajos, and Utes. With the opening in 1821 of the Santa Fe Trail linking that city with Independence, Missouri, New Mexico's commerce with the United States eclipsed trade with the rest of Mexico.

California's non-Indian population in 1821, some 3,200 missionaries, soldiers, and settlers, was vastly outnumbered by about 20,000 Indians living and working on land owned by religious missions and by 150,000 members of unsubdued tribes in the interior. In 1834, in the hope of reducing the power of the Catholic Church and attracting Mexican and foreign settlers to California, the Mexican government dissolved the great mission landholdings and emancipated Indians working for the friars. Most of the land ended up in the hands of a new class of Mexican cattle ranchers, the *Californios*, who defined their own identity in large measure against the surrounding Indian population. *Californios* referred to themselves as *gente de razón* (people capable of reason) as opposed to the *indios*, whom they called *gente sin razón* (people without reason). For the "common good," Indians were required to continue to work for the new landholders.

By 1840, California was already linked commercially with the United States. New England ships were trading with the region, as illustrated in Richard Henry Dana's popular novel *Two Years before the Mast* (1840), an account of a young man's voyage to California and his experiences there. California also

A rare photograph of wagons on their way to Oregon during the 1840s.

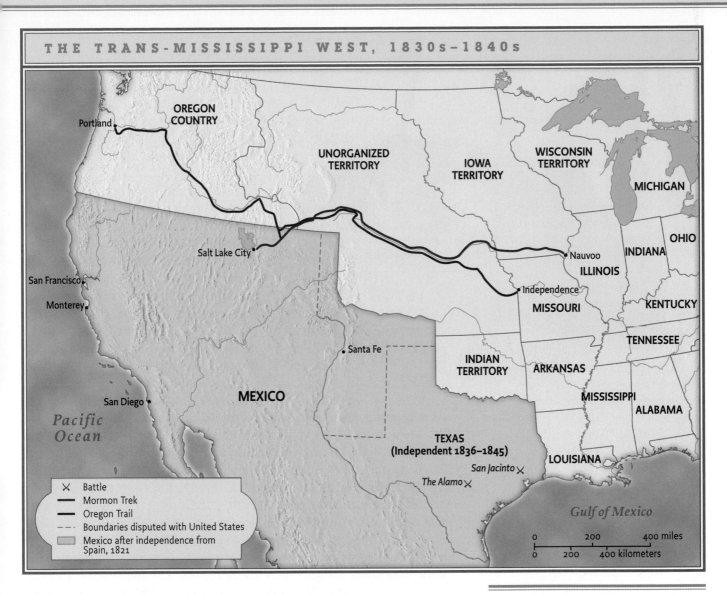

THE TRANS-MISSISSIPPI WEST, 1830s–1840s

Legend:
- ✕ Battle
- Mormon Trek
- Oregon Trail
- Boundaries disputed with United States
- Mexico after independence from Spain, 1821

Westward migration in the early and mid-1840s took American settlers across Indian country into the Oregon Territory, ownership of which was disputed with Great Britain. The Mormons migrated west to Salt Lake City, then part of Mexico.

attracted a small number of American newcomers. In 1846, Alfred Robinson, who had moved from Boston, published *Life in California*. "In this age of annexation," he wondered, "why not extend the 'area of freedom' by the annexation of California?"

THE TEXAS REVOLT

The first part of Mexico to be settled by significant numbers of Americans was Texas, whose non-Indian population of Spanish origin (called *Tejanos*) numbered only about 2,000 when Mexico became independent. In order to develop the region, the Mexican government accepted an offer by Moses Austin, a Connecticut-born farmer, to colonize it with Americans. In 1820, Austin received a large land grant. He died soon afterward and his son Stephen continued the plan, reselling land in smaller plots to American settlers at twelve cents per acre. By 1830, the population of American origin had reached around 7,000, considerably exceeding the number of *Tejanos*.

A flag carried at the Battle of San Jacinto during the Texas revolt of 1836 portrays a female figure displaying the rallying cry "Liberty or Death."

Alarmed that its grip on the area was weakening, the Mexican government in 1830 annulled existing land contracts and barred future emigration from the United States. Led by Stephen Austin, American settlers demanded greater autonomy within Mexico. Part of the area's tiny *Tejano* elite joined them. Mostly ranchers and large farmers, they had welcomed the economic boom that accompanied the settlers and formed economic alliances with American traders. The issue of slavery further exacerbated matters. Mexico had abolished slavery, but local authorities allowed American settlers to bring slaves with them. When Mexico's ruler, General Antonio López de Santa Anna, sent an army in 1835 to impose central authority, a local committee charged that his purpose was "to give liberty to our slaves and make slaves of ourselves."

The appearance of Santa Anna's army sparked a chaotic revolt in Texas. The rebels formed a provisional government that soon called for Texan independence. On March 13, 1836, Santa Anna's army stormed the Alamo, a mission compound in San Antonio, killing its 187 American and *Tejano* defenders. "Remember the Alamo" became the Texans' rallying cry. In April, forces under Sam Houston, a former governor of Tennessee, routed Santa Anna's army at the Battle of San Jacinto and forced him to recognize Texan independence. Houston was soon elected the first president of the Republic of Texas. In 1837, the Texas Congress called for union with the United States. But fearing the political disputes certain to result from an attempt to add another slave state to the Union, Presidents Andrew Jackson and Martin Van Buren shelved the question. Settlers from the United States nonetheless poured into the region, many of them slaveowners taking up fertile cotton land. By 1845, the population of Texas had reached nearly 150,000.

THE ELECTION OF 1844

Texas annexation remained on the political back burner until President John Tyler revived it in the hope of rescuing his failed administration and securing southern support for renomination in 1844. In April 1844, a letter by John C. Calhoun, whom Tyler had appointed secretary of state, was leaked to the press. It linked the idea of absorbing Texas directly to the goal of strengthening slavery in the United States. Some southern leaders, indeed, hoped that Texas could be divided into several states, thus further enhancing the South's power in Congress. Late that month, Henry Clay and former president Van Buren, the prospective Whig and Democratic candidates for president and two of the party system's most venerable leaders, met at Clay's Kentucky plantation. They agreed to issue letters rejecting immediate annexation on the grounds that it might provoke war with Mexico. Clay and Van Buren were reacting to the slavery issue in the traditional manner—by trying to keep it out of national politics.

Clay went on to receive the Whig nomination, but for Van Buren the letters proved to be a disaster. At the Democratic convention, southerners bent on annexation deserted Van Buren's cause, and he failed to receive the two-thirds majority necessary for nomination. The delegates then turned to the little-known James K. Polk, a former governor of Tennessee whose main assets were his support for annexation and his close association with Andrew Jackson, still the party's most popular figure. Like nearly all the presidents before him, Polk was a slaveholder. He owned substantial cotton plantations in Tennessee and Mississippi, where conditions were so brutal that only half of the slave children lived to the age of fifteen, and adults frequently ran away. To soothe injured feelings among northern Democrats over the rejection of Van Buren, the party platform called not only for the "reannexation" of Texas (implying that Texas had been part of the Louisiana Purchase and therefore once belonged to the United States) but also the "reoccupation" of all of Oregon. "Fifty-four forty or fight"—American control of Oregon all the way to its northern boundary at north latitude 54°40′—became a popular campaign slogan. But the bitterness of the northern Van Burenites over what they considered to be a betrayal on the part of the South would affect American politics for years to come.

Polk was the first "dark horse" candidate for president—that is, one whose nomination was completely unexpected. In the fall, he defeated Clay in an extremely close election. Polk's margin in the popular vote was less than 2 percent. Had not James G. Birney, running again as the Liberty Party candidate, received 16,000 votes in New York, mostly from antislavery Whigs, Clay would have been elected. In March 1845, only days before Polk's inauguration, Congress declared Texas part of the United States.

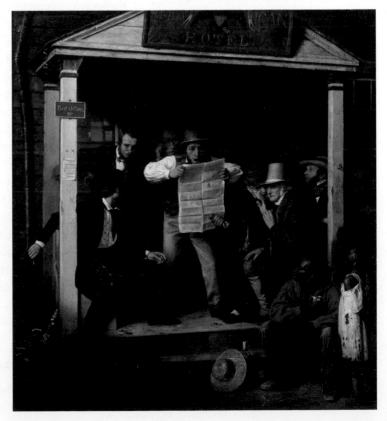

War News from Mexico, an 1848 painting by Richard C. Woodville, shows how Americans received war news through the popular press.

THE ROAD TO WAR

James K. Polk may have been virtually unknown, but he assumed the presidency with a clearly defined set of goals: to reduce the tariff, reestablish the independent treasury system, settle the dispute over ownership of Oregon, and bring California into the Union. Congress soon enacted the first two goals, and the third was accomplished in an agreement with Great Britain dividing Oregon at the forty-ninth parallel. Many northerners were bitterly disappointed by this compromise, considering it a betrayal of Polk's campaign promise not to give up any part of Oregon without a fight. But the president secured his main objectives, the Willamette Valley and the magnificent harbor of Puget Sound.

Acquiring California proved more difficult. Polk dispatched an emissary to Mexico offering to purchase the region, but the Mexican government refused to negotiate. By the spring of 1846, Polk was planning for military action. In April, American soldiers under Zachary Taylor moved into the region between the Nueces River and the Rio Grande, land claimed by both countries on the disputed border between Texas and Mexico. This action made conflict with Mexican forces inevitable. When fighting broke out, Polk claimed that the Mexicans had "shed blood upon American soil" and called for a declaration of war.

THE WAR AND ITS CRITICS

The Mexican War was the first American conflict to be fought primarily on foreign soil and the first in which American troops occupied a foreign capital. Inspired by the expansionist fervor of manifest destiny, a majority of Americans supported the war. They were convinced, as Herman Melville put it in his novel *White-Jacket* (1850), that since Americans "bear the ark of Liberties" for all mankind, "national selfishness is unbounded philanthropy . . . to the world." But a significant minority in the North dissented, fearing that far from expanding the "great empire of liberty," the administration's real aim was to acquire new land for the expansion of slavery. Ulysses S. Grant, who served with distinction in Mexico, later called the war "one of the most unjust ever waged by a stronger nation against a weaker nation," an indication that the United States was beginning to behave like "European monarchies," not a democratic republic. Henry David Thoreau was jailed in Massachusetts in 1846 for refusing to pay taxes as a protest against the war. Defending his action, Thoreau wrote an important essay, "On Civil Disobedience," which inspired such later advocates of nonviolent resistance to unjust laws as Martin Luther King Jr. "Under a government which imprisons any unjustly," wrote Thoreau, "the true place of a just man is also a prison."

Among the war's critics was Abraham Lincoln, who had been elected to Congress in 1846 from Illinois. Like many Whigs, Lincoln questioned whether the Mexicans had actually inflicted casualties on American soil, as Polk claimed, and in 1847 he introduced a resolution asking the president to specify the precise "spot" where blood had first been shed. But Lincoln was also disturbed by Polk's claiming the right to initiate an invasion of Mexico. "Allow the president to invade a neighboring country whenever he shall deem it necessary to repel an invasion," he declared, "and you allow him to make war at pleasure. . . . If today he should choose to say he thinks it necessary to invade Canada to prevent the British from invading us, how could you stop him?" Lincoln's stance proved unpopular in Illinois. He had already agreed to serve only one term in Congress, but when Democrats captured his seat in 1848, many blamed the result on Lincoln's criticism of the war. But the concerns he raised regarding the president's power to "make war at pleasure" would continue to echo in the twentieth and twenty-first centuries.

COMBAT IN MEXICO

Volunteers, over 60,000 of whom enlisted, did most of the fighting. Combat took place on three fronts. In June 1846, a band of American

THE MEXICAN WAR, 1846–1848

insurrectionists proclaimed California freed from Mexican control and named Captain John C. Frémont, head of a small scientific expedition in the West, its ruler. Their aim was California's incorporation into the United States, but for the moment they adopted a flag depicting a large bear as the symbol of the area's independence. A month later, the U.S. Navy sailed into Monterey and San Francisco Harbors, raised the American flag, and put an end to the "bear flag republic." At almost the same time, 1,600 American troops under General Stephen W. Kearney occupied Sante Fe without resistance and then set out for southern California, where they helped to put down a Mexican uprising against American rule.

The Mexican War was the first in which an American army invaded another country and occupied its capital. As a result of the war, the United States acquired a vast new area in the modern-day Southwest.

A lithograph depicting Los Angeles in 1857, nine years after the city, then quite small, became part of the United States as a result of the Treaty of Guadalupe Hidalgo.

The bulk of the fighting occurred in central Mexico. In February 1847, Taylor defeated Santa Anna's army at the Battle of Buena Vista. When the Mexican government still refused to negotiate, Polk ordered American forces under Winfield Scott to march inland from the port of Vera Cruz toward Mexico City. Scott's forces routed Mexican defenders and in September occupied the country's capital. In February 1848, the two governments agreed to the Treaty of Guadalupe Hidalgo, which confirmed the annexation of Texas and ceded California and present-day New Mexico, Arizona, Nevada, and Utah to the United States. In exchange, the United States paid Mexico $15 million. The Mexican Cession, as the land annexed from Mexico was called, established the present territorial boundaries on the North American continent except for the Gadsden Purchase, a parcel of additional land bought from Mexico in 1853, and Alaska, acquired from Russia in 1867.

The Mexican War is only a footnote in most Americans' historical memory. Unlike other wars, few public monuments celebrate the conflict. Mexicans, however, regard the war (or "the dismemberment," as it is called in that country) as a central event of their national history and a source of continued resentment over a century and a half after it was fought. As the Mexican negotiators of 1848 complained, it was unprecedented to launch a war because a country refused to sell part of its territory to a neighbor.

RACE AND MANIFEST DESTINY

With the end of the Mexican War, the United States absorbed half a million square miles of Mexico's territory, one-third of that nation's total area. A region that for centuries had been united was suddenly split in two, dividing families and severing trade routes. An estimated 75,000 to 100,000 Spanish-speaking Mexicans and over 150,000 Indians inhabited the Mexican Cession. The Treaty of Guadalupe Hidalgo guaranteed to "male citizens" of the area "the free enjoyment of their liberty and property" and "all the rights" of Americans—a provision designed to protect the property of large Mexican landowners in California. As to Indians whose homelands and hunting grounds suddenly became part of the United States, the treaty referred to them only as "savage tribes" whom the United States must prevent from launching incursions into Mexico across the new border.

The spirit of manifest destiny gave a new stridency to ideas about racial superiority. During the 1840s, territorial expansion came to be seen as proof of the innate superiority of the "Anglo-Saxon race" (a mythical construct defined largely by its opposites: blacks, Indians, Hispanics, and Catholics). "*Race*," declared John L. O'Sullivan's *Democratic Review*, was the "key" to the "history of nations" and the rise and fall of empires.

"Race" in the mid-nineteenth century was an amorphous notion involving color, culture, national origin, class, and religion. Newspapers, magazines, and scholarly works popularized the link between American freedom and the supposedly innate liberty-loving qualities of Anglo-Saxon Protestants. The annexation of Texas and conquest of much of Mexico became triumphs of civilization, progress, and liberty over the tyranny of the Catholic Church and the innate incapacity of "mongrel races." Indeed, calls by some expansionists for the United States to annex all of Mexico failed in part because of fear that the nation could not assimilate its large non-white Catholic population, supposedly unfit for citizenship in a republic.

A map of the United States from 1848 reveals how the size of the country had grown during the past four years: Texas (its western boundary still unfixed) had been annexed in 1844; the dispute with Great Britain over Oregon was settled in 1846; and the Mexican Cession—the area of present-day Arizona, New Mexico, Utah, Nevada, and California— was added in 1848 at the end of the Mexican War.

UNITED STATES
1848

A photograph of a Chinese immigrant carrying equipment used in California gold mining.

The gold rush brought thousands of fortune seekers, from nearly every corner of the globe, to California.

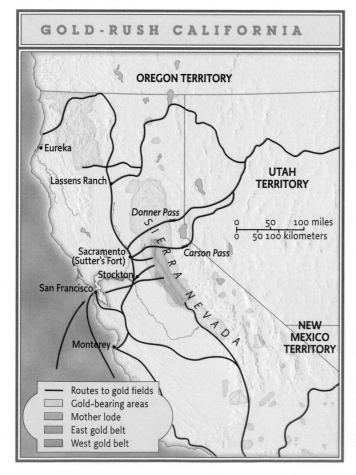

REDEFINING RACE

The imposition of the American system of race relations proved detrimental to many inhabitants of the newly acquired territories. Texas had already demonstrated as much. Mexico had abolished slavery and declared persons of Spanish, Indian, and African origin equal before the law. The Texas constitution adopted after independence not only included protections for slavery but also denied civil rights to Indians and persons of African origin. Only whites were permitted to purchase land, and the entrance of free blacks into the state was prohibited altogether. "Every privilege dear to a free man is taken away," one free black resident of Texas complained.

Local circumstances affected racial definitions in the former Mexican territories. Texas defined "Spanish" Mexicans, especially those who occupied important social positions, as white. The residents of New Mexico of both Mexican and Indian origin, on the other hand, were long deemed "too Mexican" for democratic self-government. With white migration lagging, Congress did not allow New Mexico to become a state until 1912.

GOLD-RUSH CALIFORNIA

California had a non-Indian population of under 15,000 when the Mexican War ended. For most of the 1840s, ten times as many Americans emigrated to Oregon as to California. But this changed dramatically after January 1848, when gold was discovered in the foothills of the Sierra Nevada Mountains at a sawmill owned by the Swiss immigrant Johann A. Sutter. A mania for gold spread throughout the world, fanned by newspaper accounts of instant wealth acquired by early migrants. By ship and land, newcomers poured into California. The non-Indian population rose to 200,000 by 1852 and over 360,000 eight years later.

California's gold-rush population was incredibly diverse. Experienced miners flooded in from Mexico and South America. Tens of thousands of Americans who had never seen a mine arrived from the East, and from overseas came Irish, Germans, Italians, and Australians. Nearly 25,000 Chinese landed between 1849 and 1852, almost all of them young men who had signed long-term labor contracts with Chinese merchants, who in turn leased them to mining and railroad companies and other employers. San Francisco, a town of 1,000 in 1848, became the gateway to the *El Dorado* of northern California. By 1850, it had 30,000 residents and had become perhaps the world's most racially and ethnically diverse city. Unlike farming frontiers settled by families, most of the gold-rush migrants were young men. Women played many roles in western mining communities, running restaurants and boardinghouses and working as laundresses, cooks, and prostitutes. But as late as 1860, California's male population outnumbered females by nearly three to one.

CALIFORNIA AND THE BOUNDARIES OF FREEDOM

As early surface mines quickly became exhausted, they gave way to underground mining that required a large investment of capital. This economic development worsened conflicts among California's many racial and ethnic groups engaged in fierce competition for gold. The law was very fragile in gold-rush California. In 1851 and 1856, "committees of vigilance" took control of San Francisco, sweeping aside established courts to try and execute those accused of crimes. White miners organized extralegal groups that expelled "foreign miners"—Mexicans, Chileans, Chinese, French, and American Indians—from areas with gold. The state legislature imposed a tax of twenty dollars per month on foreign miners, driving many of them from the state.

California would long remain in the American imagination a place of infinite opportunity, where newcomers could start their lives anew. But the boundaries of freedom there were tightly drawn. The state constitution of 1850 limited voting and the right to testify in court to whites, excluding Indians, Asians, and the state's few blacks (who numbered only 962 persons). California landowners who claimed Spanish descent or had intermarried with American settlers were deemed to be white. But with land titles derived from Mexican days challenged in court, many sold out to newcomers from the East.

For California's Indians, the gold rush and absorption into the United States proved to be disastrous. Gold seekers overran Indian communities. Miners, ranchers, and vigilantes murdered thousands of Indians. Determined to reduce the native population, state officials paid millions in

An 1851 daguerreotype shows ships crowding the harbor of San Francisco, a city that grew enormously as a result of the gold rush.

bounties to private militias that launched attacks on the state's Indians. Although California was a free state, thousands of Indian children, declared orphans or vagrants by local courts, were bought and sold as slaves. By 1860, California's Indian population, nearly 150,000 when the Mexican War ended, had been reduced to around 30,000.

A DOSE OF ARSENIC

By 1853, with the Gadsden Purchase, the present boundaries of the United States in North America, with the exception of Alaska, had been created.

Victory over Mexico added more than 1 million square miles to the United States—an area larger than the Louisiana Purchase. But the acquisition of this vast territory raised the fatal issue that would disrupt the political system and plunge the nation into civil war—whether slavery should be allowed to expand into the West. Events soon confirmed Ralph Waldo Emerson's prediction that if the United States gobbled up part of Mexico, "it will be as the man who swallows arsenic. . . . Mexico will poison us."

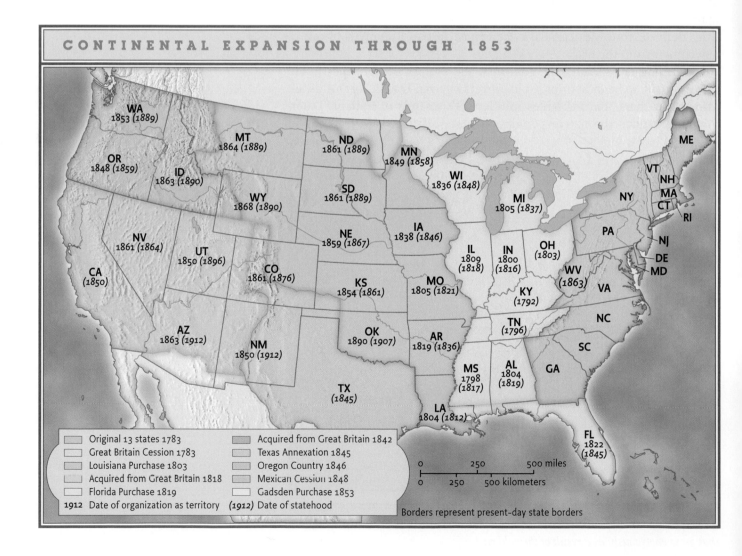

CONTINENTAL EXPANSION THROUGH 1853

WA 1853 (1889)
MT 1864 (1889)
ND 1861 (1889)
MN 1849 (1858)
ME
OR 1848 (1859)
ID 1863 (1890)
WI 1836 (1848)
VT
NH
MA
CT
WY 1868 (1890)
SD 1861 (1889)
MI 1805 (1837)
NY
RI
NV 1861 (1864)
UT 1850 (1896)
NE 1859 (1867)
IA 1838 (1846)
IL 1809 (1818)
IN 1800 (1816)
OH (1803)
PA
NJ
DE
CA (1850)
CO 1861 (1876)
KS 1854 (1861)
MO 1805 (1821)
WV (1863)
VA
MD
KY (1792)
AZ 1863 (1912)
NM 1850 (1912)
OK 1890 (1907)
AR 1819 (1836)
TN (1796)
NC
SC
TX (1845)
MS 1798 (1817)
AL 1804 (1819)
GA
LA 1804 (1812)
FL 1822 (1845)

Original 13 states 1783
Great Britain Cession 1783
Louisiana Purchase 1803
Acquired from Great Britain 1818
Florida Purchase 1819
1912 Date of organization as territory

Acquired from Great Britain 1842
Texas Annexation 1845
Oregon Country 1846
Mexican Cession 1848
Gadsden Purchase 1853
(1912) Date of statehood

0   250   500 miles
0   250   500 kilometers

Borders represent present-day state borders

THE WILMOT PROVISO

Before 1846, the status of slavery in all parts of the United States had been settled, either by state law or by the Missouri Compromise, which determined slavery's status in the Louisiana Purchase. The acquisition of new land reopened the question of slavery's expansion. The divisive potential of this issue became clear in 1846, when Congressman David Wilmot of Pennsylvania proposed a resolution prohibiting slavery from all territory acquired from Mexico. Party lines crumbled as every northerner, Democrat and Whig alike, supported what came to be known as the Wilmot Proviso, while nearly all southerners opposed it. The measure passed the House, where the more populous North possessed a majority, but failed in the Senate, with its even balance of free and slave states. The Proviso, said one newspaper, "as if by magic, brought to a head the great question that is about to divide the American people."

In 1848, opponents of slavery's expansion organized the Free Soil Party and nominated Martin Van Buren for president and Charles Francis Adams, the son of John Quincy Adams, as his running mate. Democrats nominated Lewis Cass of Michigan, who proposed that the decision on whether to allow slavery should be left to settlers in the new territories (an idea later given the name "popular sovereignty"). Van Buren was motivated in part by revenge against the South for jettisoning him in 1844. But his campaign struck a chord among northerners opposed to the expansion of slavery, and he polled some 300,000 votes, 14 percent of the northern total. Victory in 1848 went to the Whig candidate, Zachary Taylor, a hero of the Mexican War and a Louisiana sugar planter. But the fact that a former president and the son of another abandoned their parties to run on a Free Soil platform showed that antislavery sentiment had spread far beyond abolitionist ranks. "Antislavery," commented Senator William H. Seward of New York, "is at length a respectable element in politics."

THE FREE SOIL APPEAL

The Free Soil position had a popular appeal in the North that far exceeded the abolitionists' demand for immediate emancipation and equal rights for blacks. While Congress possessed no constitutional power to abolish slavery within a state, well-known precedents existed for keeping territories (areas that had not yet entered the Union as states) free from slavery. Congress had done this in 1787 in the Northwest Ordinance and again in the Missouri Compromise of 1820–1821. Many northerners had long resented what they considered southern domination of the federal government. The idea of preventing the creation of new slave states appealed to those who favored policies, such as the protective tariff and government aid to internal improvements, that the majority of southern political leaders opposed.

For thousands of northerners, moreover, the ability to move to the new western territories held out the promise of economic betterment. The depression of the early 1840s had reinforced the traditional equation of land ownership with economic freedom. The labor movement promoted access to western land as a way of combating unemployment and low wages in the East. "Freedom of the soil," declared George Henry Evans, the editor of a pro-labor newspaper, offered the only alternative to permanent economic dependence for American workers.

Such views merged easily with opposition to the expansion of slavery. If slave plantations were to occupy the fertile lands of the West, northern migration would be effectively blocked. The term "free soil" had a double meaning. The Free Soil platform of 1848 called both for barring slavery from western territories and for the federal government to provide free homesteads to settlers in the new territories. Unlike abolitionism, the "free soil" idea also appealed to the racism so widespread in northern society. Wilmot himself insisted that his controversial Proviso was motivated not by "morbid sympathy for the slaves" but to advance "the cause and rights of the free white man," in part by preventing him from having to compete with "black labor."

To white southerners, the idea of barring slavery from territory acquired from Mexico seemed a violation of their equal rights as members of the Union. Southerners had fought and died to win these territories; surely they had a right to share in the fruits of victory. To single out slavery as the one form of property barred from the West would be an affront to the South and its distinctive way of life. A majority of slaves in 1848 lived in states that had not even existed when the Constitution was adopted. Many older plantation areas already suffered from soil exhaustion. Just as northerners believed westward expansion essential to their economic well-being, southern leaders became convinced that slavery must expand or die. Moreover, the admission of new free states would overturn the delicate political balance between the sections and make the South a permanent minority. Southern interests would not be secure in a Union dominated by nonslaveholding states.

CRISIS AND COMPROMISE

In world history, the year 1848 is remembered as the "springtime of nations," a time of democratic uprisings against the monarchies of Europe and demands by ethnic minorities for national independence. American principles of liberty and self-government appeared to be triumphing in the Old World. The Chartist movement in Great Britain organized massive demonstrations in support of a proposed Charter that demanded democratic reforms. The French replaced their monarchy with a republic. Hungarians proclaimed their independence from Austrian rule. Patriots in Italy and Germany, both divided into numerous states, demanded national unification. But the revolutionary tide receded. Chartism faded away. In France, the Second Republic was soon succeeded by the reign of Emperor Napoleon III. Revolts in Budapest, Rome, and other cities were crushed. Would their own experiment in self-government, some Americans wondered, suffer the same fate as the failed revolutions of Europe?

With the slavery issue appearing more and more ominous, established party leaders moved to resolve differences between the sections. Some disputes were of long standing, but the immediate source of controversy arose from the acquisition of new lands after the Mexican War. In 1850, California asked to be admitted to the Union as a free state. Many southerners opposed the measure, fearing that it would upset the sectional balance in Congress.

Senator Henry Clay offered a plan with four main provisions that came to be known as the Compromise of 1850. California would enter the Union as a free state. The slave trade, but not slavery itself, would be abolished in the nation's capital. A stringent new law would allow southerners to reclaim runaway slaves. And the status of slavery in the remaining territories acquired from Mexico would be left to the decision of the local white inhabitants.

THE GREAT DEBATE

In the Senate debate on the Compromise, the divergent sectional positions received eloquent expression. Powerful leaders spoke for and against compromise. Daniel Webster of Massachusetts announced his willingness to abandon the Wilmot Proviso and accept a new fugitive slave law if this were the price of sectional peace. John C. Calhoun, again representing South Carolina, was too ill to speak. A colleague read his remarks rejecting the very idea of compromise. Slavery, Calhoun insisted, must be protected by the national government and extended into all the new territories. The North must yield or the Union could not survive. William H. Seward of New York also opposed compromise. To southerners' talk of their constitutional rights, Seward responded that a "higher law" than the Constitution condemned slavery—the law of morality. Here was the voice of abolitionism, now represented in the U.S. Senate.

President Zachary Taylor, like Andrew Jackson a southerner but a strong nationalist, was alarmed by talk of disunion. He accused southern leaders in Congress of holding California hostage to their own legislative aims and insisted that all Congress needed to do was admit California to the Union. But Taylor died suddenly of an intestinal infection on July 9, 1850. His successor, Millard Fillmore of New York, threw his support to Clay's proposals. Fillmore helped to break the impasse in Congress and secure adoption of the Compromise of 1850.

The Hurly-Burly Pot, *an 1850 cartoon based loosely on the witches' scenes from* Shakespeare's Macbeth, *criticizing northern and southern sectionalists said to be endangering the Union. From left to right, the figures are David Wilmot, who proposed the Proviso banning slavery from territory acquired from Mexico, abolitionist William Lloyd Garrison, Senator John C. Calhoun of South Carolina, and New York antislavery newspaper editor Horace Greeley. The traitor Benedict Arnold is visible in the flames.*

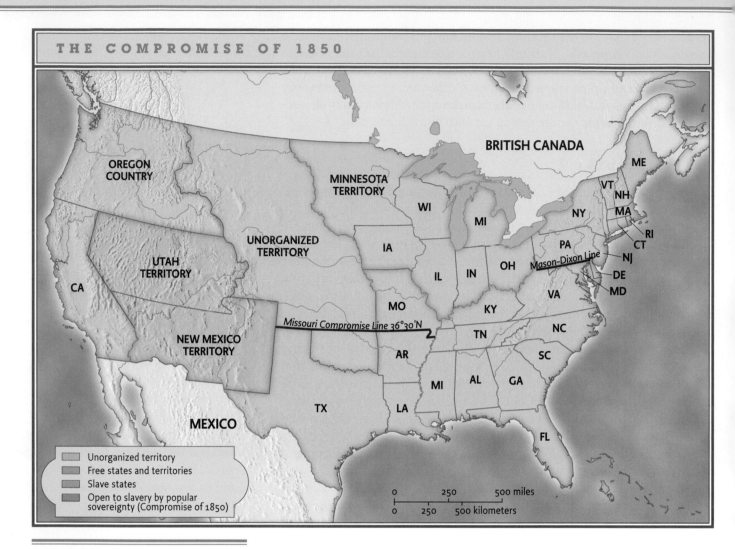

THE COMPROMISE OF 1850

The Compromise of 1850 attempted to settle issues arising from the acquisition of territory from Mexico by admitting California as a free state and providing that the status of slavery in Utah and New Mexico would be determined by the settlers.

THE FUGITIVE SLAVE ISSUE

For one last time, political leaders had removed the dangerous slavery question from congressional debate. The new Fugitive Slave Act, however, made further controversy inevitable. The law allowed special federal commissioners to determine the fate of alleged fugitives without benefit of a jury trial or even testimony by the accused individual. It prohibited local authorities from interfering with the capture of fugitives and required individual citizens to assist in such capture when called upon by federal agents. Thus, southern leaders, usually strong defenders of states' rights and local autonomy, supported a measure that brought federal agents into communities throughout the North, armed with the power to override local law enforcement and judicial procedures to secure the return of runaway slaves. The security of slavery was more important to them than states'-rights consistency.

The fugitive slave issue affected all the free states, not just those that bordered on the South. Slave catchers, for example, entered California attempting to apprehend fugitives from Texas and New Mexico who hoped to reach freedom in British Columbia. The issue drew into politics individuals like Ralph Waldo Emerson, who, while anti-slavery, had previously remained aloof from the abolitionist crusade. Emerson and others influenced by transcendentalism viewed the Fugitive Slave Act as a dangerous example of how a government doing the bidding of the South could override an individual's ability to act according to his conscience—the foundation, for Emerson, of genuine freedom.

During the 1850s, federal tribunals heard over 300 cases and ordered 157 fugitives returned to the South, many at the government's expense. But the law further widened sectional divisions. In a series of dramatic confrontations, fugitives, aided by abolitionist allies, violently resisted recapture. A large crowd in 1851 rescued the escaped slave Jerry from jail in Syracuse, New York, and spirited him off to Canada. In the same year, an owner who attempted to recapture a fugitive was killed in Christiana, Pennsylvania. Later in the decade, Margaret Garner, a Kentucky slave who had escaped with her family to Ohio, killed her own young daughter rather than see her returned to slavery by federal marshals. (At the end of the twentieth century, this incident would become the basis for Toni Morrison's celebrated novel *Beloved*.)

In the North, several thousand fugitives and free-born blacks, worried that they might be swept up in the stringent provisions of the Fugitive Slave Act, fled to safety in Canada. The sight of so many refugees seeking liberty in a foreign land challenged the familiar image of the United States as an asylum for freedom. "Families are separating," reported a Toronto newspaper in October 1850, "leaving their homes, and flying in all directions to seek in Canada, under the British flag, the protection denied to them in the free republic."

An 1855 broadside depicting the life of Anthony Burns, a runaway slave captured in Boston and returned to the South in 1854 by federal officials enforcing the Fugitive Slave Act.

DOUGLAS AND POPULAR SOVEREIGNTY

At least temporarily, the Compromise of 1850 seemed to have restored sectional peace and party unity. In the 1852 presidential election, Democrat Franklin Pierce won a sweeping victory over the Whig Winfield Scott on a platform that recognized the Compromise as a final settlement of the slavery controversy. Pierce received a broad popular mandate, winning 254 electoral votes to Scott's 42. Yet his administration turned out to be one of the most disastrous in American history. It witnessed the collapse of the party system inherited from the Age of Jackson.

In 1854, the old political order finally succumbed to the disruptive pressures of sectionalism. Early in that year, Illinois senator Stephen A. Douglas introduced a bill to provide territorial governments for Kansas and Nebraska, located within the Louisiana Purchase. With Calhoun, Clay, and Webster (the "great triumvirate") all having died between 1850 and 1852, Douglas, although only forty-one, saw himself as the new leader of the Senate. A strong believer in western development, he hoped that a transcontinental railroad could be constructed through Kansas or Nebraska. But he feared that this could not be accomplished unless formal governments had been established in these territories. Southerners in Congress, however, seemed adamant against allowing the organization of new free territories that might further upset the sectional balance. Douglas hoped to satisfy them by applying the principle of popular sovereignty, whereby the status of slavery would be determined by the votes of local settlers, not Congress. To Douglas, popular sovereignty embodied the idea of local self-government and offered a middle ground between the extremes of North and South. It was a principle on which all parts of the Democratic Party could unite, and which might enable him to capture the presidential nomination in 1856 to succeed the ineffectual Pierce.

THE KANSAS-NEBRASKA ACT

Unlike the lands taken from Mexico, Kansas and Nebraska lay in the nation's heartland, directly in the path of westward migration. Slavery, moreover, was prohibited there under the terms of the Missouri Compromise, which Douglas's bill repealed. In response to Douglas's proposal, a group of antislavery congressmen issued the *Appeal of the Independent Democrats.* Written by two abolitionists from Ohio—Congressman Joshua Giddings and Senator Salmon P. Chase—the *Appeal* proved to be one of the most effective pieces of political persuasion in American history. It arraigned Douglas's bill as a "gross violation of a sacred pledge," part and parcel of "an atrocious plot" to convert free territory into a "dreary region

The Kansas-Nebraska Act opened a vast area in the nation's heartland to the possible spread of slavery by repealing the Missouri Compromise and providing that settlers would determine the status of slavery in these territories.

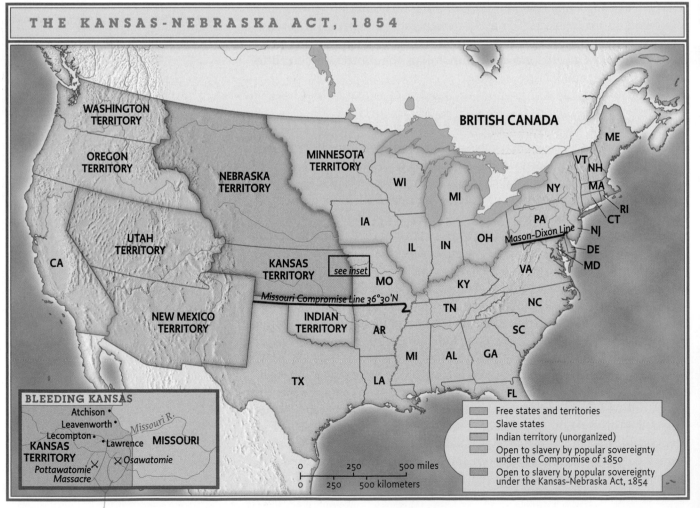

THE KANSAS-NEBRASKA ACT, 1854

BLEEDING KANSAS

Legend:
- Free states and territories
- Slave states
- Indian territory (unorganized)
- Open to slavery by popular sovereignty under the Compromise of 1850
- Open to slavery by popular sovereignty under the Kansas-Nebraska Act, 1854

of despotism, inhabited by masters and slaves." It helped to convince millions of northerners that southern leaders aimed at nothing less than extending their peculiar institution throughout the West.

Thanks to Douglas's energetic leadership, the Kansas-Nebraska Bill became law. But it shattered the Democratic Party's unity. Even as Congress debated, protest meetings sprang up throughout the North. Fearing that the bill's unpopularity among their constituents would harm their chances for reelection, half the northern Democrats in the House cast negative votes. Loyalty to Pierce, Douglas, and their party led the other half to support the measure. It is difficult to think of a piece of legislation in American history that had a more profound impact on national life. In the wake of the bill's passage, American politics underwent a profound reorganization. During the next two years, the Whig Party, unable to develop a unified response to the political crisis, collapsed. From a region divided between the two parties, the South became solidly Democratic. Most northern Whigs, augmented by thousands of disgruntled Democrats, joined a new organization, the Republican Party, dedicated to preventing the further expansion of slavery.

THE RISE OF THE REPUBLICAN PARTY

THE NORTHERN ECONOMY

The disruptive impact of slavery on the traditional parties was the immediate cause of political transformation in the mid-1850s. But the rise of the Republican Party also reflected underlying economic and social changes, notably the completion of the market revolution and the beginning of mass immigration from Europe. The period from 1843, when prosperity returned, to 1857, when another economic downturn hit, witnessed explosive economic growth, especially in the North. The catalyst was the completion of the railroad network. From 5,000 miles in 1848, railroad track mileage grew to 30,000 by 1860, with most of the construction occurring in Ohio, Illinois, and other states of the Old Northwest. Four great trunk railroads now linked eastern cities with western farming and commercial centers. The railroads completed the reorientation of the Northwest's trade from the South to the East. As late as 1850, most western farmers still shipped their produce down the Mississippi River. Ten years later, however, railroads transported nearly all their crops to the East, at a fraction of the previous cost. By 1860, for example, 60 million bushels of wheat were passing through Buffalo on their way to market in eastern cities and abroad. The economic integration of the Northwest and Northeast created the groundwork for their political unification in the Republican Party.

By 1860, the North had become a complex, integrated economy, with eastern industrialists marketing manufactured goods to the commercial farmers of the West, while residents of the region's growing cities consumed the food westerners produced. Northern society stood poised between old and new ways. The majority of the population still lived not in large cities but in small towns and rural areas, where the ideal of economic independence—owning one's own farm or shop—still lay within reach.

An 1853 broadside for one section of the Illinois Central Railroad. One of the most important new lines of the 1850s, the Illinois Central opened parts of the Old Northwest to settlement and commercial agriculture, and it helped to cement Chicago's place as the region's foremost city.

THE RAILROAD NETWORK, 1850s

The rapid expansion of the railroad network in the 1850s linked the Northeast and Northwest in a web of commerce. The South's rail network was considerably less developed.

Yet the majority of the workforce no longer labored in agriculture, and the industrial revolution was spreading rapidly.

Two great areas of industrial production had arisen. One, along the Atlantic coast, stretched from Boston to Philadelphia and Baltimore. A second was centered on or near the Great Lakes, in inland cities like Buffalo, Cleveland, Pittsburgh, and Chicago. Driven by railroad expansion, coal

The Lackawanna Valley, *an 1855 painting by George Inness commissioned by the president of the Delaware, Lackawanna, and Western Railroad. In the background is the roundhouse at Scranton, Pennsylvania. While the scene emphasizes the harmony of technological progress and nature (with a factory on the right almost entirely hidden by trees), the tree stumps in the foreground suggest some regret that the natural environment is giving way to progress.*

mining and iron manufacturing were growing rapidly. Chicago, the Northwest's major rail center and the jumping-off place for settlers heading for the Great Plains, had become a complex manufacturing center, producing 5,000 reapers each year, along with barbed wire, windmills, and prefabricated "balloon frame" houses, all of which facilitated further western settlement. New York City by 1860 had become the nation's preeminent financial, commercial, and manufacturing center. Although the southern economy was also growing and the continuing expansion of cotton production brought wealth to slaveholders, the South did not share in these broad economic changes.

THE RISE AND FALL OF THE KNOW-NOTHINGS

As noted in Chapter 9, nativism—hostility to immigrants, especially Catholics—emerged as a local political movement in the 1840s. But in 1854, with the party system in crisis, it burst on the national political scene with the sudden appearance of the American, or Know-Nothing, Party (so called because it began as a secret organization whose members, when asked about its existence, were supposed to respond, "I know nothing"). The party trumpeted its dedication to reserving political office for native-born Americans and to resisting the "aggressions" of the Catholic Church, such as its supposed efforts to undermine public school systems. The Know-Nothings swept the 1854 state elections in Massachusetts, electing the governor, all of the state's congressmen, and nearly every member of the state legislature. They captured the mayor's office in cities like Philadelphia, Chicago, and San Francisco as well. In many states, nativists emerged as a major component of victorious "anti-Nebraska" coalitions of voters opposed to the Kansas-Nebraska Act. In the North, the Know-Nothings' appeal combined anti-Catholic and antislavery sentiment, with opposition to the sale of liquor often added to the equation. After all, most Catholics, as noted in the previous chapter, vigorously opposed the reform movements inspired by evangelical Protestantism, especially antislavery

George Catlin's 1827 painting Five Points *depicts a working-class immigrant neighborhood in New York City that gained a reputation for crime, drinking, and overcrowding.*

and temperance. The 1854 elections, said one observer, revealed "a deep seated feeling in favor of human freedom and also a fine determination that hereafter none but Americans shall rule America."

Despite severe anti-Irish discrimination in jobs, housing, and education, however, it is remarkable how little came of demands that immigrants be barred from the political nation. All European immigrants benefited from being white. During the 1850s, free blacks found immigrants pushing them out of even the jobs as servants and common laborers previously available to them. The newcomers had the good fortune to arrive after white male suffrage had become the norm and automatically received the right to vote. Even as New England states sought to reduce immigrant political power (Massachusetts and Connecticut made literacy a voting requirement, and Massachusetts mandated a two-year waiting period between becoming a naturalized citizen and voting), western states desperate for labor allowed immigrants to vote well before they became citizens. In a country where the suffrage had become essential to understandings of freedom, it is significant that many white male immigrants could vote almost from the moment they landed in America, while non-whites, whose ancestors had lived in the country for centuries, could not.

THE FREE LABOR IDEOLOGY

By 1856, it was clear that the Republican Party—a coalition of antislavery Democrats, northern Whigs, Free Soilers, and Know-Nothings opposed to the further expansion of slavery—would become the major alternative to the Democratic Party in the North. Republicans managed to convince most northerners that the Slave Power, as they called the South's proslavery political leadership, posed a more immediate threat to their liberties and aspirations than "popery" and immigration. The party's appeal rested on the idea of "free labor." In Republican hands, the antithesis between "free society" and "slave society" coalesced into a comprehensive worldview that glorified the North as the home of progress, opportunity, and freedom.

The defining quality of northern society, Republicans declared, was the opportunity it offered each laborer to move up to the status of landowning farmer or independent craftsman, thus achieving the economic independence essential to freedom. Slavery, by contrast, spawned a social order consisting of degraded slaves, poor whites with no hope of advancement, and idle aristocrats. The struggle over the territories was a contest about which of two antagonistic labor systems would dominate the West and, by implication, the nation's future. If slavery were to spread into the West, northern free laborers would be barred, and their chances for social advancement severely diminished. Slavery, Republicans insisted, must be kept out of the territories so that free labor could flourish.

To southern claims that slavery was the foundation of liberty, Republicans responded with the rallying cry "freedom national"—meaning not abolition, but ending the federal government's support of slavery. Under the banner of free labor, northerners of diverse backgrounds and interests rallied in defense of the superiority of their own society. Republicans acknowledged that some northern laborers, including most Irish immigrants, were locked into jobs as factory workers and unskilled laborers and found it extremely difficult to rise in the social scale. But Republicans concluded that it was their "dependent nature"—a lack of Protestant, middle-class virtues—that explained the plight of the immigrant poor.

Republicans were not abolitionists—they focused on preventing the spread of slavery, not attacking it where it existed. Nonetheless, many party leaders viewed the nation's division into free and slave societies as an "irrepressible conflict," as Senator William H. Seward of New York put it in 1858, that eventually would have to be resolved. These "two systems" of society, Seward insisted, were "incompatible" within a single nation. The market revolution, Seward argued, by drawing the entire nation closer together in a web of transportation and commerce, heightened the tension between freedom and slavery. The United States, he predicted, "must and will, sooner or later, become either entirely a slaveholding nation, or entirely a free-labor nation."

BLEEDING KANSAS AND THE ELECTION OF 1856

Their free labor outlook, which resonated so effectively with deeply held northern values, helps to explain the Republicans' rapid rise to prominence. But dramatic events in 1855 and 1856 also fueled the party's growth. When Kansas held elections in 1854 and 1855, hundreds of proslavery Missourians crossed the border to cast fraudulent ballots. Presi-

Political Chart of the United States, *an 1856 chart graphically illustrating the division between slave and free states and providing statistics to demonstrate the superiority of free to slave society. The image underscores the Republican contention that it is essential to prevent slavery from spreading into the western territories. John C. Frémont, Republican presidential candidate, is pictured at the top.*

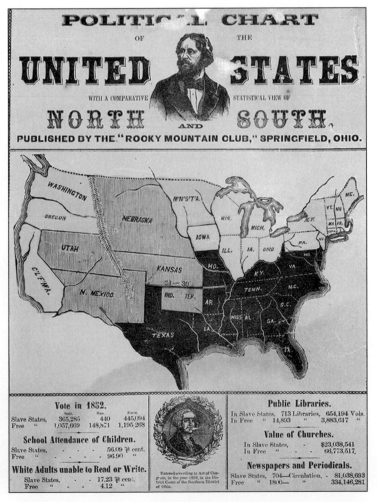

dent Franklin Pierce recognized the legitimacy of the resulting proslavery legislature and replaced the territorial governor, Andrew H. Reeder of Pennsylvania, when he dissented. Settlers from free states soon established a rival government, and a sporadic civil war broke out in Kansas in which some 200 persons eventually lost their lives. In one incident, in May 1856, a proslavery mob attacked the free-soil stronghold of Lawrence, burning public buildings and pillaging private homes.

"Bleeding Kansas" seemed to discredit Douglas's policy of leaving the decision on slavery up to the local population, thus aiding the Republicans. The party also drew strength from an unprecedented incident in the halls of Congress. South Carolina representative Preston Brooks, wielding a gold-tipped cane, beat the antislavery senator Charles Sumner of Massachusetts unconscious after Sumner delivered a denunciation of "The Crime against Kansas." Many southerners applauded Brooks, sending him canes emblazoned with the words, "hit him again!"

In the election of 1856, the Republican Party chose as its candidate John C. Frémont and drafted a platform that strongly opposed the further expansion of slavery. Stung by the northern reaction to the Kansas-Nebraska Act, the Democrats nominated James Buchanan, who had been minister to Great Britain in 1854 and thus had no direct connection with that divisive measure. The Democratic platform endorsed the principle of popular sovereignty as the only viable solution to the slavery controversy. Meanwhile, the Know-Nothings presented ex-president Millard Fillmore as their candidate. Frémont outpolled Buchanan in the North, carrying eleven of sixteen free states—a remarkable achievement for an organization that had existed for only two years. But Buchanan won the entire South and the key northern states of Illinois, Indiana, and Pennsylvania, enough to ensure his victory. Fillmore carried only Maryland. But he ran well among former Whig

Liberty, the Fair Maid of Kansas, in the Hands of the "Border Ruffians," *a cartoon blaming the Democratic Party for violence in Kansas in 1856. Leading Democrats surround the maid of liberty— from left to right, Secretary of State William L. Marcy, Democratic presidential candidate James Buchanan, President Franklin Pierce, Lewis Cass, the party's candidate for president in 1848, and Stephen A. Douglas, author of the Kansas-Nebraska Act, shown scalping an Indian.*

voters in the Upper South and more conservative areas of the North, who were reluctant to join the Democrats but feared Republican victory might threaten the Union.

The 1856 election returns made starkly clear that parties had reoriented themselves along sectional lines. One major party had been destroyed, another seriously weakened, and a new one had arisen, devoted entirely to the interests of the North.

THE EMERGENCE OF LINCOLN

The final collapse of the party system took place during the administration of a president who epitomized the old political order. Born during George Washington's presidency, James Buchanan had served in Pennsylvania's legislature, in both houses of Congress, and as secretary of state under James K. Polk. A staunch believer in the Union, he committed himself to pacifying inflamed sectional emotions. Few presidents have failed more disastrously in what they set out to accomplish.

THE DRED SCOTT DECISION

Even before his inauguration, Buchanan became aware of an impending Supreme Court decision that held out the hope of settling the slavery controversy once and for all. This was the case of Dred Scott. During the 1830s, Scott had accompanied his owner, Dr. John Emerson of Missouri, to Illinois, where slavery had been prohibited by the Northwest Ordinance of 1787 and by state law, and to Wisconsin Territory, where it was barred by the Missouri Compromise. After returning to Missouri, Scott sued for his freedom, claiming that residence on free soil had made him free.

The Dred Scott decision, one of the most famous—or infamous—rulings in the long history of the Supreme Court, was announced in March 1857, two days after Buchanan's inauguration. The justices addressed three questions. Could a black person be a citizen and therefore sue in federal court? Did residence in a free state make Scott free? Did Congress possess the power to prohibit slavery in a territory? All 9 justices issued individual opinions. But essentially, the Court divided 6–3 (with Justice Robert C. Grier of Pennsylvania, at Buchanan's behind-the-scenes urging, joining a southern majority). Speaking for the majority, Chief Justice Roger B. Taney declared that only white persons could be citizens of the United States. The nation's founders, Taney insisted, believed that blacks "had no rights which the white man was bound to respect." Descended from different ancestors and lacking a history of freedom, blacks, he continued, could never be part of the nation's "political family."

The case could have ended there, since Scott had no right to sue, but inspired by the idea of resolving the slavery issue, Taney pressed on. Scott, he declared, remained a slave. Illinois law had no effect on him after his return to Missouri. As for his residence in Wisconsin, Congress possessed no power under the Constitution to bar slavery from a territory. The Missouri Compromise, recently repealed by the Kansas-Nebraska Act, had been

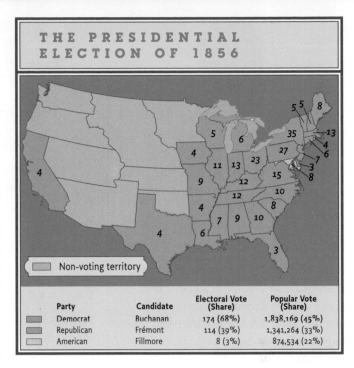

THE PRESIDENTIAL ELECTION OF 1856

	Party	Candidate	Electoral Vote (Share)	Popular Vote (Share)
	Democrat	Buchanan	174 (68%)	1,838,169 (45%)
	Republican	Frémont	114 (39%)	1,341,264 (33%)
	American	Fillmore	8 (3%)	874,534 (22%)

Non-voting territory

Dred and Harriet Scott, as pictured in Frank Leslie's Illustrated Newspaper, June 27, 1857, three months after the Supreme Court ruled that they must remain in slavery.

unconstitutional and so was any measure interfering with southerners' right to bring slaves into the western territories. The decision in effect declared unconstitutional the Republican platform of restricting slavery's expansion. It also seemed to undermine Douglas's doctrine of popular sovereignty. For if Congress lacked the power to prohibit slavery in a territory, how could a territorial legislature created by Congress do so? The Court, a Georgia newspaper exulted, "covers every question regarding slavery and settles it in favor of the South."

THE DECISION'S AFTERMATH

Perhaps the person least directly affected by the Dred Scott decision was the plaintiff himself, for a new master immediately emancipated Scott and his wife, Harriet. Both died on the eve of the Civil War, having enjoyed their freedom for only a few years. The impact on the party system was more far-reaching. Among the decision's casualties was the reputation of the Court itself, which, in the North, sank to the lowest level in all of American history. Rather than abandoning their opposition to the expansion of slavery, Republicans now viewed the Court as controlled by the Slave Power.

Slavery, announced President Buchanan, henceforth existed in all the territories, "by virtue of the Constitution." In 1858, his administration attempted to admit Kansas as a slave state under the Lecompton Constitution, which had been drafted by a pro-southern convention and never submitted to a popular vote. Outraged by this violation of popular sovereignty, Douglas formed an unlikely alliance with congressional Republicans to block the attempt. Kansas remained a territory; it would join the Union as a free state on the eve of the Civil War. The Lecompton battle convinced southern Democrats that they could not trust their party's most popular northern leader.

LINCOLN AND SLAVERY

The depth of Americans' divisions over slavery were brought into sharp focus in 1858 in one of the most storied election campaigns in the nation's history. Seeking reelection to the Senate as both a champion of popular sovereignty and the man who had prevented the administration from forcing slavery on the people of Kansas, Douglas faced an unexpectedly strong challenge from Abraham Lincoln, then little known outside of Illinois. Born into a modest farm family in Kentucky in 1809, Lincoln had moved as a youth to frontier Indiana and then Illinois. Although he began running for public office at the age of twenty-one, until the mid-1850s his career hardly seemed destined for greatness. He had served four terms as a Whig in the state legislature and one in Congress from 1847 to 1849.

Lincoln reentered politics in 1854 as a result of the Kansas-Nebraska Act. He once said that he "hated slavery as much as any abolitionist." Unlike abolitionists, however, Lincoln was willing to compromise with the South to preserve the Union. "I hate to see the poor creatures hunted down," he once wrote of fugitive slaves, "but I bite my lip and keep silent." But on one question he was inflexible—stopping the expansion of slavery.

Lincoln developed a critique of slavery and its expansion that gave voice to the central values of the emerging Republican Party and the millions of northerners whose loyalty it commanded. His speeches combined the moral fervor of the abolitionists with the respect for order and the Constitution of more conservative northerners. "I hate it," he said in 1854 of the prospect of slavery's expansion, "because of the monstrous injustice of slavery itself. I hate it because it deprives our republican example of its just influence in the world—enables the enemies of free institutions, with plausibility, to taunt us as hypocrites—causes the real friends of freedom to doubt our sincerity." If slavery were allowed to expand, he warned, the "love of liberty" would be extinguished and with it America's special mission to be a symbol of democracy for the entire world.

Even though Lincoln lived in a society firmly in the grasp of the market revolution and worked on occasion as an attorney for the Illinois Central Railroad, one of the nation's largest corporations, his America was the world of the small producer. In a sense, his own life personified the free labor ideology and the opportunities northern society offered to laboring men. During the 1850s, property-owning farmers, artisans, and shopkeepers far outnumbered wage earners in Illinois. Lincoln was fascinated and disturbed by the writings of proslavery ideologues like George Fitzhugh (discussed in Chapter 11), and he rose to the defense of northern society. "I want every man to have the chance," said Lincoln, "and I believe a black man is entitled to it, in which he *can* better his condition." Blacks might not be the equal of whites in all respects, but in their "natural right" to the fruits of their labor, they were "my equal and the equal of all others."

THE LINCOLN-DOUGLAS CAMPAIGN

The campaign against Douglas, the North's preeminent political leader, created Lincoln's national reputation. Accepting his party's nomination for the Senate in July 1858, Lincoln etched sharply the differences between them. "A house divided against itself," he announced, "cannot stand. I believe this government cannot endure, permanently half *slave* and half *free*." Lincoln's point was not that civil war was imminent, but that Americans must choose between favoring and opposing slavery. There could be no middle ground. Douglas's policy of popular sovereignty, he insisted, reflected a moral indifference that could only result in the institution's spread throughout the entire country.

The Lincoln-Douglas debates, held in seven Illinois towns and attended by tens of thousands of listeners, remain classics of American political oratory. Clashing definitions of freedom lay at their heart. To Lincoln, freedom meant opposition to slavery. The nation needed to rekindle the spirit of the founding fathers, who, he claimed, had tried to place slavery on the path to "ultimate extinction." Douglas argued that the essence of freedom lay in local self-government and individual self-determination. A large and diverse nation could only survive by respecting the right of each locality to determine its own institutions. In response to a question posed by Lincoln

A lithograph portraying Stephen A. Douglas as a gladiator. Douglas defends popular sovereignty and opposes the Buchanan administration's attempt to admit Kansas to the Union as a slave state under the Lecompton Constitution.

VOICES OF FREEDOM

FROM THE LINCOLN-DOUGLAS DEBATES (1858)

The most famous political campaign in American history, the race for the U.S. Senate between Senator Stephen A. Douglas (a former Illinois judge) and Abraham Lincoln in 1858 was highlighted by seven debates in which they discussed the politics of slavery and contrasting understandings of freedom.

DOUGLAS: Mr. Lincoln says that this government cannot endure permanently in the same condition in which it was made by its framers—divided into free and slave states. He says that it has existed for about seventy years thus divided, and yet he tells you that it cannot endure permanently on the same principles and in the same relative conditions in which our fathers made it. . . . One of the reserved rights of the states, was the right to regulate the relations between master and servant, on the slavery question.

Now, my friends, if we will only act conscientiously upon this great principle of popular sovereignty which guarantees to each state and territory the right to do as it pleases on all things local and domestic instead of Congress interfering, we will continue to be at peace one with another.

LINCOLN: Judge Douglas says, "Why can't this Union endure permanently, half slave and half free?" "Why can't we let it stand as our fathers placed it?" That is the exact difficulty between us. . . . I say when this government was first established it was the policy of its founders to prohibit the spread of slavery into the new territories of the United States, where it had not existed. But Judge Douglas and his friends have broken up that policy and placed it upon a new basis by which it is to become national and perpetual. All I have asked or desired anywhere is that it should be placed back again upon the basis that the founders of our government originally placed it—restricting it from the new territories. . . .

Judge Douglas assumes that we have no interest in them—that we have no right to interfere. . . . Do we not wish for an outlet for our surplus population, if I may so express myself? Do we not feel an interest in getting to that outlet with such institutions as we would like to have prevail there? Now irrespective of the moral aspect of this question as to whether there is a right or wrong in enslaving a negro, I am still in favor of our new territories being in such a condition that white men may find a home. I am in favor of this not merely for our own people, but as an outlet for *free white people everywhere*, the world over—in which Hans and Baptiste and Patrick, and all other men from all the world, may find new homes and better their conditions in life.

DOUGLAS: For one, I am opposed to negro citizenship in any and every form. I believe this government was made on the white basis. I believe it was made by white men, for the benefit of white men and their posterity forever . . . I do not believe that the Almighty made the negro capable of self-government. I say to you, my fellow-citizens, that in my opinion the signers of the Declaration of Independence had no reference to the negro whatever when they declared all men to be created equal. They desired to express by that phrase, white men, men of European birth and European descent . . . when they spoke of the equality of men.

LINCOLN: I have no purpose to introduce political and social equality between the white and the black races. There is a physical difference between the two, which in my judgment will probably forever forbid their living together upon the footing of perfect equality, and inasmuch as it becomes a necessity that there must be a difference, I, as well as Judge Douglas, am in favor of the race to which I belong, having the superior position. . . . But I hold that notwithstanding all this, there is no reason in the world why the negro is not entitled to all the natural rights enumerated in the Declaration of Independence, the right to life, liberty, and the pursuit of happiness. I hold that he is as much entitled to these as the white man. I agree with Judge Douglas he is not my equal in many respects—certainly not in color, perhaps not in moral or intellectual endowment. But in the right to eat the bread, without leave of anybody else, which his own hand earns, *he is my equal and the equal of Judge Douglas, and the equal of every living man.*

DOUGLAS: He tells you that I will not argue the question whether slavery is right or wrong. I tell you why I will not do it. . . . I hold that the people of the slaveholding states are civilized men as well as ourselves, that they bear consciences as well as we, and that they are accountable to God and their posterity and not to us. It is for them to decide therefore the moral and religious right of the slavery question for themselves within their own limits. . . . He says that he looks forward to a time when slavery shall be abolished everywhere. I look forward to a time when each state shall be allowed to do as it pleases.

LINCOLN: I suppose that the real difference between Judge Douglas and his friends, and the Republicans, is that the Judge is not in favor of making any difference between slavery and liberty . . . and consequently every sentiment he utters discards the idea that there is any wrong in slavery. . . . That is the real issue. That is the issue that will continue in this country when these poor tongues of Judge Douglas and myself shall be silent. It is the eternal struggle between these two principles—right and wrong—throughout the world.

QUESTIONS

1. How do Lincoln and Douglas differ on what rights black Americans are entitled to enjoy?

2. Why does Lincoln believe the nation cannot exist forever half slave and half free, whereas Douglas believes it can?

3. How does each of the speakers balance the right of each state to manage its own affairs against the right of every person to be free?

Stephen A. Douglas in a daguerreotype from around 1853.

Abraham Lincoln in 1858, the year of the Lincoln-Douglas debates.

during the Freeport debate, Douglas insisted that popular sovereignty was not incompatible with the Dred Scott decision. Although territorial legislatures could no longer exclude slavery directly, he argued, if the people wished to keep slaveholders out all they needed to do was refrain from giving the institution legal protection.

In a critique not only of the antislavery movement but of the entire reform impulse deriving from religious revivalism, Douglas insisted that politicians had no right to impose their own moral standards on society as a whole. "I deny the right of Congress," he declared, "to force a good thing upon a people who are unwilling to receive it." If a community wished to own slaves, it had a right to do so. Of course, when Douglas spoke of the "people," he meant whites alone. He spent much of his time in the debates attempting to portray Lincoln as a dangerous radical whose positions threatened to degrade white Americans by reducing them to equality with blacks. The United States government, Douglas proclaimed, had been created "by white men for the benefit of white men and their posterity for ever."

Lincoln shared many of the racial prejudices of his day. He opposed giving Illinois blacks the right to vote or serve on juries and spoke frequently of colonizing blacks overseas as the best solution to the problems of slavery and race. Yet, unlike Douglas, Lincoln did not use appeals to racism to garner votes. And he refused to exclude blacks from the human family. No less than whites, they were entitled to the inalienable rights of the Declaration of Independence, which applied to "all men, in all lands, everywhere," not merely to Europeans and their descendants.

The Illinois election returns revealed a state sharply divided, like the nation itself. Southern Illinois, settled from the South, voted strongly Democratic, while the rapidly growing northern part of the state was firmly in the Republican column. Until the adoption of the Seventeenth Amendment in the early twentieth century, each state's legislature chose its U.S. senators. In 1858, Republican candidates for the legislature won more votes statewide than Democrats. But because the apportionment of seats, based on the census of 1850, did not reflect the growth of northern Illinois since then, the Democrats emerged with a narrow margin in the legislature. Douglas was reelected. His victory was all the more remarkable because elsewhere in the North Republicans swept to victory in 1858. Resentment over the administration's Kansas policy split the Democratic Party, sometimes producing two Democratic candidates (pro-Douglas and pro-Buchanan) running against a single Republican. Coupled with the impact of the economic recession that began in 1857, this helped to produce Republican victories even in Indiana and Pennsylvania, which Democrats had carried two years earlier.

JOHN BROWN AT HARPERS FERRY

An armed assault by the abolitionist John Brown on the federal arsenal at Harpers Ferry, Virginia, further heightened sectional tensions. Brown had a long career of involvement in antislavery activities. In the 1830s and 1840s, he had befriended fugitive slaves and, although chronically in debt, helped to finance antislavery publications. Like other abolitionists, Brown was a deeply religious man. But his God was not the forgiving Jesus of the revivals, who encouraged men to save themselves through conversion, but the vengeful Father of the Old Testament. During the civil war in Kansas, Brown traveled to the territory. In May 1856, after the attack on Lawrence, he and a few followers murdered five proslavery settlers at Pottawatomie Creek. For the next two years, he traveled through the North and Canada, raising funds and enlisting followers for a war against slavery.

On October 16, 1859, with twenty-one men, seven of them black, Brown seized Harpers Ferry. Militarily, the plan made little sense. Brown's band was soon surrounded and killed or captured by a detachment of federal soldiers headed by Colonel Robert E. Lee. Placed on trial for treason to the state of Virginia, Brown conducted himself with dignity and courage, winning admiration from millions of northerners who disapproved of his violent deeds. When Virginia's governor, Henry A. Wise, spurned pleas for clemency and ordered Brown executed, he turned Brown into a martyr to much of the North. Henry David Thoreau pronounced him "a crucified hero." Since Brown's death, radicals of both the left and right have revered Brown as a man willing to take action against an institution he considered immoral. Black leaders have long hailed him as a rare white person willing to sacrifice himself for the cause of racial justice.

To the South, the failure of Brown's assault seemed less significant than the adulation he seemed to arouse from much of the northern public. His raid and execution further widened the breach between the sections. Brown's last letter was a brief, prophetic statement: "I, John Brown, am quite certain that the crimes of this guilty land will never be purged away but with blood."

John Brown in an 1847 portrait by Augustus Washington, a black photographer.

THE RISE OF SOUTHERN NATIONALISM

With the Republicans continuing to gain strength in the North, Democrats might have been expected to put a premium on party unity as the election of 1860 approached. By this time, however, a sizable group of southerners now viewed their region's prospects as more favorable outside the Union than within it. Throughout the 1850s, influential writers and political leaders kept up a drumbeat of complaints about the South's problems. The sky-high price of slaves made it impossible for many planters' sons and upwardly mobile small farmers to become planters in their own right. Many white southerners felt that the opportunity was eroding for economic independence through ownership of land and slaves—liberty as they understood it. The North, secessionists charged, reaped the benefits of the cotton trade, while southerners fell deeper and deeper into debt. To remain in the Union meant to accept "bondage" to the North. But an independent South could become the foundation of a slave empire ringing the Caribbean and embracing Cuba, other West Indian islands, Mexico, and parts of Central America.

More and more southerners were speaking openly of southward expansion. In 1854, Pierre Soulé of Louisiana, the American ambassador to Spain, had persuaded the ministers to Britain and France to join him in signing the Ostend Manifesto, which called on the United States to purchase or seize Cuba, where slavery was still legal, from Spain. Meanwhile, the military adventurer William Walker led a series of "filibustering" expeditions (the term derived from the Spanish word for pirate, *filibustero*) in Central America.

Born in Tennessee, Walker had headed to California to join the gold rush. Failing to strike it rich, he somehow decided to try to become the leader of a Latin American country. In 1853, he led a band of men who "captured" Baja California—a peninsula owned by Mexico south of California, and named himself president of an independent republic. The arrival of Mexican naval vessels forced Walker and his men to beat a hasty retreat. Walker next decided to establish himself as ruler of Nicaragua in Central America, and to open that country to slavery. Nicaragua at the time was engaged in a civil war, and one faction invited Walker to assist it by bringing 300 armed men. In 1855, Walker captured the city of Granada and in the following year proclaimed himself president. The administration of Franklin Pierce recognized Walker's government, but neighboring countries sent in troops, who forced Walker to flee. IIis activities rcpresented clear violations of American neutrality laws. But Walker won acclaim in the South, and when federal authorities placed him on trial in New Orleans in 1858, the jury acquitted him.

By the late 1850s, southern leaders were bending every effort to strengthen the bonds of slavery. "Slavery is our king," declared a South Carolina politician in 1860. "Slavery is our truth, slavery is our divine right." New state laws further restricted access to freedom. One in Louisiana stated simply: "After the passage of this act, no slave shall be emancipated in this state." Some southerners called for the reopening of the African slave trade, hoping that an influx of new slaves would lower the price, thereby increasing the number of whites with a vested interest in the peculiar institution. By early 1860, seven states of the Deep South had gone on record demanding that the Democratic Platform pledge to protect slavery in all the territories that had not yet been admitted to the Union as states. Virtually no northern politician could accept this position. For southern leaders to insist on it would guarantee the destruction of the Democratic Party as a national institution. But southern nationalists, known as "fire-eaters," hoped to split the party and the country and form an independent Southern Confederacy.

THE DEMOCRATIC SPLIT

When the Democratic convention met in April 1860, Douglas's supporters commanded a majority but not the two-thirds required for a presidential nomination. Because of his fight against Kansas's Lecompton Constitution and his refusal to support congressional laws imposing slavery on all the territories, Douglas had become unacceptable to political leaders of the Deep South. They were still determined to bring Kansas into the Union as a slave state. When the convention adopted a platform reaffirming the doctrine of popular sovereignty, delegates from the seven slave states of the Lower South walked out and the gathering recessed in confusion. Six weeks later, it reconvened, replaced the bolters with Douglas supporters, and nominated him for president. In response, southern Democrats placed their own ticket in the field, headed by John C. Breckinridge of Kentucky. Breckinridge insisted that slavery must be protected in the western territories.

The Democratic Party, the last great bond of national unity, had been shattered. National conventions had traditionally been places where party managers, mindful of the need for unity in the fall campaign, reconciled their differences. But in 1860, neither northern or southern Democrats were interested in conciliation. Southern Democrats no longer trusted their northern counterparts. Douglas's backers, for their part, would not accept a platform that doomed their party to certain defeat in the North.

THE NOMINATION OF LINCOLN

Meanwhile, Republicans gathered in Chicago and chose Lincoln as their standard-bearer. Although he entered the convention with fewer delegates than William H. Seward, Lincoln did not suffer from Seward's political liabilities. Former Know-Nothings, a majority of whom had by now joined Republican ranks, bitterly resented Seward's efforts as governor of New York to channel state funds to Catholic schools. Seward had a not entirely deserved reputation for radicalism as a result of his "higher law" and "irrepressible conflict" speeches, discussed earlier.

Lincoln's devotion to the Union appealed to moderate Republicans, and his emphasis on the moral dimension of the sectional controversy made him acceptable to Republicans from abolitionist backgrounds. Having never associated with the Know-Nothings, he could appeal to immigrant voters, and nativists preferred him to the hated Seward. Most important, coming from Illinois, Lincoln was better positioned to carry the pivotal "doubtful states" essential for Republican victory. On the third ballot, he was nominated. The party platform denied the validity of the Dred Scott decision, reaffirmed Republicans' opposition to slavery's expansion, and added economic planks designed to appeal to a broad array of northern voters—free homesteads in the West, a protective tariff, and government aid in building a transcontinental railroad.

Lincoln's nickname, "The Railsplitter," recalled his humble origins. An unknown artist created this larger-than-life portrait. The White House is visible in the distance. The painting is said to have been displayed during campaign rallies in 1860.

THE ELECTION OF 1860

In effect, two presidential campaigns took place in 1860. In the North, Lincoln and Douglas were the combatants. In the South, the Republicans had no presence and three candidates contested the election—Douglas, Breckinridge, and John Bell of Tennessee, the candidate of the hastily organized Constitutional Union Party. A haven for Unionist former Whigs, this new party adopted a platform consisting of a single pledge—to preserve "the Constitution as it is [that is, with slavery] and the Union as it was [without sectional discord]."

The most striking thing about the election returns was their sectional character. Lincoln carried all of the North except New Jersey, receiving 1.8 million popular votes (54 percent of the regional total and 40 percent of the national) and 180 electoral votes (a clear majority). Breckinridge captured most of the slave states, although Bell carried three Upper South states and about 40 percent of the southern vote as a whole. Douglas placed first only in Missouri, but his 1.3 million popular votes were second in number only to Lincoln's. Douglas was the only candidate with significant support in all parts of the country, a vindication, in a sense, of his long effort to transcend sectional divisions.

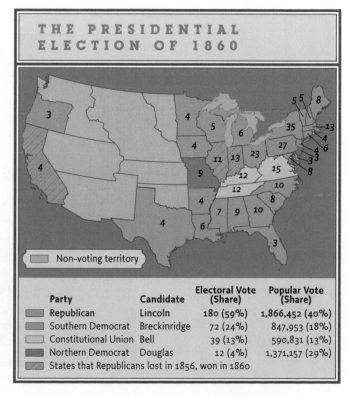

THE PRESIDENTIAL ELECTION OF 1860

Non-voting territory

Party	Candidate	Electoral Vote (Share)	Popular Vote (Share)
Republican	Lincoln	180 (59%)	1,866,452 (40%)
Southern Democrat	Breckinridge	72 (24%)	847,953 (18%)
Constitutional Union	Bell	39 (13%)	590,831 (13%)
Northern Democrat	Douglas	12 (4%)	1,371,157 (29%)
States that Republicans lost in 1856, won in 1860			

But his failure to carry either section suggested that a traditional political career based on devotion to the Union was no longer possible. Without a single vote in ten southern states, Lincoln was elected the nation's sixteenth president. He failed to secure a majority of the national popular vote. But because of the North's superiority in population, Lincoln would still have carried the electoral college and thus been elected president even if the votes of his three opponents had all been cast for a single candidate.

THE IMPENDING CRISIS

THE SECESSION MOVEMENT

In the eyes of many white southerners, Lincoln's victory placed their future at the mercy of a party avowedly hostile to their region's values and interests. Those advocating secession did not believe Lincoln's administration would take immediate steps against slavery in the states. But if, as seemed quite possible, the election of 1860 marked a fundamental shift in power, the beginning of a long period of Republican rule, who could say what the North's antislavery sentiment would demand in five years, or ten? Slaveowners, moreover, feared Republican efforts to extend their party into the South by appealing to non-slaveholders. Rather than accept permanent minority status in a nation governed by their opponents, Deep South political leaders boldly struck for their region's independence. At stake, they believed, was not a single election, but an entire way of life.

In the months that followed Lincoln's election, seven states stretching from South Carolina to Texas seceded from the Union. These were the states of the Cotton Kingdom, where slaves represented a larger part of the total population than in the Upper South. First to secede was South Carolina, the state with the highest percentage of slaves in its population and

An 1860 engraving of a mass meeting in Savannah, Georgia, shortly after Lincoln's election as president, which called for the state to secede from the Union. The banner on the obelisk at the center reads, "Our Motto State's Rights, Equality of the States, Don't Tread on Me"—the last a slogan from the American Revolution.

a long history of political radicalism. On December 20, 1860, the legislature unanimously voted to leave the Union. Its *Declaration of the Immediate Causes of Secession* placed the issue of slavery squarely at the center of the crisis. The North had "assumed the right of deciding upon the propriety of our domestic institutions." Lincoln was a man "whose opinions and purposes are hostile to slavery." Experience had proved "that slaveholding states cannot be safe in subjection to nonslaveholding states." Secessionists equated their movement with the struggle for American independence. Proslavery ideologue George Fitzhugh, however, later claimed that southern secession was even more significant than the "commonplace affair" of 1776, since the South rebelled not merely against a particular government but against the erroneous modern idea of freedom based on "human equality" and "natural liberty."

THE SECESSION CRISIS

As the Union unraveled, President Buchanan seemed paralyzed. He denied that a state could secede, but he also insisted that the federal government had no right to use force against it. Other political leaders struggled to find a formula to resolve the crisis. Senator John J. Crittenden of Kentucky, a slave state on the border between North and South, offered the most widely supported compromise plan of the secession winter. Embodied in a series of unamendable constitutional amendments, Crittenden's proposal would have guaranteed the future of slavery in the states where it existed, and extended the Missouri Compromise line to the Pacific Ocean, dividing between slavery and free soil all territories "now held, or hereafter acquired." The seceding states rejected the compromise as too little, too late. But many in the Upper South and North saw it as a way to settle sectional differences and prevent civil war.

Crittenden's plan, however, foundered on the opposition of Abraham Lincoln. Willing to conciliate the South on issues like the return of fugitive slaves, Lincoln took an unyielding stand against the expansion of slavery. Here, he informed one Republican leader, he intended to "hold firm, as with a chain of steel." A fundamental principle of democracy, Lincoln believed, was at stake. "We have just carried an election," he wrote, "on principles fairly stated to the people. Now we are told in advance that the government shall be broken up unless we surrender to those we have beaten, before we take the offices.... If we surrender, it is the end of us and the end of the government." Lincoln, moreover, feared that Crittenden's reference to land "hereafter acquired" offered the South a thinly veiled

A Richmond, Virginia, cartoonist in April 1861 depicts Lincoln as a cat seeking to catch the southern states as mice fleeing the Union, which lies dead on the left.

invitation to demand the acquisition of Cuba, Mexico, and other territory suited to slavery.

Before Lincoln assumed office on March 4, 1861, the seven seceding states formed the Confederate States of America, adopted a constitution, and chose as their president Jefferson Davis of Mississippi. With a few alterations—the president served a single six-year term; cabinet members, as in Britain, could sit in Congress—the Confederate constitution was modeled closely on that of the United States. It departed from the federal Constitution, however, in explicitly guaranteeing slave property both in the states and in any territories the new nation acquired. The "cornerstone" of the Confederacy, announced Davis's vice president, Alexander H. Stephens of Georgia, was "the great truth that the negro is not equal to the white man, that slavery, subordination to the superior race, is his natural and normal condition."

AND THE WAR CAME

Even after rejecting the Crittenden Compromise, Lincoln did not believe war inevitable. When he became president, eight slave states of the Upper South remained in the Union. Here, slaves and slaveholders made up a considerably lower proportion of the population than in the Deep South, and large parts of the white population did not believe Lincoln's election justified dissolving the Union. Even within the Confederacy, whites had divided over secession, with considerable numbers of non-slaveholding farmers in opposition. In time, Lincoln believed, secession might collapse from within.

In his inaugural address, delivered on March 4, 1861, Lincoln tried to be conciliatory. He rejected the right of secession but denied any intention of interfering with slavery in the states. He said nothing of retaking the forts, arsenals, and customs houses the Confederacy had seized, although he did promise to "hold" remaining federal property in the seceding states. But Lincoln also issued a veiled warning: "In your hands, my dissatisfied fellow countrymen, and not in mine, is the momentous issue of civil war."

In his first month as president, Lincoln walked a tightrope. He avoided any action that might drive more states from the Union, encouraged southern Unionists to assert themselves within the Confederacy, and sought to quiet a growing clamor in the North for forceful action against secession. Knowing that the risk of war existed, Lincoln strove to ensure that if hostilities did break out, the South, not the Union, would

Inauguration of Mr. Lincoln, *a photograph taken on March 4, 1861. The unfinished dome of the Capitol building symbolizes the precarious state of the Union at the time Lincoln assumed office.*

Bombardment of Fort Sumter, *a lithograph by Nathaniel Currier and James Ives depicting the beginning of the Civil War.*

fire the first shot. And that is precisely what happened on April 12, 1861, at Fort Sumter, an enclave of Union control in the harbor of Charleston, South Carolina.

A few days earlier, Lincoln had notified South Carolina's governor that he intended to replenish the garrison's dwindling food supplies. Viewing Fort Sumter's presence as an affront to southern nationhood, and perhaps hoping to force the wavering Upper South to join the Confederacy, Jefferson Davis ordered batteries to fire on the fort. On April 14, its commander surrendered. The following day, Lincoln proclaimed that an insurrection existed in the South and called for 75,000 troops to suppress it. Civil war had begun. Within weeks, Virginia, North Carolina, Tennessee, and Arkansas joined the Confederacy. "Both sides deprecated war," Lincoln later said, "but one of them would *make* war rather than let the nation survive; and the other would *accept* war rather than let it perish. And the war came."

In 1842, Henry Wadsworth Longfellow published *Poems on Slavery*, a collection that included a work entitled simply "The Warning." In it, Longfellow compared the American slave to the mighty biblical figure of Samson, who after being blinded and chained, managed to destroy the temple of his tormentors:

> There is a poor, blind Samson in this land,
> Shorn of his strength, and bound in bonds of steel,
> Who may, in some grim revel, raise his hand,
> And shake the pillars of this Commonweal,
> Till the vast Temple of our liberties
> A shapeless mass of wreck and rubbish lies.

In 1861, Longfellow's warning came to pass. The Union created by the founders lay in ruins. The struggle to rebuild it would bring about a new birth of American freedom.

Young Girl with Portrait of George Washington. *A patriotic photograph from around 1850. Ten years later, it was not clear whether the nation Washington helped to create could survive.*

SUGGESTED READING

Anbinder, Tyler. *Nativism and Slavery: The Northern Know-Nothings and the Politics of the 1850s* (1992). A detailed study of the relationship between nativism and antislavery politics in the North.

Bushman, Claudia L. and Richard L. Bushman. *Building the Kingdom: A History of Mormons in America* (2001). A survey of the history of American Mormons.

Cronon, William. *Nature's Metropolis: Chicago and the Great West* (1992). An influential account of the rise of Chicago and the city's relationship to its agricultural hinterland.

Current, Richard N. *Lincoln and the First Shot* (1963). Examines the decisions and strategy of both Lincoln and Jefferson Davis that produced the firing on Fort Sumter that began the Civil War.

Davis, William C. *Lone Star Rising: The Revolutionary Birth of the Texas Republic* (2004). An up-to-date history of the Texas war for independence.

Earle, Jonathan H. *Jacksonian Antislavery and the Politics of Free Soil, 1824–1854* (2004). Emphasizes the role of northern Jacksonians in antislavery politics.

Foner, Eric. *Free Soil, Free Labor, Free Men: The Ideology of the Republican Party before the Civil War* (1970). A discussion of the basic ideas that united Republicans in the 1850s, especially their "free labor ideology."

Haas, Lisbeth. *Conquests and Historical Identities in California, 1769–1936* (1995). Contains a detailed description of how California's acquisition by the United States affected the state's diverse population groups.

Holt, Michael F. *The Fate of Their Country: Politicians, Slavery Expansion, and the Coming of the Civil War* (2004). A brief history of the 1850s, stressing how the decisions of political leaders led the country to war.

Johannsen, Robert W. *To the Halls of Montezuma: The Mexican War in the American Imagination* (1985). A history of the Mexican War and how it was remembered after its conclusion.

Levine, Bruce. *Half Slave and Half Free: The Roots of the Civil War* (1992). A survey of the coming of the Civil War, stressing irreconcilable differences between North and South.

Potter, David M. *The Impending Crisis, 1848–1861* (1976). Still the standard account of the nation's history in the years before the Civil War.

Sinha, Manisha. *The Counterrevolution of Slavery: Politics and Ideology in Antebellum South Carolina* (2002). A detailed study of how a vigorous defense of slavery developed in South Carolina, which justified the decision for secession.

Stampp, Kenneth. *And the War Came: The North and the Secession Crisis, 1860–61* (1950). An examination of Northern actions and attitudes during the secession crisis.

Stephanson, Anders. *Manifest Destiny: American Expansionism and the Empire of Right* (1995). Considers how the idea of an American mission to spread freedom and democracy has affected American foreign policy throughout the country's history.

REVIEW QUESTIONS

1. Describe how the values and platform of the Free Soil Party differed from that of the abolitionists.

2. Analyze the significance of the Dred Scott decision in the developing sectional split.

3. What were the main factors driving continental expansion in the antebellum era?

4. Explain how the spirit of "manifest destiny" gave a new stridency to ideas of racial superiority.

5. How did Abraham Lincoln and Stephen Douglas convey their ideas of freedom during their famous debates?

KEY TERMS

slavery and the Texas Revolt (p. 466)

Fugitive Slave Act (p. 478)

Kansas-Nebraska Act (p. 481)

The Caning of Charles Sumner (p. 486)

Lecompton Constitution (p. 488)

Election of 1860 (p. 495)

REVIEW TABLE

Road Toward War

Event	Date	Explanation	Result
Compromise of 1850	1850	Southerners are concerned that congressional balance would be disrupted by California's request for free-state status	California becomes a free state; the Fugitive Slave Act is passed; and slavery in the New Mexico territory is to be decided by locals
Kansas-Nebraska Act	1854	A bill that grants statehood to the two territories and provides for slavery to be decided by popular sovereignty	"Bleeding Kansas"—civil war in Kansas over the issue of slavery in 1856
Dred Scott decision	1857	Supreme Court rules that only white persons are citizens and that Congress possesses no power to bar slavery from a territory	It in effect declared unconstitutional the Republican platform of restricting slavery's expansion
John Brown and Harpers Ferry	1859	Brown raids a federal arsenal to launch a slave rebellion and is executed for his crime	Brown becomes a martyr to many in the North
1860 Election	1860	Abraham Lincoln wins with no votes in the South	Seven states secede from the Union before Lincoln is inaugurated

CHAPTER 14

A New Birth of Freedom: The Civil War, 1861–1865

Departure of the 7th Regiment, *a lithograph from 1861 illustrating the departure of a unit of the New York State militia for service in the Civil War. A contemporary writer captured the exuberant spirit of the early days of the war: "New York was certainly raving mad with excitement. The ladies laughed, smiled, sighed, sobbed, and wept. The men cheered and shouted as never men cheered and shouted before."*

☞ FOCUS QUESTIONS

- Why is the Civil War considered to be the first modern war?

- How did a war to preserve the union become a war to end slavery?

- How did the Civil War contribute to a stronger American nation-state?

- How did the war affect the society and economy of the Confederacy?

- What were the military and political turning points of the war?

- What were the most important wartime "rehearsals for Reconstruction"?

Like hundreds of thousands of other Americans, Marcus M. Spiegel volunteered in 1861 to fight in the Civil War. Born into a Jewish family in Germany in 1829, Spiegel took part in the failed German revolution of 1848. In the following year he emigrated to Ohio, where he married the daughter of a local farmer. When the Civil War broke out, the nation's 150,000 Jews represented less than 1 percent of the total population. But Spiegel shared wholeheartedly in American patriotism. He went to war, he wrote to his brother-in-law, to defend "the flag that was ever ready to protect you and me and every one who sought its protection from oppression."

Spiegel rose to the rank of colonel in the 120th Ohio Infantry and saw action in Virginia, Mississippi, and Louisiana. He corresponded frequently with his wife, Caroline. "I have seen and learned much," he wrote in 1863. "I have seen men dying of disease and mangled by the weapons of death; I have witnessed hostile armies arrayed against each other, the charge of infantry, [and] cavalry hunting men down like beasts." But he never wavered in his commitment to the "glorious cause" of preserving the Union and its heritage of freedom.

What one Pennsylvania recruit called "the magic word *Freedom*" shaped how many Union soldiers understood the conflict. The war's purpose, wrote Samuel McIlvaine, a sergeant from Indiana, was to preserve the American nation as "the beacon light of liberty and freedom to the human race." But as the war progressed, prewar understandings of liberty gave way to something new. Millions of northerners who had not been abolitionists became convinced that preserving the Union as an embodiment of liberty required the destruction of slavery.

Marcus Spiegel's changing views mirrored the transformation of a struggle to save the Union into a war to end slavery. Spiegel was an ardent Democrat. He shared the era's racist attitudes and thought Lincoln's Emancipation Proclamation a serious mistake. Yet as the Union army penetrated the heart of the Deep South, Spiegel became increasingly opposed to slavery. "Since I am here," he wrote to his wife from Louisiana in January 1864, "I have learned and seen . . . the horrors of slavery. You know it takes me long to say anything that sounds antidemocratic [opposed to Democratic Party policies], but . . . never hereafter will I either speak or vote in favor of slavery."

Marcus Spiegel was killed in a minor engagement in Louisiana in May 1864, one of 620,000 Americans to perish in the Civil War.

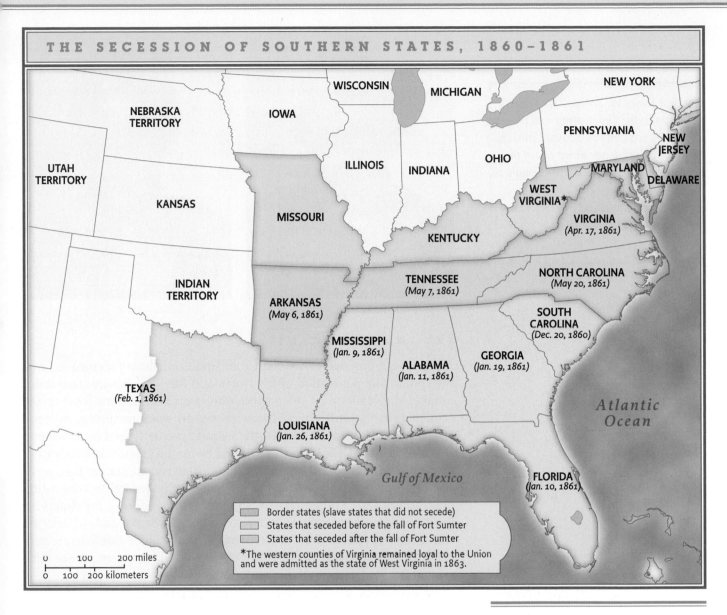

THE SECESSION OF SOUTHERN STATES, 1860–1861

Border states (slave states that did not secede)
States that seceded before the fall of Fort Sumter
States that seceded after the fall of Fort Sumter

*The western counties of Virginia remained loyal to the Union and were admitted as the state of West Virginia in 1863.

By the time secession ran its course, eleven slave states had left the Union.

THE FIRST MODERN WAR

The American Civil War is often called the first modern war. Never before had mass armies confronted each other on the battlefield with the deadly weapons created by the industrial revolution. The resulting casualties dwarfed anything in the American experience. Beginning as a battle of army versus army, the war became a conflict of society against society, in which the distinction between military and civilian targets often disappeared. In a war of this kind, the effectiveness of political leadership, the ability to mobilize economic resources, and a society's willingness to keep up the fight despite setbacks are as crucial to the outcome as success or failure on individual battlefields.

Sergeant James W. Travis, Thirty-eighth Illinois Infantry, Union army, and Private Edwin Francis Jemison, Second Louisiana Regiment, Confederate army, two of the nearly 3 million Americans who fought in the Civil War. Before going off to war, many soldiers sat for photographs like these, reproduced on small cards called cartes de visite, *which they distributed to friends and loved ones. Jemison was killed in the Battle of Malvern Hill in July 1862.*

THE TWO COMBATANTS

Almost any comparison between Union and Confederacy seemed to favor the Union. The population of the North and the loyal border slave states numbered 22 million in 1860, while only 9 million persons lived in the Confederacy, 3.3 million of them slaves. In manufacturing, railroad mileage, and financial resources, the Union far outstripped its opponent. On the other hand, the Union confronted by far the greater task. To restore the shattered nation, it had to invade and conquer an area larger than western Europe. Confederate soldiers were highly motivated fighters defending their homes and families. Like Washington's forces during the American Revolution, southern armies could lose most of the battles and still win the war if their opponent tired of the struggle. "No people," Confederate general P. G. T. Beauregard later claimed, "ever warred for independence with more relative advantages than the Confederacy."

On both sides, the outbreak of war stirred powerful feelings of patriotism. Recruits rushed to enlist, expecting a short, glorious war. Later, as enthusiasm waned, both sides resorted to a draft. The Confederacy in the spring of 1862 passed the first draft law in American history, and the North soon followed. By 1865, over 2 million men had served in the Union army and 900,000 in the Confederate army. Each was a cross section of its society: the North's was composed largely of farm boys, shopkeepers, artisans, and urban workers, while the South's consisted mostly of non-slaveholding small farmers, with slaveowners dominating the officer corps.

Few recruits had any military experience. Fifteen years had passed since the Mexican War. Ideas about war were highly romantic, based on novels, magazine articles, and lithographs of soldiers covering themselves with glory. One private wrote home in 1862 that his notion of combat had come from the pictures of battles he had seen: "they would all be in a line, all standing in a nice level field fighting, a number of ladies taking care of the wounded, etc. But it isn't so." Nor were the recruits ready for military regimentation. "It comes rather hard at first to be deprived of liberty," wrote an Illinois soldier. Initially, the constant round of drilling, ditch digging, and other chores were only occasionally interrupted by fierce bursts of fighting on the battlefield. According to one estimate, during the first two years of the war the main Union force, the Army of the Potomac, spent only thirty days in actual combat.

THE TECHNOLOGY OF WAR

Neither the soldiers nor their officers were prepared for the way technology had transformed warfare. The Civil War was the first major conflict in which the railroad transported troops and supplies and the first to see railroad junctions such as Atlanta and Petersburg become major military objectives. The famous sea battle between the Union vessel *Monitor* and the Confederate *Merrimac* in 1862 was the first demonstration of the superiority of ironclads over wooden ships, revolutionizing naval warfare. The war saw the use of the telegraph for military communication, the introduction of observation balloons to view enemy lines, and even primitive hand grenades and submarines.

Perhaps most important, a revolution in arms manufacturing had replaced the traditional musket, accurate at only a short range, with the more modern rifle, deadly at 600 yards or more because of its grooved (or "rifled") barrel. This development changed the nature of combat, emphasizing the importance of heavy fortifications and elaborate trenches and giving those on the defensive—usually southern armies—a significant advantage over attacking forces. "My men," said Confederate general Thomas "Stonewall" Jackson, "sometimes fail to drive the enemy from his position, but to hold one, never." The war of rifle and trench produced the appalling casualty statistics of Civil

Battle of the Iron-clads Monitor and Merrimac, painted in 1877 by William Torgerson, depicts the first clash between ironclad ships, which took place off the coast of Virginia on March 9, 1862. Precursors of modern battleships, ironclads were among the numerous technological advances introduced during the Civil War. The masts of a wooden naval vessel are visible on the horizon.

Confederate dead at Spotsylvania, Virginia, the site of a bloody battle in 1864.

A surgeon's kit used in the Civil War, containing amputation instruments, knives, and tourniquets. With medical knowledge and practices primitive at best, far more men died from wounds, infections, and disease than in battle.

War battles. The 620,000 who perished in the war represent the equivalent, in terms of today's population, of more than 5 million men. The death toll in the Civil War nearly equals the total number of Americans who died in all the nation's other wars, from the Revolution to the war in Iraq.

Nor was either side ready for other aspects of modern warfare. Medical care remained primitive. "I believe the doctors kill more than they cure," wrote an Alabama private in 1862. Diseases like measles, dysentery, malaria, and typhus swept through army camps, killing more men than did combat. The Civil War was the first war in which large numbers of Americans were captured by the enemy and held in dire conditions in military prisons. Some 50,000 men died in these prisons, victims of starvation and disease, including 13,000 Union soldiers at Andersonville, Georgia.

THE PUBLIC AND THE WAR

Another modern feature of the Civil War was that both sides were assisted by a vast propaganda effort to mobilize public opinion. In the Union, an outpouring of lithographs, souvenirs, sheet music, and pamphlets issued by patriotic organizations and the War Department reaffirmed northern values, tarred the Democratic Party with the brush of treason, and accused the South of numerous crimes against Union soldiers and loyal civilians. Comparable items appeared in the Confederacy.

At the same time, the war's brutal realities were brought home with unprecedented immediacy to the public at large. War correspondents

Confederate prisoners of war at Camp Douglas, Chicago, in 1864.

accompanied the armies, and newspapers reported the results of battles on the following day and quickly published long lists of casualties. The infant art of photography carried images of war into millions of American living rooms. Beginning in 1862, when photographers entered the battlefield to take shocking pictures of the dead at Antietam, the camera, in the words of one journalist, "brought the bodies and laid them in our door-yards." Mathew Brady, who organized a corps of photographers to cover the war, found the conflict a passport to fame and wealth. For photography itself, it was a turning point in its growth as an art and business enterprise.

MOBILIZING RESOURCES

The outbreak of the war found both sides unprepared. In 1861, there was no national railroad gauge (the distance separating the two tracks) so that trains built for one line could not run on another. There was no national banking system, no tax system capable of raising the enormous funds needed to finance the war, and not even accurate maps of the southern states. Soon after the firing on Fort Sumter, Lincoln proclaimed a naval blockade of the South, part of the so-called Anaconda Plan, which aimed to strangle the South economically. But the navy charged with patrolling the 3,500-mile coastline consisted of only ninety vessels, fewer than half of them steam-powered. Not until late in the war did the blockade become effective.

Then there was the problem of purchasing and distributing the food, weapons, and other supplies required by the soldiers. The Union army eventually became the best-fed and best-supplied military force in history. By the war's third year, on the other hand, southern armies were suffering from acute shortages of food, uniforms, and shoes. Yet the chief of the Confederacy's Ordnance Bureau, Josiah Gorgas (a transplanted northerner), proved brilliantly resourceful in arming southern troops. Under his direction, the Confederate government imported weapons from abroad and established arsenals of its own to turn out rifles, artillery, and ammunition.

MILITARY STRATEGIES

Each side tried to find ways to maximize its advantages. Essentially, the Confederacy adopted a defensive strategy, with occasional thrusts into the North. General Robert E. Lee, the leading southern commander, was a brilliant battlefield tactician who felt confident of his ability to fend off attacks by larger Union forces. He hoped that a series of defeats would weaken the North's resolve and lead it eventually to abandon the conflict and recognize southern independence.

Lincoln's early generals found it impossible to bring the Union's advantages in manpower and technology to bear on the battlefield. In April 1861, the regular army numbered little over 15,000 men, most of whom were stationed west of the Mississippi River. Its officers had been trained to lead small, professional forces into battle, not the crowds of untrained men who assembled in 1861. The North also suffered from narrowness of

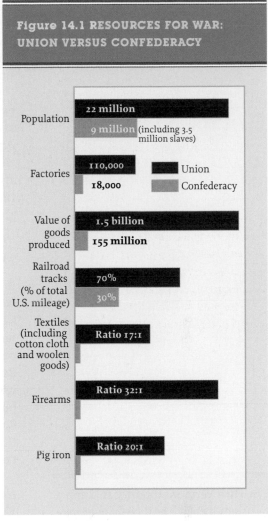

Figure 14.1 RESOURCES FOR WAR: UNION VERSUS CONFEDERACY

	Union	Confederacy
Population	22 million	9 million (including 3.5 million slaves)
Factories	110,000	18,000
Value of goods produced	1.5 billion	155 million
Railroad tracks (% of total U.S. mileage)	70%	30%
Textiles (including cotton cloth and woolen goods)	Ratio 17:1	
Firearms	Ratio 32:1	
Pig iron	Ratio 20:1	

In nearly every resource for warfare, the Union enjoyed a distinct advantage. But this did not make Union victory inevitable; as during the War of Independence, the stronger side sometimes loses.

military vision. Its generals initially concentrated on occupying southern territory and attempting to capture Richmond, the Confederate capital. They attacked sporadically and withdrew after a battle, thus sacrificing the North's manpower superiority and allowing the South to concentrate its smaller forces when an engagement impended.

Well before his generals did, Lincoln realized that simply capturing and occupying territory would not win the war, and that defeating the South's armies, not capturing its capital, had to be the North's battlefield objective. And when he came to adopt the policy of emancipation, Lincoln acknowledged what Confederate vice president Alexander H. Stephens had already affirmed: slavery was the "cornerstone" of the Confederacy. To win the war, therefore, the Union must make the institution that lay at the economic and social foundation of southern life a military target.

THE WAR BEGINS

In the East, most of the war's fighting took place in a narrow corridor between Washington and Richmond—a distance of only 100 miles—as a succession of Union generals led the Army of the Potomac (as the main northern force in the East was called) toward the Confederate capital, only to be turned back by southern forces. The first significant engagement, the first Battle of Bull Run, took place in northern Virginia on July 21, 1861. It ended with the chaotic retreat of the Union soldiers, along with the sightseers and politicians who had come to watch the battle. Almost 800 men died at Bull Run, a toll eclipsed many times in the years to come, but more Americans than had been killed in any previous battle in the nation's history. The encounter disabused both sides of the idea that the war would be a brief lark.

In the wake of Bull Run, George B. McClellan, an army engineer who had recently won a minor engagement with Confederate troops in western Virginia, assumed command of the Union's Army of the Potomac. A brilliant organizer, McClellan succeeded in welding his men into a superb fighting force. He seemed reluctant, however, to commit them to battle,

The Fifth Vermont Infantry at Camp Griffin, Virginia, 1861, *one of numerous Civil War photographs taken by the Mathew Brady studio.*

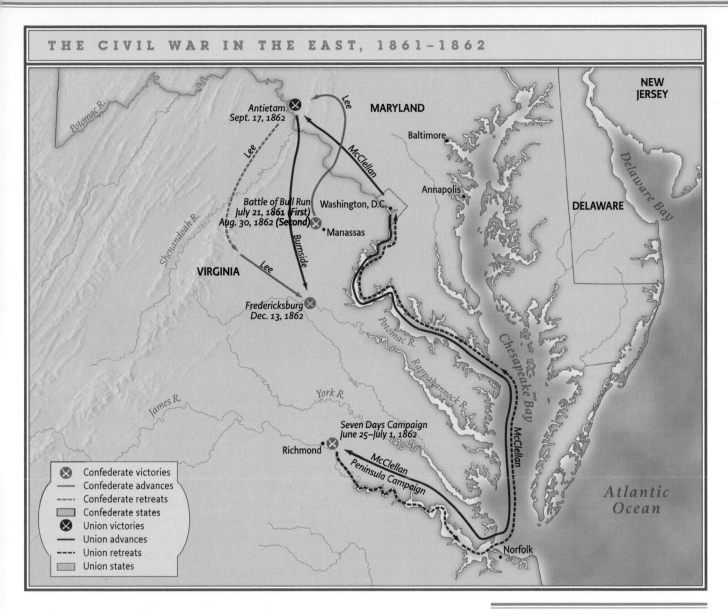

THE CIVIL WAR IN THE EAST, 1861–1862

During the first two years of the war, most of the fighting took place in Virginia and Maryland.

since he tended to overestimate the size of enemy forces. And as a Democrat, he hoped that compromise might end the war without large-scale loss of life or a weakening of slavery. Months of military inactivity followed.

THE WAR IN THE EAST, 1862

Not until the spring of 1862, after a growing clamor for action by Republican newspapers, members of Congress, and an increasingly impatient Lincoln, did McClellan lead his army of over 100,000 men into Virginia. Here they confronted the smaller Army of Northern Virginia under the command of the Confederate general Robert E. Lee. A brilliant battlefield tactician, Lee had been offered a command in the Union army but chose to fight for the Confederacy because of his devotion to Virginia. In the Seven Days' Campaign, a series of engagements in June 1862 on the peninsula south of Richmond, Lee blunted McClellan's attacks and forced him to

The Battle of Antietam, *a painting of a Union advance by Captain James Hope of the Second Vermont Volunteers. Over 4,000 men died on September 17, 1862, when the Battle of Antietam was fought.*

withdraw back to the vicinity of Washington, D.C. In August 1862, Lee again emerged victorious at the second Battle of Bull Run against Union forces under the command of General John Pope.

Successful on the defensive, Lee now launched an invasion of the North. He hoped to bring the border slave states into the Confederacy, persuade Britain and France to recognize southern independence, influence the North's fall elections, and perhaps capture Washington, D.C. At the Battle of Antietam, in Maryland, McClellan and the Army of the Potomac repelled Lee's advance. In a single day of fighting, over 4,300 men were killed and 18,000 wounded (2,000 of whom later died of their injuries). The dead, one survivor recalled, lay three deep in the field, mowed down "like grass before the scythe." More Americans died on September 17, 1862, when the battle of Antietam was fought, than on any other day in the nation's history, including D-Day in World War II and the terrorist attacks of September 11, 2001. Indeed, more American soldiers perished at Antietam than in all the other wars fought by the United States in the nineteenth century combined.

Since Lee was forced to retreat, the North could claim Antietam as a victory. It was to be the Union's last success in the East for some time. In December 1862, the Union suffered one of its most disastrous defeats of the war when General Ambrose E. Burnside, who had replaced McClellan as the head of the Army of the Potomac, assaulted Lee's army, which was entrenched on heights near Fredericksburg, Virginia. "It was not a fight," wrote one Union soldier to his mother, "it was a massacre."

THE WAR IN THE WEST

While the Union accomplished little in the East in the first two years of the war, events in the West followed a different course. Here, the architect of early success was Ulysses S. Grant. A West Point graduate who had resigned from the army in 1854 in part because of allegations of excessive drinking, Grant had been notably unsuccessful in civilian life. When the war broke out, he was working as a clerk in his brother's leather store in Galena, Illinois. But after being commissioned as a colonel in an Illinois regiment,

Most of the Union's victories in the first two years of the war occurred in the West, especially at Shiloh and New Orleans.

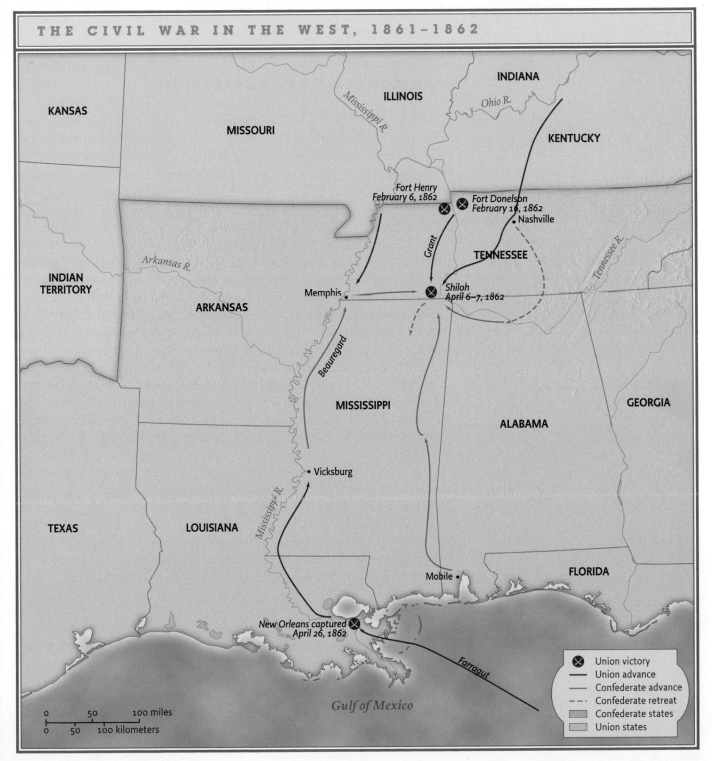

THE CIVIL WAR IN THE WEST, 1861–1862

Grant quickly displayed the daring, the logical mind, and the grasp of strategy he would demonstrate throughout the war.

In February 1862, Grant won the Union's first significant victory when he captured Forts Henry and Donelson in Tennessee. In April, naval forces under Admiral David G. Farragut steamed into New Orleans, giving the Union control of the South's largest city and the rich sugar plantation parishes to its south and west. At the same time, Grant withstood a surprise Confederate attack at Shiloh, Tennessee. But Union momentum in the West then stalled.

THE COMING OF EMANCIPATION

SLAVERY AND THE WAR

War, it has been said, is the midwife of revolution. And the Civil War produced far-reaching changes in American life. The most dramatic of these was the destruction of slavery, the central institution of southern society. Between 1831, when the British abolished slavery in their empire, and 1888, when emancipation came to Brazil, some 6 million slaves gained their freedom in the Western Hemisphere. Of these, nearly 4 million, two-thirds of the total, lived in the southern United States. In numbers, scale, and the economic power of the institution of slavery, American emancipation dwarfed that of any other country (although far more people were liberated in 1861 when Czar Alexander I abolished serfdom in the Russian empire).

At the outset of the war, Lincoln invoked time-honored northern values to mobilize public support. In a message to Congress, he identified the Union cause with the fate of democracy for the "whole family of man." He identified the differences between North and South in terms of the familiar free labor ideology: "This is essentially a people's struggle. On the side of the Union, it is a struggle for maintaining in the world, that form and substance of government, whose leading object is to elevate the condition of men . . . to afford all, an unfettered start, and a fair chance, in the race of life."

But while appealing to free labor values, Lincoln initially insisted that slavery was irrelevant to the conflict. In the war's first year, his paramount concerns were to keep the border slave states—Delaware, Maryland, Kentucky, and Missouri—in the Union and to build the broadest base of support in the North for the war effort. Action against slavery, he feared, would drive the border, with its white population of 2.6 million and nearly 500,000 slaves, into the Confederacy and alienate conservative northerners.

THE UNRAVELING OF SLAVERY

Thus, in the early days of the war, a nearly unanimous Congress adopted a resolution proposed by Senator John J. Crittenden of Kentucky, which affirmed that the Union had no intention of interfering with slavery. Northern military commanders even returned fugitive slaves to their owners, a policy that raised an outcry in antislavery circles. Yet as the Confederacy set slaves to work as military laborers and blacks began to escape to

Union lines, the policy of ignoring slavery unraveled. By the end of 1861, the military had adopted the plan, begun in Virginia by General Benjamin F. Butler, of treating escaped blacks as contraband of war—that is, property of military value subject to confiscation. Butler's order added a word to the war's vocabulary. Escaping slaves became known as "the contrabands." They were housed by the army in "contraband camps" and educated in new "contraband schools."

Meanwhile, slaves themselves took actions that helped propel a reluctant white America down the road to emancipation. Whatever the policies of the administration, blacks saw the outbreak of fighting as heralding the long-awaited end of bondage. Well before Lincoln made emancipation a war aim, blacks, in the North and the South, were calling the conflict the "freedom war." In 1861 and 1862, as the federal army occupied Confederate territory, slaves by the thousands headed for Union lines. Unlike fugitives before the war, these runaways included large numbers of women and children, as entire families abandoned the plantations. Not a few passed along military intelligence and detailed knowledge of the South's terrain. "The most valuable and reliable information of the enemy's movements in our vicinity that we have been able to get," noted the Union general Daniel E. Sickles, "derived from Negroes who came into our lines." In southern Louisiana, the arrival of the Union army in 1862 led slaves to sack plantation houses and refuse to work unless wages were paid. Slavery there, wrote a northern reporter, "is forever destroyed and worthless, no matter what Mr. Lincoln or anyone else may say on the subject."

Fugitive Slaves Crossing the Rappahannock River in Virginia, *an 1862 photograph of some of the thousands of slaves who fled to Union lines as the army entered parts of the South.*

STEPS TOWARD EMANCIPATION

At first, blacks' determination to seize the opportunity presented by the war proved a burden to the army and an embarrassment to the administration. But the failure of traditional strategies to produce victory strengthened the hand of antislavery northerners. Since slavery stood at the foundation of the southern economy, they insisted, emancipation was necessary to weaken the South's ability to sustain the war.

The most uncompromising opponents of slavery before the war, abolitionists and Radical Republicans, quickly concluded that the institution must become a target of the Union war effort. "It is plain," declared Thaddeus Stevens, a Radical Republican congressman from Pennsylvania, "that nothing approaching the present policy will subdue the rebels." Outside of

Congress, few pressed the case for emancipation more eloquently than Frederick Douglass. From the outset, he insisted that it was futile to "separate the freedom of the slave from the victory of the government." "Fire must be met with water," Douglass declared, "darkness with light, and war for the destruction of liberty must be met with war for the destruction of slavery."

These appeals won increasing support in a Congress frustrated by lack of military success. In March 1862, Congress prohibited the army from returning fugitive slaves. Then came abolition in the District of Columbia (with monetary compensation for slaveholders) and the territories, followed in July by the Second Confiscation Act, which liberated slaves of disloyal owners in Union-occupied territory, as well as slaves who escaped to Union lines.

Throughout these months, Lincoln struggled to retain control of the emancipation issue. In August 1861, John C. Frémont, commanding Union forces in Missouri, a state racked by a bitter guerrilla war between pro-northern and pro-southern bands, decreed the freedom of its slaves. Fearful of the order's impact on the border states, Lincoln swiftly rescinded it. In November, the president proposed that the border states embark on a program of gradual emancipation with the federal government paying owners for their loss of property. He also revived the idea of colonization. In August 1862, Lincoln met at the White House with a delegation of black leaders and urged them to promote emigration from the United States. "You and we are different races," he declared. "It is better for us both to be separated." As late as December, the president signed an agreement with a shady entrepreneur to settle former slaves on an island off the coast of Haiti.

LINCOLN'S DECISION
– memorize

Sometime during the summer of 1862, Lincoln concluded that emancipation had become a political and military necessity. Many factors contributed to his decision—lack of military success, hope that emancipated slaves might help meet the army's growing manpower needs, changing northern public opinion, and the calculation that making slavery a target of the war effort would counteract sentiment in Britain for recognition of the Confederacy. But on the advice of Secretary of State William H. Seward, Lincoln delayed his announcement until after a Union victory, lest it seem an act of desperation. On September 22, 1862, five days after McClellan's army forced Lee to retreat at Antietam, Lincoln issued the Preliminary Emancipation Proclamation. It warned that unless the South laid down its arms by the end of 1862, he would decree abolition.

Abe Lincoln's Last Card, *an engraving from the British magazine* Punch, *October 18, 1862, portrays the Preliminary Emancipation Proclamation as the last move of a desperate gambler.*

The initial northern reaction was not encouraging. In the fall elections of 1862, Democrats made opposition to emancipation the centerpiece of their campaign, warning that the North would be "Africanized"—inundated by freed slaves who would compete for jobs and seek to marry white women. The Republicans suffered sharp reverses. They lost control of the legislatures of Indiana and Illinois and the governorship of New York, and saw their majorities dangerously reduced in other states. In his annual message to Congress, early in December, Lincoln tried to calm northerners' racial fears, reviving the ideas of gradual emancipation and colonization. He concluded, however, on a higher note: "Fellow citizens, we cannot escape history. . . . The fiery trial through which we pass, will light us down, in honor or dishonor, to the latest generation. . . . In giving freedom to the slave, we assure freedom to the free—honorable alike in what we give, and what we preserve."

THE EMANCIPATION PROCLAMATION

On January 1, 1863, after greeting visitors at the annual White House New Year's reception, Lincoln retired to his study to sign the Emancipation Proclamation. The document did not liberate all the slaves—indeed, on the day it was issued, it applied to very few. Because its legality derived from the president's authority as military commander in chief to combat the South's rebellion, the Proclamation exempted areas firmly under Union control (where the war, in effect, had already ended). Thus, it did not apply to the loyal border slave states that had never seceded or to areas of the Confederacy occupied by Union soldiers, such as Tennessee and parts of Virginia and Louisiana. But the vast majority of the South's slaves, over 3 million men, women, and children, it declared,

Freedom to the Slave, a hand-colored lithograph from 1863 celebrating the promise of emancipation.

Freed Negroes Celebrating President Lincoln's Decree of Emancipation, a fanciful engraving from the French periodical Le Monde Illustré, *March 21, 1863.*

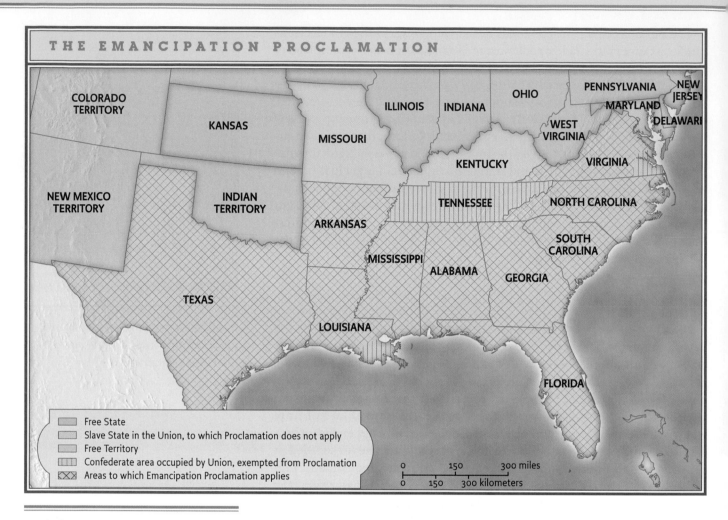

THE EMANCIPATION PROCLAMATION

Free State

Slave State in the Union, to which Proclamation does not apply

Free Territory

Confederate area occupied by Union, exempted from Proclamation

Areas to which Emancipation Proclamation applies

With the exception of the Sea Islands of South Carolina, the Emancipation Proclamation applied only to slaves in areas of the Confederacy not under Union control on January 1, 1863. Lincoln did not "free the slaves" with a stroke of his pen, but the Proclamation did change the nature of the Civil War.

"henceforward shall be free." Since most of these slaves were still behind Confederate lines, however, their liberation would have to await Union victories.

Despite its limitations, the Proclamation set off scenes of jubilation among free blacks and abolitionists in the North and "contrabands" and slaves in the South. "Sound the loud timbrel o'er Egypt's dark sea," intoned a black preacher at a celebration in Boston. "Jehovah hath triumphed, his people are free." By making the Union army an agent of emancipation and wedding the goals of Union and abolition, the Proclamation sounded the eventual death knell of slavery.

Not only did the Emancipation Proclamation alter the nature of the Civil War and the course of American history, but it also represented a turning point in Lincoln's own thinking. It contained no reference to compensation to slaveholders or to colonization of the freed people. For the first time, it committed the government to enlisting black soldiers in the Union army. Lincoln now became in his own mind the Great Emancipator—that is, he assumed the role that history had thrust upon him, and he tried to live up to it. He would later refuse suggestions that he rescind or modify the Proclamation in the interest of peace. Were he to do so, he told one visitor, "I should be damned in time and eternity."

The Civil War, which was begun to preserve the prewar Union, now portended a far-reaching transformation in southern life and a redefinition of American freedom. Decoupling emancipation from colonization meant that the freed slaves would become part of American life. A new system of labor, politics, and race relations would have to replace the shattered institution of slavery. "Up to now," wrote the socialist thinker Karl Marx, observing events from London, "we have witnessed only the first act of the Civil War—the constitutional waging of war. The second act, the revolutionary waging of war, is at hand." The evolution of Lincoln's emancipation policy displayed the hallmarks of his wartime leadership—his capacity for growth and his ability to develop broad public support for his administration.

ENLISTING BLACK TROOPS

Of the Proclamation's provisions, few were more radical in their implications than the enrollment of blacks into military service. Since sailor had been one of the few occupations open to free blacks before the war, Secretary of the Navy Gideon Welles had already allowed African-Americans to serve on Union warships. But as during the American Revolution, when George Washington initially excluded blacks from the Continental army, blacks in the Civil War had to fight for the right to fight on land. Early in the war, Harry Jarvis, a Virginia slave, escaped to Fortress Monroe and offered to enlist in the Union army. General Benjamin F. Butler, Jarvis later recalled, "said *it wasn't a black man's war.* I told him it *would* be a black man's war before they got through."

This widely reprinted recruiting poster urged African-American men to join the Union army after Congress and the president changed the policy of allowing only whites to serve.

Photographs of four anonymous black Civil War soldiers, including a sergeant (with three stripes on his uniform).

At the outset, the Union army refused to accept northern black volunteers. The administration feared that whites would not be willing to fight alongside blacks, and that enlisting black soldiers would alienate the border slave states that remained in the Union. By the end of 1861, however, the army was employing escaped slaves as cooks, laundresses, and laborers. Preliminary steps to enlist combat troops were taken in a few parts of the South in 1862. White abolitionist Thomas Wentworth Higginson was sent to the South Carolina Sea Islands, which the Union navy had seized early in the war, to enroll slaves in the First South Carolina Volunteers. But only after the Emancipation Proclamation did the recruitment of black soldiers begin in earnest.

By the end of the war, over 180,000 black men had served in the Union army, and 24,000 in the navy. One-third died in battle, or of wounds or disease. Fifteen black soldiers and eight sailors received the Congressional Medal of Honor, the highest award for military valor. Some black units won considerable notoriety, among them the Fifty-fourth Massachusetts Volunteers, a company of free blacks from throughout the North commanded by Robert Gould Shaw, a young reformer from a prominent Boston family. The bravery of the Fifty-fourth in the September 1863 attack on Fort Wagner, South Carolina, where nearly half the unit, including Shaw, perished, helped to dispel widespread doubts about blacks' ability to withstand the pressures of the Civil War battlefield. (The exploits of Shaw and the Fifty-fourth Massachusetts were popularized in the 1989 film *Glory.*)

Most black soldiers were emancipated slaves who joined the army in the South. After Union forces in 1863 seized control of the rich plantation lands of the Mississippi Valley, General Lorenzo Thomas raised fifty regiments of black soldiers—some 76,000 men in all. Another large group hailed from the border states exempted from the Emancipation Proclamation, where enlistment was, for most of the war, the only route to freedom. Here black military service undermined slavery, for Congress expanded the Emancipation Proclamation to liberate black soldiers and their families.

THE BLACK SOLDIER

For black soldiers themselves, military service proved to be a liberating experience. "No negro who has ever been a soldier," wrote a northern official in 1865, "can again be imposed upon; they have learned what it is to be free and they will infuse their feelings into others." Service in the army established men as community leaders and opened a door to political advancement. Out of the army came many of the leaders of the Reconstruction era. At least 130 former soldiers served in political office after the Civil War. In time, the memory of black military service would fade from white America's collective memory. Of the hundreds of Civil War monuments that still dot the northern landscape, fewer than a dozen contain an image of a black soldier. But well into the twentieth century, it remained a point of pride in black families throughout the United States that their fathers and grandfathers had fought for freedom.

The Union navy treated black sailors pretty much the same as white sailors. Conditions on ships made racial segregation impossible. Black and white sailors lived and dined together in the same quarters. They received equal pay and had the same promotion opportunities. Within the army, however, black soldiers received treatment that was anything but equal to their white counterparts. Organized into segregated units under sometimes abusive white officers, they initially received lower pay (ten dollars per month, compared to sixteen dollars for white soldiers). They were disproportionately assigned to labor rather than combat, and they could not rise to the rank of commissioned officer until the very end of the war. If captured by Confederate forces they faced the prospect of sale into slavery or immediate execution. In a notorious incident in 1864, 200 of 262 black soldiers died when southern troops under the command of Nathan B. Forrest overran Fort Pillow in Tennessee. Some of those who perished were killed after surrendering.

Nonetheless, black soldiers played a crucial role not only in winning the Civil War but in defining the war's consequences. "Once let a black man get upon his person the brass letters U.S.," wrote Frederick Douglass in urging blacks to enlist, "and there is no power on earth which can deny that he has earned the right to citizenship in the United States." As Douglass predicted, thanks in part to black military service many Republicans in the last two years of the war came to believe that emancipation must bring with it equal protection of the laws regardless of race. One of the first acts of the federal government to recognize this principle was the granting of retroactive equal pay to black soldiers early in 1865. Racism was hardly eliminated from national life. But, declared George William Curtis, the editor of *Harper's Weekly*, the war and emancipation had transformed a government "for white men" into one "for mankind."

The service of black soldiers affected Lincoln's own outlook. He insisted that they must be treated the same as whites when captured and suspended prisoner-of-war exchanges when the Confederacy refused to include black troops. In 1864, Lincoln, who before the war had never supported suffrage for African-Americans, urged the governor of Union-occupied Louisiana to work for the partial enfranchisement of blacks, singling out soldiers as especially deserving. At some future time, he observed, they might again be called upon to "keep the *jewel of Liberty* in the family of freedom."

THE SECOND AMERICAN REVOLUTION

"Old things are passing away," wrote a black resident of California in 1862, "and eventually old prejudices must follow. The revolution has begun, and time alone must decide where it is to end." The changing status of black Americans was only one dramatic example of what some historians call the Second American Revolution—the transformation of American government and society brought about by the Civil War.

Lincoln transform the nature of what it means to live in the USA

LIBERTY AND UNION

Never was freedom's contested nature more evident than during the Civil War. "We all declare for liberty," Lincoln observed in 1864, "but in using the same *word* we do not all mean the same *thing*." To the North, he continued, freedom meant for "each man" to enjoy "the product of his labor." To

The illustration accompanying The American Flag, *a piece of patriotic Civil War sheet music, exemplifies how the war united the ideals of liberty and nationhood.*

A portrait of Abraham Lincoln by the artist Edward D. Marchant, painted in 1863, depicts the president sitting at a desk, with a copy of the Emancipation Proclamation, in front of a statue of a freed slave with a broken chain at his feet.

southern whites, it conveyed mastership—the power to do "as they please with other men, and the product of other men's labor." The Union's triumph consolidated the northern understanding of freedom as the national norm.

The attack on Fort Sumter crystallized in northern minds the direct conflict between freedom and slavery that abolitionists had insisted upon for decades. The war, as Frederick Douglass recognized as early as 1862, merged "the cause of the slaves and the cause of the country." "Liberty and Union," he continued, "have become identical." As during the American Revolution, religious and secular understandings of freedom joined in a celebration of national destiny. "As He died to make men holy, let us die to make men free," proclaimed the popular song "Battle Hymn of the Republic," written by Julia Ward Howe and published in 1862. Emancipation offered proof of the progressive nature and global significance of the country's history. For the first time, wrote the *Chicago Tribune*, the United States could truly exist as "our fathers designed it—the home of freedom, the asylum of the oppressed, the seat of justice, the land of equal rights under the law."

LINCOLN'S VISION

But it was Lincoln himself who linked the conflict with the deepest beliefs of northern society. It is sometimes said that the American Civil War was part of a broader nineteenth-century process of nation building. Throughout the world, powerful, centralized nation-states developed in old countries like Japan, and new nations emerged where none had previously existed. Lincoln has been called the American equivalent of Giuseppe Mazzini or Otto von Bismarck, who during this same era created nation-states in Italy and Germany from disunited collections of principalities. But Lincoln's nation was different from those being constructed in Europe. They were based on the idea of unifying a particular people with a common ethnic, cultural, and linguistic heritage. To Lincoln, the American nation embodied a set of universal ideas, centered on political democracy and human liberty. The United States represented to the world the principle that government should rest on popular consent and that all men should be free. These ideals, Lincoln declared, allowed immigrants from abroad, who could not "trace their connection by blood" to the nation's birth, nonetheless to become fully American.

Lincoln summarized his conception of the war's meaning in November 1863 in brief remarks at the dedication of a military cemetery at the site of the war's greatest battle. The Gettysburg Address is considered his finest speech (see the Appendix for the full text). In less than three minutes, he identified the nation's mission with the principle that "all men are created equal," spoke of the war as bringing about a "new birth of freedom," and defined the essence of democratic government. The sacrifices of Union soldiers, he declared, would ensure that "government of the people, by the people, for the people, shall not perish from the earth."

FROM UNION TO NATION

The mobilization of the Union's resources for modern war brought into being a new American nation-state with greatly expanded powers and responsibilities. The United States remained a federal republic with sover-

The Eagle's Nest, *an 1861 antisecession cartoon promising "annihilation to traitors." The eggs representing seceding states have become rotten and are hatching monsters.*

eignty divided between the state and national governments. But the war forged a new national self-consciousness, reflected in the increasing use of the word "nation"—a unified political entity—in place of the older "Union" of separate states. In his inaugural address in 1861, Lincoln used the word "Union" twenty times, while making no mention of the "nation." By 1863, "Union" does not appear at all in the 269-word Gettysburg Address, while Lincoln referred five times to the "nation."

"Liberty, ... true liberty," the writer Francis Lieber proclaimed, "requires a country." This was the moral of one of the era's most popular works of fiction, Edward Everett Hale's short story "The Man Without a Country," published in 1863. Hale's protagonist, Philip Nolan, in a fit of anger curses the land of his birth. As punishment, he is condemned to live on a ship, never to set foot on American soil or hear the name "the United States" spoken. He learns that to be deprived of national identity is to lose one's sense of self.

LIBERTY IN WARTIME

This intense new nationalism made criticism of the war effort—or of the policies of the Lincoln administration—seem to Republicans equivalent to treason. Although there had been sporadic persecution of opponents of the Mexican War, the Civil War presented, for the first time since the Revolution, the issue of the limits of wartime dissent. During the conflict, declared the Republican *New York Times*, "the safety of the nation is the supreme law." Arbitrary arrests numbered in the thousands. They included opposition newspaper editors, Democratic politicians, individuals who discouraged enlistment in the army, and ordinary civilians like

VOICES OF FREEDOM

From Speech of Alexander H. Stephens, Vice President of the Confederacy (March 21, 1861)

A Whig leader in Georgia, Alexander H. Stephens opposed secession until his state voted to leave the Union. He then accepted the vice presidency of the Confederacy, and in a speech in Savannah in March 1861 he explained the basic premises of the new government.

The [Confederate] Constitution has put at rest forever all the agitating questions relating to our peculiar institutions—African slavery as it exists among us—the proper status of the negro in our form of civilization. This was the immediate cause of the late rupture and present revolution. . . . The prevailing ideas entertained by [Jefferson] and most of the leading statesmen at the time of the formation of the old Constitution, were, that the enslavement of the African was in violation of the laws of nature; that it was wrong in principle, socially, morally and politically. . . .

These ideas, however, were fundamentally wrong. They rested on the assumption of the equality of races. This was an error. . . . Our new Government is founded upon exactly the opposite ideas; its foundations are laid, its cornerstone rests, upon the great truth that the negro is not equal to the white man; that slavery, subordination to the superior race, is his natural and moral condition. This, our new Government, is the first, in the history of the world, based upon this great physical, philosophical, and moral truth. . . .

It is the first Government ever instituted upon principles in strict conformity to nature, and the ordination of Providence, in furnishing the materials of human society. Many Governments have been founded upon the principles of certain classes; but the classes thus enslaved, were of the same race, and in violation of the laws of nature. Our system commits no such violation of nature's laws. The negro by nature, or by the curse against Canaan, is fitted for that condition which he occupies in our system. . . . The substratum of our society is made of the material fitted by nature for it, and by experience we know that it is the best, not only for the superior but for the inferior race, that it should be so.

FROM ABRAHAM LINCOLN,
Address at Sanitary Fair, Baltimore (April 18, 1864)

Abraham Lincoln's speech at a Sanitary Fair (a grand bazaar that raised money for the care of Union soldiers) offers a dramatic illustration of the contested meaning of freedom during the Civil War.

The world has never had a good definition of the word liberty, and the American people, just now, are much in want of one. We all declare for liberty; but in using the same *word* we do not all mean the same *thing*. With some the word liberty may mean for each man to do as he pleases with himself, and the product of his labor; while with others the same word may mean for some men to do as they please with other men, and the product of other men's labor. Here are two, not only different, but incompatible things, called by the same name—liberty. And it follows that each of the things is, by the respective parties, called by two different and incompatible names—liberty and tyranny.

The shepherd drives the wolf from the sheep's throat, for which the sheep thanks the shepherd as a *liberator*, while the wolf denounces him for the same act as the destroyer of liberty, especially as the sheep was a black one. Plainly the sheep and the wolf are not agreed upon a definition of the word liberty; and precisely the same difference prevails today among us human creatures, even in the North, and all professing to love liberty. Hence we behold the process by which thousands are daily passing from under the yoke of bondage, hailed by some as the advance of liberty, and bewailed by others as the destruction of all liberty. Recently, as it seems, the people of Maryland have been doing something to define liberty [abolishing slavery in the state]; and thanks to them that, in what they have done, the wolf's dictionary, has been repudiated.

QUESTIONS

1. Why does Stephens argue that slavery in the South differs from slavery as it has existed in previous societies?

2. What does Lincoln identify as the essential difference between northern and southern definitions of freedom?

3. How do Lincoln and Stephens differ in their definition of liberty and whether it applies to African-Americans?

the Chicago man briefly imprisoned for calling the president a "damned fool." With the Constitution unclear as to who possessed the power to suspend the writ of habeas corpus (thus allowing prisoners to be held without charge), Lincoln claimed the right under the presidential war powers and twice suspended the writ throughout the entire Union for those accused of "disloyal activities."

The courts generally gave the administration a free hand. They refused to intervene when a military court convicted Clement L. Vallandigham, a leading Ohio Democrat known for his blistering antiwar speeches, of treason. On Lincoln's order, Vallandigham was banished to the Confederacy. In 1861, Chief Justice Roger B. Taney had ordered the president to release John Merryman, a civilian who had been arrested by military authorities in Maryland, but the president ignored him. Not until 1866, after the fighting had ended, did the Supreme Court, in the case *Ex parte Milligan*, declare it unconstitutional to bring accused persons before military tribunals where civil courts were operating. The Constitution, declared Justice David Davis, is not suspended in wartime—it remains "a law for rulers and people, equally in time of war and peace."

Lincoln was not a despot. Most of those arrested were quickly released, the Democratic press continued to flourish, and contested elections were held throughout the war. But the policies of the Lincoln administration offered proof—to be repeated during later wars—of the fragility of civil liberties in the face of assertive patriotism and wartime demands for national unity.

THE NORTH'S TRANSFORMATION

Even as he invoked traditional values, Lincoln presided over far-reaching changes in northern life. The effort to mobilize the resources of the Union greatly enhanced the power not only of the federal government but also of a rising class of capitalist entrepreneurs. Unlike the South, which suffered economic devastation, the North experienced the war as a time of prosperity.

Nourished by wartime inflation and government contracts, the profits of industry boomed. New England mills worked day and night to supply the army with blankets and uniforms, and Pennsylvania coal mines and ironworks rapidly expanded their production. Mechanization proceeded apace in many industries, especially those like boot and shoe production and meatpacking that supplied the army's ever-increasing needs. Agriculture also flourished, for even as farm boys by the hundreds of thousands joined the army, the frontier of cultivation pushed westward, with machinery and immigrants replacing lost labor. Wisconsin furnished 90,000 men to the Union army, yet its population, grain production, and farm income continued to grow.

GOVERNMENT AND THE ECONOMY

As in contemporary Germany and Japan, the new American nation-state that emerged during the Civil War was committed to rapid economic development. Congress adopted policies that promoted economic growth and permanently altered the nation's financial system. With the South now unrepresented, the lawmakers adopted policies long advocated by many northerners. To spur agricultural development, the Homestead Act

Sheet music for two of the best-known patriotic songs written during the Civil War.

offered 160 acres of free public land to settlers in the West. It took effect on January 1, 1863, the same day as the Emancipation Proclamation, and like the Proclamation, tried to implement a vision of freedom. By the 1930s, over 400,000 families had acquired farms under its provisions. In addition, the Land Grant College Act assisted the states in establishing "agricultural and mechanic colleges."

BUILDING THE TRANSCONTINENTAL RAILROAD

Congress also made huge grants of money and land for internal improvements, including up to 100 million acres to the Union Pacific and Central Pacific, two companies chartered in 1862 and charged with building a railroad from the Missouri River to the Pacific coast. (These were the first corporate charters issued by the federal government since the Second Bank of the United States in 1816.)

When first proposed by entrepreneur Asa Whitney in 1846, the idea of a transcontinental railroad had been considered by Congress "too gigantic" and "entirely impracticable." And, indeed, the project was monumental. The Central Pacific progressed only twenty miles a year for the first three years of construction because the Sierra Nevada range was almost impassable. It required some 20,000 men to lay the tracks across prairies and mountains, a substantial number of them immigrant Chinese contract laborers, called "coolies" by many Americans. Hundreds of Chinese workers died blasting tunnels and building bridges through this treacherous terrain. When it was completed in 1869, the transcontinental railroad, which ran from Omaha, Nebraska, to San Francisco, expanded the national market, facilitated the spread of settlement and investment in the West, and heralded the doom of the Plains Indians.

A NEW FINANCIAL SYSTEM

The need to pay for the war produced dramatic changes in financial policy. To raise money, the government increased the tariff to unprecedented

Filling Cartridges at the U. S. Arsenal of Watertown, Massachusetts, *an engraving from* Harper's Weekly, *September 21, 1861. Both men and women were drawn to work in the booming war-related industries of the North.*

heights (thus promoting the further growth of northern industry), imposed new taxes on the production and consumption of goods, and enacted the nation's first income tax. It also borrowed over $2 billion by selling interest-bearing bonds, thus creating an immense national debt. And it printed over $400 million worth of paper money, called "greenbacks," declared to be legal tender—that is, money that must be accepted for nearly all public and private payments and debts. To rationalize the banking system, Congress established a system of nationally chartered banks, which were required to purchase government bonds and were given the right to issue bank notes as currency. A heavy tax drove money issued by state banks out of existence. Thus, the United States, whose money supply before the war was a chaotic mixture of paper notes issued by state and local banks, now had essentially two kinds of national paper currency—greenbacks printed directly by the federal government, and notes issued by the new national banks.

Along with profitable contracts to supply goods for the military effort, wartime economic policies greatly benefited northern manufacturers, railroad men, and financiers. Numerous Americans who would take the lead in reshaping the nation's postwar economy created or consolidated their fortunes during the Civil War, among them iron and steel entrepreneur Andrew Carnegie, oil magnate John D. Rockefeller, financiers Jay Gould and J. P. Morgan, and Philip D. Armour, who earned millions supplying beef to the Union army. These and other "captains of industry" managed to escape military service, sometimes by purchasing exemptions or hiring substitutes, as allowed by the draft law.

Taken together, the Union's economic policies vastly increased the power and size of the federal government. The federal budget for 1865 exceeded $1 billion—nearly twenty times that of 1860. With its new army of clerks, tax collectors, and other officials, the government became the nation's largest employer. And while much of this expansion proved temporary, the government would never return to its weak and fragmented condition of the prewar period.

WOMEN AND THE WAR

For many northern women, the conflict opened new doors of opportunity. Women took advantage of the wartime labor shortage to move into jobs in factories and into certain largely male professions, particularly nursing. The expansion of the activities of the national government opened new jobs for women as clerks in government offices. Many of these wartime gains were short-lived, but in white-collar government jobs, retail sales, and nursing, women found a permanent place in the workforce.

Some northern women took a direct part in military campaigns. Clara Barton, a clerk in the Patent Office in Washington, D.C., when the war began, traveled with the Army of Northern Virginia, helping to organize supply lines and nursing wounded soldiers. Barton worked alone rather than as a part of the Department of Female Nurses, and she never received compensation from the government.

Hundreds of thousands of northern women took part in organizations that gathered money and medical supplies for soldiers and sent books,

A female nurse photographed between two wounded Union soldiers in a Nashville military hospital in 1862. Many northern women served the army as nurses during the war.

clothing, and food to freedmen. The United States Sanitary Commission emerged as a centralized national relief agency to coordinate donations on the northern home front. Although control at the national level remained in male hands, patriotic women did most of the grassroots work. Women played the leading role in organizing Sanitary Fairs—grand bazaars that displayed military banners, uniforms, and other relics of the war and sold goods to raise money for soldiers' aid. New York City's three-week fair of 1864 attracted a crowd of 30,000 and raised over $1 million.

Many men understood women's war work as an extension of their "natural" capacity for self-sacrifice. But the very act of volunteering to work in local soldiers' aid societies brought many northern women into the public sphere and offered them a taste of independence. The suffrage movement suspended operations during the war to devote itself to the Union and emancipation. But women's continuing lack of the vote seemed all the more humiliating as their involvement in war work increased.

Camp of Thirty-first Pennsylvania Infantry, Near Washington, D.C., *an 1862 photograph by the Mathew Brady studio. Many women worked for the army as laundresses. Some accompanied their husbands and even brought their children.*

From the ranks of this wartime mobilization came many of the leaders of the postwar movement for women's rights. Mary Livermore, the wife of a Chicago minister, for example, toured military hospitals to assess their needs, cared for injured and dying soldiers, and organized two Sanitary Fairs. She emerged from the war with a deep resentment of women's legal and political subordination and organized her state's first women's suffrage convention. Women, she had concluded, must "think and act for themselves." After the war, Clara Barton not only became an advocate of women's suffrage but, as president of the American National Red Cross, lobbied for the United States to endorse the First Geneva Convention of 1864, which mandated the humane treatment of battlefield casualties. Largely as a result of

Whimsical potholders expressing hope for a better life for emancipated slaves were sold at the Chicago Sanitary Fair of 1865, to raise money for soldiers' aid.

Barton's efforts, the Senate ratified the convention in 1882. (Subsequent Geneva Conventions in the twentieth century would deal with the treatment of prisoners of war and civilians during wartime.)

THE DIVIDED NORTH

Despite Lincoln's political skills, the war and his administration's policies divided northern society. Republicans labeled those opposed to the war Copperheads, after a poisonous snake that strikes without warning. Mounting casualties and rapid societal changes divided the North. Disaffection was strongest among the large southern-born population of states like Ohio, Indiana, and Illinois and working-class Catholic immigrants in eastern cities.

As the war progressed, it heightened existing social tensions and created new ones. The growing power of the federal government challenged traditional notions of local autonomy. The Union's draft law, which allowed individuals to provide a substitute or buy their way out of the army, caused widespread indignation. Workers resented manufacturers and financiers who reaped large profits while their own real incomes dwindled because of inflation. The war witnessed the rebirth of the northern labor movement, which organized numerous strikes for higher wages. The prospect of a sweeping change in the status of blacks called forth a racist reaction in many parts of the North. Throughout the war, the Democratic Party subjected Lincoln's policies to withering criticism, although it remained divided between "War Democrats," who supported the military effort while criticizing emancipation and the draft, and those who favored immediate peace.

On occasion, dissent degenerated into outright violence. In July 1863, the introduction of the draft provoked four days of rioting in New York City. The mob, composed largely of Irish immigrants, assaulted symbols of the new order being created by the war—draft offices, the mansions of wealthy Republicans, industrial establishments, and the city's black population, many of whom fled to New Jersey or took refuge in Central Park. Only the arrival of Union troops quelled the uprising, but not before over 100 persons had died.

The Riots in New York: The Mob Lynching a Negro in Clarkson Street, *an engraving from the British magazine* Illustrated London News, *August 8, 1863, reveals how the New York City draft riots escalated from an attempt to obstruct the draft into an assault on the city's black population.*

THE CONFEDERATE NATION

LEADERSHIP AND GOVERNMENT

The man charged with the task of rallying public support for the Confederacy proved unequal to the task. Born in 1808 in Kentucky, within eight months and 100 miles of Lincoln's birth, Jefferson Davis had moved to Mississippi as a youth, attended West Point, and acquired a large plantation. Aloof, stubborn, and humorless, he lacked Lincoln's common touch and political flexibility. Although known before the war as the "Cicero of the Senate" for his eloquent speeches, Davis, unlike Lincoln, proved unable to communicate the war's meaning effectively to ordinary men and women. Moreover, the Confederacy's lack of a party system proved to be a political liability. Like the founders of the American republic, southern leaders saw parties as threats to national unity. As a result, Davis lacked a counterpart to the well-organized Republican Party, which helped to mobilize support for the Lincoln administration.

Under Davis, the Confederate nation became far more centralized than the Old South had been. The government raised armies from scratch, took control of southern railroads, and built manufacturing plants. But it failed to find an effective way of utilizing the South's major economic resource, cotton. In the early part of the war, the administration tried to suppress cotton production, urging planters to grow food instead and banning cotton exports. This, it was hoped, would promote economic self-sufficiency and force Great Britain, whose textile mills could not operate without southern cotton, to intervene on the side of the Confederacy.

"King Cotton diplomacy" turned out to be ineffective. Large crops in 1859 and 1860 had created a huge stockpile in English warehouses. By the time distress hit the manufacturing districts in 1862, the government of Prime Minister Palmerston had decided not to intervene, partly because Britain needed northern wheat almost as much as southern cotton. But the Confederate policy had far-reaching global consequences. Recognizing their overdependence

The centrality of slavery to the Confederacy is illustrated by the paper money issued by state governments and private banks, which frequently juxtaposed scenes of slaves at work with other revered images. The ten-dollar note of the Eastern Bank of Alabama depicts slaves working in the field and at a port, along with an idealized portrait of southern white womanhood. Alabama's five-dollar bill includes an overseer directing slaves in the field, and a symbol of liberty.

on southern cotton, other nations moved to expand production. Britain promoted cultivation of the crop in Egypt and India, Russia in parts of Central Asia. As a result, the resumption of American cotton production after the war led directly to a worldwide crisis of overproduction that drove down the price of cotton, impoverishing farmers around the world.

Nor did Davis deal effectively with obstructionist governors like Joseph E. Brown of Georgia, who denounced the Confederate draft as "a dangerous usurpation" of states' rights and individual liberty. All in all, Davis was so inferior to Lincoln as a wartime leader that one historian has suggested that had the North and South exchanged presidents, the South would have won the war.

THE INNER CIVIL WAR

As the war progressed, social change and internal turmoil engulfed much of the Confederacy. At the outset, most white southerners rallied to the Confederate cause. No less fervently than northern troops, southern soldiers spoke of their cause in the language of freedom. "We are fighting for our liberty," wrote one volunteer, without any sense of contradiction, "against tyrants of the North . . . who are determined to destroy slavery." But public disaffection eventually became an even more serious problem for the Confederacy than for the Union.

Even as it waged a desperate struggle for independence, the South found itself increasingly divided. One grievance was the draft. Like the Union, the Confederacy allowed individuals to provide a substitute. Because of the accelerating disintegration of slavery, it also exempted one white male for every twenty slaves on a plantation (thus releasing many overseers and planters' sons from service). The "twenty-negro" provision convinced many yeomen that the struggle for southern independence had become "a rich man's war and a poor man's fight."

ECONOMIC PROBLEMS

Economic deprivation also sparked disaffection. As the blockade tightened, areas of the Confederacy came under Union occupation, and production by slaves declined, shortages arose of essential commodities such as salt, corn, and meat. The war left countless farms, plantations, businesses, and railroads in ruins. The economic crisis, which stood in glaring contrast to the North's boom, was an unavoidable result of the war. But Confederate policies exaggerated its effects. War requires sacrifice, and civilian support for war depends, in part, on the belief that sacrifice is being fairly shared. Many nonslaveholders, however, became convinced that they were bearing an unfair share of the war's burdens.

Like the Union, the Confederacy borrowed heavily to finance the war. Unlike federal lawmakers, however, the planter-dominated Confederate Congress proved unwilling to levy heavy taxes that planters would have to pay. It relied on paper money, of which it issued $1.5 billion, far more than the North's greenbacks. Congress also authorized military officers to seize farm goods to supply the army, paying with increasingly worthless Confederate money. Small farmers deeply resented this practice, known as "impressment." "The Rebel army treated us a heap worse than [Union general William T.] Sherman did," a Georgia farmer later recalled. "I had hogs, and a mule, and a horse, and they took them all." Numerous yeoman families, many of whom had gone to war to preserve their economic independence, sank into poverty and debt. Food riots broke out in many places, including Richmond, Virginia, where in 1863 a large crowd of women plundered army food supplies.

In 1862, Joshua B. Moore, a slaveholder in northern Alabama, commented on how slavery threatened the Confederate war effort: "Men who have no interest in it," he wrote, "are not going to fight through a long war to save it—never. They will tire of it and quit." As the war progressed, desertion became what one officer called a "crying evil" for the southern armies. By the war's end, over 100,000 men had deserted, almost entirely from among "the poorest class of nonslaveholders whose labor is indispensable to the daily support of their families." Men, another official noted, "cannot be expected to fight for the government that permits their wives and children to starve."

SOUTHERN UNIONISTS

By 1864, organized peace movements had appeared in several southern states, and secret societies such as the Heroes of America were actively promoting disaffection. Confederate military tribunals imprisoned hundreds of Unionists. Others were violently driven from their homes, and a few were executed by the army or civilian authorities. But southerners loyal to the Union made a significant contribution to northern victory. By the end of the war, an estimated 50,000 white southerners had fought in the Union armies.

An engraving from Frank Leslie's Illustrated Newspaper, *May 23, 1863, showing the bread riot that took place in Richmond, the capital of the Confederacy.*

One of the most celebrated Union heroes of the war was Elizabeth Van Lew of Richmond, who had persuaded her mother to free the family's slaves when her father died in 1843. During the war she frequently visited Libby Prison in the Confederate capital, bringing supplies to Union prisoners of war and helping some of them to escape. With the aid of Mary Elizabeth Bowser, a former slave of the Van Lew family who worked as a servant in the southern White House, Van Lew passed information about Confederate plans to Union forces.

WOMEN AND THE CONFEDERACY

Even more than in the North, the war placed unprecedented burdens on southern white women. Left alone on farms and plantations, they were often forced to manage business affairs and discipline slaves, previously the responsibility of men. As in the North, women mobilized to support soldiers in the field and stepped out of their traditional "sphere" to run commercial establishments and work in arms factories. In Richmond, "government girls" staffed many of the clerkships in the new Confederate bureaucracy. Rose Greenhow, the widow of a former American diplomat, headed an espionage ring in Washington that passed valuable information about Union troop movements to the Confederacy early in the war. Even after her arrest and jailing, she managed to smuggle out intelligence until she was exiled to Richmond in 1862. Jefferson Davis rewarded Greenhow with $2,500 for her services.

Southern women's self-sacrificing devotion to the cause became legendary. But as the war went on and the death toll mounted, increasing numbers of women came to believe that the goal of independence was not worth the cost. The growing disaffection of southern white women, conveyed in letters to loved ones at the front, contributed to the decline in civilian morale and encouraged desertion from the army.

BLACK SOLDIERS FOR THE CONFEDERACY

The growing shortage of white manpower eventually led Confederate authorities to a decision no one could have foreseen when the war began: they authorized the arming of slaves to fight for the South. As early as September 1863, a Mississippi newspaper had argued for freeing and enlisting able-bodied black men. "Let them," it wrote, "be declared free, placed in the ranks, and told to fight for their homes and country." But many slaveholders fiercely resisted this idea, and initially, the Confederate Senate rejected it. Not until March 1865, after Robert E. Lee had endorsed the plan, did the Confederate Congress authorize the arming of slaves.

The war ended before the recruitment of black soldiers actually began. But the Confederate army did employ numerous blacks, nearly all of them slaves, as laborers. This later led to some confusion over whether blacks actually fought for the Confederacy—apart from a handful who "passed" for white, none in fact did. But the South's decision to raise black troops illustrates how the war undermined not only slavery but also the proslavery ideology. "The day you make soldiers of them is the beginning of the end of the revolution," declared Howell Cobb, a Georgia planter and politician. "If slaves make good soldiers, our whole theory of slavery is wrong."

TURNING POINTS

GETTYSBURG AND VICKSBURG

Despite the accelerating demise of slavery and the decline of morale in the South, the war's outcome remained very much in doubt for much of its third and fourth years. In April 1863, "Fighting Joe" Hooker, who had succeeded Ambrose E. Burnside as the Union comander in the East, brought the Army of the Potomac into central Virginia to confront Lee. Outnumbered two to one, Lee repelled Hooker's attack at Chancellorsville, although he lost his ablest lieutenant, "Stonewall" Jackson, mistakenly killed by fire from his own soldiers.

Lee now gambled on another invasion of the North, although his strategic objective remains unclear. Perhaps he believed a defeat on its own territory would destroy the morale of the northern army and public. In any event, the two armies, with Union soldiers now under the command of General George

In July 1863, the Union won major victories at Gettysburg and Vicksburg.

THE CIVIL WAR, 1863

G. Meade, met at Gettysburg, Pennsylvania, on the first three days of July 1863. With 165,000 troops involved, Gettysburg remains the largest battle ever fought on the North American continent. Lee found himself in the unusual position of confronting entrenched Union forces. After two days of failing to dislodge them, he decided to attack the center of the Union line. On July 3, Confederate forces, led by Major General George E. Pickett's crack division, marched across an open field toward Union forces. Withering artillery and rifle fire met the charge, and most of Pickett's soldiers never reached Union lines. Of the 14,000 men who made the advance—the flower of Lee's army—fewer than half returned. Later remembered as "the high tide of the Confederacy," Pickett's Charge was also Lee's greatest blunder. His army retreated to Virginia, never again to set foot on northern soil.

On the same day that Lee began his retreat from Gettysburg, the Union achieved a significant victory in the West. Late in 1862, Grant had moved into Mississippi toward the city of Vicksburg. From its heights, defended by miles of trenches and earthworks, the Confederacy commanded the central Mississippi River. When direct attacks failed, as did an attempt to divert the river by digging a canal, Grant launched a siege. On July 4, 1863, Vicksburg surrendered, and with it John C. Pemberton's army of 30,000 men, a loss the Confederacy could ill afford. The entire Mississippi Valley now lay in Union hands. The simultaneous defeats at Gettysburg and Vicksburg dealt a heavy blow to southern morale. "Today absolute ruin seems our portion," one official wrote in his diary. "The Confederacy totters to its destruction."

1864

Nearly two years, however, would pass before the war ended. Brought east to take command of Union forces, Grant in 1864 began a war of attrition against Lee's army in Virginia. That is, he was willing to accept high numbers of casualties, knowing that the North could replace its manpower losses while the South could not. Grant understood that to bring the North's manpower advantage into play, he must attack continuously "all along the line," thereby preventing the enemy from concentrating its forces or retreating to safety after an engagement.

In May 1864, the 115,000-man Army of the Potomac crossed the Rapidan River to do battle with Lee's forces in Virginia. A month of the war's bloodiest fighting followed. Grant and Lee first encountered each other in the Wilderness, a wild, shrub-covered region where, one participant recalled, "it was as though Christian men had turned to fiends, and hell itself had usurped the place of earth." Grant's army suffered 18,000 casualties, while Lee's far smaller forces incurred 7,500. Previous Union generals had broken off engagements after losses of this magnitude. But Grant continued to press forward, attacking again at Spotsylvania and then at Cold Harbor. At the end of six weeks of fighting, Grant's casualties stood at 60,000—almost the size of Lee's entire army—while Lee had lost 30,000 men. The sustained fighting in Virginia was a turning point in modern warfare. With daily combat and a fearsome casualty toll, it had far more in common with the trench warfare of World War I (discussed

Generals Robert E. Lee and Ulysses S. Grant, leaders of the opposing armies in the East, 1864–1865.

in Chapter 19) than the almost gentlemanly fighting with which the Civil War began.

Grant had become the only Union general to maintain the initiative against Lee, but at a cost that led critics to label him a "butcher of men." Victory still eluded him. Grant attempted to capture Petersburg, which controlled the railway link to Richmond, but Lee got to Petersburg first, and Grant settled in for a prolonged siege. Meanwhile, General William T. Sherman, who had moved his forces into Georgia from Tennessee, encountered dogged resistance from Confederate troops. Not until September 1864 did he finally enter Atlanta, seizing Georgia's main railroad center.

As casualty rolls mounted in the spring and summer of 1864, northern morale sank to its lowest point of the war. Lincoln for a time believed he would be unable to win reelection. In May, hoping to force Lincoln to step aside, Radical Republicans nominated John C. Frémont on a platform calling for a constitutional amendment to abolish slavery, federal protection of the freedmen's rights, and confiscation of the land of leading Confederates. The Democratic candidate for president, General George B. McClellan, was hampered from the outset of the campaign by a platform calling for an immediate cease-fire and peace conference—a plan that even war-weary northerners viewed as equivalent to surrender. In the end, Frémont withdrew, and buoyed by Sherman's capture of Atlanta, Lincoln won a sweeping victory. He captured every state but Kentucky, Delaware, and New Jersey. The result ensured that the war would continue until the Confederacy's defeat.

REHEARSALS FOR RECONSTRUCTION AND THE END OF THE WAR

As the war drew toward a close and more and more parts of the Confederacy came under Union control, federal authorities found themselves presiding over the transition from slavery to freedom. In South Carolina, Louisiana, and other parts of the South, debates took place over issues—access to land, control of labor, and the new structure of political power—that would reverberate in the postwar world.

THE SEA ISLAND EXPERIMENT

The most famous "rehearsal for Reconstruction" took place on the Sea Islands just off the coast of South Carolina. The war was only a few months old when, in November 1861, the Union navy occupied the islands. Nearly the entire white population fled, leaving behind some 10,000 slaves. The navy was soon followed by other northerners—army officers, treasury agents, prospective investors in cotton land, and a group known as Gideon's Band, which included black and white reformers and teachers committed to uplifting the freed slaves. Each of these groups, in addition to the islands' black population, had its own view of how the transition to freedom should be organized. And journalists reported every development on the islands to an eager reading public in the North.

Diagram of plots selected by former slaves on Port Royal Island, South Carolina, January 25, 1864. Taking advantage of a sale of abandoned property, eighteen blacks (seventeen men and one woman) selected plots on a Sea Island plantation for purchase.

Teachers in the Freedmen's Schools in Norfolk, 1863, *a photograph of a group of black and white teachers who brought education to former slaves in a Union-occupied part of Virginia.*

Convinced that education was the key to making self-reliant, productive citizens of the former slaves, northern-born teachers like Charlotte Forten, a member of one of Philadelphia's most prominent black families, and Laura M. Towne, a white native of Pittsburgh, devoted themselves to teaching the freed blacks. Towne, who in 1862 helped to establish Penn school on St. Helena Island, remained there as a teacher until her death in 1901. Like many of the Gideonites, Towne and Forten assumed that blacks needed outside guidance to appreciate freedom. But they sympathized with the former slaves' aspirations, central to which was the desire for land.

Other northerners, however, believed that the transition from slave to free labor meant not giving blacks land but enabling them to work for wages in more humane conditions than under slavery. When the federal government put land on the islands up for sale, most was acquired not by former slaves but by northern investors bent upon demonstrating the superiority of free wage labor and turning a tidy profit at the same time. By 1865, the Sea Island experiment was widely held to be a success. Black families were working for wages, acquiring education, and enjoying better shelter and clothing and a more varied diet than under slavery. But the experiment also bequeathed to postwar Reconstruction the contentious issue of whether land ownership should accompany black freedom.

WARTIME RECONSTRUCTION IN THE WEST

A very different rehearsal for Reconstruction, involving a far larger area and population than the Sea Islands, took place in Louisiana and the Mississippi Valley. After the capture of Vicksburg, the Union army established regulations for plantation labor. Military authorities insisted that the emancipated slaves must sign labor contracts with plantation owners who took an oath of loyalty. But, unlike before the war, they would be paid wages and provided with education, physical punishment was prohibited, and their families were safe from disruption by sale.

Neither side was satisfied with the new labor system. Blacks resented having to resume working for whites and being forced to sign labor contracts. Planters complained that their workers were insubordinate. Without the whip, they insisted, discipline could not be enforced. But only occasionally did army officers seek to implement a different vision of freedom. At Davis Bend, Mississippi, site of the cotton plantations of Jefferson Davis and his brother Joseph, General Grant decided to establish a "negro paradise." Here, rather than being forced to labor for white owners, the emancipated slaves saw the land divided among themselves. In addition, a system of government was established with the former slaves electing their own judges and sheriffs.

THE POLITICS OF WARTIME RECONSTRUCTION

As the Civil War progressed, the future political status of African-Americans emerged as a key dividing line in public debates. Events in Union-occupied Louisiana brought the issue to national attention. Hoping to establish a functioning civilian government in the state, Lincoln in 1863 announced his Ten-Percent Plan of Reconstruction. He essentially offered an amnesty and full restoration of rights, including property except for slaves, to nearly all white southerners who took an oath affirming loyalty to the Union and support for emancipation. When 10 percent of the voters of 1860 had taken the oath, they could elect a new state government, which would be required to abolish slavery. Lincoln's plan offered no role to blacks in shaping the post-slavery order. His leniency toward southern whites seems to have been based on the assumption that many former slaveholders would come forward to accept his terms, thus weakening the Confederacy, shortening the war, and gaining white support for the ending of slavery.

Another group now stepped onto the stage of politics—the free blacks of New Orleans, who saw the Union occupation as a golden opportunity to press for equality before the law and a role in government for themselves. Their complaints at being excluded under Lincoln's Reconstruction plan won a sympathetic hearing from Radical Republicans in Congress. By the summer of 1864, dissatisfaction with events in Louisiana helped to inspire the Wade-Davis Bill, named for two leading Republican members of Congress. This bill required a majority (not one-tenth) of white male southerners to pledge support for the Union before Reconstruction could begin in any state, and it guaranteed blacks equality before the law, although not the right to vote. The bill passed Congress only to die when Lincoln refused to sign it and Congress adjourned. As the war drew to a close, it was clear that while slavery was dead, no agreement existed as to what social and political system should take its place.

VICTORY AT LAST

After Lincoln's reelection, the war hastened to its conclusion. In November 1864, Sherman and his army of 60,000 set out from Atlanta on their March to the Sea. Cutting a sixty-mile-wide swath through the heart of Georgia, they destroyed railroads, buildings, and all the food and supplies they could not use. His aim, Sherman wrote, was "to whip the rebels, to humble

General William T. Sherman photographed in 1864.

The Evacuation of Richmond, *a Currier and Ives lithograph from 1865, dramatically depicts the last days of the Civil War. Residents flee the Confederate capital as fires set by retreating troops to destroy ammunition supplies consume parts of the city.*

their pride, to follow them to their innermost recesses, and make them fear and dread us." Here was modern war in all its destructiveness, even though few civilians were physically harmed. In January 1865, after capturing Savannah, Sherman moved into South Carolina, bringing even greater destruction. Anarchy reigned on the plantations as slaves drove off remaining overseers, destroyed planters' homes, plundered smokehouses and storerooms, and claimed the land for themselves.

On January 31, 1865, Congress approved the Thirteenth Amendment, which abolished slavery throughout the entire Union—and in so doing, introduced the word "slavery" into the Constitution for the first time. In March, in his second inaugural address, Lincoln called for reconciliation: "with malice toward none, with charity for all, . . . let us . . . bind up the nation's wounds." Yet he also leveled a harsh judgment on the nation's past. "This terrible war," the president declared, was God's punishment for the sin of slavery. And if God willed that it continue until all the wealth created by 250 years of slave labor had been destroyed, and "every drop of blood drawn with the lash shall be paid by another drawn with the sword," this too would be an act of justice (see the Appendix for the full text).

April 1865 brought some of the most momentous events in American history. On April 2, Grant finally broke through Lee's lines at Petersburg, forcing the Army of Northern Virginia to abandon the city and leaving Richmond defenseless. The following day, Union soldiers occupied the southern capital. At the head of one black army unit marched its chaplain, Garland H. White, a former fugitive from slavery. Called upon by a large crowd to make a speech, White, as he later recalled, proclaimed "for the first time in that city freedom to all mankind." Then, the "doors of all the slave pens were thrown open and thousands came out shouting and praising God, and Father, or Master Abe."

On April 4, heedless of his own safety, Lincoln walked the streets of Richmond accompanied only by a dozen sailors. At every step he was besieged by former slaves, some of whom fell on their knees before the embarrassed

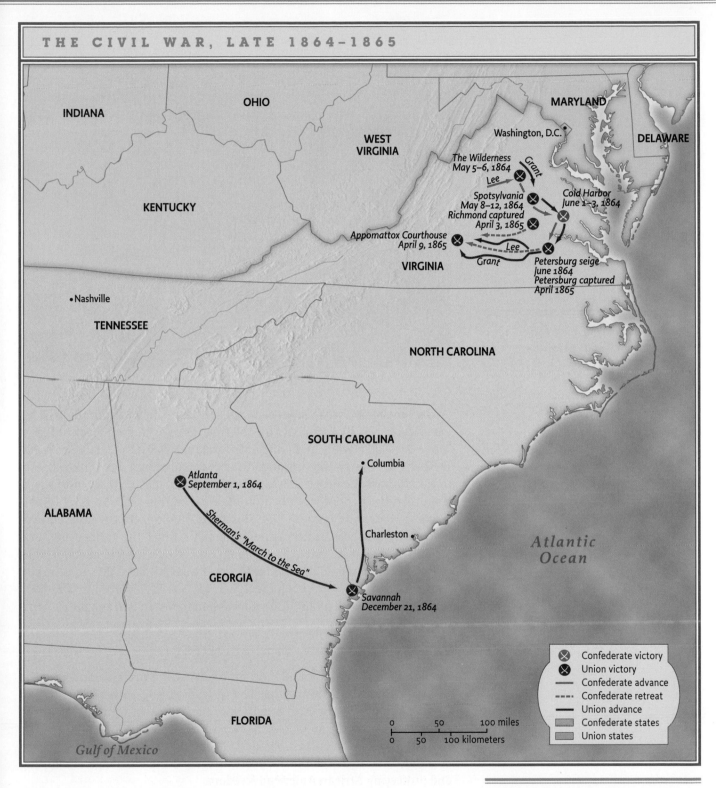

THE CIVIL WAR, LATE 1864–1865

INDIANA

OHIO

MARYLAND

Washington, D.C.

WEST VIRGINIA

DELAWARE

The Wilderness
May 5–6, 1864

Grant

Lee

Spotsylvania
May 8–12, 1864

Cold Harbor
June 1–3, 1864

KENTUCKY

Richmond captured
April 3, 1865

Appomattox Courthouse
April 9, 1865

Lee

VIRGINIA

Grant

Petersburg seige
June 1864
Petersburg captured
April 1865

Nashville

TENNESSEE

NORTH CAROLINA

SOUTH CAROLINA

Columbia

ALABAMA

Atlanta
September 1, 1864

Sherman's "March to the Sea"

Charleston

Atlantic
Ocean

GEORGIA

Savannah
December 21, 1864

FLORIDA

Gulf of Mexico

⊗	Confederate victory
⊗	Union victory
—	Confederate advance
---	Confederate retreat
—	Union advance
▦	Confederate states
▦	Union states

0   50   100 miles
0   50   100 kilometers

president, who urged them to remain standing. Meanwhile, Lee and his army headed west, only to be encircled by Grant's forces. Realizing that further resistance was useless, Lee surrendered at Appomattox Court House, Virginia, on April 9. Although some Confederate units remained in the field, the Civil War was over.

The military defeat of the Confederacy came in the East, with Sherman's March to the Sea, Grant's occupation of Richmond, and the surrender of Robert E. Lee's army.

The ruins of Richmond, in an 1865 photograph by Alexander Gardner.

Lincoln did not live to savor victory. On April 11, in what proved to be his last speech, he called publicly for the first time for limited black suffrage. Three days later, while attending a performance at Ford's Theatre in Washington, D.C., the president was mortally wounded by John Wilkes Booth, one of the nation's most celebrated actors. Lincoln died the next morning. A train carried the president's body to its final resting place in Illinois on a winding 1,600-mile journey that illustrated how tightly the railroad now bound the northern states. Grieving crowds lined the train route, and solemn processions carried the president's body to lie in state in major cities so that mourners could pay their respects. It was estimated that 300,000 persons passed by the coffin in Philadelphia, 500,000 in New York, and 200,000 in Chicago. On May 4, 1865, Lincoln was laid to rest in Springfield.

THE WAR IN AMERICAN HISTORY

The Civil War laid the foundation for modern America, guaranteeing the Union's permanence, destroying slavery, and shifting power in the nation from the South to the North (and, more specifically, from slaveowning planters to northern capitalists). It dramatically increased the power of the federal government and accelerated the modernization of the northern economy. And it placed on the postwar agenda the challenge of defining and protecting African-American freedom.

Paradoxically, both sides lost something they had gone to war to defend. Slavery was the cornerstone of the Confederacy, but the war led inexorably to slavery's destruction. In the North, the war hastened the transformation of Lincoln's America—the world of free labor, of the small shop and independent farmer—into an industrial giant. Americans, in the words of the abolitionist Wendell Phillips, would "never again . . . see the republic in which we were born."

Late in May 1865, a little over a month after Lincoln's death, some 200,000 veterans paraded through Washington, D.C., for the Grand Review of the Union armies, a final celebration of the nation's triumph. The scene inspired the poet Bret Harte to imagine a very different parade—a "phantom army" of the Union dead:

> The martyred heroes of Malvern Hill,
> Of Gettysburg and Chancellorsville,
> The men whose wasted figures fill
> The patriot graves of the nation. . . .
> And marching beside the others,
> Came the dusky martyrs of Pillow's fight.

To Harte, the war's meaning ultimately lay in the sacrifices of individual soldiers. He included in his reverie the black troops, including those massacred at Fort Pillow. Blacks, Harte seemed to be saying, had achieved equality in death. Could the nation give it to them in life?

Here was the problem that confronted the United States as the postwar era known as Reconstruction began. "Verily," as Frederick Douglass declared, "the work does not *end* with the abolition of slavery, but only *begins*."

SUGGESTED READING

Ayers, Edward L. *In the Presence of Mine Enemies: War in the Heart of America, 1859–1863* (2003). A study of the experiences of Americans in two counties, one in Pennsylvania, one in Virginia, in the early years of the Civil War.

Berlin, Ira, ed. *Slaves No More: Three Essays on Emancipation and the Civil War* (1992). A careful account of the causes and consequences of emancipation during the war.

Faust, Drew G. *Mothers of Invention: Women of the Slaveholding South during the American Civil War* (1996). Explores how the waning enthusiasm of southern women for the war effort weakened the Confederacy.

Freehling, William W. *The South vs. the South: How Anti-Confederate Southerners Shaped the Course of the Civil War* (2001). An examination of internal disunion within the Confederacy and how it affected the struggle for southern independence.

Glatthaar, Joseph T. *Forged in Battle: The Civil War Alliance of Black Soldiers and White Officers* (1990). Relates the complex experience of black Civil War soldiers and their officers.

Lawson, Melinda. *Patriot Fires: Forging a New Nationalism in the Civil War North* (2002). Considers how both public and private groups, in order to mobilize support for the war effort, promoted a new idea of American nationalism.

McPherson, James M. *Battle Cry of Freedom: The Civil War Era* (1988). The standard account of the coming of the war, its conduct, and its consequences.

Mitchell, Reid. *Civil War Soldiers* (1988). A look at the Civil War from the point of view of the experience of ordinary soldiers.

Neely, Mark E. *The Fate of Liberty: Abraham Lincoln and Civil Liberties* (1991). Explores how the Lincoln administration did and did not meet the challenge of preserving civil liberties while fighting the war.

Quarles, Benjamin. *Lincoln and the Negro* (1962). A judicious account of the evolution of Lincoln's policies regarding slavery, emancipation, and the rights of African-Americans.

Richardson, Heather C. *Greatest Nation of the Earth: Republican Economic Policies during the Civil War* (1997). Considers the far-reaching impact of the economic measures adopted by the Union during the war.

Rose, Willie Lee. *Rehearsal for Reconstruction: The Port Royal Experiment* (1964). Traces the unfolding of the issues of Reconstruction in the Sea Islands of South Carolina in the midst of the war.

Rubin, Anne S. *Shattered Nation: The Rise and Fall of the Confederacy, 1861–1868* (2005). An up-to-date account of the Confederate experience.

Silber, Nina. *Daughters of the Union: Northern Women Fight the Civil War* (2005). Examines the participation of northern women in the war effort and how this did and did not alter their lives.

Weigley, Russell F. *A Great Civil War: A Political and Military History, 1861–1865* (2000). A comprehensive account of the war's military history.

REVIEW QUESTIONS

1. Describe how blacks played a crucial role in both winning the Civil War and in defining the war's consequences.

2. What material advantages did the North have over the South?

3. Describe how Lincoln's war aims evolved between 1861 and 1863, changing from preserving the Union to ending slavery .

4. How did the Gettysburg Address express ideas of freedom and liberty?

5. In what ways did Lincoln restrict liberty during the war?

KEY TERMS

railroads (p. 507)

Lincoln and colonization (p. 516)

black sailors (p. 520)

Ex parte Milligan (p. 526)

women and work (p. 528)

Southern Unionism (p. 533)

women in the Confederacy (p. 534)

Election of 1864 (p. 537)

REVIEW TABLE

Rehearsals for Reconstruction

Event	Explanation	Result
Sea Island experiment, 1861–1865	Union takes islands and northerners bring their ideas for education, land distribution, and employment for blacks	Black families work for wages, getting an education and enjoying better food and shelter than under slavery
"Negro paradise"	General Grant seizes the cotton plantations of Jefferson Davis and his brother	Grant divides the land among the freed slaves, rather than have them work for white owners
Ten-Percent Plan	Lincoln's lenient plan toward the South, which offered no role for blacks	Rejected by many black Southerners and the Radical Republicans in Congress
Wade-Davis Bill	Stricter reconstruction plan that guarantees blacks equality before the law	Pocket vetoed by Lincoln

Chapter 15

"What Is Freedom?": Reconstruction, 1865–1877

The Shackle Broken—by the Genius of Freedom, *an 1874 lithograph celebrating the progress of black freedom during the Civil War and Reconstruction. At the center, Robert B. Elliott, a black congressman from South Carolina, delivers a celebrated speech supporting the bill that became the Civil Rights Act of 1875. Elliott is surrounded by images of black soldiers and sailors, as well as Abraham Lincoln, Senator Charles Sumner (the bill's author), and a scene of black family life. The print illustrates the centrality of military service to black claims to citizenship, and the linkage of the ideals of emancipation, equality, and free labor during the Reconstruction era that followed the Civil War.*

FOCUS QUESTIONS

• What visions of freedom did the former slaves and slaveholders pursue in the postwar South?

• What were the sources and the significance of radical Reconstruction?

• What were the social and political effects of radical Reconstruction in the South?

• What were the main reasons for the defeat of Reconstruction in the South?

On the evening of January 12, 1865, less than a month after Union forces captured Savannah, Georgia, twenty leaders of the city's black community gathered for a discussion with General William T. Sherman and Secretary of War Edwin M. Stanton. Mostly Baptist and Methodist ministers, the group included several men who within a few years would assume prominent positions during the era of Reconstruction that followed the Civil War. Ulysses S. Houston, pastor of the city's Third African Baptist Church, and James Porter, an episcopal religious leader who had operated a secret school for black children before the war, in a few years would win election to the Georgia legislature. James D. Lynch, who had been born free in Baltimore and educated in New Hampshire, went on to serve as secretary of state of Mississippi.

The conversation revealed that the black leaders brought out of slavery a clear definition of freedom. Asked what he understood by slavery, Garrison Frazier, a Baptist minister chosen as the group's spokesman, responded that it meant one person's "receiving by irresistible power the work of another man, and not by his consent." Freedom he defined as "placing us where we could reap the fruit of our own labor, and take care of ourselves." The way to accomplish this was "to have land, and turn it and till it by our own labor." Frazier insisted that blacks possessed "sufficient intelligence" to maintain themselves in freedom and enjoy the equal protection of the laws.

Sherman's meeting with the black leaders foreshadowed some of the radical changes that would take place during the era known as Reconstruction (meaning, literally, the rebuilding of the shattered nation). In the years following the Civil War, former slaves and their white allies, North and South, would seek to redefine the meaning and boundaries of American freedom. Previously an entitlement of whites, freedom would be expanded to include black Americans. The laws and Constitution would be rewritten to guarantee African-Americans, for the first time in the nation's history, recognition as citizens and equality before the law. Black men would be granted the right to vote, ushering in a period of interracial democracy throughout the South. Black schools, churches, and other institutions would flourish, laying the foundation for the modern African-American community. Many of the advances of Reconstruction would prove temporary, swept away during a campaign of violence in the South, and the North's retreat from the ideal of equality. But Reconstruction laid the foundation for future struggles to extend freedom to all Americans.

All this, however, lay in the future in January 1865. Four days after the meeting, Sherman responded to the black delegation by issuing Special Field Order 15. This set aside the Sea Islands and a large area along the South Carolina and Georgia coasts for the settlement of black families on forty-acre plots of land. He also offered them broken-down mules that the army could no longer use. In Sherman's order lay the origins of the phrase, "forty acres and a mule," that would reverberate across the South in the next few years. By June, some 40,000 freed slaves had been settled on "Sherman land." Among the emancipated slaves, Sherman's order raised hopes that the end of slavery would be accompanied by the economic independence that they, like other Americans, believed essential to genuine freedom.

THE MEANING OF FREEDOM

With the end of the Civil War, declared an Illinois congressman in 1865, the United States was a "new nation," for the first time "wholly free." The destruction of slavery, however, made the definition of freedom the central question on the nation's agenda. "What is freedom?" asked Congressman James A. Garfield in 1865. "Is it the bare privilege of not being chained? If this is all, then freedom is a bitter mockery, a cruel delusion." Did freedom mean simply the absence of slavery, or did it imply other rights for the former slaves, and if so, which ones: equal civil rights, the vote, ownership of property? During Reconstruction, freedom became a terrain of conflict, its substance open to different, often contradictory interpretations. Out of the conflict over the meaning of freedom arose new kinds of relations between black and white southerners, and a new definition of the rights of all Americans.

BLACKS AND THE MEANING OF FREEDOM

African-Americans' understanding of freedom was shaped by their experiences as slaves and their observation of the free society around them. To begin with, freedom meant escaping the numerous injustices of slavery—punishment by the lash, the separation of families, denial of access to education, the sexual exploitation of black women by their owners—and sharing in the rights and opportunities of American citizens. "If I cannot do like a white man," Henry Adams, an emancipated slave in Louisiana, told his former master in 1865, "I am not free."

Blacks relished the opportunity to demonstrate their liberation from the regulations, significant and trivial, associated with slavery. They openly held mass meetings and religious services free of white supervision, and they acquired dogs, guns, and liquor, all barred to them under slavery. No longer required to obtain a pass from their owners to travel, former slaves throughout the South left the plantations in search of better jobs, family members, or simply a taste of personal liberty. Many moved to southern towns and cities, where, it seemed, "freedom was free-er."

Family Record, a lithograph marketed to former slaves after the Civil War, centers on an idealized portrait of a middle-class black family, with scenes of slavery and freedom.

A post–Civil War photograph of an unidentified black family, seated before their humble home, possibly a former slave cabin.

Mother and Daughter Reading, Mt. Meigs, Alabama, *an 1890 photograph by Rudolph Eickemeyer. During Reconstruction and for years thereafter, former slaves exhibited a deep desire for education, and learning took place outside of school as well as within.*

FAMILIES IN FREEDOM

With slavery dead, institutions that had existed before the war, like the black family, free blacks' churches and schools, and the secret slave church, were strengthened, expanded, and freed from white supervision. The family was central to the postemancipation black community. Former slaves made remarkable efforts to locate loved ones from whom they had been separated under slavery. One northern reporter in 1865 encountered a freedman who had walked more than 600 miles from Georgia to North Carolina, searching for the wife and children from whom he had been sold away before the war. Meanwhile, widows of black soldiers successfully claimed survivors' pensions, forcing the federal government to acknowledge the validity of prewar relationships that slavery had attempted to deny.

But while Reconstruction witnessed the stabilization of family life, freedom subtly altered relationships within the family. Emancipation increased the power of black men and brought to many black families the nineteenth-century notion that men and women should inhabit separate "spheres." Immediately after the Civil War, planters complained that freedwomen had "withdrawn" from field labor and work as house servants. Many black women preferred to devote more time to their families than had been possible under slavery, and men considered it a badge of honor to see their wives remain at home. Eventually, the dire poverty of the black community would compel a far higher proportion of black women than white women to go to work for wages.

CHURCH AND SCHOOL

At the same time, blacks abandoned white-controlled religious institutions to create churches of their own. On the eve of the Civil War, 42,000 black Methodists worshiped in biracial South Carolina churches; by the end of Reconstruction, only 600 remained. The rise of the independent black church, with Methodists and Baptists commanding the largest followings, redrew the religious map of the South. As the major institution independent of white control, the church played a central role in the black community. A place of worship, it also housed schools, social events, and political gatherings. Black ministers came to play a major role in politics. Some 250 held public office during Reconstruction.

Another striking example of the freedpeople's quest for individual and community improvement was their desire for education. Education, declared a Mississippi freedman, was "the next best thing to liberty." The thirst for learning sprang from many sources—a desire to read the Bible, the need to prepare for the economic marketplace, and the opportunity, which arose in 1867, to take part in politics. Blacks of all ages flocked to the schools established by northern missionary societies, the Freedmen's

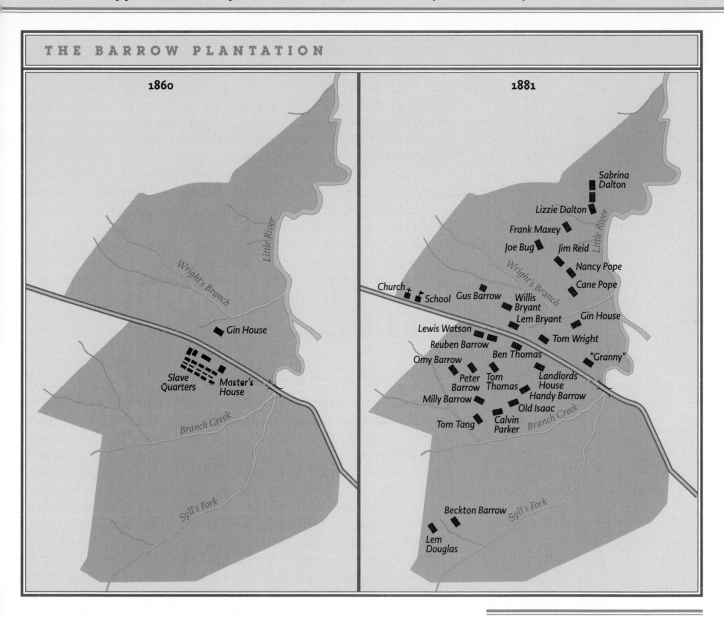

THE BARROW PLANTATION

1860

Little River

Wright's Branch

Gin House

Slave Quarters   Master's House

Branch Creek

Syll's Fork

1881

Sabrina Dalton

Lizzie Dalton

Frank Maxey

Joe Bug   Jim Reid

Nancy Pope

Cane Pope

Church +   Little River

School   Gus Barrow   Willis Bryant   Wright's Branch

Lem Bryant   Gin House

Lewis Watson   Tom Wright

Reuben Barrow

Omy Barrow   Ben Thomas   "Granny"

Peter   Tom   Landlords House
Barrow   Thomas

Milly Barrow   Handy Barrow

Old Isaac

Tom Tang   Calvin   Branch Creek
Parker

Beckton Barrow   Syll's Fork

Lem Douglas

Bureau, and groups of ex-slaves themselves. Northern journalist Sidney Andrews, who toured the South in 1865, was impressed by how much education also took place outside of the classroom: "I had occasion very frequently to notice that porters in stores and laboring men in warehouses, and cart drivers on the streets, had spelling books with them, and were studying them during the time they were not occupied with their work." Reconstruction also witnessed the creation of the nation's first black colleges, including Fisk University in Tennessee, Hampton Institute in Virginia, and Howard University in the nation's capital.

Two maps of the Barrow plantation illustrate the effects of emancipation on rural life in the South. In 1860, slaves lived in communal quarters near the owner's house. Twenty years later, former slaves working as sharecroppers lived scattered across the plantation and had their own church and school.

POLITICAL FREEDOM

In a society that had made political participation a core element of freedom, the right to vote inevitably became central to the former slaves' desire for empowerment and equality. As Frederick Douglass put it soon after the South's surrender in 1865, "Slavery is not abolished until the black man has the ballot." In a "monarchial government," Douglass explained, no "special" disgrace applied to those denied the right to vote. But in a democracy, "where universal suffrage is the rule," excluding any group meant branding them with "the stigma of inferiority." As soon as the Civil War ended, and in some parts of the South even earlier, free blacks and emancipated slaves claimed a place in the public sphere. They came together in conventions, parades, and petition drives to demand the right to vote and, on occasion, to organize their own "freedom ballots."

Anything less than full citizenship, black spokesmen insisted, would betray the nation's democratic promise and the war's meaning. Speakers at black conventions reminded the nation of Crispus Attucks, who fell at the Boston Massacre, and of black soldiers' contribution to the War of 1812 and during "the bloody struggle through which we have just passed." To demonstrate their patriotism, blacks throughout the South organized Fourth of July celebrations. For years after the Civil War, white southerners would "shut themselves within doors" on Independence Day, as a white resident of Charleston recorded in her diary, while former slaves commemorated the holiday themselves.

LAND, LABOR, AND FREEDOM

Like rural people throughout the world, former slaves' ideas of freedom were directly related to land ownership. Only land, wrote Merrimon Howard, a freedman from Mississippi, would enable "the poor class to enjoy the sweet boon of freedom." On the land they would develop independent communities free of white control. Many former slaves insisted that through their unpaid labor, they had acquired a right to the land. "The property which they hold," declared an Alabama black convention, "was nearly all earned by the sweat of *our* brows." In some parts of the South, blacks in 1865 seized property, insisting that it belonged to them. On one Tennessee plantation, former slaves claimed to be "joint heirs" to the estate and, the owner complained, took up residence "in the rooms of my house."

In its individual elements and much of its language, former slaves' definition of freedom resembled that of white Americans—self-ownership, family stability, religious liberty, political participation, and economic autonomy. But these elements combined to form a vision very much their own. For whites, freedom, no matter how defined, was a given, a birthright to be defended. For African-Americans, it was an open-ended process, a transformation of every aspect of their lives and of the society and culture that had sustained slavery in the first place. Although the freedpeople failed to achieve full freedom as they understood it, their definition did much to shape national debate during the turbulent era of Reconstruction.

MASTERS WITHOUT SLAVES

Most white southerners reacted to military defeat and emancipation with dismay, not only because of the widespread devastation but also because they must now submit to northern demands. "The demoralization is complete," wrote a Georgia girl. "We are whipped, there is no doubt about it." The appalling loss of life, a disaster without parallel in the American experience, affected all classes of southerners. Nearly 260,000 men died for the Confederacy—over one-fifth of the South's adult male white population. The widespread destruction of work animals, farm buildings, and machinery ensured that economic revival would be slow and painful. In 1870, the value of property in the South, not counting that represented by slaves, was 30 percent lower than before the war.

Planter families faced profound changes in the war's aftermath. Many lost not only their slaves but their life savings, which they had patriotically invested in now-worthless Confederate bonds. Some, whose slaves departed the plantation, for the first time found themselves compelled to do physical labor. General Braxton Bragg returned to his "once prosperous" Alabama home to find "*all, all* was lost, except my debts." Bragg and his wife, a woman "raised in affluence," lived for a time in a slave cabin.

The Great Labor Question from a Southern Point of View, *a cartoon by the artist Winslow Homer, published in* Harper's Weekly, *July 29, 1865. Homer satirizes the attitudes of many white southerners. While blacks labor in the fields, an idle planter warns a former slave, "My boy, we've toiled and taken care of you long enough—now you've got to work!"*

Southern planters sought to implement an understanding of freedom quite different from that of the former slaves. As they struggled to accept the reality of emancipation, most planters defined black freedom in the narrowest manner. As journalist Sidney Andrews discovered late in 1865, "The whites seem wholly unable to comprehend that freedom for the negro means the same thing as freedom for them. They readily enough admit that the government has made him free, but appear to believe that they have the right to exercise the same old control." Southern leaders sought to revive the antebellum definition of freedom as if nothing had changed. Freedom still meant hierarchy and mastery; it was a privilege, not a right, a carefully defined legal status rather than an open-ended entitlement. Certainly, it implied neither economic autonomy nor civil and political equality. "A man may be free and yet not independent," Mississippi planter Samuel Agnew observed in his diary in 1865. A Kentucky newspaper summed up the stance of much of the white South: the former slave was "*free*, but free only to labor."

THE FREE LABOR VISION

Along with former slaves and former masters, the victorious Republican North tried to implement its own vision of freedom. Central to its definition was the antebellum principle of free labor, now further strengthened as a definition of the good society by the Union's triumph. In the free-labor vision of a reconstructed South, emancipated blacks, enjoying the same opportunities for advancement as northern workers, would labor more productively than they had as slaves. At the same time, northern capital and migrants would energize the economy. The South would eventually come to resemble the "free society" of the North, complete with public schools, small towns, and independent farmers. Unified on the basis of free labor, proclaimed Carl Schurz, a refugee from the failed German revolution of 1848 who rose to become a leader of the Republican Party, America would become "a republic, greater, more populous, freer, more prosperous, and more powerful" than any in history.

With planters seeking to establish a labor system as close to slavery as possible, and former slaves demanding economic autonomy and access to land, a long period of conflict over the organization and control of labor followed on plantations throughout the South. It fell to the Freedmen's Bureau, an agency established by Congress in March 1865, to attempt to establish a working free labor system.

THE FREEDMEN'S BUREAU

Under the direction of O. O. Howard, a graduate of Bowdoin College in Maine and a veteran of the Civil War, the Bureau took on responsibilities that can only be described as daunting. The Bureau was an experiment in government social policy that seems to belong more comfortably to the New Deal of the 1930s or the Great Society of the 1960s (see Chapters 21 and 25, respectively) than to nineteenth-century America. Bureau agents were supposed to establish schools, provide aid to the poor and aged, settle disputes between whites and blacks and among the freedpeople, and secure for former slaves and white Unionists equal treatment before the courts. "It is not . . . in your power to fulfill one-tenth of the expectations of those who framed the Bureau," General William T. Sherman wrote to Howard. "I fear you have Hercules' task."

The Bureau lasted from 1865 to 1870. Even at its peak, there were fewer than 1,000 agents in the entire South. Nonetheless, the Bureau's achieve-

The Freedmen's Bureau, *an engraving from* Harper's Weekly, *July 25, 1868, depicts the Bureau agent as a promoter of racial peace in the violent postwar South.*

ments in some areas, notably education and health care, were striking. While the Bureau did not establish schools itself, it coordinated and helped to finance the activities of northern societies committed to black education. By 1869, nearly 3,000 schools, serving over 150,000 pupils in the South, reported to the Bureau. Bureau agents also assumed control of hospitals established by the army during the war, and expanded the system into new communities. They provided medical care and drugs to both black and white southerners. In economic relations, however, the Bureau's activities proved far more problematic.

THE FAILURE OF LAND REFORM

The idea of free labor, wrote one Bureau agent, was "the noblest principle on earth." All that was required to harmonize race relations in the South was fair wages, good working conditions, and the opportunity to improve the laborer's situation in life. But blacks wanted land of their own, not jobs on plantations. One provision of the law establishing the Bureau gave it the authority to divide abandoned and confiscated land into forty-acre plots for rental and eventual sale to the former slaves.

In the summer of 1865, however, President Andrew Johnson, who had succeeded Lincoln, ordered nearly all land in federal hands returned to its former owners. A series of confrontations followed, notably in South Carolina and Georgia, where the army forcibly evicted blacks who had settled on "Sherman land." When O. O. Howard, head of the Freedmen's Bureau, traveled to the Sea Islands to inform blacks of the new policy, he was greeted with disbelief and protest. A committee of former slaves drew up petitions to Howard and President Johnson. "We want Homesteads," they declared, "we were promised Homesteads by the government." Land, the freedmen insisted, was essential to the meaning of freedom. Without it, they declared, "we have not bettered our condition" from the days of slavery—"you will see, this is not the condition of really free men."

Because no land distribution took place, the vast majority of rural freedpeople remained poor and without property during Reconstruction. They had no alternative but to work on white-owned plantations, often for their former owners. Far from being able to rise in the social scale through hard work, black men were largely confined to farm work, unskilled labor, and service jobs, and black women to positions in private homes as cooks and maids. Their wages remained too low to allow for any accumulation. By the turn of the century, a significant number of southern African-Americans had managed to acquire small parcels of land. But the failure of land reform produced a deep sense of betrayal that survived among the former slaves and their descendants long after the end of Reconstruction. "No sir," Mary Gaffney, an elderly ex-slave, recalled in the 1930s, "we were not given a thing but freedom."

TOWARD A NEW SOUTH

Out of the conflict on the plantations, new systems of labor emerged in the different regions of the South. The task system, under which workers were

A black family in the cotton fields after the Civil War, photographed in 1867.

VOICES OF FREEDOM

FROM

Petition of Committee in Behalf of the Freedmen to Andrew Johnson (1865)

In the summer of 1865, President Andrew Johnson ordered land that had been distributed to freed slaves in South Carolina and Georgia returned to its former owners. A committee of freedmen drafted a petition asking for the right to obtain land. Johnson did not, however, change his policy.

We the freedmen of Edisto Island, South Carolina, have learned from you through Major General O. O. Howard . . . with deep sorrow and painful hearts of the possibility of [the] government restoring these lands to the former owners. We are well aware of the many perplexing and trying questions that burden your mind, and therefore pray to god (the preserver of all, and who has through our late and beloved President [Lincoln's] proclamation and the war made us a free people) that he may guide you in making your decisions and give you that wisdom that cometh from above to settle these great and important questions for the best interests of the country and the colored race.

Here is where secession was born and nurtured.

Here is where we have toiled nearly all our lives as slaves and treated like dumb driven cattle. This is our home, we have made these lands what they were, we are the only true and loyal people that were found in possession of these lands. We have been always ready to strike for liberty and humanity, yea to fight if need be to preserve this glorious Union. Shall not we who are freedmen and have always been true to this Union have the same rights as are enjoyed by others? . . . Are not our rights as a free people and good citizens of these United States to be considered before those who were found in rebellion against this good and just government? . . .

[Are] we who have been abused and oppressed for many long years not to be allowed the privilege of purchasing land but be subject to the will of these large land owners? God forbid. Land monopoly is injurious to the advancement of the course of freedom, and if government does not make some provision by which we as freedmen can obtain a homestead, we have not bettered our condition. . . .

We look to you . . . for protection and equal rights with the privilege of purchasing a homestead—a homestead right here in the heart of South Carolina.

FROM Article by Elizabeth Cady Stanton on Women's Suffrage, *The Revolution* (January 14, 1869)

One of the most prominent leaders of the nineteenth-century women's suffrage movement, Elizabeth Cady Stanton was bitterly disappointed both that the Reconstruction Congress extended the right to vote to black men but not to women, and that many leading abolitionists who had previously supported votes for women proclaimed Reconstruction the "Negro's hour" and supported the congressional policy. In this article, she chastises the abolitionist Gerrit Smith for refusing to sign a women's suffrage petition.

The above is a petition to which our friend Gerrit Smith, as an abolitionist, can not conscientiously put his name.... He does not clearly read the signs of the times, or he would see that there is to be no reconstruction of this nation, except on the basis of universal suffrage, as the natural, inalienable right of every citizen.... As the aristocracy in this country is the "male sex," and as Mr. Smith belongs to the privileged order, he naturally considers it important for the best interests of the nation, that every type and shade of degraded, ignorant manhood should be enfranchised, before even the higher classes of womanhood should be admitted to the polls. This does not surprise us. Men always judge more wisely of objective wrongs and oppressions, than of those in which they are themselves involved. Tyranny on a Southern plantation is far more easily seen by white men at the North than the wrongs of the women of their own households....

Again; Mr. Smith refuses to sign the petition because he thinks the broader question of "universal suffrage" would defeat the partial one of "manhood suffrage"; in other words, to demand protection for woman against her oppressors, would jeopardize the black men's chance of securing protection against his oppressors. If it is a question of precedence merely, on what principle of justice or courtesy should woman yield her right of enfranchisement to the negro? If men cannot be trusted to legislate for their own sex, how can they legislate for the oppose sex, of whose wants and needs they know nothing?...

Mr. Smith ... would undoubtedly plead the necessity of the ballot for the negro at the south for his protection, and point us to innumerable acts of cruelty he suffers today. But all these things fall as heavily on the women of the black race, yea far more so, for no man can ever know the deep, the damning degradation to which woman is subject in her youth, in helplessness and poverty. The enfranchisement of the men of her race, Mr. Smith would say, is her protection. Our Saxon men have held the ballot in this country for a century, and what honest man can claim that it has been used for woman's protection?... Women everywhere are waking up to their own God-given rights, to their true dignity as citizens of a republic, as mothers of the race.... End all this talk of class legislation, bury the negro in the citizen, and claim the suffrage for all men and women, as a natural, inalienable right.

QUESTIONS

1. Why do the black petitioners believe that owning land is essential to the enjoyment of freedom?

2. Why does Stanton believe that women need and deserve the right to vote?

3. What do these documents suggest about the boundaries of freedom in the Reconstruction era?

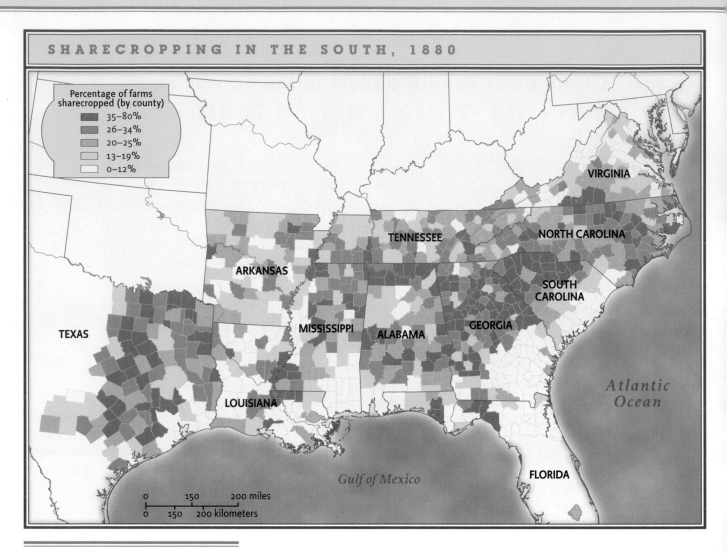

SHARECROPPING IN THE SOUTH, 1880

Percentage of farms
sharecropped (by county)

- 35–80%
- 26–34%
- 20–25%
- 13–19%
- 0–12%

By 1880, sharecropping had become the dominant form of agricultural labor in large parts of the South. The system involved both white and black farmers.

assigned daily tasks, completion of which ended their responsibilities for that day, survived in the rice kingdom of South Carolina and Georgia. Closely supervised wage labor predominated on the sugar plantations of southern Louisiana. Sharecropping came to dominate the Cotton Belt and much of the Tobacco Belt of Virginia and North Carolina.

Sharecropping initially arose as a compromise between blacks' desire for land and planters' demand for labor discipline. The system allowed each black family to rent a part of a plantation, with the crop divided between worker and owner at the end of the year. Sharecropping guaranteed the planters a stable resident labor force. Former slaves preferred it to gang labor because it offered them the prospect of working without day-to-day white supervision. But as the years went on, sharecropping became more and more oppressive. Sharecroppers' economic opportunities were severely limited by a world market in which the price of farm products suffered a prolonged decline.

THE WHITE FARMER

The plight of the small farmer was not confined to blacks in the postwar South. Wartime devastation set in motion a train of events that permanently altered the independent way of life of white yeomen, leading to what they considered a loss of freedom. Before the war, most small farmers had concentrated on raising food for their families and grew little cotton. With much of their property destroyed, many yeomen saw their economic condition worsened by successive crop failures after the war. To obtain supplies from merchants, farmers were forced to take up the growing of cotton and pledge a part of the crop as collateral (property the creditor can seize if a debt is not paid). This system became known as the "crop lien." Since interest rates were extremely high and the price of cotton fell steadily, many farmers found themselves still in debt after marketing their portion of the crop at year's end. They had no choice but to continue to plant cotton to obtain new loans. By the mid-1870s, white farmers, who cultivated only 10 percent of the South's cotton crop in 1860, were growing 40 percent, and many who had owned their land had fallen into dependency as sharecroppers, who now rented land owned by others.

Both black and white farmers found themselves caught in the sharecropping and crop-lien systems. A far higher percentage of black than white farmers in the South rented land rather than owned it. But every census from 1880 to 1940 counted more white than black sharecroppers. The workings of sharecropping and the crop-lien system are illustrated by the case of Matt Brown, a Mississippi farmer who borrowed money each year from a local merchant. He began 1892 with a debt of $226 held over from the previous year. By 1893, although he produced cotton worth $171, Brown's debt had increased to $402, because he had borrowed $33 for food, $29 for clothing, $173 for supplies, and $112 for other items. Brown never succeeded in getting out of debt. He died in 1905; the last entry under his name in the merchant's account book is a coffin.

Farmers with Cotton in the Courthouse Square, *an 1880 photograph from Marietta, Georgia. After the Civil War, more and more white farmers began growing cotton to support their families, permanently altering their formerly self-sufficient way of life.*

THE URBAN SOUTH

Even as the rural South stagnated economically, southern cities experienced remarkable growth after the Civil War. As railroads penetrated the interior, they enabled merchants in market centers like Atlanta to trade directly with the North, bypassing coastal cities that had traditionally monopolized southern commerce. A new urban middle class of merchants, railroad promoters, and bankers reaped the benefits of the spread of cotton production in the postwar South.

Thus, Reconstruction witnessed profound changes in the lives of southerners, black and white, rich and poor. In place of the prewar world of master, slave, and self-sufficient yeoman, the postwar South was peopled by new social classes—landowning employers, black and white sharecroppers, cotton-producing white farmers, wage-earning black laborers, and urban entrepreneurs. Each of these groups turned to Reconstruction politics in an attempt to shape to its own advantage the aftermath of emancipation.

THE MAKING OF RADICAL RECONSTRUCTION

Between 1865 and 1868, the United States confronted one of the greatest political crises of its history—the battle between President Andrew Johnson and Congress over Reconstruction. The struggle resulted in profound changes in the nature of citizenship, the structure of constitutional authority, and the meaning of American freedom.

ANDREW JOHNSON

To Lincoln's successor, Andrew Johnson, fell the task of overseeing the restoration of the Union. Born in poverty in North Carolina, as a youth Johnson worked as a tailor's apprentice. After moving to Tennessee, he achieved success through politics. Beginning as an alderman (a town official), he rose to serve in the state legislature, the U.S. Congress, and for two terms as governor of Tennessee. Johnson identified himself as the champion of his state's "honest yeomen" and a foe of large planters, whom he described as a "bloated, corrupted aristocracy." A strong defender of the Union, he became the only senator from a seceding state to remain at his post in Washington, D.C., when the Civil War began in 1861. When northern forces occupied Tennessee, Abraham Lincoln named him military governor. In 1864, Republicans nominated him to run for vice president as a symbol of the party's hope of extending its organization into the South.

In personality and outlook, Johnson proved unsuited for the responsibilities he shouldered after Lincoln's death. A lonely, stubborn man, he was intolerant of criticism and unable to compromise. He lacked Lincoln's political skills and keen sense of public opinion. A fervent believer in states' rights, Johnson insisted that since secession was illegal, the southern states had never actually left the Union or surrendered the right to govern their own affairs. Moreover, while Johnson had supported emancipation once Lincoln made it a goal of the war effort, he held deeply racist views. African-Americans, Johnson believed, had no role to play in Reconstruction.

THE FAILURE OF PRESIDENTIAL RECONSTRUCTION

A little over a month after Lee's surrender at Appomattox, and with Congress out of session until December, Johnson in May 1865 outlined his plan for reuniting the nation. He issued a series of proclamations that began the period of Presidential Reconstruction (1865–1867). Johnson offered a pardon (which restored political and property rights, except for slaves) to nearly all white southerners who took an oath of allegiance. He excluded Confederate leaders and wealthy planters whose prewar property had been valued at more than $20,000. This exemption suggested at first that Johnson planned a more punitive Reconstruction than Lincoln had intended. Most of those exempted, however, soon received individual pardons from the president. Johnson also appointed provisional governors and ordered them to call state conventions, elected by whites alone, that would establish loyal governments in the South. Apart from the requirement that they abolish slavery, repudiate secession, and refuse to pay the Confederate debt—all unavoidable consequences of southern defeat—he granted the new governments a free hand in managing local affairs.

At first, most northerners believed Johnson's policy deserved a chance to succeed. The conduct of the southern governments elected under his program, however, turned most of the Republican North against the president. By and large, white voters returned prominent Confederates and members of the old elite to power. Reports of violence directed against former slaves and northern visitors in the South further alarmed Republicans.

THE BLACK CODES

But what aroused the most opposition to Johnson's Reconstruction policy were the Black Codes, laws passed by the new southern governments that attempted to regulate the lives of the former slaves. These laws granted blacks certain rights, such as legalized marriage, ownership of property, and limited access to the courts. But they denied them the rights to testify against whites, to serve on juries or in state militias, or to vote. And in response to planters' demands that the freedpeople be required to work on the plantations, the Black Codes declared that those who failed to sign yearly labor contracts could be arrested and hired out to white landowners. Some states limited the occupations open to blacks and barred them from acquiring land, and others provided that judges could assign black children to work for their former owners without the consent of the parents.

Clearly, the death of slavery did not automatically mean the birth of freedom. But the Black Codes so completely violated free labor principles that they called forth a vigorous response from the Republican North. Wars—especially civil wars—often generate hostility and bitterness. But few groups of rebels in history have been treated more leniently than the

Selling a Freeman to Pay His Fine at Monticello, Florida, *an engraving from* Frank Leslie's Illustrated Newspaper, *January 19, 1867. Under the Black Codes enacted by southern legislatures immediately after the Civil War, blacks convicted of "vagrancy"—often because they refused to sign contracts to work on plantations—were fined and, if unable to pay, auctioned off to work for the person who paid the fine.*

defeated Confederates. A handful of southern leaders were arrested but most were quickly released. Only one was executed—Henry Wirz, the commander of Andersonville prison, where thousands of Union prisoners of war had died. Most of the Union army was swiftly demobilized. What motivated the North's turn against Johnson's policies was not a desire to "punish" the white South, but the inability of the South's political leaders to accept the reality of emancipation. "We must see to it," announced Republican senator William Stewart of Nevada, "that the man made free by the Constitution of the United States is a freeman indeed."

THE RADICAL REPUBLICANS

When Congress assembled in December 1865, Johnson announced that with loyal governments functioning in all the southern states, the nation had been reunited. In response, Radical Republicans, who had grown increasingly disenchanted with Johnson during the summer and fall, called for the dissolution of these governments and the establishment of new ones with "rebels" excluded from power and black men guaranteed the right to vote. Radicals tended to represent constituencies in New England and the "burned-over" districts of the rural North that had been home to religious revivalism, abolitionism, and other reform movements. Although they differed on many issues, Radicals shared the conviction that Union victory created a golden opportunity to institutionalize the principle of equal rights for all, regardless of race.

The Radicals fully embraced the expanded powers of the federal government born during the Civil War. Traditions of federalism and states' rights, they insisted, must not obstruct a sweeping national effort to protect the rights of all Americans. The most prominent Radicals in Congress were Charles Sumner, a senator from Massachusetts, and Thaddeus Stevens, a lawyer and iron manufacturer who represented Pennsylvania in the House of Representatives. Before the Civil War, both had been outspoken foes of slavery and defenders of black rights. Early in the Civil War, both had urged Lincoln to free and arm the slaves, and both in 1865 favored black suffrage in the South. "The same national authority," declared Sumner, "that destroyed slavery must see that this other pretension [racial inequality] is not permitted to survive."

Thaddeus Stevens's most cherished aim was to confiscate the land of disloyal planters and divide it among former slaves and northern migrants to the South. "The whole fabric of southern society," he declared, "*must* be changed. Without this, this Government can never be, as it has never been, a true republic." But his plan to make "small independent landholders" of the former slaves proved too radical even for many of his Radical colleagues. Congress, to be sure, had already offered free land to settlers in the West in the Homestead Act of 1862. But this land had been in the possession of the federal government, not private individuals (although originally, of course, it had been occupied by Indians). Most congressmen believed too deeply in the sanctity of property rights to be willing to take land from one group of owners and distribute it to others. Stevens's proposal failed to pass.

Thaddeus Stevens, leader of the Radical Republicans in the House of Representatives during Reconstruction.

THE ORIGINS OF CIVIL RIGHTS

With the South unrepresented, Republicans enjoyed an overwhelming majority in Congress. But the party was internally divided. Most Republicans were moderates, not Radicals. Moderates believed that Johnson's plan was flawed, but they desired to work with the president to modify it. They feared that neither northern nor southern whites would accept black suffrage. Moderates and Radicals joined in refusing to seat the southerners recently elected to Congress, but moderates broke with the Radicals by leaving the Johnson governments in place.

Early in 1866, Senator Lyman Trumbull of Illinois proposed two bills, reflecting the moderates' belief that Johnson's policy required modification. The first extended the life of the Freedmen's Bureau, which had been originally established for only one year. The second, the Civil Rights Bill, was described by one congressman as "one of the most important bills ever presented to the House for its action." It defined all persons born in the United States as citizens and spelled out rights they were to enjoy without regard to race. Equality before the law was central to the measure—no longer could states enact laws like the Black Codes discriminating between white and black citizens. So were free labor values. According to the law, no state could deprive any citizen of the right to make contracts, bring lawsuits, or enjoy equal protection of one's person and property. These, said Trumbull, were the "fundamental rights belonging to every man as a free man." The bill made no mention of the right to vote for blacks. In constitutional terms, the Civil Rights Bill represented the first attempt to give concrete meaning to the Thirteenth Amendment, which had abolished slavery, to define in law the essence of freedom.

To the surprise of Congress, Johnson vetoed both bills. Both, he said, would centralize power in the national government and deprive the states of the authority to regulate their own affairs. Moreover, he argued, blacks did not deserve the rights of citizenship. By acting to secure their rights, Congress was discriminating "against the white race." The vetoes made a breach between the president and nearly the entire Republican Party inevitable. Congress failed by a single vote to muster the two-thirds majority necessary to override the veto of the Freedmen's Bureau Bill (although later in 1866, it did extend the Bureau's life to 1870). But in April 1866, the Civil Rights Bill became the first major law in American history to be passed over a presidential veto.

THE FOURTEENTH AMENDMENT

Congress now proceeded to adopt its own plan of Reconstruction. In June, it approved and sent to the states for ratification the Fourteenth Amendment, which placed in the Constitution the principle of citizenship for all persons born in the United States, and which empowered the federal government to protect the rights of all Americans. The amendment prohibited the states from abridging the "privileges and immunities" of citizens or denying them the "equal protection of the law." This broad language opened the door for future Congresses and the federal courts to breathe meaning into the guarantee of legal equality.

President Andrew Johnson, in an 1868 lithograph by Currier and Ives. Because of Johnson's stubborn opposition to the congressional Reconstruction policy, one disgruntled citizen drew a crown on his head with the words, "I am King."

A Democratic Party broadside from the election of 1866 in Pennsylvania uses racist imagery to argue that government assistance aids lazy former slaves at the expense of hardworking whites.

In a compromise between the radical and moderate positions on black suffrage, the amendment did not grant blacks the right to vote. But it did provide that if a state denied the vote to any group of men, that state's representation in Congress would be reduced. (This provision did not apply when states barred women from voting.) The abolition of slavery threatened to increase southern political power, since now all blacks, not merely three-fifths as in the case of slaves, would be counted in determining a state's representation in Congress. The Fourteenth Amendment offered the leaders of the white South a choice—allow black men to vote and keep their state's full representation in the House of Representatives, or limit the vote to whites and sacrifice part of their political power.

The Fourteenth Amendment produced an intense division between the parties. Not a single Democrat in Congress voted in its favor, and only 4 of 175 Republicans were opposed. Radicals, to be sure, expressed their disappointment that the amendment did not guarantee black suffrage. (It was far from perfect, Stevens told the House, but he intended to vote for it, "because I live among men and not among angels.") Nonetheless, by writing into the Constitution the principle that equality before the law regardless of race is a fundamental right of all American citizens, the amendment made the most important change in that document since the adoption of the Bill of Rights.

THE RECONSTRUCTION ACT

The Fourteenth Amendment became the central issue of the political campaign of 1866. Johnson embarked on a speaking tour of the North, called by journalists the "swing around the circle," to urge voters to elect members of Congress committed to his own Reconstruction program. Denouncing his critics, the president made wild accusations that the Radicals were plotting to assassinate him. His behavior further undermined public support for his policies, as did riots that broke out in Memphis and New Orleans, in which white policemen and citizens killed dozens of blacks.

In the northern congressional elections that fall, Republicans opposed to Johnson's policies won a sweeping victory. Nonetheless, at the president's urging, every southern state but Tennessee refused to ratify the Fourteenth Amendment. The intransigence of Johnson and the bulk of the white South pushed moderate Republicans toward the Radicals. In March 1867, over Johnson's veto, Congress adopted the Reconstruction Act, which temporarily divided the South into five military districts and called for the creation of new state governments, with black men given the right to vote. Thus began the period of Radical Reconstruction, which lasted until 1877.

A variety of motives combined to produce Radical Reconstruction—demands by former slaves for the right to vote, the Radicals' commitment to the idea of equality, widespread disgust with Johnson's policies, the desire to fortify the Republican Party in the South, and the determination to keep ex-Confederates from office. But the conflict between President Johnson and Congress did not end with the passage of the Reconstruction Act.

IMPEACHMENT AND THE ELECTION OF GRANT

In March 1867, Congress adopted the Tenure of Office Act, barring the president from removing certain officeholders, including cabinet members, without the consent of the Senate. Johnson considered this an unconstitutional restriction on his authority. In February 1868, he removed Secretary of War Edwin M. Stanton, an ally of the Radicals. The House of Representatives responded by approving articles of impeachment—that is, it presented charges against Johnson to the Senate, which had to decide whether to remove him from office.

That spring, for the first time in American history, a president was placed on trial before the Senate for "high crimes and misdemeanors." By this point, virtually all Republicans considered Johnson a failure as president. But some moderates disliked Benjamin F. Wade, a Radical who, as temporary president of the Senate, would become president if Johnson were removed. Others feared that conviction would damage the constitutional separation of powers between Congress and the executive. Johnson's lawyers assured moderate Republicans that, if acquitted, he would stop interfering with Reconstruction policy. The final tally was 35–19 to convict Johnson, one vote short of the two-thirds necessary to remove him. Seven Republicans had joined the Democrats in voting to acquit the president.

A few days after the vote, Republicans nominated Ulysses S. Grant, the Union's most prominent military hero, as their candidate for president. Grant's Democratic opponent was Horatio Seymour, the former governor of New York. Reconstruction became the central issue of the bitterly fought 1868 campaign. Republicans identified their opponents with secession and treason, a tactic known as "waving the bloody shirt." Democrats denounced Reconstruction as unconstitutional and condemned black suffrage as a violation of America's political traditions. They appealed openly to racism. Seymour's running mate Francis P. Blair Jr., charged Republicans with placing the South under the rule of "a semi-barbarous race" who longed to "subject the white women to their unbridled lust."

THE FIFTEENTH AMENDMENT

Grant won the election of 1868, although by a margin—300,000 of 6 million votes cast—that many Republicans found uncomfortably slim. The result led Congress to adopt the era's third and final amendment to the Constitution. In February 1869, it approved the Fifteenth Amendment, which prohibited the federal and state governments from denying any citizen the right to vote because of race. Bitterly opposed by the Democratic Party, it was ratified in 1870.

A Democratic ribbon from the election of 1868, with Horatio Seymour and Francis P. Blair Jr., the party's candidates for president and vice president. The ribbon illustrates the explicit appeals to racism that marked the campaign.

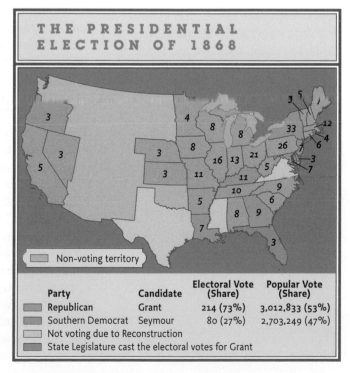

THE PRESIDENTIAL ELECTION OF 1868

Non-voting territory

Party	Candidate	Electoral Vote (Share)	Popular Vote (Share)
Republican	Grant	214 (73%)	3,012,833 (53%)
Southern Democrat	Seymour	80 (27%)	2,703,249 (47%)
Not voting due to Reconstruction			
State Legislature cast the electoral votes for Grant			

The Fifteenth Amendment, *an 1870 lithograph marking the ratification of the constitutional amendment prohibiting states from denying citizens the right to vote because of race. Surrounding an image of a celebration parade are portraits of Abraham Lincoln; President Ulysses S. Grant and his vice president, Schuyler Colfax; abolitionists John Brown, Martin R. Delany, and Frederick Douglass; and Hiram Revels, the first black to serve in the United States Senate. At the bottom are scenes of freedom—education, family, political representation, and church life.*

Although the Fifteenth Amendment opened the door to suffrage restrictions not explicitly based on race—literacy tests, property qualifications, and poll taxes—and did not extend the right to vote to women, it marked the culmination of four decades of abolitionist agitation. As late as 1868, even after Congress had enfranchised black men in the South, only eight northern states allowed African-American men to vote. With the Fifteenth Amendment, the American Anti-Slavery Society disbanded, its work, its members believed, now complete. "Nothing in all history," exclaimed veteran abolitionist William Lloyd Garrison, equaled "this wonderful, quiet, sudden transformation of four millions of human beings from . . . the auction-block to the ballot-box."

THE "GREAT CONSTITUTIONAL REVOLUTION"

The laws and amendments of Reconstruction reflected the intersection of two products of the Civil War era—a newly empowered national state, and the idea of a national citizenry enjoying equality before the law. What Republican leader Carl Schurz called the "great Constitutional revolution" of Reconstruction transformed the federal system and with it, the language of freedom so central to American political culture.

Before the Civil War, American citizenship had been closely linked to race. The first Congress, in 1790, had limited to whites the right to become a naturalized citizen when immigrating from abroad. No black person, free or slave, the Supreme Court had declared in the *Dred Scott* decision of 1857, could be a citizen of the United States. The laws and amendments of Reconstruction repudiated the idea that citizenship was an entitlement of whites alone. The principle of equality before the law, moreover, did not apply only to the South. The Reconstruction amendments voided many northern laws discriminating on the basis of race. And, as one congressman noted, the amendments expanded the liberty of whites as well as blacks, including "the millions of people of foreign birth who will flock to our shores."

The new amendments also transformed the relationship between the federal government and the states. The Bill of Rights had linked civil liberties to the autonomy of the states. Its language—"Congress shall make no law"—reflected the belief that concentrated national power posed the greatest threat to freedom. The authors of the Reconstruction amendments assumed that rights required national power to enforce them. Rather than a threat to liberty, the federal government, in Charles Sumner's words, had become "the custodian of freedom."

The Reconstruction amendments transformed the Constitution from a document primarily concerned with federal-state relations and the rights of property into a vehicle through which members of vulnerable minorities could stake a claim to freedom and seek protection against misconduct by all levels of government. In the twentieth century, many of the Supreme Court's most important decisions expanding the rights of American citizens were based on the Fourteenth Amendment, perhaps most notably the 1954 *Brown* ruling that outlawed school segregation (see Chapter 24).

Uncle Sam's Thanksgiving Dinner, *an engraving by Thomas Nast from* Harper's Weekly, *November 20, 1868, shortly after the election of Ulysses S. Grant, graphically illustrates how the boundaries of freedom had expanded during Reconstruction. The guests include, among others, African-Americans, Asian-Americans, and Native Americans, all enjoying a harmonious feast. The table's centerpiece contains the slogan, "universal suffrage."*

BOUNDARIES OF FREEDOM

Reconstruction redrew the boundaries of American freedom. Lines of exclusion that limited the privileges of citizenship to white men had long been central to the practice of American democracy. Only in an unparalleled crisis could they have been replaced, even temporarily, by the vision of a republic of equals embracing black Americans as well as white. That the United States was a "white man's government" had been a widespread belief before the Civil War. It is not difficult to understand why Andrew Johnson, in one of his veto messages, claimed that federal protection of blacks' civil rights violated "all our experience as a people."

Reconstruction Republicans' belief in universal rights also had its limits. In his remarkable "Composite Nation" speech of 1869, Frederick Douglass condemned prejudice against immigrants from China. America's destiny, he declared, was to transcend race by serving as an asylum for people "gathered here from all corners of the globe by a common aspiration for national liberty." A year later, Charles Sumner moved to strike the word "white" from naturalization requirements. Senators from the western states objected. At their insistence, the naturalization law was amended to make Africans eligible to obtain citizenship when migrating from abroad. But Asians remained ineligible. The racial boundaries of nationality had been redrawn, but not eliminated. The juxtaposition of the amended naturalization law and the Fourteenth Amendment created a significant division in the Asian-American community. Well into the twentieth century, Asian immigrants could not become citizens, but their native-born children automatically did so.

THE RIGHTS OF WOMEN

"The contest with the South that destroyed slavery," wrote the Philadelphia lawyer Sidney George Fisher in his diary, "has caused an immense increase in the popular passion for liberty and equality." But advocates of women's rights encountered the limits of the Reconstruction commitment to equality. Women activists saw Reconstruction as the moment to claim their own emancipation. No less than blacks, proclaimed Elizabeth Cady Stanton, women had arrived at a "transition period, from slavery to freedom." The rewriting of the Constitution, declared suffrage leader Olympia Brown, offered the opportunity to sever the blessings of freedom from sex as well as race and to "bury the black man and the woman in the citizen."

The destruction of slavery led feminists to search for ways to make the promise of free labor real for women. Every issue of the new women's rights journal, *The Agitator*, edited by Mary

A Delegation of Advocates of Women's Suffrage Addressing the House Judiciary Committee, *an engraving from* Frank Leslie's Illustrated Newspaper, *February 4, 1871. The group includes Elizabeth Cady Stanton, seated just to the right of the speaker, and Susan B. Anthony, at the table on the extreme right.*

Livermore, who had led fund-raising efforts for aid to Union soldiers during the war, carried stories complaining of the limited job opportunities and unequal pay for females who entered the labor market. Other feminists debated how to achieve "liberty for married women." Demands for liberalizing divorce laws (which generally required evidence of adultery, desertion, or extreme abuse to terminate a marriage) and for recognizing "woman's control over her own body" (including protection against domestic violence and access to what later generations would call birth control) moved to the center of many feminists' concerns. "Our rotten marriage institution," one Ohio woman wrote, "is the main obstacle in the way of woman's freedom."

FEMINISTS AND RADICALS

Talk of women's suffrage and redesigning marriage found few sympathetic male listeners. Even Radical Republicans insisted that Reconstruction was the "Negro's hour" (the hour, that is, of the black male). The Fourteenth Amendment for the first time introduced the word "male" into the Constitution, in its clause penalizing a state for denying any group of men the right to vote. The Fifteenth Amendment outlawed discrimination in voting based on race but not gender. These measures produced a bitter split both between feminists and Radical Republicans, and within feminist circles.

Some leaders, like Stanton and Susan B. Anthony, opposed the Fifteenth Amendment because it did nothing to enfranchise women. They denounced their former abolitionist allies and moved to sever the women's rights movement from its earlier moorings in the antislavery tradition. On occasion, they appealed to racial and ethnic prejudices, arguing that native-born white women deserved the vote more than non-whites and immigrants. "Patrick and Sambo and Hans and Yung Tung, who do not know the difference between a monarchy and a republic," declared Stanton, had no right to be "making laws for [feminist leader] Lucretia Mott." But other abolitionist-feminists, like Abby Kelley and Lucy Stone, insisted that despite their limitations, the Reconstruction amendments represented steps in the direction of truly universal suffrage and should be supported. The result was a split in the movement and the creation in 1869 of two hostile women's rights organizations—the National Woman Suffrage Association, led by Stanton, and the American Woman Suffrage Association, with Lucy Stone as president. They would not reunite until the 1890s.

Thus, even as it rejected the racial definition of freedom that had emerged in the first half of the nineteenth century, Reconstruction left the gender boundary largely intact. When women tried to use the rewritten legal code and Constitution to claim equal rights, they found the courts unreceptive. Myra Bradwell invoked the idea of free labor in challenging an Illinois statute limiting the practice of law to men, but the Supreme Court in 1873 rebuffed her claim. Free labor principles, the justices declared, did not apply to women, since "the law of the Creator" had assigned them to "the domestic sphere."

Despite their limitations, the Fourteenth and Fifteenth Amendments and the Reconstruction Act of 1867 marked a radical departure in American and world history. Alone among the nations that abolished slavery in the nineteenth century, the United States, within a few years of emancipation, clothed its former slaves with citizenship rights equal to those of whites. "We have cut loose from the whole dead past," wrote Timothy Howe, a Republican senator from Wisconsin, "and have cast our anchor out a hundred years" into the future. The Reconstruction Act of 1867 inaugurated America's first real experiment in interracial democracy.

RADICAL RECONSTRUCTION IN THE SOUTH

"THE TOCSIN OF FREEDOM"

Among the former slaves, the passage of the Reconstruction Act inspired an outburst of political organization. At mass political meetings—community gatherings attended by men, women, and children—African-Americans staked their claim to equal citizenship. Blacks, declared an Alabama meeting, deserved "exactly the same rights, privileges and immunities as are enjoyed by white men. We ask for nothing more and will be content with nothing less."

These gatherings inspired direct action to remedy long-standing grievances. Hundreds took part in sit-ins that integrated horse-drawn public streetcars in cities across the South. Plantation workers organized strikes for higher wages. Speakers, male and female, fanned out across the South. Frances Ellen Watkins Harper, a black veteran of the abolitionist movement, embarked on a two-year tour, lecturing on "Literacy, Land, and Liberation." James D. Lynch, a member of the group that met with General Sherman in 1865, organized Republican meetings. He became known, in the words of a white contemporary, as "a great orator, fluid and graceful," who "stirred the emotions" of his listeners "as no other man could do."

Determined to exercise their new rights as citizens, thousands joined the Union League, an organization closely linked to the Republican Party, and the vast majority of eligible African-Americans registered to vote. James K. Green, a former slave in Hale County, Alabama and a League organizer, went on to serve eight years in the Alabama legislature. In the 1880s, Green looked back on his political career. Before the war, he declared, "I was entirely ignorant; I knew nothing more than to obey my master; and there were thousands of us in the same attitude. . . . But the tocsin [warning bell] of freedom sounded and knocked at the door and we walked out like free men and shouldered the responsibilities."

By 1870, all the former Confederate states had been readmitted to the Union, and in a region where the Republican Party had not existed before the war, nearly all were under Republican control.

Electioneering at the South, *an engraving from* Harper's Weekly, *July 25, 1868, depicts a speaker at a political meeting in the rural South. Women as well as men took part in these grassroots gatherings.*

Their new state constitutions, drafted in 1868 and 1869 by the first public bodies in American history with substantial black representation, marked a considerable improvement over those they replaced. The constitutions greatly expanded public responsibilities. They established the region's first state-funded systems of free public education, and they created new penitentiaries, orphan asylums, and homes for the insane. The constitutions guaranteed equality of civil and political rights and abolished practices of the antebellum era such as whipping as a punishment for crime, property qualifications for officeholding, and imprisonment for debt. A few states initially barred former Confederates from voting, but this policy was quickly abandoned by the new state governments.

THE BLACK OFFICEHOLDER

Throughout Reconstruction, black voters provided the bulk of the Republican Party's support. But African-Americans did not control Reconstruction politics, as their opponents frequently charged. The highest offices remained almost entirely in white hands, and only in South Carolina, where blacks made up 60 percent of the population, did they form a majority of the legislature. Nonetheless, the fact that some 2,000 African-Americans occupied public offices during Reconstruction represented a fundamental shift of power in the South and a radical departure in American government.

African-Americans were represented at every level of government. Fourteen were elected to the national House of Representatives. Two blacks served in the U.S. Senate during Reconstruction, both representing Mississippi. Hiram Revels, who had been born free in North Carolina, was

The First Vote, *an engraving from* Harper's Weekly, *November 16, 1867, depicts the first biracial elections in southern history. The voters represent key sources of the black political leadership that emerged during Reconstruction—the artisan carrying his tools, the well-dressed city person (probably free before the war), and the soldier.*

Black and white members of the Mississippi Senate, 1874–1875, shortly before the end of Reconstruction in the state. The woman in the bottom row is a postmistress.

The Operations of the Registration Laws and Negro Suffrage in the South, *an engraving in* Frank Leslie's Illustrated Newspaper, *November 30, 1867, shows blacks and whites for the first time serving together on a southern jury.*

educated in Illinois, and served as a chaplain in the wartime Union army, in 1870 became the first black senator in American history. The second, Blanche K. Bruce, a former slave, was elected in 1875. Since then, only three African-Americans—Edward W. Brooke of Massachusetts (who served 1967–1978), Carol Moseley Braun of Illinois (1993–1998), and Barack Obama of Illinois (2005–)—have held seats in the Senate.

Pinckney B. S. Pinchback of Louisiana, the Georgia-born son of a white planter and a free black woman, served briefly during the winter of 1872–1873 as America's first black governor. Over a century would pass before L. Douglas Wilder of Virginia, elected in 1989, became the second. Some 700 blacks sat in state legislatures during Reconstruction, and scores held local offices ranging from justice of the peace to sheriff, tax assessor, and policeman. The presence of black officeholders and their white allies made a real difference in southern life, ensuring that blacks accused of crimes would be tried before juries of their peers and enforcing fairness in such aspects of local government as road repair, tax assessment, and poor relief.

In South Carolina and Louisiana, homes of the South's wealthiest and best-educated free black communities, most prominent Reconstruction officeholders had never experienced slavery. In addition, a number of black Reconstruction officials, like Pennsylvania-born Jonathan J. Wright, who served on the South Carolina Supreme Court, had come from the North after the Civil War. The majority, however, were former slaves who had established their leadership in the black community by serving in the Union army, working as ministers, teachers, or skilled craftsmen, or engaging in Union League organizing. Among the most celebrated black officeholders was Robert Smalls, who had worked as a slave on the Charleston docks before the Civil War and who won national fame in 1862 by secretly guiding the *Planter*, a Confederate vessel, out of the harbor and delivering it to Union forces. Smalls became a powerful political leader on the South Carolina Sea Islands and was elected to five terms in Congress.

CARPETBAGGERS AND SCALAWAGS

The new southern governments also brought to power new groups of whites. Many Reconstruction officials were northerners who for one reason or another had made their homes in the South after the war. Their opponents dubbed them "carpetbaggers," implying that they had packed all their belongings in a suitcase and left their homes in order to reap the spoils of office in the South. Some carpetbaggers were undoubtedly corrupt adventurers. The large majority, however, were former Union soldiers who decided to remain in the South when the war ended, before there was any prospect of going into politics. Others were investors in land and railroads who saw in the postwar South an opportunity to combine personal economic advancement with a role in helping to substitute, as one wrote, "the civilization of freedom for that of slavery." Teachers, Freedmen's Bureau officers, and others who came to the region genuinely hoping to assist the former slaves represented another large group of "carpetbaggers."

Most white Republicans, however, had been born in the South. Former Confederates reserved their greatest scorn for these "scalawags," whom they considered traitors to their race and region. Some southern-born Republicans were men of stature and wealth, like James L. Alcorn, the owner of one of Mississippi's largest plantations and the state's first Republican governor.

Most "scalawags," however, were non-slaveholding white farmers from the southern upcountry. Many had been wartime Unionists, and they now cooperated with the Republicans in order to prevent "rebels" from returning to power. Others hoped Reconstruction governments would help them recover from wartime economic losses by suspending the collection of debts and enacting laws protecting small property holders from losing their homes to creditors. In states like North Carolina, Tennessee, and Arkansas, Republicans initially commanded a significant minority of the white vote. Even in the Deep South, the small white Republican vote was important, because the population remained almost evenly divided between blacks (almost all of whom voted for the party of Lincoln) and whites (overwhelmingly Democratic).

SOUTHERN REPUBLICANS IN POWER

In view of the daunting challenges they faced, the remarkable thing is not that Reconstruction governments in many respects failed, but how much they did accomplish. Perhaps their greatest achievement lay in establishing the South's first state-supported public schools. The new educational systems served both black and white children, although generally in schools segregated by race. Only in New Orleans were the public schools integrated during Reconstruction, and only in South Carolina did the state university admit black students (elsewhere, separate colleges were established). By the 1870s, in a region whose prewar leaders had made it illegal for slaves to learn and had done little to provide education for poorer whites, over half the children, black and white, were attending public schools. The new governments also pioneered civil rights legislation. Their laws made it illegal for railroads,

Emancipation, an 1865 lithograph, is unusual because along with the familiar images of Lincoln and emancipated slaves, it also portrays a poor white family, suggesting that all Americans will benefit from the end of slavery and Reconstruction.

Black students outside a schoolhouse in a post-Civil War photograph. The teacher is seated at the far right.

hotels, and other institutions to discriminate on the basis of race. Enforcement varied considerably from locality to locality, but Reconstruction established for the first time at the state level a standard of equal citizenship and a recognition of blacks' right to a share of public services.

Republican governments also took steps to strengthen the position of rural laborers and promote the South's economic recovery. They passed laws to ensure that agricultural laborers and sharecroppers had the first claim on harvested crops, rather than merchants to whom the landowner owed money. South Carolina created a state Land Commission, which by 1876 had settled 14,000 black families and a few poor whites on their own farms.

THE QUEST FOR PROSPERITY

Rather than land distribution, however, the Reconstruction governments pinned their hopes for southern economic growth and opportunity for African-Americans and poor whites alike on regional economic development. Railroad construction, they believed, was the key to transforming the South into a society of booming factories, bustling towns, and diversified agriculture. "A free and living republic," declared a Tennessee Republican, would "spring up in the track of the railroad." Every state during Reconstruction helped to finance railroad construction, and through tax reductions and other incentives tried to attract northern manufacturers to invest in the region. The program had mixed results. Economic development in general remained weak. With abundant opportunities existing in the West, few northern investors ventured to the Reconstruction South.

To their supporters, the governments of Radical Reconstruction presented a complex pattern of disappointment and accomplishment. A revitalized southern economy failed to materialize, and most African-Americans remained locked in poverty. On the other hand, biracial democratic government, a thing unknown in American history, for the first time functioned effectively in many parts of the South. Public facilities were rebuilt and expanded, school systems established, and legal codes purged of racism. The conservative elite that had dominated southern government from colonial times to 1867 found itself excluded from political power, while poor whites, newcomers from the North, and former slaves cast ballots, sat on juries, and enacted and administered laws. "We have gone through one of the most remarkable changes in our relations to each other," declared a white South Carolina lawyer in 1871, "that has been known, perhaps, in the history of the world." It is a measure of how far change had progressed that the reaction against Reconstruction proved so extreme.

THE OVERTHROW OF RECONSTRUCTION

RECONSTRUCTION'S OPPONENTS

The South's traditional leaders—planters, merchants, and Democratic politicians—bitterly opposed the new governments. They denounced them as corrupt, inefficient, and examples of "black supremacy." "Intelligence, virtue, and patriotism" in public life, declared a protest by prominent southern Democrats, had given way to "ignorance, stupidity, and vice." Corruption did exist during Reconstruction, but it was confined to no race, region, or party. The rapid growth of state budgets and the benefits to be gained from public aid led in some states to a scramble for influence that produced bribery, insider dealing, and a get-rich-quick atmosphere. Southern frauds, however, were dwarfed by those practiced in these years by the Whiskey Ring, which involved high officials of the Grant administration, and by New York's Tweed Ring, controlled by the Democrats, whose thefts ran into the tens of millions of dollars. (These are discussed in the next chapter.) The rising taxes needed to pay for schools and other new public facilities and to assist railroad development were another cause of opposition to Reconstruction. Many poor whites who had initially supported the Republican Party turned against it when it became clear that their economic situation was not improving.

The most basic reason for opposition to Reconstruction, however, was that most white southerners could not accept the idea of former slaves voting, holding office, and enjoying equality before the law. In order to restore white supremacy in southern public life and to ensure planters a disciplined, reliable labor force, they believed, Reconstruction must be overthrown. Opponents launched a campaign of violence in an

Murder of Louisiana, an 1873 cartoon, illustrates the intensity of the opposition to Reconstruction. President Ulysses S. Grant, depicted as an emperor advised by Attorney General George H. Williams in the form of the devil, prepares to sacrifice the state on the "altar of radicalism." The victim, held by two black men, has already had her heart cut out by Republican governor William P. Kellogg. The other southern states, with South Carolina kneeling in chains, look on.

effort to end Republican rule. Their actions posed a fundamental challenge both for Reconstruction governments in the South and for policymakers in Washington, D.C.

"A REIGN OF TERROR"

The Civil War ended in 1865, but violence remained widespread in large parts of the postwar South. In the early years of Reconstruction, violence was mostly local and unorganized. Blacks were assaulted and murdered for refusing to give way to whites on city sidewalks, using "insolent" language, challenging end-of-year contract settlements, and attempting to buy land. The violence that greeted the advent of Republican governments after 1867, however, was far more pervasive and more directly motivated by politics. In wide areas of the South, secret societies sprang up with the aim of preventing blacks from voting and destroying the organization of the Republican Party by assassinating local leaders and public officials.

The most notorious such organization was the Ku Klux Klan, which in effect served as a military arm of the Democratic Party in the South. From its founding in 1866 in Tennessee, the Klan was a terrorist organization. It quickly spread into nearly every southern state. Led by planters, merchants, and Democratic politicians, men who liked to style themselves the South's "respectable citizens," the Klan committed some of the most brutal criminal acts in American history. In many counties, it launched what one victim called a "reign of terror" against Republican leaders, black and white.

The Klan's victims included white Republicans, among them wartime Unionists and local officeholders, teachers, and party organizers. William Luke, an Irish-born teacher in a black school, was lynched in 1870. But African-Americans—local political leaders, those who managed to acquire land, and others who in one way or another defied the norms of white supremacy—bore the brunt of the violence. In York County, South Carolina, where nearly the entire white male population joined the Klan (and women participated by sewing the robes and hoods Klansmen wore as disguises), the organization committed eleven murders and hundreds of whippings.

On occasion, violence escalated from assaults on individuals to mass terrorism and even local insurrections. In Meridian, Mississippi, in 1871, some thirty blacks were murdered in cold blood, along with a white Republican judge. The bloodiest act of violence during Reconstruction took place in Colfax, Louisiana, in 1873, where armed whites assaulted the town with a small cannon. Hundreds of former slaves were murdered, including fifty members of a black militia unit after they had surrendered.

Unable to suppress the Klan, the new southern governments appealed to Washington for help. In 1870 and 1871, Congress adopted three Enforcement Acts, outlawing terrorist societies and allowing the president to use the army against them. These laws continued the expansion of national authority during Reconstruction. They defined crimes that aimed to deprive citizens of their civil and political rights as federal offenses rather than violations of state law. In 1871,

A Prospective Scene in the City of Oaks, *a cartoon in the September 1, 1868, issue of the* Independent Monitor, *a Democratic newspaper published in Tuscaloosa, Alabama. The cartoon sent a warning to the Reverend A. S. Lakin, who had moved from Ohio to become president of the University of Alabama, and Dr. N. B. Cloud, a southern-born Republican serving as Alabama's superintendent of public education. The Ku Klux Klan forced both men from their positions.*

President Grant dispatched federal marshals, backed up by troops in some areas, to arrest hundreds of accused Klansmen. Many Klan leaders fled the South. After a series of well-publicized trials, the Klan went out of existence. In 1872, for the first time since the Civil War, peace reigned in most of the former Confederacy.

THE LIBERAL REPUBLICANS

Despite the Grant administration's effective response to Klan terrorism, the North's commitment to Reconstruction waned during the 1870s. Many Radicals, including Thaddeus Stevens, who died in 1868, had passed from the scene. Within the Republican Party, their place was taken by politicians less committed to the ideal of equal rights for blacks. Northerners increasingly felt that the South should be able to solve its own problems without constant interference from Washington. The federal government had freed the slaves, made them citizens, and given them the right to vote. Now, blacks should rely on their own resources, not demand further assistance.

In 1872, an influential group of Republicans, alienated by corruption within the Grant administration and believing that the growth of federal power during and after the war needed to be curtailed, formed their own party. They included Republican founders like Lyman Trumbull and prominent editors and journalists such as E. L. Godkin of *The Nation*. Calling themselves Liberal Republicans, they nominated Horace Greeley, editor of the *New York Tribune*, for president.

The Liberals' alienation from the Grant administration initially had little to do with Reconstruction. They claimed that corrupt politicians had come to power in the North by manipulating the votes of immigrants and workingmen, while men of talent and education like themselves had been pushed aside. Democratic criticisms of Reconstruction, however, found a receptive audience among the Liberals. As in the North, they became convinced, the "best men" of the South had been excluded from power while "ignorant" voters controlled politics, producing corruption and misgovernment. Power in the South should be returned to the region's "natural leaders." During the campaign of 1872, Greeley repeatedly called on Americans to "clasp hands across the bloody chasm" by putting the Civil War and Reconstruction behind them.

Greeley had spent most of his career, first as a Whig and then as a Republican, denouncing the Democratic Party. But with the Republican split presenting an opportunity to repair their political fortunes, Democratic leaders endorsed Greeley as their candidate. Many rank and file Democrats, unable to bring themselves to vote for Greeley, stayed at home on election day. As a result, Greeley suffered a devastating defeat by Grant, whose margin of over 700,000 popular votes was the largest in a nineteenth-century presidential contest. But Greeley's campaign placed on the northern agenda the one issue on which the Liberal reformers and the Democrats could agree—a new policy toward the South.

THE NORTH'S RETREAT

The Liberal attack on Reconstruction, which continued after 1872, contributed to a resurgence of racism in the North. Journalist James S. Pike, a

A Mississippi member of the Ku Klux Klan, photographed in his hooded disguise in 1871.

leading Greeley supporter, in 1874 published *The Prostrate State*, an influential account of a visit to South Carolina. The book depicted a state engulfed by political corruption, drained by governmental extravagance, and under the control of "a mass of black barbarism." The South's problems, he insisted, arose from "Negro government." The solution was to restore leading whites to political power. Newspapers that had long supported Reconstruction now began to condemn black participation in southern government. They expressed their views visually as well. Engravings depicting the former slaves as heroic Civil War veterans, upstanding citizens, or victims of violence were increasingly replaced by caricatures presenting them as little more than unbridled animals. Resurgent racism offered a convenient explanation for the alleged "failure" of Reconstruction.

Other factors also weakened northern support for Reconstruction. In 1873, the country plunged into a severe economic depression. Distracted by economic problems, Republicans were in no mood to devote further attention to the South. The depression dealt the South a severe blow and further weakened the prospect that Republicans could revitalize the region's economy. Democrats made substantial gains throughout the nation in the elections of 1874. For the first time since the Civil War, their party took control of the House of Representatives. Before the new Congress met, the old one enacted a final piece of Reconstruction legislation, the Civil Rights Act of 1875. This outlawed racial discrimination in places of public accommodation like hotels and theaters. But it was clear that the northern public was retreating from Reconstruction.

The Supreme Court whittled away at the guarantees of black rights Congress had adopted. In the *Slaughterhouse Cases* (1873), butchers excluded from a state-sponsored monopoly in Louisiana went to court, claiming that their right to equality before the law guaranteed by the Fourteenth Amendment had been violated. The justices rejected their claim, ruling that the amendment had not altered traditional federalism. Most of the rights of cit-

The Old Plantation Home, a lithograph from 1872 produced by the prominent firm of Currier and Ives in New York City, illustrates how a nostalgic image of slavery as a time of carefree happiness for African-Americans was being promoted even as Reconstruction took place.

Changes in graphic artist Thomas Nast's depiction of blacks in Harper's Weekly *mirrored the evolution of Republican sentiment in the North.* And Not This Man, *August 5, 1865, shows the black soldier as an upstanding citizen deserving of the vote.* Colored Rule in a Reconstructed (?) State, *March 14, 1874, suggests that Reconstruction legislatures had become travesties of democratic government.*

izens, it declared, remained under state control. Three years later, in *U.S. v. Cruikshank*, the Court gutted the Enforcement Acts by throwing out the convictions of some of those responsible for the Colfax Massacre of 1873.

THE TRIUMPH OF THE REDEEMERS

By the mid-1870s, Reconstruction was clearly on the defensive. Democrats had already regained control of states with substantial white voting majorities such as Tennessee, North Carolina, and Texas. The victorious Democrats called themselves Redeemers, since they claimed to have "redeemed" the white South from corruption, misgovernment, and northern and black control.

In those states where Reconstruction governments survived, violence again erupted. This time, the Grant administration showed no desire to intervene. In contrast to the Klan's activities—conducted at night by disguised men—the violence of 1875 and 1876 took place in broad daylight, as if to underscore Democrats' conviction that they had nothing to fear from Washington. In Mississippi, in 1875, white rifle clubs drilled in public and openly assaulted and murdered Republicans. When Governor Adelbert Ames, a Maine-born Union general, frantically appealed to the federal government for assistance, President Grant responded that the northern

Of Course He Wants to Vote the Democratic Ticket, *a cartoon from* Harper's Weekly, October 21, 1876, *comments on the campaign of terror launched by South Carolina Democrats in an attempt to carry the election of 1876.*

public was "tired out" by southern problems. On election day, armed Democrats destroyed ballot boxes and drove former slaves from the polls. The result was a Democratic landslide and the end of Reconstruction in Mississippi. "A revolution has taken place," wrote Ames, "and a race are disfranchised—they are to be returned to . . . an era of second slavery."

Similar events took place in South Carolina in 1876. Democrats nominated for governor former Confederate general Wade Hampton. Hampton promised to respect the rights of all citizens of the state, but his supporters, inspired by Democratic tactics in Mississippi, launched a wave of intimidation. Democrats intended to carry the election, one planter told a black official, "if we have to wade in blood knee-deep."

THE DISPUTED ELECTION AND BARGAIN OF 1877

Events in South Carolina directly affected the outcome of the presidential campaign of 1876. To succeed Grant, the Republicans nominated Governor Rutherford B. Hayes of Ohio. Democrats chose as his opponent New York's governor, Samuel J. Tilden. By this time, only South Carolina, Florida, and Louisiana remained under Republican control. The election turned out to be so close that whoever captured these states—which both parties claimed to have carried—would become the next president.

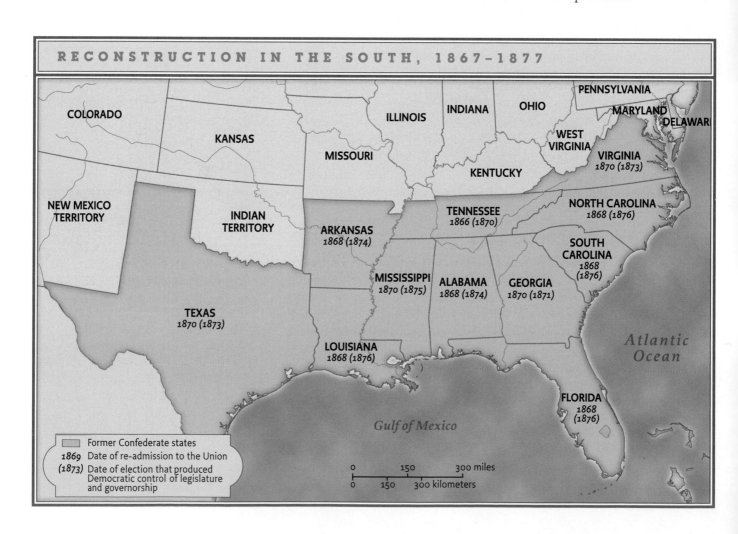

RECONSTRUCTION IN THE SOUTH, 1867–1877

Former Confederate states
1869 Date of re-admission to the Union
(1873) Date of election that produced Democratic control of legislature and governorship

Unable to resolve the impasse on its own, Congress in January 1877 appointed a fifteen-member Electoral Commission, composed of senators, representatives, and Supreme Court justices. Republicans enjoyed an 8–7 majority on the commission, and to no one's surprise, the members decided by that margin that Hayes had carried the disputed southern states and had been elected president. Even as the commission deliberated, however, behind-the-scenes negotiations took place between leaders of the two parties. Hayes's representatives agreed to recognize Democratic control of the entire South and to avoid further intervention in local affairs. They also pledged that Hayes would place a southerner in the cabinet position of postmaster general and that he would work for federal aid to the Texas and Pacific railroad, a transcontinental line projected to follow a southern route. For their part, Democrats promised not to dispute Hayes's right to office and to respect the civil and political rights of blacks.

Thus was concluded the Bargain of 1877. Not all of its parts were fulfilled. But Hayes became president, and he did appoint David M. Key of Tennessee as postmaster general. Hayes quickly ordered federal troops to stop guarding the state houses in Louisiana and South Carolina, allowing Democratic claimants to become governor. (Contrary to legend, Hayes did not remove the last soldiers from the South—he simply ordered them to return to their barracks.) But the Texas and Pacific never did get its land grant. Of far more significance, the triumphant southern Democrats failed to live up to their pledge to recognize blacks as equal citizens.

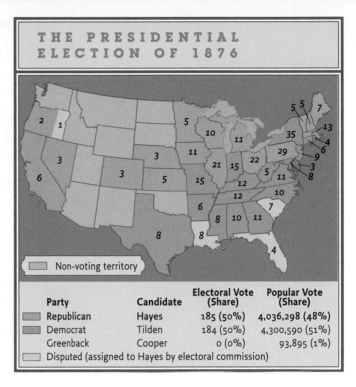

THE PRESIDENTIAL ELECTION OF 1876

Non-voting territory

Party	Candidate	Electoral Vote (Share)	Popular Vote (Share)
Republican	Hayes	185 (50%)	4,036,298 (48%)
Democrat	Tilden	184 (50%)	4,300,590 (51%)
Greenback	Cooper	0 (0%)	93,895 (1%)
Disputed (assigned to Hayes by electoral commission)			

THE END OF RECONSTRUCTION

As a historical process—the nation's adjustment to the destruction of slavery—Reconstruction continued well after 1877. Blacks continued to vote and, in some states, hold office into the 1890s. But as a distinct era of national history—when Republicans controlled much of the South, blacks exercised significant political power, and the federal government accepted the responsibility for protecting the fundamental rights of all American citizens—Reconstruction had come to an end. Despite its limitations, Reconstruction was a remarkable chapter in the story of American freedom. Nearly a century would pass before the nation again tried to bring equal rights to the descendants of slaves. The civil rights era of the 1950s and 1960s would sometimes be called the Second Reconstruction.

Even while it lasted, however, Reconstruction revealed some of the tensions inherent in nineteenth-century discussions of freedom. The policy of granting black men the vote while denying them the benefits of land ownership strengthened the idea that the free citizen could be a poor, dependent laborer. Reconstruction placed on the national agenda a problem that would dominate political discussion for the next half-century—how, in a modern society, to define the economic essence of freedom.

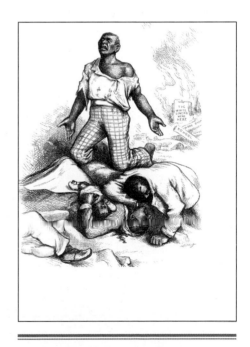

Is This a Republican Form of Government?, *a cartoon by Thomas Nast in* Harper's Weekly, *September 2, 1876, illustrates his conviction that the overthrow of Reconstruction meant that the United States was not prepared to live up to its democratic ideals or protect the rights of black citizens threatened by violence.*

SUGGESTED READING

Carter, Dan T. *When the War Was Over: The Failure of Self-Reconstruction in the South, 1865–1867* (1985). A careful study of the South during the period of presidential Reconstruction.

Du Bois, W. E. B. *Black Reconstruction in America* (1935). The first comprehensive refutation of the "traditional" view of Reconstruction as an era of misgovernment, which originated with opponents of black rights, and of racism in historical writing on the era.

DuBois, Ellen C. *Feminism and Suffrage: The Emergence of an Independent Women's Movement in America, 1848–1869* (1978). Explores how the split over the exclusion of women from the Fourteenth and Fifteenth Amendments gave rise to a movement for women's suffrage no longer tied to the abolitionist tradition.

Edwards, Laura. *Gendered Strife and Confusion: The Political Culture of Reconstruction* (1997). Considers how issues relating to gender relations affected the course of southern Reconstruction.

Fields, Barbara J. *Slavery and Freedom on the Middle Ground: Maryland during the Nineteenth Century* (1985). A study of slavery and emancipation in a key border state.

Foner, Eric. *Reconstruction: America's Unfinished Revolution, 1863–1877* (1988). The most comprehensive recent account of the Reconstruction era.

Hahn, Steven. *A Nation under Our Feet: Black Political Struggles in the Rural South from Slavery to the Great Migration* (2003). A detailed study of black political activism, stressing nationalist consciousness and emigration movements.

Hyman, Harold M. *A More Perfect Union: The Impact of the Civil War and Reconstruction on the Constitution* (1973). Analyzes how the laws and constitutional amendments of Reconstruction changed the Constitution and the rights of all Americans.

Litwack, Leon F. *Been in the Storm So Long: The Aftermath of Slavery* (1979). A detailed look at the immediate aftermath of the end of slavery and the variety of black and white responses to emancipation.

Rable, George C. *But There Was No Peace: The Role of Violence in the Politics of Reconstruction* (1984). The only full-scale study of violence in the Reconstruction South.

Ransom, Roger L., and Richard Sutch. *One Kind of Freedom: The Economic Consequences of Emancipation* (1977). Two economic historians examine the transition from slavery to sharecropping in the cotton South.

Richardson, Heather C. *The Death of Reconstruction: Race, Labor, and Politics in the Post–Civil War North* (2001). An examination of the numerous causes of the North's retreat from Reconstruction.

Rodrigue, John C. *Reconstruction in the Cane Fields: From Slavery to Free Labor in Louisiana's Sugar Parishes, 1862–1880* (2001). A study of how an often-neglected part of the South experienced the aftermath of slavery.

Summers, Mark W. *Railroads, Reconstruction, and the Gospel of Prosperity: Aid under the Radical Republicans, 1865–1877* (1984). A detailed look at southern governments' efforts to promote economic development, and the political corruption that sometimes accompanied it.

Trefousse, Hans L. *The Radical Republicans: Lincoln's Vanguard for Racial Justice* (1969). An account of the political history of the Radical Republicans, from the pre–Civil War period through the end of Reconstruction.

REVIEW QUESTIONS

1. Frederick Douglass insisted that "slavery is not abolished until the black man has the ballot." What did Douglass mean by this?

2. The women's movement split into two separate national organizations in part because the Fifteenth Amendment did not give women the vote. Explain why the two groups split.

3. What meanings of freedom were most important to the freed slaves?

4. What were the arguments for and against land distribution for the freed slaves?

5. Why was Reconstruction brought to an end in 1877?

KEY TERMS

black families (p. 550)

presidential pardons (p. 561)

"swing around the circle" (p. 564)

literacy tests (p. 566)

Bradwell v. Illinois (p. 569)

Enforcement Acts (p. 576)

Civil Rights Act of 1875 (p. 578)

Slaughterhouse Cases (p. 578)

REVIEW TABLE

Reconstruction Constitutional Amendments

Amendment	Date Ratified	Provisions
Thirteenth	1865	Ends slavery
Fourteenth	1868	Guarantees federal protection of citizenship
Fifteenth	1870	Prohibits voting restrictions based on race, color, or previous conditions of servitude

Appendix

DOCUMENTS

TABLES AND FIGURES

The Declaration of Independence (1776)

When in the course of human events, it becomes necessary for one people to dissolve the political bands which have connected them with another, and to assume among the Powers of the earth, the separate and equal station to which the Laws of Nature and of Nature's God entitle them, a decent respect to the opinions of mankind requires that they should declare the causes which impel them to the separation.

We hold these truths to be self-evident, that all men are created equal, that they are endowed by their Creator with certain unalienable rights, that among these are Life, Liberty, and the pursuit of Happiness. That to secure these rights, Governments are instituted among Men, deriving their just powers from the consent of the governed. That whenever any Form of Government becomes destructive of these ends, it is the Right of the People to alter or to abolish it, and to institute new Government, laying its foundation on such principles and organizing its powers in such form, as to them shall seem most likely to effect their Safety and Happiness. Prudence, indeed, will dictate that Governments long established should not be changed for light and transient causes; and accordingly all experience hath shown, that mankind are more disposed to suffer, while evils are sufferable, than to right themselves by abolishing the forms to which they are accustomed. But when a long train of abuses and usurpations, pursuing invariably the same Object evinces a design to reduce them under absolute Despotism, it is their right, it is their duty, to throw off such Government, and to provide new Guards for their future security.—Such has been the patient sufferance of these Colonies; and such is now the necessity which constrains them to alter their former Systems of Government. The history of the present King of Great Britain is a history of repeated injuries and usurpations, all having in direct object the establishment of an absolute Tyranny over these States. To prove this, let Facts be submitted to a candid world.

He has refused his Assent to Laws, the most wholesome and necessary for the public good.

He has forbidden his Governors to pass Laws of immediate and pressing importance, unless suspended in their operation till his Assent should be obtained; and when so suspended, he has utterly neglected to attend to them.

He has refused to pass other Laws for the accommodation of large districts of people, unless those people would relinquish the right of Representation in the Legislature, a right inestimable to them and formidable to tyrants only.

He has called together legislative bodies at places unusual, uncomfortable, and distant from the depository of their public Records, for the sole purpose of fatiguing them into compliance with his measures.

He has dissolved Representative Houses repeatedly, for opposing with manly firmness his invasions on the rights of the people.

He has refused for a long time, after such dissolutions, to cause others to be elected; whereby the Legislative powers, incapable of Annihilation, have returned to the People at large for their exercise; the State remaining in the mean time exposed to all dangers of invasion from without, and convulsions within.

He has endeavoured to prevent the population of these States; for that purpose obstructing the Laws of Naturalization of Foreigners; refusing to pass others to encourage their migrations hither, and raising the conditions of new Appropriations of Lands.

He has obstructed the Administration of Justice, by refusing his Assent to Laws for establishing Judiciary powers.

He has made Judges dependent on his Will alone, for the tenure of their offices, and the amount and payment of their salaries.

He has erected a multitude of New Offices, and sent hither swarms of Officers to harass our People, and eat out their substance.

He has kept among us, in times of peace, Standing Armies without the Consent of our legislatures.

He has affected to render the Military independent of and superior to the Civil Power.

He has combined with others to subject us to a jurisdiction foreign to our constitution, and unacknowledged by our laws; giving his Assent to their Acts of pretended Legislation:

For quartering large bodies of armed troops among us:

For protecting them, by a mock Trial, from Punishment for any Murders which they should commit on the Inhabitants of these States:

For cutting off our Trade with all parts of the world:

For imposing taxes on us without our Consent:

For depriving us of many cases, of the benefits of Trial by jury:

For transporting us beyond Seas to be tried for pretended offences:

For abolishing the free System of English Laws in a neighbouring Province, establishing therein an Arbitrary government, and enlarging its Boundaries so as to render it at once an example and fit instrument for introducing the same absolute rule into these Colonies:

For taking away our Charters, abolishing our most valuable Laws, and altering fundamentally the Forms of our Governments:

For suspending our own Legislatures, and declaring themselves invested with Power to legislate for us in all cases whatsoever.

He has abdicated Government here, by declaring us out of his Protection and waging War against us.

He has plundered our seas, ravaged our Coasts, burnt our towns, and destroyed the lives of our people.

He is at this time transporting large armies of foreign mercenaries to compleat the works of death, desolation, and tyranny, already begun with circumstances of Cruelty & perfidy scarcely paralleled in the most barbarous ages, and totally unworthy the Head of a civilized nation.

He has constrained our fellow Citizens taken Captive on the high Seas to bear Arms against their Country, to become the executioners of their friends and Brethren, or to fall themselves by their Hands.

He has excited domestic insurrections amongst us, and has endeavoured to bring on the inhabitants of our frontiers, the merciless Indian Savages, whose known rule of warfare, is an undistinguished destruction of all ages, sexes, and conditions.

In every stage of these Oppressions We have Petitioned for Redress in the most humble terms: Our repeated Petitions have been answered only by repeated injury. A Prince, whose character is thus marked by every act which may define a Tyrant, is unfit to be the ruler of a free people.

Nor have We been wanting in attention to our British brethren. We have warned them from time to time of attempts by their legislature to extend an unwarrantable jurisdiction over us. We have reminded them of the circumstances of our emigration and settlement here. We have appealed to their native justice and magnanimity, and we have conjured them by the ties of our common kindred to disavow these usurpations, which, would inevitably interrupt our connections and correspondence. They too must have been deaf to the voice of justice and of consanguinity. We must, therefore, acquiesce in the necessity, which denounces our Separation, and hold them, as we hold the rest of mankind, Enemies in War, in Peace Friends.

WE, THEREFORE, the Representatives of the UNITED STATES OF AMERICA, in General Congress, Assembled, appealing to the Supreme Judge of the world for the rectitude of our intentions, do, in the Name, and by Authority of the good People of these Colonies, solemnly publish and declare, That these United Colonies are, and of Right ought to be FREE AND INDEPENDENT STATES; that they are Absolved from all Allegiance to the British Crown, and that all political connection between them and the State of Great Britain, is and ought to be totally dissolved; and that as Free and Independent States, they have full Power to levy War, conclude Peace, contract Alliances, establish Commerce, and to do all other Acts and Things which Independent States may of right do. And for the support of this Declaration, with a firm reliance on the Protection of Divine Providence, we mutually pledge to each other our Lives, our Fortunes, and our sacred Honor.

The foregoing Declaration was, by order of Congress, engrossed, and signed by the following members:

John Hancock

NEW HAMPSHIRE
Josiah Bartlett
William Whipple
Matthew Thornton

MASSACHUSETTS BAY
Samuel Adams
John Adams
Robert Treat Paine
Elbridge Gerry

RHODE ISLAND
Stephen Hopkins
William Ellery

CONNECTICUT
Roger Sherman
Samuel Huntington
William Williams
Oliver Wolcott

NEW YORK
William Floyd
Philip Livingston
Francis Lewis
Lewis Morris

NEW JERSEY
Richard Stockton
John Witherspoon
Francis Hopkinson
John Hart
Abraham Clark

PENNSYLVANIA
Robert Morris
Benjamin Rush
Benjamin Franklin
John Morton
George Clymer
James Smith
George Taylor
James Wilson
George Ross

DELAWARE
Caesar Rodney
George Read
Thomas M'Kean

MARYLAND
Samuel Chase
William Paca
Thomas Stone
Charles Carroll, of Carrollton

VIRGINIA
George Wythe
Richard Henry Lee
Thomas Jefferson
Benjamin Harrison
Thomas Nelson, Jr.
Francis Lightfoot Lee
Carter Braxton

NORTH CAROLINA
William Hooper
Joseph Hewes
John Penn

SOUTH CAROLINA
Edward Rutledge
Thomas Heyward, Jr.
Thomas Lynch, Jr.
Arthur Middleton

GEORGIA
Button Gwinnett
Lyman Hall
George Walton

Resolved, That copies of the Declaration be sent to the several assemblies, conventions, and committees, or councils of safety, and to the several commanding officers of the continental troops; that it be proclaimed in each of the United States, at the head of the army.

The Constitution of the United States (1787)

We the People of the United States, in order to form a more perfect Union, establish Justice, insure domestic Tranquility, provide for the common defence, promote the general Welfare, and secure the Blessings of Liberty to ourselves and our Posterity, do ordain and establish this Constitution for the United States of America.

ARTICLE. I.

Section. 1. All legislative Powers herein granted shall be vested in a Congress of the United States, which shall consist of a Senate and House of Representatives.

Section. 2. The House of Representatives shall be composed of Members chosen every second Year by the People of the several States, and the Electors in each State shall have the Qualifications requisite for Electors of the most numerous Branch of the State Legislature.

No Person shall be a Representative who shall not have attained to the Age of twenty five Years, and been seven Years a Citizen of the United States, and who shall not, when elected, be an Inhabitant of that State in which he shall be chosen.

Representatives and direct Taxes shall be apportioned among the several States which may be included within this Union, according to their respective Numbers, which shall be determined by adding to the whole Number of free Persons, including those bound to Service for a Term of Years, and excluding Indians not taxed, three fifths of all other Persons. The actual Enumeration shall be made within three Years after the first Meeting of the Congress of the United States, and within every subsequent Term of ten Years, in such Manner as they shall by Law direct. The Number of Representatives shall not exceed one for every thirty Thousand, but each State shall have at Least one Representative; and until such enumeration shall be made, the State of New Hampshire shall be entitled to chuse three, Massachusetts eight, Rhode-Island and Providence Plantations one, Connecticut five, New York six, New Jersey four, Pennsylvania eight, Delaware one, Maryland six, Virginia ten, North Carolina five, South Carolina five, and Georgia three.

When vacancies happen in the Representation from any state, the Executive Authority thereof shall issue Writs of Election to fill such Vacancies.

The House of Representatives shall chuse their Speaker and other Officers; and shall have the sole Power of Impeachment.

Section. 3. The Senate of the United States shall be composed of two Senators from each State, chosen by the legislature thereof, for six Years; and each Senator shall have one Vote.

Immediately after they shall be assembled in Consequence of the first Election, they shall be divided as equally as may be into three Classes. The Seats of the Senators of the first Class shall be vacated at the Expiration of the second Year, of the second Class at the Expiration of the fourth Year, and of the third Class at the Expiration of the sixth Year, so that one third may be chosen every second Year; and if Vacancies happen by Resignation, or otherwise, during the Recess of the Legislature of any State, the Executive thereof may make temporary Appointments until the next Meeting of the Legislature, which shall then fill such Vacancies.

No Person shall be a Senator who shall not have attained to the Age of thirty Years, and been nine Years a Citizen of the United States, and who shall not, when elected, be an Inhabitant of that State for which he shall be chosen.

The Vice President of the United States shall be President of the Senate, but shall have no Vote, unless they be equally divided.

The Senate shall chuse their other Officers, and also a President pro tempore, in the Absence of the Vice President, or when he shall exercise the Office of President of the United States.

The Senate shall have the sole Power to try all Impeachments. When sitting for that Purpose, they shall be on Oath or Affirmation. When the President of the United States is tried, the Chief Justice shall preside: And no Person shall be convicted without the Concurrence of two thirds of the Members present.

Judgment in Cases of Impeachment shall not extend further than to removal from Office, and disqualification to hold and enjoy any Office of honor, Trust or Profit under the United States: but the Party convicted shall nevertheless be liable and subject to Indictment, Trial, Judgment and Punishment, according to Law.

Section. 4. The Times, Places and Manner of holding Elections for Senators and Representatives, shall be prescribed in each State by the Legislature thereof; but the Congress may at any time by Law make or alter such Regulations, except as to the Places of chusing Senators.

The Congress shall assemble at least once in every Year, and such Meeting shall be on the first Monday in December, unless they shall by Law appoint a different Day.

Section. 5. Each House shall be the Judge of the Elections, Returns and Qualifications of its own Members, and a Majority of each shall constitute a Quorum to do Business; but a smaller Number may adjourn from day to day, and may be authorized to compel the Attendance of absent Members, in such Manner, and under such Penalties as each House may provide.

Each House may determine the Rules of its Proceedings, punish its Members for disorderly Behaviour, and, with the Concurrence of two thirds, expel a Member.

Each House shall keep a Journal of its Proceedings, and from time to time publish the same, excepting such Parts as may in their Judgment require Secrecy; and the Yeas and Nays of the Members of either House on any question shall, at the Desire of one fifth of those Present, be entered on the Journal.

Neither House, during the Session of Congress, shall, without the Consent of the other, adjourn for more than three days, not to any other Place than that in which the two Houses shall be sitting.

Section. 6. The Senators and Representatives shall receive a Compensation for their Services, to be ascertained by Law, and paid out of the Treasury of the United States. They shall in all Cases, except Treason, Felony and Breach of the Peace, be privileged from Arrest during their Attendance at the Session of their respective Houses, and in going to and returning from the same; and for any Speech or Debate in either House, they shall not be questioned in any other Place.

No Senator or Representative shall, during the Time for which he was elected, be appointed to any civil Office under the Authority of the United States, which shall have been created, or the Emoluments whereof shall have been encreased during such time; and no Person holding any Office under the United States, shall be a Member of either House during his Continuance in Office.

Section. 7. All Bills for raising Revenue shall originate in the House of Representatives; but the Senate may propose or concur with Amendments as on other Bills.

Every Bill which shall have passed the House of Representatives and the Senate shall, before it become a Law, be presented to the President of the United States; If he approve he shall sign it, but if not he shall return it, with his Objections to that House in which it shall have originated, who shall enter the Objections at large on their Journal, and proceed to reconsider it. If after such Reconsideration two thirds of that House shall agree to pass the Bill, it shall be sent, together with the Objections, to the other House, by which it shall likewise be reconsidered, and if approved by two thirds of that House, it shall become a Law. But in all such Cases the Votes of both Houses shall be determined by Yeas and Nays, and the Names of the Persons voting for and against the Bill shall be entered on the Journal of each House respectively. If any Bill shall not be returned by the President within ten Days (Sundays excepted) after it shall have been presented to him, the Same shall be a Law, in like Manner as if he had signed it, unless the Congress by their Adjournment prevent its Return, in which Case it shall not be a Law.

Every Order, Resolution, or Vote to which the Concurrence of the Senate and House of Representatives may be necessary (except on a question of Adjournment) shall be presented to the President of the United States; and before the Same shall take Effect, shall be approved by him, or being disapproved by him, shall be repassed by two thirds of the Senate and House of Representatives, according to the Rules and Limitations prescribed in the Case of a Bill.

Section. 8. The Congress shall have Power To lay and collect Taxes, Duties, Imposts and Excises, to pay the Debts and provide for the common Defence and general Welfare of the United States; but all Duties, Imposts and Excises shall be uniform throughout the United States;

To borrow Money on the credit of the United States;

To regulate Commerce with foreign Nations, and among the several States, and with the Indian Tribes;

To establish an uniform Rule of Naturalization, and uniform Laws on the subject of Bankruptcies throughout the United States;

To coin Money, regulate the Value thereof, and of foreign Coin, and fix the Standard of Weights and Measures;

To provide for the Punishment of counterfeiting the Securities and current Coin of the United States;

To establish Post Offices and Post Roads;

To promote the Progress of Science and useful Arts, by securing for limited Times to Authors and Inventors the exclusive Right to their respective Writings and Discoveries;

To constitute Tribunals inferior to the supreme Court;

To define and punish Piracies and Felonies committed on the high Seas, and Offences against the Law of Nations;

To declare War, grant Letters of Marque and Reprisal, and make Rules concerning Captures on Land and Water;

To raise and support Armies, but no Appropriation of Money to that Use shall be for a longer Term than two Years;

To provide and maintain a Navy;

To make Rules for the Government and Regulation of the land and naval Forces;

To provide for calling forth the Militia to execute the Laws of the Union, suppress Insurrections and repel Invasions;

To provide for organizing, arming, and disciplining, the Militia, and for governing such Part of them as may be employed in the Service of the United States, reserving to the States respectively, the Appointment of the Officers, and the Authority of training the Militia according to the discipline prescribed by Congress;

To exercise exclusive Legislation in all Cases whatsoever, over such District (not exceeding ten Miles square) as may, by Cession of Particular States, and the Acceptance of Congress, become the Seat of the Government of the United States, and to exercise like Authority over all Places purchased by the Consent of the Legislature of the State in which the Same shall be, for the Erection of Forts, Magazines, Arsenals, dock-Yards, and other needful Buildings;—And

To make all Laws which shall be necessary and proper for carrying into Execution the foregoing Powers, and all other Powers vested by this Constitution in the Government of the United States, or in any Department or Officer thereof.

Section. 9. The Migration or Importation of such Persons as any of the States now existing shall think proper to admit, shall not be prohibited by the Congress prior to the Year one thousand eight hundred and eight, but a Tax or duty may be imposed on such Importation, not exceeding ten dollars for each Person.

The Privilege of the Writ of Habeas Corpus shall not be suspended, unless when in Cases of Rebellion or Invasion the public Safety may require it.

No Bill of Attainder or ex post facto Law shall be passed.

No Capitation, or other direct, Tax shall be laid, unless in Proportion to the Census or Enumeration herein before directed to be taken.

No Tax or Duty shall be laid on Articles exported from any State.

No Preference shall be given by any Regulation of Commerce or Revenue to the Ports of one State over those of another: nor shall Vessels bound to, or from, one State, be obliged to enter, clear, or pay Duties in another.

No Money shall be drawn from the Treasury, but in Consequence of Appropriations made by Law; and a regular Statement and Account of the Receipts and Expenditures of all public Money shall be published from time to time.

No Title of Nobility shall be granted by the United States: And no Person holding any Office of Profit or Trust under them, shall, without the Consent of the Congress, accept of any present, Emolument, Office, or Title, of any kind whatever, from any King, Prince, or foreign State.

Section. 10. No State shall enter into any Treaty, Alliance, or Confederation; grant Letters of Marque and Reprisal; coin Money; emit Bills of Credit; make any Thing but gold and silver Coin a Tender in Payment of Debts; pass any Bill of Attainder, ex post facto Law, or Law impairing the Obligation of Contracts, or grant any Title of Nobility.

No State shall, without the Consent of the Congress, lay any Imposts or Duties on Imports or Exports, except what may be absolutely necessary for executing its inspection Laws: and the net Produce of all Duties and Imposts, laid by any State on Imports or Exports, shall be for the Use of the Treasury of the United States; and all such Laws shall be subject to the Revision and Controul of the Congress.

No State shall, without the Consent of Congress, lay any Duty of Tonnage, keep Troops, or Ships of War in time of Peace, enter into any Agreement or Compact with another State, or with a foreign Power, or engage in War, unless actually invaded, or in such imminent Danger as will not admit of delay.

ARTICLE. II.

Section. 1. The executive Power shall be vested in a President of the United States of America. He shall hold his Office during the term of four Years, and, together with the Vice President, chosen for the same Term, be elected, as follows:

Each State shall appoint, in such Manner as the Legislature thereof may direct, a Number of Electors, equal to the whole Number of Senators and Representatives to which the State may be entitled in the Congress: but no Senator or Representative, or Person holding an Office of Trust or Profit under the United States, shall be appointed an Elector.

The Electors shall meet in their respective States, and vote by Ballot for two Persons, of whom one at least shall not be an Inhabitant of the same State with themselves. And they shall make a List of all the Persons voted for, and of the Number of Votes for each; which List they shall sign and certify, and transmit sealed to the Seat of the Government of the United States, directed to the President of the Senate. The President of the Senate shall, in the Presence of the Senate and House of Representatives, open all the Certificates, and the Votes shall then be counted. The Person having the greatest Number of Votes shall be the President, if such Number be a Majority of the whole Number of Electors appointed; and if there be more than one who have such Majority, and have an equal Number of Votes, then the House of Representatives shall immediately chuse by Ballot one of them for President; and if no Person have a Majority, then from the five highest on the List the said House shall in like Manner chuse the President. But in chusing the President, the Votes shall be taken by States, the Representation from each State having one Vote; A quorum for this Purpose shall consist of a Member or Members from two thirds of the States, and a Majority of all the States shall be necessary to a Choice. In every Case, after the Choice of the President, the Person having the greatest Number of Votes of the Electors shall be the Vice President. But if there should remain two or more who have equal Votes, the Senate shall chuse from them by Ballot the Vice President.

The Congress may determine the Time of chusing the Electors, and the Day on which they shall give their Votes; which Day shall be the same throughout the United States.

No Person except a natural born Citizen, or a Citizen of the United States, at the time of the Adoption of this Constitution, shall be eligible to the Office of President; neither shall any Person be eligible to that Office who shall not have attained to the Age of thirty five Years, and been fourteen Years a Resident within the United States.

In Case of the Removal of the President from Office, or of his Death, Resignation, or Inability to discharge the Powers and Duties of the said Office, the Same shall devolve on the Vice President, and the Congress may by Law provide for the Case of Removal, Death, Resignation or Inability, both of the President and Vice President, declaring what Officer shall then act as President, and such Officer shall act accordingly, until the Disability be removed, or a President shall be elected.

The President shall, at stated Times, receive for his Services, a Compensation, which shall neither be encreased or diminished during the Period for which he shall have been elected, and he shall not receive within that Period any other Emolument from the United States, or any of them.

Before he enters on the Execution of his Office, he shall take the following Oath or Affirmation:—"I do solemnly swear (or affirm) that I will faithfully execute the Office of President of the United States, and will to the best of my Ability, preserve, protect and defend the Constitution of the United States."

Section. 2. The President shall be Commander in Chief of the Army and Navy of the United States, and of the Militia of the several States, when called into the actual Service of the United States; he may require the Opinion, in writing, of the principal Officer in each of the executive Departments, upon any Subject relating to the Duties of their respective Offices, and he shall have Power to grant Reprieves and Pardons for Offences against the United States, except in Cases of Impeachment.

He shall have Power, by and with the Advice and Consent of the Senate, to make Treaties, provided two thirds of the Senators present concur; and he shall nominate, and by and with the Advice and Consent of the Senate, shall appoint Ambassadors, other public Ministers and Consuls, Judges of the supreme Court, and all other Officers of the United States, whose Appointments are not herein otherwise provided for, and which shall be established by Law; but the Congress may by Law vest the Appointment of such inferior Officers, as they think proper, in the President alone, in the Courts of Law, or in the Heads of Departments.

The President shall have Power to fill up all Vacancies that may happen during the Recess of the Senate, by granting Commissions which shall expire at the End of their next Session.

Section. 3. He shall from time to time give to the Congress Information of the State of the Union, and recommend to their Consideration such Measures as he shall judge necessary and expedient; he may, on extraordinary Occasions, convene both Houses, or either of them, and in Case of Disagreement between them, with Respect to the Time of Adjournment, he may adjourn them to such Time as he shall think proper; he shall receive Ambassadors and other public Ministers; he shall take Care that the Laws be faithfully executed, and shall Commission all the Officers of the United States.

Section. 4. The President, Vice President and all civil Officers of the United States, shall be removed from Office on Impeachment for, and Conviction of, Treason, Bribery, or other high Crimes and Misdemeanors.

ARTICLE. III.

Section. 1. The judicial Power of the United States, shall be vested in one supreme Court, and in such inferior Courts as the Congress may from time to time ordain and establish. The Judges, both of the supreme and inferior Courts, shall hold their Offices during good Behavior, and shall, at stated Times, receive for their Services, a Compensation, which shall not be diminished during their Continuance in Office.

Section. 2. The judicial Power shall extend to all Cases, in Law and Equity, arising under this Constitution, the Laws of the United States, and Treaties made, or which shall be made, under their Authority;—to all Cases affecting Ambassadors, other public Ministers and Consuls;—to all Cases of admiralty and maritime Jurisdiction;—the Controversies to which the United States shall be a Party;—to Controversies between two or more States;—between a State and Citizens of another State;—between Citizens of different States;—between Citizens of the same State claiming Lands under Grants of different States, and between a State, or the Citizens thereof, and foreign States, Citizens or Subjects.

In all cases affecting Ambassadors, other public Ministers and Consuls, and those in which a State shall be Party, the supreme Court shall have original Jurisdiction. In all the other Cases before mentioned, the supreme Court shall have appellate Jurisdiction, both as to Law and Fact, with such Exceptions, and under such Regulations as the Congress shall make.

The Trial of all Crimes, except in Cases of Impeachment, shall be by Jury; and such Trial shall be held in the State where the said Crimes shall have been committed; but when not committed within any State, the Trial shall be at such Place or Places as the Congress may by Law have directed.

Section. 3. Treason against the United States, shall consist only in levying War against them, or in adhering to their Enemies, giving them Aid and Comfort. No Person shall be convicted of Treason unless on the Testimony of two Witnesses to the same overt Act, or on Confession in open Court.

The Congress shall have Power to declare the Punishment of Treason, but no Attainder of Treason shall work Corruption of Blood, or Forfeiture except during the Life of the Person attainted.

ARTICLE. IV.

Section. 1. Full Faith and Credit shall be given in each State to the public Acts, Records, and judicial Proceedings of every other State. And the Congress may by general Laws prescribe the Manner in which such Acts, Records and Proceedings shall be proved, and the Effect thereof.

Section. 2. The Citizens of each State shall be entitled to all Privileges and Immunities of Citizens in the several States.

A Person charged in any State with Treason, Felony, or other Crime, who shall flee from Justice, and be found in another State, shall on Demand of the executive Authority of the State from which he fled, be delivered up, to be removed to the State having Jurisdiction of the Crime.

No Person held to Service or Labour in one State, under the Laws thereof, escaping into another, shall, in Consequence of any Law or Regulation therein, be discharged from such Service or Labour, but shall be delivered up on Claim of the Party to whom such Service or Labour may be due.

Section. 3. New States may be admitted by the Congress into this Union; but no new State shall be formed or erected within the Jurisdiction of any other State; nor any State be formed by the Junction of two or more States, or Parts of States, without the consent of the Legislatures of the States concerned as well as of the Congress.

The Congress shall have Power to dispose of and make all needful Rules and Regulations respecting the Territory or other Property belonging to the United States; and nothing in this Constitution shall be so construed as to Prejudice any Claims of the United States, or of any particular States.

Section. 4. The United States shall guarantee to every State in this Union a Republican Form of Government, and shall protect each of them against Invasion; and on Application of the Legislature, or of the Executive (when the Legislature cannot be convened) against domestic Violence.

ARTICLE. V.

The Congress, whenever two thirds of both Houses shall deem it necessary, shall propose Amendments to this Constitution, or, on the Application of the Legislatures of two thirds of the several States, shall call a Convention for proposing Amendments, which, in either Case, shall be valid to all Intents and Purposes, as Part of this Constitution, when ratified by the Legislatures of three fourths of the several States, or by Conventions in three fourths thereof, as the one or the other Mode of Ratification may be proposed by the Congress; Provided that no Amendment which may be made prior to the Year One thousand eight hundred and eight shall in any Manner affect the first and fourth Clauses in the Ninth Section of the first Article; and that no State, without its Consent, shall be deprived of its equal Suffrage in the Senate.

ARTICLE. VI.

All Debts contracted and Engagements entered into, before the Adoption of this Constitution, shall be as valid against the United States under this Constitution, as under the Confederation.

This Constitution, and the Laws of the United States which shall be made in Pursuance thereof; and all Treaties made, or which shall be made, under the Authority of the United States, shall be the supreme Law of the Land; and the Judges in every State shall be bound thereby, any Thing in the Constitution or Laws of any State to the Contrary notwithstanding.

The Senators and Representatives before mentioned, and the Members of the several State Legislatures, and all executive and judicial Officers, both of the United States and of the several States, shall be bound by Oath or Affirmation, to support this Constitution; but no religious Test shall ever be required as a Qualification to any Office or public Trust under the United States.

ARTICLE. VII.

The Ratification of the Conventions of nine States, shall be sufficient for the Establishment of this Constitution between the States so ratifying the Same.

Done in Convention by the Unanimous Consent of the States present the Seventeenth Day of September in the Year of our Lord one thousand seven hundred and Eighty seven and of the Independence of the United States of America the Twelfth. In witness thereof We have hereunto subscribed our Names,

G°. WASHINGTON—Presd[t].
and deputy from Virginia

NEW HAMPSHIRE
John Langdon
Nicholas Gilman

MASSACHUSETTS
Nathaniel Gorham
Rufus King

CONNECTICUT
W[m] Sam[l] Johnson
Roger Sherman

NEW YORK
Alexander Hamilton

NEW JERSEY
Wil: Livingston
David A. Brearley
W[m] Paterson
Jona: Dayton

PENNSYLVANIA
B Franklin
Thomas Mifflin
Rob[t] Morris
Geo. Clymer
Tho[s] FitzSimons
Jared Ingersoll
James Wilson
Gouv Morris

DELAWARE
Geo: Read
Gunning Bedford jun
John Dickinson
Richard Bassett
Jaco: Broom

MARYLAND
James M[c]Henry
Dan of S[t] Tho[s] Jenifer
Dan[l] Carroll

VIRGINIA
John Blair—
James Madison Jr.

NORTH CAROLINA
W[m] Blount
Rich[d] Dobbs Spaight
Hu Williamson

SOUTH CAROLINA
J. Rutledge
Charles Cotesworth
Pinckney
Charles Pinckney
Pierce Butler

GEORGIA
William Few
Abr Baldwin

AMENDMENTS TO THE CONSTITUTION

Articles in addition to, and Amendment of the Constitution of the United States of America, proposed by Congress, and ratified by the Legislatures of the several States, pursuant to the fifth Article of the original Constitution.

AMENDMENT I.*

Congress shall make no law respecting an establishment of religion, or prohibiting the free exercise thereof; or abridging the freedom of speech, or of the press; or the right of the people peaceably to assemble, and to petition the Government for a redress of grievances.

AMENDMENT II.

A well regulated Militia, being necessary to the security of a free State, the right of the people to keep and bear Arms, shall not be infringed.

AMENDMENT III.

No Soldier shall, in time of peace be quartered in any house, without the consent of the Owner, nor in time of war, but in a manner to be prescribed by law.

AMENDMENT IV.

The right of the people to be secure in their persons, houses, papers, and effects, against unreasonable searches and seizures, shall not be violated, and no Warrants shall issue, but upon probable cause, supported by Oath or affirmation, and particularly describing the place to be searched, and the persons or things to be seized.

AMENDMENT V.

No person shall be held to answer for a capital, or otherwise infamous crime, unless on a presentment or indictment of a Grand Jury, except in cases arising in the land or naval forces, or in the Militia, when in actual service in time of War or public danger; nor shall any person be subject for the same offence to be twice put in jeopardy of life or limb; nor shall be compelled in any criminal case to be a witness against himself, nor be deprived of life, liberty, or property, without due process of law; nor shall private property be taken for public use, without just compensation.

AMENDMENT VI.

In all criminal prosecutions, the accused shall enjoy the right to a speedy and public trial, by an impartial jury of the State and district wherein the crime shall have been committed, which district shall have been previously ascertained by law, and to be informed of the nature and cause of the accusation; to be confronted with the witnesses against him; to have compulsory process for obtaining witnesses in his favor, and to have the Assistance of Counsel for his defence.

AMENDMENT VII.

In Suits at common law, where the value in controversy shall exceed twenty dollars, the right of trial by jury shall be preserved, and no fact tried by a jury, shall be otherwise re-examined in any Court of the United States, than according to the rules of the common law.

AMENDMENT VIII.

Excessive bail shall not be required, nor excessive fines imposed, nor cruel and unusual punishments inflicted.

AMENDMENT IX.

The enumeration in the Constitution, of certain rights, shall not be construed to deny or disparage others retained by the people.

AMENDMENT X.

The powers not delegated to the United States by the Constitution, nor prohibited by it to the States, are reserved to the States respectively, or to the people.

AMENDMENT XI.

The Judicial power of the United States shall not be construed to extend to any suit in law or equity, commenced or prosecuted against one of the United States by Citizens of another State, or by Citizens or Subjects of any Foreign State. [January 8, 1798]

AMENDMENT XII.

The Electors shall meet in their respective states, and vote by ballot for President and Vice-President, one of whom, at least, shall not be an inhabitant of the same state with themselves; they shall name in their ballots the person voted for as President, and in distinct ballots the person voted for as Vice-President, and they shall make distinct lists of all persons voted for as President, and of all persons voted for as Vice President, and of the number of votes for each, which lists they shall sign and certify, and transmit sealed to the seat of the government of the United States, directed to the President of the Senate;—The President of the Senate shall, in the presence of the Senate and

*The first ten Amendments (the Bill of Rights) were ratified in 1791.

House of Representatives, open all the certificates and the votes shall then be counted;—The person having the greatest number of votes for President, shall be the President, if such number be a majority of the whole number of Electors appointed; and if no person have such majority, then from the persons having the highest numbers not exceeding three on the list of those voted for as President, the House of Representatives shall choose immediately, by ballot, the President. But in choosing the President, the votes shall be taken by states, the representation from each state having one vote; a quorum for this purpose shall consist of a member or members from two-thirds of the states, and a majority of all the states shall be necessary to a choice. And if the House of Representatives shall not choose a President whenever the right of choice shall devolve upon them, before the fourth day of March next following, then the Vice-President shall act as President, as in the case of the death or other constitutional disability of the President.—The person having the greatest number of votes as Vice-President, shall be the Vice-President, if such number be a majority of the whole number of Electors appointed, and if no person have a majority, then from the two highest numbers on the list, the Senate shall choose the Vice-President; a quorum for the purpose shall consist of two-thirds of the whole number of Senators, and a majority of the whole number shall be necessary to a choice. But no person constitutionally ineligible to the office of President shall be eligible to that of Vice-President of the United States. [September 25, 1804]

AMENDMENT XIII.

Section 1. Neither slavery nor involuntary servitude, except as a punishment for crime whereof the party shall have been duly convicted, shall exist within the United States, or any place subject to their jurisdiction.

Section 2. Congress shall have power to enforce this article by appropriate legislation. [December 18, 1865]

AMENDMENT XIV.

Section 1. All persons born or naturalized in the United States, and subject to the jurisdiction thereof, are citizens of the United States and of the State wherein they reside. No State shall make or enforce any law which shall abridge the privileges or immunities of citizens of the United States; nor shall any State deprive any person of life, liberty, or property, without due process of law; nor deny to any person within its jurisdiction the equal protection of the laws.

Section 2. Representatives shall be apportioned among the several States according to their respective numbers, counting the whole number of persons in each State, excluding Indians not taxed. But when the right to vote at any election for the choice of electors for President and Vice President of the United States, Representatives in Congress, the Executive and Judicial officers of a State, or the members of the Legislature thereof, is denied to any of the male inhabitants of such State, being twenty-one years of age, and citizens of the United States, or in any way abridged, except for participation in rebellion, or other crime, the basis of representation therein shall be reduced in the proportion which the number of such male citizens shall bear to the whole number of male citizens twenty-one years of age in such State.

Section 3. No person shall be a Senator or Representative in Congress, or elector of President and Vice President, or hold any office, civil or military, under the United States, or under any State, who, having previously taken an oath, as a member of Congress, or as an officer of the United States, or as a member of any State legislature, or as an executive or judicial officer of any State, to support the Constitution of the United States, shall have engaged in insurrection or rebellion against the same, or given aid or comfort to the enemies thereof. But Congress may by a vote of two-thirds of each House, remove such disability.

Section 4. The validity of the public debt of the United States, authorized by law, including debts incurred for payment of pensions and bounties for services in suppressing insurrection or rebellion, shall not be questioned. But neither the United States nor any State shall assume or pay any debt or obligation incurred in aid of insurrection or rebellion against the United States, or any claim for the loss or emancipation of any slave; but all such debts, obligations and claims shall be held illegal and void.

Section 5. The Congress shall have power to enforce, by appropriate legislation, the provisions of this article. [July 28, 1868]

AMENDMENT XV.

Section 1. The right of citizens of the United States to vote shall not be denied or abridged by the United States or by any State on account of race, color, or previous condition of servitude—

Section 2. The Congress shall have power to enforce this article by appropriate legislation. [March 30, 1870]

AMENDMENT XVI.

The Congress shall have power to lay and collect taxes on incomes, from whatever source derived, without apportionment among the several States, and without regard to any census or enumeration. [February 25, 1913]

AMENDMENT XVII.

The Senate of the United States shall be composed of two senators from each State, elected by the people thereof, for six years; and each Senator shall have one vote. The electors in each State shall have the qualifications requisite for electors of the most numerous branch of the State legislatures.

When vacancies happen in the representation of any State in the Senate, the executive authority of such State shall issue writs of election to fill such vacancies: *Provided,* That the legislature of any State may empower the executive thereof to make temporary appointments until the people fill the vacancies by election as the legislature may direct.

This amendment shall not be so construed as to affect the election or term of any senator chosen before it becomes valid as part of the Constitution. [May 31, 1913]

AMENDMENT XVIII.

After one year from the ratification of this article, the manufacture, sale, or transportation of intoxicating liquors within, the importation thereof into, or the exportation thereof from the United States and all territory subject to the jurisdiction thereof for beverage purposes is hereby prohibited.

The Congress and the several States shall have concurrent power to enforce this article by appropriate legislation.

This article shall be inoperative unless it shall have been ratified as an amendment to the Constitution by the legislatures of the several States, as provided in the Constitution, within seven years from the date of the submission thereof to the States by Congress. [January 29, 1919]

AMENDMENT XIX.

The right of citizens of the United States to vote shall not be denied or abridged by the United States or by any State on account of sex.

The Congress shall have power by appropriate legislation to enforce the provisions of this article. [August 26, 1920]

AMENDMENT XX.

Section 1. The terms of the President and Vice-President shall end at noon on the twentieth day of January, and the terms of Senators and Representatives at noon on the third day of January, of the years in which such terms would have ended if this article had not been ratified; and the terms of their successors shall then begin.

Section 2. The Congress shall assemble at least once in every year, and such meeting shall begin at noon on the third day of January, unless they shall by law appoint a different day.

Section 3. If, at the time fixed for the beginning of the term of the President, the President-elect shall have died, the Vice-President-elect shall become President. If a President shall not have been chosen before the time fixed for the beginning of his term, or if the President-elect shall have failed to qualify,

then the Vice-President-elect shall act as President until a President shall have qualified; and the Congress may by law provide for the case wherein neither a President-elect nor a Vice-President-elect shall have qualified, declaring who shall then act as President, or the manner in which one who is to act shall be selected, and such person shall act accordingly until a President or Vice-President shall have qualified.

Section 4. The Congress may by law provide for the case of the death of any of the persons from whom the House of Representatives may choose a President whenever the right of choice shall have devolved upon them, and for the case of the death of any of the persons from whom the Senate may choose a Vice-President whenever the right of choice shall have devolved upon them.

Section 5. Sections 1 and 2 shall take effect on the 15th day of October following the ratification of this article.

Section 6. This article shall be inoperative unless it shall have been ratified as an amendment to the Constitution by the legislatures of three-fourths of the several States within seven years from the date of its submission. [February 6, 1933]

AMENDMENT XXI.

Section 1. The eighteenth article of amendment to the Constitution of the United States is hereby repealed.

Section 2. The transportation or importation into any State, Territory or possession of the United States for delivery or use therein of intoxicating liquors, in violation of the laws thereof, is hereby prohibited.

Section 3. This article shall be inoperative unless it shall have been ratified as an amendment to the Constitution by convention in the several States, as provided in the Constitution, within seven years from the date of the submission thereof to the States by the Congress. [December 5, 1933]

AMENDMENT XXII.

Section 1. No person shall be elected to the office of the President more than twice, and no person who has held the office of President, or acted as President, for more than two years of a term to which some other person was elected President shall be elected to the office of the President more than once. But this Article shall not apply to any person holding the office of President when this Article was proposed by the Congress, and shall not prevent any person who may be holding the office of President, or acting as President, during the term within which this Article becomes operative from holding the office of President or acting as President during the remainder of such term.

Section 2. This article shall be inoperative unless it shall have been ratified as an amendment to the Constitution by the legislatures of three-fourths of the several States within seven years from the date of its submission to the States by the Congress. [February 27, 1951]

Amendment XXIII.

Section 1. The District constituting the seat of government of the United States shall appoint in such manner as the Congress may direct:

A number of electors of President and Vice-President equal to the whole number of Senators and Representatives in Congress to which the District would be entitled if it were a State, but in no event more than the least populous State; they shall be in addition to those appointed by the States, but they shall be considered, for the purposes of the election of President and Vice-President, to be electors appointed by a State; and they shall meet in the District and perform such duties as provided by the twelfth article of amendment.

Section 2. The Congress shall have the power to enforce this article by appropriate legislation. [March 29, 1961]

Amendment XXIV.

Section 1. The right of citizens of the United States to vote in any primary or other election for President or Vice President, for electors for President or Vice President, or for Senator or Representative in Congress, shall not be denied or abridged by the United States or any State by reason of failure to pay any poll tax or other tax.

Section 2. The Congress shall have power to enforce this article by appropriate legislation. [January 23, 1964]

Amendment XXV.

Section 1. In case of the removal of the President from office or of his death or resignation, the Vice President shall become President.

Section 2. Whenever there is a vacancy in the office of Vice President, the President shall nominate a Vice President who shall take office upon confirmation by a majority vote of both Houses of Congress.

Section 3. Whenever the President transmits to the President pro tempore of the Senate and the Speaker of the House of Representatives his written declaration that he is unable to discharge the powers and duties of his office, and until he transmits to them a written declaration to the contrary, such powers and duties shall be discharged by the Vice President as Acting President.

Section 4. Whenever the Vice President and a majority of either the principal officers of the executive departments or of such other body as Congress may by law provide, transmit to the President pro tempore of the Senate and the Speaker of the House of Representatives their written declaration that the President is unable to discharge the powers and duties of his office, the Vice President shall immediately assume the powers and duties of the office as Acting President.

Thereafter, when the President transmits to the President pro tempore of the Senate and the Speaker of the House of Representatives his written declaration that no inability exists, he shall resume the powers and duties of his office unless the Vice President and a majority of either the principal officers of the executive departments or of such other body as Congress may by law provide, transmit within four days to the President pro tempore of the Senate and the Speaker of the House of Representatives their written declaration that the President is unable to discharge the powers and duties of his office. Thereupon Congress shall decide the issue, assembling within forty-eight hours for that purpose if not in session. If the Congress, within twenty-one days after receipt of the latter written declaration, or, if Congress is not in session, within twenty-one days after Congress is required to assemble, determines by two-thirds vote of both Houses that the President is unable to discharge the powers and duties of his office, the Vice President shall continue to discharge the same as Acting President; otherwise, the President shall resume the powers and duties of his office. [February 10, 1967]

Amendment XXVI.

Section 1. The right of citizens of the United States, who are eighteen years of age or older, to vote shall not be denied or abridged by the United States or by any State on account of age.

Section 2. The Congress shall have power to enforce this article by appropriate legislation. [June 30, 1971]

Amendment XXVII.

No law, varying the compensation for the services of the Senators and Representatives shall take effect, until an election of Representatives shall have intervened. [May 8, 1992]

FROM GEORGE WASHINGTON'S FAREWELL ADDRESS (1796)

Friends and Citizens:

The period for a new election of a citizen to administer the executive government of the United States being not far distant, and the time actually arrived when your thoughts must be employed in designating the person who is to be clothed with that important trust, it appears to me proper, especially as it may conduce to a more distinct expression of the public voice, that I should now apprise you of the resolution I have formed, to decline being considered among the number of those out of whom a choice is to be made.

* * *

In looking forward to the moment which is intended to terminate the career of my public life, my feelings do not permit me to suspend the deep acknowledgment of that debt of gratitude which I owe to my beloved country for the many honors it has conferred upon me; still more for the steadfast confidence with which it has supported me; and for the opportunities I have thence enjoyed of manifesting my inviolable attachment, by services faithful and persevering, though in usefulness unequal to my zeal. If benefits have resulted to our country from these services, let it always be remembered to your praise, and as an instructive example in our annals, that under circumstances in which the passions, agitated in every direction, were liable to mislead, amidst appearances sometimes dubious, vicissitudes of fortune often discouraging, in situations in which not unfrequently want of success has countenanced the spirit of criticism, the constancy of your support was the essential prop of the efforts, and a guarantee of the plans by which they were effected. Profoundly penetrated with this idea, I shall carry it with me to my grave, as a strong incitement to unceasing vows that heaven may continue to you the choicest tokens of its beneficence; that your union and brotherly affection may be perpetual; that the free Constitution, which is the work of your hands, may be sacredly maintained; that its administration in every department may be stamped with wisdom and virtue; that, in fine, the happiness of the people of these States, under the auspices of liberty, may be made complete by so careful a preservation and so prudent a use of this blessing as will acquire to them the glory of recommending it to the applause, the affection, and adoption of every nation which is yet a stranger to it.

Here, perhaps, I ought to stop. But a solicitude for your welfare, which cannot end but with my life, and the apprehension of danger, natural to that solicitude, urge me, on an occasion like the present, to offer to your solemn contemplation, and to recommend to your frequent review, some sentiments which are the result of much reflection, of no inconsiderable observation, and which appear to me all-important to the permanency of your felicity as a people. These will be offered to you with the more freedom, as you can only see in them the disinterested warnings of a parting friend, who can possibly have no personal motive to bias his counsel. Nor can I forget, as an encouragement to it, your indulgent reception of my sentiments on a former and not dissimilar occasion.

Interwoven as is the love of liberty with every ligament of your hearts, no recommendation of mine is necessary to fortify or confirm the attachment.

The unity of government which constitutes you one people is also now dear to you. It is justly so, for it is a main pillar in the edifice of your real independence, the support of your tranquility at home, your peace abroad; of your safety; of your prosperity; of that very liberty which you so highly prize. But as it is easy to foresee that, from different causes and from different quarters, much pains will be taken, many artifices employed to weaken in your minds the conviction of this truth; as this is the point in your political fortress against which the batteries of internal and external enemies will be most constantly and actively (though often covertly and insidiously) directed, it is of infinite moment that you should properly estimate the immense value of your national union to your collective and individual happiness; that you should cherish a cordial, habitual, and immovable attachment to it; accustoming yourselves to think and speak of it as of the palladium of your political safety and prosperity; watching for its preservation with jealous anxiety; discountenancing whatever may suggest even a suspicion that it can in any event be abandoned; and indignantly frowning upon the first dawning of every attempt to alienate any portion of our country from the rest, or to enfeeble the sacred ties which now link together the various parts.

For this you have every inducement of sympathy and interest. Citizens, by birth or choice, of a common country, that country has a right to concentrate your affections. The name of American, which belongs to you in your national capacity, must always exalt the just pride of patriotism more than any appellation derived from local discriminations. With slight shades of difference, you have the same religion, manners, habits, and political principles. You have in a common cause fought and triumphed together; the independence and liberty you possess are the work of joint counsels, and joint efforts of common dangers, sufferings, and successes.

But these considerations, however powerfully they address themselves to your sensibility, are greatly outweighed by those which apply more immediately to your interest. Here every portion of our country finds the most commanding motives for carefully guarding and preserving the union of the whole.

The North, in an unrestrained intercourse with the South, protected by the equal laws of a common government, finds in the productions of the latter great additional resources of maritime and commercial enterprise and precious materials of manufacturing industry. The South, in the same intercourse, benefiting by the agency of the North, sees its agriculture grow and its commerce expand. Turning partly into its own channels the seamen of the North, it finds its particular navigation invigorated; and, while it contributes, in different ways, to nourish and increase the general mass of the national navigation, it looks forward to the protection of a maritime strength, to which itself is unequally adapted. The East, in a like intercourse with the West, already finds, and in the progressive improvement of interior communications by land and water, will more and more find a valuable vent for the commodities which it brings from abroad, or manufactures at home. The West derives from the East supplies requisite to its growth and comfort, and, what is perhaps of still greater consequence, it must of necessity owe the secure enjoyment of indispensable outlets for its own productions to the weight, influence, and the future maritime strength of the Atlantic side of the Union, directed by an indissoluble community of interest as one nation. Any other tenure by which the West can hold this essential advantage, whether derived from its own separate strength, or from an apostate and unnatural connection with any foreign power, must be intrinsically precarious.

While, then, every part of our country thus feels an immediate and particular interest in union, all the parts combined cannot fail to find in the united mass of means and efforts greater strength, greater resource, proportionably greater security from external danger, a less frequent interruption of their peace by foreign nations; and, what is of inestimable value, they must derive from union an exemption from those broils and wars between themselves, which so frequently afflict neighboring countries not tied together by the same governments, which their own rival ships alone would be sufficient to produce, but which opposite foreign alliances, attachments, and intrigues would stimulate and embitter. Hence, likewise, they will avoid the necessity of those overgrown military establishments which, under any form of government, are inauspicious to liberty, and which are to be regarded as particularly hostile to republican liberty. In this sense it is that your union ought to be considered as a main prop of your liberty, and that the love of the one ought to endear to you the preservation of the other.

These considerations speak a persuasive language to every reflecting and virtuous mind, and exhibit the continuance of the Union as a primary object of patriotic desire. Is there a doubt whether a common government can embrace so large a sphere? Let experience solve it. To listen to mere speculation in such a case were criminal. We are authorized to hope that a proper organization of the whole with the auxiliary agency of governments for the respective subdivisions, will afford a happy issue to the experiment. It is well worth a fair and full experiment. With such powerful and obvious motives to union, affecting all parts of our country, while experience

shall not have demonstrated its impracticability, there will always be reason to distrust the patriotism of those who in any quarter may endeavor to weaken its bands.

* * *

To the efficacy and permanency of your Union, a government for the whole is indispensable. No alliance, however strict, between the parts can be an adequate substitute; they must inevitably experience the infractions and interruptions which all alliances in all times have experienced. Sensible of this momentous truth, you have improved upon your first essay, by the adoption of a constitution of government better calculated than your former for an intimate union, and for the efficacious management of your common concerns. This government, the offspring of our own choice, uninfluenced and unawed, adopted upon full investigation and mature deliberation, completely free in its principles, in the distribution of its powers, uniting security with energy, and containing within itself a provision for its own amendment, has a just claim to your confidence and your support. Respect for its authority, compliance with its laws, acquiescence in its measures, are duties enjoined by the fundamental maxims of true liberty. The basis of our political systems is the right of the people to make and to alter their constitutions of government. But the Constitution which at any time exists, till changed by an explicit and authentic act of the whole people, is sacredly obligatory upon all. The very idea of the power and the right of the people to establish government presupposes the duty of every individual to obey the established government.

* * *

I have already intimated to you the danger of parties in the State, with particular reference to the founding of them on geographical discriminations. Let me now take a more comprehensive view, and warn you in the most solemn manner against the baneful effects of the spirit of party generally.

This spirit, unfortunately, is inseparable from our nature, having its root in the strongest passions of the human mind. It exists under different shapes in all governments, more or less stifled, controlled, or repressed; but, in those of the popular form, it is seen in its greatest rankness, and is truly their worst enemy.

The alternate domination of one faction over another, sharpened by the spirit of revenge, natural to party dissension, which in different ages and countries has perpetrated the most horrid enormities, is itself a frightful despotism. But this leads at length to a more formal and permanent despotism. The disorders and miseries which result gradually incline the minds of men to seek security and repose in the absolute power of an individual; and sooner or later the chief of some prevailing faction, more able or more fortunate than his competitors, turns this disposition to the purposes of his own elevation, on the ruins of public liberty.

Without looking forward to an extremity of this kind (which nevertheless ought not to be entirely out of sight), the common and continual mischiefs of the spirit of party are sufficient to make it the interest and duty of a wise people to discourage and restrain it.

It serves always to distract the public councils and enfeeble the public administration. It agitates the community with ill-founded jealousies and false alarms, kindles the animosity of one part against another, foments occasionally riot and insurrection. It opens the door to foreign influence and corruption, which finds a facilitated access to the government itself through the channels of party passions. Thus the policy and the will of one country are subjected to the policy and will of another.

There is an opinion that parties in free countries are useful checks upon the administration of the government and serve to keep alive the spirit of liberty. This within certain limits is probably true; and in governments of a monarchical cast, patriotism may look with indulgence, if not with favor, upon the spirit of party. But in those of the popular character, in governments purely elective, it is a spirit not to be encouraged. From their natural tendency, it is certain there will always be enough of that spirit for every salutary purpose. And there being constant danger of excess, the effort ought to be by force of public opinion, to mitigate and assuage it. A fire not to be quenched, it demands a uniform vigilance to prevent its bursting into a flame, lest, instead of warming, it should consume.

It is important, likewise, that the habits of thinking in a free country should inspire caution in those entrusted with its administration, to confine themselves within their respective constitutional spheres, avoiding in the exercise of the powers of one department to encroach upon another. The spirit of encroachment tends to consolidate the powers of all the departments in one, and thus to create, whatever the form of government, a real despotism. A just estimate of that love of power, and proneness to abuse it, which predominates in the human heart, is sufficient to satisfy us of the truth of this position. The necessity of reciprocal checks in the exercise of political power, by dividing and distributing it into different depositaries, and constituting each the guardian of the public weal against invasions by the others, has been evinced by experiments ancient and modern; some of them in our country and under our own eyes. To preserve them must be as necessary as to institute them. If, in the opinion of the people, the distribution or modification of the constitutional powers be in any particular wrong, let it be corrected by an amendment in the way which the Constitution designates. But let there be no change by usurpation; for though this, in one instance, may be the instrument of good, it is the customary weapon by which free governments are destroyed. The precedent must always greatly overbalance in permanent evil any partial or transient benefit, which the use can at any time yield.

* * *

Observe good faith and justice towards all nations; cultivate peace and harmony with all. Religion and morality enjoin this conduct; and can it be, that good policy does not equally enjoin it? It will be worthy of a free, enlightened, and at no dis-

tant period, a great nation, to give to mankind the magnanimous and too novel example of a people always guided by an exalted justice and benevolence. Who can doubt that, in the course of time and things, the fruits of such a plan would richly repay any temporary advantages which might be lost by a steady adherence to it? Can it be that Providence has not connected the permanent felicity of a nation with its virtue? The experiment, at least, is recommended by every sentiment which ennobles human nature. Alas! is it rendered impossible by its vices?

In the execution of such a plan, nothing is more essential than that permanent, inveterate antipathies against particular nations, and passionate attachments for others, should be excluded; and that, in place of them, just and amicable feelings towards all should be cultivated. The nation which indulges towards another a habitual hatred or a habitual fondness is in some degree a slave. It is a slave to its animosity or to its affection, either of which is sufficient to lead it astray from its duty and its interest. Antipathy in one nation against another disposes each more readily to offer insult and injury, to lay hold of slight causes of umbrage, and to be haughty and intractable, when accidental or trifling occasions of dispute occur. Hence, frequent collisions, obstinate, envenomed, and bloody contests. The nation, prompted by ill-will and resentment, sometimes impels to war the government, contrary to the best calculations of policy. The government sometimes participates in the national propensity, and adopts through passion what reason would reject; at other times it makes the animosity of the nation subservient to projects of hostility instigated by pride, ambition, and other sinister and pernicious motives. The peace often, sometimes perhaps the liberty, of nations, has been the victim.

* * *

The great rule of conduct for us in regard to foreign nations is in extending our commercial relations, to have with them as little political connection as possible. So far as we have already formed engagements, let them be fulfilled with perfect good faith. Here let us stop. Europe has a set of primary interests which to us have none; or a very remote relation. Hence she must be engaged in frequent controversies, the causes of which are essentially foreign to our concerns. Hence, therefore, it must be unwise in us to implicate ourselves by artificial ties in the ordinary vicissitudes of her politics, or the ordinary combinations and collisions of her friendships or enmities.

Our detached and distant situation invites and enables us to pursue a different course. If we remain one people under an efficient government, the period is not far off when we may defy material injury from external annoyance; when we may take such an attitude as will cause the neutrality we may at any time resolve upon to be scrupulously respected; when belligerent nations, under the impossibility of making acquisitions upon us, will not lightly hazard the giving us provocation; when we may choose peace or war, as our interest, guided by justice, shall counsel.

Why forego the advantages of so peculiar a situation? Why quit our own to stand upon foreign ground? Why, by interweaving our destiny with that of any part of Europe, entangle our peace and prosperity in the toils of European ambition, rivalship, interest, humor or caprice?

It is our true policy to steer clear of permanent alliances with any portion of the foreign world; so far, I mean, as we are now at liberty to do it; for let me not be understood as capable of patronizing infidelity to existing engagements. I hold the maxim no less applicable to public than to private affairs, that honesty is always the best policy. I repeat it, therefore, let those engagements be observed in their genuine sense. But, in my opinion, it is unnecessary and would be unwise to extend them.

Taking care always to keep ourselves by suitable establishments on a respectable defensive posture, we may safely trust to temporary alliances for extraordinary emergencies.

Harmony, liberal intercourse with all nations, are recommended by policy, humanity, and interest. But even our commercial policy should hold an equal and impartial hand; neither seeking nor granting exclusive favors or preferences; consulting the natural course of things; diffusing and diversifying by gentle means the streams of commerce, but forcing nothing; establishing (with powers so disposed, in order to give trade a stable course, to define the rights of our merchants, and to enable the government to support them) conventional rules of intercourse, the best that present circumstances and mutual opinion will permit, but temporary, and liable to be from time to time abandoned or varied, as experience and circumstances shall dictate; constantly keeping in view that it is folly in one nation to look for disinterested favors from another; that it must pay with a portion of its independence for whatever it may accept under that character; that, by such acceptance, it may place itself in the condition of having given equivalents for nominal favors, and yet of being reproached with ingratitude for not giving more.

* * *

Relying on its kindness in this as in other things, and actuated by that fervent love towards it, which is so natural to a man who views in it the native soil of himself and his progenitors for several generations, I anticipate with pleasing expectation that retreat in which I promise myself to realize, without alloy, the sweet enjoyment of partaking, in the midst of my fellow-citizens, the benign influence of good laws under a free government, the ever-favorite object of my heart, and the happy reward, as I trust, of our mutual cares, labors, and dangers.

Geo. Washington

The Seneca Falls Declaration of Sentiments and Resolutions (1848)

1. Declaration of Sentiments

When, in the course of human events, it becomes necessary for one portion of the family of man to assume among the people of the earth a position different from that which they have hitherto occupied, but one to which the laws of nature and of nature's God entitle them, a decent respect to the opinions of mankind requires that they should declare the causes that impel them to such a course.

We hold these truths to be self-evident: that all men and women are created equal; that they are endowed by their Creator with certain inalienable rights; that among these are life, liberty, and the pursuit of happiness; that to secure these rights governments are instituted, deriving their just powers from the consent of the governed. Whenever any form of government becomes destructive of these ends, it is the right of those who suffer from it to refuse allegiance to it, and to insist upon the institution of a new government, laying its foundation on such principles, and organizing its powers in such form, as to them shall seem most likely to effect their safety and happiness. Prudence, indeed, will dictate that governments long established should not be changed for light and transient causes; and accordingly all experience hath shown that mankind are more disposed to suffer, while evils are sufferable, than to right themselves by abolishing the forms to which they are accustomed. But when a long train of abuses and usurpations, pursuing invariably the same object, evinces a design to reduce them under absolute despotism, it is their duty to throw off such government, and to provide new guards for their future security. Such has been the patient sufferance of the women under this government, and such is now the necessity which constrains them to demand the equal station to which they are entitled. The history of mankind is a history of repeated injuries and usurpations on the part of man toward woman, having in direct object the establishment of an absolute tyranny over her. To prove this, let facts be submitted to a candid world.

He has never permitted her to exercise her inalienable right to the elective franchise.

He has compelled her to submit to laws, in the formation of which she had no voice.

He has withheld from her rights which are given to the most ignorant and degraded men—both natives and foreigners.

Having deprived her of this first right of a citizen, the elective franchise, thereby leaving her without representation in the halls of legislation, he has oppressed her on all sides.

He has made her, if married, in the eye of the law, civilly dead. He has taken from her all right in property, even to the wages she earns.

He has made her, morally, an irresponsible being, as she can commit many crimes with impunity, provided they be done in the presence of her husband.

In the covenant of marriage, she is compelled to promise obedience to her husband, he becoming, to all intents and purposes, her master—the law giving him power to deprive her of her liberty, and to administer chastisement.

He has so framed the laws of divorce, as to what shall be the proper causes, and in case of separation, to whom the guardianship of the children shall be given, as to be wholly regardless of the happiness of women—the law, in all cases, going upon a false supposition of the supremacy of man, and giving all power into his hands.

After depriving her of all rights as a married woman, if single, and the owner of property, he has taxed her to support a government which recognizes her only when her property can be made profitable to it.

He has monopolized nearly all the profitable employments, and from those she is permitted to follow, she receives but a scanty remuneration. He closes against her all the avenues to wealth and distinction which he considers most honorable to himself. As a teacher of theology, medicine, or law, she is not known.

He has denied her the facilities for obtaining a thorough education, all colleges being closed against her.

He allows her in Church, as well as State, but a subordinate position, claiming Apostolic authority for her exclusion from the ministry, and, with some exceptions, from any public participation in the affairs of the Church.

He has created a false public sentiment by giving to the world a different code of morals for men and women, by which moral delinquencies which exclude women from society, are not only tolerated, but deemed of little account in man.

He has usurped the prerogative of Jehovah himself, claiming it as his right to assign for her a sphere of action, when that belongs to her conscience and to her God.

He has endeavored, in every way that he could, to destroy her confidence in her own powers, to lessen her self-respect and to make her willing to lead a dependent and abject life.

Now, in view of this entire disfranchisement of one-half the people of this country, their social and religious degradation—in view of the unjust laws above mentioned, and because women do feel themselves aggrieved, oppressed, and fraudulently deprived of their most sacred rights, we insist that they have immediate admission to all the rights and privileges which belong to them as citizens of the United States.

In entering upon the great work before us, we anticipate no small amount of misconception, misrepresentation, and ridicule; but we shall use every instrumentality within our power to effect our object. We shall employ agents, circulate tracts, petition the State and National legislatures, and endeavor to enlist the pulpit and the press in our behalf. We hope this Convention will be followed by a series of Conventions embracing every part of the country.

2. RESOLUTIONS

WHEREAS, The great precept of nature is conceded to be, that "man shall pursue his own true and substantial happiness." Blackstone in his Commentaries remarks, that this law of Nature being coeval with mankind, and dictated by God himself, is of course superior in obligation to any other. It is binding over all the globe, in all countries and at all times; no human laws are of any validity if contrary to this, and such of them as are valid, derive all their force, and all their validity, and all their authority, mediately and immediately, from this original; therefore,

Resolved, That such laws as conflict, in any way, with the true and substantial happiness of woman, are contrary to the great precept of nature and of no validity, for this is "superior in obligation to any other."

Resolved, That all laws which prevent woman from occupying such a station in society as her conscience shall dictate, or which place her in a position inferior to that of man, are contrary to the great precept of nature, and therefore of no force or authority.

Resolved, That woman is man's equal—was intended to be so by the Creator, and the highest good of the race demands that she should be recognized as such.

Resolved, That the women of this country ought to be enlightened in regard to the laws under which they live, that they may no longer publish their degradation by declaring themselves satisfied with their present position, nor their ignorance, by asserting that they have all the rights they want.

Resolved, That inasmuch as man, while claiming for himself intellectual superiority, does accord to woman moral superiority, it is pre-eminently his duty to encourage her to speak and teach, as she has an opportunity, in all religious assemblies.

Resolved, That the same amount of virtue, delicacy, and refinement of behavior that is required of woman in the social state, should also be required of man, and the same transgressions should be visited with equal severity on both man and woman.

Resolved, That the objection of indelicacy and impropriety, which is so often brought against woman when she addresses a public audience, comes with a very ill-grace from those who encourage, by their attendance, her appearance on the stage, in the concert. Or in feats of the circus.

Resolved, That woman has too long rested satisfied in the circumscribed limits which corrupt customs and a perverted application of the Scriptures have marked out for her, and that it is time she should move in the enlarged sphere which her great Creator has assigned her.

Resolved, That it is the duty of the women of this country to secure to themselves their sacred right to the elective franchise.

Resolved, That the equality of human rights results necessarily from the fact of the identity of the race in capabilities and responsibilities.

Resolved, therefore, That, being invested by the Creator with the same capabilities, and the same consciousness of responsibility for their exercise, it is demonstrably the right and duty of woman, equally with man, to promote every righteous cause by every righteous means; and especially in regard to the great subjects of morals and religion, it is self-evidently her right to participate with her brother in teaching them, both in private and in public, by writing and by speaking, by any instrumentalities proper to be used, and in any assemblies proper to be held; and this being a self-evident truth growing out of the divinely implanted principles of human nature, any custom or authority adverse to it, whether modern or wearing the hoary sanction of antiquity, is to be regarded as a self-evident falsehood, and at war with mankind.

Resolved, That the speedy success of our cause depends upon the zealous and untiring efforts of both men and women, for the overthrow of the monopoly of the pulpit, and for the securing to women an equal participation with men in the various trades, professions, and commerce.

FROM FREDERICK DOUGLASS'S "WHAT, TO THE SLAVE, IS THE FOURTH OF JULY?" SPEECH (1852)

* * *

This, for the purpose of this celebration, is the Fourth of July. It is the birthday of your National Independence, and of your political freedom. This, to you, is what the Passover was to the emancipated people of God. It carries your minds back to the day, and to the act of your great deliverance; and to the signs and to the wonders associated with that act and that day. This celebration also marks the beginning of another year of your national life; and reminds you that the Republic of America is now seventy-six years old. I am glad, fellow citizens, that your nation is so young. Seventy-six years, though a good old age for a man, is but a mere speck in the life of a nation. Three score years and ten is the allotted time for individual men; but nations number their years by thousands. According to this fact, you are, even now, only in the beginning of your national career, still lingering in the period of childhood. I repeat, I am glad this is so. There is hope in the thought, and hope is much needed, under the dark clouds which lower above the horizon. The eye of the reformer is met with angry flashes, portending disastrous times; but his heart may well beat lighter at the thought that America is young, and that she is still in the impressible stage of her existence. May he not hope that high lessons of wisdom, of justice and of truth, will yet give direction to her destiny? Were the nation older, the patriot's heart might be sadder and the reformer's brow heavier. Its future might be shrouded in gloom and the hope of its prophets go out in sorrow. There is consolation in the thought that America is young. Great streams are not easily turned from channels worn deep in the course of ages. They may sometimes rise in quiet and stately majesty, and inundate the land, refreshing and fertilizing the earth with their mysterious properties. They may also rise in wrath and fury, and bear away on their angry waves the accumulated wealth of years of toil and hardship. They, however, gradually flow back to the same old channel and flow on as serenely as ever. But, while the river may not be turned aside, it may dry up and leave nothing behind but the withered branch and the unsightly rock, to howl in the abyss-sweeping wind, the sad tale of departed glory. As with rivers, so with nations.

Fellow citizens, I shall not presume to dwell at length on the associations that cluster about this day. The simple story of it is, that seventy-six years ago the people of this country were British subjects. The style and title of your "sovereign people" (in which you now glory) was not then born. You were under the British Crown. Your fathers esteemed the English government as the home government, and England as the fatherland. This home government, you know, although a considerable distance from your home, did, in the exercise of its parental prerogatives, impose upon its colonial children such restraints, burdens and limitations as, in its mature judgment, it deemed wise, right and proper.

* * *

Feeling themselves harshly and unjustly treated by the home government, your fathers, like men of honesty and men of spirit, earnestly sought redress. They petitioned and remonstrated, they did so in a decorous, respectful and loyal manner. Their conduct was wholly unexceptionable. This, however, did not answer the purpose. They saw themselves treated with sovereign indifference, coldness and scorn. Yet they persevered. They were not the men to look back.

* * *

Citizens, your fathers . . . succeeded; and today you reap the fruits of their success. The freedom gained is yours; and you, therefore, may properly celebrate this anniversary. The Fourth of July is the first great fact in your nation's history—the very ringbolt in the chain of your yet undeveloped destiny.

Pride and patriotism, not less than gratitude, prompt you to celebrate and to hold it in perpetual remembrance. I have said that the Declaration of Independence is the ringbolt to the chain of your nation's destiny; so, indeed, I regard it. The principles contained in that instrument are saving principles. Stand by those principles, be true to them on all occasions, in all places, against all foes, and at whatever cost.

* * *

[The fathers of this republic] were peace men, but they preferred revolution to peaceful submission to bondage. They were quiet men; but they did not shrink from agitating against oppression. They showed forbearance, but that they knew its limits. They believed in order, but not in the order of tyranny. With them, nothing was "settled" that was not right. With them, justice, liberty and humanity were "final," not slavery and oppression. You may well cherish the memory of such men. They were great in their day and generation. Their solid manhood stands out the more as we contrast it with these degenerate times.

* * *

Fellow citizens, pardon me, allow me to ask, why am I called upon to speak here today? What have I, or those I represent, to do with your national independence? Are the great principles of political freedom and of natural justice, embodied in that Declaration of Independence, extended to us? and am I, therefore, called upon to bring our humble offering to the national altar and to confess the benefits and express devout gratitude for the blessings resulting from your independence to us?

* * *

But such is not the state of the case. I say it with a sad sense of the disparity between us. I am not included within the pale of this glorious anniversary! Your high independence only reveals the immeasurable distance between us. The blessings in which you, this day, rejoice, are not enjoyed in common. The rich inheritance of justice, liberty, prosperity and independence, bequeathed by your fathers, is shared by you, not by me. The sunlight that brought light and healing to you, has brought stripes and death to me. This Fourth of July is *yours*, not *mine. You* may rejoice, *I* must mourn.

* * *

Fellow citizens, above your national, tumultuous joy I hear the mournful wail of millions! whose chains, heavy and grievous yesterday, are today rendered more intolerable by the jubilee shouts that reach them. If I do forget, if I do not faithfully remember those bleeding children of sorrow this day, "may my right hand forget her cunning, and may my tongue cleave to the roof of my mouth!" To forget them, to pass lightly over their wrongs and to chime in with the popular theme would be treason most scandalous and shocking and would make me a reproach before God and the world. My subject, then, fellow citizens, is American slavery. I shall see this day and its popular characteristics from the slave's point of view. Standing there identified with the American bondman, making his wrongs mine, I do not hesitate to declare, with all my soul, that the character and conduct of this nation never looked blacker to me than on this Fourth of July. Whether we turn to the declarations of the past or to the professions of the present, the conduct of the nation seems equally hideous and revolting. America is false to the past, false to the present, and solemnly binds herself to be false to the future.

* * *

For the present, it is enough to affirm the equal manhood of the Negro race. It is not astonishing that, while we are plowing, planting and reaping, using all kinds of mechanical tools, erecting houses, constructing bridges, building ships, working in metals of brass, iron, copper, silver and gold; that, while we are reading, writing and ciphering, acting as clerks, merchants and secretaries, having among us lawyers, doctors, ministers, poets, authors, editors, orators and teachers; that, while we are engaged in all manner of enterprises common to other men, digging gold in California, capturing the whale in the Pacific, feeding sheep and cattle on the hillside, living, moving, acting, thinking, planning, living in families as husbands, wives and children, and, above all, confessing and worshiping the Christian's God and looking hopefully for life and immortality beyond the grave, we are called upon to prove that we are men!

Would you have me argue that man is entitled to liberty? that he is the rightful owner of his own body? You have already declared it. Must I argue the wrongfulness of slavery?

Is that a question for republicans? Is it to be settled by the rules of logic and argumentation, as a matter beset with great difficulty, involving a doubtful application of the principle of justice, hard to be understood? How should I look today, in the presence of Americans, dividing and subdividing a discourse, to show that men have a natural right to freedom, speaking of it relatively and positively, negatively and affirmatively? To do so would be to make myself ridiculous and to offer an insult to your understanding. There is not a man beneath the canopy of heaven that does not know that slavery is wrong *for him*.

* * *

What, to the American slave, is your Fourth of July? I answer: a day that reveals to him, more than all other days in the year, the gross injustice and cruelty to which he is the constant victim. To him, your celebration is a sham; your boasted liberty an unholy license; your national greatness swelling vanity; your sounds of rejoicing are empty and heartless; your denunciation of tyrants brass-fronted impudence; your shouts of liberty and equality hollow mockery; your prayers and hymns, your sermons and thanksgivings, with all your religious parade and solemnity, are to Him mere bombast, fraud, deception, impiety and hypocrisy—a thin veil to cover up crimes which would disgrace a nation of savages. There is not a nation on the earth guilty of practices more shocking and bloody than are the people of the United States at this very hour.

Go where you may, search where you will, roam through all the monarchies and despotisms of the Old World, travel through South America, search out every abuse, and when you have found the last, lay your facts by the side of the everyday practices of this nation, and you will say with me, that, for revolting barbarity and shameless hypocrisy, America reigns without a rival.

* * *

Americans! your republican politics, not less than your republican religion, are flagrantly inconsistent. You boast of your love of liberty, your superior civilization and your pure Christianity, while the whole political power of the nation (as embodied in the two great political parties) is solemnly pledged to support and perpetuate the enslavement of three millions of your countrymen. You hurl your anathemas at the crowned-headed tyrants of Russia and Austria and pride yourselves on your democratic institutions, while you yourselves consent to be the mere *tools* and *bodyguards* of the tyrants of Virginia and Carolina. You invite to your shores fugitives of oppression from abroad, honor them with banquets, greet them with ovations, cheer them, toast them, salute them, protect them, and pour out your money to them like water; but the fugitives from your own land you advertise, hunt, arrest, shoot and kill. You glory in your refinement and your universal education; yet you maintain a system as barbarous and dreadful as ever stained the character of a nation—a system begun in avarice, supported in pride, and perpetuated in cruelty. You shed tears over fallen Hungary, and make the sad story of her wrongs the theme of your poets, statesmen and orators, till your gallant sons are ready to fly to arms to vindicate her cause against the oppressor;* but, in regard to the ten thousand wrongs of the American slave, you would enforce the strictest silence and would hail him as an enemy of the nation who dares to make those wrongs the subject of public discourse! You are all on fire at the mention of liberty for France or for Ireland, but are as cold as an iceberg at the thought of liberty for the enslaved of America. You discourse eloquently on the dignity of labor; yet, you sustain a system which, in its very essence, casts a stigma upon labor. You can bare your bosom to the storm of British artillery to throw off a three-penny tax on tea, and yet wring the last hard-earned farthing from the grasp of the black laborers of your country. You profess to believe "that of one blood God made all nations of men to dwell on the face of all the earth"† and hath commanded all men, everywhere, to love one another; yet you notoriously hate (and glory in your hatred) all men whose skins are not colored like your own. You declare before the world, and are understood by the world to declare, that you "*hold these truths to be self-evident, that all men are created equal;*

*The fledgling Hungarian republic was invaded by Austria and Russia in 1849.
†Acts 17:26.

and are endowed by their Creator with certain unalienable rights; and that among these are, life, liberty and the pursuit of happiness"; and yet, you hold securely, in a bondage which, according to your own Thomas Jefferson, "*is worse than ages of that which your fathers rose in rebellion to oppose,*" *a seventh part* of the inhabitants of your country.

Fellow citizens, I will not enlarge further on your national inconsistencies. The existence of slavery in this country brands your republicanism as a sham, your humanity as a base pretense, and your Christianity as a lie. It destroys your moral power abroad; it corrupts your politicians at home. It saps the foundation of religion; it makes your name a hissing and a byword to a mocking earth. It is the antagonistic force in your government, the only thing that seriously disturbs and endangers your union. It fetters your progress; it is the enemy of improvement; the deadly foe of education; it fosters pride; it breeds insolence; it promotes vice; it shelters crime; it is a curse to the earth that supports it; and yet you cling to it as if it were the sheet anchor of all your hopes.

* * *

Allow me to say, in conclusion, notwithstanding the dark picture I have this day presented, of the state of the nation, I do not despair of this country. There are forces in operation which must inevitably work the downfall of slavery.

* * *

The Gettysburg Address (1863)

Four score and seven years ago our fathers brought forth on this continent, a new nation, conceived in Liberty, and dedicated to the proposition that all men are created equal.

Now we are engaged in a great civil war, testing whether that nation, or any nation so conceived and so dedicated, can long endure. We are met on a great battle field of that war. We have come to dedicate a portion of that field, as a final resting place for those who here gave their lives that that nation might live. It is altogether fitting and proper that we should do this.

But, in a larger sense, we can not dedicate—we can not consecrate—we can not hallow—this ground. The brave men, living and dead, who struggled here, have consecrated it, far above our poor power to add or detract. The world will little note, nor long remember what we say here, but it can never forget what they did here. It is for us the living, rather, to be dedicated here to the unfinished work which they who fought here have thus far so nobly advanced. It is rather for us to be here dedicated to the great task remaining before us—that from these honored dead we take increased devotion to that cause for which they gave the last full measure of devotion—that we here highly resolve that these dead shall not have died in vain—that this nation, under God, shall have a new birth of freedom—and that government of the people, by the people, for the people, shall not perish from the earth.

Abraham Lincoln
November 19, 1863

Abraham Lincoln's Second Inaugural Address (1865)

Fellow Countrymen:

At this second appearing to take the oath of the presidential office, there is less occasion for an extended address than there was at the first. Then a statement, somewhat in detail, of a course to be pursued, seemed fitting and proper. Now, at the expiration of four years, during which public declarations have been constantly called forth on every point and phase of the great contest which still absorbs the attention, and engrosses the energies of the nation, little that is new could be presented. The progress of our arms, upon which all else chiefly depends, is as well known to the public as to myself; and it is, I trust, reasonably satisfactory and encouraging to all. With high hope for the future, no prediction in regard to it is ventured.

On the occasion corresponding to this four years ago, all thoughts were anxiously directed to an impending civil war. All dreaded it—all sought to avert it. While the inaugural address was being delivered from this place, devoted altogether to *saving* the Union without war, insurgent agents were in the city seeking to *destroy* it without war—seeking to dissolve the Union, and divide effects, by negotiation. Both parties deprecated war; but one of them would *make* war rather than let the nation survive; and the other would *accept* war rather than let it perish. And the war came.

One eighth of the whole population were colored slaves, not distributed generally over the Union, but localized in the southern part of it. These slaves constituted a peculiar and powerful interest. All knew that this interest was, somehow, the cause of the war. To strengthen, perpetuate, and extend this interest was the object for which the insurgents would rend the Union, even by war; while the government claimed no right to do more than to restrict the territorial enlargement of it. Neither party expected for the war, the magnitude, or the duration, which it has already attained. Neither anticipated that the *cause* of the conflict might cease with, or even before, the conflict itself should cease. Each looked for an easier triumph, and a result less fundamental and astounding. Both read the same Bible, and pray to the same God; and each invokes His aid against the other. It may seem strange that any men should dare to ask a just God's assistance in wringing their bread from the sweat of other men's faces; but let us judge not that we be not judged. The prayers of both could not be answered; that of neither has been answered fully. The Almighty has His own purposes. "Woe unto the world because of offences! for it must needs be that offences come; but woe to that man by whom the offence cometh." If we shall suppose that American slavery is one of those offences which, in the providence of God, must needs come, but which, having continued through His appointed time, He now wills to remove, and that He gives to both North and South, this terrible war, as the woe due to those by whom the offence came, shall we discern therein any departure from those divine attributes which the believers in a living God always ascribe to Him? Fondly do we hope, fervently do we pray—that this mighty scourge of war may speedily pass away. Yet, if God wills that it continue until all the wealth piled by the bondsman's two hundred and fifty years of unrequited toil shall be sunk, and until every drop of blood drawn with the lash shall be paid by another drawn with the sword, as was said three thousand years ago, so still it must be said "the judgments of the Lord are true and righteous altogether."

With malice toward none; with charity for all; with firmness in the right as God gives us to see the right, let us strive on to finish the work we are in; to bind up the nation's wounds; to care for him who shall have borne the battle and for his widow and his orphan, to do all which may achieve and cherish a just and a lasting peace, among ourselves and with all nations.

THE POPULIST PLATFORM OF 1892

Assembled upon the 116th anniversary of the Declaration of Independence, the People's Party of America, in their first national convention, invoking upon their action the blessing of Almighty God, puts forth in the name and on behalf of the people of this country, the following preamble and declaration of principles:

PREAMBLE

The conditions which surround us best justify our cooperation; we meet in the midst of a nation brought to the verge of moral, political, and material ruin. Corruption dominates the ballot-box, the Legislatures, the Congress, and touches even the ermine of the bench. The people are demoralized; most of the States have been compelled to isolate the voters at the polling places to prevent universal intimidation and bribery. The newspapers are largely subsidized or muzzled, public opinion silenced, business prostrated, homes covered with mortgages, labor impoverished, and the land concentrating in the hands of the capitalists. The urban workmen are denied the right to organize for self-protection, imported pauperized labor beats down their wages, a hireling standing army, unrecognized by our laws, is established to shoot them down, and they are rapidly degenerating into European conditions. The fruits of the toil of millions are boldly stolen to build up the fortunes for a few, unprecedented in the history of mankind; and the possessors of these, in turn, despise the Republic and endanger liberty. From the same prolific womb of governmental injustice we breed the two great classes—tramps and millionaires.

The national power to create money is appropriated to enrich bondholders; a vast public debt, payable in legal tender currency, has been funded into gold-bearing bonds, thereby adding millions to the burdens of the people. Silver, which has been accepted as coin since the dawn of history, has been demonetized to add to the purchasing power of gold by decreasing the value of all forms of property as well as human labor, and the supply of currency is purposely abridged to fatten usurers, bankrupt enterprise, and enslave industry. A vast conspiracy against mankind has been organized on two continents, and it is rapidly taking possession of the world. If not met and overthrown at once it forebodes terrible social convulsions, the destruction of civilization, or the establishment of an absolute despotism.

We have witnessed for more than a quarter of a century the struggles of the two great political parties for power and plunder, while grievous wrongs have been inflicted upon the suffering people. We charge that the controlling influences dominating both these parties have permitted the existing dreadful conditions to develop without serious effort to prevent or restrain them. Neither do they now promise us any substantial reform. They have agreed together to ignore in the coming campaign every issue but one. They propose to drown the outcries of a plundered people with the uproar of a sham battle over the tariff, so that capitalists, corporations, national banks, rings, trusts, watered stock, the demonetization of silver, and the oppressions of the usurers may all be lost sight of. They propose to sacrifice our homes, lives, and children on the altar of mammon; to destroy the multitude in order to secure corruption funds from the millionaires.

Assembled on the anniversary of the birthday of the nation, and filled with the spirit of the grand general and chief who established our independence, we seek to restore the government of the Republic to the hands of "the plain people," with which class it originated. We assert our purpose to be identical with the purposes of the National Constitution, "to form a more perfect union and establish justice, insure domestic tranquility, provide for the common defense, promote the general welfare, and secure the blessings of liberty for ourselves and our posterity." We declare that this Republic can only endure as a free government while built upon the love of the whole people for each other and for the nation; that it cannot be pinned together by bayonets; that the civil war is over, and that every passion and resentment which grew out of it must die with it; and that we must be in fact, as we are in name, one united brotherhood of free men.

Our country finds itself confronted by conditions for which there is no precedent in the history of the world; our annual agricultural productions amount to billions of dollars in value, which must, within a few weeks or months, be exchanged for billions of dollars of commodities consumed in their production; the existing currency supply is wholly inadequate to make this exchange; the results are falling prices, the formation of combines and rings, the impoverishment of the producing class. We pledge ourselves, if given power, we will labor to correct these evils by wise and reasonable legislation, in accordance with the terms of our platform. We believe that the power of government—in other words, of the people—should be expanded (as in the case of the postal service) as rapidly and as far as the good sense of an intelligent people and the teaching of experience shall justify, to the end that oppression, injustice, and poverty shall eventually cease in the land.

While our sympathies as a party of reform are naturally upon the side of every proposition which will tend to make men intelligent, virtuous, and temperate, we nevertheless regard these questions—important as they are—as secondary to the great issues now pressing for solution, and upon which not only our individual prosperity but the very existence of free institutions depend; and we ask all men to first help us to determine whether we are to have a republic to administer before we differ as to the conditions upon which it is to be administered, believing that the forces of reform this day organized will never cease to move forward until every wrong is remedied, and equal rights and equal privileges securely established for all the men and women of this country.

PLATFORM

We declare, therefore—

First.—That the union of the labor forces of the United States this day consummated shall be permanent and perpetual; may its spirit enter into all hearts for the salvation of the Republic and the uplifting of mankind!

Second.—Wealth belongs to him who creates it, and every dollar taken from industry without an equivalent is robbery. "If any will not work, neither shall he eat." The interests of rural and civic labor are the same; their enemies are identical.

Third.—We believe that the time has come when the railroad corporations will either own the people or the people must own the railroads; and, should the government enter upon the work of owning and managing all railroads, we should favor an amendment to the Constitution by which all persons engaged in the government service shall be placed under a civil-service regulation of the most rigid character, so as to prevent the increase of the power of the national administration by the use of such additional government employees.

FINANCE.—We demand a national currency, safe, sound, and flexible, issued by the general government only, a full legal tender for all debts, public and private, and that without the use of banking corporations, a just, equitable, and efficient means of distribution direct to the people, at a tax not to exceed two per cent per annum, to be provided as set forth in the sub-treasury plan of the Farmers' Alliance, or a better system; also by payments in discharge of its obligations for public improvements.

1. We demand free and unlimited coinage of silver and gold at the present legal ratio of 16 to 1.

2. We demand that the amount of circulating medium be speedily increased to not less than $50 per capita.

3. We demand a graduated income tax.

4. We believe that the money of the country should be kept as much as possible in the hands of the people, and hence we demand that all State and national revenues shall be limited to the necessary expenses of the government, economically and honestly administered.

5. We demand that postal savings banks be established by the government for the safe deposit of the earnings of the people and to facilitate exchange.

TRANSPORTATION.—Transportation being a means of exchange and a public necessity, the government should own and operate the railroads in the interest of the people. The telegraph and telephone, like the post-office system, being a necessity for the transmission of news, should be owned and operated by the government in the interest of the people.

LAND.—The land, including all the natural sources of wealth, is the heritage of the people, and should not be monopolized for speculative purposes, and alien ownership of land should be prohibited. All land now held by railroads and other corporations in excess of their actual needs, and all lands now owned by aliens should be reclaimed by the government and held for actual settlers only.

EXPRESSION OF SENTIMENTS

Your committee on Platform and Resolutions beg leave unanimously to report the following:

Whereas, Other questions have been presented for our consideration, we hereby submit the following, not as a part of the Platform of the People's Party, but as resolutions expressive of the sentiment of this Convention:

1. *Resolved*, That we demand a free ballot and a fair count in all elections, and pledge ourselves to secure it to every legal voter without federal intervention, through the adoption by the States of the unperverted Australian or secret ballot system.

2. *Resolved*, That the revenue derived from a graduated income tax should be applied to the reduction of the burden of taxation now levied upon the domestic industries of this country.

3. *Resolved*, That we pledge our support to fair and liberal pensions to ex-Union soldiers and sailors.

4. *Resolved*, That we condemn the fallacy of protecting American labor under the present system, which opens our ports to the pauper and criminal classes of the world, and crowds out our wage-earners; and we denounce the present ineffective laws against contract labor, and demand the further restriction of undesirable emigration.

5. *Resolved*, that we cordially sympathize with the efforts of organized workingmen to shorten the hours of labor, and demand a rigid enforcement of the existing eight-hour law on Government work, and ask that a penalty clause be added to the said law.

6. *Resolved*, That we regard the maintenance of a large standing army of mercenaries, known as the Pinkerton system, as a menace to our liberties, and we demand its abolition; and we condemn the recent invasion of the Territory of Wyoming by the hired assassins of plutocracy, assisted by federal officers.

7. *Resolved*, That we commend to the favorable consideration of the people and the reform press the legislative system known as the initiative and referendum.

8. *Resolved,* That we favor a constitutional provision limiting the office of President and Vice-President to one term, and providing for the election of Senators of the United States by a direct vote of the people.

9. *Resolved,* That we oppose any subsidy or national aid to any private corporation for any purpose.

10. *Resolved,* That this convention sympathizes with the Knights of Labor and their righteous contest with the tyrannical combine of clothing manufacturers of Rochester, and declare it to be the duty of all who hate tyranny and oppression to refuse to purchase the goods made by the said manufacturers, or to patronize any merchants who sell such goods.

I am certain that my fellow Americans expect that on my induction into the Presidency I will address them with a candor and a decision which the present situation of our Nation impels. This is preeminently the time to speak the truth, the whole truth, frankly and boldly. Nor need we shrink from honestly facing conditions in our country today. This great Nation will endure as it has endured, will revive and will prosper. So, first of all, let me assert my firm belief that the only thing we have to fear is fear itself—nameless, unreasoning, unjustified terror which paralyzes needed efforts to convert retreat into advance. In every dark hour of our national life a leadership of frankness and vigor has met with that understanding and support of the people themselves which is essential to victory. I am convinced that you will again give that support to leadership in these critical days.

In such a spirit on my part and on yours we face our common difficulties. They concern, thank God, only material things. Values have shrunken to fantastic levels; taxes have risen; our ability to pay has fallen; government of all kinds is faced by serious curtailment of income; the means of exchange are frozen in the currents of trade; the withered leaves of industrial enterprise lie on every side; farmers find no markets for their produce; the savings of many years in thousands of families are gone.

More important, a host of unemployed citizens face the grim problem of existence, and an equally great number toil with little return. Only a foolish optimist can deny the dark realities of the moment.

Yet our distress comes from no failure of substance. We are stricken by no plague of locusts. Compared with the perils which our forefathers conquered because they believed and were not afraid, we have still much to be thankful for. Nature still offers her bounty and human efforts have multiplied it. Plenty is at our doorstep, but a generous use of it languishes in the very sight of the supply. Primarily this is because the rulers of the exchange of mankind's goods have failed, through their own stubbornness and their own incompetence, have admitted their failure, and abdicated. Practices of the unscrupulous money changers stand indicted in the court of public opinion, rejected by the hearts and minds of men.

True they have tried, but their efforts have been cast in the pattern of an outworn tradition. Faced by failure of credit they have proposed only the lending of more money. Stripped of the lure of profit by which to induce our people to follow their false leadership, they have resorted to exhortations, pleading tearfully for restored confidence. They know only the rules of a generation of self-seekers. They have no vision, and when there is no vision the people perish.

The money changers have fled from their high seats in the temple of our civilization. We may now restore that temple to the ancient truths. The measure of the restoration lies in the extent to which we apply social values more noble than mere monetary profit.

Happiness lies not in the mere possession of money; it lies in the joy of achievement, in the thrill of creative effort. The joy and moral stimulation of work no longer must be forgotten in the mad chase of evanescent profits. These dark days will be worth all they cost us if they teach us that our true destiny is not to be ministered unto but to minister to ourselves and to our fellow men.

Recognition of the falsity of material wealth as the standard of success goes hand in hand with the abandonment of the false belief that public office and high political position are to be valued only by the standards of pride of place and personal profit; and there must be an end to a conduct in banking and in business which too often has given to a sacred trust the likeness of callous and selfish wrongdoing. Small wonder that confidence languishes, for it thrives only on honesty, on honor, on the sacredness of obligations, on faithful protection, on unselfish performance; without them it cannot live.

Restoration calls, however, not for changes in ethics alone. This Nation asks for action, and action now.

Our greatest primary task is to put people to work. This is no unsolvable problem if we face it wisely and courageously. It can be accomplished in part by direct recruiting by the Government itself, treating the task as we would treat the emergency of a war, but at the same time, through this employment, accomplishing greatly needed projects to stimulate and reorganize the use of our natural resources.

Hand in hand with this we must frankly recognize the overbalance of population in our industrial centers and, by engaging on a national scale in a redistribution, endeavor to provide a better use of the land for those best fitted for the land. The task can be helped by definite efforts to raise the values of agricultural products and with this the power to purchase the output of our cities. It can be helped by preventing realistically the tragedy of the growing loss through foreclosure of our small homes and our farms. It can be helped by insistence that the Federal, State, and local governments act forthwith on the demand that their cost be drastically reduced. It can be helped by the unifying of relief activities which today are often scattered, uneconomical, and unequal. It can be helped by national planning for and supervision of all forms of transportation and of communications and other utilities which have a definitely public character. There are many ways in which it can be helped, but it can never be helped merely by talking about it. We must act and act quickly.

Finally, in our progress toward a resumption of work we require two safeguards against a return of the evils of the old order; there must be a strict supervision of all banking and credits and investments; there must be an end to speculation with other people's money, and there must be provision for an adequate but sound currency.

There are the lines of attack. I shall presently urge upon a new Congress, in special session, detailed measures for their fulfillment, and I shall seek the immediate assistance of the several States.

Through this program of action we address ourselves to putting our own national house in order and making income balance outgo. Our international trade relations, though vastly important, are in point of time and necessity secondary to the establishment of a sound national economy. I favor as a practical policy the putting of first things first. I shall spare no effort to restore world trade by international economic readjustment, but the emergency at home cannot wait on that accomplishment.

The basic thought that guides these specific means of national recovery is not narrowly nationalistic. It is the insistence, as a first consideration, upon the interdependence of the various elements in all parts of the United States—a recognition of the old and permanently important manifestation of the American spirit of the pioneer. It is the way to recovery. It is the immediate way. It is the strongest assurance that the recovery will endure.

In the field of world policy I would dedicate this Nation to the policy of the good neighbor—the neighbor who resolutely respects himself and, because he does so, respects the rights of others—the neighbor who respects his obligations and respects the sanctity of his agreements in and with a world of neighbors.

If I read the temper of our people correctly, we now realize as we have never realized before our interdependence on each other; that we cannot merely take but we must give as well; that if we are to go forward, we must move as a trained and loyal army willing to sacrifice for the good of a common discipline, because without such discipline no progress is made, no leadership becomes effective. We are, I know, ready and willing to submit our lives and property to such discipline, because it makes possible a leadership which aims at a larger good. This I propose to offer, pledging that the larger purposes will bind upon us all as a sacred obligation with a unity of duty hitherto evoked only in time of armed strife.

With this pledge taken, I assume unhesitatingly the leadership of this great army of our people dedicated to a disciplined attack upon our common problems.

Action in this image and to this end is feasible under the form of government which we have inherited from our ancestors. Our Constitution is so simple and practical that it is possible always to meet extraordinary needs by changes in emphasis and arrangement without loss of essential form. That is why our constitutional system has proved itself the most superbly enduring political mechanism the modern world has produced. It has met every stress of vast expansion of territory, of foreign wars, of bitter internal strife, of world relations.

It is to be hoped that the normal balance of executive and legislative authority may be wholly adequate to meet the unprecedented task before us. But it may be that an unprecedented demand and need for undelayed action may call for temporary departure from that normal balance of public procedure.

I am prepared under my constitutional duty to recommend the measures that a stricken nation in the midst of a stricken world may require. These measures, or such other measures as the Congress may build out of its experience and wisdom, I shall seek, within my constitutional authority, to bring to speedy adoption.

But in the event that the Congress shall fail to take one of these two courses, and in the event that the national emergency is still critical, I shall not evade the clear course of duty that will then confront me. I shall ask the Congress for the one remaining instrument to meet the crisis—broad Executive power to wage a war against the emergency, as great as the power that would be given to me if we were in fact invaded by a foreign foe.

For the trust reposed in me I will return the courage and the devotion that befit the time. I can do no less.

We face the arduous days that lie before us in the warm courage of national unity; with the clear consciousness of seeking old and precious moral values; with the clean satisfaction that comes from the stern performance of duty by old and young alike. We aim at the assurance of a rounded and permanent national life.

We do not distrust the future of essential democracy. The people of the United States have not failed. In their need they have registered a mandate that they want direct, vigorous action. They have asked for discipline and direction under leadership. They have made me the present instrument of their wishes. In the spirit of the gift I take it.

In this dedication of a Nation we humbly ask the blessing of God. May He protect each and every one of us. May He guide me in the days to come.

Martin Luther King Jr.'s, "I Have a Dream" Speech (1963)

I am happy to join with you today in what will go down in history as the greatest demonstration for freedom in the history of our nation.

Five score years ago, a great American, in whose symbolic shadow we stand today, signed the Emancipation Proclamation. This momentous decree came as a great beacon light of hope to millions of Negro slaves who had been seared in the flames of withering injustice. It came as a joyous daybreak to end the long night of captivity.

But one hundred years later, the Negro still is not free. One hundred years later, the life of the Negro is still sadly crippled by the manacles of segregation and the chains of discrimination. One hundred years later, the Negro is still languishing in the corners of American society and finds himself an exile in his own land. And so we've come here today to dramatize a shameful condition.

In a sense we have come to our nation's capital to cash a check. When the architects of our republic wrote the magnificent words of the Constitution and the Declaration of Independence, they were signing a promissory note to which every American was to fall heir. This note was a promise that all men, yes black men as well as white men, would be guaranteed the "unalienable Rights of Life, Liberty, and the pursuit of Happiness." It is obvious today that America has defaulted on this promissory note insofar as her citizens of color are concerned. Instead of honoring this sacred obligation, America has given the Negro people a bad check,—a check which has come back marked "insufficient funds."

But we refuse to believe that the bank of justice is bankrupt. We refuse to believe that there are insufficient funds in the great vaults of opportunity of this nation. And so we've come to cash this check,—a check that will give us upon demand the riches of freedom and the security of justice.

We have also come to this hallowed spot to remind America of the fierce urgency of now. This is no time to engage in the luxury of cooling off or to take the tranquilizing drug of gradualism. Now is the time to make real the promises of democracy. Now is the time to rise from the dark and desolate valley of segregation to the sunlit path of racial justice. Now is the time to lift our nation from the quicksands of racial injustice to the solid rock of brotherhood. Now is the time to make justice a reality for all of God's children.

It would be fatal for the nation to overlook the urgency of the moment. This sweltering summer of the Negro's legitimate discontent will not pass until there is an invigorating autumn of freedom and equality. Nineteen sixty-three is not an end, but a beginning. And those who hope that the Negro needed to blow off steam and will now be content will have a rude awakening if the nation returns to business as usual. There will be neither rest nor tranquility in America until the Negro is granted his citizenship rights. The whirlwinds of revolt will continue to shake the foundation of our nation until the bright day of justice emerges.

But there is something that I must say to my people, who stand on the warm threshold which leads into the palace of justice: In the process of gaining our rightful place, we must not be guilty of wrongful deeds. Let us not seek to satisfy our thirst for freedom by drinking from the cup of bitterness and hatred. We must forever conduct our struggle on the high plane of dignity and discipline. We must not allow our creative protest to degenerate into physical violence. Again and again, we must rise to the majestic heights of meeting physical force with soul force. The marvelous new militancy which has engulfed the Negro community must not lead us to a distrust of all white people, for many of our white brothers, as evidenced by their presence here today, have come to realize that their destiny is tied up with our destiny. And they have come to realize that their freedom is inextricably bound to our freedom. We cannot walk alone.

And as we walk, we must make the pledge that we shall march ahead. We cannot turn back. There are those who are asking the devotees of civil rights, "When will you be satisfied?"

We can never be satisfied as long as the Negro is the victim of unspeakable horrors of police brutality. We can never be satisfied as long as our bodies, heavy with the fatigue of travel, cannot gain lodging in the motels of the highways and the hotels of the cities. We cannot be satisfied as long as the Negro's basic mobility is from a smaller ghetto to a larger one. We can never be satisfied as long as our children are stripped of their selfhood and robbed of their dignity by signs stating "for whites only." We cannot be satisfied as long as a Negro in Mississippi cannot vote and a Negro in New York believes he has nothing for which to vote. No, no, we are not satisfied, and we will not be satisfied until, "justice rolls down like waters and righteousness like a mighty stream."

I am not unmindful that some of you have come here out of great trials and tribulations. Some of you have come fresh from narrow jail cells. Some of you have come from areas where your quest for freedom left you battered by the storms of persecution and staggered by the winds of police brutality. You have been the veterans of creative suffering. Continue to work with the faith that unearned suffering is redemptive.

Go back to Mississippi, go back to Alabama, go back to South Carolina, go back to Georgia, go back to Louisiana, go back to the slums and ghettos of our northern cities, knowing that somehow this situation can and will be changed. Let us not wallow in the valley of despair.

I say to you today, my friends, so even though we face the difficulties of today and tomorrow, I still have a dream. It is a dream deeply rooted in the American dream.

I have a dream that one day this nation will rise up and live out the true meaning of its creed: "We hold these truths to be self-evident, that all men are created equal."

I have a dream that one day on the red hills of Georgia, the sons of former slaves and the sons of former slave owners will be able to sit down together at the table of brotherhood.

I have a dream that one day even the state of Mississippi, a state sweltering with the heat of injustice, sweltering with the heat of oppression, will be transformed into an oasis of freedom and justice.

I have a dream that my four little children will one day live in a nation where they will not be judged by the color of their skin but by the content of their character. I have a dream today.

I have a dream that one day down in Alabama, with its vicious racists, with its governor having his lips dripping with the words of "interposition" and "nullification," one day right there in Alabama little black boys and black girls will be able to join hands with little white boys and white girls as sisters and brothers. I have a dream today.

I have a dream that one day "every valley shall be exalted, and every hill and mountain shall be made low; the rough places will be made plain, and the crooked places will be made straight; and the glory of the Lord shall be revealed, and all flesh shall see it together."

This is our hope. This is the faith that I go back to the South with. With this faith we will be able to hew out of the mountain of despair a stone of hope. With this faith will be able to transform the jangling discords of our nation into a beautiful symphony of brotherhood. With this faith we will be able to work together, to pray together, to struggle together, to go to jail together, to stand up for freedom together, knowing that we will be free one day. This will be the day, this will be the day when all of God's children will be able to sing with a new meaning:

> *My country, 'tis of thee, sweet land of liberty, of thee I sing.*
> *Land where my fathers died, land of the pilgrim's pride,*
> *From every mountainside, let freedom ring.*

And if America is to be a great nation this must become true.

And so let freedom ring from the prodigious hilltops of New Hampshire.

Let freedom ring from the mighty mountains of New York.

Let freedom ring from the heightening Alleghenies of Pennsylvania.

Let freedom ring from the snowcapped Rockies of Colorado.

Let freedom ring from the curvaceous peaks of California.

But not only that: let freedom ring from Stone Mountain of Georgia.

Let freedom ring from Lookout Mountain of Tennessee.

Let freedom ring from every hill and molehill of Mississippi. From every mountainside, let freedom ring.

And when this happens, when we allow freedom to ring, when we let it ring from every village and every hamlet, from every state and every city, we will be able to speed up that day when all of God's children, black men and white men, Jews and Gentiles, Protestants and Catholics, will be able to join hands and sing in the words of the old Negro spiritual:

> *Free at last! Free at last!*
> *Thank God Almighty, we are free at last!*

Ronald Reagan's First Inaugural Address (1981)

**WEST FRONT OF THE U.S. CAPITOL
JANUARY 20, 1981**

Senator Hatfield, Mr. Chief Justice, Mr. President, Vice President Bush, Vice President Mondale, Senator Baker, Speaker O'Neill, Reverend Moomaw, and my fellow citizens.

To a few of us here today this is a solemn and most momentous occasion, and yet in the history of our nation it is a commonplace occurrence. The orderly transfer of authority as called for in the Constitution routinely takes place, as it has for almost two centuries, and few of us stop to think how unique we really are. In the eyes of many in the world, this every-four-year ceremony we accept as normal is nothing less than a miracle.

Mr. President, I want our fellow citizens to know how much you did to carry on this tradition. By your gracious cooperation in the transition process, you have shown a watching world that we are a united people pledged to maintaining a political system which guarantees individual liberty to a greater degree than any other, and I thank you and your people for all your help in maintaining the continuity which is the bulwark of our republic. The business of our nation goes forward. These United States are confronted with an economic affliction of great proportions. We suffer from the longest and one of the worst sustained inflations in our national history. It distorts our economic decisions, penalizes thrift, and crushes the struggling young and the fixed-income elderly alike. It threatens to shatter the lives of millions of our people.

Idle industries have cast workers into unemployment, human misery, and personal indignity. Those who do work are denied a fair return for their labor by a tax system which penalizes successful achievement and keeps us from maintaining full productivity. But great as our tax burden is, it has not kept pace with public spending. For decades we have piled deficit upon deficit, mortgaging our future and our children's future for the temporary convenience of the present. To continue this long trend is to guarantee tremendous social, cultural, political, and economic upheavals.

You and I, as individuals, can, by borrowing, live beyond our means, but for only a limited period of time. Why, then, should we think that collectively, as a nation, we're not bound by that same limitation? We must act today in order to preserve tomorrow. And let there be no misunderstanding: We are going to begin to act, beginning today. The economic ills we suffer have come upon us over several decades. They will not go away in days, weeks, or months, but they will go away. They will go away because we as Americans have the capacity now, as we've had in the past, to do whatever needs to be done to preserve this last and greatest bastion of freedom.

In this present crisis, government is not the solution to our problem; government is the problem. From time to time we've been tempted to believe that society has become too complex to be managed by self-rule, that government by an elite group is superior to government for, by, and of the people. Well, if no one among us is capable of governing himself, then who among us has the capacity to govern someone else? All of us together, in and out of government, must bear the burden. The solutions we seek must be equitable, with no one group singled out to pay a higher price.

We hear much of special interest groups. Well, our concern must be for a special interest group that has been too long neglected. It knows no sectional boundaries or ethnic and racial divisions, and it crosses political party lines. It is made up of men and women who raise our food, patrol our streets, man our mines and factories, teach our children, keep our homes, and heal us when we're sick—professionals, industrialists, shopkeepers, clerks, cabbies, and truck drivers. They are, in short, "we the people," this breed called Americans.

Well, this administration's objective will be a healthy, vigorous, growing economy that provides equal opportunities for all Americans, with no barriers born of bigotry or discrimination. Putting America back to work means putting all Americans back to work. Ending inflation means freeing all Americans from the terror of runaway living costs. All must share in the productive work of this "new beginning," and all must share in the bounty of a revived economy. With the idealism and fair play which are the core of our system and our strength, we can have a strong and prosperous America, at peace with itself and the world.

So, as we begin, let us take inventory. We are a nation that has a government—not the other way around. And this makes us special among the nations of the Earth. Our government has no power except that granted it by the people. It is time to check and reverse the growth of government, which shows signs of having grown beyond the consent of the governed.

It is my intention to curb the size and influence of the federal establishment and to demand recognition of the distinction between the powers granted to the federal government and those reserved to the states or to the people. All of us need to be reminded that the federal government did not create the states; the states created the federal government.

Now, so there will be no misunderstanding, it's not my intention to do away with government. It is rather to make it work—work with us, not over us; to stand by our side, not ride on our back. Government can and must provide opportunity, not smother it; foster productivity, not stifle it.

If we look to the answer as to why for so many years we achieved so much, prospered as no other people on earth, it was because here in this land we unleashed the energy and individual genius of man to a greater extent than has ever been done before. Freedom and the dignity of the individual have been more available and assured here than in any other place on earth. The price for this freedom at times has been high, but we have never been unwilling to pay the price.

It is no coincidence that our present troubles parallel and are proportionate to the intervention and intrusion in our lives that result from unnecessary and excessive growth of government. It is time for us to realize that we're too great a nation to limit ourselves to small dreams. We're not, as some would have us believe, doomed to an inevitable decline. I do not believe in a fate that will fall on us no matter what we do. I do believe in a fate that will fall on us if we do nothing. So, with all the creative energy at our command, let us begin an era of national renewal. Let us renew our determination, our courage, and our strength. And let us renew our faith and our hope.

We have every right to dream heroic dreams. Those who say that we're in a time when there are no heroes, they just don't know where to look. You can see heroes every day going in and out of factory gates. Others, a handful in number, produce enough food to feed all of us and then the world beyond. You meet heroes across a counter, and they're on both sides of that counter. There are entrepreneurs with faith in themselves and faith in an idea who create new jobs, new wealth and opportunity. They're individuals and families whose taxes support the government and whose voluntary gifts support church, charity, culture, art, and education. Their patri-

otism is quiet, but deep. Their values sustain our national life.

Now, I have used the words "they" and "their" in speaking of these heroes. I could say "you" and "your," because I'm addressing the heroes of whom I speak—you, the citizens of this blessed land. Your dreams, your hopes, your goals are going to be the dreams, the hopes, and the goals of this administration, so help me God.

We shall reflect the compassion that is so much a part of your makeup. How can we love our country and not love our countrymen; and loving them, reach out a hand when they fall, heal them when they're sick, and provide opportunity to make them self-sufficient so they will be equal in fact and not just in theory?

Can we solve the problems confronting us? Well, the answer is an unequivocal and emphatic "yes." To paraphrase Winston Churchill, I did not take the oath I've just taken with the intention of presiding over the dissolution of the world's strongest economy.

In the days ahead I will propose removing the roadblocks that have slowed our economy and reduced productivity. Steps will be taken aimed at restoring the balance between the various levels of government. Progress may be slow, measured in inches and feet, not miles, but we will progress. It is time to reawaken this industrial giant, to get government back within its means, and to lighten our punitive tax burden. And these will be our first priorities, and on these principles there will be no compromise.

On the eve of our struggle for independence a man who might have been one of the greatest among the Founding Fathers, Dr. Joseph Warren, president of the Massachusetts Congress, said to his fellow Americans, "Our country is in danger, but not to be despaired of . . . On you depend the fortunes of America. You are to decide the important questions upon which rests the happiness and the liberty of millions yet unborn. Act worthy of yourselves." Well, I believe we, the Americans of today, are ready to act worthy of ourselves, ready to do what must be done to ensure happiness and liberty for ourselves, our children, and our children's children. And as we renew ourselves here in our own land, we will be seen as having greater strength throughout the world. We will again be the exemplar of freedom and a beacon of hope for those who do not now have freedom.

To those neighbors and allies who share our freedom, we will strengthen our historic ties and assure them of our support and firm commitment. We will match loyalty with loyalty. We will strive for mutually beneficial relations. We will not use our friendship to impose on their sovereignty, for our own sovereignty is not for sale. As for the enemies of freedom, those who are potential adversaries, they will be reminded that peace is the highest aspiration of the American people. We will negotiate for it, sacrifice for it; we will not surrender for it, now or ever.

Our forbearance should never be misunderstood. Our reluctance for conflict should not be misjudged as a failure of will. When action is required to preserve our national security, we will act. We will maintain sufficient strength to prevail if need be, knowing that if we do so we have the best chance of never having to use that strength. Above all, we must realize that no arsenal or no weapon in the arsenals of the world is so formidable as the will and moral courage of free men and women. It is a weapon our adversaries in today's world do not have. It is a weapon that we as Americans do have. Let that be understood by those who practice terrorism and prey upon their neighbors. I'm told that tens of thousands of prayer meetings are being held on this day, and for that I'm deeply grateful. We are a nation under God, and I believe God intended for us to be free. It would be fitting and good, I think, if on each Inaugural Day in future years it should be declared a day of prayer.

This is the first time in our history that this ceremony has been held, as you've been told, on the West Front of the Capitol. Standing here, one faces a magnificent vista, opening up on the city's special beauty and history. At the end of this open mall are those shrines to the giants on whose shoulders we stand.

Directly in front of me, the monument to a monumental man, George Washington, father of our country. A man of humility who came to greatness reluctantly. He led Americans out of revolutionary victory into infant nationhood. Off to one side, the stately memorial to Thomas Jefferson. The Declaration of Independence flames with his eloquence. And then, beyond the Reflecting Pool, the dignified columns of the Lincoln Memorial. Whoever would understand in his heart the meaning of America will find it in the life of Abraham Lincoln.

Beyond those monuments to heroism is the Potomac River, and on the far shore the sloping hills of Arlington National Cemetery, with its row upon row of simple white markers bearing crosses of Stars of David. They add up to only a tiny fraction of the price that has been paid for our freedom. Each one of those markers is a monument to the kind of hero I spoke of earlier. Their lives ended in places called Belleau Wood, the Argonne, Omaha Beach, Salerno, and halfway around the world on Guadalcanal, Tarawa, Pork Chop Hill, the Chosin Reservoir, and in a hundred rice paddies and jungles of a place called Vietnam.

Under one such marker lies a young man, Martin Treptow, who left his job in a small town barbershop in 1917 to go to France with the famed Rainbow Division. There, on the western front, he was killed trying to carry a message between battalions under heavy artillery fire.

We're told that on his body was found a diary. On the flyleaf under the heading "My Pledge," he had written these words: "America must win this war. Therefore I will work, I will save, I will sacrifice, I will endure, I will fight cheerfully and do my utmost, as if the issue of the whole struggle depended on me alone."

The crisis we are facing today does not require of us the kind of sacrifice that Martin Treptow and so many thousands of others were called upon to make. It does require, however, our best effort and our willingness to believe in ourselves and to believe in our capacity to perform great deeds, to believe that together with God's help we can and will resolve the problems which now confront us.

And after all, why shouldn't we believe that? We are Americans.

God bless you, and thank you.

PRESIDENTIAL ELECTIONS

Year	Number of States	Candidates	Parties	Popular Vote	% of Popular Vote	Electoral Vote	% Voter Participation
1789	11	**GEORGE WASHINGTON** John Adams Other candidates	NO PARTY DESIGNATIONS			69 34 35	
1792	15	**GEORGE WASHINGTON** John Adams George Clinton Other candidates	NO PARTY DESIGNATIONS			132 77 50 5	
1796	16	**JOHN ADAMS** Thomas Jefferson Thomas Pinckney Aaron Burr Other candidates	FEDERALIST Republican Federalist Republican			71 68 59 30 48	
1800	16	**THOMAS JEFFERSON** Aaron Burr John Adams Charles C. Pinckney John Jay	REPUBLICAN Republican Federalist Federalist Federalist			73 73 65 64 1	
1804	17	**THOMAS JEFFERSON** Charles C. Pinckney	REPUBLICAN Federalist			162 14	
1808	17	**JAMES MADISON** Charles C. Pinckney George Clinton	REPUBLICAN Federalist Republican			122 47 6	
1812	18	**JAMES MADISON** DeWitt Clinton	REPUBLICAN Federalist			128 89	

Year	Number of States	Candidates	Parties	Popular Vote	% of Popular Vote	Electoral Vote	% Voter Participation
1816	19	**JAMES MONROE**	REPUBLICAN			183	
		Rufus King	Federalist			34	
1820	24	**JAMES MONROE**	REPUBLICAN			231	
		John Quincy Adams	Independent			1	
1824	24	**JOHN QUINCY ADAMS**	NO PARTY	108,740	31.0	84	26.9
		Andrew Jackson	DESIGNATIONS	153,544	43.0	99	
		William H. Crawford		46,618	13.0	41	
		Henry Clay		47,136	13.0	37	
1828	24	**ANDREW JACKSON**	DEMOCRAT	647,286	56.0	178	57.6
		John Quincy Adams	National Republican	508,064	44.0	83	
1832	24	**ANDREW JACKSON**	DEMOCRAT	687,502	54.5	219	55.4
		Henry Clay	National Republican	530,189	37.5	49	
		William Wirt	Anti-Masonic	101,051	8.0	7	
		John Floyd	Democrat			11	
1836	26	**MARTIN VAN BUREN**	DEMOCRAT	765,483	51.0	170	57.8
		William H. Harrison	Whig			73	
		Hugh L. White	Whig	739,795	49.0	26	
		Daniel Webster	Whig			14	
		William P. Mangum	Whig			11	
1840	26	**WILLIAM H. HARRISON**	WHIG	1,274,624	53.0	234	80.2
		Martin Van Buren	Democrat	1,127,781	47.0	60	

Year	Number of States	Candidates	Parties	Popular Vote	% of Popular Vote	Electoral Vote	% Voter Participation
1844	26	**JAMES K. POLK** Henry Clay James G. Birney	DEMOCRAT Whig Liberty	1,338,464 1,300,097 62,300	50.0 48.0 2.0	170 105	78.9
1848	30	**ZACHARY TAYLOR** Lewis Cass Martin Van Buren	WHIG Democrat Free Soil	1,360,967 1,222,342 291,263	47.5 42.5 10.0	163 127	72.7
1852	31	**FRANKLIN PIERCE** Winfield Scott John P. Hale	DEMOCRAT Whig Free Soil	1,601,117 1,385,453 155,825	51.0 44.0 5.0	254 42	69.6
1856	31	**JAMES BUCHANAN** John C. Frémont Millard Fillmore	DEMOCRAT Republican American	1,832,955 1,339,932 871,731	45.0 33.0 22.0	174 114 8	78.9
1860	33	**ABRAHAM LINCOLN** Stephen A. Douglas John C. Breckinridge John Bell	REPUBLICAN Northern Democrat Southern Democrat Constitutional Union	1,865,593 1,382,713 848,356 592,906	40.0 29.0 18.0 13.0	180 12 72 39	81.2
1864	36	**ABRAHAM LINCOLN** George B. McClellan	REPUBLICAN Democrat	2,206,938 1,803,787	55.0 45.0	212 21	73.8
1868	37	**ULYSSES S. GRANT** Horatio Seymour	REPUBLICAN Democrat	3,013,421 2,706,829	53.0 47.0	214 80	78.1

Year	Number of States	Candidates	Parties	Popular Vote	% of Popular Vote	Electoral Vote	% Voter Participation
1872	37	**ULYSSES S. GRANT**	REPUBLICAN	3,596,745	55.6	286	71.3
		Horace Greeley	Democrat	2,843,446	43.9	66	
1876	38	**RUTHERFORD B. HAYES**	REPUBLICAN	4,036,572	48.0	185	81.8
		Samuel J. Tilden	Democrat	4,284,020	51.0	184	
1880	38	**JAMES A. GARFIELD**	REPUBLICAN	4,453,295	48.4	214	79.4
		Winfield S. Hancock	Democrat	4,414,082	48.3	155	
		James B. Weaver	Greenback-Labor	308,578	3.5		
1884	38	**GROVER CLEVELAND**	DEMOCRAT	4,879,507	48.5	219	77.5
		James G. Blaine	Republican	4,850,293	48.2	182	
		Benjamin F. Butler	Greenback-Labor	175,370	1.8		
		John P. St. John	Prohibition	150,369	1.5		
1888	38	**BENJAMIN HARRISON**	REPUBLICAN	5,447,129	47.9	233	79.3
		Grover Cleveland	Democrat	5,537,857	48.6	168	
		Clinton B. Fisk	Prohibition	249,506	2.2		
		Anson J. Streeter	Union Labor	146,935	1.3		
1892	44	**GROVER CLEVELAND**	DEMOCRAT	5,555,426	46.1	277	74.7
		Benjamin Harrison	Republican	5,182,690	43.0	145	
		James B. Weaver	People's	1,029,846	8.5	22	
		John Bidwell	Prohibition	264,133	2.2		
1896	45	**WILLIAM McKINLEY**	REPUBLICAN	7,102,246	51.0	271	79.3
		William J. Bryan	Democrat	6,492,559	47.0	176	

Year	Number of States	Candidates	Parties	Popular Vote	% of Popular Vote	Electoral Vote	% Voter Participation
1900	45	WILLIAM McKINLEY	REPUBLICAN	7,218,491	52.0	292	73.2
		William J. Bryan	Democrat; Populist	6,356,734	46.0	155	
		John C. Wooley	Prohibition	208,914	1.5		
1904	45	THEODORE ROOSEVELT	REPUBLICAN	7,628,461	56.4	336	65.2
		Alton B. Parker	Democrat	5,084,223	37.6	140	
		Eugene V. Debs	Socialist	402,283	3.0		
		Silas C. Swallow	Prohibition	258,536	1.9		
1908	46	WILLIAM H. TAFT	REPUBLICAN	7,675,320	52.0	321	65.4
		William J. Bryan	Democrat	6,412,294	43.4	162	
		Eugene V. Debs	Socialist	420,793	2.8		
		Eugene W. Chafin	Prohibition	253,840	1.7		
1912	48	WOODROW WILSON	DEMOCRAT	6,296,547	41.9	435	58.8
		Theodore Roosevelt	Progressive	4,118,571	27.4	88	
		William H. Taft	Republican	3,486,720	23.2	8	
		Eugene V. Debs	Socialist	900,672	6.0		
		Eugene W. Chafin	Prohibition	206,275	1.4		
1916	48	WOODROW WILSON	DEMOCRAT	9,127,695	49.4	277	61.6
		Charles E. Hughes	Republican	8,533,507	46.2	254	
		A. L. Benson	Socialist	585,113	3.2		
		J. Frank Hanly	Prohibition	220,506	1.2		
1920	48	WARREN G. HARDING	REPUBLICAN	16,153,115	60.6	404	49.2
		James M. Cox	Democrat	9,133,092	34.3	127	
		Eugene V. Debs	Socialist	915,490	3.4		
		P. P. Christensen	Farmer-Labor	265,229	1.0		
1924	48	CALVIN COOLIDGE	REPUBLICAN	15,719,921	54.0	382	48.9
		John W. Davis	Democrat	8,386,704	29.0	136	
		Robert M. La Follette	Progressive	4,832,532	16.5	13	

Year	Number of States	Candidates	Parties	Popular Vote	% of Popular Vote	Electoral Vote	% Voter Participation
1928	48	**HERBERT C. HOOVER**	REPUBLICAN	21,437,277	58.2	444	56.9
		Alfred E. Smith	Democrat	15,007,698	40.9	87	
1932	48	**FRANKLIN D. ROOSEVELT**	DEMOCRAT	22,829,501	57.7	472	56.9
		Herbert C. Hoover	Republican	15,760,684	39.8	59	
		Norman Thomas	Socialist	884,649	2.2		
1936	48	**FRANKLIN D. ROOSEVELT**	DEMOCRAT	27,757,333	60.8	523	61.0
		Alfred M. Landon	Republican	16,684,231	36.6	8	
		William Lemke	Union	892,267	2.0		
1940	48	**FRANKLIN D. ROOSEVELT**	DEMOCRAT	27,313,041	54.9	449	62.5
		Wendell L. Willkie	Republican	22,348,480	44.9	82	
1944	48	**FRANKLIN D. ROOSEVELT**	DEMOCRAT	25,612,610	53.5	432	55.9
		Thomas E. Dewey	Republican	22,017,617	46.0	99	
1948	48	**HARRY S. TRUMAN**	DEMOCRAT	24,179,345	49.7	303	53.0
		Thomas E. Dewey	Republican	21,991,291	45.3	189	
		J. Strom Thurmond	States' Rights	1,176,125	2.4	39	
		Henry A. Wallace	Progressive	1,157,326	2.4		
1952	48	**DWIGHT D. EISENHOWER**	REPUBLICAN	33,936,234	55.1	442	63.3
		Adlai E. Stevenson	Democrat	27,314,992	44.4	89	

Year	Number of States	Candidates	Parties	Popular Vote	% of Popular Vote	Electoral Vote	% Voter Participation
1956	48	**DWIGHT D. EISENHOWER**	REPUBLICAN	35,590,472	57.6	457	60.6
		Adlai E. Stevenson	Democrat	26,022,752	42.1	73	
1960	50	**JOHN F. KENNEDY**	DEMOCRAT	34,226,731	49.7	303	62.8
		Richard M. Nixon	Republican	34,108,157	49.6	219	
1964	50	**LYNDON B. JOHNSON**	DEMOCRAT	43,129,566	61.0	486	61.9
		Barry M. Goldwater	Republican	27,178,188	38.4	52	
1968	50	**RICHARD M. NIXON**	REPUBLICAN	31,785,480	43.2	301	60.9
		Hubert H. Humphrey	Democrat	31,275,166	42.6	191	
		George C. Wallace	American Independent	9,906,473	12.9	46	
1972	50	**RICHARD M. NIXON**	REPUBLICAN	47,169,911	60.7	520	55.2
		George S. McGovern	Democrat	29,170,383	37.5	17	
		John G. Schmitz	American	1,099,482	1.4		
1976	50	**JIMMY CARTER**	DEMOCRAT	40,830,763	50.0	297	53.5
		Gerald R. Ford	Republican	39,147,793	48.0	240	
1980	50	**RONALD REAGAN**	REPUBLICAN	43,904,153	50.9	489	52.6
		Jimmy Carter	Democrat	35,483,883	41.1	49	
		John B. Anderson	Independent	5,720,060	6.6		
		Ed Clark	Libertarian	921,299	1.1		

Year	Number of States	Candidates	Parties	Popular Vote	% of Popular Vote	Electoral Vote	% Voter Participation
1984	50	**RONALD REAGAN**	REPUBLICAN	54,455,075	58.8	525	53.1
		Walter F. Mondale	Democrat	37,577,185	40.5	13	
1988	50	**GEORGE H. BUSH**	REPUBLICAN	48,886,097	53.4	426	50.1
		Michael Dukakis	Democrat	41,809,074	45.6	111	
1992	50	**BILL CLINTON**	DEMOCRAT	44,909,326	42.9	370	55.0
		George H. Bush	Republican	39,103,882	37.4	168	
		H. Ross Perot	Independent	19,741,657	18.9		
1996	50	**BILL CLINTON**	DEMOCRAT	47,402,357	49.2	379	49.0
		Bob Dole	Republican	39,198,755	40.7	159	
		H. Ross Perot	Reform Party	8,085,402	8.4		
2000	50	**GEORGE W. BUSH**	REPUBLICAN	50,455,156	47.9	271	50.4
		Albert Gore	Democrat	50,992,335	48.4	266	
		Ralph Nader	Green Party	2,882,738	2.7		
2004	50	**GEORGE W. BUSH**	REPUBLICAN	62,040,610	50.7	286	56.2
		John F. Kerry	Democrat	59,028,111	48.3	251	

Candidates receiving less than 1 percent of the popular vote have been omitted. Thus, the percentage of popular vote given for any election year may not total 100 percent. Before the passage of the Twelfth Amendment in 1804, the electoral college voted for two presidential candidates; the runner-up became vice president.

ADMISSION OF STATES

Order of Admission	State	Date of Admission	Order of Admission	State	Date of Admission
1	Delaware	December 7, 1787	26	Michigan	January 26, 1837
2	Pennsylvania	December 12, 1787	27	Florida	March 3, 1845
3	New Jersey	December 18, 1787	28	Texas	December 29, 1845
4	Georgia	January 2, 1788	29	Iowa	December 28, 1846
5	Connecticut	January 9, 1788	30	Wisconsin	May 29, 1848
6	Massachusetts	February 7, 1788	31	California	September 9, 1850
7	Maryland	April 28, 1788	32	Minnesota	May 11, 1858
8	South Carolina	May 23, 1788	33	Oregon	February 14, 1859
9	New Hampshire	June 21, 1788	34	Kansas	January 29, 1861
10	Virginia	June 25, 1788	35	West Virginia	June 30, 1863
11	New York	July 26, 1788	36	Nevada	October 31, 1864
12	North Carolina	November 21, 1789	37	Nebraska	March 1, 1867
13	Rhode Island	May 29, 1790	38	Colorado	August 1, 1876
14	Vermont	March 4, 1791	39	North Dakota	November 2, 1889
15	Kentucky	June 1, 1792	40	South Dakota	November 2, 1889
16	Tennessee	June 1, 1796	41	Montana	November 8, 1889
17	Ohio	March 1, 1803	42	Washington	November 11, 1889
18	Louisiana	April 30, 1812	43	Idaho	July 3, 1890
19	Indiana	December 11, 1816	44	Wyoming	July 10, 1890
20	Mississippi	December 10, 1817	45	Utah	January 4, 1896
21	Illinois	December 3, 1818	46	Oklahoma	November 16, 1907
22	Alabama	December 14, 1819	47	New Mexico	January 6, 1912
23	Maine	March 15, 1820	48	Arizona	February 14, 1912
24	Missouri	August 10, 1821	49	Alaska	January 3, 1959
25	Arkansas	June 15, 1836	50	Hawaii	August 21, 1959

POPULATION OF THE UNITED STATES

Year	Number of States	Population	% Increase	Population per Square Mile
1790	13	3,929,214		4.5
1800	16	5,308,483	35.1	6.1
1810	17	7,239,881	36.4	4.3
1820	23	9,638,453	33.1	5.5
1830	24	12,866,020	33.5	7.4
1840	26	17,069,453	32.7	9.8
1850	31	23,191,876	35.9	7.9
1860	33	31,443,321	35.6	10.6
1870	37	39,818,449	26.6	13.4
1880	38	50,155,783	26.0	16.9
1890	44	62,947,714	25.5	21.1
1900	45	75,994,575	20.7	25.6
1910	46	91,972,266	21.0	31.0
1920	48	105,710,620	14.9	35.6
1930	48	122,775,046	16.1	41.2
1940	48	131,669,275	7.2	44.2
1950	48	150,697,361	14.5	50.7
1960	50	179,323,175	19.0	50.6
1970	50	203,235,298	13.3	57.5
1980	50	226,504,825	11.4	64.0
1985	50	237,839,000	5.0	67.2
1990	50	250,122,000	5.2	70.6
1995	50	263,411,707	5.3	74.4
2000	50	281,421,906	6.8	77.0

HISTORICAL STATISTICS OF THE UNITED STATES

LABOR FORCE—SELECTED CHARACTERISTICS EXPRESSED AS A PERCENTAGE OF THE LABOR FORCE: 1800–2000

Year	Agriculture	Manufacturing	Domestic service	Clerical, sales, and service	Professions	Slave	Nonwhite	Foreign-born	Female
1800	74.4	—	2.4	—	—	30.2	32.6	—	21.4
1860	55.8	13.8	5.4	4.8[1]	3.0[1]	21.7	23.6	24.5[1]	19.6
1910	30.7	20.8	5.5	14.1	4.7	—	13.4	22.0	20.8
1950	12.0	26.4	2.5	27.3	8.9	—	10.0	8.7	27.9
2000	2.4	14.7	0.6	38.0[2]	15.6	—	16.5	10.3[2]	46.6

[1]Values for 1870 are presented here because the available data for 1860 exclude slaves.
[2]1990.
Note: "Clerical, sales, and service" excludes domestic service.

IMMIGRATION, BY ORIGIN (in thousands)

Period	Europe	Americas	Asia
1820–30	106	12	—
1831–40	496	33	—
1841–50	1,597	62	—
1851–60	2,453	75	42
1861–70	2,065	167	65
1871–80	2,272	404	70
1881–90	4,735	427	70
1891–1900	3,555	39	75
1901–10	8,065	362	324
1911–20	4,322	1,144	247
1921–30	2,463	1,517	112
1931–40	348	160	16
1941–50	621	355	32
1951–60	1,326	997	150
1961–70	1,123	1,716	590
1971–80	800	1,983	1,588
1981–90	762	3,616	2,738
1991–2000	1,100	3,800	2,200

UNEMPLOYMENT RATE, 1890–2000

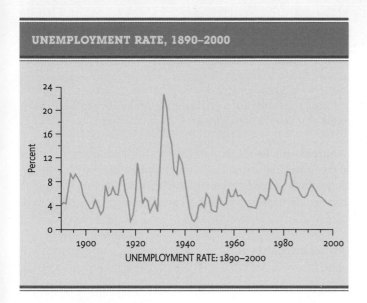

UNEMPLOYMENT RATE: 1890–2000

VOTER PARTICIPATION IN PRESIDENTIAL ELECTIONS, 1824–2000

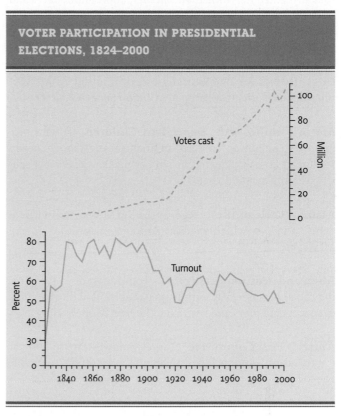

UNION MEMBERSHIP AS A PERCENTAGE OF NONAGRICULTURAL EMPLOYMENT, 1880–1999

Abolitionism Social movement of the pre–Civil War era that advocated the immediate emancipation of the slaves and their incorporation into American society as equal citizens.

Agricultural Adjustment Act (1933) New Deal legislation that established the Agricultural Adjustment Administration (AAA) to improve agricultural prices by limiting market supplies; declared unconstitutional in *United States v. Butler* (1936).

Aid to Families with Dependent Children Federal program, also known as "welfare," of financial assistance to needy American families; created in 1935 as part of the Social Security Act; abolished in 1996.

Alamo, Battle of the Siege in the Texas War for Independence, 1836, in which the San Antonio mission fell to the Mexicans.

Alien and Sedition Acts (1798) Four measures passed during the undeclared war with France that limited the freedoms of speech and press and restricted the liberty of noncitizens.

America First Committee Largely midwestern isolationist organization supported by many prominent citizens, 1940–1941.

American Civil Liberties Union Organization founded during World War I to protest the suppression of freedom of expression in wartime; played a major role in court cases that achieved judicial recognition of Americans' civil liberties.

American Colonization Society Organized in 1816 to encourage colonization of free blacks to Africa; West African nation of Liberia founded in 1822 to serve as a homeland for them.

American Federation of Labor Founded in 1881 as a federation of trade unions composed mostly of skilled, white, native-born workers; its long-term president was Samuel Gompers.

American System Program of internal improvements and protective tariffs promoted by Speaker of the House Henry Clay in his presidential campaign of 1824; his proposals formed the core of Whig ideology in the 1830s and 1840s.

Amistad Ship that transported slaves from one port in Cuba to another, seized by the slaves in 1839. They made their way northward to the United States, where the status of the slaves became the subject of a celebrated court case; eventually most were able to return to Africa.

Anarchism Belief that all institutions that exercise power over individuals, especially government, are illegitimate; it flourished among certain native-born individualists in the nineteenth century and radical immigrants in the early twentieth century.

Antietam, Battle of One of the bloodiest battles of the Civil War, fought to a standoff on September 17, 1862, in western Maryland.

Antifederalists Opponents of the Constitution who saw it as a limitation on individual and states' rights; their demands led to the addition of a Bill of Rights to the document.

Appomattox Court House, Virginia Site of the surrender of Confederate general Robert E. Lee to Union general Ulysses S. Grant on April 9, 1865, marking the end of the Civil War.

Army-McCarthy hearings Televised U.S. Senate hearings in 1954 on Senator Joseph McCarthy's charges of disloyalty in the Army; his tactics contributed to his censure by the Senate.

Articles of Confederation First frame of government for the United States; in effect from 1781 to 1788, it provided for a weak central authority and was soon replaced by the Constitution.

Atlanta Compromise Speech to the Cotton States and International Exposition in 1895 by educator Booker T. Washington, the leading black spokesman of the day; black scholar W. E. B. Du Bois gave the speech its derisive name and criticized Washington for encouraging blacks to accommodate segregation and disenfranchisement.

Atlantic Charter Issued August 12, 1941, following meetings in Newfoundland between President Franklin D. Roosevelt and British prime minister Winston Churchill, the charter signaled the allies' cooperation and stated their war aims.

Atomic Energy Commission Created in 1946 to supervise peacetime uses of atomic energy.

Axis powers In World War II, the nations of Germany, Italy, and Japan.

Aztec   Mesoamerican people who were conquered by the Spanish under Hernán Cortés, 1519–1528.

Baby boom   Markedly higher birthrate in the years following World War II; led to the biggest demographic "bubble" in American history.

Bacon's Rebellion   Unsuccessful 1676 revolt led by planter Nathaniel Bacon against Virginia governor William Berkeley's administration because of governmental corruption and because Berkeley had failed to protect settlers from Indian raids and did not allow them to occupy Indian lands.

***Baker v. Carr* (1962)**   U.S. Supreme Court decision that established the principle of "one man, one vote," that is, that legislative districts must be equal in population.

***Bakke v. Regents of the University of California* (1978)**   Case in which the U.S. Supreme Court ruled against the California university system's use of racial quotas in admissions but allowed the use of race as one factor in admissions decisions.

Balance of trade   Ratio of imports to exports.

Bank of the United States   Proposed by the first secretary of the treasury, Alexander Hamilton, the bank opened in 1791 and operated until 1811 to issue a uniform currency, make business loans, and collect tax monies. The Second Bank of the United States was chartered in 1816 but President Andrew Jackson vetoed the recharter bill in 1832.

Barbary pirates   Plundering pirates off the Mediterranean coast of Africa; President Thomas Jefferson's refusal to pay them tribute to protect American ships sparked an undeclared naval war with North African nations, 1801–1805.

Barbed wire   First practical fencing material for the Great Plains was invented in 1873 and rapidly spelled the end of the open range.

Bay of Pigs Invasion   Hoping to inspire a revolt against Fidel Castro, the CIA sent 1,500 Cuban exiles to invade their homeland on April 17, 1961, but the mission was a spectacular failure.

Bill of Rights   First ten amendments to the U.S. Constitution, adopted in 1791 to guarantee individual rights against infringement by the federal government.

Black Codes (1865–1866)   Laws passed in southern states to restrict the rights of former slaves; to nullify the codes, Congress passed the Civil Rights Act of 1866 and the Fourteenth Amendment.

Black Legend   Idea that the Spanish New World empire was more oppressive toward the Indians than other European empires; was used as a justification for English imperial expansion.

Black Power   Post-1966 rallying cry of a more militant civil rights movement.

Bland-Allison Act (1878)   Passed over President Rutherford B. Hayes's veto, the inflationary measure authorized the purchase each month of 2 to 4 million dollars' worth of silver for coinage.

"Bleeding Kansas"   Violence between pro- and antislavery settlers in the Kansas Territory, 1856.

Boston Massacre   Clash between British soldiers and a Boston mob, March 5, 1770, in which five colonists were killed.

Boston Tea Party   On December 16, 1773, the Sons of Liberty, dressed as Indians, dumped hundreds of chests of tea into Boston harbor to protest the Tea Act of 1773, under which the British exported to the colonies millions of pounds of cheap— but still taxed—tea, thereby undercutting the price of smuggled tea and forcing payment of the tea duty.

Boxer Rebellion   Chinese nationalist protest against Western commercial domination and cultural influence, 1900; a coalition of American, European, and Japanese forces put down the rebellion and reclaimed captured embassies in Peking (Beijing) within the year.

***Bracero* program**   System agreed to by Mexican and American governments in 1942 under which tens of thousands of Mexicans entered the United States to work temporarily in agricultural jobs in the Southwest; lasted until 1964 and inhibited labor organization among farm workers since *braceros* could be deported at any time.

Brains trust   Group of advisers—many of them academics— assembled by Franklin D. Roosevelt to recommend New Deal policies during the early months of his presidency.

Bretton Woods   Town in New Hampshire and site of international agreement in 1944 by which the American dollar replaced the British pound as the most important international currency, and the World Bank and World Trade Organization were created to promote rebuilding after World War II and to insure that countries did not devalue their currencies.

Brook Farm   Transcendentalist commune in West Roxbury, Massachusetts, populated from 1841 to 1847 principally by writers (Nathaniel Hawthorne, for one) and other intellectuals.

Brown v. Board of Education of Topeka **(1954)** U.S. Supreme Court decision that struck down racial segregation in public education and declared "separate but equal" unconstitutional.

Bull Run, Battles of (First and Second Manassas) First land engagement of the Civil War took place on July 21, 1861, at Manassas Junction, Virginia, at which Union troops quickly retreated; one year later, on August 29–30, Confederates captured the federal supply depot and forced Union troops back to Washington.

Bunker Hill, Battle of First major battle of the Revolutionary War; it actually took place at nearby Breed's Hill, Massachusetts, on June 17, 1775.

"Burned-over district" Area of western New York strongly influenced by the revivalist fervor of the Second Great Awakening; Disciples of Christ and Mormons are among the many sects that trace their roots to the phenomenon.

Bush v. Gore **(2000)** U.S. Supreme Court case that determined the winner of the disputed 2000 presidential election.

Calvinism Doctrine of predestination expounded by Swiss theologian John Calvin in 1536; influenced the Puritan, Presbyterian, German and Dutch Reformed, and Huguenot churches in the colonies.

Camp David accords Peace agreement between the leaders of Israel and Egypt, brokered by President Jimmy Carter in 1978.

Carpetbaggers Derisive term for northern emigrants who participated in the Republican governments of the Reconstruction South.

Chancellorsville, Battle of Confederate general Robert E. Lee won his last major victory and General "Stonewall" Jackson died in this Civil War battle in northern Virginia on May 1–4, 1863.

Chinese Exclusion Act (1882) Halted Chinese immigration to the United States.

Civil Rights Act of 1866 Along with the Fourteenth Amendment, guaranteed the rights of citizenship to former slaves.

Civil Rights Act of 1957 First federal civil rights law since Reconstruction; established the Civil Rights Commission and the Civil Rights Division of the Department of Justice.

Civil Rights Act of 1964 Outlawed discrimination in public accommodations and employment.

Closed shop Hiring requirement that all workers in a business must be union members.

Coercive Acts/Intolerable Acts (1774) Four parliamentary measures in reaction to the Boston Tea Party that forced payment for the tea, disallowed colonial trials of British soldiers, forced their quartering in private homes, and reduced the number of elected officials in Massachusetts.

Cold War Term for tensions, 1945–1989, between the Soviet Union and the United States, the two major world powers after World War II.

Commonwealth v. Hunt **(1842)** Landmark ruling of the Massachusetts Supreme Court establishing the legality of labor unions.

Communitarianism Social reform movement of the nineteenth century driven by the belief that by establishing small communities based on common ownership of property, a less competitive and individualistic society could be developed.

Compromise of 1850 Complex compromise devised by Senator Henry Clay that admitted California as a free state, included a stronger fugitive slave law, and delayed determination of the slave status of the New Mexico and Utah territories.

Compromise of 1877 Deal made by a Republican and Demo-cratic special congressional commission to resolve the disputed presidential election of 1876; Republican Rutherford B. Hayes, who had lost the popular vote, was declared the winner in exchange for the withdrawal of federal troops from involvement in politics in the South, marking the end of Reconstruction.

Congress of Industrial Organizations (CIO) Umbrella organization of semiskilled industrial unions, formed in 1935 as the Committee for Industrial Organization and renamed in 1938.

Congress of Racial Equality (CORE) Civil rights organization started in 1942 and best known for its Freedom Rides, bus journeys challenging racial segregation in the South in 1961.

Conspicuous consumption Phrase referring to extravagant spending to raise social standing, coined by Thorstein Veblen in *The Theory of the Leisure Class* (1899).

Constitutional Convention Meeting in Philadelphia, May 25–September 17, 1787, of representatives from twelve colonies—excepting Rhode Island—to revise the existing Articles of Confederation; convention soon resolved to produce an entirely new constitution.

Containment General U.S. strategy in the Cold War that called for containing Soviet expansion; originally devised by U.S. diplomat George F. Kennan.

Continental army Army authorized by the Continental Congress in 1775 to fight the British; commanded by General George Washington.

Continental Congress Representatives of the colonies met first in Philadelphia in 1774 to formulate actions against British policies; the Second Continental Congress (1775–1789) conducted the war and adopted the Declaration of Independence and the Articles of Confederation.

Convict leasing System developed in the post–Civil War South that generated income for the states and satisfied planters' need for cheap labor by renting prisoners out; the convicts were often treated poorly.

Copperheads Republican term for northerners opposed to the Civil War; it derived from the name of a poisonous snake.

Coral Sea, Battle of the Fought on May 7–8, 1942, near the eastern coast of Australia, it was the first U.S. naval victory over Japan in World War II.

Cotton gin Invented by Eli Whitney in 1793, the machine separated cotton seed from cotton fiber, speeding cotton processing and making profitable the cultivation of the more hardy, but difficult to clean, short-staple cotton; led directly to the dramatic nineteenth-century expansion of slavery in the South.

Counterculture "Hippie" youth culture of the 1960s, which rejected the values of the dominant culture in favor of illicit drugs, communes, free sex, and rock music.

Court-packing plan President Franklin D. Roosevelt's failed 1937 attempt to increase the number of U.S. Supreme Court justices from nine to fifteen in order to save his Second New Deal programs from constitutional challenges.

Coverture Principle in English and American law that a married woman lost her legal identity, which became "covered" by that of her husband, who therefore controlled her person and the family's economic resources.

Credit Mobilier scandal Millions of dollars in overcharges for building the Union Pacific Railroad were exposed; high officials of the Ulysses S. Grant administration were implicated but never charged.

Creoles (*Criollos* in Spanish) Persons born in the New World of European ancestry.

Cuban missile crisis Caused when the United States discovered Soviet offensive missile sites in Cuba in October 1962; the U.S.-Soviet confrontation was the Cold War's closest brush with nuclear war.

Crop-lien system Merchants extended credit to tenants based on their future crops, but high interest rates and the uncertainties of farming often led to inescapable debts.

D-Day June 6, 1944, when an Allied amphibious assault landed on the Normandy coast and established a foothold in Europe, leading to the liberation of France from German occupation.

***Dartmouth College v. Woodward* (1819)** U.S. Supreme Court upheld the original charter of the college against New Hampshire's attempt to alter the board of trustees; set precedent of support of contracts against state interference.

Dawes Act Law passed in 1887 meant to encourage adoption of white norms among Indians; broke up tribal holdings into small farms for Indian families, with the remainder sold to white purchasers.

Declaration of Independence Document adopted on July 4, 1776, that made the break with Britain official; drafted by a committee of the Second Continental Congress, including principal writer Thomas Jefferson.

Deindustrialization Term describing decline of manufacturing in old industrial areas in the late twentieth century as companies shifted production to low-wage centers in the South and West or in other countries.

Deism Enlightenment thought applied to religion; emphasized reason, morality, and natural law.

Democratic-Republican Societies Organizations created in the mid-1790s by opponents of the policies of the Washington administration and supporters of the French Revolution.

Department of Homeland Security Created to coordinate federal antiterrorist activity following the 2001 terrorist attacks on the World Trade Center and Pentagon.

Depression Period in which economic output declines sharply and unemployment rises; it applied especially to the Great Depression of the 1930s.

Depression of 1893 Worst depression of the nineteenth century, set off by a railroad failure, too much speculation on Wall Street, and low agricultural prices.

Disenfranchise To deprive of the right to vote; in the United States, exclusionary policies were used to deny groups, especially African-Americans and women, their voting rights.

Division of Powers The division of political power between the state and federal governments under the U.S. Constitution (also known as federalism).

Dixiecrats Deep South delegates who walked out of the 1948 Democratic National Convention in protest of the party's support for civil rights legislation and later formed the States' Rights Democratic (Dixiecrat) Party, which nominated Strom Thurmond of South Carolina for president.

Dominion of New England Consolidation into a single colony of the New England colonies—and later New York and New Jersey—by royal governor Edmund Andros in 1686; dominion reverted to individual colonial governments three years later.

Dred Scott v. Sandford (1857) U.S. Supreme Court decision in which Chief Justice Roger B. Taney ruled that Congress could not prohibit slavery in the territories, on the grounds that such a prohibition would violate the Fifth Amendment rights of slaveholders, and that no black person could be a citizen of the United States.

Due-process clause Clause in the Fifth and the Fourteenth Amendments to the U.S. Constitution guaranteeing that states could not "deprive any person of life, liberty, or property, without due process of law."

Dust Bowl Great Plains counties where millions of tons of topsoil were blown away from parched farmland in the 1930s; massive migration of farm families followed.

Eighteenth Amendment (1919) Prohibition amendment that made illegal the manufacture, sale, or transportation of alcoholic beverages; repealed in 1933.

Ellis Island Reception center in New York Harbor through which most European immigrants to America were processed from 1892 to 1954.

Emancipation Proclamation (1863) President Abraham Lincoln issued a preliminary proclamation on September 22, 1862, freeing the slaves in areas under Confederate control as of January 1, 1863, the date of the final proclamation, which also authorized the enrollment of black soldiers into the Union army.

Embargo Act of 1807 Attempt to exert economic pressure by prohibiting all exports from the United States, instead of waging war in reaction to continued British impressment of American sailors; smugglers easily circumvented the embargo, and it was repealed two years later.

Emergency Banking Relief Act (1933) First New Deal measure that provided for reopening the banks under strict conditions and took the United States off the gold standard.

Emergency Immigration Act of 1921 Limited U.S. immigration to 3 percent of each foreign-born nationality in the 1910 census; three years later, Congress restricted immigration even further.

Encomienda System under which officers of the Spanish conquistadores gained ownership of Indian land.

Enlightenment Revolution in thought in the eighteenth century that emphasized reason and science over the authority of traditional religion.

Environmental Protection Agency (EPA) Created in 1970 during the first administration of President Richard M. Nixon to oversee federal pollution control efforts.

Equal Rights Amendment Amendment to guarantee equal rights for women, introduced in 1923 but not passed by Congress until 1972; it failed to be ratified by the states.

Era of Good Feelings Contemporary characterization of the administration of popular Republican president James Monroe, 1817–1825.

Erie Canal Most important and profitable of the canals of the 1820s and 1830s; stretched from Buffalo to Albany, New York, connecting the Great Lakes to the East Coast and making New York City the nation's largest port.

Espionage and Sedition Acts (1917–1918) Limited criticism of government leaders and policies by imposing fines and prison terms on those who opposed American participation in the First World War.

Eugenics "Science" of improving the human race by regulating who can bear children; flourished in early twentieth century and led to laws for involuntary sterilization of the "feeble-minded."

Fair Deal Domestic reform proposals of the Truman administration; included civil rights legislation, national health insurance, and repeal of the Taft-Hartley Act, but only extensions of some New Deal programs were enacted.

Fair Employment Practices Commission Created in 1941 by executive order, the FEPC sought to eliminate racial discrimination in jobs; it possessed little power but represented a step toward civil rights for African-Americans.

Family Wage Idea that male workers should earn a wage sufficient to enable them to support their entire family without their wives having to work outside the home.

Federal Trade Commission Act (1914) Established the Federal Trade Commission to enforce existing antitrust laws that prohibited business combinations in restraint of trade.

The Federalist   Collection of eighty-five essays that appeared in the New York press in 1787–1788 in support of the Constitution; written by Alexander Hamilton, James Madison, and John Jay and published under the pseudonym "Publius."

Federalist Party   One of the two first national political parties; led by George Washington, John Adams, and Alexander Hamilton, it favored a strong central government.

Feminism   Term that entered the lexicon in the early twentieth century to describe the movement for full equality for women, in political, social, and personal life.

Fifteenth Amendment   Constitutional Amendment ratified in 1870, which prohibited states from discriminating in voting privileges on the basis of race.

"Fifty-four forty or fight"   Democratic campaign slogan in the presidential election of 1844, urging that the northern border of Oregon be fixed at 54°40′ north latitude.

Filibuster   In the nineteenth century, invasions of Central American countries launched privately by groups of Americans seeking to establish personal rule and spread slavery; in the twentieth century, term for the practice of members of the U.S. Senate delivering interminable speeches in order to prevent voting on legislation.

***Fletcher v. Peck* (1810)**   U.S. Supreme Court decision in which Chief Justice John Marshall upheld the initial fraudulent sale contracts in the Yazoo Fraud cases; it upheld the principle of sanctity of a contract.

Fordism   Early twentieth-century term describing the economic system pioneered by Ford Motor Company based on high wages and mass consumption.

Fort McHenry   Fort in Baltimore Harbor unsuccessfully bombarded by the British in September 1814, Francis Scott Key, a witness to the battle, was moved to write the words to "The Star-Spangled Banner."

Fort Sumter   First battle of the Civil War, in which the federal fort in Charleston (South Carolina) Harbor was captured by the Confederates on April 14, 1861, after two days of shelling.

Fourteen Points   President Woodrow Wilson's 1918 plan for peace after World War I; at the Versailles peace conference, however, he failed to incorporate all of the points into the treaty.

Fourteenth Amendment (1868)   Guaranteed rights of citizenship to former slaves, in words similar to those of the Civil Rights Act of 1866.

Franchise   The right to vote.

"Free person of color"   Negro or mulatto person not held in slavery; immediately before the Civil War, there were nearly a half million in the United States, split almost evenly between North and South.

Free Soil Party   Formed in 1848 to oppose slavery in the territory acquired in the Mexican War; nominated Martin Van Buren for president in 1848. By 1854 most of the party's members had joined the Republican Party.

Free Speech Movement   Founded in 1964 at the University of California at Berkeley by student radicals protesting restrictions on their right to distribute political publications.

Freedmen's Bureau   Reconstruction agency established in 1865 to protect the legal rights of former slaves and to assist with their education, jobs, health care, and landowning.

French and Indian War   Known in Europe as the Seven Years' War, the last (1755–1763) of four colonial wars fought between England and France for control of North America east of the Mississippi River.

Fugitive Slave Act of 1850   Gave federal government authority in cases involving runaway slaves; aroused considerable opposition in the North.

Fundamentalism   Anti-modernist Protestant movement started in the early twentieth century that proclaimed the literal truth of the Bible; the name came from *The Fundamentals*, published by conservative leaders.

Gadsden Purchase (1853)   Thirty thousand square miles in present-day Arizona and New Mexico bought by Congress from Mexico primarily for the Southern Pacific Railroad's transcontinental route.

Gag Rule   Rule adopted by House of Representatives in 1836 prohibiting consideration of abolitionist petitions; opposition, led by former president John Quincy Adams, succeeded in having it repealed in 1844.

Gentlemen's Agreement (1907)   The United States would not exclude Japanese immigrants if Japan would voluntarily limit the number of immigrants coming to the United States.

Gettysburg, Battle of   Fought in southern Pennsylvania, July 1–3, 1863; the Confederate defeat and the simultaneous loss at Vicksburg marked the military turning point of the Civil War.

***Gibbons v. Ogden* (1824)**   U.S. Supreme Court decision reinforcing the "commerce clause" (the federal government's right to regulate interstate commerce) of the Constitution; Chief Justice John Marshall ruled against the State of New York's granting of steamboat monopolies.

Gideon v. Wainwright (1963)   U.S. Supreme Court decision guaranteeing legal counsel for indigent felony defendants.

The Gilded Age   Mark Twain and Charles Dudley Warner's 1873 novel, the title of which became the popular name for the period from the end of the Civil War to the turn of the century.

Glass-Steagall Act (Banking Act of 1933)   Established the Federal Deposit Insurance Corporation and included banking reforms, some designed to control speculation. Repealed in 1999, opening the door to scandals involving banks and stock investment companies.

Globalization   Term that became prominent in the 1990s to describe the rapid acceleration of international flows of commerce, financial resources, labor, and cultural products.

Gold Standard   Policy at various points in American history by which the value of a dollar is set at a fixed price in terms of gold (in the post–World War II era, for example, $35 per ounce of gold).

Good Neighbor Policy   Proclaimed by President Franklin D. Roosevelt in his first inaugural address in 1933, it sought improved diplomatic relations between the United States and its Latin American neighbors.

Grandfather clause   Loophole created by southern disfranchising legislatures of the 1890s for illiterate white males whose grandfathers had been eligible to vote in 1867.

Granger movement   Political movement that grew out of the Patrons of Husbandry, an educational and social organization for farmers founded in 1867; the Grange had its greatest success in the Midwest of the 1870s, lobbying for government control of railroad and grain elevator rates and establishing farmers' cooperatives.

Great Awakening   Fervent religious revival movement in the 1720s through the 1740s that was spread throughout the colonies by ministers like New England Congregationalist Jonathan Edwards and English revivalist George Whitefield.

Great Compromise (Connecticut Compromise)   Settled the differences between the New Jersey and Virginia delegations to the Constitutional Convention by providing for a bicameral legislature, the upper house of which would have equal representation for each state and the lower house of which would be apportioned by population.

Great Depression   Worst economic depression in American history; it was spurred by the stock market crash of 1929 and lasted until World War II.

Great Migration   Large-scale migration of southern blacks during and after World War I to the North, where jobs had become available during the labor shortage of the war years.

Great Society   Term coined by President Lyndon B. Johnson in his 1965 State of the Union address, in which he proposed legislation to address problems of voting rights, poverty, diseases, education, immigration, and the environment.

Greenback-Labor Party   Formed in 1876 in reaction to economic depression, the party favored issuance of unsecured paper money to help farmers repay debts; the movement for free coinage of silver took the place of the greenback movement by the 1880s.

Griswold v. Connecticut (1965)   Supreme Court decision that, in overturning Connecticut law prohibiting the use of contraceptives, established a constitutional right to privacy.

Gulf War   Military action in 1991 in which an international coalition led by the United States drove Iraq from Kuwait, which it had occupied the previous year.

Habeas corpus, Writ of   An essential component of English common law and of the U.S. Constitution that guarantees that citizens may not be imprisoned without due process of law; literally means, "you may have the body"; suspended by President Lincoln during the Civil War and limited by President Bush after the attacks of September 11, 2001.

Hacienda   Large-scale farm in the Spanish New World empire worked by Indian laborers.

Harlem Renaissance   African-American literary and artistic movement of the 1920s centered in New York City's Harlem district; writers Langston Hughes, Jean Toomer, Zora Neale Hurston, and Countee Cullen were among those active in the movement.

Harpers Ferry, Virginia   Site of abolitionist John Brown's failed raid on the federal arsenal, October 16–17, 1859; Brown became a martyr to his cause after his capture and execution.

Hart-Celler Act (1965)   Eliminated the national origins quota system for immigration established by laws in 1921 and 1924; led to radical change in the origins of immigrants to the United States, with Asians and Latin Americans outnumbering Europeans.

Hartford Convention   Meeting of New England Federalists on December 15, 1814, to protest the War of 1812; proposed seven constitutional amendments (limiting embargoes and changing requirements for officeholding, declaration of war, and admission of new states), but the war ended before Congress could respond.

Hawley-Smoot Tariff Act (1930)   Raised tariffs to an unprecedented level and worsened the Great Depression by raising prices and discouraging foreign trade.

Haymarket affair   Violence during an anarchist protest at Haymarket Square in Chicago on May 4, 1886; the deaths of eight, including seven policemen, led to the trial of eight anarchist leaders for conspiracy to commit murder.

Hessians   German soldiers, most from Hesse-Cassel principality (hence the name), paid to fight for the British in the Revolutionary War.

Holding company   Investment company that holds controlling interest in the securities of other companies.

Homestead Act (1862)   Authorized Congress to grant 160 acres of public land to a western settler, who had to live on the land for five years to establish title.

Homestead Strike   Violent strike at the Carnegie Steel Company near Pittsburgh in 1892 that culminated in the defeat of the Amalgamated Association of Iron and Steel Workers, the first steelworkers' union.

House Un-American Activities Committee (HUAC)   Formed in 1938 to investigate subversives in the government and holders of radical ideas more generally; best-known investigations were of Hollywood notables and of former State Department official Alger Hiss, who was accused in 1948 of espionage and Communist Party membership. Abolished in 1975.

Hundred Days   Extraordinarily productive first three months of President Franklin D. Roosevelt's administration in which a special session of Congress enacted fifteen of his New Deal proposals.

Impeachment   Bringing charges against a public official; for example, the House of Representatives can impeach a president for "treason, bribery, or other high crimes and misdemeanors" by majority vote, and after the trial the Senate can remove the president by a vote of two-thirds. Two presidents, Andrew Johnson and Bill Clinton, have been impeached and tried before the Senate; neither was convicted.

Implied powers   Federal powers beyond those specifically enumerated in the U.S. Constitution; based on the "elastic clause" of Article I, Section 8, of the Constitution that allows Congress to enact laws that promote the "general welfare."

"In God We Trust"   Phrase placed on all new U.S. currency as of 1954.

Indentured servant   Settler who signed on for a temporary period of servitude to a master in exchange for passage to the New World; Virginia and Pennsylvania were largely peopled in the seventeenth and eighteenth centuries by English and German indentured servants.

Indian Removal Act (1830)   Signed by President Andrew Jackson, the law permitted the negotiation of treaties to obtain the Indians' lands in exchange for their relocation to what would become Oklahoma.

Individualism   Term that entered the language in the 1820s to describe the increasing emphasis on the pursuit of personal advancement and private fulfillment free of outside interference.

Industrial Workers of the World   Radical union organized in Chicago in 1905 and nicknamed the Wobblies; its opposition to World War I led to its destruction by the federal government under the Espionage Act.

Inflation   An economic condition in which prices rise continuously.

Insular Cases   Series of cases between 1901 and 1904 in which the Supreme Court ruled that constitutional protection of individual rights did not fully apply to residents of "insular" territories acquired by the United States in the Spanish-American War, such as Puerto Rico and the Philippines.

Interstate Commerce Commission   Reacting to the U.S. Supreme Court's ruling in *Wabash Railroad v. Illinois* (1886), Congress established the ICC to curb abuses in the railroad industry by regulating rates.

Iran-Contra affair   Scandal of the second Reagan administration involving sales of arms to Iran in partial exchange for release of hostages in Lebanon and use of the arms money to aid the Contras in Nicaragua, which had been expressly forbidden by Congress.

Iraq War   Military campaign in 2003 in which the United States, unable to gain approval by the United Nations, unilaterally occupied Iraq and removed dictator Saddam Hussein from power.

Iron Curtain   Term coined by Winston Churchill to describe the Cold War divide between western Europe and the Soviet Union's eastern European satellites.

Jamestown, Virginia Site in 1607 of the first permanent English settlement in the New World.

Japanese-American Internment Policy adopted by the Roosevelt administration in 1942 under which 110,000 persons of Japanese descent, most of them American citizens, were removed from the West Coast and forced to spend most of World War II in internment camps; it was the largest violation of American civil liberties in the twentieth century.

Jay's Treaty Treaty with Britain negotiated in 1794 by Chief Justice John Jay; Britain agreed to vacate forts in the Northwest Territories, and festering disagreements (border with Canada, prewar debts, shipping claims) would be settled by commission.

Jim Crow Minstrel show character whose name became synonymous with racial segregation.

Kansas-Nebraska Act (1854) Law sponsored by Illinois senator Stephen A. Douglas to allow settlers in newly organized territories north of the Missouri border to decide the slavery issue for themselves; fury over the resulting repeal of the Missouri Compromise of 1820 led to violence in Kansas and to the formation of the Republican Party.

Kellogg-Briand Pact Representatives of sixty-two nations in 1928 signed the pact (also called the Pact of Paris) to outlaw war.

Keynesianism Economic theory derived from the writings of British economist John Maynard Keynes, which rejected the laissez-faire approach in favor of public spending to stimulate economic growth, even at the cost of federal deficits; dominated economic policies of administrations from the 1940s to the mid-1970s.

Knights of Labor Founded in 1869, the first national union lasted, under the leadership of Terence V. Powderly, only into the 1890s; supplanted by the American Federation of Labor.

Know-Nothing (American) Party Nativist, anti-Catholic third party organized in 1854 in reaction to large-scale German and Irish immigration; the party's only presidential candidate was Millard Fillmore in 1856.

Korean War Conflict touched off in 1950 when Communist North Korea invaded South Korea; fighting, largely by U.S. forces, continued until 1953.

Ku Klux Klan Organized in Pulaski, Tennessee, in 1866 to terrorize former slaves who voted and held political offices during Reconstruction; a revived organization in the 1910s and 1920s stressed white, Anglo-Saxon, fundamentalist Protestant supremacy; the Klan revived a third time to fight the civil rights movement of the 1950s and 1960s in the South.

Laissez-faire Term adopted from French, meaning "let people do as they choose," describing opposition to government action to regulate economic or personal behavior.

Land Ordinance of 1785 Directed surveying of the Northwest Territory into townships of thirty-six sections (square miles) each, the sale of the sixteenth section of which was to be used to finance public education.

League of Nations Organization of nations to mediate disputes and avoid war established after World War I as part of the Treaty of Versailles; President Woodrow Wilson's "Fourteen Points" speech to Congress in 1918 proposed the formation of the league, which the United States never joined.

Lend-Lease Act (1941) Permitted the United States to lend or lease arms and other supplies to the Allies, signifying increasing likelihood of American involvement in World War II.

Levittown Low-cost, mass-produced developments of suburban tract housing built by William Levitt after World War II on Long Island and elsewhere.

Lexington and Concord, Battle of The first shots fired in the Revolutionary War, on April 19, 1775, near Boston; approximately 100 minutemen and 250 British soldiers were killed.

Leyte Gulf, Battle of Largest sea battle in history, fought on October 25, 1944, and won by the United States off the Philippine island of Leyte; Japanese losses were so great that they could not rebound.

Liberalism Originally, political philosophy that emphasized the protection of liberty by limiting the power of government to interfere with the natural rights of citizens; in the twentieth century, belief in an activist government promoting greater social and economic equality.

Liberty Party Abolitionist political party that nominated James G. Birney for president in 1840 and 1844; merged with the Free Soil Party in 1848.

Lincoln-Douglas debates Series of senatorial campaign debates in 1858 focusing on the issue of slavery in the territories; held in Illinois between Republican Abraham Lincoln, who made a national reputation for himself, and incumbent Democratic senator Stephen A. Douglas, who managed to hold onto his seat.

Little Bighorn, Battle of   Most famous battle of the Great Sioux War took place in 1876 in the Montana Territory; combined Sioux and Cheyenne warriors massacred a vastly outnumbered U.S. Cavalry commanded by Lieutenant Colonel George Armstrong Custer.

Lochner v. New York **(1905)**   Decision by Supreme Court overturning a New York law establishing a limit on the number of hours per week bakers could be compelled to work; "Lochnerism" became a way of describing the liberty of contract jurisprudence, which opposed all governmental intervention in the economy.

Louisiana Purchase   President Thomas Jefferson's 1803 purchase from France of the important port of New Orleans and 828,000 square miles west of the Mississippi River to the Rocky Mountains; it more than doubled the territory of the United States at a cost of only $15 million.

Loyalists   Colonists who remained loyal to Great Britain during the War of Independence.

Lusitania   British passenger liner sunk by a German U-boat, May 7, 1915, creating a diplomatic crisis and public outrage at the loss of 128 Americans (roughly 10 percent of the total aboard); Germany agreed to pay reparations, and the United States waited two more years to enter World War I.

Lyceum movement   Founded in 1826, the movement promoted adult public education through lectures and performances.

Lynching   Practice, particularly widespread in the South between 1890 and 1940, in which persons (usually black) accused of a crime were murdered by mobs before standing trial. Lynchings often took place before large crowds, with law enforcement authorities not intervening.

Manhattan Project   Secret American program during World War II to develop an atomic bomb; J. Robert Oppenheimer led the team of physicists at Los Alamos, New Mexico.

Manifest Destiny   Phrase first used in 1845 to urge annexation of Texas; used thereafter to encourage American settlement of European colonial and Indian lands in the Great Plains and the West and, more generally, as a justification for American empire.

Marbury v. Madison **(1803)**   First U.S. Supreme Court decision to declare a federal law—the Judiciary Act of 1801—unconstitutional.

March on Washington   Civil rights demonstration on August 28, 1963, where the Reverend Martin Luther King Jr., gave his "I Have a Dream" speech on the steps of the Lincoln Memorial.

Marshall Plan   U.S. program for the reconstruction of post–World War II Europe through massive aid to former enemy nations as well as allies; proposed by General George C. Marshall in 1947.

Massive resistance   In reaction to the *Brown* decision of 1954, effort by southern states to defy federally mandated school integration.

Maya   Pre-Columbian society in Mesoamerica before about A.D. 900.

Mayflower Compact   Signed in 1620 aboard the *Mayflower* before the Pilgrims landed at Plymouth, the document committed the group to majority-rule government.

McCarran Internal Security Act (1950)   Passed over President Harry S. Truman's veto, the law required registration of American Communist Party members, denied them passports, and allowed them to be detained as suspected subversives.

McCarthyism   Post–World War II Red Scare focused on the fear of Communists in U.S. government positions; peaked during the Korean War; most closely associated with Joseph McCarthy, a major instigator of the hysteria.

McCulloch v. Maryland **(1819)**   U.S. Supreme Court decision in which Chief Justice John Marshall, holding that Maryland could not tax the Second Bank of the United States, supported the authority of the federal government versus the states.

McNary-Haugen Bill   Vetoed by President Calvin Coolidge in 1927 and 1928, the bill to aid farmers would have artificially raised agricultural prices by selling surpluses overseas for low prices and selling the reduced supply in the United States for higher prices.

Meat Inspection Act (1906)   Passed largely in reaction to Upton Sinclair's *The Jungle*, the law set strict standards of cleanliness in the meatpacking industry.

Medicaid   Great Society program established in 1965 that provided free medical care to the poor.

Medicare   Key component of Great Society of Lyndon B. Johnson; government program created in 1965 to pay medical costs of elderly and disabled Americans.

Mercantilism   Policy of Great Britain and other imperial powers of regulating the economies of colonies to benefit the mother country.

Mestizo   Spanish word for person of mixed Native American and European ancestry.

Mexican War   Controversial war with Mexico for control of California and New Mexico, 1846–1848; the Treaty of Guadalupe Hidalgo fixed the border at the Rio Grande and extended the United States to the Pacific coast, annexing more than a half-million square miles of Mexican territory.

Midway, Battle of   Decisive American victory near Midway Island in the South Pacific on June 4, 1942; the Japanese navy never recovered its superiority over the U.S. navy.

Minstrel show   Blackface vaudeville entertainment popular in the decades surrounding the Civil War.

***Miranda v. Arizona* (1966)**   U.S. Supreme Court decision required police to advise persons in custody of their rights to legal counsel and against self-incrimination.

Missouri Compromise   Deal proposed by Kentucky senator Henry Clay in 1820 to resolve the slave/free imbalance in Congress that would result from Missouri's admission as a slave state; Maine's admission as a free state offset Missouri, and slavery was prohibited in the remainder of the Louisiana Territory north of the southern border of Missouri.

Molly Maguires   Secret organization of Irish coal miners that used violence to intimidate mine officials in the 1870s.

***Monitor* and *Merrimac,* Battle of the**   First engagement between ironclad ships; fought at Hampton Roads, Virginia, on March 9, 1862.

Monroe Doctrine   President James Monroe's declaration to Congress on December 2, 1823, that the American continents would be thenceforth closed to European colonization, and that the United States would not interfere in European affairs.

Moral Majority   Televangelist Jerry Falwell's political lobbying organization, the name of which became synonymous with the Religious Right—conservative evangelical Protestants who helped ensure President Ronald Reagan's 1980 victory.

Mormons   Founded in 1830 by Joseph Smith, the sect (officially, the Church of Jesus Christ of Latter-day Saints) was a product of the intense revivalism of the "burned-over district" of New York; Smith's successor Brigham Young led 15,000 followers to Utah in 1847 to escape persecution.

Montgomery bus boycott   Sparked by Rosa Parks's arrest on December 1, 1955, for refusing to surrender her seat to a white passenger, a successful year-long boycott protesting segregation on city buses; led by the Reverend Martin Luther King Jr.

Muckrakers   Writers who exposed corruption and abuses in politics, business, meatpacking, child labor, and more, primarily in the first decade of the twentieth century; their popular books and magazine articles spurred public interest in reform.

Mugwumps   Reform wing of the Republican Party that supported Democrat Grover Cleveland for president in 1884 over Republican James G. Blaine, whose influence peddling had been revealed in the Mulligan letters of 1876.

Multiculturalism   Term that became prominent in the 1990s to describe a growing emphasis on group racial and ethnic identity and demands that jobs, education, and politics reflect the increasingly diverse nature of American society.

***Munn v. Illinois* (1877)**   U.S. Supreme Court ruling that upheld a Granger law allowing the state to regulate grain elevators.

NAFTA   Approved in 1993, the North American Free Trade Agreement with Canada and Mexico allowed goods to travel across their borders free of tariffs; critics argued that American workers would lose their jobs to cheaper Mexican labor.

Nat Turner Rebellion   Most important slave uprising in nineteenth-century America, led by a slave preacher who, with his followers, killed about sixty white persons in Southampton County, Virginia, in 1831.

National Association for the Advancement of Colored People (NAACP)   Founded in 1910, this civil rights organization brought lawsuits against discriminatory practices and published *The Crisis*, a journal edited by African-American scholar W. E. B. Du Bois.

National Defense Education Act (1958)   Passed in reaction to America's perceived inferiority in the space race; encouraged education in science and modern languages through student loans, university research grants, and aid to public schools.

National Industrial Recovery Act (1933)   Passed on the last of the Hundred Days, it created public-works jobs through the Federal Emergency Relief Administration and established a system of self-regulation for industry through the National Recovery Administration, which was ruled unconstitutional in 1935.

National Organization for Women   Founded in 1966 by writer Betty Friedan and other feminists, NOW pushed for abortion rights, nondiscrimination in the workplace, and other forms of equality for women.

National Road   First federal interstate road, built between 1811 and 1838 and stretching from Cumberland, Maryland, to Vandalia, Illinois.

National Security Act (1947) Authorized the reorganization of government to coordinate military branches and security agencies; created the National Security Council, the Central Intelligence Agency, and the National Military Establishment (later renamed the Department of Defense).

National Youth Administration Created in 1935 as part of the Works Progress Administration, it employed millions of youths who had left school.

Nativism Anti-immigrant and anti-Catholic feeling especially prominent in the 1830s through the 1850s; the largest group was New York's Order of the Star-Spangled Banner, which expanded into the American (Know-Nothing) Party in 1854.

Naval stores Tar, pitch, and turpentine made from pine resin and used in shipbuilding; an important industry in the southern colonies, especially North Carolina.

Navigation Acts Passed by the English Parliament to control colonial trade and bolster the mercantile system, 1650–1775; enforcement of the acts led to growing resentment by colonists.

Neutrality Acts Series of laws passed between 1935 and 1939 to keep the United States from becoming involved in war by prohibiting American trade and travel to warring nations.

New Deal Franklin D. Roosevelt's campaign promise, in his speech to the Democratic National Convention of 1932, to combat the Great Depression with a "new deal for the American people"; the phrase became a catchword for his ambitious plan of economic programs.

New Freedom Democrat Woodrow Wilson's political slogan in the presidential campaign of 1912; Wilson wanted to improve the banking system, lower tariffs, and, by breaking up monopolies, give small businesses freedom to compete.

New Frontier John F. Kennedy's program, stymied by a Republican Congress and his abbreviated term; his successor Lyndon B. Johnson had greater success with many of the same concepts.

New Harmony Founded in Indiana by British industrialist Robert Owen in 1825, the short-lived New Harmony Community of Equality was one of the few nineteenth-century communal experiments not based on religious ideology.

New Left Radical youth protest movement of the 1960s, named by leader Tom Hayden to distinguish it from the Old (Marxist-Leninist) Left of the 1930s.

New Nationalism Platform of the Progressive Party and slogan of former president Theodore Roosevelt in the presidential campaign of 1912; stressed government activism, including regulation of trusts, conservation, and recall of state court decisions that had nullified progressive programs.

New Orleans, Battle of Last battle of the War of 1812, fought on January 8, 1815, weeks after the peace treaty was signed but prior to the news reaching America; General Andrew Jackson led the victorious American troops.

New South *Atlanta Constitution* editor Henry W. Grady's 1886 term for the prosperous post–Civil War South he envisioned: democratic, industrial, urban, and free of nostalgia for the defeated plantation South.

Nineteenth Amendment (1920) Granted women the right to vote.

Nisei Japanese-Americans; literally, "second generation."

Normalcy Word coined by future president Warren G. Harding as part of a 1920 campaign speech—"not nostrums, but normalcy"—signifying public weariness with Woodrow Wilson's internationalism and domestic reforms.

North Atlantic Treaty Organization (NATO) Alliance founded in 1949 by ten western European nations, the United States, and Canada to deter Soviet expansion in Europe.

Northwest Ordinance of 1787 Created the Northwest Territory (area north of the Ohio River and west of Pennsylvania), established conditions for self-government and statehood, included a Bill of Rights, and permanently prohibited slavery.

Nullification Concept of invalidation of a federal law within the borders of a state; first expounded in Thomas Jefferson's draft of Kentucky resolution against Alien and Sedition Acts (1798); cited by South Carolina in its Ordinance of Nullification (1832) of the Tariff of Abominations, used by southern states to explain their secession from the Union (1861), and cited again by southern states to oppose the *Brown v. Board of Education* decision (1954).

Office of Price Administration Created in 1941 to control wartime inflation and price fixing resulting from shortages of many consumer goods, the OPA imposed wage and price freezes and administered a rationing system.

Okies Displaced farm families from the Oklahoma dust bowl who migrated to California during the 1930s in search of jobs.

Oneida Community Utopian community founded in 1848; the Perfectionist religious group practiced "complex marriage" under leader John Humphrey Noyes.

OPEC   Organization of Petroleum Exporting Countries.

Open Door Policy   In hopes of protecting the Chinese market for U.S. exports, Secretary of State John Hay demanded in 1899 that Chinese trade be open to all nations.

Open Shop   Situation in which union membership is not a condition of employment in a factory or other business.

Operation Dixie   CIO's largely ineffective post–World War II campaign to unionize southern workers.

Oregon Trail   Route of wagon trains bearing settlers from Independence, Missouri, to the Oregon Country in the 1840s through the 1860s.

Ostend Manifesto   Memorandum written in 1854 from Ostend, Belgium, by the U.S. ministers to England, France, and Spain recommending purchase or seizure of Cuba in order to increase the United States' slaveholding territory.

Panic of 1819   Financial collapse brought on by sharply falling cotton prices, declining demand for American exports, and reckless western land speculation.

Panic of 1837   Beginning of major economic depression lasting about six years; touched off by a British financial crisis and made worse by falling cotton prices, credit and currency problems, and speculation in land, canals, and railroads.

Panic of 1857   Beginning of economic depression lasting about two years and brought on by falling grain prices and a weak financial system; the South was largely protected by international demand for its cotton.

Panic of 1873   Onset of severe six-year depression marked by bank failures and railroad and insurance bankruptcies.

Peace of Paris   Signed on September 3, 1783, the treaty ending the Revolutionary War and recognizing American independence from Britain also established the border between Canada and the United States, fixed the western border at the Mississippi River, and ceded Florida to Spain.

Pendleton Civil Service Act (1883)   Established the Civil Service Commission and marked the end of the spoils system.

Pentagon Papers   Informal name for the Defense Department's secret history of the Vietnam conflict; leaked to the press by former official Daniel Ellsberg and published in the *New York Times* in 1971.

Philippine War   American military campaign that suppressed the movement for Philippine independence after the Spanish-American War; America's death toll was over 4,000 and the Philippine's was far higher.

Pilgrims   Puritan Separatists who broke completely with the Church of England and sailed to the New World aboard the *Mayflower*, founding Plymouth Colony on Cape Cod in 1620.

Pinckney's Treaty   Treaty with Spain negotiated by Thomas Pinckney in 1795; established United States boundaries at the Mississippi River and the thirty-first parallel and allowed open transportation on the Mississippi.

Plantation   An early word for a colony, a settlement "planted" from abroad among an alien population in Ireland or the New World. Later, a large agricultural enterprise that used unfree labor to produce a crop for the world market.

Planter   In the antebellum South, the owner of a large farm worked by twenty or more slaves.

Platt Amendment (1901)   Amendment to Cuban constitution that reserved the United States' right to intervene in Cuban affairs and forced newly independent Cuba to host American naval bases on the island.

***Plessy v. Ferguson* (1896)**   U.S. Supreme Court decision supporting the legality of Jim Crow laws that permitted or required "separate but equal" facilities for blacks and whites.

Poll tax   Tax that must be paid in order to be eligible to vote; used as an effective means of disenfranchising black citizens after Reconstruction, since they often could not afford even a modest fee.

Popular sovereignty   Allowed settlers in a disputed territory to decide the slavery issue for themselves; program most closely associated with Senator Stephen A. Douglas of Illinois.

Populist Party   Founded in 1892, it advocated a variety of reform issues, including free coinage of silver, income tax, postal savings, regulation of railroads, and direct election of U.S. senators.

Potsdam Conference   Last meeting of the major Allied powers, the conference took place outside Berlin from July 17 to August 2, 1945; United States president Harry Truman, Soviet dictator Joseph Stalin, and British prime minister Clement Attlee finalized plans begun at Yalta.

Proclamation of Amnesty and Reconstruction   President Lincoln's proposal for reconstruction, issued in 1863, allowed southern states to rejoin the Union if 10 percent of the 1860 electorate signed loyalty pledges, accepted emancipation, and had received presidential pardons.

Proclamation of 1763 Royal directive issued after the French and Indian War prohibiting settlement, surveys, and land grants west of the Appalachian Mountains; caused considerable resentment among colonists hoping to move west.

Progressive Party Created when former president Theodore Roosevelt broke away from the Republican Party to run for president again in 1912; the party supported progressive reforms similar to the Democrats but stopped short of seeking to eliminate trusts. Also the name of party backing Robert La Follette for president in 1924.

Progressivism Broad-based reform movement, 1900–1917, that sought governmental action in solving problems in many areas of American life, including education, public health, the economy, the environment, labor, transportation, and politics.

Proposition 13 Measure approved by California voters in 1978 prohibiting future increases in property taxes; marked beginning of "tax revolt" as major political impulse.

Public sphere The world of political organization and debate in private associations and publications outside the control of government.

Pueblo Revolt Uprising in 1680 in which Pueblo Indians temporarily drove Spanish colonists out of modern-day New Mexico.

Pullman Strike Strike against the Pullman Palace Car Company in the company town of Pullman, Illinois, on May 11, 1894, by the American Railway Union under Eugene V. Debs; the strike was crushed by court injunctions and federal troops two months later.

Pure Food and Drug Act (1906) First law to regulate manufacturing of food and medicines; prohibited dangerous additives and inaccurate labeling

Puritans English religious group that sought to purify the Church of England; founded the Massachusetts Bay Colony under John Winthrop in 1630.

Quakers (Society of Friends) Religious group in England and America whose members believed all persons possessed the "inner light" or spirit of God; they were early proponents of abolition of slavery and equal rights for women.

Radical Republicans Group within the Republican Party in the 1850s and 1860s that advocated strong resistance to the expansion of slavery, opposition to compromise with the South in the secession crisis of 1860–1861, emancipation and arming of black soldiers during the Civil War, and equal civil and political rights for blacks during Reconstruction.

Railroad Strike of 1877 Interstate strike, crushed by federal troops, which resulted in extensive property damage and many deaths.

Reaganomics Popular name for President Ronald Reagan's philosophy of "supply-side" economics, which combined tax cuts with an unregulated marketplace.

Reconstruction Act (1867) Established temporary military governments in ten Confederate states—excepting Tennessee—and required that the states ratify the Fourteenth Amendment and permit freedmen to vote.

Reconstruction Finance Corporation Federal program established in 1932 under President Herbert Hoover to loan money to banks and other institutions to help them avert bankruptcy.

Red Scare Fear among many Americans after World War I of Communists in particular and noncitizens in general, a reaction to the Russian Revolution, mail bombs, strikes, and riots.

Redeemers Conservative white Democrats, many of them planters or businessmen, who reclaimed control of the South following the end of Reconstruction.

Regulators Groups of backcountry Carolina settlers who protested colonial policies.

Republican Party Organized in 1854 by antislavery Whigs, Democrats, and Free Soilers in response to the passage of the Kansas-Nebraska Act; nominated John C. Frémont for president in 1856 and Abraham Lincoln in 1860; also the name of the party formed by Thomas Jefferson and James Madison in the 1790s.

Republicanism Political theory in eighteenth-century England and America that celebrated active participation in public life by economically independent citizens as central to freedom.

Revolution of 1800 First time that an American political party surrendered power to the opposition party; Jefferson, a Republican, had defeated incumbent Adams, a Federalist, for president.

Right-to-work State laws enacted to prevent imposition of the closed shop; any worker, whether or not a union member, could be hired.

Roe v. Wade (1973) U.S. Supreme Court decision requiring states to permit first-trimester abortions.

Roosevelt Corollary (1904) President Theodore Roosevelt announced in what was essentially a corollary to the Monroe

Doctrine that the United States could intervene militarily to prevent interference from European powers in the Western Hemisphere.

Rough Riders The first U.S. Volunteer Cavalry, led in battle in the Spanish-American War by Theodore Roosevelt; they were victorious in their only battle near Santiago, Cuba, and Roosevelt used the notoriety to aid his political career.

Santa Fe Trail Beginning in the 1820s, a major trade route from St. Louis, Missouri, to Santa Fe, New Mexico Territory.

Saratoga, Battle of Major defeat of British general John Burgoyne and more than 5,000 British troops at Saratoga, New York, on October 17, 1777.

Scalawags Southern white Republicans—some former Unionists—who supported Reconstruction governments.

Schenck v. U.S. **(1919)** U.S. Supreme Court decision upholding the wartime Espionage and Sedition Acts; in the opinion he wrote for the case, Justice Oliver Wendell Holmes set the now-familiar "clear and present danger" standard.

Scientific management Management campaign to improve worker efficiency using measurements like "time and motion" studies to achieve greater productivity; introduced by Frederick Winslow Taylor in 1911.

Scopes Trial (1925) Trial of John Scopes, Tennessee teacher accused of violating state law prohibiting teaching of the theory of evolution; it became a nationally celebrated confrontation between religious fundamentalism and civil liberties.

Scottsboro case (1931) In overturning verdicts against nine black youths accused of raping two white women, the U.S. Supreme Court established precedents in *Powell v. Alabama* (1932), that adequate counsel must be appointed in capital cases, and in *Norris v. Alabama* (1935), that African-Americans cannot be excluded from juries.

Second Great Awakening Religious revival movement of the early decades of the nineteenth century, in reaction to the growth of secularism and rationalist religion; began the predominance of the Baptist and Methodist churches.

Segregation Policy of separating persons on the basis of race in schools, transportation, and other public facilities; *de facto* segregation refers to social customs that accomplish this, *de jure* segregation to laws requiring it.

Seneca Falls Convention First women's rights meeting and the genesis of the women's suffrage movement; held in July 1848 in a church in Seneca Falls, New York, organized by Elizabeth Cady Stanton and Lucretia Coffin Mott.

"Separate but equal" Principle underlying legal racial segregation, upheld in *Plessy v. Ferguson* (1896) and struck down in *Brown v. Board of Education* (1954).

Separation of Powers Feature of the United States Constitution, sometimes called "checks and balances," in which power is divided between executive, legislative, and judicial branches of the national government so that no one can dominate the other two and endanger citizens' liberties.

Servicemen's Readjustment Act (1944) The "GI Bill of Rights" provided money for education and other benefits to military personnel returning from World War II.

Settlement houses Late-nineteenth-century movement to offer a broad array of social services in urban immigrant neighborhoods; Chicago's Hull House was one of hundreds of settlement houses that operated by the early twentieth century.

Seventeenth Amendment (1913) Progressive reform that required U.S. senators to be elected directly by voters; previously, senators were chosen by state legislatures.

Shakers Founded by Mother Ann Lee in England, the United Society of Believers in Christ's Second Appearing settled in Watervliet, New York, in 1774 and subsequently established eighteen additional communes in the Northeast, Indiana, and Kentucky.

Sharecropping Type of farm tenancy that developed after the Civil War in which landless workers—often former slaves—farmed land in exchange for farm supplies and a share of the crop.

Shays's Rebellion (1787) Massachusetts farmer Daniel Shays and 1,200 compatriots, seeking debt relief through issuance of paper currency and lower taxes, attempted to prevent courts from seizing property from indebted farmers.

Sherman Antitrust Act (1890) First law to restrict monopolistic trusts and business combinations; extended by the Clayton Antitrust Act of 1914.

Sherman Silver Purchase Act (1890) In replacing and extending the provisions of the Bland-Allison Act of 1878, it increased the amount of silver periodically bought for coinage.

Single tax Concept of taxing only landowners as a remedy for poverty, promulgated by Henry George in *Progress and Poverty* (1879).

Sit-down strikes Tactic adopted by labor unions in the mid- and late 1930s, whereby striking workers refused to leave factories, making production impossible; proved highly effective in the organizing drive of the Congress of Industrial Organizations.

Sit-ins Tactic adopted by young civil rights activists, beginning in 1960, of demanding service at lunch counters or public accommodations and refusing to leave if denied access; marked the beginning of the most militant phase of the civil rights struggle.

Sixteenth Amendment (1913) Legalized the federal income tax.

Smith v. Allwright (1944) U.S. Supreme Court decision that outlawed all-white Democratic Party primaries in Texas.

Social Darwinism Application of Charles Darwin's theory of natural selection to society; used the concept of the "survival of the fittest" to justify class distinctions and to explain poverty.

Social Gospel Preached by liberal Protestant clergymen in the late nineteenth and early twentieth centuries; advocated the application of Christian principles to social problems generated by industrialization.

Social Security Act (1935) Created the Social Security system with provisions for a retirement pension, unemployment insurance, disability insurance, and public assistance (welfare).

Socialist Party Political party demanding public ownership of major economic enterprises in the United States as well as reforms like recognition of labor unions and women's suffrage; reached peak of influence in 1912 when presidential candidate Eugene V. Debs received over 900,000 votes.

Sons of Liberty Organizations formed by Samuel Adams, John Hancock, and other radicals in response to the Stamp Act.

South Carolina Exposition and Protest Written in 1828 by Vice-President John C. Calhoun of South Carolina to protest the so-called Tariff of Abominations, which seemed to favor northern industry; introduced the concept of state interposition and became the basis for South Carolina's Nullification Doctrine of 1833.

Southeast Asia Treaty Organization (SEATO) Pact among mostly Western nations signed in 1954; designed to deter Communist expansion and cited as a justification for U.S. involvement in Vietnam.

Southern Christian Leadership Conference (SCLC) Civil rights organization founded in 1957 by the Reverend Martin Luther King Jr., and other civil rights leaders.

Spoils system The term—meaning the filling of federal government jobs with persons loyal to the party of the president—originated in Andrew Jackson's first term.

Sputnik First artificial satellite to orbit the earth; launched October 4, 1957, by the Soviet Union.

Stalwarts Conservative Republican Party faction during the presidency of Rutherford B. Hayes, 1877–1881; led by Senator Roscoe B. Conkling of New York, Stalwarts opposed civil service reform and favored a third term for President Ulysses S. Grant.

Stamp Act (1765) Parliament required that revenue stamps be affixed to all colonial printed matter, documents, and playing cards; the Stamp Act Congress met to formulate a response, and the act was repealed the following year.

Standard Oil Company Founded in 1870 by John D. Rockefeller in Cleveland, Ohio, it soon grew into the nation's first industry-dominating trust; the Sherman Antitrust Act (1890) was enacted in part to combat abuses by Standard Oil.

Staple crop Important cash crop, for example, cotton or tobacco.

Steamboats Paddlewheelers that could travel both up- and down-river in deep or shallow waters; they became commercially viable early in the nineteenth century and soon developed into America's first inland freight and passenger service network.

Strategic Defense Initiative ("Star Wars") Defense Department's plan during the Reagan administration to build a system to destroy incoming missiles in space.

Student Nonviolent Coordinating Committee (SNCC) Founded in 1960 to coordinate civil rights sit-ins and other forms of grassroots protest.

Students for a Democratic Society (SDS) Major organization of the New Left, founded at the University of Michigan in 1960 by Tom Hayden and Al Haber.

Sugar Act (Revenue Act of 1764) Parliament's tax on refined sugar and many other colonial products.

Taft-Hartley Act (1947) Passed over President Harry Truman's veto, the law contained a number of provisions to weaken labor unions, including the banning of closed shops.

Tariff   Federal tax on imported goods.

Tariff of Abominations (Tariff of 1828)   Taxed imported goods at a very high rate; aroused strong opposition in the South.

Tariff of 1816   First true protective tariff, intended to protect certain American goods against foreign competition.

Tax Reform Act (1986)   Lowered federal income tax rates to 1920s levels and eliminated many loopholes.

Teapot Dome   Harding administration scandal in which Secretary of the Interior Albert B. Fall profited from secret leasing to private oil companies of government oil reserves at Teapot Dome, Wyoming, and Elk Hills, California.

Tennessee Valley Authority   Created in 1933 to control flooding in the Tennessee River valley, provide work for the region's unemployed, and produce inexpensive electric power for the region.

Tenure of Office Act (1867)   Required the president to obtain Senate approval to remove any official whose appointment had also required Senate approval; President Andrew Johnson's violation of the law by firing Secretary of War Edwin Stanton led to Johnson's impeachment.

Tet Offensive   Surprise attack by the Viet Cong and North Vietnamese during the Vietnamese New Year of 1968; turned American public opinion strongly against the war in Vietnam.

Thirteenth Amendment   Constitutional amendment adopted in 1865 that irrevocably abolished slavery throughout the United States.

Three Mile Island   Nuclear power plant near Harrisburg, Pennsylvania, site of 1979 accident that released radioactive steam into the air; public reaction ended the nuclear power industry's expansion.

Title IX   Part of the Educational Amendments Act of 1972 that banned gender discrimination in higher education.

Tonkin Gulf Resolution (1964)   Passed by Congress in reaction to supposedly unprovoked attacks on American warships off the coast of North Vietnam; it gave the president unlimited authority to defend U.S. forces and members of SEATO.

Townshend Acts (1767)   Parliamentary measures (named for the chancellor of the Exchequer) that taxed tea and other commodities, and established a Board of Customs Commissioners and colonial vice-admiralty courts.

Trail of Tears   Cherokees' own term for their forced removal, 1838–1839, from the Southeast to Indian lands (later Oklahoma); of 15,000 forced to march, 4,000 died on the way.

Transcendentalism   Philosophy of a small group of mid-nineteenth-century New England writers and thinkers, including Ralph Waldo Emerson, Henry David Thoreau, and Margaret Fuller; they stressed personal and intellectual self-reliance.

Transcontinental railroad   First line across the continent from Omaha, Nebraska, to Sacramento, California, established in 1869 with the linkage of the Union Pacific and Central Pacific railroads at Promontory, Utah.

Truman Doctrine   President Harry S. Truman's program announced in 1947 of aid to European countries—particularly Greece and Turkey—threatened by communism.

Trust   Companies combined to limit competition.

Twenty-first Amendment (1933)   Repealed the prohibition of the manufacture, sale, and transportation of alcoholic beverages, effectively nullifying the Eighteenth Amendment.

Twenty-second Amendment (1951)   Limited presidents to two full terms of office or two terms plus two years of an assumed term; passed in reaction to President Franklin D. Roosevelt's unprecedented four elected terms.

Twenty-sixth Amendment (1971)   Lowered the voting age from twenty-one to eighteen.

U.S.S. *Maine*   Battleship that exploded in Havana Harbor on February 15, 1898, resulting in 266 deaths; the American public, assuming that the Spanish had mined the ship, clamored for war, and the Spanish-American War was declared two months later.

Uncle Tom's Cabin   Harriet Beecher Stowe's 1852 antislavery novel popularized the abolitionist position.

Underground Railroad   Operating in the decades before the Civil War, the "railroad" was a clandestine system of routes and safehouses through which slaves were led to freedom in the North.

Understanding clause   Added to southern state constitutions in the late nineteenth century, it allowed illiterate whites to circumvent literacy tests for voting by demonstrating that they understood a passage in the Constitution; black citizens would be judged by white registrars to have failed.

Unitarianism   Late-eighteenth-century liberal offshoot of the New England Congregationalist Church; rejecting the Trinity, Unitarianism professed the oneness of God and the goodness of rational man.

United Farm Workers   Union for the predominantly Mexican-American migrant laborers of the Southwest, organized by César Chavez in 1962.

United Nations   Organization of nations to maintain world peace, established in 1945 and headquartered in New York.

Universal Negro Improvement Association   Black nationalist movement active in the United States from 1916 to 1923, led by Marcus Garvey.

V-E Day   May 8, 1945, the day World War II officially ended in Europe.

Vertical integration   Company's avoidance of middlemen by producing its own supplies and providing for distribution of its product.

Veto   President's constitutional power to reject legislation passed by Congress; a two-thirds vote in both houses of Congress can override a veto.

Vicksburg, Battle of   The fall of Vicksburg, Mississippi, to General Ulysses S. Grant's army on July 4, 1863, after two months of siege was a turning point in the war because it gave the Union control of the Mississippi River.

Vietnam War   Longest war in which the United States has been involved; began with giving American financial assistance to France, who sought to maintain control over Vietnam colony; moved to dispatching advisers to bolster the government of South Vietnam; and finally sent over 500,000 American soldiers by the mid-1960s; resulted in massive antiwar movement, eventual American withdrawal, and communist victory in 1975; only war the United States has lost.

Virginia and Kentucky Resolutions (1798–1799)   Passed by the Virginia and the Kentucky legislatures; written by James Madison and Thomas Jefferson in response to the Alien and Sedition Acts, the resolutions advanced the state compact theory of the Constitution. Virginia's resolution called on the federal courts to protect free speech. Jefferson's draft for Kentucky stated that a state could nullify federal law, but this was deleted.

Virginia and New Jersey Plans   Differing opinions of delegations to the Constitutional Convention: New Jersey wanted one legislative body with equal representation for each state; Virginia's plan called for a strong central government and a two-house legislature apportioned by population.

Volstead Act (1919)   Enforced the Prohibition amendment, beginning January 1920.

Voting Rights Act of 1965   Passed in the wake of Martin Luther King Jr.'s, Selma to Montgomery March, it authorized federal protection of the right to vote and permitted federal enforcement of minority voting rights in individual counties, mostly in the South.

Wabash Railroad v. Illinois (1886)   Reversing the U.S. Supreme Court's ruling in *Munn v. Illinois*, the decision disallowed state regulation of interstate commerce.

Wade-Davis Bill (1864)   Radical Republicans' plan for reconstruction that required loyalty oaths, abolition of slavery, repudiation of war debts, and denial of political rights to high-ranking Confederate officials; President Lincoln refused to sign the bill.

Wagner Act (National Labor Relations Act of 1935)   Established the National Labor Relations Board and facilitated unionization by regulating employment and bargaining practices.

War Industries Board   Run by financier Bernard Baruch, the board planned production and allocation of war materiel, supervised purchasing, and fixed prices, 1917–1919.

War of 1812   Fought with Britain, 1812–1814, over issues that included impressment of American sailors, interference with shipping, and collusion with Northwest Territory Indians; settled by the Treaty of Ghent in 1814.

War on Poverty   Announced by President Lyndon B. Johnson in his 1964 State of the Union address; under the Economic Opportunity Bill signed later that year, Head Start, VISTA, and the Jobs Corps were created, and programs were created for students, farmers, and businesses in efforts to eliminate poverty.

War Powers Act   Law passed in 1973, reflecting growing opposition to American involvement in Vietnam War; required congressional approval before president sent troops abroad.

War Production Board   Created in 1942 to coordinate industrial efforts in World War II; similar to the War Industries Board in World War I.

Warren Court   The U.S. Supreme Court under Chief Justice Earl Warren, 1953–1969, decided such landmark cases as *Brown v. Board of Education* (school desegregation), *Baker v. Carr* (legislative redistricting), and *Gideon v. Wainwright* and *Miranda v. Arizona* (rights of criminal defendants).

Washington Armaments Conference   Leaders of nine world powers met in 1921–1922 to discuss the naval race; resulting treaties limited to a specific ratio the carrier and battleship tonnage of each nation (Five-Power Naval Treaty), formally ratified the Open Door to China (Nine-Power Treaty), and agreed to respect each other's Pacific territories (Four-Power Treaty).

Watergate   Washington office and apartment complex that lent its name to the 1972–1974 scandal of the Nixon administration; when his knowledge of the break-in at the Watergate and subsequent coverup was revealed, Nixon resigned the presidency under threat of impeachment.

Webster-Hayne debate   U.S. Senate debate of January 1830 between Daniel Webster of Massachusetts and Robert Hayne of South Carolina over nullification and states' rights.

Whig Party   Founded in 1834 to unite factions opposed to President Andrew Jackson, the party favored federal responsibility for internal improvements; the party ceased to exist by the late 1850s, when party members divided over the slavery issue.

Whiskey Rebellion   Violent protest by western Pennsylvania farmers against the federal excise tax on whiskey, 1794.

Wilmot Proviso   Proposal to prohibit slavery in any land acquired in the Mexican War, but southern senators, led by John C. Calhoun of South Carolina, defeated the measure in 1846 and 1847.

Women's Christian Temperance Union   Largest female reform society of the late nineteenth century; it moved from opposing sale of liquor to demanding the right to vote for women.

Works Progress Administration (WPA)   Part of the Second New Deal, it provided jobs for millions of the unemployed on construction and arts projects.

Wounded Knee, Battle of   Last incident of the Indian Wars took place in 1890 in the Dakota Territory, where the U.S. Cavalry killed over 200 Sioux men, women, and children.

Writs of assistance   One of the colonies' main complaints against Britain, the writs allowed unlimited search warrants without cause to look for evidence of smuggling.

XYZ affair   French foreign minister Tallyrand's three anonymous agents demanded payments to stop French plundering of American ships in 1797; refusal to pay the bribe was followed by two years of undeclared sea war with France (1798–1800).

Yalta conference   Meeting of Franklin D. Roosevelt, Winston Churchill, and Joseph Stalin at a Crimean resort to discuss the postwar world on February 4–11, 1945; Joseph Stalin claimed large areas in eastern Europe for Soviet domination.

Yellow journalism   Sensationalism in newspaper publishing that reached a peak in the circulation war between Joseph Pulitzer's *New York World* and William Randolph Hearst's *New York Journal* in the 1890s; the papers' accounts of events in Havana Harbor in 1898 led directly to the Spanish-American War.

Yeoman farmers   Small landowners (the majority of white families in the Old South) who farmed their own land and usually did not own slaves.

Yick Wo v. Hopkins   Supreme Court decision in 1886 overturning San Francisco law that, as enforced, discriminated against Chinese-owned laundries; established principle that equal protection of the law embodied in Fourteenth Amendment applied to all Americans, not just former slaves.

Yorktown, Battle of   Last battle of the Revolutionary War; General Lord Charles Cornwallis along with over 7,000 British troops surrendered at Yorktown, Virginia, on October 17, 1781.

Young Americans for Freedom   Organization of conservative students founded in 1960; played major role in 1964 presidential campaign of Barry Goldwater and in rebirth of conservatism in the 1960s.

Zimmermann Telegram   From the German foreign secretary to the German minister in Mexico, February 1917, instructing him to offer to recover Texas, New Mexico, and Arizona for Mexico if it would fight the United States to divert attention from Germany in the event that the United States joined the war.

CREDITS

PHOTOS

Half Title Courtesy of the Massachusetts Historical Society. Banner, William Lloyd Garrison (1805–1879) "Proclaim Liberty Throughout all the Land unto all the inhabitants thereof." MHS image #332; **Title Page** Reproduced from the collections of the Library of Congress, Prints & Photographs Division, P&P LC-USZC2-3794; **Title Page** American Social History Project, NY; **Title Page** George Eastman House; **Title Page** Cecil J. Williams; **2 (left)** The Maryland Historical Society, Baltimore, Maryland; **2–3 (bottom)** © The Trustees of The British Museum; **3 (top)** This item is reproduced by permission of The Huntington Library, San Marino, California; **3 (bottom)** Unidentified artist, British, 18th century or first quarter 19th century; *Quaker Meeting*; Oil on canvas; 64.1 × 76.2cm (25 1/4 × 30in.); Museum of Fine Arts, Boston; Bequest of Maxim Karolik; 64.456; **4–5** © The Trustees of The British Museum; **7** Cliché Bibliothèque nationale de France, Paris; **10** Photo Courtesy of Edward E. Ayer Collection, The Newberry Library, Chicago; **11 (top)** Library of Congress; **11 (bottom)** Timothy O'Sullivan, *Ancient Ruins in the Canon de Chelle, N.M. in a Niche 50 Feet above Present Canon Bed*, albumen silver print, 1873; Amon Carter Museum, Fort Worth, Texas P1982.27.38; **12** © The British Museum; **14** British National Archives; **15** © The British Museum; **16** Courtesy Lilly Library, Indiana University, Bloomington, IN; **17** Reproduced from the collections of the Library of Congress, LC-DIG-PPMSCA-02937; **21** The Mariners' Museum, Newport News, VA; **22** Biblioteca Estense Universitaria, Modena; **23** Museu Nacional de Arte Antiga; **24** By permission of the British Library; **26 (top)** Florence, Library Medicea Laurenziana, ms. Med. Palat. 220. By permission of the Ministero per I Beni e le Attivita' Culturali; **26 (bottom)** The Granger Collection, NY; **28** Courtesy of the Library of Congress, Huexotzinco Codex, Painting V, Manuscript 1531; **29** Museo de América; **30** Instituto Nacional de Antropologia e Historia, Chapultepec Castle, Mexico City; **31** Rare Books Division, The New York Public Library, Astor, Lenox, and Tilden Foundations; **32** The Library of Congress; **33** Museo Naval, Madrid; **36** The Library of Congress, Prints & Photographs Division, Edward S. Curtis Collection, LC-USZ62-102168; **37** Bettmann/Corbis; **42** Collection du monastère des Ursulines de Québec, Musée des Ursulines de Québec (1997.1017); **43** Library and Archives, Canada; **44** © Bettmann/Corbis; **45** The J. Clarence Davies Collection, Museum of the City of New York; **46** Museum of the City of New York; **47** The Colonial Williamsburg Foundation; **50–51** *Self-Portrait*, by Thomas Smith, 1948.19, Worcester Art Museum, Worcester, Massachusetts; **53** © Archivo Iconografico, S.A. / Corbis; **55** By kind permission of His Grace the Duke of Bedford and the Trustees of the Bedford Estates; **56** The John Carter Brown Library at Brown University; **57** The Library Company of Philadelphia; **58** This item is reproduced by permission of The Huntington Library, San Marino, California; **59** GLC 4110. Document signed: contracts relating to the indenture of James Mahony, 31 March 1773. (The Gilder Lehrman Collection, courtesy of the Gilder Lehrman Institute of American History, New York.); **60** The British Museum; **61** Museum of Art, Rhode Island School of Design. Gift of Robert Winthrop. Photography by Erik Gould; **63 (top)** © Corbis; **63 (bottom)** National Portrait Gallery, Smithsonian Institution/Art Resource, NY; **64** Reproduced from the collections of the Library of Congress, LC-USZ62-73206; **65 (top)** Reproduced from the collections of the Library of Congress, LC-USZC4-5306; **65 (bottom)** Ingham Fosler Collection, Imperial Tobacco Limited; **66** © Corbis; **68** The Library of Congress; **69** Courtesy American Antiquarian Society; **70** The Granger Collection, NY; **71** Courtesy of the Massachusetts Archives; **72** *The Savage Family*, by Edward Savage, 1964.7, Worcester Art Museum, Worcester, Massachusetts; **73** Massachusetts Historical Society; **77** Annenberg Rare Book and Manuscript Library, Van Pelt-Dietrich Library Center, University of Pennsylvania; **78** The Library of Congress; **80** *Mrs. Elizabeth Freake and Baby Mary*, unknown artist, 1963.134, Worcester Art Museum, Worcester, Massachusetts; **81** © Historical Picture Archive/Corbis; **82** *An Eyewitness Representation of the Execution of King Charles I (1600–49) of England*, 1649 (oil on canvas), Weesop (fl.1641–49)/Private Collection/www.bridgeman.co.uk; **83** By permission of the British Library; **87** The Cromwell Museum, Huntingdon; **90–91** The Colonial Williamsburg Foundation; **92** The John Carter Brown Library at Brown University; **96** Reproduced from the collections of the Library of Congress, MSS E58.L16; **98** The Historical Society of Pennsylvania; **99** Unidentified artist, British, 18th century or first quarter 19th century; Quaker Meeting; Oil on canvas; 64.1 × 76.2cm (25 1/4 × 30in.); Museum of Fine Arts, Boston; Bequest of Maxim Karolik; 64.456; **101** By permission of the British Library; **102 (top)** The John Carter Brown Library at Brown University; **102 (bottom)** The Colonial Williamsburg Foundation; **105** National Maritime Museum, London; **107** *King William III (1650–1702)* (oil on canvas), English School, (18th century)/Springhill, County Londonderry, Northern Ireland, National Trust Photographic Library/Derrick E. Witty/www.bridgeman.co.uk; **110** Rare Books Division, The New York Public Library, Astor, Lenox and Tilden Foundations; **114** National Archives; **115** The Historical Society of Pennsylvania; **119** Benjamin West, Pennsylvania Academy of the Fine Arts; Joseph and Sarah Harrison Collection; **120** The Library Company of Philadelphia; **122** Courtesy of The Maryland Historical Society; **123** Virginia Historical Society, Richmond, Virginia; **124** The Colonial Williamsburg Foundation; **126** Fenimore Art Museum, Cooperstown, New York; **127** Gift of Edgar William and Bernice Chrysler Garbisch, Image © 2006 Board of Trustees, National Gallery of Art, Washington; **130–131** Abby Aldrich Rockefeller Folk Art Museum, Colonial Williamsburg Foundation, Williamsburg, VA; **133** Reproduced from the collections of the Library of Congress, LC-USZ62-54026; **134** By permission of the British Library; **137** Reproduced from the collections of the Library of Congress, LC-USZ62-44000; **138 (top)** The Maryland Historical Society, Baltimore, Maryland; **138 (bottom)** The Colonial Williamsburg Foundation; **139** The Maryland Historical Society, Baltimore, Maryland; **140** Courtesy, American Antiquarian Society; **141** Newport Historical Society (53.3); **144** Charleston Library Society; **146** By courtesy of the National Portrait Gallery, London; **147** Chicago Historical Society; **148** By courtesy of the Trustees of Sir John Soane's Museum; **149** Reproduced from the collections of the Library of Congress, LC-USZ62-82852; **150** The Library Company of Philadelphia; **153** This item is reproduced by permission of The Huntington Library, San Marino, California; **154** © Bettmann/Corbis; **155** Library of Congress; **157** National Portrait Gallery, London; **160** Courtesy of the Bancroft Library, University of California, Berkeley; **161** Courtesy of Tulane University; **162** Reproduced from the collections of the Library of Congress, LC-USZC4-5309; **169** The Library of Congress; **173 (top)** Courtesy of Picture History; **173 (bottom)** The Library of Congress; **174 (top)** Courtesy of the Beineke Rare Book and Manuscript Library, Yale University; **174 (bottom left)** Print Collection, Miriam and Ira D. Wallach Division of Art, Prints, and Photographs, The New York Public Library; Astor, Lenox, and Tilden Foundations; **174 (bottom right)** © New Bedford Whaling Museum; **175** © Bettmann/Corbis; **176–177** GLC 2873. Paul Revere. Print: A View of Boston and British Ships of

TEXT, TABLES, AND FIGURES

Page numbers in *italics* refer to illustrations.

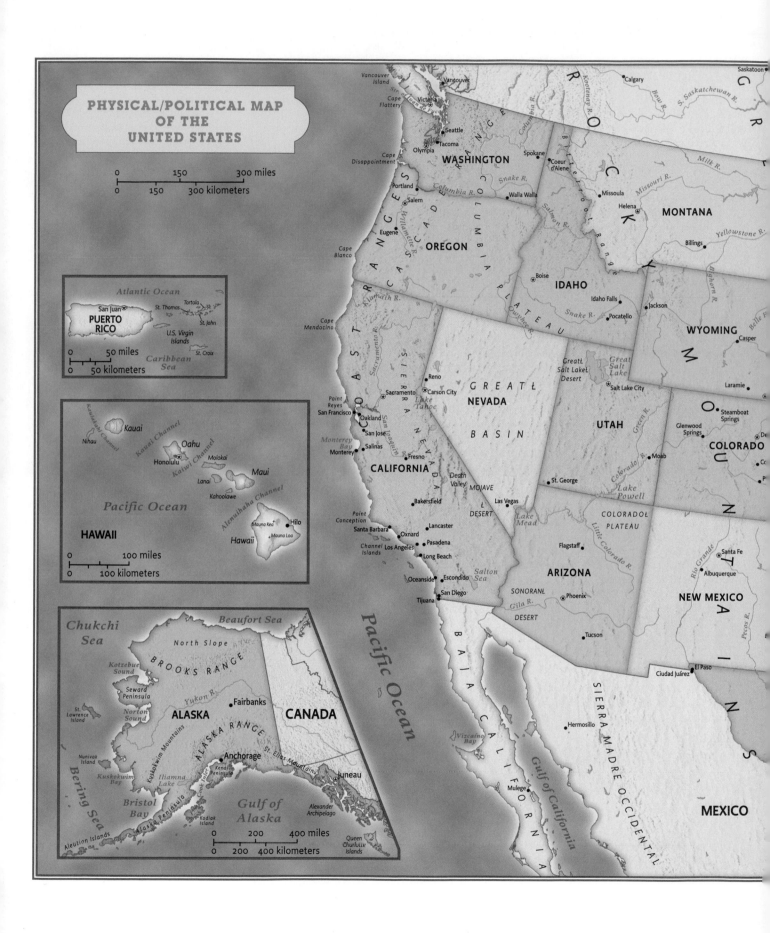

PHYSICAL/POLITICAL MAP OF THE UNITED STATES

0   150   300 miles
0   150   300 kilometers

PUERTO RICO

Atlantic Ocean
San Juan ✪   St. Thomas   Tortola
                              St. John
                U.S. Virgin
                Islands
                        St. Croix
Caribbean Sea
0   50 miles
0   50 kilometers

HAWAII

Kauai Channel
Nihau   Kauai
Kaiwi Channel   Oahu   Molokai
Honolulu ✪   Lanai   Maui
Pacific Ocean   Kahoolawe   Alenuihaha Channel
                        Mauna Kea   Hawaii
                        Mauna Loa   Hilo
0   100 miles
0   100 kilometers

ALASKA

Chukchi Sea   Beaufort Sea
North Slope
Kotzebue Sound   BROOKS RANGE
Seward Peninsula   Yukon R.
St. Lawrence Island   Norton Sound   ALASKA   CANADA
Nunivak Island   Kuskokwim Mountains   ALASKA RANGE   Fairbanks
Bering Sea   Iliamna Lake   St. Elias Mountains
Kuskokwim Bay   Anchorage   Juneau
Bristol Bay   Kenai Peninsula   Cook Inlet   Alexander Archipelago
Aleutian Islands   Kodiak Island   Gulf of Alaska   Queen Charlotte Islands
0   200   400 miles
0   200   400 kilometers

Main map labels

Vancouver Island   Vancouver   Calgary   Saskatoon
Cape Flatterly   Strait of Juan de Fuca   Victoria   Columbia R.   Kootenay R.   Bow R.   S. Saskatchewan R.
Seattle   Tacoma   Spokane   Milk R.
Olympia   WASHINGTON   Coeur d'Alene
Cape Disappointment   Salmon R.   Missoula   Missouri R.   MONTANA
Portland   Columbia R.   Snake R.   Helena   Billings   Yellowstone R.
Salem   Walla Walla
Eugene   OREGON   Boise
Cape Blanco   COLUMBIA PLATEAU   IDAHO   Idaho Falls   Jackson   Bighorn R.
Klamath R.   Pocatello   Snake R.   WYOMING
Cape Mendocino   Owyhee R.   Casper
CASCADE RANGES   Great Salt Lake Desert   Great Salt Lake   Laramie
Sacramento R.   Reno   GREAT   Salt Lake City   Steamboat Springs
Point Reyes   Sacramento   Carson City   NEVADA   Glenwood Springs   COLORADO
San Francisco   SIERRA   Lake Tahoe   BASIN   UTAH   Green R.   Moab
Oakland   San Joaquin   St. George   Lake Powell
San Jose   NEVADA   Death Valley   Colorado R.   COLORADO PLATEAU
Monterey Bay   Salinas   Fresno   MOJAVE   Lake Mead   Flagstaff   Little Colorado R.
Monterey   CALIFORNIA   Bakersfield   DESERT   Las Vegas   Santa Fe
Point Conception   Lancaster   ARIZONA   Rio Grande   Albuquerque
Santa Barbara   Oxnard   Pasadena   Phoenix   Gila R.   NEW MEXICO   Pecos R.
Channel Islands   Los Angeles   Long Beach   SONORAN DESERT   Tucson
Oceanside   Escondido   Salton Sea   El Paso
San Diego   Ciudad Juárez
Tijuana   BAJA CALIFORNIA   Hermosillo   SIERRA MADRE OCCIDENTAL
Pacific Ocean   Vizcaino Bay   Gulf of California   MEXICO
Mulege

Scale at equator

| 0 | 750 | 1,500 miles |
| 0 | 750 | 1,500 kilometers |

Arctic Ocean

Ellesmere Island

Queen Elizabeth Islands

Banks Island

Beaufort Sea

Amundsen Gulf

Victoria Island

Baffin Island

Greenland (Denmark)

Baffin Bay

Denmark Strait

ICELAND

Reykjavík

Chukchi Sea

RUSSIA

Bering Sea

Alaska (U.S.)

Gulf of Alaska

Foxe Basin

Hudson Strait

Hudson Bay

Labrador Sea

Aleutian Islands

CANADA

IRELAND

North Atlantic Ocean

Ottawa   Montréal

Toronto

Chicago

New York
Washington, D.C.

PORTUGAL

Azores (Por.)

Lisbon

North Pacific Ocean

UNITED STATES

San Francisco

Los Angeles

Dallas

Bermuda (U.K.)

Madeira Islands (Por.)

Rabat

Canary Islands (Sp.)

MOROCCO

Hawaii (U.S.)

MEXICO

Gulf of Mexico

Nassau
BAHAMAS
Havana   CUBA   HAITI   DOMINICAN REPUBLIC
Mexico City   Puerto Rico (U.S.)
BELIZE   ST. KITTS AND NEVIS
JAMAICA   DOMINICA
GUATEMALA   ST. LUCIA
EL SALVADOR   ST. VINCENT AND THE GRENADINES
HONDURAS   BARBADOS
NICARAGUA   Caribbean Sea TRINIDAD AND TOBAGO
COSTA RICA
PANAMA   Caracas
             VENEZUELA   GUYANA
Bogotá   French Guiana (Fr.)
COLOMBIA
Galapagos Islands (Ecuador)   Quito
ECUADOR   SURINAME

Western Sahara (Mor.)

MAURITANIA

Nouakchott

CAPE VERDE

SENEGAL
GAMBIA
GUINEA-BISSAU   GUINEA
SIERRA LEONE   CÔTE D'IVOIRE
LIBERIA

São

Kiritimati (Kiribati)

Phoenix Islands

KIRIBATI

Marquesas Islands (Fr.)

PERU

Lima

BRAZIL

Brasília

Ascension

SAMOA
Apia Pago Pago

FIJI

Nuku'alofa

TONGA

Cook Islands

Papeete

French Polynesia (Fr.)

South Pacific Ocean

La Paz
BOLIVIA
Sucre

Rio de Janeiro

South Atlantic Ocean

Pitcairn Islands (U.K.)

Adamstown

Easter Island (Chile)

PARAGUAY
Asunción

Juan Fernandez Archipelago (Chile)

Santiago

URUGUAY
Buenos Aires   Montevideo

CHILE   ARGENTINA

Tristan da Cunha Group

Atlantic Ocean
Southern Ocean
SOUTH AMERICA
ANTARCTICA
Pacific Ocean
Southern Ocean
Indian Ocean

Pacific Ocean
NORTH AMERICA
Arctic Ocean
ASIA
EUROPE
Atlantic Ocean

| 0 | 1,500 miles |
| 0 | 1,500 kilometers |

Falkland Islands (U.K.)

South Georgia

South Sandwich Islands

Scotia Sea

South Shetland Islands

South Orkney Islands

Southern

Arctic Ocean

Franz Josef Land

Severnaya
Zemlya

New Siberian
Islands

Laptev Sea

East Siberian
Sea

Wrangel
Island

Svalbard
(Norway)

Kara Sea

Barents Sea

Novaya Zemlya

Bering
Sea

SWEDEN
FINLAND

RUSSIA

Oslo
Stockholm
ESTONIA
LATVIA
LITHUANIA
RUS.

Moscow

Sea of
Okhotsk

Aleutian Islands

Berlin
NY
POLAND
BELARUS
CZECH
REP.
SLOVAKIA
HUNGARY
MOLDOVA
UKRAINE
AUSTRIA
ROMANIA
ITALY
SL.
CROATIA
B.H.
SERBIA
BULGARIA
Rome
MONT.
MAC.
ALBANIA
GREECE
Black Sea

Astana

KAZAKHSTAN

Lake
Baikal

Ulan Bator

MONGOLIA

NORTH
KOREA

Kuril Islands

JAPAN

North Pacific
Ocean

GEORGIA
ARMENIA
AZERBAIJAN

Aral
Sea
UZBEKISTAN
KYRGYZSTAN

Lake
Balkhash

Beijing

Sea of
Japan

Mediterranean Sea
TURKEY
CYPRUS
LEBANON
ISRAEL
SYRIA
Tehran
TURKMENISTAN
TAJIKISTAN

Seoul
SOUTH
KOREA

Tokyo

Tripoli
JORDAN
IRAQ
IRAN

Kabul
AFGHANISTAN
Islamabad

Yellow
Sea

Cairo
KUWAIT
BAHRAIN
QATAR

PAKISTAN
New Delhi

NEPAL
Kathmandu
BHUTAN
Thimphu

East
China
Sea

TAIWAN

LIBYA
EGYPT
SAUDI
ARABIA
UNITED
ARAB
EMIRATES
Persian Gulf
OMAN

Muscat

BANGLADESH
Dhaka

Red Sea

CHAD
N'Djamena
Khartoum
SUDAN
ERITREA
YEMEN
DJIBOUTI

Arabian
Sea

Socotra
(Yemen)

INDIA

MYANMAR
LAOS

South
China
Sea

Philippine
Sea

Northern
Mariana
Islands
(U.S.)

MARSHALL
ISLANDS

Bay of
Bengal
Andaman
Islands
(India)
THAILAND
VIETNAM
CAMBODIA
Manila

Guam
(U.S.)

CENTRAL
AFRICAN
REP.
Adis Ababa
ETHIOPIA

SRI
LANKA

PHILIPPINES

PALAU

FEDERATED STATES OF MICRONESIA

CAMEROON
UGANDA
KENYA
SOMALIA
Mogadishu

MALDIVES

BRUNEI
MALAYSIA
SINGAPORE

Celebes
Sea

KIRIBATI

CONGO
RWANDA
DEMOCRATIC
REP. OF
CONGO
BURUNDI
TANZANIA
Nairobi
Dar es Salaam

SEYCHELLES

Chagos
Archipelago
(U.K.)

Sumatra
Borneo

NAURU

SOLOMON
ISLANDS

Luanda

Diego Garcia

Jakarta
Java Sea
INDONESIA
Java

PAPUA
NEW GUINEA

TUVALU

ANGOLA
ZAMBIA
MALAWI
COMOROS

EAST
TIMOR
Arafura Sea
Timor Sea

Coral
Sea

VANUATU

FIJI

NAMIBIA
ZIMBABWE
BOTSWANA
MOZAMBIQUE
Antananarivo
MADAGASCAR
MAURITIUS
Réunion
(Fr.)

Indian Ocean

New
Caledonia
(Fr.)

South
Pacific
Ocean

Windhoek
Gaborone
Pretoria
Johannesburg
SWAZILAND
Maseru
LESOTHO
SOUTH
AFRICA
Cape Town

Mozambique Channel

AUSTRALIA

Norfolk
Island
(Aus.)

Kermadec
Islands
(N.Z.)

Great
Australian
Bight

Sydney
Canberra, A.C.T.

Tasman
Sea

North
Island

NEW
ZEALAND

Tasmania

Prince
Edward
Islands
(So. Africa)

Crozet Islands

French Southern and
Antarctic Lands (Fr.)

Kerguélen
Islands

South
Island

Heard Island and
McDonald Islands
(Aus.)

Southern
Ocean